ENVIRONMENTAL HEALTH LAW

AUSTRALIA

The Law Book Company
Brisbane · Sydney · Melbourne · Perth

CANADA

Carswell
Ottawa · Toronto · Calgary · Montreal · Vancouver

AGENTS

Steimatzky's Agency Ltd., Tel Aviv
N.M. Tripathi (Private) Ltd., Bombay
Eastern Law House (Private) Ltd., Calcutta
M.P.P. House, Bangalore
Universal Book Traders, Delhi
Aditya Books, Delhi
MacMillan Shuppan KK, Tokyo
Pakistan Law House, Karachi, Lahore

ENVIRONMENTAL HEALTH LAW

PROFESSOR NEIL HAWKE
LL.B.(Hon.) (Hull), Ph.D. (Nottingham), FRSA
Professor of Environmental Law
Environmental Law Institute
De Montfort University, Leicester

LONDON
SWEET & MAXWELL
1995

Published in 1995 by
Sweet & Maxwell Limited of
South Quay Plaza, 183 Marsh Wall, London E14 9FT.
Typeset by Mendip Communications Ltd, Frome, Somerset
Printed in Great Britain by The Bath Press, Bath, Avon

No natural forests were destroyed to make this product:
only farmed timber was used and replanted

A CIP catalogue record for this book is available from the British Library

ISBN 0 421 46550 6

ACKNOWLEDGEMENT

The author acknowledges, with thanks, the permission of Barry Rose Periodicals to reproduce part of his article "New British Pesticides Law and North American Perspectives" published in volume 15, no. 3 of the Anglo-American Law Review.

PREFACE

The law of Environmental Health poses any commentator with a considerable challenge given the width, depth and rapid movement of the subject. The present work seeks to discipline this difficult body of law in the space of fourteen chapters recognising the equal difficulty of knowing what to exclude. Apart from the fact that the law here is undoubtedly different in scope to that found in many other Member States of the European Community the work seeks to recognise that some areas of law are either peripheral to the concerns of the local authority (such as the law relating to pharmaceutical products) or may be so extensive as to be more suitably researched in more specialised works (such as the substantive law of Health and Safety at Work).

Such is the recent development of Environmental law through statutes such as the Environmental Protection Act that it is no longer a matter of difficulty to identify the impact on health of different environmental occurrences. The explosion in such legislation—and the attendant explosion in relevant European Community law—has undoubtedly extended the frontiers of Environmental Health law. Such contemporary legislation does put into perspective the changing structure of regulatory control of environmental health. It is undoubtedly the case that older regulatory patterns in legislation are being replaced by newer techniques, some of which are developing from important perceptions about market and product-based controls. The next decade will see important developments here as well as in relation to another very significant element relating to the need for ever better identification and definition of scientific data for the purpose of initiating—and enforcing—environmental health controls.

The essential task of this work is to provide environmental health professionals—Environmental Health officers in particular—as well as lawyers with a detailed definition and analysis of the relevant law. At particular points reference is also made to the interrelationship between different strands of the law. Frequent reference is also made to the growing body of relevant European Community law. The background to this ever important European dimension is to be found in the Introduction that follows.

The genesis of this work lies in the author's teaching, research and publication in the area of Environmental Health law over the years. As General Editor of the Encyclopedia of Environmental Health Law and Practice the author owes a considerable debt of gratitude for the support and encouragement of the publisher, Sweet and Maxwell. Thanks are also due to Charles Cross for his enthusiastic encouragement as well as to colleagues from the Environmental Law Institute at De Montfort University. The author's gratitude is also due to his secretary, Liz Steward, for her tireless efforts in getting the book to press and to his wife and family for their unfailing support during its writing.

The law is intended to be stated as it was on May 20, 1994.

Leicester

Neil Hawke

CONTENTS

TABLE OF CASES

Table of Cases

TABLE OF U.K. STATUTES

TABLE OF STATUTORY INSTRUMENTS

TABLE OF DEPARTMENT OF ENVIRONMENT CIRCULARS

E.E.C. TREATIES

E.C. REGULATIONS

E.C. DIRECTIVES

INTRODUCTION

ENVIRONMENTAL HEALTH LAW

Environmental health is an elusive category of law in some respects. For the purpose of this work, the subject is broken down into 14 areas, 13 of them concerned with substantive areas of law as described below. The remaining area relates to an increasingly important matter in practice: access to environmental health information. Many but not all of the areas covered by this work are governed or influenced significantly by European Community law (E.C. law) whose framework is dealt with elsewhere in this Introduction and further developed in detail through the substantive areas of environmental health law.

The Substantive Areas of Environmental Health Law

The 13 substantive areas dealt with in the following chapters are as follows:

(a) water resources and supply;
(b) sewage effluent and disposal;
(c) land drainage and flood defence;
(d) water pollution;
(e) land pollution;
(f) atmospheric pollution;
(g) integrated pollution control;
(h) noise pollution;
(i) statutory nuisance;
(j) building control;
(k) housing;
(l) food safety; and
(m) miscellaneous controls.

Interposed between the chapters on noise pollution and statutory nuisance is the chapter dealing with access to environmental health information. Access to information by the public in particular may be a greater priority in practice in the areas of environmental health covered in the chapters preceding this chapter on access compared with the areas covered in the chapters that follow. Nevertheless, to the extent that access to information is significant for the purposes of regulatory enforcement, treatment of the law on information access is of course important for a variety of other purposes in all areas.

Water resources and supply

The essence of this first chapter is the management and care of water resources for the purpose of maintaining a supply. The general supply duties and responsibilities of the water undertakers under the Water Industry Act 1991 are dealt with, together with water abstraction and the enforcement of quality standards. This is set in the context of a privatised water industry subject to considerable regulatory control and governed to an equally considerable extent by E.C. legal requirements.

Sewage and effluent disposal

Again in the context of a privatised water industry, the emphasis of this chapter is the range of regulatory responsibilities of the sewerage undertakers in containing, regulating and facilitating the treatment of defined categories of effluent in collaboration with agencies and organisations in the public and private sectors. Again, the influence of E.C. legal requirements is considerable, particularly in setting limits on the toxic substances that may or may not be discharged to sewer under the Water Industry Act.

Land drainage and flood defence

Land drainage is concerned essentially with the removal of unwanted water from land to the sea, primarily to facilitate agriculture. In an area that is not subject to any particular E.C. influence, the regulatory framework of the Land Drainage Act 1991 and (to a lesser extent) the Water Resources Act 1991 confers various statutory responsibilities on internal drainage boards and the National Rivers Authority.

Water pollution

The civil and criminal enforcement of water quality standards in this chapter is directly referable to the opening chapters on water resources and supply, and sewage and effluent disposal. Water pollution law is governed both by the regulatory requirements of the Water Resources Act and by the common law, with its concern for the identification and distribution of relevant liabilities.

Land pollution

This large, generic category accommodates waste management, contaminated land, litter control, pesticides and the environmental release of genetically modified organisms. Certain areas—contaminated land in particular—attract reference to common law liabilities and the difficult task of their identification and distribution. With the exception of the law governing pesticides, the statutory regulatory framework is to be found in the Environmental Protection

Act 1990. The regulation of pesticides is dealt with by the Food and Environment Protection Act 1985. Again, many of the areas encompassed are subject to E.C. legal standards and requirements.

Atmospheric pollution

In an area of difficult and diverse environmental impact, the law's control is divided between a statutory regulatory regime found in the Clean Air Act 1993, the Environmental Protection Act and (to a lesser extent) the Control of Pollution Act 1974, and the common law. A key feature of the Environmental Protection Act is local authority air pollution control, whose counterpart—integrated pollution control—is dealt with in the chapter following. Again, E.C. legal standards and requirements are crucial factors.

Integrated pollution control

Heavily influenced by E.C. law and policy, integrated pollution control is driven by the need to subject multi-media pollution to regulatory rationalisation in a manner that permits continuous recognition of improving technology and techniques of process control through best available techniques not entailing excessive cost under the Environmental Protection Act. At the time of writing, the intention is to establish a new Environment Agency, bringing together many of the foregoing functions of environmental regulation and control presently undertaken by the National Rivers Authority, Her Majesty's Inspectorate of Pollution and the waste regulation authorities.

Noise pollution

Like atmospheric pollution, noise may be characterised as a particularly difficult, diverse pollutant. Although subject to an increasing number of E.C. legal standards and requirements, noise control is still governed primarily by statute and common law which owes very little to the European influence. Statutory regulation ranges across area-based controls in the Control of Pollution Act and the control of noise from premises and streets under the statutory nuisance provisions of the Environmental Protection Act to a variety of provisions covering matters such as compensation schemes for noise disturbance under various items of legislation.

Access to environmental health information

The law governing access to environmental health information has particular significance in relation to information availability to the public as a characteristic of many regulatory statutes in environmental health. However, information access serves a number of purposes, not the least of which is the process of enforcement. Access to environmental information is heavily influenced by E.C.

requirements, especially in so far as any regulatory information requirement less generous than that prescribed by the European Community is assumed to be on a par with these latter requirements.

Statutory nuisance

Within the framework of the Environmental Protection Act, both local authorities and individuals aggrieved by a statutory nuisance (whose definition is heavily influenced by the requirements for a common law nuisance) may take summary proceedings to remedy its adverse environmental impact. With a considerable historical pedigree, the measures to deal with a statutory nuisance have considerable merit, in being cheap, expeditious and localised.

Building control

The essence of the law (confined mainly in the Building Act 1984) is its concern for the regulatory control of health and safety of buildings, implemented and enforced primarily by local authorities. A significant element of the law is its concern with fire safety in buildings.

Housing

The focus of environmental health in housing under the Housing Act 1985 is with disrepair and standards of fitness for occupation. Standards and requirements here are relative, at least to the extent that the law's requirements may vary according to a number of factors, including mode of occupation and locality.

Food safety

Statutory regulation of food safety under the Food Safety Act 1990, influenced in some significant areas by E.C. standards and requirements, is concerned essentially with the integrity and safety of food and its broader environment as administered and enforced primarily by the food authorities. The chapter also examines additional controls over the quality and wholesomeness of milk and meat.

Miscellaneous controls

The final chapter examines a broad range of controls including health and safety at work. This area is dealt with primarily from the general standpoint of local authority participation in enforcement of the Health and Safety at Work Act 1974 but does not deal with detailed areas of substantive law, for which the reader should turn to specialised works on the subject. The miscellaneous controls dealt with focus primarily on local authority functions and responsibilities. The other controls dealt with relate to:

(a) the control of disease and environmental intrusions;
(b) the control of pests;
(c) entertainment, theatre, cinema and sex establishment licensing;
(d) animal welfare;
(e) street trading;
(f) scrap metal dealing;
(g) rag flock;
(h) skin piercing;
(i) nursing agencies; and
(j) camps and caravan sites.

In this latter area, the Criminal Justice and Public Order Act 1994 repeals Part II of the Caravan Sites Act 1968. Part V of the Act confers a variety of powers on the police to deal with public order matters as they are manifested by collective trespass or nuisance on land. Two sections directly affect local authorities. The first empowers a local authority (principally a county, district or London borough council) to direct unauthorised campers to leave land. The second provides for orders (to be made by a magistrates' court on application by any local authority) for the removal of persons and their vehicles unlawfully on land.

Sources and Status of E.C. Environmental Health Law

At numerous points in this work, reference is made to E.C. law, its implementation and enforcement in relation to environmental health. Accordingly there is an important need to stress the sources—and status—of E.C. environmental health law, particularly as it affects municipal law. Originally "the Community" was the "European Economic Community": an economic union of Member States according to the original terms of the main source of Community law, the EEC Treaty, dating back to 1957. Subsequently, there has been a considerable expansion in the size of the Community and an equally considerable expansion in the objectives of the Community which, since the Maastricht Treaty of 1992, may also be referred to as the "European Union". Reference throughout this work is to the "European Community".

Environmental objectives

Until recently, it was only indirectly that environmental objectives could be accommodated within the law-making competence of the Community, usually as a consequence of provisions seeking to harmonise the terms of trade as between Member States. Even now, it is not uncommon to find that there is a dichotomy between trade and environmental priorities.[1]

The EEC Treaty[2] authorises the legislation of directives for the approximation of laws, regulations and administrative provisions in Member States affecting the

[1] Case 302/86, *E.C. Commission v. Denmark*: [1988] E.C.R. 4607; [1989] 1 C.M.L.R. 619.
[2] Art.100.

establishment and functioning of the Community.[3] The Treaty also provides for general powers to further Community objectives where there is an absence of express competence.

Matters of public health and the environment are now provided for in the Treaty, as follows. It is stated in general terms that the activities of the Community shall include "... a contribution to the attainment of a high level of health protection". More specifically Article 129 [Title X: Public Health] and Article 130 [Title XVI: Environment] make the following provision: Article 129 states that the Community shall contribute towards ensuring a high level of human health protection by encouraging co-operation between the Member States and, if necessary, lending support to their action. Community action is to be directed towards the prevention of diseases and, in particular, the major health scourges. Health protection requirements also form a constituent part of the Community's other policies. For these purposes, Article 129 also declares that Member States, while liaising with the Commission, shall co-ordinate amongst themselves their policies and programmes. Article 130R goes on to stipulate that Community policy on the environment shall contribute to, *inter alia*, pursuit of the objectives of preserving, protecting and improving the environment and protecting human health. Reference may also be made to other fundamentals of E.C. environmental policy, to be found in various "action programmes". The first of these programmes, dating back to 1973, is particularly influential, referring as it does to the "precautionary principle" (preventing environmental damage at source rather than after the event) and the "polluter pays principle" (imposing the cost of avoiding and removing environmental nuisance (in principle) on the person causing such nuisance).

Finally, in relation to environmental objectives, the matter of subsidiarity must be taken into account. Subsidiarity is embodied in Article 130R, referred to previously. By virtue of the Maastricht Treaty, it is stated that the Community shall act only if and in so far as the objectives of action proposed cannot be achieved sufficiently—by virtue of the scale or effect of proposed action—in Member States acting independently.

Sources

The fundamental source of Community law for present purposes is the EEC Treaty which provides for the matter of competence in the making of subordinate legislation.[4] Community regulations apply generally across Member States, are binding in their entirety and are directly applicable, requiring no further action to bring them into force. Although little used in relation to implementation of environmental policy, nevertheless the regulation has the considerable merit of allowing universal legal requirements to be binding throughout the Community immediately. The directive, on the other hand, is the normal vehicle for implementation of environmental policy. Any directive is

[3] As extended by the Single European Act 1986: see Arts.100–102 of the Treaty.
[4] EEC Treaty, Art.189; *cf.* revised Arts.130s, 189b and c.

binding in terms of the objective or objectives set: the mode of implementation is a matter for the individual Member State. In practice, any controversy here (which may ultimately be resolved by litigation involving the Member State in the European Court of Justice) will usually relate to an alleged failure to implement within the prescribed time limit, or a failure to meet the required objectives of the directive. Another source—the decision—is binding in its entirety on those to whom it is addressed by the Commission, for example. Recommendations and opinions, on the other hand, have no binding force.

The adoption of Community law

Unlike the situation in some other countries, there is no immediate effect in law for treaties under English law unless and until expressly recognised by municipal legislation. The starting point for this process in relation to membership of the European Community was through the European Communities Act 1972[5] which, in turn, was further extended following the Single European Act 1986 and the Maastricht Treaty of 1992. Fundamentally, any Member State is bound by Community law according to various judgments of the Court of Justice, so that Community law will prevail over inconsistent municipal law.[6]

The European Communities Act, s.2(2), empowers the making of subordinate legislation enabling, in turn, the implementation in English law of Community measures which are not directly applicable. Additionally, the power can be used to supplement some measures which are directly applicable. More generally, however, section 2(2) remains a very important vehicle for the implementation of many requirements flowing from the E.C. directives on the environment.

The enforcement of directives

Where it is said that a Community measure has "direct effect", that measure will permit an individual to enforce it as long as the measure in question is clear and precise, unconditional and requires no further action for implementation by a Member State.[7] Another fundamental assumption here is that direct effect will operate only "vertically" against "the State" but not "horizontally" against another individual.[8] Consequently, an important inquiry here is whether a particular organisation or agency is sufficiently well identified with "the State". Almost inevitably, the privatised water industry comes to mind, with water and sewerage undertaker PLCs operating as companies under the Companies Act

[5] See in particular s.2(1), allowing adoption of Treaty provisions as well as the requirements of regulations, decisions and judgments of the European Court of Justice.

[6] Case 26/62, *Van Gend en Loos v. Nederlandse Administratie der Belastingen*: [1963] E.C.R. 1; [1963] C.M.L.R. 105. *Cf.* s.2(4) of the Act of 1972.

[7] *Ibid.* As to other instances of direct effect, see Case 41/74, *van Duyn v. Home Office*: [1974] E.C.R. 1337; [1975] 1 C.M.L.R. 1.

[8] Case 152/84, *Marshall v. Southampton Area Health Authority*: [1986] E.C.R. 723; [1986] 1 C.M.L.R. 688.

1985 but within a tightly prescribed statutory framework and subject to considerable direction by government.[9]

From the foregoing, it is important to stress that directives impose obligations on individual Member States although, again, a challenge may be available for alleged failure to implement, either as a matter of chronology or as a matter of substance, where it is argued that purported Member State implementation does not in fact measure up to the directive's requirements and obligations. All of this may be subject to any argument that there is sufficient scope for direct effect in favour of the plaintiff. Whatever the circumstances, it is the case that an English court will presume that municipal legislation is to be interpreted and applied consistently with Community law,[10] although the point is not without difficulty in relation to municipal measures having the force of law before the subject directive.[11]

It appears that in some circumstances a Member State's failure to take all necessary measures to achieve the objective prescribed by a directive may attract liability for compensation.[12] There are three prerequisites for present purposes:

(a) the result identified by the directive must involve rights conferred on individuals;
(b) the content of the rights must be identifiable on the basis of the directive's provisions; and
(c) there must be some causal link between the failure of a Member State to fulfil its obligations and the damage suffered by the individual affected.

A case based on any alleged breach of Community law will normally be brought before the courts of the United Kingdom. Resort to the European Court of Justice is closely circumscribed.[13] Nevertheless, there is an opportunity for a municipal court to refer issues of Community law to the Court of Justice.[14] Finally, it should be noted that a facility exists for a complaint to be made to the Commission, usually where there is no legally enforceable cause of action.[15]

Public Health Exemptions in E.C. Law

In three areas of Community law, relating to the free movement of goods under Articles 30 to 34 of the EEC Treaty, the right of establishment under Article 52

[9] See, in particular, case C–188/89, *Foster v. British Gas*: [1990] I E.C.R. 331; [1990] 2 C.M.L.R. 833 on the position in the privatised gas industry. *Cf. Griffin and Others v. South West Water Services Ltd*, 236 ENDS Report 38.

[10] *Garland v. BRE* [1983] A.C. 751.

[11] Case 106/89, *Marleasing S.A. v. Commercial Internacional de Alimentacion S.A.*: [1990] I E.C.R. 4135; [1992] 1 C.M.L.R. 305.

[12] Case C–6 & 9/90, *Francovich v. Italian Republic*: [1991] I E.C.R. 5357; [1993] 2 C.M.L.R. 66; [1992] I.R.L.R. 84.

[13] EEC Treaty, Art.173.

[14] *Ibid.* Art.177.

[15] *Ibid.* Art.169.

and the right of free movement for workers under Article 48, there exist exemptions, or derogations, including exemptions based on public health grounds.

The free movement of goods

There are tightly defined exceptions to the Treaty provisions on the free movement of goods, including the protection of health. Any such exception must be capable of justification. To prove necessity here is by no means easy and cases often fail on the ground of proportionality. A number of factors were influential before the European Court in *E.C. Commission v. United Kingdom*,[16] where the United Kingdom was unsuccessful in attempting to defend import restrictions on poultry, meat and eggs. The Court commented on the absence of any strategic health policy, the speed with which the restrictions were imposed and a failure to consult the Commission and other Member States. Although there is no necessity to identify conclusive evidence of public health threats, nevertheless a great deal depends on the way in which the evidence (and the response to it) is managed. In many situations, the technical, scientific evidence may be equivocal in circumstances where what is being claimed by a Member State is a prima facie risk to public health. Rigorous monitoring of the evidence will be expected, and a Member State will have to point to its own arrangements, such as strategic measures, to deal with contingencies affecting public health. Against this background, Community law appears to operate by reference to certain presumptions, including:

(a) the need for measures which are only minimally disruptive;
(b) the need to promote efficient cross-border transactions where (for example) the integrity of certain, sealed products may eliminate many checking processes[17];
(c) the assumption of integrity among Member States in their respective testing requirements; and
(d) the assumption that relevant standards and requirements (relating, say, to the inspection of meat and milk) are sufficiently harmonised across the Community to smoothe the cross-border transactions referred to previously.

In some instances, public health issues may be sufficiently sensitive to allow a rather easier derogation or exception.[18]

[16] Case 40/82: [1982] E.C.R. 2793.
[17] Case 251/78, *Denkavit Futtermittel v. Minister fur Ernahrung, Landswirtschaft und Forsten*: [1979] E.C.R. 3369.
[18] Case 271/92, *Société Laboratoire de Prothoses Oculaires v. Union Nationale des Syndicats d'Opticiens de France* (1993).

The right of establishment

Exceptions or derogations from the right of establishment under Article 52 also extend to public health. However, any exception here may extend only to matters of residence or entry to a Member State, not the terms and conditions on which (say) a particular professional career is undertaken.

The right of free movement of workers

The Annex to Directive 64/221,[19] which deals with this right, refers very specifically to public health factors that may operate as an exception in the present case. The diseases and disabilities mentioned in the Annex are the only diseases and disabilities justifying refusal of entry to the territory of a Member State or a refusal to issue a first residence permit.

[19] [1964] O.J. Spec. Ed. 850.

CHAPTER 1

WATER RESOURCES AND SUPPLY

Introduction

The present chapter divides into three parts, covering the supply of water by abstraction, the supply of water by water undertakers from the point of abstraction to the point where it may be exploited for consumption and, finally, the quality standards and expectations affecting that water. For these purposes, most of the law is concentrated in the Water Resources Act 1991 and the Water Industry Act 1991 which, in turn, are influenced by European Community legislation, which is also referred to, particularly in relation to the quality of water for human consumption. Although there is a need to stress the centrality of drinking water standards, incidental reference is also made to E.C. standards that can also be connected with concerns associated with human consumption in its wider sense. Accordingly, reference is also made to E.C. Directives on water for fisheries (including shellfish fisheries) and bathing which are fully discussed in Chapter 4.

Water Resources and Abstraction

The general statutory background

Despite frequent references to "water resources", the term receives no definition in the principal legislation, the Water Resources Act. On the other hand, in Part II of the Act, dealing with water resources management, there are numerous references to sources of supply. For example, the starting point for the law governing abstraction refers to the fact that ". . . no person shall . . . abstract water from any source of supply . . . except in pursuance of a licence . . . granted by . . ." the National Rivers Authority (NRA hereafter).[1] Here, then, is a critical framework within which the law governing abstraction operates. The term "source of supply" is defined[2] to mean any inland waters, except those[3] which are "discrete waters", and also to mean any underground strata[4] in which water is or at any time may be contained. "Discrete waters" refers to inland waters so far as

[1] s.24(1)(a).
[2] Water Resources Act, s.221(1).
[3] Note the qualification: *ibid.* subs.(3).
[4] Strata subjacent to the surface of any land: *ibid.*

they comprise a lake, pond or reservoir which does not discharge to any other inland waters, or one of a group of two or more lakes, ponds or reservoirs (whether near to or distant from each other), and of watercourses or mains connecting them, where none of the inland waters in the group discharges to any inland waters outside the group.[5]

Water resources management

NRA has prime statutory responsibility for water resources management under the Water Resources Act. The statutory duty is defined in fairly broad terms, requiring NRA "... to take all such action as it may from time to time consider, in accordance ... with the directions of the Secretary of State, to be necessary or expedient ..." for the purpose of conserving, redistributing or otherwise augmenting water resources in England and Wales and of securing the proper use of water resources in those areas.[6] This duty, in largely similar terms, was previously exercised by the former water authorities.[7] The Secretary of State is empowered[8] to give NRA general or specific directions in relation to the fulfilment of its functions, including its water resources functions, *inter alia.*[9] Directions may also be given for the purpose of enabling effect to be given to any European Community obligations and any international agreement to which the United Kingdom is a party.[10] NRA is subject to a duty to comply with any direction given to it,[11] although any power here to give a direction requires prior consultation with NRA, except in an emergency.[12]

Although NRA is subject to the foregoing duty in relation to water resources management, it does not detract from the obligation of water undertakers to develop water resources for the purpose of the general duty to maintain an economical and efficient water supply system under section 37 of the Water Industry Act 1991.[13] Accordingly, water undertakers' strategic planning should not be confused with NRA duties in the present context. However, the most important inter-relationship of functions between NRA and the water undertakers is recognised in statutory provision which is made for water resources management schemes.[14] Such schemes enable a measure of reciprocity between the agencies, in so far as NRA may contribute towards any benefit derived from use of water undertakers' facilities while undertakers may be able to utilise any relevant facilities provided by NRA in the exercise of its various powers. The onus appears to fall fairly positively on NRA, in so far as it is subject to a duty

[5] *Ibid.*
[6] *Ibid.* s.19(1).
[7] Water Act 1973, s.10.
[8] Water Resources Act, s.5.
[9] *Ibid.* subs.(1).
[10] *Ibid.* subs(2).
[11] *Ibid.* subs.(5).
[12] *Ibid.* subs.(3).
[13] *Ibid.* s.19(2).
[14] *Ibid.* s.20.

"... so far as [is] reasonably practicable to enter into and maintain such arrangements with water undertakers for securing the proper management or operation of..." a variety of facilities, as considered appropriate by NRA for or in connection with the execution of its functions of general water resource management.[15] Those facilities relate to waters available to water undertakers for the discharge of their functions, together with any reservoirs, apparatus or other works belonging to or controlled by water undertakers for the discharge of their functions.[16] Any questions arising from such arrangements are referable to the Secretary of State or the Director-General of Water Services.[17] A copy of any arrangement here must be sent to the Secretary of State by NRA.[18] Interestingly, the obligations of any water undertaker by virtue of an arrangement here is enforceable under section 18 of the Water Industry Act,[19] prescribing an administrative framework for enforcement.[20]

Allied to NRA's general water resources management is the NRA power, supplementing general, incidental powers in section 4 of the Water Resources Act, to enter works agreements with both water and sewerage undertakers, local authorities, joint planning boards or the owners or occupiers of land.[21] Any such agreement may cover a variety of matters:

(a) works considered by NRA to be necessary or expedient in connection with the performance of its functions;
(b) the maintenance of such works;
(c) provision of access to land or the use of such land for the performance of NRA functions; and
(d) the mode of operation of reservoirs.[22]

The Secretary of State is able, by direction, to require that NRA does not enter a works agreement without his consent.[23] Provision is made in the case of both registered and unregistered land for relevant terms of any works agreement concluded under these powers to run with the subject land, so binding successive owners.[24] In some cases, such provision will of course be unnecessary, in so far as any covenant or other similar requirement will have been performed completely by the "original" parties.

Where any works have been conducted by a navigation, harbour or

[15] *Ibid.* subs.(1).
[16] *Ibid.*
[17] *Ibid.* subs.(2)(c).
[18] *Ibid.* subs.(3).
[19] *Ibid.*
[20] Described later in the present chapter in relation to general water supply duties under s.37, Water Industry Act.
[21] Water Resources Act, s.158.
[22] *Ibid.* subs.(1): any agreement for these purposes may contain incidental and consequential provisions, including financial provision: subs.(3).
[23] *Ibid.* subs.(2).
[24] *Ibid.* subss.(4), (5).

conservancy authority and it appears to NRA that those works have made or will make a beneficial contribution to fulfilment of its water resources functions, NRA is obliged to make a contribution to those works.[25] The reverse situation is also provided for, in relation to any NRA works.[26] The contribution will be determined by agreement between the parties: any disputes are referable to the Secretary of State who, in turn, may decide to refer the dispute to arbitration.[27]

The foregoing arrangements, as well as numerous other matters relating to water resources and their management, may give rise to disagreement or other matters of concern. Even where there is no disagreement or other matters of concern, each of the Ministers (the Secretary of State or the Minister of Agriculture) has a wide power to convene a local inquiry in connection with water resources management or otherwise in connection with NRA functions.[28] In so far as any such inquiry is convened, it will be governed by the provisions of section 250 of the Local Government Act 1972.

Resource definition

NRA has a broad-based duty to make arrangements to undertake research and related activities in connection with the performance of its functions, including water resources functions.[29] This task may be undertaken by NRA, or it may be undertaken by others, through sub-contract arrangements, for example.[30] Allied to this responsibility is a further duty[31] to collate and publish information from which assessments can be made of the actual and prospective demand for water, as well as actual and prospective water resources, in England and Wales, and (so far as NRA considers it appropriate to do so) to collaborate with others in collating and publishing information relating to places outside England and Wales.

The search for water resources is aided by statutory provision[32] which empowers those authorised by NRA to enter premises to conduct surveys or tests to determine whether land should be acquired or compulsory works orders sought.[33] The power to enter premises here is stated to include, *inter alia*, the power to conduct experimental borings, install monitoring apparatus and to take away and analyse samples.[34] In so far as NRA provides a building, plant or machinery or apparatus in, on, over or under land for the purpose of survey or investigation as part of its general functions here[35] or, more specifically, as part of its water functions,[36] permitted development rights indicate that planning

[25] *Ibid.* s.120(1).
[26] *Ibid.* subs.(2).
[27] *Ibid.* subss.(3), (4), (5).
[28] *Ibid.* s.213(1).
[29] *Ibid.* s.2(3).
[30] *Ibid.*
[31] *Ibid.* s.188.
[32] *Ibid.* s.171(1), (2).
[33] *Ibid.* s.168 (compulsory works orders).
[34] *Ibid.* s.171(3). *Cf.* the limits set by subss.(4), (5).
[35] Town and Country Planning General Development Order 1988, Sched. 2, Pt. 15, Class A(d).
[36] *Ibid.* Pt. 17, Class C(e).

permission is not normally required. Where an abstraction of water is involved, a licence for that purpose is not required.[37] However, if an abstraction for present purposes is being undertaken on land, NRA may, by direction, require the provision of information.[38] If the requirement for information is considered unduly onerous or unreasonable, representations can be made to the Secretary of State, who may then require NRA to revoke or modify the subject direction.[39] However, the Secretary of State's power to require revocation or modification of a direction will not apply on those occasions when an occupier is required to disclose the quantity or quality of water abstracted by him, or on his behalf, from any source of supply.[40] Failure to comply with a direction here is an offence, punishable on summary conviction.[41]

Any person other than NRA who proposes to install a gauge for measuring and recording the flow, level or volume of any inland waters other than discrete waters[42] is required to give notice to NRA and to desist from installation works before the end of a period of three months from the date of the notice, or any shorter period allowed by NRA.[43] Within one month of the completion of those installation works, NRA must be notified of the whereabouts of the records generated by the measurements.[44] Any contravention of these requirements is a summary offence.[45] However, these requirements do not apply to any gauge installed for the sole purpose of indicating the level of inland waters for the benefit of those who fish them and any gauge which is removed at or before the end of a period of 28 days beginning with the date of installation.[46]

Availability of information about the flow, level or volume of inland waters or any water in underground strata, as well as information about rainfall or any fall of snow, hail or sleet, or water evaporation, is the subject of reciprocal duties between NRA and water undertakers.[47] In so far as NRA maintains any records containing this information, there is a further duty to make it available to any person.[48] The duty to provide NRA with this information on the part of a water undertaker is enforceable under section 18 of the Water Industry Act.[49] If any other person maintains records of the flow, level and volume of inland waters except "discrete waters", NRA has a statutory right to inspect and take copies of the subject information: failure to make the information available without reasonable excuse is a summary offence.[50]

[37] Water Resources Act, s.32. *Cf.* s.64 in relation to NRA abstractions.
[38] *Ibid.* s.201.
[39] *Ibid.* subss.(2), (3).
[40] *Ibid.* subs.(4).
[41] *Ibid.* subs.(5).
[42] *Ibid.* s.221(1).
[43] *Ibid.* s.200(1).
[44] *Ibid.* subs.(2).
[45] *Ibid.* subs.(4).
[46] *Ibid.* subs.(3).
[47] *Ibid.* s.197(1), (2).
[48] *Ibid.* subs.(1).
[49] *Ibid.* subs.(6).
[50] *Ibid.* subs.(3).

Abstraction

Abstraction of water in any source of supply is defined as:

> "... the doing of anything whereby any of that water is removed from that source of supply, whether temporarily or permanently, including anything whereby the water is so removed for the purpose of being transferred to another source of supply ..."[51]

The process of abstraction of water and the licensing of that process is controlled by NRA, by virtue of Part II of the Water Resources Act. Much of Part II is taken up with regulatory licensing of abstractions by private individuals and organisations as well as water undertakers, although provision is made also for the regulation of abstraction by NRA.[52] Provision is also made for abstractions by the British Waterways Board[53] and in respect of ecclesiastical property.[54] The licensing requirements in Part II of the Act do not apply to land in which there is a Crown interest or an interest enjoyed by the Duchy of Lancaster.[55]

Exceptional provision

The foregoing reference to NRA, British Waterways Board, ecclesiastical property and Crown property indicate a range of potentially important exceptions to the normal licensing requirements in Part II of the Act. Exceptional treatment also applies to water undertakers and their abstraction requirements. Each case is summarised below.

In the case of NRA, abstraction of water for the purpose of water resources functions requires a licence. The terms on which any such licence is granted or deemed to be granted by the Secretary of State will be set out in regulations made for the purpose.[56]

Abstractions by the British Waterways Board as governed by section 66 of the Water Resources Act relate to all inland water owned or managed by the Board, subject to any exceptions determined (by statutory instrument) by the Secretary of State.[57] There is no requirement that it have control of land, or access to it, that is contiguous to the inland waters in question. Furthermore, normal publicity requirements will not apply to the processing of an abstraction application from it.[58]

[51] *Ibid.* s.221(2). *Cf. British Waterways Board v. National Rivers Authority* [1993] Env.L.R. 239.
[52] Water Resources Act, s.64 and *cf.* n.37, *supra.*
[53] *Ibid.* s.66. Note that the British Waterways Board is not required to have control of land contiguous to subject inland waters, or even access to it: s.35.
[54] *Ibid.* s.67.
[55] *Ibid.* s.222.
[56] *Ibid.* s.64(1), (2).
[57] *Ibid.* s.66(1).
[58] *Ibid.* subs.(2).

Provision for abstraction from ecclesiastical property is taken up with specification of those (either an incumbent of the Church of England or the Church Commissioners, in the usual case) who may apply for abstraction licences and be regarded as the licence holder.[59] Provision is also made for the purpose of determining the recipient of any compensation payable under the Part II provisions relating to abstraction and impounding.[60]

Where the Crown or the Duchy of Lancaster has an interest in land, the present provisions in Part II of the Act do not apply to anything done by or on behalf of the Crown, or to any land which is in the occupation of a government department, or any other land in which there is a Crown or Duchy interest and which is occupied in right of that interest.[61]

In the case of water undertakers, the power to undertake works for the purpose of water abstraction will have been gained from a variety of statutory sources before and after the enactment of the Water Act 1989. Many authorisations for this purpose will have come from Local Acts, although more recently the powers in section 167 of the Water Industry Act have assumed a far greater significance. This provision relates to compulsory works orders, approved by the Secretary of State for the purpose of or in connection with the carrying out of any prescribed functions. Among other things, a compulsory works order may provide powers to acquire land compulsorily and even facilitate the repeal or amendment of any local statutory provision.[62] The present provision clearly recognises that a water undertaker may not have power to take water[63] and stipulates that nothing in a compulsory works order shall exempt an undertaker from the requirement to obtain a licence for any relevant abstraction of water.[64] Unless a water undertaker has obtained a licence as a successor to one of the old water authorities,[65] an application for any new licence will in broad terms accord with the normal licensing regime found in Part II of the Water Resources Act. However, the water undertaker will put before NRA either a confirmed compulsory purchase order or other evidence to indicate that any draft order, if confirmed, will authorise compulsory acquisition of the subject land.[66] Once granted, the licence in this case is not required to specify the land on which and the purposes for which the abstracted water is to be used.[67] Where any engineering or building operations are authorised by a compulsory works order and a licence or deemed licence for abstraction is granted, compensation is not payable in so far as there is injurious affection to land attributable to the operations and the abstraction of water.[68]

[59] *Ibid.* s.167(2), (3).
[60] *Ibid.* subss.(4), (5), (6).
[61] *Ibid.* s.222(2).
[62] *Ibid.* s.167(4).
[63] *Ibid.* subs.(7).
[64] *Ibid.* subs.(6).
[65] Water Act 1989, Sched. 2 and Sched. 26, para. 29(1).
[66] Water Resources Act, s.35(4), (5).
[67] *Ibid.* s.46(4).
[68] Water Industry Act, Sched. 11, para. 7. *Cf.* Water Resources Act, Sched. 19, para. 7, in relation to NRA.

Enforcement of Part II

The provisions of Chapter II of Part II of the Act relating to abstraction and impounding are enforceable by NRA but without prejudice to its powers of enforcement in relation to other provisions of the Water Resources Act governing enforcement powers.[69] NRA is under a duty to enforce this area of the Act, a duty enforceable by mandamus,[70] at least to the extent that the order may require NRA to consider the merits of enforcement action.[71] No proceedings for any offence can be instituted except by NRA or the DPP. Any other individual or organisation may institute such proceedings only with the consent of the DPP.[72]

Abstraction licences

Apart from any requirements for an environmental assessment in respect of abstraction works on land,[73] any such works undertaken on agricultural land which are reasonably necessary for the purposes of agriculture within the subject agricultural unit may not require planning permission, having attained permitted development rights under the Town and Country Planning General Development Order 1988.[74] Any other type of development on land for water abstraction would normally require planning permission under the Town and Country Planning Act 1990.[75]

No person is permitted to abstract water from any source of supply or to cause or permit any other person so to abstract any water without an abstraction licence granted by NRA, and then only within the terms of that licence.[76] Special provision applies to the abstraction of water from any underground strata. Where such abstraction is prohibited, no person except in pursuance of a licence, can begin, or cause or permit any other person to begin, defined works unless other specified requirements are satisfied. The defined works comprise the construction of wells, boreholes and other works to facilitate extraction, the extension of such works, and the installation or modification of facilities permitting the abstraction of additional quantities of water. The specified requirements to be satisfied relate to a need for authorisation by the licence of the abstraction or the abstraction of additional quantities, as well as a need for the defined works to fulfil requirements laid down in the licence.[77] Failure to comply with the foregoing requirements is an offence. It is also an offence, as a licence holder, not to comply with any condition or requirement imposed by the

[69] Water Resources Act, s.216(1).
[70] R.S.C., Ord. 53.
[71] *R. v. Kerrier District Council, ex p. Guppys (Bridport) Ltd* (1977) 75 L.G.R. 129.
[72] Water Resources Act, s.216(2).
[73] Town and Country Planning (Assessment of Environmental Effects) Regulations 1988 (S.I. 1988 No. 1199), Sched. 2.
[74] Sched. 2, Part 6.
[75] s.57.
[76] Water Resources Act, s.24.
[77] *Ibid.* subss.(2), (3).

provisions of the licence, even if there is no contravention of the foregoing requirements.[78] Any person guilty of these offences is punishable, on summary conviction, with a fine not exceeding the statutory maximum and, on indictment, a fine.[79]

The status of an abstraction licence

Any abstraction licence granted under the Act must specify the person to whom the licence is granted.[80] Any such person can be regarded in law as the holder of the licence, as is any person receiving a licence to obstruct or impede any inland waters for present purposes.[81] The foregoing definition of the term "holder" is subject to other provisions of the Act governing succession to abstraction licences[82] and rights of abstraction in relation to ecclesiastical property,[83] as well as statutory provision for licence variation.

The requirements for succession distinguish between a licence which is held by a person who is occupier of the whole of the land specified in the licence and a person who is occupier of part only of the subject land. In the first case, if the occupier dies or ceases to be in occupation of the whole or any part of the land and another person becomes the occupier, the "prior holder" ceases to be the licence holder, to be replaced by his successor.[84] If, before the expiration of 15 months from this change, the successor has not advised NRA of the change, the successor ceases to be the licence holder.[85] Whatever the circumstances, if no person succeeds to occupation of the land, the abstraction licence lapses.[86] In so far as a successor notifies NRA of a change of occupier within the period of 15 months, NRA is obliged to vary the licence accordingly.[87] Subject to any powers of variation or revocation elsewhere in the Act, under this provision NRA has no control over factors relating to the successor, which may in turn relate to the licence. Succession rights where a person becomes occupier of part of the subject land only vary from a right to become holder of the licence to a right to apply for and be granted a new licence.[88] Regulations here may provide for both the prior holder and a successor to receive an abstraction licence and for NRA to vary any licence accordingly.[89]

Once granted, an abstraction licence is declaratory of the fact that

> "... a person who is for the time being the holder of a licence ... to abstract

[78] *Ibid.* subs.(4).
[79] *Ibid.* subs.(5).
[80] *Ibid.* s.47.
[81] *Ibid.* subss.(1), (2).
[82] *Ibid.* ss.49 and 50.
[83] *Ibid.* s.167. *Cf.* nn.59 and 60, *supra.*
[84] *Ibid.* s.49(1), (2).
[85] *Ibid.* subs.(3).
[86] *Ibid.* subs.(5).
[87] *Ibid.* subs.(4).
[88] *Ibid.* s.50.
[89] *Ibid.* subss.(4), (5).

> water shall be taken to have a right to abstract water to the extent authorised by the licence and in accordance with the provisions in it".[90]

In any action, it is therefore a defence to prove that the water was abstracted in pursuance of a licence and that the licence provisions were complied with.[91] If the action is in respect of the obstruction or any impediment to the flow of inland waters by means of impounding works, it is a defence to prove that the flow was obstructed or impeded in pursuance of a licence, that the obstruction or impediment was in the manner specified by and did not exceed the licence requirements, and that any other (relevant) licence requirements were complied with.[92] However, neither of these foregoing sets of defences will exonerate a person from any action in negligence or for breach of contract.[93] Every licence granted must provide for the determination, by measurement or assessment, of the quantity of water authorised for abstraction from the particular source.[94] If a quantity of water has been determined in accordance with abstraction measurement or assessment methods contained in the licence, that is conclusive evidence of the matters to which it relates,[95] for example, in relation to proceedings anticipated previously by section 48 of the Water Resources Act.

Protected rights

Protected rights are important considerations in the determination of applications. NRA may not, except with the consent of any person entitled to such rights, to grant a licence authorising abstraction or the obstruction or impediment of the flow of inland waters by impounding works.[96] A right is a "protected right" if it is a right to abstract small quantities for domestic or agricultural use,[97] or is a right to abstract represented by the terms of a licence.[98] By way of contrast, where a licence application relates to abstraction from underground strata, NRA is merely obliged to have regard to the requirements of existing lawful uses of water abstracted from those strata, whether for agriculture, industry, water supply or other purposes.[99] For these purposes, NRA is entitled but not bound to treat as lawful any existing use of water, unless it has been determined to be unlawful in any legal proceedings in circumstances where that decision has not been quashed or reversed.[1]

[90] *Ibid.* s.48(1). As to a possible defence of statutory authority for abstraction as against a riparian owner, see *Allen v. Gulf Oil Refining Co.* [1981] 2 W.L.R. 188 and *Gillingham Borough Council v. Medway (Chatham Docks) Co. Ltd* [1992] Env.L.R. 98.
[91] Water Resources Act, s.48(2), but subject to Sched. 7, para. 2.
[92] *Ibid.* subs.(3).
[93] *Ibid.* subs.(4).
[94] *Ibid.* s.46(2), (6).
[95] *Ibid.* s.209(3).
[96] *Ibid.* s.39(1).
[97] *Ibid.* s.27(6).
[98] *Ibid.* s.48(1). *Cf.* n.90, *supra.*
[99] *Ibid.* s.39(2).
[1] *Ibid.* subs.(5).

There are limited possibilities in relation to any remedy in law for a breach of NRA's duty in relation to the foregoing protected rights. Breach of the duty does not invalidate the grant or variation of a licence. Furthermore, any breach is not enforceable by criminal proceedings, by prohibition or injunction, or by action against any person other than NRA.[2] Any person with a protected right has one remedy only: an action against NRA for damages for breach of statutory duty.[3] That same remedy is again the sole remedy against NRA where any grant or variation of a licence occurs at the direction of the Secretary of State.[4] However, whatever the origin of an action against NRA here, it has a defence in so far as it is shown as a fact that the authorised abstraction derogated from protected rights, or that any authorised obstruction of or impediment to the flow of inland waters similarly did not derogate.[5] Where NRA is liable for damages for breach of statutory duty under the above provisions by virtue of the requirement to comply with a direction to grant or vary a licence in breach of protected rights, the Secretary of State may, if he thinks fit, pay to NRA the whole or part of the damages paid, or liable to have been paid if an action had been pursued.[6] Similarly, if proposals for a licence revocation or variation are formulated by NRA and these lead to revocation or variation and compensation is payable by NRA,[7] the Secretary of State may, if he thinks fit, pay the whole or some part of that amount.[8]

Abstraction restrictions: the exceptions

Provision is made to take a number of minor abstractions out of the framework of regulatory licensing under Part II of the Act. The restriction on abstraction will not apply to any abstraction of water not exceeding five cubic metres.[9] If the amount in question is not to exceed 20 cubic metres, again the restriction will not apply, but NRA consent is required.[10] Both these stipulations will apply only so long as abstraction does not form part of a continuous operation or a series of operations by which the aggregate quantity of water extracted exceeds these two amounts.[11] The restriction again will not apply where an occupier of land which is contiguous to inland waters abstracts up to 20 cubic metres every 24 hours for use on a holding, which is part of the contiguous land, for domestic or agricultural purposes.[12] Such purposes cannot include use of the water for spray irrigation. Spray irrigation is the irrigation of land or plants (including seeds) by means of water or other liquid emerging (in whatever form) from apparatus designed or

[2] *Ibid.* s.60(1).
[3] *Ibid.* subs.(2).
[4] *Ibid.* subs.(3).
[5] *Ibid.* subs.(5). *Cf.* Sched. 7.
[6] *Ibid.* s.63(1).
[7] *Ibid.* s.61.
[8] *Ibid.* s.63(2). As to the relevant amounts payable for the purposes of subs.(1) and (2), see subs.(4).
[9] *Ibid.* s.27(1).
[10] *Ibid.* subs.(2).
[11] *Ibid.*.
[12] *Ibid.* subs.(3).

adapted to eject liquid into the air in the form of jets or spray.[13] There are similar provisions governing abstraction from underground strata. Abstraction of quantities of water not exceeding 20 cubic metres every 24 hours can be undertaken, but only for domestic purposes.[14] If a well or borehole is constructed for domestic purposes alone, abstraction of a quantity of water not exceeding 20 cubic metres every 24 hours will also not require a licence.[15]

A potentially significant restriction is provided for in relation to the situation outlined above, in which a protected right is conferred on an occupier whose land is contiguous to inland waters and up to 20 cubic metres is extracted every 24 hours for use on the holding for domestic or agricultural purposes.[16] The restriction anticipates a situation where the subject holding is of a size that land over a considerable area may be irrigated, compared with the land able to be irrigated on adjacent holdings that enjoy similar rights. In these circumstances, NRA may serve a notice on the occupier of the subject holding, indicating the "relevant" restricted area over which the rights may be exercised.[17] The occupier has an appeal to the county court, which may confirm, quash or vary the NRA notice.[18]

In the case of abstraction from a source of supply in the course of or resulting from any operations for the purposes of land drainage, restrictions under the Act again will not apply,[19] in the same way that they will not apply to works relating to the drainage of mines, quarries or other land subject to engineering, building or other operations.[20] In these latter cases, beyond land drainage, it must be shown that abstraction is necessary to prevent interference with or damage to the subject works or operations.[21] This latter right of abstraction is unaffected by any use of the water which is abstracted and used for the purpose of the works or operations, where the water is abstracted from any excavation into underground strata.[22] It was seen previously, under section 24(2),[23] that there is a restriction on the construction and other works associated with well, borehole and other similar facilities if the abstraction of water from underground strata is prohibited. In so far as any water is abstracted from underground strata in relation to the land drainage or other works or operations just referred to, the foregoing restriction under section 24(2) will not apply.[24] It should also be noted that, for the purposes of the present section 29, "land drainage" is defined to include the protection of land

[13] *Ibid.* s.72(1). As to restrictions on the definition, see the Spray Irrigation (Definition) Order 1992 (S.I. 1992 No. 1096).

[14] Water Resources Act, s.72(7).

[15] *Ibid.*.

[16] *See* n.12, *supra*.

[17] Water Resources Act, s.28(1), (2).

[18] *Ibid.* subs.(4).

[19] *Ibid.* s.29(1).

[20] *Ibid.* subs.(2).

[21] *Ibid.*.

[22] *Ibid.* subs.(3).

[23] *See* n.77, *supra*.

[24] Water Resources Act, s.29(4).

against erosion or encroachment by water (whether from inland waters or from the sea) and also includes warping and irrigation, other than spray irrigation.[25]

It was seen previously that works associated with the sinking of a well or borehole may lie outside abstraction licensing requirements, even though there may be a separate need for planning permission under the Town and Country Planning Act. However, there is still a need to notify NRA of any relevant works here.[26] Subject to any appeal, NRA may respond to the notification by serving on the individual concerned a conservation notice requiring "... such reasonable measures for conserving water as are specified in the notice".[27] Such measures are those which, in the opinion of NRA, will not interfere with the protection of the underground works in question.[28] Failure to comply with any of these requirements renders the defendant punishable summarily or on indictment.[29] The appeal here is to the Secretary of State on either or both of two grounds: that the measures required are not reasonable and that the measures would interfere with the protection of the underground works in question.[30] Prior to a determination of the appeal, the Secretary of State may convene a local inquiry or hearing, whereupon he may exercise broad powers to confirm, quash or vary the notice: ultimately his decision is final.[31]

The restriction on abstraction will not apply to any transfer of water from one area of inland waters to another in the course of or resulting from the operations of any navigation, harbour or conservancy authority. The restriction on impounding works also does not apply to the construction or alteration of such works by these authorities in the performance of their functions.[32]

Miscellaneous abstraction rights

Where apparatus or machinery installed on a vessel is used to abstract water for use on that or any other vessel, the foregoing restriction on abstraction will not apply,[33] in the same way as it will not apply to fire-fighting and related purposes.[34] If the purpose of any abstraction is to ascertain the presence of water in any underground strata or its quality or quantity, or the effect of abstraction from a well, borehole or other work on abstraction or water level in any other well, borehole or work, the restriction on abstraction will not apply to any such abstraction, the construction or extension of any well, borehole or other work or the installation or modification of machinery or other apparatus.[35]

[25] *Ibid.* subs.(5).
[26] *Ibid.* s.30(1).
[27] *Ibid.* subs.(2).
[28] *Ibid.* subs.(3).
[29] *Ibid.* subs.(4).
[30] *Ibid.* s.31(1).
[31] *Ibid.* subss.(3), (4), (5).
[32] *Ibid.* s.126.
[33] *Ibid.* s.32(1). *Cf.* n.37, *supra.*
[34] *Ibid.* subs.(2).
[35] *Ibid.* subss.(3), (4).

The provision of further rights to abstract

On those occasions when it is considered that the restriction on abstraction is not needed in relation to a particular source, or sources, of supply, NRA or (in relation to inland waters) any harbour, navigation or conservancy authority may apply to the Secretary of State for an order excepting the source or sources of supply.[36] After consultation with NRA, where no application has been made, the Secretary of State may direct that such an application should be made in respect of any source of supply.[37] Where an order comes into force here, certain of the restrictions in section 24[38] cease to apply and any licence for abstraction ceases to have effect.[39]

Licence applications

The application for consent to abstract must be made in the prescribed manner[40] and dealt with by NRA in the prescribed manner. The regulations for these purposes must also indicate facilities for notice of applications in favour of national park planning authorities, as well as the matters to which NRA or, in appropriate cases, the Secretary of State is to have regard, which should include representations made by such authorities.[41]

Applicants' status

There is a strict statutory entitlement in relation to the submission of applications, indicating that, in the case of any inland waters, there is entitlement to make an application if, at the place where abstraction will occur, the applicant is the occupier of land contiguous to the inland waters, or where the applicant satisfies NRA that he has, or at the time when the proposed licence is to take effect will have, a right of access to the subject land.[42] If the application refers to abstraction from underground strata, again the applicant must show status as an occupier, but of land consisting of or comprising those underground strata or, alternatively, he must be able to satisfy two conditions relating to land which is excavated and filled with water from surrounding strata.[43] For present purposes, an "occupier" includes anyone who is able to satisfy NRA that negotiations have been entered that would give an interest in land sufficient for occupation, as well as anyone with powers of compulsory acquisition where such acquisition has been authorised or can be authorised and has been initiated.[44]

[36] *Ibid.* s.33(1), (3). As to orders under this section, see Sched. 6.
[37] *Ibid.* subs.(4).
[38] *Ibid.* s.24(2).
[39] *Ibid.* s.33(6).
[40] Water Resources (Licences) Regulations 1965 (S.I. 1965 No. 534).
[41] Water Resources Act, s.34. *Cf.* s.17.
[42] *Ibid.* s.35(2).
[43] *Ibid.* subs.(3).
[44] *Ibid.* subs.(4). As to whether such acquisition has been "initiated", see subs.(5) and *cf.* n.66, *supra.*

Combined abstraction and impounding licences

Impounding works may involve the construction of any dam, weir or other works in any inland waters for the impounding of water, and any works for diversion of the flow of inland waters in connection with the construction or alteration of a dam, weir or other works.[45] Subject to some exceptions, including the issue of a licence for the purpose by NRA, no person is able to begin or cause or permit any other person to begin, to construct or to alter any impounding works.[46] Failure to comply with the restrictions under this set of provisions, including any failure to comply with the terms on which any licence is issued, is an offence which is punishable, summarily or on indictment.[47] If an impounding application is to be made to NRA, a combined application may be made, in so far as the purpose of the impounding is the abstraction of water at or near the point of impounding.[48] In accepting the application, NRA is able to deal with it and grant the application if the factors prescribed by the Act are taken into account.[49]

Charging

NRA is able to charge in respect of the present abstraction licensing functions[50] by virtue of a charging scheme approved by the Secretary of State.[51] The scope of charging is potentially quite wide, extending to applications, the grant of licences or their variation (including the variation of any attached conditions), as well as the continuation of any such licence in force.[52] In this latter case, among the possibilities is a single charge made in respect of the whole period for which the licence is in force.[53] Whatever the format of the scheme it is subject to:

(a) provision for revocation for non-payment of charges[54];
(b) specific exemptions[55];
(c) agreements between NRA and persons liable to charges for exemptions from those charges[56];
(d) special charges in respect of spray irrigation[57]; and
(e) the waiver or reduction of charges where the British Waterways Board abstracts water from inland waters in its ownership or management.[58]

45 *Ibid.* s.25(8).
46 *Ibid.* subs.(1).
47 *Ibid.* subss.(2), (3).
48 *Ibid.* s.36.
49 *Ibid.*.
50 *Ibid.* s.123.
51 *Ibid.* s.124.
52 *Ibid.* s.123(1).
53 *Ibid.* subs.(3).
54 *Ibid.* s.58. See nn.13–15, *infra.*
55 *Ibid.* s.125.
56 *Ibid.* s.126.
57 *Ibid.* ss.127–129.
58 *Ibid.* s.130.

Proposals for a charging scheme from NRA must be publicised and any representations taken into account before the Secretary of State arrives at a decision. In arriving at a decision on a proposed scheme, the Secretary of State must have regard to the need to avoid a situation in which the product of the charges for present purposes does not subsidise other NRA functions, although other NRA water resources functions may be so subsidised.[59]

Publication of licence applications

It is provided that NRA shall not entertain an application for abstracting or impounding water or a combined licence unless the application is accompanied by a copy of a notice, published in the *London Gazette* and at least one local newspaper and copied to any appropriate agency such as a drainage board, and prescribed evidence that the necessary notices have been given.[60] The prescribed notice must contain a variety of detail, including facilities for access to details of the application and advice to the effect that representations may be made in writing to NRA.[61]

The requirement that NRA shall not entertain an application that does not comply with the foregoing requirements is ostensibly a mandatory requirement. However, by analogy with the similar publicity requirement in the Town and Country Planning Act 1990,[62] it would appear that the impact of any informality is by no means clear-cut.[63] Only in the most flagrant case of failure to comply with this procedural requirement would the court's discretion be exercised, usually in favour of an applicant who could establish substantial prejudice.

The call-in of applications

The Secretary of State is able to give NRA directions, requiring the reference of any application to him for determination, as well as any class of application.[64] The Secretary of State has wide powers of decision for present purposes, and any decision in favour of the grant of a licence is in the form of a direction to NRA to grant that licence.[65] Prior to any determination of the application, the Secretary of State may convene a local inquiry or hearing and is obliged so to do if requested by NRA or the applicant.[66] Provisions on publicity for applications, the general consideration of applications, the consideration of existing lawful uses of water in underground strata and the obligation to take river flows into account all apply to the consideration of called-in applications.[67] The Secretary of State is also obliged

[59] *Ibid.* s.124.
[60] *Ibid.* s.37(1), (2).
[61] *Ibid.* subss.(4), (5).
[62] *Ibid.* s.66.
[63] *R. v. Swansea City Council, ex p. Main* (1985) 49 P. & C.R. 26.
[64] Water Resources Act, s.41.
[65] *Ibid.* s.42(1), (5).
[66] *Ibid.* subs.(2).
[67] *Ibid.* ss.37, 38(1), (3), 39(2) and 40, respectively.

to consider any derogation from protected rights that may occur if NRA is directed to grant a licence.[68]

Decisions

NRA is obliged to arrive at a decision within three months of receipt of the application or to advise the applicant that the application has been called in by the Secretary of State.[69] In arriving at a decision, there may be a requirement to consult with the planning authority for a national park for abstractions occurring in such areas, or the Nature Conservancy Council, where NRA has been previously notified of the sensitivity of any particular site of special scientific interest.[70] If an application has been called in, the applicant must be advised of the reason for any direction to that effect. Where NRA fails to notify any decision of its own or to the effect that the application has been called in, there is a right of appeal to the Secretary of State.[71]

It has been seen previously that NRA is subject to statutory limitations in so far as protected rights may be affected by the licensing process.[72] A further statutory limitation in more general terms indicates that NRA may not determine an application before the expiration of the period prescribed for notices of applications; which is at least 28 days from the date of receipt of the application.[73] NRA is required to have regard to any representations made in writing before the end of the prescribed period, as well as the applicant's requirements, in so far as they appear to be reasonable requirements.[74] Having considered an application, NRA may grant a licence containing such provisions (such as conditions) as it considers appropriate or alternatively, may refuse a licence if considered necessary or expedient.[75]

Factors to be considered in the decision-making process

NRA's decision-making powers relating to licence applications are governed by various requirements already examined, namely the so-called general environmental duty under section 16 of the Water Resources Act and the limit on "protected rights" found in section 27,[76] together with representations received and the applicant's requirements, as referred to in section 38. However, there is one other factor that may be significant here and that relates to minimum acceptable flows.

[68] *Ibid.* s.42(4).
[69] *See* nn.64 and 65, *supra.*
[70] *See* n.41, *supra.*
[71] Water Resources Act, s.43(2).
[72] *Ibid.* s.39(1): see n.96, *supra.*
[73] *Ibid.* s.38(1). As to prescribed notice periods, see s.37(5).
[74] *Ibid.* subs.(3).
[75] *Ibid.* subs.(2).
[76] *cf. ibid.* s.39(2).

Minimum acceptable flows

NRA has a wide discretion to submit to the Secretary of State a draft statement for approval, indicating what are the minimum acceptable flows for inland waters other than "discrete" waters.[77] The Act also sets down considerable detail on matters of calculation[78] and allows the Secretary of State to direct NRA to consider the matter of minimum acceptable flows.[79] Hitherto, minimum acceptable flows have not been particularly significant elements of this or related regulatory schemes. The advent of water quality objectives and changing climatic conditions may suggest greater reliance on the process of abstraction licensing by NRA.

The licence: form and content

Any regulations that the Secretary of State is empowered to make in relation to the form and content of a licence are subject to the terms of the Water Resources Act.[80] The licence granted must provide for the quantity of water to be abstracted from the subject source, as well as the approach to measurement for the purpose of determining the quantities extracted during the period or periods covered by the licence,[81] in addition to the means to be used for the abstraction.[82] Normally, the land on which the water is to be used will be specified in the licence, together with the purposes for which it will be used.[83]

The appeals process

The facility for an appeal to the Secretary of State is drawn very widely, either because the applicant is "dissatisfied" with the NRA decision or NRA, within the prescribed period, fails to give notice of its decision to the applicant or notice that the application has been referred to the Secretary of State under a section 41 direction.[84] The applicant is required to serve a notice of appeal on NRA[85] which, in turn, is obliged at the requirement of the Secretary of State to serve notice of appeal on any person who made representations about the original application.[86]

The Secretary of State has a widely drawn appeal jurisdiction, to the extent that he may allow or dismiss the appeal or reverse or vary any part of the decision (whether or not it is subject to appeal), dealing with the matter as though it were referred to him in the first instance.[87] However, prior to the determination of an

[77] *Ibid.* s.21, Sched. 5.
[78] *Ibid.* ss.21 and 23.
[79] *Ibid.* s.22.
[80] *Ibid.* s.46(1).
[81] *Ibid.* subs.(2).
[82] *Ibid.* subs.(3).
[83] *Ibid.* subs.(4). *Cf.* n.67, *supra.*
[84] *Ibid.* s.43(1), (2).
[85] *Ibid.* subs.(4).
[86] *Ibid.* subs.(5).
[87] *Ibid.* s.44(1).

appeal, the Secretary of State may convene a local inquiry[88] or afford the parties a hearing,[89] but is required to act here if so requested by the applicant or NRA. In approaching his decision, the Secretary of State is obliged to take into account any further representations made to him within the period prescribed, together with the applicant's reasonable requirements.[90] If the decision is that a licence should be granted, varied or revoked, the Secretary of State will give an appropriate direction to NRA.[91] The Secretary of State more generally here is obliged to consider whether any right to abstract or to impede the flow of inland waters by the means of impounding works would derogate from protected rights.[92] As a result, the Secretary of State's decision, which is final,[93] may have a considerable adverse impact on protected rights. However, in view of the status of protected rights (as discussed previously)[94] it may be argued that even if enforcement of the law here is worthwhile, particularly in relation to limited quantities of water, the opportunities for effective enforcement against NRA may be very limited indeed.

The validity of decisions by the Secretary of State

The Water Resources Act contains a fairly standard provision,[95] which stipulates that, except within certain limits, the decision of the Secretary of State on appeal or in respect of a call-in or reference relating to a proposed licence revocation or variation shall not be questioned in any legal proceedings whatsoever.[96] Any proposed challenge by way of review here can be undertaken only within a period of six weeks from the date on which the decision was made, either on the ground that the decision is not within the powers of the Act or that any procedural requirements have not been complied with.[97] The High Court, to whom any such application is made, is empowered to quash the decision (which includes any direction from the Secretary of State) if it is considered substantively not to be within the powers of the Act or that any failure to comply with procedural requirements has substantially prejudiced the interests of the applicant for review under this provision. Any such applicant is barred from the present proceedings beyond the period of six weeks, which is an absolute period.[98]

[88] Subject to the provisions of the Local Government Act 1972, s.250.
[89] Water Resources Act, s.44(2).
[90] *Ibid.* s.44(3).
[91] *Ibid.* subs.(6).
[92] *Ibid.* subs.(4).
[93] *Ibid.* subs.(7).
[94] *See* nn.96–98, *supra.*
[95] s.69.
[96] Water Resources Act, s.69(1).
[97] *Ibid.* subs.(2).
[98] *Smith v. East Elloe RDC* [1956] A.C. 736.

The modification of licences

"Modification", for present purposes, refers to the possible revocation or variation of a licence granted by NRA. Modification may be initiated by the licence holder, NRA, the Secretary of State or the owner of fishing rights in inland waters where there has been no determination of a minimum acceptable flow. Special provision is made for the emergency variation of licences for spray irrigation purposes.[99] The Secretary of State is empowered to make regulations governing the making of applications for revocation or variation of licences.[1]

Where it is the licence holder who applies to NRA for revocation of a licence, NRA is required to accede and revoke the licence accordingly.[2] However, in the case of a request from the licence holder for variation, all of the Act's provisions relating to publicity for applications and so on[3] will apply unless variation is to permit the abstraction of lesser amounts of water.[4]

Three sections of the Act govern any modification proposed by NRA or the Secretary of State.[5] Where the Secretary of State is concerned, he has powers to direct NRA to formulate proposals for revocation or variation.[6] Notice of any proposal here is served on the licence holder and publicised, as in the case of a normal application. The notice will specify the whereabouts of a copy of the proposal and supporting documents, and allow objections by the licence holder and representations by any other parties within the time limit prescribed.[7] In the absence of objections, NRA will be free to adopt the proposal.[8] If NRA chooses to proceed to vary a licence in the absence of any objection, it will be obliged to have regard to any written representations and the applicant's reasonable requirements and the rights of any existing licence holder as well as being obliged to take account of any impact on river flow.[9] If there are objections to variation or revocation proposals, the Secretary of State must consider the proposal and any such objections, as well as any wider public representations.[10] For these purposes, the Secretary of State may convene a local inquiry or hearing, and must so act if requested by one of the parties involved.[11] The rights of other licence holders must be considered, along with the impact on users of water from underground strata and the impact on river flow.[12]

NRA is able to revoke a licence if charges are not paid within 28 days of a

[99] Water Resources Act, s.57.
[1] *Ibid.* s.59.
[2] *Ibid.* s.51(1).
[3] *Ibid.* ss.37–44, 51(2), (3).
[4] *Ibid.* s.51(4).
[5] *Ibid.* ss.52–54.
[6] *Ibid.* subss.(2), (3).
[7] *Ibid.* subss.(6), (7).
[8] *Ibid.* s.53(3).
[9] *Ibid.* subs.(5).
[10] *Ibid.* s.54(1).
[11] *Ibid.* subs.(2). Section 250 of the Local Government Act 1972 will apply.
[12] Water Resources Act, s.54(4).

notice demanding payment of such charges being served on the licence holder.[13] The demand notice will refer to the sanction of revocation and its effect, and further advise the licence holder that no compensation is payable in respect of a revocation under this section.[14] Failure to pay within any permitted period will empower NRA to serve a revocation notice advising the licence holder of the reasons for revocation, and further advising him that the notice will take effect if payment is not tendered before the end of the period specified, which is at least 28 days from the date when the notice was served on the licence holder.[15]

If the owner of fishing rights on inland waters sustains loss or damage directly attributable to the abstraction of water under a licence, that person may request that the Secretary of State revoke or vary that licence, but only after the licence has been in force for one year in circumstances where there has been no determination of a minimum acceptable flow.[16] It should be noted, however, that any loss or damage must be sustained in the person's capacity as owner of the fishing rights, for example, where water levels are much reduced. Even then, an application here will be invalidated in so far as the applicant is shown to enjoy "protected rights" in respect of the inland waters, or that the loss or damage is attributable to a breach of statutory duty for derogation from such rights.[17] An applicant is required to serve notice on NRA and the licence holder, advising them of their right to make written representations to the Secretary of State within 28 days of the notice.[18] In dealing with an application here, the Secretary of State may convene a local inquiry or hearing, and must so act if requested by any of the parties involved. In considering the applicant's case and any representations advanced by NRA and the licence holder, the Secretary of State has to bear in mind that the onus of proof in respect of any loss or damage is on the applicant, and has to be satisfied that the extent of the loss or damage sustained by the applicant is such as to justify revocation or variation.[19] There can be no revocation or variation if the Secretary of State is satisfied that the loss or damage sustained was wholly or mainly attributable to an exceptional shortage of rain or to an accident or other unforeseen act or event not caused by and outside the control of NRA.[20] In so far as a variation is deemed appropriate, that variation is to be limited to that which is requisite having regard to the loss or damage sustained.[21] Any decision to vary or revoke (which is final)[22] must include a direction to NRA to revoke or vary the licence, as the case may be.[23]

The licence holder or holders abstracting water from a source of supply for the

[13] *Ibid.* s.58(1).
[14] *Ibid.* subs.(2).
[15] *Ibid.* subss.(3), (4).
[16] *Ibid.* s.55(1), (2).
[17] *Ibid.* subs.(3).
[18] *Ibid.* subs.(4).
[19] *Ibid.* s.56(1), (2), (3).
[20] *Ibid.* subs.(4).
[21] *Ibid.* subs.(5).
[22] *Ibid.* subs.(7).
[23] *Ibid.* subs.(6).

purpose of spray irrigation may be served with a notice reducing the quantity of water to be abstracted for any specified period. NRA is able to serve such a notice in aid of a temporary restriction by reason of exceptional shortage of rain or other emergency.[24] Similar restrictions may apply to licences to abstract water from underground strata but these are rather more limited, in so far as they may only be imposed if it appears likely that such abstraction will affect the level of inland waters which are neither discrete waters nor inland waters, abstraction from which is not restricted.[25] Where there are two or more closely related abstractions by different licence holders, NRA is obliged to ensure proportionate fairness between them for present purposes.[26] Overall, the present provisions on spray irrigation abstraction have effect without prejudice to the exercise of the various powers of licence modification dealt with previously.[27]

Compensation for licence modification

The Water Resources Act divides compensation provision into two, according to whether it is a matter of modification on the Secretary of State's direction or, on the other hand, payment of compensation to the owner of fishing rights who has applied for modification.[28] In the first case, the licence holder may be compensated by NRA for abortive expenditure occasioned by the modification, or any directly attributable loss or damage.[29] Preparatory planning work may be compensated, but any expenditure prior to the grant of the licence is not.[30] Any licence holder who has not abstracted water for a period of seven years is excluded from claiming compensation here.[31]

In the case of a modification arising from the application of an owner of fishing rights, compensation is payable for any loss or damage sustained on the terms described by section 55.[32] If the Secretary of State determines that the grounds of the section 55 application have been established to his satisfaction but that there will be no revocation or variation, he is obliged to so certify.[33] Assuming that within six months of that certification no notice to treat to acquire the applicant's fishing rights has been served by NRA, or that no offer has been made by NRA to compulsorily acquire those rights from their owner, that owner is entitled to compensation from NRA.[34] The amount of the compensation payable will depend on the extent to which the value of the rights or, where they subsist only as rights included in an interest in land, the value of that interest, has been

[24] *Ibid.* s.57(1), (2).
[25] *Ibid.* subs.(3).
[26] *Ibid.* subs.(4).
[27] *Ibid.* subs.(5).
[28] ss.61 and 62, respectively.
[29] Water Resources Act, s.61(1).
[30] *Ibid.* subss.(2), (3).
[31] *Ibid.* subs.(4). See n.17, *supra.*
[32] *Ibid.* subs.(3).
[33] *Ibid.* s.62(2).
[34] *Ibid.* subs.(3).

depreciated by exploitation of the abstraction rights in the licence.[35] Matters of disputed compensation in both areas are dealt with by the Lands Tribunal.[36] In both areas, the Secretary of State may indemnify NRA in respect of compensation payments here.[37]

Registers of licences

NRA is obliged to maintain a register open to public inspection and containing information relating to applications for the grant, revocation or variation of licences and including details of the way in which the applications were disposed of.[38] The register should also include information about those who are successors to licences, together with details of licences granted or deemed to be granted, varied or revoked in respect of abstraction or impounding works by NRA.[39]

There are restrictions on the disclosure of information relating to any particular business which has been obtained by virtue of the Water Resources Act and relates to the affairs of any individual or that business. Those restrictions require that this information is not disclosed except with the consent of the individual or person carrying on the business in question during the individual's lifetime, or for as long as the business is carried on.[40] However, the restrictions do not apply for the purposes of NRA functions. Accordingly, the important question for NRA is whether any information is disclosed through the register or otherwise in fulfilment of the Act's licensing functions.[41] This in turn raises the question of whether the information is pertinent to the objects of the regulatory process. In practice, the legal requirements here would tend to suggest a need to exclude what appears to be peripheral information about the affairs of individuals or businesses connected with the present regulatory function. Any contravention of the restrictions is an offence punishable in summary proceedings or on indictment.[42]

Civil liability

The Water Resources Act seeks to cut down the potential scope of civil liability under the present provisions governing restrictions on abstraction.[43] on impounding[44] and borings not requiring licences.[45] While the Act may provide for civil liability—in section 60(2), relating to damages against NRA for breach of

[35] *Ibid.* subs.(4).
[36] *Ibid.* ss.61(5), 62(5).
[37] *Ibid.* s.63(2), (3).
[38] *Ibid.* s.189(1), (4).
[39] *Ibid.* subs.(2).
[40] *Ibid.* s.204(1).
[41] *Ibid.* subs.(2).
[42] *Ibid.* subs.(6).
[43] *Ibid.* s.24. *Cf.* n.76, *supra.*
[44] *Ibid.* s.25. *Cf.* n.46, *supra.*
[45] *Ibid.* s.30. *Cf.* n.26, *supra.*

statutory duty,[46] for example—there is no further right of action in any civil proceedings, other than proceedings for the recovery of a fine imposed for contravention of the above restrictions.[47] Furthermore, those restrictions do not affect restrictions which may arise by virtue of any other Public, Private or Local Act and do not derogate from any right of action or other remedy, civil or criminal, in proceedings outside the present provisions on abstraction and impounding.[48] The present provisions also apply the rule against double jeopardy in relation to criminal offences.[49]

Protection against pollution

The functions of NRA are stated to include the protection from pollution of any waters, whether on the surface or underground, which belong to it or any water undertaker or from which it or any undertaker is authorised to take water.[50] That protection also extends to any reservoir owned or operated by NRA or any water undertaker, as well as any underground strata from which it or any water undertaker is authorised to abstract water.[51] Directly related to this statement of function is the authorisation that may be given to NRA by the Secretary of State for the Environment or the Minister of Agriculture for the compulsory purchase of land for the purposes of or in connection with the execution of those functions.[52]

Where it appears to NRA that any poisonous, noxious or polluting matter or any solid waste matter is likely to enter, or to be or to have been present in, any controlled waters, it is empowered to carry out various works or operations, whether or not the foregoing powers of compulsory purchase have been used.[53] "Controlled waters" are defined[54] to include relevant territorial waters, coastal waters, inland freshwaters and ground waters. Although NRA has powers in this context, they cannot be used to impede or prevent the making of a discharge to controlled waters under a consent granted by Part III of the Act.[55]

The true scope of the present powers under section 161 can be seen in relation to the range of works and operations that may be undertaken in almost any appropriate location. In the first place, if matter appears likely to enter any controlled waters, works and operations may be undertaken for the purpose of preventing it from doing so. Secondly, if matter appears to be or to have been present in any controlled waters, works and operations can be undertaken for the purpose of removing or disposing of it, remedying or mitigating any pollution caused by its presence in the waters or (so far as it is reasonably practicable to do

[46] *Ibid.* s.39. *Cf.* n.96, *supra.*
[47] *Ibid.* s.70.
[48] *Ibid.*
[49] *Ibid.* (Interpretation Act 1978, s.18).
[50] Water Resources Act s.3(2)(a).
[51] *Ibid.* subs.(2)(b), (c).
[52] *Ibid.* s.154.
[53] *Ibid.* s.161.
[54] *Ibid.* s.104.
[55] *Ibid.* s.161(2).

so) restoring the waters, including any dependent flora and fauna, to the state they were in immediately before the matter became present in the waters.[56] Wide powers of entry for these and various other similar purposes are provided by the Act.[57]

Expenses reasonably incurred by NRA in undertaking these works and operations are recoverable. However, the power of recovery here is not referable to anyone who is the owner or occupier of particular land. In fact, the cost recovery powers operate, as the case may be, against any person who caused or knowingly permitted the matter to be present at a place where, in the opinion of NRA, it was likely to enter controlled waters, or to be present in those waters.[58] Accordingly, the recovery of costs will be dependent on proof of a person's active operation, without any need to prove intention or negligence or that, having control over any subject land or operation so as to be in a position to stop matter entering controlled waters, such a person failed to exert that control.[59]

In addition to these anti-pollution powers, NRA has powers to construct and maintain drains, sewers, watercourses, catchpits and other works for the purpose of intercepting, treating or disposing of any foul water arising or flowing on land in its ownership or over which it has easements or rights.[60]

Drought

The statutory regulation of drought situations is divided between the Water Resources Act and the Water Industry Act. While the provisions of the former Act are the more directly apposite, the latter Act provides a complementary regime, dealing with measures to prevent waste[61] and temporary hosepipe bans,[62] as well as powers of entry to premises.[63] The Water Resources Act, on the other hand, provides a series of provisions[64] built around the drought order as a means of regulation and control. These provisions will be resorted to, usually when arrangements made between the water undertakers and NRA can no longer accommodate the relevant shortages of water.[65]

Drought orders

Provision is made in the Water Resources Act[66] for drought orders, comprising "ordinary" drought orders and "emergency" drought orders. It is open to a water undertaker or NRA to apply to the Secretary of State for the making of an

[56] *Ibid.* subs.(1).
[57] *Ibid.* ss.169–173, Sched. 20.
[58] *Ibid.* s.161(3).
[59] *Alphacell Ltd v. Woodward* [1972] A.C. 824 and *Price v. Cromack* [1975] 1 W.L.R. 988, respectively.
[60] Water Resources Act, s.162(1).
[61] Water Industry Act 1991, s.75.
[62] *Ibid.* s.76.
[63] *Ibid.* s.170.
[64] ss.73–81.
[65] Water Resources Act, s.20.
[66] *See* n.64, *supra.*

ordinary drought order. The Secretary of State must be "... satisfied that, by reason of an exceptional shortage of rain, a serious deficiency of supplies of water in any area exists or is threatened ..."[67] Procedures governing drought orders are described elsewhere in the Act, requiring publication of draft orders in local newspapers, and opportunities to make representations being given to local authorities, various interested individuals and public agencies.[68] Despite this elaborate procedure, it is noticeable that the Act simply indicates that a drought order shall not be made by the Secretary of State except on an application by NRA or the water undertaker supplying water to the area in question. The process is therefore without any facility for consultation between or collaboration with neighbouring undertakers, or even NRA itself.[69] The only apparent statutory gesture here arises from another provision of the Act[70] by which NRA is under a duty to have particular regard to, *inter alia*, the duties of any water undertaker.

Various matters may be provided for in an order that comes into effect, in each case through the medium of a statutory instrument. The matters provided for are widely defined so that, for example, a water undertaker may be authorised to take water from any source specified in the order, subject to any specified conditions or restrictions, while NRA may be authorised to discharge water to any place specified in the order.[71] An order may have effect even to restrict or prevent the taking of water where a person is otherwise entitled to take water by virtue of rights at common law or by statute.[72] Failure to comply with the requirements of an order is an offence punishable summarily or on indictment.[73]

There are broad similarities in relation to the making of emergency drought orders, although in this case the Secretary of State is also obliged to be satisfied that "... the deficiency is such as to be likely to impair the economic or social well-being of persons in the area".[74] The provisions of an emergency drought order are comparable with those for ordinary drought orders, but it should be noted that any such order obtained on an application from a water undertaker may contain provision "... authorising the water undertaker to prohibit or limit the use of water for such purposes as the water undertaker thinks fit", and for the supply of water by stand-pipes or water tanks.[75] However, compared with the ordinary drought order, compensation rights are limited.[76] Any emergency order has a life of three months, but this is subject to extension by the Secretary of State.[77]

Matters of compensation are dealt with through a division of the provisions

[67] Water Resources Act, s.73(1).
[68] *Ibid.* Sched. 8.
[69] *Ibid.* s.73(3).
[70] *Ibid.* s.15.
[71] *Ibid.* s.74(1), (2).
[72] *Ibid.* s.77(2).
[73] *Ibid.* s.80.
[74] *Ibid.* s.73(2)(b).
[75] *Ibid.* s.75(2)(b), (c).
[76] *Ibid.* s.79, Sched. 9.
[77] *Ibid.* s.75(3).

between, on the one hand, all drought orders and, on the other, ordinary drought orders.[78] In the case of all drought orders, compensation in respect of entry upon or occupation or use of land is made by the applicant for the order, for loss or damage sustained by reason of entry upon, occupation of or use of the land.[79] In the case of an ordinary drought order, compensation in respect of the taking of water from a source, or its taking from a source otherwise than in accordance with a restriction or obligation which has been suspended or modified, is made by the applicant for the order for loss or damage sustained by reason of the taking of the water.[80]

The Supply of Water

The water undertakers

The appointment and regulation of the undertakers is provided for by Part II of the Water Industry Act 1991. A company may be appointed as a water undertaker by the Secretary of State or, in accordance with his general authorisation, the Director-General of Water Services, whose primary responsibility is regulation of the activities of the water and sewerage undertakers under section 1 of the Act of 1991.[81] The terms of any such appointment are set out in an instrument of appointment, including the "water supply area" to be served by the undertaker. Although specific powers associated with a company's water supply functions will be found in the memorandum and articles of association,[82] general powers for present purposes are to be found in the relevant legislation.[83] It is of course assumed from the instrument of appointment for a company that it will carry out its water supply and related functions in its own area. However, the company may be able to operate in the area of other undertakers, subject to limitations affecting the property and works of the other undertakers.[84] Undertakers have an explicit right to exercise their powers both within and outside their respective areas.[85] Contrast this position with that relating to compulsory works orders, where the section fails to refer to such orders being able to be exercised outside the undertaker's area.[86]

78 *Ibid.* Sched. 9, paras. (1) and (2).
79 *Ibid.* para. (1).
80 *Ibid.* para. (2).
81 Water Industry Act, s.6(1). As to functions in connection with the resolution of certain disputes, see s.30A.
82 Statutory Water Companies Act 1991, ss.11–13.
83 *Ibid.* s.1.
84 Water Industry Act, Sched. 13.
85 *Ibid.* s.192(3).
86 *Ibid.* s.167.

Private water supplies

Private supplies comprise any supply provided otherwise than by a water undertaker.[87] Included in the definition is water abstracted from a source on the premises on which it is used or consumed. Regulations made under the Water Industry Act—the Private Water Supplies Regulations 1991[88]—deal with the wholesomeness of supplies and prescribe the monitoring of supplies to be undertaken by local authorities. The Drinking Water Inspectorate, as technical assessor to the Secretary of State, is responsible for checking that the local authorities are complying with the requirements under the Regulations.

It is the task of the local authorities to identify private supplies in their area and to allocate each supply to one of the 11 classes specified in the Regulations.[89] The Regulations[90] prescribe legal standards for private water supplies, although there are circumstances in which they may be relaxed.[91] However, action may be necessary to improve a private supply, in which case statutory powers are available to the local authority. The principal powers are those under the Water Industry Act,[92] although others powers exist under the Local Government and Housing Act 1989 and the Public Health Act 1936. Under the former Act, the quality of a private supply may be such that a property is deemed to be unfit for human habitation. In these circumstances, the local authority may serve a compulsory repair notice or a demolition or closing order, or even include the property in a clearance order.[93] Under the Public Health Act, local authority powers may be used where a water supply is, or is considered likely to become, so polluted as to be prejudicial to health.[94]

Water undertakers' supplies

It is the duty of every undertaker under section 37 of the Water Industry Act to develop and maintain an efficient and economical system of water supply within its area, and to ensure that arrangements have been made for providing a supply to premises and making a supply available. The duty here is drawn very broadly, suggesting that it is not amenable to enforcement through the order of mandamus under R.S.C., Ord. 53. Despite the appearance of the remedy's non-availability where discretionary powers are in issue, in cases such as *Padfield v. Minister of Agriculture*[95] and *R. v. Hanley Revising Barrister*[96] the foregoing duty under section 37 set around with broader, discretionary issues falls into the mould of statutory duties subject (initially at least) to administrative control only. This is the case in

[87] *Ibid.* s.93.
[88] S.I. 1991 No. 2790.
[89] Department of the Environment Circular 24/91, para. 2.
[90] S.I. 1991 No. 2790, Pt. II.
[91] Water Resources Act, s.48(2), but subject to Sched. 7, para. 2.
[92] Water Industry Act, ss.77–82 (covered later in the present chapter).
[93] *cf.* n.62, *infra.*
[94] s.140.
[95] [1968] A.C. 997.
[96] [1912] 3 K.B. 518, *per* Darling J. at 529.

relation to section 37 and a variety of other duties in this legislation: enforcement is by reference to a special regime to be found in sections 18–22 of the present Act. Each undertaker is obliged, by section 86A, to establish a procedure for dealing with complaints about supply.

Enforcement orders

Confirmation that the enforcement of a number of the statutory requirements is by reference to an exclusive regime in the hands of the Secretary of State and, for some purposes, the Director-General of Water Services, is found in the Act.[97] The exclusivity of the enforcement process undoubtedly eliminates third party challenge through judicial review under R.S.C., Ord. 53. On the other hand, the duties that are enforceable under the Act—section 37 in particular—are often widely defined, and probably go beyond anything that would be legally enforceable in other circumstances.

At the outset, the Secretary of State (or the Director) must be satisfied that there has been contravention of any one of a number of requirements, including any condition of a company's appointment or any statutory requirement enforceable under section 18 where the Secretary of State (or the Director) is the enforcing authority.[98] If so satisfied, there is a duty to proceed to enforcement. However, there is no requirement that an enforcement order should be made or that a provisional enforcement order should be confirmed if the Secretary of State (or Director) be satisfied that there are only trivial contraventions involved, that reliable undertakings to comply have been forthcoming or that overriding duties under Part I of the Act preclude the making of any enforcement order.[99]

The Act provides for a final and a provisional enforcement order. The provisional order is essentially anticipatory, to the extent that any person is likely to sustain loss or damage as a consequence of a failure to comply with statutory requirements, for example, before a final order can be made.[1] Such an order has immediate effect and endures for a maximum period of three months[2] unless other requirements have been complied with.[3] Any final order may not be made and any provisional order may not be confirmed until various publicity and notification requirements are satisfied and any resulting representations or objections considered.[4]

The facility to acquire information for enforcement purposes is expressly provided for by the Act, but only in so far as it appears to the Secretary of State or the Director that a corporate water undertaker is contravening or may have

[97] Water Industry Act, s.18(8).
[98] *Ibid.* subs.(1).
[99] *Ibid.* s.19. As to undertakings that may be sufficient to fulfil E.C. requirements leaving reserve powers of enforcement under the Act, see *R. v. Secretary of State for the Environment, ex p. Friends of the Earth Ltd*, *The Times*, April 4, 1994.
[1] Water Industry Act, s.18(3).
[2] *Ibid.* subs.(7).
[3] *Ibid.* subs.(4).
[4] *Ibid.* s.20.

contravened any condition of appointment or any statutory or other requirement enforceable under section 18,[5] such as the general duty to maintain a water supply system.[6] By notice, the water undertaker can be compelled to provide any information sought.[7]

Reference was made previously to final and provisional orders. Both the Secretary of State and the Director are required to comply with notification requirements before a final order is made or a provisional order is confirmed.[8] However, the notification requirement is limited and does not extend to those agencies who might otherwise have claimed to be statutory consultees, such as NRA or local authorities. As a result of the notification process, the Secretary of State or the Director, as the case may be, is obliged to consider any representations or objections duly made before proceeding to a decision.

When an enforcement order is in force, any company to which it relates and which is aggrieved by the order may challenge its legality before the High Court within a period of 42 days on certain specified grounds.[9] If the High Court is satisfied that the order is beyond the powers provided by section 18 or that a company is substantially prejudiced by a failure to comply with the procedures found in section 20, the order may be quashed.[10]

The Act creates a statutory duty, owed to the person who may be affected by contravention of an enforcement order, binding on the subject company and enforceable to the extent that the plaintiff has sustained loss or damage.[11] In any proceedings for these purposes, the company may rely on the defence that it took all reasonable steps and exercised all due diligence to avoid contravention of the order.[12] Despite the availability of proceedings for breach of statutory duty, the Secretary of State or the Director, as the case may be, can take enforcement action by seeking an injunction or any other appropriate relief.[13]

Performance standards

The Secretary of State is empowered by the Act[14] to make regulations prescribing performance standards. Perhaps significantly, the regulations may prescribe the extent to which breaches of Part III of the Act on water supply constitute a breach of the section 37 duty described previously. The added significance of this provision is seen in the context of the enforcement powers available under the Act, which were examined above.

[5] *Ibid.* s.203(1).
[6] *Ibid.* s.37.
[7] *Ibid.* s.203(2).
[8] *Ibid.* s.20(1). *Cf.* s.195(2)(c).
[9] *Ibid.* s.21(1).
[10] *Ibid.* subs.(2).
[11] *Ibid.* s.22(1), (2).
[12] *Ibid.* subs.(3).
[13] *Ibid.* subss.(4), (5).
[14] *Ibid.* ss.38 and 39. See Water Supply and Sewerage Services (Customer Service Standards) Regulations 1989 (S.I. 1989 No. 1147), as amended by S.I. 1989 No. 1383 and *cf.* s.38A on information about performance standards.

Domestic water supply

For a variety of purposes, including differential charging rates for domestic water supply and the water undertaker's statutory duty[15] to connect its mains to premises for domestic use, *inter alia*, the term "domestic purposes" is defined by the Act to refer to drinking, washing, cooking, central heating and sanitary purposes.[16] Significantly, the legislation makes no reference to any need for a water supply to be made to "domestic premises", so that use of a supply of water may be for domestic purposes in premises other than a dwelling. It was held in *Metropolitan Water Board v. Avery*[17] that water supplied to the licensee of a public house where luncheons were served was used for domestic purposes. Lord Atkinson considered that

> "... water supplied for domestic purposes would mean water supplied to satisfy or help satisfy the needs, or perform or help in performing services, which, according to the ordinary habits of civilised life, are commonly satisfied and performed in people's homes, as distinguished from those needs and services which are satisfied or performed outside those homes and are not connected with, nor incidental to, the occupation of them."[18]

Where plans are submitted to a local authority for approval under the Building Regulations in respect of the construction of a house, the authority is obliged to reject those plans unless it appears that satisfactory provision is made for the supply of wholesome water to the occupants, sufficient for their domestic purposes.[19] Matters of water quality are dealt with later in the present chapter but, for the moment, it should be noted that wholesomeness of water for most domestic purposes is defined by regulation.[20]

Whatever the premises, the Water Industry Act[21] defines the varieties of pipe that may be used in fulfilment of the water supply duty. A water main is a pipe vested in a water undertaker for the purpose of making a general supply of water available to customers or potential customers, as opposed to particular customers. A trunk main, on the other hand, is a water main used by a water undertaker to convey water from a source of supply to a filter or reservoir, or to convey water in bulk. Finally, a service pipe is so much of a pipe as is connected with a water main for the purpose of supplying premises. Any such pipe will comprise two parts: the communication pipe in the street and the service pipe on the premises receiving the supply, the supply pipe.

[15] Water Industry Act, s.45.
[16] *Ibid.* s.218.
[17] [1914] A.C. 118.
[18] *Ibid.* at 126, 127.
[19] Building Act 1984, s.25.
[20] Water Supply (Water Quality) Regulations 1989 (S.I. 1989 No. 1147), reg. 3(2), (3). *Cf.* Water Industry Act, s.93(1).
[21] s.219(1).

A water undertaker is able to disconnect a service pipe or otherwise cut off a water supply to any premises if it is reasonable for the purpose of carrying out "necessary works"[22] by virtue of statutory authority. The power also extends to a reduction of supply.[23] Except in case of emergencies, reasonable notice must be given to the consumer and the undertaker is obliged to execute the works with reasonable dispatch, failing which the consumer may pursue an action against the undertaker for any loss or damage sustained.[24]

Fulfilment of the general duty to provide a water supply for its area by virtue of section 37 may be anticipated by a requirement from an owner, an occupier or a local authority for the water undertaker to furnish a water main to facilitate a domestic supply. Again, any breach of the duty is actionable at the initiative of the person who sustains loss or damage, although there is a defence in so far as the undertaker can show that it took all reasonable steps and exercised all due diligence to avoid the breach.[25] Among the prerequisites that will trigger this duty[26] is a financial condition that allows the undertaker to proceed on the basis of a payment reflecting the extra costs of provision. In the case of owners and occupiers, the water undertaker may demand security in advance in respect of the works for provision of the main.[27] Detailed prescriptions are provided by the Act to enable a calculation of the amount due from the requisitioner to the water undertaker, including an identification of those costs "reasonably incurred" in providing the water main.[28]

Domestic mains connections

An owner or occupier may by notice require an undertaker to connect its water main to premises for the purpose of facilitating a domestic supply.[29] This duty extends to the connection of a service pipe to any main, which is neither a trunk nor a water main, to be used for the supply of water for non-domestic purposes.[30] The undertaker is able to respond to any notice, subject to conditions stipulated by the Act.[31] Failure to comply with the present statutory duty is actionable by any owner or occupier who has sustained loss or damage as the result of a breach of the duty. There is, however, a defence in so far as the undertaker can show that he has taken all reasonable steps and exercised all due diligence to avoid the breach.[32] On the analogy of the defence of "reasonable excuse", it seems likely that the undertaker may avoid liability here in respect of those matters or occurrences that are genuinely beyond its control. Elsewhere in this Part of the

[22] Note the extension of this term to bodies other than water undertakers: Water Industry Act, s.93(1).
[23] *Ibid.* s.60(1).
[24] *Ibid.* subss.(3)–(5).
[25] *Ibid.* s.41.
[26] *Ibid.* subs.(1).
[27] *Ibid.* s.42.
[28] *Ibid.* s.43.
[29] *Ibid.* s.45. As to the nature of ownership or occupation required here, see subs.(1).
[30] *Ibid.* s.45(2).
[31] *Ibid.* ss.46, 47 and 51.
[32] *Ibid.* s.45(4), (5).

Act,[33] there is a specification of some of the circumstances in which an undertaker may be liable for breach of duty, referable to time limits for the discharge of the statutory duty.

The domestic supply duty

Once the connection of a supply pipe has occurred, as previously indicated, the Act goes on the prescribe the water undertaker's general duty to provide "... such a supply of water as (so far as those premises are concerned) is sufficient for domestic purposes ...".[34] The domestic supply duty will apply where particular conditions apply, such as the making of a demand for domestic supply, unless certain exceptions apply, as where, for example, the water undertaker has relied on its statutory powers of disconnection.[35] Breach of the duty again entitles the person to whom the duty is owed to claim compensation from the undertaker, subject to the defence that that undertaker took all reasonable steps and exercised all due diligence to avoid the breach.[36] Where the undertaker lawfully exercises his power of disconnection referred to previously as a response to contamination of supply, for example, the supply duty is suspended.[37]

The non-domestic supply duty

A water undertaker's duty in relation to non-domestic supplies is heavily circumscribed and applies to any "new" supply only in so far as that undertaker is able to avoid unreasonable expenditure or the risk of being unable to satisfy existing and future domestic and non-domestic supply obligations. Assuming that these constraints can be avoided, the undertaker will be obliged to respond to a request for non-domestic supplies from the owner or occupier of premises to be supplied.[38] The foregoing constraints will not be available to the undertaker as a means of avoiding the non-domestic supply duty where requests are made for increases in existing supplies. However, it may be argued that an increase in an existing supply may be so excessive, as a matter of fact and degree, as to constitute a proposal for a "new" supply, so attracting the opportunity for the undertaker to resist on the above grounds of unreasonable expenditure or prejudice to future supply obligations. As with the domestic supply duty, there are situations where the non-domestic supply duty may not apply because the undertaker seeks lawfully to exercise its power of disconnection, for example.[39] If the duty is to be performed but subject to terms and conditions, any dispute concerning those terms and conditions will be resolved by the Director-General of Water Services, unless the matter is referred by him to arbitration.[40]

[33] *Ibid.* s.51.
[34] *Ibid.* s.52(1). As to the meaning of "premises" here, see subss.(3), (4).
[35] *Ibid.* subss.(2) and (6), respectively.
[36] *Ibid.* s.54.
[37] *Ibid.* s.52(8).
[38] *Ibid.* s.55.
[39] *Ibid.* subs.(8).
[40] *Ibid.* s.56.

In addition to the above non-domestic supply duty, a water undertaker is also obliged to supply water at the request of any sewerage undertaker, highway authority or local authority, for a variety of relevant purposes. Those purposes are, respectively, the cleansing of sewers and drains, the watering of highways and the supply of public pumps, baths or wash-houses.[41] Other provisions in the Act[42] place a duty on water undertakers to supply water for fire-fighting and to provide fire hydrants at the request of owners or occupiers of factories or other places of business.

Constancy and pressure

A water undertaker is subject to a duty to ensure that water in its water mains and other pipes used to supply water for domestic purposes, including those to which fire hydrants are attached, is laid on constantly and is at such pressure that the water can reach the topmost storey of every building in its area.[43] The duty extends only to the undertaker's own water mains and other pipes and is enforceable by virtue of section 18.[44] Additionally, breach of this duty is an offence, although the undertaker has a defence if able to prove that all reasonable steps were taken and all due diligence exercised in order to avoid commission of the offence.[45]

Liability for escape

The Act[46] imposes strict liability on a water undertaker where an escape of water, however caused, from a pipe vested in that undertaker causes loss or damage. This strict liability regime is one that avoids the problem of establishing negligence. A further and equally significant provision occurs in the New Roads and Street Works Act 1991.[47] Here, it is provided that an undertaker is obliged to compensate the street or any other relevant authority in respect of any damage or loss suffered by the authority in their capacity as such, as well as any other person having apparatus in the street, in respect of any expense reasonably incurred in making good damage to that apparatus. The "events" included for the purpose of this provision include the discharge of water from pipes. The undertaker's liability here arises whether or not the damage was attributable to negligence and notwithstanding that action had been taken in pursuance of a statutory duty. Significantly, it is stated by the Water Industry Act[48] that the undertaker shall not incur strict liability under that Act for any loss or damage sustained by a person

[41] *Ibid.* s.59.
[42] *Ibid.* ss.57 and 58.
[43] *Ibid.* s.65.
[44] *Ibid.* subs.(1). *Cf.* n.97, *supra.*
[45] *Ibid.* subss.(10), (11).
[46] *Ibid.* s.209.
[47] s.82.
[48] s.209(3).

with a right to compensation under the above provision of the New Roads and Street Works Act. What, therefore, is the relative status and effect of the two provisions? The predecessor provision of the New Roads and Street Works Act, section 18 of the Public Utilities Street Works Act 1950, was in issue before the House of Lords in *Department of Transport v. North West Water Authority.*[49] The question at issue was whether the section had the effect of imposing strict liability on the water authority for a nuisance caused by them in the course of performing their statutory duty (to supply water under pressure), so that there may be liability in nuisance notwithstanding the absence of negligence. It was concluded by the House of Lords that the provision was not intended to alter the existing law that a body is not liable for a nuisance attributable to its performance of a statutory duty, even though the statute makes it liable expressly, or does not exempt it from liability. Significantly, it was further concluded that the burst in question occurred in the discharge of the authority's *duty* to supply water under pressure. The provision "... is simply a non-exoneration clause of general application to undertakers acting in the exercise of a power but not in the performance of a duty . . ."[50]

Bulk supply

The Water Industry Act[51] empowers every water undertaker to provide supplies of water in bulk, in other words, to supply water for distribution by the undertaker taking the supply.[52] A disputed refusal to supply in bulk may be referred to and dealt with by the Director-General of Water Services. The statutory powers available for this purpose[53] permit resolution of the dispute on the basis of a wide discretion as to terms and conditions for supply, but only where the Director-General considers that it is necessary or expedient for water supply purposes that a supply should be made and that such a supply will not be facilitated by agreement.

Water mains

The term "water main" refers to any pipe vested in a water undertaker used for the purpose of making a general supply of water available to customers at large.[54] By way of contrast, a service pipe comprises two parts: the communication pipe in the street and the service pipe on the premises receiving the supply, the supply pipe. The undertaker is empowered to insist that separate service pipes are provided to a house or other building under separate occupation.[55]

Each water undertaker is obliged to keep and maintain a record of the location of every resource main, water main or discharge pipe, as well as any other

[49] [1984] A.C. 336.
[50] *Ibid. Per* Lord Fraser at 360.
[51] s.217(6).
[52] Water Industry Act, s.219(1).
[53] *Ibid.* s.40. As to the variation and termination of bulk supply agreements, see s.40A.
[54] *Ibid.* s.219(1).
[55] *Ibid.* s.64. *Cf.* s.170, prescribing powers of entry.

underground works, other than a service pipe.[56] The duty here is enforceable under section 18, described previously.

A water undertaker has various powers to maintain pipes in, under or over any street.[57] This power also extends to the maintenance of pipes in any land comprised elsewhere than in a street.[58] Wherever references to maintenance occur in relation to pipes, this is taken to include the process of cleansing.[59] Apart from maintenance, the foregoing provisions extend to the laying of pipes and their inspection, adjustment, repair or alteration, as well as the execution of any works "requisite for or incidental to, these purposes".[60]

Further powers are conferred on a water undertaker supplying water to premises where, for example, there is reason for the undertaker to believe that water in any pipe connected with any main or other pipe is being, or is likely to be, contaminated before use. In an emergency, the pipe may be disconnected, while in any other case the consumer will be notified of necessary remedial action.[61]

Whether a dwelling-house is fit for human habitation in the opinion of a local housing authority may be determined by reference to its failure to meet one or more requirements and to the fact that, by reason of that failure, the dwelling-house is not reasonably suitable for occupation. Among those requirements is the need for an adequate piped supply of wholesome water.[62]

Waste, misuse and contamination of water

Any person who causes or allows any underground water to run to waste from any well, borehole or other work, or abstracts from any well, borehole or other work water in excess of his reasonable requirements, commits an offence. There are various exemptions provided for, including action taken to test the quality of water. If a conviction occurs in other circumstances provided for, the court may make a variety of orders, including an order to prevent the waste of water. NRA enjoys powers to act in default if there is failure to comply with such an order.[63]

A second offence in this area arises where the defendant is guilty of any act or neglect whereby the water in any "waterworks" (defined to include any spring, well, adit, borehole, service reservoir or tank, and any main or other pipe or conduit of a water undertaker) which is used or likely to be used for human consumption or domestic purposes, or for manufacturing food or drink for human consumption, is polluted or likely to be polluted. Again, the Act provides for a number of exemptions from the offence.[64]

[56] *Ibid.* s.198. As to the meaning of the term "discharge pipe", see s.192(1).
[57] *Ibid.* s.158.
[58] *Ibid.* s.159.
[59] *Ibid.* s.192(2).
[60] *Ibid.* ss.158 and 159.
[61] *Ibid.* s.75.
[62] Housing Act 1985, s.604(1). *Cf.* provision for service of a defective premises notice under the Building Act 1984, s.76.
[63] Water Industry Act, s.71.
[64] *Ibid.* s.72.

A third offence applies to an owner or occupier of premises provided with a water supply by an undertaker. The offence arises if that person intentionally or negligently causes or suffers any "water fittings" (defined to include pipes (other than water mains), taps, cocks and valves, among other facilities for supplying water)[65] for which he has responsibility to be or remain defective, as a result of which water in a main or other pipe connected to the premises is likely to be contaminated by the return of substances to the main or pipe, or water supplied to the premises is likely to be contaminated before use, or is or is likely to be wasted, misused or unduly consumed. Commission of the offence entitles recovery by the water undertaker of a reasonable amount, reflecting the value of the water wasted, misused or improperly consumed as a consequence of the offence.[66]

Regulatory support in the present context is also provided by the Act, which empowers the Secretary of State to make regulations for the prevention of contamination, waste and misuse of water. Breach of any such regulations (which may also relate to water fittings) may attract default powers in favour of a water undertaker or local authority. The regulations may indicate that breach of any particular regulation constitutes a summary offence.[67]

Finally, in the present context, additional measures beyond the regulation-making power in section 74 are provided by the Act, allowing any water undertaker, in a variety of stated circumstances, to act to prevent the contamination or waste of water. Normally, the undertaker would be obliged to provide notification of measures to be taken here, but an emergency may justify dispensation with this requirement. The undertaker may also take action in default and recover any costs reasonably incurred.[68] Allied to this power is the availability of criminal enforcement where a person, without the consent of a water undertaker, attaches a pipe or other apparatus to any water main or pipe supplying premises.[69]

Quality Standards

Drinking water quality

Water quality standards now relate to water as used for a wide variety of purposes, one of the most important of which is drinking. Elsewhere in the present work, reference is made to legal standards for waters devoted, *inter alia*, to fisheries and bathing. The establishment, implementation and enforcement of quality standards for drinking water necessitates reference to European Community law, together with municipal statute and common law.

[65] *Ibid.* s.93.
[66] *Ibid.* s.73.
[67] *Ibid.* s.74.
[68] *Ibid.* s.75.
[69] *Ibid.* s.174(3).

European Community legal requirements

Two sets of Community directives merit attention for present purposes: Directive 75/440[69a] and 79/869,[69b] on the quality of surface water to be abstracted for use as drinking water, together with methods of measurement and frequency of sampling and analysis, and Directive 80/778,[69c] on the quality of water intended for human consumption. The requirements of these Directives demand an adequate response in municipal law: in English law, this involves a series of detailed statutory provisions, carried into effect mainly through the medium of subordinate legislation.

Surface water quality

Directive 75/440 requires that water which is abstracted for the purpose of drinking should conform to labelled categories A1, A2 and A3, referable to the level of treatment needed to bring such water to drinking quality. The lower "extreme" is A3, indicating that water falling into this category would require extensive treatment and disinfection. The Directive stipulates that water falling below this standard or level should not be abstracted for drinking.[70] At the other end of the scale, A1 level indicates that minimal treatment and disinfection will be required. The Directive sets down a number of mandatory limits for drinking water quality where 25 per cent. of samples must comply with those limits. Other, less stringent, limits are set by the Directive, requiring compliance in 90 per cent. of samples.[71] Despite these detailed prescriptions, the Directive does not require detailed legislative definition of sample points, although there is a need for precise definition of quality values for each sampling point actually selected and used.[72]

The Water Resources Act[73] provides the authority for regulations prescribing standards for surface waters, supplemented by further provisions[74] which allow water quality objectives to be set, achieved and maintained. Having arrived at a classification of the quality of waters for the purpose of setting, achieving and maintaining water quality objectives, a framework is thereby provided for important regulatory functions in determining applications for consent to discharge effluents and other substances to controlled waters under the present Act.[75] The prescription of classifications may be undertaken by the Secretary of State in relation to "any description of controlled waters" and by reference to quite general criteria referable to any one or more of the following: the purposes

[69a] [1975] O.J. L194.
[69b] [1979] O.J. L271.
[69c] [1980] O.J. L229.
[70] Art.4. This provision includes an improvement programme for such water.
[71] Art.5.
[72] Case C–237/90, *E.C. Commission v. Germany*: [1994] Env.L.R. 1.
[73] s.82.
[74] Water Resources Act, ss.83 and 84.
[75] *Ibid.* s.88, Sched. 10.

for which the waters are to be suitable, the presence or absence of particular substances in the waters and any specific requirements relating to other characteristics of the waters.[76]

The quality values found in the Directive are now found in the Surface Waters (Classification) Regulations 1989.[77] The threefold classification system prescribes detailed concentrations of a number of critical substances. Elsewhere it is stipulated that, in carrying out its statutory function to supply water for drinking, washing, cooking or food production, a water undertaker shall not supply water from any source which consists of or includes raw water without disinfection and further treatment as defined by Directive 75/440.

The protection of human health is the essential purpose behind the second major directive in this area, Directive 80/778, which prescribes quality standards where water is to be used for drinking and the manufacture of food and drink.

Drinking water quality

Directive 80/778 is concerned with standards applicable where water is used for drinking and food and drink manufacture. Any source devoted to the extraction of such water must be capable of producing water for present purposes that requires minimal treatment only. Sampling must be undertaken at points to be identified by the competent agency in each Member State and must be at a point where the water is available to the consumer. There are numerous quality standards in the Directive, to be found in Annex I, while Annex II deals with monitoring and Annex III defines methods of water analysis. The standards in Annex I may be subject to derogation according to various criteria, including geological conditions and emergencies. Article 10(1) permits a Member State to authorise values in excess of the maximum permitted concentrations in emergencies. The European Court of Justice has construed the term "emergencies" as meaning urgent situations in which the competent authorities are required to cope suddenly with difficulties in water supply for human consumption. Supplies exceeding the maximum permitted concentrations are allowed only for a limited period, corresponding to the time normally required to restore normal supplies. Ultimately, it is for the national courts of a Member State to decide whether its domestic legislation contains provisions restricting the possibilities for derogation as anticipated by the Directive.[78]

The requirements of the Directive were implemented originally under the Water Act 1989 and now by the Water Industry Act 1991. Under this legislation, the Water Supply (Water Quality) Regulations 1989[79] have been made. Among other things, the Regulations define standards of wholesomeness in respect of water supplied privately and by water undertakers for drinking, washing or

[76] *Ibid.* s.82(1).
[77] S.I. 1989 No. 1148.
[78] *Pretura Unificata Di Torino v. Persons Unknown* [1990] 1 C.M.L.R. 716. *Cf.* Case 237/90, *E.C. Commission v. Germany, supra.*
[79] S.I. 1989 No. 1147, as amended by S.I. 1991 No. 1837: note regs. 3 and 5 in particular.

cooking.[80] However, the Regulations also stipulate the circumstances in which wholesomeness standards may be relaxed. Relaxations are the responsibility of the Secretary of State for the Environment, but subject to restrictions. In any decision in this context, it is necessary for the Secretary of State to adhere to the constraint of time required to restore normal supplies, even though it is stipulated that any "relaxation" authorisation shall specify the date on which it ceases to have effect.[81]

Part II of the Regulations governing wholesomeness provides that water is to be regarded as being wholesome if it contains concentrations or values in respect of various properties, elements, organisms or substances which do not contravene prescribed maxima and, in some cases, minimum concentrations or values referred to principally by Annex I of the Directive. Part IV deals with monitoring through analysis of samples from consumers' taps. Water undertakers are required to identify, by reference to "water supply zones", so many suitably located taps such that samples will be representative of quality in each zone. The standard number of samples required is detailed by the Regulations. The treatment of water is dealt with in Part VI, and regulates the substances, processes and products that may be used by water undertakers in supplying water. Requirements for disinfection are defined, along with the treatment of surface water, and there is a prohibition on any abstraction for the supply of drinking water of water below category A3 under Directive 75/440, on the quality of surface water. Water undertakers are obliged to make certain categories of information available under Part VIII. Records must be prepared and maintained concerning the quality of water supplied in each water supply zone. Such information must be supplied to relevant local authorities, as well as being made available for public inspection. There is a further obligation to provide local authorities—and district health authorities—with information that may affect the health of residents. Finally, water undertakers are required to publish annual reports on water quality in their respective areas. Local authorities are also bound by certain obligations under the Regulations in relation to the quality of water supplied by the undertakers. Arrangements must be made, between a local authority and an undertaker, about the provision of information. Local authorities are also empowered to take such samples of water as may be reasonably required.

Municipal legal requirements

The foregoing provisions of the Water Supply (Water Quality) Regulations represent detailed implementation of European Community legal requirements via the statutory authority of the Water Industry Act 1991.[82] The Regulations were made under the predecessor to sections 67 and 69 of the Act. A water undertaker is under a duty, in supplying water for domestic or food production purposes to any premises, to supply only water which is wholesome "at the time

[80] As to the impact of E.C. directives on standards of wholesomeness, see *Cambridge Water Co. Ltd v. Eastern Counties Leatherwork Plc* [1993] Env.L.R. 287, *per* Mann L.J. at 289, C.A.

[81] Water Industry Act Pt. III, Chap. III, ss.67–86.

[82] *Ibid.*

of supply".[83] Water is to be regarded as wholesome where it complies with the standards specified in the Regulations.[84] The undertaker is also under a duty, so far as reasonably practicable, to ensure (in relation to any source or combination of sources from which there is provided a supply for domestic or food production purposes) that there is, in general, no deterioration in quality of water produced from the source or combination of sources. These duties are enforceable by the Secretary of State under section 18 of the Act.[85] The above provision refers to a supply to "any premises" of the consumer in conformity with the long-held view that the supplier's duty extends only to the consumer's premises but no further. However, the present duties extend to requiring an undertaker to secure the elimination, or reduction to a minimum, of any risk of contamination once a supply enters the consumer's premises.[86] If there is a risk that water would not meet statutory requirements for wholesomeness, in these circumstances the water undertaker is subject to specific duties to remedy the particular contamination.[87]

The supply of water unfit for human consumption

Where a water undertaker, by means of pipes, supplies water to any premises which is unfit for human consumption, an offence is committed which may be subject to summary proceedings or proceedings on indictment.[88] There is no reference to what is to be regarded as "unfit for human consumption" in the Act, although standards of wholesomeness may be indicative of the law's attitude to this offence, which was introduced under the influence of the controversy surrounding the water contamination at Camelford in Cornwall in 1988. It should be noted that, under the Water Supply (Water Quality) Regulations,[89] it is stated that water supplied to any premises for drinking, washing, cooking or food production purposes is to be regarded as being "unwholesome" if it contains concentrations of various substances in excess of prescribed concentrations. Arguably, this definition of "unwholesomeness" is restricted and therefore not conclusively indicative of unfitness. Such unfitness is likely to be of some considerable moment, taking the case beyond the process of "administrative" enforcement under section 18 of the Act. Proceedings for an offence under the section, which appears to be a strict liability offence, are limited to the Secretary of State and the DPP.[90]

[83] *Ibid.* s.68(1). *Cf.* subss.(2), (3) on the meaning of "at the time of supply".
[84] Water Supply (Water Quality) Regulations 1989, reg.3(2). *Cf.* reg.3(7) for the circumstances where water is to be regarded as unwholesome, and see *McColl v. Strathclyde Regional Council* [1984] J.P.L. 351, O.H. and Department of the Environment Circular 20/82 (Welsh Office Circular 33/82).
[85] See nn.97 *et seq.*, *supra.*
[86] Water Industry Act, s.68(3).
[87] Water Supply (Water Quality) Regulations 1989, reg.24(1).
[88] Water Industry Act 1991, s.70.
[89] Reg.3(7) and Sched. 2, Table C.
[90] Water Industry Act 1991, s.70(4). As to defences, see subs.(3).

Water waste, contamination and misuse

A series of provisions referred to previously in this chapter—sections 71–76 of the Water Industry Act—deal with these problems, in a variety of different ways.

For the purpose of dealing with any person who causes or allows any underground water to run to waste from any well, borehole or other work, or any person who abstracts in excess of reasonable requirements from the same sources, the Act creates what again appears to be an offence of strict liability, punishable as a result of summary proceedings.[91] On conviction, the court may order various remedial works which could include, for example, a requirement that a borehole be sealed. Failure to comply empowers NRA, without prejudice to any penalty that may be imposed for contempt of court, to apply to the court to execute the court's order and to recover the costs from the person convicted.[92]

Another offence arises where, through a person's act or neglect, water in "any waterworks" used or likely to be used for human consumption or domestic purposes, or for manufacturing food or drink for human consumption, is polluted or likely to be polluted.[93] The offence may be tried summarily or by way of indictment. Both in this and any other context in which the expression "domestic purposes" appears, that expression means "... drinking, washing, cooking, central heating and sanitary purposes ..." for which water is supplied to particular premises.[94]

Whereas the foregoing offences are probably offences of strict liability, a third offence refers to any owner or occupier of premises who, in receiving a water supply from an undertaker, intentionally or negligently "causes or suffers" any water fitting—defined to include pipes, taps, cocks, valves and meters, etc.[95]—for which he is responsible to be or remain so out of order, so in need of repair or so constructed or adapted, or to be so used, that certain consequences ensue.[96] Those consequences are defined[97] to include contamination and wasting of water supplied. The offence attracts summary conviction, as does a second offence in the same context: that of using water supplied to premises by a water undertaker for a purpose other than that for which it was supplied, unless the purpose is extinguishment of a fire.[98]

Complementary powers are conferred on the Secretary of State for the purpose of making regulations:

(a) to secure that water in an undertaker's main or pipe is not contaminated and that its quality is not prejudiced;
(b) to secure the same requirements for water in any pipe connected to such a main or pipe;

[91] *Ibid.* s.71.
[92] *Ibid.* subss.(5), (6).
[93] *Ibid.* s.72. As to the scope of "any waterworks", see subs.(5).
[94] *Ibid.* s.218.
[95] *Ibid.* s.93(1).
[96] *Ibid.* s.73.
[97] *Ibid.* subs.(1).
[98] *Ibid.* subs.(2).

(c) to prevent waste, undue consumption and misuse of water as it leaves the undertaker's pipes as a supply to premises; and
(d) to secure that water fittings installed and used by any person to whom a supply is made are safe and satisfy other performance standards.[99]

Any regulations relating to water fittings may make provision for a variety of requirements, including the penalty for contravention as a result of summary conviction. Such regulations may also make provision for modification of section 73 and its definition of offences of contaminating, wasting and misusing water, together with section 75 which (as will be seen below) describes various powers for the prevention of damage and the execution of measures to prevent contamination and waste. This power of modification permits detailed alignment between the two sets of provisions, in the light of requirements emerging from particular regulations made under the powers in section 74.

Considerable powers are given to a water undertaker by section 75, beyond any section 74 regulations, where that undertaker has reason to believe that:

(a) damage to persons or property is being or is likely to be caused by a damaged or defective water fitting;
(b) water in the undertaker's main or pipe is being or is likely to be contaminated by the return of any substance from the consumer's premises;
(c) water that has been supplied to premises is being or is likely to be contaminated prior to use; or
(d) water supplied or to be supplied is being or is likely to be wasted or (having regard to the purposes for which it is supplied) misused or unduly consumed.

If the undertaker is confronted by an emergency, the present provisions permit disconnection without notice. In any other situation, strict notice requirements apply and, in all cases, the undertaker has wide-ranging remedial powers, with the facility to recover any costs reasonably incurred.

If a water undertaker is of the opinion that there is an actual or threatened deficiency of water available for distribution and that that deficiency is "serious", the undertaker may impose a temporary hosepipe ban.[1] There are strict requirements for notification before the ban comes into force. Failure to comply with any prohibition or restriction for present purposes is subject to a penalty on summary conviction.

Legal liabilities for failure of wholesome supply

The incident at Camelford in Cornwall in 1988 concerned the introduction of 20 tonnes of aluminium sulphate into the system at a water treatment works. In criminal proceedings for public nuisance, the water undertaker was convicted.

[99] *Ibid.* s.74.
[1] *Ibid.* s.76.

While it seems clear that compensatory damages may be payable in proceedings for nuisance, whether public or private, it appears that any breach of duty to supply wholesome water will not, in these proceedings, give rise to exemplary or aggravated damages.[2]

There remains also the possibility of proceedings for breach of statutory duty. In *Read v. Croydon Corporation*[3] the failure of a wholesome supply led to the contraction of typhoid and a limitation by the court of the categories of plaintiff (in this case the ratepayer) who could be regarded as "beneficiaries" of the statutory duty. Such a restriction is likely to remain when it is borne in mind that the statutory duty is now far broader.[4] The scope of statutory liabilities is also significantly extended, in so far as a supplier, whether a water undertaker or private supplier, may be liable under the strict liability regime of the Consumer Protection Act 1987. The damage caused by an unwholesome supply may be compensated. Because water is a substance,[5] it is defined as "goods" and, as such, is a "product" under the Act. The fact that a supply is provided brings a supplier within the Act by virtue of the fact that a service is undertaken through which water may be consumed on the consumer's premises.

Even if water is not unwholesome, the water undertaker or other private supplier may be subject to a duty of care in negligence. If, for example, water supplied becomes poisonous on the consumer's premises because of its passage through lead pipes, the undertaker may be liable in negligence for failure to warn of the consequences of consumption. In these circumstances it has been said that ". . . the plaintiffs . . . [are] entirely dependent upon the supplier of the water to see that it [is] water which [is] not in its nature poisonous".[6]

Local authority functions

A district council or a London borough council is subject to a duty to take "all such steps as they consider appropriate" for keeping itself informed about the wholesomeness and sufficiency of water supplies provided to premises in the area, including every private supply.[7] The requirements here, which extend to directions from the Secretary of State to local authorities in connection with private supplies, may be extended by regulations.[8] Closely allied to local authority functions and duties are the provisions of the Water Supply (Water Quality) Regulations and, more particularly, the duty of any water undertaker to advise a local authority of any threat to a supply.[9] If a local authority considers that there is a threat to wholesomeness or supply, it is obliged to advise the water undertaker accordingly. Failure to provide remedial action to the satisfaction of the local authority empowers that authority to refer the matter to the Secretary of State

[2] *Gibbons v. South West Water Services Ltd* [1993] Env.L.R. 266.
[3] [1938] 4 All E.R. 631.
[4] Water Industry Act, s.68(1)(a).
[5] For the purposes of s.45(1) of the Act of 1987.
[6] Slesser L.J. in *Barnes v. Irwell Valley Water Board* [1938] 2 All E.R. 650 at 659.
[7] Water Industry Act 1991, s.77.
[8] See nn.83 *et seq., supra.*
[9] Reg.30(5)–(7).

who, no doubt, will consider the merits of enforcement action under section 18 of the Act.[10]

Where it is not practicable at reasonable cost for an undertaker to provide or maintain a supply of wholesome water to any particular premises in an area sufficient for domestic purposes, the local authority is subject to a duty to require the undertaker to provide a supply to the premises, otherwise than in pipes. The undertaker is able to recover costs from the local authority and, in turn, the authority may recover its costs from the owners or occupiers of the benefiting premises. The undertaker's duty is again enforceable under section 18 of the Act.[11]

Rights of entry are provided for local authorities, for a variety of purposes under section 84. Those purposes are as follows:

(a) to ascertain whether any breach of section 72 has occurred;[12]
(b) to ascertain whether, in respect of water fittings, any waste or misuse of water is occurring; and
(c) for the discharge of functions and responsibilities in relation to private supplies.

Functions in relation to private supplies

Each responsible authority has statutory powers to notify persons that information is reasonably required for the purpose of enabling discharge of statutory functions relating to private supplies.[13] The matter of private supplies has been examined previously,[14] but not the specific statutory powers available to the local authorities.[15]

Where a local authority is satisfied that premises are not receiving wholesome supplies for domestic or food production purposes, a notice may be served on the owners or occupiers of the premises requiring appropriate remedial action.[16] One possibility is that a water undertaker or "other person" may be required to supply water to the premises in question.[17] The procedures governing such notices indicate that private supply notices are subject to confirmation by the Secretary of State.[18] The local authority may take action in default if the notice is not complied with, and any costs reasonably incurred may be recovered from the owners or occupiers. Successive owners or occupiers of the premises will be bound by the notice if it has been registered as a local land charge.[19]

[10] Water Industry Act 1991, s.78.
[11] *Ibid.* s.79.
[12] See, n.93, *supra.*
[13] Water Industry Act, s.85.
[14] See n.87, *supra.*
[15] See n.92, *supra.*
[16] Water Industry Act, s.80. *Cf.* s.83 as to the nature of remedial action available.
[17] *Ibid.* subs.(6).
[18] *Ibid.* s.81.
[19] *Ibid.* s.82.

CHAPTER 2

SEWAGE AND EFFLUENT DISPOSAL

The Effluent Chain

The need to deal with large quantities of sewage, trade and other effluents may be best understood through an appreciation of the line that joins the point of generation, in the home or factory, for example, to the point of discharge. Although this final point in the effluent chain may be reached without any intermediate treatment of the effluent, leaving the aquatic environment to absorb the pollution, increasingly environmental laws and the E.C. directive concerning urban waste water treatment, Directive 91/271,[1] in particular, are requiring focus on a need for treatment with the aim of reducing the quantity of "raw" effluent that does reach the environment outside, beyond the point of discharge. The essential purposes of the law to be examined in this chapter are to contain, regulate and facilitate treatment of defined categories of effluent in the context of a division of legal responsibilities between the private and public "sectors". These purposes may be achieved in a variety of different ways, such as discharge (perhaps controversially) directly into the aquatic environment. However, the concern of the present chapter is with sewerage and drainage as a means of containing, regulating and treating effluent generated from a wide range of activity. Accordingly, the distinction between a sewer and a drain is critically important for present purposes.

Definitions

The essential distinction between a sewer and a drain to be drawn from the definitions found in the Public Health Act 1936[1a] is that while a drain is usually a pipe draining one building, a sewer is usually a pipe that drains more than one building. More specifically, a "drain" is defined by the foregoing provision of the Public Health Act as follows: ". . . a drain used for the drainage of one building or of any buildings or yards appurtenant to buildings within the same curtilage". On the other hand, the same provision goes on to say that a sewer ". . . does not include a drain as defined by this section but, save as aforesaid, includes all sewers and drains used for the drainage of buildings and yards appurtenant to buildings". Although a pipe may be serving as a drain or a sewer, the law does recognise other

[1] [1991] O.J. L135.
[1a] s.343(1).

means of effluent "conveyance", although if, say, the "conveyance" is a culvert, it must be functioning as a drain or sewer, as the case may be.[2] Bearing in mind the very specific statutory definition of a drain, it seems clear that a land drain is excluded, again by reference to matters of function.

Drains

Considerable difficulties occur in any attempt to determine the existence of a drain by reference to the foregoing statutory definition. Ultimately, the matter of whether there is "one building" or "buildings within the same curtilage" can only be a question of fact, taking account of a variety of factors, such as the unity of ownership and structure.[3] The High Court has decided that two cottages, occupied separately, amounted to a single building for drainage purposes, a decision influenced possibly by one owner's consent to the connection of drainage pipes leading to a sewer laid by the local authority. For this purpose at least, the appearance of the cottages was as an "enclosure" of dwellings with integrated drainage arrangements.[4]

Sewers

It should be noted that the definition here is prefaced by the word "include", allowing the inclusion of any conduit that falls naturally within the definition. Even a drain could fall within the definition, as long as it does not fall into the pre-existing definition of the term "drain" just examined. Reconstruction may, of course, lead to a change of status, so that what was once a sewer could become a drain.[5] However, even if a pipe no longer functions as a sewer because it has been sealed off, for example, it retains its status as a sewer[6]: "Once it is conceded that a sewer is a pipe to drain buildings, it becomes a sewer and in my judgment it remains a sewer in this case notwithstanding that the actual use has ceased."[7]

Assessment of "sewer functions" is clearly crucial in any determination of the question whether a pipe is a sewer. In practice, the question whether such a pipe will be adopted as a public sewer by a sewerage undertaker, with all the attendant legal obligations examined below, is dependent on a number of factors. The powers of vesting and adoption for present purposes are to be found in the Water Industry Act 1991.[8] Significantly, in deciding whether a declaration of adoption should be made, the undertaker is obliged to have regard to "all the circumstances", as well as a number of particular considerations, including the state of repair of the sewer. In these circumstances, a culvert acting as a sewer and which is out of repair may well remain unadopted.

[2] *British Railways Board v. Tonbridge and Malling District Council* (1981) 79 L.G.R. 565, C.A.
[3] *Weaver v. Family Housing Association (York) Ltd* (1975) 74 L.G.R. 255, H.L.
[4] *Cook v. Minion* [1979] J.P.L. 305.
[5] *Kershaw v. Smith* [1913] 2 K.B. 455.
[6] *Blackdown Properties v. Minister of Housing and Local Government* [1965] 2 All E.R. 345.
[7] *Ibid. per* Stamp J. at 348.
[8] ss.102 (adoption) and 179 (vesting).

Statutory Sewerage Undertakers

The Water Industry Act[9] provides for the appointment by the Secretary of State, or, with the consent of or in accordance with the Secretary of State's general authorisation, the Director-General of Water Services, of a limited company as a statutory sewerage undertaker. The terms of the appointment are laid out in an instrument of appointment indicating, *inter alia*, the area over which the undertaker will operate in the provision of sewerage services, defined to include "... the disposal of sewage and any other services which are required to be provided by a sewerage undertaker for the purpose of carrying out its functions".[10]

General duties

The sewerage undertaker is subject to a general duty to provide, improve, extend and empty its public sewers. The core of this duty is aimed at ensuring that the undertaker's area in particular is effectually drained.[11] In the performance of this duty, the undertaker must have regard to existing and future obligations to allow the discharge of trade effluent into its public sewers, as well as the need to provide for the disposal of such trade effluent.[12] The duty here is enforceable under section 18 of the Act[13] by the Secretary of State or the Director-General for Water Services. If there has been or is likely to be contravention of what is referred to as "any principal duty" (which includes the above duty, as well as the duty under section 37 requiring a water undertaker to maintain a water supply system), the Secretary of State or the Director-General may apply to the High Court for a special administration order, the effect of which is to empower the court to appoint an administrator who will take over the management of the company holding the appointment as sewerage undertaker.[14] Such an application to the court would no doubt arise from a grave problem associated with a very clear failure to perform the relevant statutory duty. Significantly, this facility is available without any necessity for seeking an enforcement order under section 18 as a prerequisite, emphasising the gravity of the section 94 duty.

Beyond the facility for statutory enforcement of the general duty, the notable absence of any facility for the statutory undertaker's liability where flooding from a sewer causes loss, damage or injury focuses attention on the common law of nuisance. In the absence of negligence, it is the case that, most commonly, sewerage overload is not regarded as the legal responsibility of the undertaker except in the most extreme circumstances. The matter was described thus by Upjohn J. in *Smeaton v. Ilford Corporation*[15]:

[9] s.6.

[10] Water Industry Act, s.219(1). *Cf.* s.217, concerning the construction of any enactment relating to undertakers' functions, including (with NRA) anti-pollution functions.

[11] *Ibid.* s.94(1).

[12] *Ibid.* subs.(2).

[13] See Chap. 1, "Water Resources and Supply", nn.97–13, *supra.*

[14] Water Industry Act, ss.23 and 24.

[15] [1954] 1 All E.R. 923.

> "... the defendants' whole sewerage system has now become totally inadequate to deal with the increased volume of sewage which it now has to carry, but that cannot give rise to a claim for nuisance; the only remedy of the injured party is to complain to the Minister ... No doubt the defendants are bound to provide and maintain the sewers ... but they are not thereby causing or adopting the nuisance. It is not the sewers that constitute the nuisance; it is the fact that they are overloaded. That overloading, however, arises not from any act of the defendants but because under [statutory requirements] they are bound to permit occupiers of premises to make connections to the sewer and to discharge their sewage therein ..."[16]

Determination of the extent to which breaches of various statutory obligations relating to the provision of sewerage services amount to breach of the above general duty is in accordance with regulations to be made by the Secretary of State. The same regulation-making power may be used for the purpose of supplementing the general duty through the establishment of overall standards of performance in relation to the provision of sewerage services.[17]

Local authority agencies

A number of so-called "relevant" authorities, including local authorities (district councils and London borough councils), may, individually, be parties to arrangements with statutory undertakers for the performance of sewerage functions. Such functions are defined to exclude sewage disposal and trade effluent discharges to the public sewer. However, any such arrangement—which may be defined in very wide terms—does not provide the statutory undertaker with immunity from any of the remedies that may be available in respect of the execution of functions, or any failure in execution.[18]

Public Sewers

While a private sewer is a sewer that drains more than one building, a public sewer is a sewer that is vested in the statutory undertaker.[19] A private sewer is capable of being in the ownership of a statutory undertaker or any other private ownership, in the former case otherwise than for the purpose of a discharge of its functions *qua* statutory undertaker. The process of vesting will normally occur by means of a prescribed statutory procedure, but it is possible that vesting may occur by means of agreed acquisition. Indeed, acquisition may occur in as many

[16] *Ibid.* at 927–928. *Cf.* Denning L.J. in *Pride of Derby and Derbyshire Angling Association Ltd v. British Celanese Ltd* [1953] 1 All E.R. 179 at 203.

[17] Water Industry Act, ss.95 and 96: *cf.* the Water Supply and Sewerage Services (Customer Service Standards) Regulations 1989 (S.I. 1989 No. 1159) and the amending regulations (S.I. 1989 No. 1383).

[18] *Ibid.* s.97. *Cf. King v. Harrow London Borough Council* [1994] E.G.C.S. 76 and *R. v. Yorkshire Water Services Ltd, The Times*, July 8, 1994.

[19] *Ibid.* s.219(1).

circumstances as a local authority may acquire property. In *Royco Homes Ltd v. Eatonwill Construction Ltd*,[20] for example, it was held that a pipe may attain the status of a public sewer if constructed in land belonging to the local authority and used as a highway, and despite the absence of any formal adoption. By analogy, it seems to be the case that the same principle will now apply to any sewerage undertaker.

Vesting

Vesting of a public sewer in a statutory sewerage undertaker following the enactment of the Water Act 1989 depended on the question of whether the subject sewer was vested previously in any one of the former water authorities. Most sewers constructed before October 1, 1937 were vested in the predecessor's local authorities.[21] In the case of sewers constructed after that date, the law now prescribes[22] that any sewer constructed at its own expense by or vested in a former water authority, any sewer laid by virtue of powers in Part XI of the Highways Act 1989 (except those referable to any road which is maintained by the highway authority), and any sewer that has vested as a result of a declaration formerly made under Part II of the Public Health Act 1936, vests. By way of contrast, any new sewer constructed by an undertaker using statutory powers[23] vests automatically in that undertaker.

Adoption

Except in the case of sewers or other associated disposal works constructed before October 1, 1937, a sewerage undertaker has the power to make a declaration to vest a sewer or other works in itself. While on the one hand the undertaker may take the initiative for the purpose of adoption, it is also provided that the owner (or any of the owners) of a sewer or disposal works may apply for a declaration to the undertaker. Where the undertaker intends to make a declaration for present purposes, notice of its proposal must be given to the owner or owners and no further action may be taken until a period of two months has elapsed without an appeal (under section 105 of the Act) being lodged, or until any such appeal has been determined.[24]

A crucial part of the undertaker's decision-making process is seen, both in the requirement to "have regard to all the circumstances of the case" and in a number of specific considerations in section 102(5). The Act lists five such specific considerations, the first one of which raises the question of whether the sewers or works are adapted to or required for any general system of sewerage or disposal provided, or proposed to be provided, for the whole or part of the area in question. The second consideration is whether the sewer is constructed under a

[20] (1978) 76 L.G.R. 515.

[21] The former water authorities succeeded the local authorities for present purposes on April 1, 1974.

[22] Water Industry Act 1991, s.179.

[23] *Ibid.*

[24] *Ibid.* s.102(1)–(4) and (7).

highway or under land reserved by a planning scheme for a street. This consideration may be significant by reference to ease of access for the purpose of maintenance and associated works in connection with the sewer or other disposal works. The third consideration relates to the number of buildings to be served and the potential need for the sewer to service additional buildings in the same proximity. The fourth consideration is the method of construction and state of repair of the sewer or works. Of particular significance here is the potential for additional capital investment,[25] either by reference to standards of construction that do not match the undertaker's higher standards or the need, following adoption, to bring a sewer or works up to a particular standard of repair. Finally, the undertaker must have regard to whether an adoption declaration would be seriously detrimental to any objecting owner. The potential for flooding from an overflowing sewer is clearly detrimental, probably seriously so, to an owner. However, some of the foregoing considerations necessarily emphasise that the act of adoption by declaration could suggest an adoption of legal liabilities that may arise from a defective sewer or disposal works, for example.

The foregoing reference to appeals is a reference in section 105 to an owner's right of appeal in respect of an undertaker's proposal to adopt a sewer or disposal works, or a refusal to adopt by the undertaker on an application by the owner; in both cases, any such appeal is dealt with by the Secretary of State for the Environment. The section also extends to deal with the situation in which any person has constructed or is proposing to construct a drain, sewer or any sewage disposal works.[26] An appeal to the Secretary of State is available in these circumstances, in three situations:

(a) on a refusal under section 104 (empowering sewerage undertakers to enter into adoption agreements);
(b) on an indication of an offer to grant an application to which there is objection; and
(c) a refusal to indicate, within two months of the making of the application, whether there is to be a grant or refusal of the application.

In determining an appeal under section 105, the Secretary of State has a widely drawn jurisdiction so that, for example, in making any declaration that the undertaker would have been empowered to make, the Secretary of State may "... specify conditions, including conditions as to payment of compensation by the sewerage undertaker.[27] Similarly wide powers relate to appeals in the area of

[25] The decision of the High Court in *R. v. Secretary of State for Wales, ex p. A. B. Hutton* [1987] J.P.L. 711 raises but does not answer the question whether financial obligation is relevant. The likelihood is that the primary consideration is always to be the physical condition and capacity of the sewer or disposal works in question.

[26] Water Industry Act, s.105(2). *Cf.* subs.(7) and the relevant considerations in s.102(5).

[27] *Ibid.* subs.(5). Compensation is (exceptionally) referable to some tangible loss suffered by the owner in relation to some more specific use of the sewer identifiable with his ownership: *cf.* Public Health Act 1936, s.278(3), excluding compensation.

adoption by agreement, described above. In determining appeals here, the Secretary of State may, *inter alia*, make an agreement on behalf of the undertaker "... on such terms as he considers reasonable".[28] However, in determining any appeal in connection with a declaration or agreement, the Secretary of State is obliged to have regard to all the circumstances of the case, as well as the considerations referred to previously in section 102(5).

Where a declaration has been made for adoption of a sewer, the remaining issue concerns entitlement to continued use by those entitled to be users up to that point. The Act[29] stipulates that *any* person "... who immediately before the making of a declaration ... was entitled to use the sewer in question shall be entitled to use it, or any sewer substituted for it, to the same extent as if the declaration had not been made".

Requisition

A sewerage undertaker is under a duty to provide a public sewer for the drainage for domestic purposes of premises in a particular locality in its area, in certain circumstances defined by the Act.[30] Those circumstances fall into three categories, requiring that:

(a) a notice is served on the undertaker by a person entitled to require the provision of a sewer for the particular locality;
(b) the "premises" in question have buildings upon them or will have when building proposals are carried out; and
(c) certain financial conditions are satisfied.[31]

Those who are entitled to require the provision of a public sewer for any locality are:

(a) the owner or occupier of any premises in the locality;
(b) any local authority whose area comprises the whole of or part of the locality;
(c) certain administrative agencies responsible for new towns; and
(d) any urban development corporation whose area comprises the whole of or part of the locality in question.[32]

At the core of the present duty is a requirement for the drainage of premises for "domestic purposes", defined by the Act[33] by reference to "... such domestic sewerage purposes as are specified ..." in the requirement for existing buildings, or as may be specified for buildings to be erected. This contrasts with what may be

[28] Water Industry Act, s.105(6).
[29] *Ibid.* s.102(6).
[30] *Ibid.* ss.98–101.
[31] *Ibid.* s.98(1).
[32] *Ibid.* subs.(2).
[33] *Ibid.* subs.(5).

the slightly more specific definition of "domestic purposes" in relation to water supply, to be found elsewhere in the Act.[34]

The duty arising from the present provision on requisition is owed by an undertaker to the person requiring provision or, as the case may be, a number of persons joining together for the purpose of requiring provision of a sewer. Any loss or damage caused by a breach of this duty is actionable by the person to whom the duty is owed, although there is a defence that the undertaker took all reasonable steps and exercised all due diligence to avoid the breach.[35] The importance of requisition should be recognised in these provisions for enforcement, in contrast with the more generally enforced duty occurring in section 94 of the Act, relating to the sewerage undertaker's general duty to provide a system of sewerage, enforceable by the Secretary of State under section 18.

Reference was made earlier to three categories of circumstances in which a duty to comply with a requisition would arise. One of those circumstances involves satisfaction of certain financial conditions, set out in section 99 of the Act. Essentially, these financial conditions are satisfied if the person seeking requisition provides an appropriate undertaking for the undertaker and also provides appropriate security for the benefit of the undertaker. Any such undertaking is defined by the Act as any undertaking for the payment of an amount that does not exceed "the relevant deficit"[36] (as defined by section 99 of the Act) on the sewer "... in each of the twelve years following the provision of the sewer". If the requisition is undertaken by two or more persons, the undertakings will bind jointly and severally.[37]

The remaining issues relating to requisition concern the determination of a completion date for the requisitioned sewer, as well as its route: both of these are covered by the provisions of section 101. The first issue focuses on the circumstances in which the section 98 duty is deemed to be satisfactorily discharged. The undertaker is not in breach of the section 98 duty if, in response to a requisition, it has laid the public sewer within a period of six months from the "relevant day" (as defined by the Act[38]), so that communication can be effected for the purpose of domestic drainage.[39] This latter requirement is expressed by the Act[40] by reference to a public sewer "... so laid ... as to enable drains and private sewers to be used for the drainage of premises ... to communicate with the public sewer ..." at places to be determined by agreement or arbitration. Any such communication must be effective: the absence of any or insufficient gravity to enable the communication to fulfil its essential function suggests ineffectiveness for this purpose.[41]

[34] *Ibid.* s.218(1).
[35] *Ibid.* s.98(3), (4).
[36] An equation seeking to reflect the full value of any investment.
[37] Water Industry Act, s.99.
[38] *Ibid.* s.101(5).
[39] *Ibid.* subs.(1).
[40] *Ibid.* subs.(1)(b).
[41] *Leech (William) Ltd v. Severn-Trent Water Authority* [1980] J.P.L. 753.

The laying of sewers

A sewerage undertaker has express statutory powers to lay sewers by virtue of Part VI of the Act[42]: local authorities may also exercise such powers on the terms provided for by the Act.[43] There may be circumstances in which the Secretary of State is willing to provide grant-aid to a sewerage undertaker to make "... adequate provision for the sewerage of a rural locality or for the disposal of such a locality's sewerage".[44]

The powers divide broadly into two categories. The first category relates to the power to lay pipes in streets under section 158 of the Act, which refers to "a relevant pipe"; this is, for present purposes, a reference to any sewer or disposal main.[45] The scope of the powers is seen in the following extract from the section[46]:

> "... to lay a relevant pipe in, under or over any street and to keep that pipe there; ... to inspect, maintain, adjust, repair or alter any relevant pipe which is in; under or over any street; and ... to carry out any works requisite for or incidental to, the purposes of [the foregoing works], including, for those purposes the following kinds of works, that is to say—
> (i) the breaking up or opening a street;
> (ii) tunnelling or boring under a street;
> (iii) breaking up or opening a sewer, drain or tunnel;
> (iv) moving or removing earth and other materials."

The second category of powers is found in section 159 and relates to the laying of pipes in "other" land which is not in, under or over a street. With the exception of the latter "inclusive" words just quoted from the previous section, the powers conferred here are similar to those in section 158.[47] The present powers may only be exercised after stipulated notice has been given, except in the event of an emergency.[48]

In relation to any works on "other" land for the purposes of both section 159 and section 161 (the latter provision empowering a sewerage undertaker to carry out work on land in a street or otherwise for the purpose of securing that any water in a waterworks is not polluted or otherwise contaminated), the Director-General of Water Services has a duty to investigate any complaint concerning the exercise of these powers.[49] If the Director-General, having accepted a complaint and investigated, finds that the undertaker had failed

[42] Water Industry Act, ss.158–161.
[43] *Ibid.* s.97(3). *Cf.* n.18, *supra.*
[44] *Ibid.* s.151.
[45] *Ibid.* s.158(7): as to a disposal main, see s.219(1).
[46] *Ibid.* subs.(1). *Cf.* s.161.
[47] *Ibid.* s.159(1).
[48] *Ibid.* subss.(5), (6).
[49] *Ibid.* s.181(1).

adequately to consult the complainant before and in the course of exercising the powers, or had caused loss or damage to the complainant by acting unreasonably in the exercise of the powers, an award of compensation up to £5,000 may be made in respect of any "... failure, loss, damage or inconvenience".[50]

The maintenance of sewers

In dealing previously with an undertaker's general duty to provide a system of sewerage under section 94 of the Act, it was seen that one of the incidental effects of that duty is the resulting duty to maintain any public sewer.[51] Specifically, the duty is defined, in part, as follows: "... to provide, improve and extend such a system of public sewers ... and so to cleanse and maintain those sewers as to ensure that that area is and continues to be effectually drained..."[52] The maintenance duty is one that is associated with all those incidents of repair that may reasonably be associated with the continuation of public sewer functions. As to the limits of this maintenance duty, it is clear from the first instance decision in *Radstock Cooperative and Industrial Society v. Norton–Radstock UDC*[53] that that duty does not, for example, extend to the maintenance of land or property beyond the sewer, or to the welfare of any person who is not concerned with the sewer. Different considerations would, of course, apply if the sewer in question was found to be defective and, in turn, the cause of some loss, damage of injury amounting, say, to a nuisance at common law.

While the duty to maintain is referable to the above duty to repair, the duty to cleanse necessarily includes the removal of stoppages and other blockages. Again, the scope of the duty is necessarily defined by the need for the public sewer to continue performance of its essential functions.

Standards of performance in relation to maintenance, cleansing and other duties are subject to statutory prescription. The scope of the system of performance recognition has been described previously in the present chapter.[54]

Sewer maps

A sewerage undertaker is obliged to keep records of the location and "other relevant particulars" of every public sewer or disposal main vested in that undertaker, every sewer in respect of which a declaration of vesting has been made and every drain or sewer subject to an agreement for future adoption. Among other things, the "relevant particulars" must indicate each one's status as a drain, sewer or disposal main, as well as the descriptions of effluent for the disposal of which it will be used. Records here are kept separately by reference to the area of each local authority. The undertaker is further obliged to ensure reasonable

[50] *Ibid.* subs.(4). *Cf.* s.180 and Sched. 12, providing for compensation in respect of pipe-laying and other works.
[51] See nn.11–13, *supra.*
[52] Water Industry Act, s.94(1)(a).
[53] [1967] Ch. 1094.
[54] See n.17, *supra.*

access to the records for the public. The records must be in the form of maps, although the Act does not indicate that maps here have to comply with any particular specification. No doubt the purposes for which the maps may be used—including local authority building control and town and country planning functions—will be important indicators of the format of such maps. Normally, the undertaker is not obliged to keep the above records in respect of any drain, sewer or disposal main laid before September 1, 1989 if it is not known of, or there are no reasonable grounds for suspecting its existence, or if it is not reasonably practicable for the undertaker to discover the course of the drain, sewer or disposal main.[55]

Failure by the undertaker to make any necessary modification of records here is a breach of the duty (enforceable by the Secretary of State under section 18 of the Act).[56] However, the Act indicates that the duty "... shall be taken to require any modification of the records to be made as soon as reasonably practicable after the completion of the works which make the modification necessary ...".[57] A further duty (again enforceable under section 18 by the Secretary of State) obliges the undertaker to provide local authorities, free of charge, with copies of the sewer map records held, as well as any modifications of those records.[58]

Sewer protection

The well-known categories of remedy are available in the event of a trespass: the owner of a private sewer could, for example, seek damages and perhaps, an injunction where a person seeks to connect to such a sewer.[59] Equally, building over a public sewer which causes that sewer to be damaged may attract the same remedies in favour of the sewerage undertaker *qua* owner of the sewer in question.[60]

Statutory protection under the Building Act 1984 extends to any drain, sewer or disposal main shown on the map of sewers. Where plans are submitted to the local authority under the Building Regulations and they relate to a building or extension to a building, the authority may reject the plans in certain circumstances, unless they may properly be consented to either unconditionally or subject to certain specified requirements. There are three such circumstances in which the authority's discretion may be exercised here:

(a) any proposal to erect the building or extension over the drain, sewer or disposal main;
(b) any such proposal which would result in interference with the use of the drain, sewer or disposal main; or

[55] Water Industry Act, s.199(1)–(5).
[56] *Ibid.* subss.(6), (9).
[57] *Ibid.* subs.(6).
[58] *Ibid.* s.200.
[59] *Royco Homes Ltd v. Eatonwill Construction Ltd* (1978) 76 L.G.R. 515: see n.20, *supra.*
[60] *Cleckheaton UDC v. Firth* (1898) 62 J.P. 536: the proceedings in this case were unsuccessful on the facts.

(c) any such proposal which would result in obstruction of access to the drain, sewer or disposal main.

In these circumstances, the local authority is obliged to advise the undertaker of the proposal submitted to it. Where the undertaker's requirements relating to its drains, sewers or disposal mains are communicated to the local authority in these circumstances and are "reasonable", it is the local authority's duty to exercise its functions here in accordance with those requirements.[61] A variety of questions arising between the local authority and the person submitting the subject plans, including questions whether a building when constructed will be over a particular sewer and whether and on what conditions a consent ought to be granted by the local authority, may be determined by the magistrates' court on application by the person making the submission.[62]

Despite ownership of any drain, sewer or disposal main vesting in the undertaker, significant powers of remedial action remain, by statute, with the local authority by virtue of the Building Act. The Act[63] empowers the local authority to serve a so-called "section 36" notice on an owner where there has been a contravention, for example, because plans have not been deposited, or because certain safeguards stipulated for the purpose of permitting building over a sewer have been ignored. The notice may require that any work completed is pulled down or removed, or that some other requirement (which could have been the subject of a condition) is substituted and complied with. Any such notice cannot be given if 12 months have expired from the date of completion of the subject work. Failure to comply with a section 36 notice allows the local authority to act in default and to recover costs from the owner. However, nothing in the section overall affects the power of the local authority (or the Attorney-General) to pursue injunctive proceedings as a means of enforcement.[64]

The process of sewer protection will, in many cases, necessitate street works. Unless there exists some statutory right, or a street works licence, it is an offence for any person other than the street authority[65] to place "apparatus" (which is stated to include a sewer, drain or tunnel[66]) in a street or

> "... to break up or open a street, or a sewer, drain or tunnel under it, or to tunnel or bore under a street, for the purpose of placing, inspecting, maintaining, adjusting, repairing, altering or renewing apparatus, or of changing the position of apparatus or removing it ...".[67]

The street authority may grant a street works licence permitting the placing or retention of apparatus in a street and, thereafter, its inspection, maintenance,

[61] Building Act 1984, s.18(1)–(3).
[62] *Ibid.* subs.(4).
[63] s.36.
[64] Building Act 1984, s.36(2)–(4) and (6).
[65] New Roads and Street Works Act 1991, s.49.
[66] *Ibid.* s.89(3).
[67] *Ibid.* s.51(1).

adjustment, repair, alteration or removal, as well as any change of position or removal.[68] Where any undertaker is proposing to execute street works affecting a public sewer, he is obliged to consult the "sewer authority"—the sewerage undertaker—before giving statutory notice of a starting date[69] in relation to the works.[70] Any undertaker is obliged here not only to ensure reinstatement of the street in question, but also reinstatement of any sewer, drain or tunnel which has been broken up or opened. The responsible authority in the case of a public sewer—the sewerage undertaker—may enforce any non-compliance with the present duty by requiring necessary remedial works. Any failure to comply with the notice requiring those remedial works empowers the sewerage undertaker in this case to execute the works in default and recover reasonably incurred costs. There exists also a "summary" procedure in this context, not involving service of any notice, where the sewerage undertaker considers that failure of the undertaker to reinstate is causing danger to users of the street.[71]

Sewer closure

Reference was made previously to the general duty on sewerage undertakers to provide a system of sewerage, as defined by section 94 of the Water Industry Act.[72] Although there is no explicit reference to closure in that provision, it is the case that sewer closure by an undertaker may be necessary for the purpose of ensuring (as the Act puts it) that the area is "effectually drained". Elsewhere, the Act makes explicit the right of an undertaker to close any public sewer, permitting any such undertaker to "discontinue and prohibit the use" of "any" public sewer. That discontinuance or prohibition may be for all purposes, or for the purpose of foul water or surface water drainage. However, before any lawful user of the sewer is deprived of his right to use it, the undertaker is obliged to provide a sewer which is equally effective for use for the purpose, and (at the undertaker's own expense) carry out any work necessary to make the user's drains or sewers communicate with the replacement sewer.[73]

Private Sewers and Drains

Development control decisions of the local planning authority may legitimately take account of drainage, usually in the immediate locality of the proposed development. Any conditions imposed (which may flow from or be suggested by the relevant development plan) must, *inter alia*, fairly and reasonably relate to the planning permission granted. As an alternative to or in support of such conditions, drainage may be the subject of a planning agreement or obligation

[68] *Ibid.* s.50 and Sched. 3.
[69] *Ibid.* s.55.
[70] *Ibid.* s.89(2).
[71] *Ibid.* s.90.
[72] See n.11, *supra.*
[73] Water Industry Act, s.116. As to matters of retention of status, see n.6, *supra.*

indicating, for example, that occupation of the subject development will not occur until agreed drainage specifications are satisfied. Specific statutory requirements beyond the Town and Country Planning Act 1990 are to be found in the Building Act 1984.

Building Act and associated drainage requirements

In exercising its powers for the purpose of approval under the Building Regulations, a local authority is able to require that a new building or an extension to an existing building is provided with a satisfactory system of drainage. The Building Act requires that the local authority should reject plans submitted if no satisfactory provision is made in the plans, unless it is considered that any such requirement can be waived.[74] At the core of this provision is the requirement that "... satisfactory provision will be made for the drainage of the building", a requirement that refers to the drains of the particular building and their connection to a sewer or discharge to a cesspool, and not to any more extensive system of drainage.[75] This more limited requirement is clearly a significant limitation on the local authority's powers in considering plans submitted for approval under the Building Regulations.

The powers just described under section 21 are extended under the next section, section 22. In an appropriate case, the local authority is able to require that two or more buildings are drained in combination. This power is seemingly available only in respect of buildings and not extensions, where plans are required to be deposited under the Act and Building Regulations. The power is available only where the owners agree to its exercise in relation to each building, prior to the approval of submitted plans. The power is available in respect of an "existing sewer", which may not be a public sewer. Whether there is appropriate provision in this case probably depends on the local authority's view of the economics and efficiency of drainage in combination. The essence of this provision is that buildings are drained in combination into the existing sewer by means of a private sewer, to be constructed either by the owners of the buildings (as directed by the authority) or by the authority on behalf of the owners. The authority will determine (subject to an appeal to the magistrates' court) the division of expenses relating to the construction, maintenance and repair of the private sewer. Local authorities share the statutory powers available to sewerage undertakers for the laying of pipes in streets, powers that are extended to any person other than a local authority.[76]

Private sewer construction

A sewerage undertaker has statutory powers to compel construction of a drain or sewer according to its own specification, but only where a developer or other

[74] Building Act 1984, s.21.
[75] *Chesterton RDC v. Thompson* [1947] 1 K.B. 300.
[76] Water Industry Act, s.158. *Cf.* the Building Act 1984, s.101.

person "proposes" such construction and the undertaker considers that the drain or sewer is, or is likely to be, needed to form part of a general sewerage system. Any such requirement is subject to appeal to the Secretary of State. The duty to comply with this requirement for construction is owed to the undertaker, so that any breach causing loss or damage to that undertaker is actionable. Compliance with the duty may attract "extra expenses reasonably incurred" and (until the drain or sewer becomes a public sewer) other expenses reasonably incurred for the purpose of repair or maintenance attributable to the undertaker's requirements. In these circumstances, the undertaker is obliged to repay such expenses.[77]

If the undertaker agrees with a person who is constructing or proposing to construct any sewer or sewage disposal works that the sewer or works will accord with the requirements of an agreement, such an agreement may include a stipulation that, at a specified date or on the occurrence of some identified contingency, the sewer or works will be vested in the undertaker. This facility extends also to drains, but in this case it must be a condition of the agreement that any "vesting declaration" does not occur until the drain has become a sewer. Whatever the circumstances, the person who is constructing or proposing to construct the sewer or disposal works may apply to the undertaker requesting that an agreement made under the present provision will run with the land, to the extent that it will be enforceable against an undertaker by the owner or occupier for the time being of any premises served by the sewer or works to which it relates.[78]

Many of the transactions discussed above will be undertaken by developers in the course of estate development of all kinds. In this context, it is important to appreciate the significance of the parcel of provisions just examined in this section, along with the Building Act provisions set out in the previous section of this chapter. Overall, this parcel of provisions can be said to provide aid and encouragement to the provision of private sewers, in the absence of any mandatory power by statute to compel their provision and construction. The process of construction will require planning permission, but the application will not attract the need for prior publicity; the laying of sewers is expressly excluded.[79] Nevertheless, the laying of sewers in a street will require a street works licence.[80]

Sewer Connection

The tort of trespass will determine liabilities on those occasions when an unlawful connection of drains to public or private sewers occurs. In *Cook v. Minion*,[81] the

[77] *Ibid.*
[78] *Ibid.* s.104.
[79] Town and Country Planning Act 1990, s.65; Town and Country Planning General Development Order 1988, art.11(1)(d).
[80] See nn.65–71, *supra.*
[81] [1979] J.P.L. 305: see n.4, *supra.*

judge found[82] that one pair of cottages had been connected to another owner's drain with his consent and that expense had been incurred by the owner of the pair of cottages in reliance on the permission by the installation of water closets. In these circumstances, the owner of the pair of cottages acquired a permanent equitable right of drainage.[83] On the other hand, another cottage's drain was found to have been connected without consent, giving the plaintiff a prima facie claim in equity for an injunction. Normally, in these circumstances, any triviality in a trespass claim would lead to a refusal to grant an injunction. On the facts of the present case, the judge was not prepared to categorise the claim as trivial. Nevertheless, the court in these circumstances will normally consider exercising its discretion to award damages in lieu of an injunction. On the facts of the present case, Goulding J. concluded that it would be oppressive to the defendant to require him to alter his drainage arrangements without securing anything tangible for the plaintiff in return. Accordingly, damages were assessed in lieu of an injunction.

The owner or occupier of any premises in the undertaker's area or the owner of any private sewer draining premises in that area has a statutory right to have any such drains or sewer communicate with the undertaker's public sewer for the purpose of discharging foul and surface water.[84] However, this right is subject to three primary restrictions.[85] First, there is no entitlement to discharge, directly or indirectly, into any public sewer any liquid (apart from domestic sewage or surface or storm water) from a factory or a manufacturing process, or any liquid whose passage into a public sewer is prohibited by any statute. This latter restriction includes the detailed restrictions set out in section 111 of the Water Industry Act, aimed at avoiding the passage in a sewerage system of any matter which is likely to injure a sewer or drain or interfere with the flow of the contents of the system, including a treatment system. Failure to comply with the restrictions is an offence punishable summarily, or on indictment, with a daily penalty for any continuing contravention. The second restriction prohibits foul water discharges to surface water sewers and (except with the undertaker's approval) surface water discharges to foul water sewers, where separate sewers are provided.[85a] Finally, a person's drains or sewer cannot be made to communicate directly with a stormwater overflow sewer.

Where a person wishes to exercise the right of connection discussed above, notice of any such proposal is required to be given to the undertaker. That undertaker, within a period of 21 days from the date of notification, may advise the applicant that the communication cannot be permitted because it appears that the mode of construction or condition of the drain or sewer is such that the making of the communication would be prejudicial to the sewerage system. To enable an evaluation of these matters, the undertaker is empowered to require the

[82] *Ibid.* at 307.
[83] *Ward v. Kirkland* [1967] Ch. 194; *E.R. Ives Investment Ltd v. High* [1967] 2 Q.B. 379.
[84] Water Industry Act, s.106(1).
[85] *Ibid.* subs.(2).
[85a] *cf.* s.115, enabling highway authorities to enter agreements with sewerage undertakers for the use of highway drains as sewers, and vice versa.

drain or sewer concerned to be laid open for inspection.[86] Any question relating to an undertaker's refusal to permit communication, or the reasonableness of a requirement to lay open a drain or sewer, may be determined by a magistrates' court.[87]

Three further and significant issues arise from the operation of the section 106 provisions on communication. First, the law presumes the freedom of the sewerage undertaker to determine the precise location where a connection may be made.[88] Secondly, a landowner's consent is necessary if a connection necessitates use of that person's land. In *Wood v. Ealing Tenants Ltd*,[89] a local authority was requested by the owner of premises to construct a drain for the purpose of connecting his premises to a main sewer. It was held by the court that the local authority had no further rights beyond those enjoyed by the owner of the premises for the purpose of laying a drain in land owned by a third party. Finally, the sewerage undertaker is unable to refuse consent for a connection by reference to a perceived overloading of the sewerage system, which is essentially a matter to be taken into account at any preliminary, planning stage.[90]

If consent is granted for the purpose of making a communication, notice must be given to the undertaker so that arrangements can be made for supervision of the work. Thereafter, "all reasonable facilities" must be provided to enable the work to be supervised. To enable any person to exercise the right prescribed by section 106 and to enable necessary works of examination, repair or renewal, the owner or occupier of the subject premises enjoys the undertaker's powers under section 158 (relating to the laying of pipes in streets) and section 161(1) (relating to works for the purpose of dealing with foul water and pollution).[91]

The owner or occupier of the premises in question may seek the assistance of the sewerage undertaker for the purpose of establishing communication. This may be achieved by means of section 275 of the Public Health Act 1936 or section 107 of the Water Industry Act. By virtue of section 107, the undertaker, following service of a notice under section 106, may complete the communication with the public sewer itself, with all the rights in law that are normally enjoyed by the person serving the notice. It is in response to such a notice, served under section 106, that the undertaker will indicate (within 14 days of receipt of the notice) that it will complete the connection itself. If, despite this indication from the undertaker, the person serving the original notice proceeds with the communication, he commits an offence. Where there are no such irregularities, the undertaker may determine that work commence only on receipt of reasonable estimated expenses, or some security in respect of the costs of the work.[92] Under section 275, the undertaker may, by agreement with the

[86] *Ibid.* subss.(4), (5).

[87] *Ibid.* subs.(6). Subs.(7) applies ss.300–302 of the Public Health Act 1936 to the magistrates' court jurisdiction under the present provisions.

[88] *Beech Properties Ltd v. Wallis (G.E.) & Sons* (1976) 241 E.G. 685.

[89] [1907] 2 K.B. 390.

[90] See n.15, *supra*.

[91] Water Industry Act, s.108.

[92] *Ibid.* s.107.

owner or occupier, execute at his expense the completion of a communication with the public sewer.

If any person causes a drain or sewer to communicate with a public sewer in contravention of the requirements just examined under section 106 or 108, or before the expiration of the 21-day period allowed to the undertaker for a response under section 106, an offence (triable summarily) is committed. Whether or not proceedings have been taken by the undertaker in these circumstances, resort may be had to default powers, through the closure of any communication made and recovery of reasonably incurred expenses.[93]

Even where a drain or sewer connects with a public sewer in a manner which is sufficient for the effectual drainage of the premises, it may not be adapted to the area's general sewerage system or may be otherwise objectionable. In these circumstances, the undertaker may, at its own expense, close the drain or sewer and fill any cesspool. However, these powers may be used by the undertaker only where equally convenient facilities are first provided by that undertaker. Accordingly, any proposal for a disconnection can only be pursued if the notice requirement of this provision is followed.[94]

Repairs to Sewers and Drains

Responsibility for the repair of public sewers lies with the sewerage undertaker.[95] Nevertheless, the Public Health Acts 1936–61 and the Building Act 1984 empower the supervision of private sewers and drains, albeit that local authorities here may have status and functions *qua* agent of any sewerage undertaker. The owner or occupier of "any premises" is able to exercise the same powers as any sewerage undertaker under section 158 (the laying of pipes in streets) and section 161(1) (works for the purpose of dealing with foul water and pollution) for the purpose, *inter alia,* of repairing any drain or private sewer draining those premises into a public sewer.[96] Furthermore, local authorities and other persons who have the right to lay and maintain sewers and drains have the same power to break open streets as is enjoyed by sewerage undertakers in this context.[97]

Both local authorities (in relation to a drain or private sewer, *inter alia*)[98] and sewerage undertakers (in relation to any drain connecting with a public sewer, or any private sewer so connecting),[99] having reasonable grounds for suspecting that any of these facilities is defective or is in such a condition as to be "prejudicial to health or a nuisance"[1] or "injurious or likely to cause injury to health or as to be a nuisance",[2] many examine the facility or apply a test (other than by water

[93] *Ibid.* s.109.
[94] *Ibid.* s.113.
[95] *Ibid.* s.94.
[96] *Ibid.* s.108 and *cf.* n.91, *supra.*
[97] Building Act 1984, s.101.
[98] Public Health Act 1936, s.48. The powers extend to cesspools, as defined by s.90.
[99] Water Industry Act, s.114.
[1] Public Health Act 1936, s.48.
[2] Water Industry Act, s.114.

pressure) and, if necessary, open the ground. However, the ground must be reinstated as soon as possible and any damage made good if the facility is found to be in "proper condition". If a person has sustained damage by reason of an exercise of these powers, where he himself is not in default in respect of the matter under investigation, there is a statutory liability to make "full compensation".[3] An undertaker's duties in relation to street works is to be found in the New Roads and Street Works Act 1991.[4]

Reference was made previously in this section to the individual's repair powers in relation to drains and private sewers by virtue of section 108 of the Water Industry Act. However, except in the case of an emergency, no person is able to repair, reconstruct or alter the course of an underground drain that communicates with a sewer without giving the local authority 24 hours' notice of his intention. During the execution of such works, an authorised officer of the local authority must be permitted free access to them. Failure to comply with these requirements is an offence, triable summarily.[5] Furthermore, if a drain is so constructed or repaired as to be prejudicial to health or a nuisance, the person who undertook or executed the construction or repair commits an offence, triable summarily, unless it can be shown that the prejudice to health or nuisance could not have been avoided by the exercise of reasonable care.[6]

If it appears to a local authority that a drain or private sewer, *inter alia*, is not sufficiently maintained and kept in good repair and can be sufficiently repaired at a cost not exceeding £250, the local authority may[7] (after giving the person concerned not less than seven days' notice) cause the drain or private sewer to be repaired.[8] The local authority may recover any reasonably incurred expenses not exceeding the limit of £250,[9] although the court may apportion liability for these expenses.[10] Such circumstances could arise where an environmental health inspector has validly served a notice under the present provisions, even where it emerges that the blockage was not on the land of the person served.[11] If a notice has not been validly served because the court can find no justification for the local authority's view that a drain or private sewer was insufficiently maintained and kept in good repair, no expenses can be recovered by the local authority.[12] The foregoing provision may also apply to a further local authority power in the present context: the power to serve a notice on an owner or occupier if it appears that a drain or private sewer, *inter alia*, is stopped up. The notice will require

[3] Public Health Act 1936, s.278.
[4] ss.70–73.
[5] Building Act 1984, s.61.
[6] *Ibid.* s.63(1). *Cf.* subss.(2) and (3), allowing the defendant to plead the act or default of some other person.
[7] Public Health Act 1961, s.17(2).
[8] *Ibid.* subs.(1).
[9] *Ibid.*
[10] *Ibid.* subs.(6).
[11] *Rotherham MBC v. Dodds* [1986] 2 All E.R. 867, C.A.
[12] Public Health Act 1961, s.17(8).

remedial action, but again subject to default action and the possible recovery of reasonably incurred expenses by the local authority.[13]

The foregoing powers under section 17 of the Public Health 1961 are without prejudice to other powers available to a local authority under section 59 of the Building Act.[14] The Building Act provision refers, *inter alia*, to private sewers and drains and indicates that a local authority "shall by notice require . . . either the owner or the occupier of the building" to undertake any necessary works of repair. As such, these powers are wider than those described in section 17 of the Act of 1961 for present purposes, referring as they do to owners of premises alone.[15] Where a private sewer is in such a condition as to be prejudicial to health or a nuisance, a local authority may act under section 59 by serving a notice of repair on the owners of the property above the defect, rather than on all those who are served by the drainage system.[16] There is a potential overlap between the present powers and those available to the local authority under the statutory nuisance provisions of the Environmental Protection Act 1990.[17] In practice, the more specific powers (particularly in section 59) are to be preferred. In order to establish a case for action under section 59, it may be necessary to carry out a smoke or other test using the powers in section 48 of the Public Health Act 1936,[18] together with the powers of entry under section 287 of the same Act. If the wrong party, as between owner or occupier, is chosen as recipient of the notice, this may form the basis for an appeal to the magistrates' court under section 102. The local authority must exercise a reasonable discretion, according to the nature and probable cause of the defect, in choosing between owner and occupier. However, the authority cannot be expected to investigate the respective liabilities of a landlord and tenant under the terms of a lease, prior to service of a section 59 notice. Normally, an occupier will be liable for defective drains unless any defect is of a structural character.[19] Any section 59 notice must indicate the nature of the works to be executed, as well as the period of time within which they are to be executed. Subject to any appeal just referred to, the local authority may act in default and recover any reasonably incurred expenses if the works are not executed within the time stipulated by the notice. Without prejudice to this default power, the local authority may take summary criminal proceedings for default. Provision is also made in the Act for a continuing fine for each day following conviction when the default continues.[20]

[13] *Ibid.* subs.(3). *Cf.* s.35 of the Local Government (Miscellaneous Provisions) Act 1976, which now authorises service of a notice on owners or occupiers of premises served by the sewer who may therefore be liable for the remedial works, so mitigating a possible unfairness arising from the operation of s.17(3) of the Act of 1961.

[14] Subs.(15).

[15] Public Health Act 1961, s.17(2)(b).

[16] *Swansea City Council v. Jenkins*, *The Times*, April 1, 1994.

[17] Pt. III.

[18] See, n.98, *supra*.

[19] *Russell v. Shenton* (1842) 3 Q.B. 449.

[20] Building Act 1984, s.102.

Disconnection of Drains and Sewers

Any person who undertakes works resulting in a drain being put out of use is required to disconnect and seal up any unused drain or portion of a drain at such points (not necessarily on the owner's own premises) as the local authority may reasonably require. Determination of the reasonableness of any such local authority requirement is a matter for the magistrates' court. The Building Act provides that 48 hours' notice of works to comply with the requirement must be given to the local authority: failure to comply with present requirements is an offence, triable summarily, with provision also for continuing fines for every day when default occurs.[21] However, the requirement set out in this provision does not apply in relation to anything done in the course of the demolition of a building or part of a building. In these circumstances, the local authority is empowered to serve a notice requiring, *inter alia*, that:

(a) any sewer or drain in or under the building to be demolished is disconnected and sealed, at such points as the local authority may reasonably require;
(b) any such sewer or drain is removed, sealing off any sewer or drain with which the removed sewer or drain is connected, and
(c) the surface of the ground disturbed for these purposes is made good, to the satisfaction of the local authority.[22]

Supporting powers giving an option of disconnection are also to be found in section 59.[23]

Sanitary Conveniences

The provision and maintenance of sanitary conveniences is governed by two Acts, the Public Health Act 1936 and the Building Act 1984. The present section of this chapter is concerned with matters of provision and maintenance only in relation to existing buildings: new buildings and their sanitary facilities are governed by the Building Regulations 1985–91, dealt with elsewhere in this book.

In the case of existing buildings, local authorities enjoy two important sets of powers under section 45 of the Public Health Act 1936 (defective closets[24] capable of repair) and section 64 of the Building Act (provision of sufficient closets[25] in buildings). Under section 45, if it appears to the local authority that any closets provided for or in connection with a building are in such a state as to be prejudicial to health or a nuisance but that they can be put into a satisfactory

[21] *Ibid.* s.62.
[22] *Ibid.* s.82. *Cf.* s.81.
[23] See n.14, *supra.*
[24] As defined by s.90(1): note the definition of "water closet".
[25] As defined by s.126(1): note the definition of "water closet".

condition without reconstruction, the local authority is obliged to serve a notice on the owner or occupier requiring the completion of necessary remedial works which may cover both repair and cleansing. Failure to comply with any cleansing requirements is an offence punishable summarily: the penalties include a continuing fine for every day when default occurs following conviction. In any such criminal proceedings, it is open to the defendant to question the reasonableness of the authority's requirements or the fact that the notice was addressed to him and not the owner, or occupier, as the case may be. This and various other matters may be raised on appeal to the magistrates' court under section 290 of the Act. Section 64 of the Building Act enables the local authority to deal with buildings without sufficient closet accommodation or with closets that cannot be put right without reconstruction. The authority is obliged by the section to serve a notice on the owner only, although there is provision for an appeal to the magistrates' court[26] that includes questions relating to disputed occupation and responsibility. The local authority is able to take action in default in the event of non-compliance with a notice, but, without prejudice to such proceedings, summary criminal proceedings may be taken[27] with additional provision being made for a continuing fine for every day of non-compliance beyond conviction. The provisions of section 64 do not apply to a factory or other workplace or other premises, to which the Offices, Shops and Railway Premises Act 1963 applies.[28] Various other provisions apply to sanitary conveniences in these and other premises.[29]

The Acts of 1936 and 1984 contain a range of supplementary provisions. In brief, the Public Health Act provisions are to be found in:

(a) section 49 (restriction on the use of rooms situated over certain types of closet other than a water or earth closet);
(b) section 50 (overflowing and leaking cesspools);
(c) section 51 (care of closets); and
(d) section 52 (care of sanitary conveniences used in common).

Enforcement of these provisions is essentially a matter for the local authority.

The Act of 1984 provides for:

(a) the replacement of earth closets with water closets (section 66);
(b) the loan of temporary sanitary conveniences by a local authority (section 67); and
(c) local authority consent requirements in relation to the erection of public conveniences (section 68).

[26] Public Health Act 1936, s.102.

[27] *Ibid.* s.99.

[28] *Ibid.* s.64(6).

[29] See, in particular, Housing Act 1985, s.604 (criteria for fitness for human habitation of houses); Building Act 1984, s.65 (workplaces); Factories Act 1961, s.7 (factories); Offices, Shops and Railway Premises Act 1963, s.9; Local Government (Miscellaneous Provisions) Act 1976, s.20 (places of entertainment).

Discharges to a Sewer

Discharges to the public sewer are subject to qualifications that fall into three broad categories, relating to the statutory right of connection under section 106 of the Water Industry Act,[30] prohibitions arising by virtue of section 111 of the same Act,[31] and restrictions on the generation of trade effluent. Each of these categories is dealt with in turn.

The statutory right of connection

It will be recalled that the owner or occupier of any premises in the area of a sewerage undertaker, or the owner of any private sewer draining premises in any such area, is entitled to have his drains or sewers communicate with the relevant public sewer "... and thereby to discharge foul water and surface water from those premises or that private sewer".[32] Reference has been made already to the three "primary" restrictions on this right.[33]

Injurious matter or substances

Subject to the Water Industry Act provisions on trade effluent discharges, dealt with below, there is a statutory prohibition on the discharge to a public sewer (or any drain or private sewer communicating with it) of any matter falling into any one of three categories.[34] The first category refers to "matter" likely to injure the sewer or drain, to interfere with the free flow of its contents or to affect prejudicially the treatment and disposal of its contents. The second category refers to any such chemical refuse or waste stream, or any such liquid of a temperature higher than 110°F, as to be a "prohibited substance". Any of these may be a prohibited substance alone or in combination with the contents of any sewer or drain (or, in the case of a liquid, when heated) if it is dangerous, the cause of a nuisance or injurious, or likely to cause injury to health. The third category comprises any petroleum spirit or carbide of calcium. For present purposes, the term "petroleum spirit" receives a broad definition, meaning any crude petroleum and any oil made from petroleum or from coal, shale, peat or other bituminous substances, or any product of petroleum or mixture containing petroleum. Whether for these purposes any substance or matter is "dangerous" is necessarily a matter of fact, supported by any appropriate scientific evidence. In *Liverpool Corporation v. Coghill (H.) and Son Ltd*,[35] the adverse impact of sewage effluent on land where it was spread was sufficient for the purpose of the present provision.

Contravention of any of the foregoing provisions is a criminal offence, triable

[30] See n.84, *supra.*
[31] See section entitled "Sewer Connection", *supra.*
[32] Water Industry Act, s.106(1).
[33] See n.85, *supra.*
[34] Water Industry Act, s.111(1).
[35] [1918] 1 Ch. 307.

summarily or on indictment. Although provision is made for continuing fines following summary conviction, injunctive enforcement may be available where, for example, the scale of penalties may not be a deterrent to the individual or company that regards those penalties as a "legitimate" business expense.[36]

Trade effluents

Restrictions on the discharge of trade effluents to the public sewer are defined by statute as an important contribution to environmental quality. The restrictions contribute to an overall need to comply with quality standards for the aquatic environment in the main, focusing on the legal responsibilities of the sewerage undertakers and their task of providing safe, adequate treatment for effluent prior to discharge, usually to that aquatic environment. Such is the significance of this subject that it occupies its own section of the present chapter.

Trade Effluent Discharges

Within the area a sewerage undertaker, any occupier of trade premises may not discharge trade effluent to the public sewer without the consent of that undertaker. Contravention of this requirement is an offence, triable summarily or on indictment. Furthermore, any effluent may be discharged to the public sewer only by means of a drain or sewer. More generally, some of the foregoing provisions of the Water Industry Act[37] will not apply as long as a lawful discharge occurs in compliance with the present provision.[38] For the purpose of this provision, "effluent" means any liquid, including particles of matter and other substances in suspension in the liquid.[39] On the other hand, "trade effluent" does not include domestic sewage but refers to any liquid, either with or without particles of matter in suspension within it, which is wholly or partly produced in the course of any trade or industry carried on at trade premises, and (in relation to trade premises) means any such liquid which is so produced in the course of any trade or industry carried on at those premises.[40] Included in the definition of "trade premises" (any premises used or intended to be used for carrying on any trade or industry) are premises used for agricultural or horticultural purposes, or scientific research or experiment.[41] The effluent from a laundry or launderette, although more readily associated with domestic sewage, nevertheless remains as "trade effluent" by virtue of its generation in the course of a trade or industry.[42]

[36] *A.-G. v. Sharp* [1931] 1 Ch. 121.
[37] ss.106(2)(a), (b) and 111(1)(a), (b).
[38] Water Industry Act, s.118.
[39] *Ibid.* s.219(1).
[40] *Ibid.* s.141(1). *Cf.* the statutory power to extend the categories of effluent here, under s.139.
[41] *Ibid.* s.141(2).
[42] *Thames Water Authority v. Blue and White Launderettes* [1980] 1 W.L.R. 700, C.A.

Consents and conditions

An application for a consent to discharge trade effluent to the public sewer must be made in writing, by notice served on the sewerage undertaker.[43] The application must indicate the nature and composition of the effluent, the maximum quantity to be discharged on any one day and the highest rate of discharge.[44] The sewerage undertaker may grant a consent unconditionally or subject to such conditions as are thought fit to be imposed in relation to:

(a) the receiving sewer or sewers;
(b) the nature and composition of the trade effluent;
(c) the maximum quantity of trade effluent which may be discharged on any one day; and
(d) the highest rate at which the effluent will be discharged.

A variety of other conditions may be attached to the consent, governing such matters as:

(a) the timing of discharges;
(b) the temperature of the effluent;
(c) the payment of charges for discharge and disposal;
(d) monitoring;
(e) inspection; and
(f) record-keeping.

In exercising the power to impose charges, the sewerage undertaker is obliged to have regard to a variety of matters, including the composition of the effluent, its volume and its rate of discharge, together with the additional expenses (if any) arising from reception and disposal, and any revenue to be derived from the trade effluent. If the sewerage undertaker chooses to impose a condition relating to the elimination or diminution of any specified constituent of the trade effluent before it enters the sewer, the undertaker must be satisfied that there would be injury or obstruction to the sewer or difficulty or expense in treatment or disposal, or that there would be injury or obstruction to navigation on or the use of a harbour or tidal water where there is an outfall to such locations. Contravention of conditions is, once again (as in the case of contravention of the basic consent requirement in section 118), triable summarily or on indictment.[45] The consent granted by a sewerage undertaker operates for the benefit of the subject trade

[43] Water Industry Act, ss.119(1), 141(3).
[44] *Ibid.* s.119(2).
[45] *Ibid.* s.121. *Cf.* s.136, by which it is to be presumed in legal proceedings that any measuring or similar apparatus has registered accurately.

premises, even where new drainage or sewerage arrangements are substituted by the sewerage undertaker.[46]

Referring to the second part of the definition of "trade effluent"[47] in *Yorkshire Dyeing and Proofing Co. v. Middleton Borough Council*,[48] it was considered that:

> "... the object [of that part of the definition] was to restrict the trade effluent to the particular premises on which the trade is carried on, and it would not bear a construction which would enable the effluent from the new premises, which were not covered by [the statutory exemption from licensing], to be discharged under the umbrella of the exemption which the old premises acquired ..."[49]

Any such new trade premises would require a fresh consent from the sewerage undertaker.

Variation

Significant powers of variation are available to the sewerage undertaker, in two sets of circumstance: the first relates to the variation of conditions (usually beyond specified time limits), while the second extends the facility, but subject to certain safeguards.

In the first set of circumstances, the undertaker may give a variation direction, subject to notice specifying a right of appeal and the date when variation takes effect, but not within two years from the date of the consent or the date of any previous notice of a variation direction, unless the owner and occupier of the trade premises consent.[50] In the second set of circumstances, the variation direction may be given within the above time limits and without any consent if the undertaker considers it necessary to act for the "proper protection" of persons likely to be affected by discharges which, otherwise, could be made quite lawfully. The undertaker is liable to pay compensation to the owner and the occupier of the trade premises unless that undertaker is of the view that variation is required because of a change of circumstances, *inter alia*. Notice of the reasons justifying the undertaker's view must be given to the owner and occupier.[51]

If a direction has been given and it requires that trade effluent should not be discharged until a specified date, the undertaker may conclude that a later date should be substituted. If that conclusion is formed in consequence of a failure to complete reception and disposal works or by reference to any other exceptional consequences, the undertaker may apply to the Director-General of Water Services for the substitution. The undertaker is obliged to give notice of the

[46] *Ibid.* s.113: *Cf.* n.94, *supra.*
[47] See n.40, *supra.*
[48] [1953] 1 All E.R. 540.
[49] *Ibid. per* Lynskey J. at 543.
[50] Water Industry Act, ss.124 and 125.
[51] *Ibid.* s.125.

application to the owner and occupier and, in turn, the Director-General is obliged to take their representations into account in arriving at a decision.[52]

Special category effluent

An application for consent is subject to different considerations if the proposed discharge is of so-called "special category" effluent. In these circumstances, it is the noxious quality of the discharge that obliges the sewerage undertaker to refer the application to the Secretary of State (unless it is intended to refuse the application) in connection with the questions of whether the proposed discharges should be prohibited or, if not, whether any requirements as to conditions should be imposed. No decision can be made by the undertaker until the Secretary of State has determined the reference. The duty of the undertaker to make a reference is enforceable under section 18[53] of the Act and, instead of making an order under that section, the Secretary of State may proceed as if the subject application was in fact a reference. Where the decision-making process remains unaffected by any such informality, the requirements relating to conditions will apply but, of course, subject to any special measures reflecting the noxious character of the subject discharge.[54]

The present provisions represent an important legislative and enforcement framework in relation to the toxic "red list" substances prescribed by E.C. environmental legislation, particularly by reference to the so-called "precautionary" principle of Community environmental policy. These provisions in Part IV of the Water Industry Act represent the implementation of two central E.C. Directives: 76/464[54a] (pollution caused by certain dangerous substances discharged into the aquatic environment) and 91/271[54b] (urban waste water treatment). The substances—and processes—prescribed by Directive 76/464 are reflected in the provisions of the Trade Effluent (Prescribed Processes and Substances) Regulations 1989,[55] with Schedule 1 prescribing the Directive's list of substances and Schedule 2 prescribing five categories of process. Directly linked to Directive 76/464 on a broader scale is the later Directive 91/271, which requires the provision of treatment facilities for urban waste water. The Directive does not seek to identify the quality of the "receiving" waters but rather defines the means to be used against a background of the "precautionary" approach, mentioned previously. Nevertheless, there is some recognition of the condition of the "receiving" waters through a defined relationship between levels of treatment, according to whether the waters are in "sensitive" or less than sensitive areas.[56]

[52] *Ibid.* s.128.
[53] See n.13, *supra*. *Cf.* s.132.
[54] Water Industry Act, s.120.
[54a] [1976] O.J. L129.
[54b] [1991] O.J. L135.
[55] S.I. 1989 No. 1156, as amended by S.I. 1990 No. 1629.
[56] As to implementation, see the Water Resources Act, s.88, and S.I. 1989 No. 1156, as amended by S.I. 1990 No. 1629.

The Water Industry Act defines special category effluent by reference to the foregoing categories of "substances" and effluents derived from prescribed "processes".[57] However, there is an exclusion that operates by reference to the regulatory regime of integrated pollution control under the Environmental Protection Act 1990. Accordingly, trade effluent is not a special category effluent for present licensing purposes "... if it is produced, or to be produced, in any process which is a prescribed process designated for central control..." by Her Majesty's Inspectorate of Pollution in relation to integrated pollution control, discussed in Chapter 7.[58]

Where a consent is in force the Secretary of State is empowered to conduct a review of that consent, either for the purpose of considering whether the authorised discharges should be prohibited or, if not, whether any requirements should be imposed in relation to subject conditions. A review may be undertaken for the purpose of enabling effect to be given to a European Community obligation or other international agreement, or for the protection of public health, or that of flora and fauna dependent on an aquatic environment. Otherwise, the present review powers may not be used unless circumstances fall within a small range of categories, including any situation where a consent has not previously been subject to review and was given before September 1, 1989.[59]

Appeals

A range of appeal provisions is provided by the Act, in relation to decisions on applications,[60] in relation to the disposal of appeals on matters affecting special category effluents[61] and in relation to decisions on variation of consents.[62]

Any person who is aggrieved by the refusal of a consent by a sewerage undertaker under section 119, a failure to give a consent within two months of an application, or any condition attached to a consent, may appeal to the Director-General of Water Services. In the second case, the Director-General has wide powers to grant a consent unconditionally or subject to conditions. If the appeal relates to conditions attached to a consent, the Director-General is empowered to review all of the conditions and even substitute new conditions, including stipulations about the payment of charges. The Director-General may and shall, if so directed by the High Court, state a special case for the court's decision on any question of law arising at any stage in the appeal proceedings.[63]

The foregoing appeal facility may not be used if it appears to the Director-General that the case is one in which a reference under section 120 is

[57] Water Industry Act, s.138.
[58] *Ibid.* subs.(2).
[59] *Ibid.* s.127.
[60] *Ibid.* s.122. Conditions for payment of charges to an undertaker are not to be determined on an appeal here and under s.126 except in so far as there is no charging scheme in force under s.143: s.135.
[61] *Ibid.* s.123.
[62] *Ibid.* s.126.
[63] *Ibid.* s.137.

necessary prior to any decision[64] and that the undertaker has not made that reference, unless the Director-General has made the reference and received notice of the Secretary of State's decision.[65]

Appeals in relation to variation of consents fall into two categories. In the first, an appeal to the Director-General is available within two months of notice of a direction of variation,[66] or at any later time, with his written consent. The Director-General has wide powers to annul or substitute a decision.[67] The facility to state a case to the High Court also applies to this first category of appeal.[68] The second category of appeal, again to the Director-General, relates to directions to vary a consent within the time limits defined by the Act.[69] The ground of appeal allowed by the Act is that compensation should be paid as a consequence of the direction and the Director-General may direct that the undertaker was not of the opinion to which the notice relates.[70]

Agreements for trade effluent disposal

A sewerage undertaker is empowered to enter and carry into effect with any owner or occupier of trade premises an agreement for the reception and disposal of trade effluent from those premises, or for the removal and disposal of substances produced in the course of treating trade effluent on or in connection with those premises. The agreement may also make provision for a number of other obligations, as well as authorising a discharge which would otherwise require a consent, as previously described.[71]

Any proposal to enter such an agreement with respect to, or to any matter connected with, the reception or disposal of any special category effluent puts the undertaker under a duty to refer certain questions to the Secretary of State. Those questions are whether the agreement should be prohibited or, if not, subject to any requirements governing the conditions for the execution of the agreement. The duty is enforceable under section 18 of the Act.[72] The Secretary of State also enjoys powers to review such agreements relating to special category effluents, again for the purpose of deciding whether operations should be prohibited or, if not, subject to particular requirements. The powers available are similar to those available to the Secretary of State on any review of consents for the discharge of special category effluent.[73]

[64] See n.54, *supra*.
[65] Water Industry Act, s.123.
[66] See n.50, *supra*.
[67] Water Industry Act, s.126(1).
[68] *Ibid*. s.137.
[69] *Ibid*. s.125; see n.51, *supra*.
[70] *Ibid*. subs.(2).
[71] *Ibid*. s.129.
[72] *Ibid*. s.130. *Cf*. n.13, *supra*.
[73] *Ibid*. s.131. *Cf*. n.59, *supra*.

References and reviews relating to special category effluent

Elsewhere in this section of the chapter, there are descriptions of the references to the Secretary of State under section 120, 123 or 130 and reviews by virtue of sections 127 and 131, all in relation to special category effluents. In conducting any consideration of a reference for these purposes, the Secretary of State is obliged to permit any objections or representations from the sewerage undertaker, the person intending to undertake a discharge to the public sewer or (as the case may be) a would-be party to an agreement. In making a determination for the purpose of delivering his notice of decision, the Secretary of State enjoys wide powers to permit or prohibit subject operations or to impose conditions, as well as power to vary or revoke any relevant notice, consent or agreement.[74] Thereafter the sewerage undertaker and the Director-General are obliged to ensure that the requirements of the Secretary of State's notice are complied with.[75] If the Secretary of State's conclusions as a result of a section 132 reference are founded on the protection of public health or that of flora and fauna dependent on an aquatic environment in circumstances[76] where a review would otherwise have been prohibited an owner or occupier of trade premises will be entitled to compensation.[77] However, there will be no compensation entitlement if the reference and its determination arose from a change of circumstances that was not reasonably forseeable, or because material information was not reasonably available to the Secretary of State at the time of that determination.[78]

Transitional provision

Many trade effluent discharges occur by virtue of provision made prior to the coming into force of the Water Act 1989. Transitional provision in these circumstances is made by Schedule 8 to the Act. Disputes in relation to these arrangements are determined by the Director-General.[79]

Charges

Reference has been made to the imposition of conditions, including the power to include a condition requiring the payment of trade effluent charges to the sewerage undertaker.[80] In addition, the agreements provided for by the legislation may incorporate charging requirements.[81]

Charges schemes are provided for by the Water Industry Act.[82] Such schemes may provide for the fixing of charges for the provision of sewerage services by an

[74] *Ibid.* s.132.
[75] *Ibid.* s.133.
[76] *Ibid.* ss.127(2) and 131(2).
[77] *Ibid.* s.134.
[78] *Ibid.* subs.(2).
[79] *Ibid.* Sched. 8, para. 4.
[80] *Ibid.* s.121 and *cf.* n.45, *supra.*
[81] *Ibid.* ss.129–131 and *cf.* nn.71–73, *supra. Cf.* s.142(2), (3).
[82] *Ibid.* ss.142 and 143.

undertaker, for the payment to that undertaker of the prescribed charge in the circumstances prescribed by the scheme and for the time and method of payment. The "prescribed circumstances" just referred to cover any application for consent[83] and a consent granted by an undertaker, as well as a discharge made in pursuance of such a consent.[84] Each sewerage undertaker is required, as a condition of appointment, to maintain a charges scheme and to make it available to consumers, on request. If any agreement exists with the sewerage undertaker, it is possible for any charging provision in that agreement to supersede any scheme as prescribed above.[85] However, in so far as any scheme does govern the payment of charges, the liability for those charges is borne by the occupier of the benefiting premises.[86]

Trade effluent registers

Each sewerage undertaker is obliged to maintain a trade effluent register containing details of each consent granted, direction given, agreement entered into and notices served under section 132 in relation to references and reviews. Each register must be kept available, at all reasonable times, for inspection by the public free of charge, at the offices of the undertaker. The undertaker is under a duty to furnish a copy of, or extract from, anything on the register on payment of a reasonable sum.[87] The duties here are enforceable by the Director-General of Water Services.[88]

Agency Arrangements with Local Authorities

A sewerage undertaker is able to arrange with a local authority for the discharge of sewerage functions in the whole or any part of that local authority's area. However, any such arrangements do not affect the availability to any individual of any remedy in respect of responsibility for the discharge of sewerage functions, or any failure to discharge such functions. For the purpose of these agency arrangements and the discharge by the local authority of the undertaker's functions, that local authority may exercise any power for those purposes granted by statute to the undertaker.[89]

There are two significant limitations on the sewerage functions which may be the subject of agency arrangements. Under such arrangements, a local authority is unable to deal with sewerage disposal and trade effluent regulatory functions.[90]

[83] *Ibid.* s.119 and *cf.* nn.43 and 44, *supra.*

[84] *Ibid.* s.143(1).

[85] *Ibid.* s.143(5).

[86] *Ibid.* s.144.

[87] *Ibid.* s.196. *Cf.* s.204, requiring an owner or occupier of land from which a discharge of trade effluent is made, or is intended to be made, to provide relevant information to the undertaker.

[88] *Ibid.* s.18. *Cf.* n.13, *supra.*

[89] *Ibid.* s.97. *Cf.* s.179(5). *Cf.* n.18, *supra.*

[90] *Ibid.* subs.(5). *Cf.* n.18, *supra.*

Sewerage Disposal Operations

Any reference to disposal in relation to sewage includes treatment.[91] Works constructed for sewage disposal will vest in the sewerage undertaker, including works constructed by the undertaker, as well as works vested in the undertaker, by virtue of sections 102 and 104 of the Water Industry Act.[92] There may be circumstances in which sewage disposal works can be regarded as part of an indivisible whole with sewers and, as such, vested in the undertaker. This was the case in *Solihull RDC v. Ford.*[93] The judge, Mackinnon J., took the view that:

> "... the whole of the works that were constructed pursuant to [the] licence constituted the sewer—not only the line of pipes but also the disposal plant, which is really a necessary part of the sewer and without which it would never have been authorised and could in fact never have been constructed."[94]

Construction

The sewerage functions to be undertaken include the sewerage undertaker's responsibility for the construction of sewage disposal works.[95] However unlike the relative freedom to lay pipes in land in private ownership,[96] the power to construct disposal works on land is dependent on acquisition of land, not already in the ownership of the undertaker, by compulsory purchase.[97] The critical issue, therefore is whether or not any works fall within the framework of pipe-laying. In *Kings College Cambridge v. Uxbridge RDC,*[98] it was held that the works in question could only be executed on land which was first acquired for the purpose. Byrne J. giving judgment thought:

> "... it would be a great stretch of the imagination to hold that a large independent building, outside and over the surface, or partly over the surface and partly underneath, meant to be used as an engine house and works [for lifting and forcing along a rising main the sewage of a district] was part of a sewer."[99]

The construction of works for sewage disposal will require planning permission as a building or engineering operation under the Town and Country Planning Act. Furthermore, prior notification of and publicity for the application will be required under the Act,[1] since what is involved here is "...the

[91] *Ibid.* s.219(1).
[92] *Ibid.* s.179.
[93] (1932) 30 L.G.R. 483.
[94] *Ibid.* at 484.
[95] Water Industry Act, ss.6(2)(b), 219(1).
[96] *Ibid.* s.159. *Cf.* n.48, *supra.*
[97] *Ibid.* s.155.
[98] [1901] 2 Ch. 768.
[99] *Ibid.* at 773.
[1] s.65. *Cf.* n.79, *supra.*

construction of buildings or other operations or the use of land for retaining, treating or disposing of sewage, trade waste or sludge . . .".[2]

Sewage as controlled waste

Whether sewage is "controlled" waste for the purpose of the Environmental Protection Act 1990, Pt. II, is a matter of significance for a variety of purposes, but more particularly for the purpose of the offence of unlawful deposition of controlled waste, the duty of care in relation to controlled waste and the requirement of a waste management licence for the treatment, keeping or disposal of controlled waste.[3] Controlled waste is defined to include household, commercial and industrial waste.[4]

Normally, sewage is not to be included in the definition of any of these categories of waste unless regulations stipulate otherwise.[5] Of greatest significance for present purposes is the prescription that the following waste is not to be regarded as industrial or commercial waste:

(a) sewage, sludge or septic tank sludge which is treated, kept or disposed of within the curtilage of a sewage treatment works as an integral part of the operation of those works;
(b) sludge supplied or used in accordance with the Sludge (Use in Agriculture) Regulations 1989; or
(c) septic tank sludge used in accordance with these 1989 Regulations.[6]

Operational limits

The operation of sewage disposal works will be subject to limitation by law in five main respects where environmental and amenity considerations are concerned. Those environmental and amenity considerations focus on:

(a) generation of offensive odours by sewage disposal and treatment operations;
(b) discharge of sewage effluent to controlled waters;
(c) incineration;
(d) disposal of effluent to land; and
(e) sea disposal of effluent.

[2] Town and Country Planning General Development Order 1988, art.11(1)(d). *Cf.* art.18(r), requiring consultation with NRA.
[3] Respectively, ss.33, 34 and 35, Environmental Protection Act.
[4] *Ibid.* s.75.
[5] *Ibid.* subs.(8).
[6] Controlled Waste Regulations 1992 (S.I. 1992 No. 588), art.7.

Offensive odours

In the provision of a range of sewerage services,[7] it is provided by the Water Industry Act that a sewerage undertaker should carry out its functions so as not to create a nuisance.[8] Whether liability in nuisance will arise in these circumstances really depends on whether any interference with the use and enjoyment of the plaintiff's land (in the case of private nuisance, for example) is the inevitable consequence of the exercise of statutory powers justifying the performance of any particular function.[9] If it is found by the court that the interference was not the inevitable consequence of the statutory authority performing the function or activity in question, or that there was negligence (in the operation of the system for treatment and disposal, for example), then the court may be disposed to grant an injunction with or without damages, or simply to grant damages. In *Bainbridge v. Chertsey UDC*,[10] for example, the plaintiffs owned and occupied a dwelling-house. The plaintiffs obtained an injunction against the defendants, owners of a sewage farm about 800 yards away, restraining the conduct of activities on the farm which had caused offensive smells and vapours on the plaintiffs' land.

Also of practical significance are proceedings in these circumstances for a statutory nuisance under the Environmental Protection Act.[11] It is likely that the statutory nuisance for present purposes would arise from the fact that the premises being used for sewage treatment and disposal are "prejudicial to health or a nuisance". Of greater significance, no doubt would be the reference to "nuisance", essentially a common law nuisance.[12] Although there has been reluctance in the courts to characterise sewers as "premises" for the purpose of enforcing statutory nuisance provisions, it may be argued that such an objection could not be sustained against premises comprising sewage disposal works.[13] A defence of "best practicable means" may be available in proceedings here, but only in relation to trade industrial or business premises. It may be argued that "privatised" sewerage undertakers are indeed operating such premises for the purpose of sewage disposal.

Discharges to controlled waters

Reference has been made previously[14] to the requirement that a sewerage undertaker should carry out its functions so as not to create a nuisance. Those particular functions relate to activities concerning mainly the development and maintenance of a system of sewers and drains. In addition, there is a statutory declaration that an undertaker should not be seen as being authorised to construct or use any public or other sewer, or any drain or outfall, in contravention of "any"

[7] Water Industry Act, ss.102–105, 112, 115 and 116.
[8] *Ibid.* s.117(6).
[9] *Allen v. Gulf Oil Refining Ltd* [1981] A.C. 101, H.L.
[10] (1914) 13 L.G.R. 935. *Cf. Cornford v. Havant and Waterloo UDC* (1933) 31 L.G.R. 142.
[11] Pt. III.
[12] *National Coal Board v. Thorne* [1976] 1 W.L.R. 543.
[13] *Fulham Vestry v. London County Council* [1897] 2 Q.B. 76. *Cf. R. v. Parlby* (1889) 22 Q.B.D. 520.
[14] See nn.7, 8, *supra*.

applicable provisions in the Water Resources Act 1991[15] (particularly those governing the licensing of discharges to "controlled" waters), or for the purpose of conveying fouled water into any natural or artificial stream, watercourse, canal, pond or lake without the water having been treated so as not to affect prejudicially the purity and quality of the water in those locations.[16] The essential concern here is whether any discharge from sewage disposal works is authorised by a consent issued by NRA (the National Rivers Authority),[17] a licensing system enforced by reference to criminal sanctions.

The criminal enforcement measures found in the Water Resources Act[18] are based on a person's contravention where he "... causes or knowingly permits any poisonous, noxious or polluting matter or any solid waste matter to enter any controlled waters".[19] However, a more specifically relevant provision stipulates a contravention where a person causes or knowingly permits "... any trade effluent or sewage effluent to be discharged into any controlled waters; or from land in England and Wales, through a pipe, into the sea outside the seaward limits of controlled waters".[20] In very similar terms, a further offence is committed where there is contravention of a specified prohibition issued by NRA and trade or sewage effluent is discharged from a building or any fixed plant onto or into any land or into any waters of a lake or pond which are not inland fresh waters.[21]

These two situations relating to the discharge of trade or sewage effluent may be of concern where the sewerage undertaker did not cause or knowingly permit the discharge but was bound to receive into the sewer or sewage disposal works matter included in the discharge. In these circumstances, the undertaker, for the purpose of the offences in section 85(3) and (4), is deemed to have caused the discharge.[22] On the other hand, the undertaker will not be guilty of an offence here by reason only of the fact that a discharge from its sewer or sewage disposal works contravenes discharge consent conditions where three conditions are satisfied. Those conditions are that the contravention arises from a discharge to the sewer or works caused or permitted by another person where the undertaker was not bound to receive it, or to receive it only in conformity with conditions that were not observed, in circumstances where that undertaker could not reasonably have been expected to prevent the discharge into the sewer or works.[23] Finally, in the present context, the Act allows a further exemption from criminal liability under section 85 where a person has caused or permitted a discharge into a sewer or sewage disposal works of an undertaker where that undertaker was bound to receive the discharge either unconditionally or subject to conditions which were observed.[24]

[15] s.88 and Sched. 10. *Cf. Cook v. South West Water Plc* [1992] Env. L.R. D1.
[16] Water Industry Act, s.117(5).
[17] *Cf.* Chap. 4, "Water Pollution".
[18] s.85. See, *e.g. Wychavon District Council v. NRA* [1993] Env. L.R. 330
[19] Water Resources Act, s.85(1).
[20] *Ibid.* subs.(3).
[21] *Ibid.* subs.(4).
[22] *Ibid.* s.87(1). *Cf. NRA v. North West Water* (1992) 205 ENDS Rep. 39.
[23] *Ibid.* subs.(2). *Cf. NRA v. Yorkshire Water* (1992) 209 ENDS Rep. 39.
[24] *Ibid.* subs.(3).

Sampling requirements for present purposes stipulate a need to divide any sample into three parts, one part going to the occupier. In present circumstances, sampling of discharges from sewers or sewage works vested in an undertaker necessitates that "one-third" part goes to that undertaker as the "occupier of the land" for present purposes.[25] The present provisions refer to "any sample", a much wider reference than that found in the predecessor Water Resources Act 1963 which referred to samples of "effluent".[26]

Incineration

"About 30% of [sewage] sludge is sent to sea. Of the remainder 45% is spread on agricultural land, about 20% goes to landfill and the remainder is incinerated on land."[27] The drastic reduction in sea dumping (dealt with below) has focused attention on a number of alternative methods of disposal, one of the more expensive of which may be incineration.

The regulation and control of incineration is governed by two E.C. directives.[28] Municipal waste incinerators with a capacity of under one tonne per hour are subject to local authority air pollution control under the Environmental Protection Act 1990.[29] Larger incinerators are subject to integrated pollution control, administered and enforced by Her Majesty's Inspectorate of Pollution, under the same Act. Both enforcing agencies are required to include conditions in authorisations, giving effect to the above E.C. directives which set combustion controls, emission limit values and operating requirements to reduce air pollution from new and existing incinerators.[30]

Effluent disposal to land

Reference has been made already to the legal status of sewage in relation to statutory controls on "controlled" waste for the purposes of the Environmental Protection Act.[31] An important area of exemption from control concerns the use of sludge in agriculture.[32] For present purposes, "sludge" is defined as ". . . residual sludge from sewage plants treating domestic or urban waste waters and from other sewage plants treating waste waters of a composition similar to domestic and urban waste waters".[33] The Sludge (Use in Agriculture) Regulations implement E.C. Directive 86/278[33a] and, as such, seek to safeguard

[25] *Ibid.* s.209(1), (4).

[26] *NRA v. Harcross Timber and Building Supplies* [1993] Env. L.R. 172. *Cf. Attorney-General's Reference (No. 2 of 1994), The Times*, August 4, 1994 and *R. v. CPC (UK) Ltd, The Times*, August 4, 1994.

[27] Ministry of Agriculture Report on The Disposal of Waste at Sea, 1986 and 1987 (1989).

[28] Directive 89/369: [1989] O.J. L163 and Directive 89/429: [1989] O.J. L203.

[29] Pt. I.

[30] Municipal Waste Incineration Directions 1991, made under s.7(2)(b) of the Act of 1990.

[31] See nn.3–6, *supra*.

[32] Sludge (Use in Agriculture) Regulations 1989 (S.I. 1989 No. 1263), as amended by S.I. 1990 No. 880.

[33] *Ibid.* reg.2(1).

[33a] [1986] O.J. L181.

humans, animals, plants and the environment generally from any adverse effects of uncontrolled sludge spreading and to encourage the proper application of sewage sludge. Under the Regulations, no person shall cause or knowingly permit sludge to be used on agricultural land unless certain requirements are fulfilled. Similarly, no person shall supply such sludge if he knows or has reason to believe that those requirements will not be fulfilled. Those requirements include modes of treatment for the sludge, application to the land and the presence of restricted categories of crops at the time of application.[34] The Regulations also time limit certain uses of the land for agricultural purposes following sludge application,[35] require the occupier of the land where sludge has been used to advise the sludge producer of details of that user[36] and require the sludge producer to maintain a register, open to inspection by the Secretary of State, of details of production, supply and use.[37] Any failure to comply with these requirements is an offence, triable summarily.[38]

Apart from incineration, spreading of sludge on agricultural land and disposal at sea, it has been seen already that a good deal of sewage sludge is landfilled. For this purpose, sewage sludge will be regarded as "controlled" waste, necessitating a waste management licence for disposal.[39]

Effluent disposal at sea

So-called "long sea" outfalls for the discharge of sewage constructed by NRA will first require the consent of the Secretary of State.[40] It was seen previously that the discharge of trade or sewage effluent from land, through a pipe, to the sea outside the seaward limits of controlled waters is an offence.[41] This area of statutory regulation is complemented by the Food and Environment Protection Act 1985 that requires a licence from the Minister of Agriculture in respect of various acts, including the deposit of "substances or articles" anywhere in the sea or under the sea bed within or outside the United Kingdom waters from vessels, aircraft, hovercraft or marine structures.[42] Licensing requirements also extend to marine incineration.[43] In determining any application for a licence, the Minister is obliged to have regard, *inter alia*, to the need to protect the marine environment, the living resources which it supports and human health, and to prevent

[34] S.I. 1989 No. 1263, reg.3.
[35] *Ibid.* reg.4.
[36] *Ibid.* reg.5.
[37] *Ibid.* regs.6 and 7.
[38] *Ibid.* reg.9.
[39] See nn.3–5, *supra.*
[40] Water Resources Act, s.181.
[41] *Ibid.* s.85(3): see n.20, *supra.*
[42] s.5.
[43] Food and Environment Protection Act 1985, s.6.

interference with legitimate uses of the sea.[44] With the aid of considerable powers of entry and inspection,[45] the Act's requirements are subject to criminal enforcement,[46] together with default powers.[47]

Effluent Control Liabilities

An enormous variety of facts may lead to a loss of control of effluent, the responsibility for which, in law, may rest with an individual *qua* owner or occupier of land or a sewerage undertaker. In these circumstances, attention is focused on liabilities in private law, usually where sewage effluent has damaged the plaintiff's land. Previously, in the present chapter, reference has been made to the problem of sewerage overload and the fact that, except in the most extreme circumstances, this will not attract liability in nuisance to the sewerage undertaker.[48]

Strict liability in nuisance

There is no doubt that liability is strict, in accordance with *Rylands v. Fletcher*, if the contents of a person's sewer or drain escape and damage the plaintiff's land or property. The principle has been described thus:

> "I think it is clear that the principle of *Rylands v. Fletcher* would apply to the owner of a sewer, whether he made the sewer or not ... His duty at common law would be to see that the sewage in his sewer did not escape to the injury of others and mere neglect of this duty would give any person injured a good cause of action".[49]

Such is the strictness of the principle that any drainage of the defendant's land across that of the plaintiff's assumes that the line of the sewer or drain will adequately control the effluent: the defendant's ignorance of any defect in the drain or sewer is no defence.[50]

Liability in nuisance and trespass may arise where the defendant knows that effluent from his sewer or drain is out of control and damaging the plaintiff's land. Foreseeability of harm or injury of the type complained of is now a prerequisite for strict liability, assuming that any subject effluent is still within the defendant's control.[51] Failure to take measures to deal with the situation may be regarded as a

[44] *Ibid.* s.8.
[45] *Ibid.* s.11 and Sched. 2.
[46] *Ibid.* s.9.
[47] *Ibid.* s.10.
[48] See nn.15 and 16, *supra.*
[49] *per* Parker J. in *Jones v. Llanwrst UDC* [1911] 1 Ch. 393 at 405.
[50] *Humphries v. Cousins* (1877) 2 C.P.D. 239. Contrast *Ilford UDC v. Beal* [1925] 1 K.B. 671, where it was found that the defendant did not know of and could not reasonably have discovered the sewer running under his house: *per* Branson J. at 679.
[51] *Cambridge Water Co. v. Eastern Counties Leather* [1994] 2 W.L.R. 53.

contamination or adoption of the nuisance, particularly if the defendant utilises any facility that "constitutes" the nuisance.[52] Such an adoption occurred in *Pearce v. Croydon RDC*,[53] where the defendant allowed surface drainage from certain roads to flow across the plaintiff's land, arguing that there was a watercourse running across the land or that a sewer ran across the land, into which they were entitled to discharge the water. It was held that although there was a "bourne course" of underground water from chalk which had often flooded the plaintiff's land, it was not a watercourse and not a sewer, so that the plaintiff could claim damages for trespass and an injunction.

Reference has been made previously to the statutory requirement that a sewerage undertaker should carry out its functions so as not to create a nuisance.[54] One very influential view of the undertaker's position is seen in *Smeaton*,[55] a position confirmed in the earlier case of *Glossop v. Heston and Isleworth Local Board*,[56] where the plaintiff complained that for some time before and since the defendant became the sanitary authority, sewage was allowed to fall into a stream passing near his residence so as to pollute it and cause a nuisance to him. The plaintiff sought damages and a mandatory injunction, claims rejected by the court essentially on the ground that there was no cause of action against an authority that had done no wrong, the evidence indicating that the authority had neither acted to create nor increase the nuisance:

> "It is not said they have done any act the consequence of which has been to bring sewage down to the [stream]. If that were so, unless they could show that act, causing a nuisance to the plaintiff, as in my opinion it has done, was protected by the Act, then of course it would be the duty of this court . . . to restrain the defendants from creating a nuisance; and although they are a public body having public duties and powers to perform those duties, that would not exempt them from legal liability in consequence of a nuisance caused by them. On the evidence there is no ground for saying they have done that."[57]

It is difficult to say whether the legislation provides immunity in favour of the undertaker: a lot depends on the court's view of the line that divides the proper though perhaps "non-feasant" performance of the section 94 duties, as opposed to a more proactive, probably negligent, approach, for example, in the implementation of sewer design. A strong case for this purpose is *Fleming v. Manchester Corporation*,[58] where the defendant authority was found to have been ignorant of defects in the sewer, dating back to construction. Those defects might have been discovered with reasonable, diligent investigation. It was held that the

52 *Sedleigh Denfield v. O'Callaghan* [1940] A.C. 880, H.L.
53 (1910) 74 J.P. 429; 8 L.G.R. 909.
54 Water Industry Act, s.117(6); see n.8, *supra*.
55 See nn.15 and 16, *supra*.
56 [1874–80] All E.R. Rep. 840.
57 *Ibid. per* Cotton L.J. at 845.
58 *The Times*, June 27, 1882.

authority was obliged to acquaint itself from time to time with the condition of its sewers in connection with cleansing and repair, for example. In these circumstances, the authority was found to be liable in negligence. In a second case—*Barrhead Burgh v. James Brownlie & Sons*[59]—the House of Lords found that flooding was due to insufficiency and faulty design of sewers. The authority's defence was based on "natural" flooding of two adjoining watercourses. It was held that the inadequacy of the sewers materially contributed to the company's loss.

Mere incapacity, allied to the undertaker's obligation to accept communications to and discharges into the public sewer, will usually suggest immunity from liability in law but subject to possible "administrative" enforcement by the Secretary of State under section 18.[60] Beyond this situation, evidence of negligence may suggest an unreasonable failure to provide adequately designed sewers capable of avoiding loss or damage which here will be far more directly referable to the sewerage undertaker. In these circumstances, matters of limitation may be of little concern to the plaintiff:

> "There must, I think, be a fresh cause of action in *Rylands v. Fletcher* whenever a fresh escape occurs. Nuisance can be continuous, or fresh causes of action for it can arise whenever new damage or interference occurs as a result of it."[61]

Where an injunction is granted against the sewerage undertaker, it is probable that the terms of the injunction would reflect the practicalities, in relation to capital spending, for example, of implementing measures to defeat the nuisance in question.

[59] (1925) 89 J.P. 157.
[60] See n.13, *supra*.
[61] *per* Judge Newey Q.C. in *Ryeford Homes Ltd v. Sevenoaks District Council* (1989) 46 B.L.R. at 47.

CHAPTER 3

LAND DRAINAGE AND FLOOD DEFENCE

The Dimensions of Land Drainage

The essence of land drainage is the removal of unwanted water from the land to the sea. The present chapter also examines the related matters of flood defence and coast protection. The Land Drainage Act 1991 (a consolidating Act covering the law on internal drainage boards, their functions and the related functions of local authorities in this context) defines drainage widely to include "... defence against water (including sea water), irrigation, other than spray irrigation, and warping".[1] Warping is a process whereby silt suspended in water is permitted to wash over land until the silt is deposited by settlement to permit fertilisation.

The statutory regulation of land drainage is scattered widely through a range of statutory provisions. Reference has been made already to the Land Drainage Act 1991, dealing with internal drainage boards and their inter-relationship with local authorities and the National Rivers Authority (NRA hereafter), and the processes necessary for the drainage of land, together with attendant financial requirements, including particularly the raising of drainage rates. Additional powers relating to drainage and flood defence works are given to the NRA by the Water Resources Act 1991, and the organisation of flood defence responsibilities is also set out in the latter Act.

Coast protection is dealt with by the Coast Protection Act 1949. Elsewhere, a wide variety of statutory provisions touch and affect the present area, including the town and country planning legislation, the highways legislation and legislation affecting the coal mining industry.

The Administrative Agencies

The Ministers

For many purposes, administration and enforcement is in the hands of the Minister of Agriculture, Fisheries and Food and, in Wales, the Secretary of State for Wales. The Ministers' functions, individually or (in the case of functions

[1] s.72(1).

straddling borders) jointly, fall into several categories, to be examined in more detail in the body of this chapter. The first category relates to flood defence and includes:

(a) supervision of NRA flood defence functions;
(b) composition of flood defence committees;
(c) provision of regulations for flood defence functions;
(d) the giving of directions to NRA;
(e) demands for information for the financing of flood defence functions; and
(f) the provision of grants for flood warning schemes.

The second category of functions relates to:

(a) supervision of the areas and constitutions of internal drainage boards;
(b) approval of internal drainage board and NRA bye laws;
(c) determination of land drainage appeals and inquiries;
(d) the making of financial grants to the drainage authorities.

In a third, broader category of financial functions there is included:

(a) approval of borrowing by NRA;
(b) approval of loans raised by internal drainage boards; and
(c) a variety of responsibilities in connection with determination of drainage charges, rates and levies for the funding of land drainage.

Finally, the Ministers have a number of miscellaneous functions, including the approval of different schemes for the transfer of so-called "main river", conservancy and navigation functions to NRA, as well as the approval of compulsory works orders for NRA.

The Ministers also enjoy considerable powers in relation to coast protection under the Coast Protection Act 1949, particularly in a supervisory capacity over the local authorities who act as coast protection authorities. Of special significance, potentially, are powers of default and direction, as well as broad powers to provide grant-aid for coast protection work.

The drainage bodies

A drainage body under the Land Drainage Act 1991 is defined to include the NRA, an internal drainage board "... or any other body having power to make or maintain works for the drainage of land".[2] A local authority may be included in this definition, for example, on the basis of maintenance of drainage works "... in connection with any watercourse" under section 17 of the Land Drainage Act where NRA consent has been given. Also included are regional flood defence committees and the local flood defence committees created under the Water

[2] *Ibid.*

Resources Act 1991, which requires that the NRA "... shall arrange for all its functions relating to flood defence ..." under this Act and the Land Drainage Act 1991 to be carried out by the regional committees.[3]

National Rivers Authority

Section 105 of the Water Resources Act requires NRA to exercise a general supervision over all matters relating to flood defence and to execute surveys from time to time of areas over which it has responsibility. Despite its responsibility to arrange for discharge of flood defence functions by the regional flood defence committees, NRA cannot devolve its responsibilities in relation to the issue of drainage levies and the making of drainage charges.[4] Exceptionally, NRA may become a drainage board under the Land Drainage Act,[5] which states that there shall continue to be internal drainage districts and internal drainage boards.[6]

Regional flood defence committees

As will be seen, the regional flood defence committees enjoy a rather complex status in relation to NRA and the Minister, although essentially they undertake the discharge of flood defence functions as NRA's agent. NRA members are excluded from membership of any regional committee,[7] which shall comprise a chairman, a number of members appointed by the relevant Minister, two members appointed by NRA and a number of members appointed by or on behalf of the constituent councils.[8] Those councils comprise the councils of every county, metropolitan district or London borough any part of which is in the area of a regional flood defence committee including (where geographically appropriate) the Common Council of the City of London.[9] Schedule 4 to the Water Resources Act governs matters of membership and proceedings both in relation to regional and local flood defence committees. Such committees are permitted to carry out any of their functions through a sub-committee, an under sub-committee of the committee, or an officer of NRA.[10]

Local flood defence committees

The basis for the creation and operation of a local flood defence committee is a local flood defence scheme made by NRA, relating to one or more districts within the regional committee's area, with a local flood defence committee for such district. It is open to the regional committee at any time to propose to NRA a local flood defence scheme for any part of their area not then covered by such a

[3] Water Resources Act, s.106(1).
[4] *Ibid.* s.106(2).
[5] s.4.
[6] Land Drainage Act, s.1(1).
[7] Water Resources Act, s.10(1).
[8] *Ibid.*
[9] *Ibid.* subs. (5).
[10] *Ibid.* Sched. 4, para. 12.

scheme or, alternatively, a scheme varying or revoking a pre-existing scheme. However, prior to submission of any such scheme for consideration by NRA, the regional committee is required to consult each local authority whose area may be affected, together with "... such organisations representative of persons interested in flood defence[11] ... or agriculture as the regional flood defence committee consider to be appropriate". Ultimately, NRA is obliged to submit the scheme to the appropriate Minister for approval.[12] A local flood defence committee comprises a chairman appointed from among their number by the regional committee, other members appointed by that regional committee, and members appointed by or on behalf of the constituent councils as previously defined in relation to the regional committees. A local committee comprises not fewer than 11 members and not more than 15.[13]

Internal drainage boards

The essential purpose of any internal drainage district, administered by an internal drainage board, is that it derives benefit or avoids danger as a result of drainage operations as an area comprising part of a regional flood defence committee area.[14] The Land Drainage Act stipulates that each board shall exercise general supervision over all matters concerning the drainage of land in its district and have other powers and responsibility for other duties as indicated by the terms of the Act.[15] An internal drainage board is a body corporate and comprises elected members and members appointed by the so-called "charging" authorities, which are authorities against whom the board has the power to issue a special drainage levy.[16] Matters of election and appointment of members are dealt with in Schedule 1 to the Land Drainage Act, while Schedule 2 deals with board proceedings.

Internal drainage boards are subject to NRA supervision, to the extent that it may give "... such general or special directions as it considers reasonable for the guidance of ... boards ..." for the purpose of securing "... the efficient working and maintenance of existing drainage works; and ... the construction of such new drainage works as may be necessary ..."[17] Detailed requirements also affect the power of boards to interfere with other boards' drainage works and to undertake works for the discharge of water into a main river,[18] referable to a need for NRA approval in the first case and NRA agreement in the second, failing which, the Minister shall determine the matter.[19] Failure by an internal drainage board to comply with these requirements may attract an exercise of default powers by

[11] As defined by *ibid.* s.113.
[12] *Ibid.* s.12.
[13] *Ibid.* s.13.
[14] Land Drainage Act, s.1(1).
[15] *Ibid.* s.1(2).
[16] *Ibid.* s.36(1) and Local Government Finance Act 1988, s.75.
[17] Land Drainage Act, s.7(1).
[18] As defined by s.113(1), Water Resources Act.
[19] Land Drainage Act, s.7(2)–(6).

NRA. There are further and more extensive default powers in the Act if NRA is of the opinion that any land is injured or likely to be injured by flooding or inadequate drainage that might be remedied wholly or partially by the exercise of an internal drainage board's powers which either are not being exercised or, in the opinion of NRA, are not being exercised to the necessary extent.[20] In some circumstances, these default powers may be exercised by a local authority on application to NRA. An adverse decision by NRA may be appealed to the relevant Minister.[21]

The Land Drainage Act confers powers on internal drainage boards to acquire land compulsorily or by agreement, to dispose of land and to exercise powers of entry to land.[22] The Act also empowers NRA to enter an agreement with an internal drainage board whereby that board carries out work on a main river. The Water Resources Act[23] defines the extent of NRA responsibilities for flood defence in respect of "main rivers".

Local authorities

Apart from functions and responsibilities of a perhaps limited nature under the Public Health Act 1936 in relation to statutory nuisances affecting the drainage of land, local authorities have other limited functions and responsibilities in the present context. There are, for example, powers to appoint persons to the membership of regional and local flood defence committees, as well as a right to be consulted by NRA in respect of a scheme to re-organise internal drainage districts prior to submission of the scheme to the relevant Minister for approval.[24] Reference was made previously[25] to local authorities' default powers, although beyond these categories there are various specific powers available to local authorities. General drainage powers are conferred on local authorities[26] by section 14, either when acting under section 18 powers for the drainage of small areas where designation of an internal drainage district would not be practicable, or where action is deemed to be necessary for the purpose of preventing flooding or for mitigating any damage caused by flooding in their areas.[27] Local authorities here have the power to maintain and improve existing works and to construct new works.[28] Powers are also provided (subject to possible compensation for injury) permitting local authorities to dispose of spoil obtained from works carried out on watercourses.[29] In so far as any of the foregoing powers under sections 14 and 15 are conferred on a non-metropolitan district council, they can be exercised by the county council at the request of the district council or in the

[20] *Ibid.* s.9.
[21] *Ibid.* s.10.
[22] ss.62–64.
[23] ss.107–111.
[24] Land Drainage Act, s.3(4).
[25] See nn.20 and 21, *supra.*
[26] As defined in s.72 of the Land Drainage Act.
[27] *Ibid.* s.14(1).
[28] *Ibid.* subs.(2).
[29] *Ibid.* s.15.

event of its default.[30] However, none of the powers in sections 14–16 can be used for drainage works in respect of any watercourse without NRA consent.[31]

In so far as a local authority, other than a district council, is of the opinion that land is capable of improvement by drainage works where it would be impracticable to constitute an internal drainage district, a scheme approved by the relevant Minister may permit that authority to undertake the requisite drainage works.[32] Any local authority, other than a non-metropolitan district, may by agreement with any person and at his expense carry out within its area drainage works that person is entitled to carry out.[33]

A final set of provisions relate to local authorities' powers to act where an ordinary watercourse[34] is impeded. The authority may by notice require the situation to be remedied and may act in default if there is a failure to comply.[35] Such powers may only be exercised after notification of any internal drainage board or NRA within whose area the watercourse is wholly or partially located. On the other hand, the local authority's agreement may be required if it has powers apart from section 25 for securing an appropriate flow in any watercourse and another body seeks to act to secure a remedy.[36]

Works and related powers of drainage bodies

Normally, the NRA will exercise its various powers in relation to "main rivers" as governed by the Water Resources Act 1991,[37] dealt with elsewhere in the present chapter. Nevertheless, the Land Drainage Act[38] does recognise the need for reciprocity by permitting NRA to undertake works in the area of an internal drainage board and vice versa.[39] The critical dividing line, however, is found in section 14 of the Land Drainage Act, referred to previously in connection with the land drainage powers of local authorities. The specified local authorities and drainage boards acting within any internal drainage district have a variety of powers referable to any watercourse or drainage work, but not a main river or the banks of such a river: hence the reference above to a "critical" distinction. The powers which sit at the centre of section 14 relate to the maintenance of existing works, allowing the drainage body ". . . to cleanse, repair or otherwise maintain in a due state of efficiency any existing watercourse or drainage work"; the improvement of any existing works allowing the drainage body ". . . to deepen, widen, straighten or otherwise improve any existing watercourse or remove or

[30] *Ibid.* s.16.
[31] *Ibid.* s.17.
[32] *Ibid.* s.18.
[33] *Ibid.* s.20.
[34] Such a watercourse does not form part of a main river: s.72(1).
[35] *Ibid.* s.25.
[36] *Ibid.* s.26.
[37] ss.107–111. *Cf.* ss.2 and 9, empowering NRA to execute sea defence work on either side of the low-water mark.
[38] s.11.
[39] Land Drainage Act, s.11.

alter mill dams, weirs or other obstructions to watercourses, or raise, widen or otherwise improve any existing drainage work", and (finally) the construction of new works allowing the drainage body to "... make any new watercourse or drainage work or erect any machinery or do any other act (not included above) required for the drainage of any land".[40] These powers are exercisable by every drainage board in its district and every local authority in pursuance of a scheme under section 18 for the drainage of small areas[41] or "... so far as may be necessary for the purpose of preventing flooding or mitigating any damage caused by flooding in their area". The powers may be exercised outside the area of the board or local authority "... for the benefit of their district or area ..." but subject to particular requirements.[42] However, whenever the powers are exercised, the board or authority is liable to make full compensation to any person who sustains injury by reason of an exercise of these powers.[43] In the case of a local authority's exercise of the powers in section 14, NRA consent will be required.[44]

Previously, in the section on local authorities' land drainage functions,[45] it was seen that drainage works may be undertaken on behalf of persons entitled to execute such works. The same powers are available to any internal drainage board, although in this case there is an express exception excluding an exercise of the powers in relation to a main river, the banks of such a river or any drainage works in connection with a main river.[46] The same exclusion appears again in section 19, which empowers an internal drainage board to make arrangements with navigation and conservancy authorities for three purposes.[47] An arrangement may provide for:

(a) the transfer to the board of the whole or any part of the undertaking of the navigation or conservancy authority[48] or any of its rights, powers, duties, liabilities and obligations and any property vested in it;
(b) the alteration or improvement by the board of any of the navigation or conservancy authority's works; and
(c) payments from the board to the navigation or conservancy authority, or vice versa, in connection with an arrangement under this provision.

Any arrangement here requires the consent of the appropriate Minister or Secretary of State.[49]

The drainage board for a district and NRA may apply to either of the relevant Ministers seeking a variation of navigation rights. Such an application can only be granted if it appears to the Minister that the navigation authority is not exercising

[40] *Ibid.* s.14(2).
[41] See n.32, *supra.*
[42] s.14(3).
[43] Land Drainage Act, s.14(5), (6).
[44] *Ibid.* s.17 and *cf.* n.31, *supra.*
[45] See n.33, *supra.*
[46] Land Drainage Act, 20(3).
[47] *Ibid.* s.19(1).
[48] As defined by *ibid.* s.72(1).
[49] *Ibid.* s.19(3).

at all, or is not exercising to the necessary extent, the powers vested in it and it appears desirable for the purpose of securing the better drainage of land.[50] In granting the application, the resulting statutory instrument may revoke, vary or amend the provisions of any local Act relating to navigation rights over any canal, river or navigable waters.[51]

A particularly important element in the enforcement of different powers and requirements by the drainage bodies is the byelaw. The byelaw-making powers are divided into two in the present context: a set of powers in section 66 of the Land Drainage Act 1991, relating to internal drainage boards and local authorities, and a further set of powers, in favour of NRA, in the Water Resources Act.[52] In the first category, internal drainage boards and local authorities are empowered to make byelaws "... as they consider necessary for securing the efficient working of the drainage system in their area".[53] However, without prejudice to the generality of this byelaw-making power, a board or a local authority may make byelaws for a variety of purposes, including regulation of the use of watercourses.[54] However, both the general and the specific powers just described are not exercisable by an internal drainage board in relation to "main rivers" and are exercisable by a local authority "... only so far as may be necessary for the purpose of preventing flooding or remedying or mitigating any damage caused by flooding".[55] Subject to some exceptions, the byelaw-making powers here are not available to a county council.[56] Bye laws made under the section attain their validity on confirmation by the relevant Minister or Secretary of State.[57] Contravention of or failure to comply with a byelaw made under section 66 is an offence, triable summarily. If contravention or failure is continued after conviction, a continuing fine applies on every day when contravention or failure is continued.[58] Without prejudice to these criminal proceedings, the board or the local authority may take such action as may be necessary to remedy the effect of contravention or failure and recover any expenses from the person acting in default.[59] In the second category, NRA may make byelaws where it appears to it to be necessary or expedient to do so for the purposes of various functions, including flood defence functions and land drainage.[60] Such byelaws may make provision in relation to any particular locality or localities as NRA considers necessary to secure the efficient working of any drainage system, including the proper defence of any land against sea or tidal water. Without prejudice to this general power, NRA may make byelaws preventing the improper use of

[50] *Ibid.* s.35.
[51] *Ibid.*
[52] Sched. 25, para. 1.
[53] Land Drainage Act, s.66(1).
[54] *Ibid.* subs.(2), but *cf.* subs.(4).
[55] *Ibid.* subs.(3).
[56] *Ibid.* subss.(1) and (8).
[57] Sched. 5 to the Act applies to these byelaws, together with the procedure in s.236 of the Local Government Act 1972.
[58] s.66(6).
[59] *Ibid.* subs.(7).
[60] Water Resources Act, Sched. 25, para. 5.

watercourses, *inter alia.*[61] Failure to comply with any such byelaw is a summary offence, attracting a fine and with a continuing fine for every day when contravention continues.[62] NRA is empowered to take "... such action as may be necessary to remedy the effect of any person's contravention ..." of byelaws made for present purposes and to recover any reasonable expenses arising from action in default.[63] Finally, NRA byelaws are enforceable by reference to a limitation period of 12 rather than six months, and do not restrict any other liabilities and offences. Furthermore, any breach of byelaws here does not give rise to civil liability.[64]

Land Drainage Works

General works: private sector

The opening sections of the present chapter have stressed, by way of introduction, the public regulatory framework. The present section focuses on works in relation to any watercourse that may have implications under both common law and statute. Such works may require planning permission under the Town and Country Planning Act 1990. However, development by a drainage body[65] in, on or under the watercourse or land drainage works in connection with the improvement, maintenance or repair of the watercourse or works is permitted development for the purpose of the Town and Country Planning General Development Order 1988.[66] Also included in the definition of permitted development is development authorised by a Local or Private Act of Parliament.[67] If the development involves the carrying out of works or operations in the bed of or on the banks of a river or stream, the local planning authority is obliged to consult NRA before granting any planning permission.[68] The Land Drainage Act 1991 provides that whether or not in the course of any works it is proposed to obstruct a watercourse with (say) a structure or a culvert the consent of the drainage board concerned must be sought and obtained.[69] The Water Resources Act 1991 contains three important prohibitions in the context of a main river, all of which relate to obstructions and all of which require NRA approval.[70] Other issues at common law may arise, in so far as a defendant owner of land which is crossed by a watercourse may seek, by some obstruction, for example, to deny an adjacent plaintiff landowner's enjoyment of that watercourse. Despite any interruption within 20 years of an action to enforce the right such plaintiff can sue

[61] *Ibid.*
[62] *Ibid.* s.211.
[63] *Ibid.* subs.(5).
[64] *Ibid.* subs.(7).
[65] Land Drainage Act, s.72(1).
[66] S.I. 1988 No. 1813, art.3 and Sched. 2, Pt. 14.
[67] *Ibid.* Pt. 11.
[68] *Ibid.* art.18(1), para. (o).
[69] ss.23 and 24.
[70] s.109.

to establish his claim, which is not lost by the defendant's alteration of its course.[71] Tindal C.J. said[72]:

> "... it would be very dangerous to hold that a party should lose his right in consequence of ... an interruption; if such were the rule, the accident of a dry season, or other causes over which the party could have no control, might deprive him of a right established by the longest course of enjoyment."

Any attempt by a third party to undertake works in relation to a watercourse on the plaintiff's land can be justified only by reference to the plaintiff's sufficient agreement or the authority of legislative provision. Such third party intervention may require planning permission, although the local planning authority shall not entertain the application without the requisite certificate indicating, *inter alia*, notification of the application to the owner of the subject land.[73]

Where the owner of land develops a watercourse on that land, he will be constrained only in so far as there is infraction of some specific rule of law or breach of some contractual obligation.[74] Particular problems may arise in so far as a landowner permits, under the terms of a licence, for example, works on his land by another for the development of a watercourse where, ultimately, the landowner finds it necessary to abort the works. According to Blackburn J. in *Roberts v. Rose*,[75] the principle is as follows:

> "... where a person attempts to justify an interference with the property of another in order to abate a nuisance, he may justify himself against the wrongdoer so far as his interference is positively necessary ... In abating the nuisance, if there are two ways of doing it, he must choose the least mischievous of the two ... If by one of these alternative methods some wrong would be done to an innocent third party or to the public, then the method cannot be justified at all, although an interference with the wrongdoer himself might be justified. Therefore, where the alternative method involves such an interference it must not be adopted; and it may become necessary to abate the nuisance in a manner more onerous to the wrongdoer."[76]

The works associated with the development of a watercourse will usually amount to an "engineering" or "other" operation for the purpose of the Town and Country Planning Act 1990,[77] thus requiring planning permission. Typically, the creation of an entirely new watercourse or waterway, or the deepening of a river or the straightening of its banks would fall within the requirements of

[71] *Hall v. Swift* (1838) 6 Bing. N.C. 381; 132 E.R. 834.
[72] *Ibid.* at 835.
[73] Town and Country Planning Act 1990, s.66.
[74] *Wilson v. Waddell* (1876) 2 App. Cas. 95; 35 L.T. 639; 42 J.P. 116, H.L.
[75] (1865) L.R. 1 Ex. 82.
[76] *Ibid.* at 89.
[77] s.55.

development control here. A rather more limited category of works is likely to attract a requirement for an environmental assessment by virtue of E.C. Directive 85/337[77a] through regulations governing assessments. These regulations are, principally, the Town and Country Planning (Assessment of Environmental Effects) Regulations 1988[78] and the Land Drainage Improvement Works (Assessment of Environmental Effects) Regulations 1988.[79] The former Regulations would apply where planning permission is required, whereas the latter Regulations apply to improvement works by drainage bodies (normally regarded as "permitted development"[80]) comprising works which

> "... deepen, widen, straighten or otherwise improve any existing watercourse or remove or alter mill dams, weirs or other obstructions to watercourses, or raise, widen or otherwise improve any existing drainage work".[81]

By virtue of the Town and Country Planning (Assessment of Environmental Effects) Regulations, development falling within Schedule 1 to these Regulations will attract a mandatory environmental assessment as part of the development control process, involving an application for planning permission. The only category of development that appears to be relevant for present purposes in Schedule 1 is the provision of "A trading port, an inland waterway which permits the passage of vessels of over 1,350 tons or a port for inland waterway traffic capable of handling such vessels". Under Schedule 2, development will require an environmental assessment to accompany the application for planning permission, in so far as it "... would be likely to have significant effects on the environment by virtue of factors such as its nature, size or location".[82] It would appear that judgments on this matter lie exclusively within the jurisdiction of the local planning authority.[83] Under Schedule 2, there are some instances of developments that may require environmental assessment: note "water management for agriculture" and "reclamation of land from the sea"[84]; "... construction of a harbour ... not being development within Schedule 1", "canalisation or flood relief works" and "a dam or other installation designed to hold water or store it on a long term basis"[85]; "and a site for depositing sludge".[86]

Although any necessary grant of planning permission (along with any accompanying planning agreement or obligation)[87] may anticipate problems and

[77a] [1985] O.J. L175.
[78] S.I. 1988 No. 1199.
[79] S.I. 1988 No. 1217.
[80] See nn.65 and 66, *supra.*
[81] S.I. 1988 No. 1217, reg.2(1).
[82] S.I. 1988 No. 1199, reg.2(1).
[83] *R. v. Swale Borough Council and Medway Ports Authority, ex p. RSPB* [1991] P.L.R. 6 and *R. v. Poole Borough Council, ex p. Beebee* [1991] J.P.L. 643.
[84] S.I. 1988 No. 1199, Sched. 2, para. 1, "Agriculture".
[85] *Ibid.* para. 10, "Intrastructure projects".
[86] *Ibid.* para. 11, "Other projects".
[87] Town and Country Planning Act 1990, s.106.

constraints, such as the reliability of watercourse works against the escape of water, the initial risks and how they may be met through (say) the engineering of the project may be anticipated by any environmental assessment that may be demanded. Beyond the four corners of such "public law" control, in so far as it is relevant, identification and distribution of any liabilities through a failure of the project will be a matter for private, common law. In one instance,[88] the owner of land on a riverbank, for the purpose of bringing water from a river to the mill that he had constructed, developed a watercourse with a shuttle at its head to control the flow of water from the river to the watercourse. Subsequently, the landowner conveyed a portion of adjoining land and, even later, his own successor in title granted to the owner of that adjacent land a right to use the water for the purposes of his own mill. It was held by the court that the existence of that right did not affect the obligation of the landowner (the owner of the watercourse) towards the owner of the adjoining land to keep the shuttle in repair so as to prevent flood water from the river getting into the watercourse and overflowing on to the plaintiff's land. Rigby L.J. said:

> "When the defendants' predecessor in title . . . conveyed to the plaintiff's predecessors in title the property now belonging to the plaintiffs, he became liable to his grantees to prevent the goit which he had made for his own purposes on land which continued to belong to him from becoming a source of danger to them."[89]

Equally, the landowner who collects water on his land in a "non-natural" artifically constructed channel which is defective may be liable in negligence and nuisance and subject to injunctive proceedings if the water escapes on to a neighbour's land. In a New Zealand case, *Spear v. Newman*,[90] the basis of the court's approach is clearly indicated in the words of one member of that court, MacGregor J.[91]:

> ". . . the defendants have not only concentrated the flow of the rainwater in a non-natural channel towards the plaintiff's land, but have allowed that channel to get out of repair, and, thus have allowed the water flowing through the channel to escape there from by faulty construction and want of repair and to discharge on to the plaintiff's land in such volume as to do the damage complained of . . ."

However, different considerations apply, in so far as there is some shared benefit from the works in question or evidence of the plaintiff's consent to any other works. In *Gill v. Edouin*,[92] for example, a facility was provided on a flat roof

[88] *R.H. Buckley & Sons Ltd. v. N. Buckley & Sons* [1898] 2 Q.B. 608.
[89] *Ibid.* at 613.
[90] [1926] N.Z.L.R. 897. *Cf. Whalley v. Lancashire and Yorkshire Railway Co.* (1884) 13 Q.B.D. 131 and *Crisp v. Snowsill* [1917] N.Z.L.R. 252.
[91] *Ibid.* at 904.
[92] (1894) 71 L.T. 762.

adjacent to property in the ownership of the plaintiff and defendant, for the purpose of allowing rain water to escape. The plaintiff had a right to use this facility but the defendant (having originally provided the flat roof) had not maintained the gully on the roof for the escape of the rainwater. It was held that, in the absence of any negligence, the defendant was not liable for damage from accumulated rainwater affecting the plaintiff's premises, on the ground that he did no more that was ordinary and reasonable in conducting his own rainwater from the roof to the gully and also on the further ground that the gully had been provided for the mutual benefit of plaintiff and defendant. The judge, Wright J., found that the defendant fell within two exceptions to *Rylands v. Fletcher* strict liability, namely that the subject land was being used in an ordinary and reasonable manner, the plaintiff being affected *qua* neighbour without wilfulness or negligence, and that the plaintiff had consented to what was brought on to the subject land.

General works: public sector

Reference has been made already to the status of drainage works in planning law when such works are undertaken by drainage bodies.[93] However, a variety of other public authorities may have cause to carry out works on or affecting watercourses. For present purposes, the more significant works are those relating to navigation and dredging, culverting, mining and highways. In some cases, the works in question may involve diversion of a watercourse or, perhaps, the obstruction of available navigation in the watercourse. A public authority will seek to justify diversion or obstruction by reference to statutory authority. However, it appears that the courts will operate a presumption against any claim of wholesale obstruction or complete diversion. Similarly, in any deliberations about statutory authority, the court will be influenced both by the plaintiff's *locus standi* and the true nature of any alleged diversion or obstruction. This is seen in *Abraham and Story v. Great Northern Railway Co.*,[94] where the railway company had statutory authority only to alter the course of non-navigable rivers. Two passages from the judgment of Patterson J. are particularly significant. In the first passage, he observes that:

> "... as against the plaintiffs ... who had no interest in the soil in the bed of the river, but have only the right of passage on the navigable highway common to all the Queen's subjects, it was not necessary for the defendants to aver and prove that they had taken the proper steps to vest in them the ownership of the bed of the river."[95]

Secondly, Patterson J. indicates that:

> "The erecting of anything in a navigable river ... which would be a

[93] See nn.65 and 66, *supra*.

[94] (1851) 16 Q.B. 586; 117 E.R. 1004.

[95] *Ibid.* at 1008.

nuisance if not authorised by an Act of Parliament, cannot by any reasonable construction of language be considered as diverting or altering the course of such a river ... No doubt such an erection in a navigable river, by preventing the water from flowing at all along the site of the erection, would prevent the water of the river from flowing in its accustomed channels and course in so ample a manner as it otherwise would have done ... but that is a very different thing from diverting or altering the course of the river ..."[96]

Navigation and dredging

The various harbour, navigation and conservancy authorities will usually operate under permissive powers for the purpose of enhancing and improving navigation of areas within their jurisdiction. While permitted development rights benefit drainage bodies in their various activities as defined,[97] statutory undertakers dealing with water-borne transport in harbours or on inland waterways have permitted development rights in relation also to "operational land", "... for the purposes of shipping, or in connection ... with the movement of traffic by ... inland navigation".[98] If a watercourse controlled by an internal drainage board, passes under or interferes with, or with the improvement or alteration of, any river, canal, dock, harbour, basin or other work belong to or under the jurisdiction of any navigation, harbour or conservancy authority, that authority has wide powers to substitute equally effective watercourses following the taking up, diversion or alteration to the level of any such watercourse.[99] Reciprocal compensation is permitted as between, on the one hand, NRA and, on the other, navigation, harbour and conservancy authorities, in so far as the one undertakes works to the benefit of the other.[1]

Whether or not the purpose of a dredging operation is to enhance or improve navigation, any statutory undertaker has permitted development rights to use land for the spreading of dredged material.[2] Such a site may also attract a requirement for an environmental assessment.[3] Authority to undertake dredging is found in the Local Acts governing navigation, harbour and conservancy authorities. In the case of an internal drainage board, or for the purpose of a scheme under section 18 of the Land Drainage Act 1991, or so far as may be necessary for the purpose of preventing flooding or mitigating flood damage in their area, a local authority, the authority to dredge is found in the Act of 1991.[4] While it is normally the case that protective provision will be made in legislation authorising dredging operations, in favour of the other public authorities whose

[96] *Ibid.* at 1009.
[97] See n.66, *supra.*
[98] S.I. 1988 No. 1813, art.3 and Sched. 2, Pt. 17.
[99] Land Drainage Act, s.68.
[1] Water Resources Act, s.120.
[2] S.I. 1988 No. 1813, art.3 and Sched. 2, Pt. 17, Class D. *Cf. R. v. Medway Ports Authority, ex p. RSPB, supra,* where there was a suggestion, *obiter,* that the MPA had these permitted development rights.
[3] See n.85, *supra.*
[4] s.14(1)(2). *Cf.* s.165, Water Resources Act, repeating the power for the NRA.

rights may be adversely affected, the courts in other situations are always likely to be alive to the issue, for example, if the dredging may affect the construction of a river tunnel by virtue of statutory powers.[5] Furthermore, the courts will look carefully at the limits of the authority to dredge, as in *Conservators of the River Thames v. Smeed, Dean & Co.*[6] where it was stressed that "... the conservators ... [had] power to dredge if they [did] so for the purpose of preserving, improving and maintaining the navigation of the Thames ..."[7]

The product of the dredging operation—spoil—may be deposited on the banks of a watercourse by an internal drainage board and by a local authority, by virtue of the Land Drainage Act 1991,[8] or by NRA, by virtue of the Water Resources Act 1991.[9] It has been seen already that land may be used for the deposit of dredged spoil by a statutory undertaker, by virtue of permitted development rights under the Town and Country Planning General Development Order and that in some, perhaps exceptional, circumstances the spreading of dredged spoil on land may attract a requirement for an environmental assessment, in addition to any planning permission that may be necessary for someone other than a statutory undertaker. Dredged spoil may be "industrial waste" for the purpose of water management licensing under Part II of the Environmental Protection Act 1990. Unless subject to any exemption, deposit of the spoil would require an appropriate licence under the Act.[10] If, on the other hand, the proposal is to deposit dredged spoil in the sea (rather than on the seashore), the consent of the Minister of Transport is not required, by virtue of the Coast Protection Act 1949.[11] However, a licence is required if dumping at sea is to be undertaken.[12] On the other hand, any deposit "... in the maintenance of harbour, coast protection ... drainage or flood control works, if made on the site of the works" will be exempt from the licensing requirement.[13]

Culverting

Particular requirements apply to the process of providing and maintaining an artificial channel for the passage of a watercourse, usually a stream. Any such culvert enables passage of the watercourse underneath a road, for example. A matter of some importance is to ensure that there is a clear distinction between a culvert and a sewer: if the channel attains the "status" of a sewer then, *inter alia*, various obligations will arise, including repair and maintenance, on the part of any sewerage undertaker. The fact that more than one property is drained by a pipe will give that pipe the status of a private sewer and, in turn, a public sewer if

[5] *East London Railway Co. v. Conservators of the River Thames* [1904] L.T. 347.
[6] [1897] 2 Q.B. 334.
[7] A.L. Smith L.J. at 342, 343.
[8] s.15.
[9] s.167.
[10] s.35.
[11] s.34.
[12] Food and Environment Protection Act 1985, Pt. II.
[13] Deposits in the Sea (Exemptions) Order 1985 (S.I. 1985 No. 1699), art.3 and Sched., para. 20.

adopted by the sewerage undertaker, so attracting the aforementioned obligations of, *inter alia*, repair and maintenance. It was against this background that Parker J. in *Shepherd v. Croft*[14] confirmed that "... the mere fact that a natural watercourse is culverted or piped by several owners of ... lands which are intersected by it does not make it a drain or sewer ..."[15]

Ultimately, whether a culvert becomes a sewer depends on whether the channel conveys sewage or water drained from more than one building. Oliver L.J. observed in *British Railways Board v. Tonbridge and West Malling District Council*[16]:

> "... something very much more than the mere discharge of sewage into a stream (and *a fortiori*, the mere discharge of pure surface water) is required before its status is changed to that of a sewer."

Local authorites undertake important regulatory responsibilities in relation to the works that may be associated with the culverting of watercourses, whether through the creation of culverts or their repair.[17] A local authority is able to empower an owner of land laid out for building to culvert any watercourse on that land or on land abutting. However, works cannot be required on land not belonging to the developer, or which prejudicially affect the rights of any person other than the developer.[18] Throughout the district of every local authority, any stream or watercourse cannot be covered or culverted except in accordance with plans and sections submitted to and approved by the local authority.[19] Furthermore, all local authorities are empowered to require the repair and cleansing of culverts as long as there is no requirement for enlargement of the culvert.[20] In so far as the erection or alteration of any culvert would be likely to affect the flow of any ordinary watercourse,[21] the consent in writing of the internal drainage board will be required.[22] These powers cannot be exercised by the local authority in question until there has been consultation with the appropriate internal drainage board.[23] The statutory powers do not authorise the local authority injuriously to affect the subject watercourse without the consent of any person who, but for the Act, would have been entitled by law to prevent or be relieved from the injurious affection arising.[24] This represents a saving of common law rights and cannot therefore give the plaintiff any new cause of action.[25] Any difference on the subject of whether the supply, quality or fall

[14] [1911] Ch. 521.
[15] *Ibid.* at 526–527.
[16] (1981) 79 L.G.R. 565 at 573.
[17] Public Health Act 1936.
[18] *Ibid.* s.262.
[19] *Ibid.* s.263.
[20] *Ibid.* s.264.
[21] Land Drainage Act, s.72(1).
[22] *Ibid.* s.23(1), (6).
[23] Public Health Act 1936, s.266(1).
[24] *Ibid.* s.331.
[25] *Radstock Co-operative Society Ltd. v. Norton Radstock UDC* [1968] 2 W.L.R. 1214.

of water in a watercourse is injuriously affected by the exercise of powers just described is subject to arbitration.[26]

The repair of a culvert may require interference with the course of a watercourse. If this is the case, the common law position is outlined in *Corporation of Greenock v. Caledonian Railway Co.*[27] Lord Finlay L.C. said:

> "It is the duty of anyone who interferes with the course of a stream to see that the works which he substitutes for the channel provided by nature are adequate to carry off the water brought down even by extraordinary rainfall, and if damage results from the deficiency of the substitute which he has provided for the natural channel he will be liable.[28]

The strictness of this requirement extends to the responsibilities of the landowner over whose land the watercourse extends, in terms of maintenance of that watercourse and any culverting that relates to it. Failure here could attract liability in nuisance unless there is evidence of "adoption" by the plaintiff: the plaintiff adopts a nuisance if he

> ". . . makes use of the erection, building, bank or artificial contrivance which constitutes the nuisance . . . [The respondents] adopted the nuisance for they continued during all that time to use the artificial contrivance of the conduit for the purpose of getting rid of water from their property without taking the proper means for rendering it safe."[29]

In the absence of any such adoption, the owner of the subject land may be liable in negligence if he fails reasonably to foresee and to deal with any defect in the culverting of the watercourse as a consequence of which the plaintiff suffers loss, damage or injury that is reasonably foreseeable.[30] The liability may of course be liability in nuisance:

> ". . . the defenders used their land in a way which they knew interfered with the natural state of things in respect that the stream, instead of beng open, was culverted and that they continued this situation . . . in maintaining on the land, in a position over the natural watercourse, substantial quantities of material extracted by earlier colliery operations and which was not a natural feature of the ground. In that situation I am of opinion that they are in law responsible . . . for the flooding of the pursuers' site caused by the obstruction of the natural watercourse resulting from the collapse of the culvert which the defenders were using."[31]

[26] Public Health Act 1936, s.332.

[27] [1917] A.C. 556.

[28] *Ibid.* at 572.

[29] *Per* Viscount Maugham in *Sedleigh-Denfield v. O'Callaghan* [1940] A.C. 880 at 894, 895.

[30] *Booth v. Thomas* [1926] 1 Ch. 397, *per* Lord Pollock at 404.

[31] *Per* Lord Mackay in *Plean Precast Ltd. v. National Coal Board*, 1986 S.L.T. 78, Court of Session, Outer House.

In the above circumstances, it may be open to the local authority to intervene under Public Health Act powers.[32] However, if the local authority intervenes in circumstances where it is found that the owner or occupier of the land is not in default, that local authority may be liable for compensation for any injury sustained by reason of the exercise of the particular powers.[33] The present statutory powers requiring repair, maintenance and cleansing of culverts are enforceable by means of local authority action in default and recovery of expenses reasonably incurred, together with summary proceedings.[34] Any culvert that is impeded so as to affect the proper flow of water may be treated by service of the requisite notice by the drainage board or local authority concerned.[35]

Mining and minerals exploitation

Mining operations may adversely affect a watercourse, so attracting to any plaintiff who suffers loss, damage or injury as a consequence remedies provided by the common law or statute. At common law the position is described by Lord Campbell C.J. in *Humphries v. Brogden*[36] thus:

> "... where there are separate freeholds from the surface of the land and the minerals belonging to different owners, we are of opinion that the owner of the surface, while unencumbered by buildings and in its natural state, is entitled to have it supported by the subjacent mineral strata."[37]

As far as statutory remedies are concerned, it is provided by the Coal Mining (Subsidence) Act 1957 that, subject to work being undertaken by agreement by the appropriate drainage authority (NRA or the internal drainage board for the district in question), the Board of British Coal

> "... shall from time to time carry out such, if any, measures [in this section referred to as 'remedial measures'] for remedying, mitigating or preventing any deterioration in any land drainage system by reason of subsidence damage which has occurred or appears likely to occur, being a drainage system maintainable by a drainage authority, as may be agreed between the Board and the appropriate drainage authority ... to be in all the circumstances reasonably required and not unjustifiable on economic grounds ..."[38]

However, the Coal Industry Act 1975 stipulates:

> "... so far as may be reasonably requisite for the working of any coal, the

[32] See n.20, *supra*.
[33] Public Health Act 1936, s.278.
[34] *Ibid*. s.290(6). *Cf.* ss.291 and 293.
[35] Land Drainage Act, s.25. *Cf.* s.28, relating to culverted ditches.
[36] (1850) 116 E.R. 1048.
[37] *Ibid*. at 1050.
[38] s.5.

> Board shall be entitled, after the expiry of the period of three months beginning with the relevant date of publication of a notice under this section, to withdraw support from any land to which the notice relates . . ."[39]

Elsewhere in the section, there are protective provisions so that, for example, nothing in the section affects rights found in section 34(1) of the Coal Act 1938, such as the rights vested in local authorities by virtue of the Public Health Act 1875 (Support of Sewers) Amendment Act 1883.[40]

Special drainage problems arise in relation to opencast mining and are anticipated by the Opencast Coal Act 1958. For the purpose of draining land covered by an opencast authorisation granted to British Coal by virtue of section 1 of the Act:

> ". . . the Minister may authorise the Board to purchase compulsorily a right to place drainage works on any other land, whether above or below ground, and to use, repair and maintain those works, without purchasing any other interest in that land."[41]

However, nothing in this provision can be construed as authorising any interference with the exercise of a public right of way, or any contravention of a prohibition or restriction imposed by or under any enactment.[42] Although drainage requirements may be recognised in the planning permission for opencast mining, they must be rooted clearly in requirement that any "planning" consideration must relate to ". . . the use and development" of the subject land.[43]

Whatever the form of minerals exploitation, any relevant planning permission since 1982 is likely to be subject to an "aftercare" provision in the shape of a condition. Any such planning permission may be granted

> ". . . subject . . . to any such condition as the mineral planning authority think fit requiring that such steps be taken as may be necessary to bring the land to the required standard for whichever of the following uses is specified in the condition, namely— . . . (iii) use for amenity."[44]

Furthermore, "the steps that may be specified in an aftercare condition . . . may consist of . . . draining . . . the land".[45] Drainage as an element of site aftercare following minerals exploitation is specifically addressed by a Department of the Environment Circular,[46] which also addresses the utility of agreements under section 20 of the Land Drainage Act 1991. Except in relation to a main river, an

[39] s.2(1).
[40] *Ibid.* s.2(8)(d).
[41] Opencast Coal Act 1958, s.16(1). *Cf.* subs.(7), defining "drainage works".
[42] *Ibid.* subs.(8).
[43] *Per* Cooke J. in *Stringer v. Minister of Housing and Local Government* [1971] All E.R. 65 at 77.
[44] Town and Country Planning Act 1990, Sched. 5, para. 2(1).
[45] *Ibid.* para. 2(5).
[46] Circular 25/85, *Mineral Workings—Legal Aspects*, relating to restoration of sites with a high water table.

internal drainage board is able to make a section 20 agreement with any person whereby, at that person's expense, the board carries out and maintains even outside its district any drainage works which that person is entitled to carry out and maintain. Such an agreement, the Circular recognises, may be sufficient to ensure low level restoration, although it would be binding against successors in title only with their agreement.[47] Referring to section 106 agreements under the Town and Country Planning Act 1990, the Circular emphasises that drainage authorities have no statutory powers enabling them to be parties to such agreements, even though drainage, water level and water pollution aspects will be major considerations in such agreements:

> "Where any such agreement is contemplated, and certainly before it is finalised between, for instance, a mineral planning authority and a landowner or mineral operator, there should be the closest consultation with the [NRA] and, where different, the drainage authority . . . to ensure that all the necessary requirements are taken into account."[48]

Highways

The Highways Act 1980 contains a range of requirements governing highway operations that may affect watercourses. A navigable watercourse may be diverted in connection with the construction, improvement and alteration of highways, the provision of new means of access and the provision and maintenance of compounds and service areas.[49] Land may also be acquired for the carrying out of any works in connection with the diversion of a navigable watercourse, authorised by an order made under section 108 of the Act.[50] Safeguards for rights of navigation are built into the legislation. Provision is made for compensation where any person suffers damage or depreciation to any interest in land by reason of a diversion order made under section 108 of the Highways Act. There is no provision, though, for compensation if in fact the waterway is less navigable than before by reason of the diversion.[51] Compensation disputes are dealt with by the Lands Tribunal.[52]

Non-navigable watercourses may also be diverted or works done to them in connection with highway works or the construction, improvement or alteration of a highway, as well as the provision of new accesses, maintenance compounds, and so on. Compensation disputes against are dealt with by the Lands Tribunal.[53]

Highway authorities are empowered to acquire land compulsorily or by agreement for the construction of roads[54] and the improvement of highways.[55]

[47] *Ibid.* para. 15.
[48] *Ibid.* para. 20.
[49] Highways Act 1980, s.108.
[50] *Ibid.* s.240(2)(a).
[51] *Ibid.* s.109.
[52] *Ibid.* s.307.
[53] *Ibid.* s.110.
[54] *Ibid.* s.239(1), (2).
[55] *Ibid.* subss(3), (4).

Powers of compulsory purchase here, and in the extended provisions under section 240, are subject to distance limits, limiting the acquisition of land to that within a certain prescribed distance of the middle of the highway. However, land acquired for the diversion of a watercourse under sections 108 and 110 is not subject to this restrictive requirement.[56] The authority may acquire rights over subject land, rather than the freehold of the land itself.[57]

An important protective provision[58] stipulates that nothing in the provisions of the Act to which this provision applies[59] authorises a highway authority, or any other person, to use or interfere with any watercourse (including the banks thereof) or any drainage or other works under the control of a drainage body without its consent.[60] Three of the provisions referred to by section 339 are sections 45, 100 and 101 dealing, respectively, with powers to obtain materials for the repair of publicly maintained highways, the drainage of highways and the power to fill in roadside ditches.

Private works

Any owner of a land's freehold or any tenant within the terms of a lease of the land may undertake drainage works on that land, in some cases without any requirement for planning permission. Permitted development rights here operate in so far as there is carried out on agricultural land comprised in an agricultural unit "... any excavation or engineering operations, reasonably necessary for the purposes of agriculture within that unit".[61] If the drainage works in question cannot be executed except through works on land not in the individual's ownership or control, the requirements of the Land Drainage Act must be satisfied.[62] Those requirements centre on the need for an application to be made to the appropriate Minister for a consent, but not before the application and details of facilities are notified to those whose land will be affected, the NRA and any relevant internal drainage board for the district in question. The Minister may convene an inquiry into the application. If granted consent, that consent allows the applicant "... to carry out the works and to maintain them for ever thereafter".[63] However, every person interested in the land affected by the Minister's order granting consent is entitled to compensation for any injury suffered by him in respect of that interest by reason of the works: disputes are adjudicated by the Lands Tribunal.[64]

[56] *Ibid.* s.249(3).
[57] *Ibid.* s.250.
[58] *Ibid.* s.339.
[59] *Ibid.* ss.45, 100, 101, 110, 294 and 299.
[60] *cf.* the reference to navigation authorities under s.339(4).
[61] Town and Country Planning General Development Order 1988, art.3, Sched. 2, Pt. 6, Class A.
[62] s.22. Note restrictions in relation to Crown Land in s.74(3).
[63] Land Drainage Act, s.22(6).
[64] *Ibid.* subs.(7).

Works relating to ditches

Although perhaps not on the same scale as many land drainage works, statutory provision is made in the Land Drainage Act 1991 and the Public Health Act 1936 for works in relation to ditches. The Land Drainage Act 1991 contains a small parcel of provisions relating to the cleansing of ditches.[65]

If a ditch is in such a condition as to cause injury to land or to prevent the improvement of the drainage of any land, the Agricultural Land Tribunal, on the application of the owner or occupier of the land, may, if they think fit, make an order requiring the person or persons named in the order to carry out the specified remedial work. For the purpose of the reference to "injury to land", because the term "land" in the Interpretation Act 1978 applies to this Act, it seems that damage to buildings such as mills would be within section 28.[66] The term "ditch" in the section does not include a watercourse vested in or under the control of a drainage body.[67] Such an excluded watercourse is dealt with by virtue of the powers in section 25 of the Act. Any order which is made for present purposes is sufficient authority to undertake the works specified and, so far as may be necessary for that purpose, to enter any land specified.[68] Powers to act in default are given to the appropriate Minister or any drainage body authorised by him.[69] This power includes a power to recover any expenses reasonably incurred in acting in default.[70] If any person sustains injury, compensation is payable by the person exercising the power only if it can be shown that the power was exercised otherwise than for the purpose of carrying out any work required to be undertaken by virtue of the section 28 order.[71] Disputes on such compensation claims are adjudicated by the Lands Tribunal.[72] The Agricultural Land Tribunal also has power to authorise drainage works in connection with a ditch passing through land other than land of the owner or occupier making the application.[73] It would appear that only in the most exceptional circumstances could a successful application come from someone whose land does not benefit directly from any works which may be authorised by the Tribunal. The line between this provision and section 22[74] may be difficult to define, particularly in view of the fact that the present section seemingly permits new construction, as does section 22. However, it would appear that section 22 will apply in so far as the scale of drainage works takes the operation beyond mere ditch construction. Furthermore, even if the proposed drainage works comprise only ditch construction, resort to section 30 appears to be inappropriate in circumstances

[65] ss.28–31.

[66] Compare *Finch v. Bannister* [1908] 2 K.B. 441, which was decided under s.14 of the Land Drainage Act 1847, to which the statutory definition of "land" did not apply.

[67] Land Drainage Act 1991, s.28(5).

[68] *Ibid.* s.29(1).

[69] *Ibid.* subs.(2).

[70] *Ibid.*

[71] *Ibid.* subs.(5).

[72] *Ibid.* subs.(6).

[73] *Ibid.* s.30.

[74] See n.62, *supra*.

where there may be objections from third parties. Such objections are expressly provided for under section 22.[75]

Three sections of the Public Health Act 1936 also deal with ditches: sections 259, 260 and 261. The first of these provisions stipulates that certain matters are to be regarded as statutory nuisances for the purpose of Part III of the Environmental Protection Act 1990.[76] In these circumstances, a local authority may take summary proceedings through the service of an abatement notice.[77] It is also possible for any person aggrieved by the statutory nuisance to take summary proceedings through a complaint directly to the magistrates' court.[78] The conditions referred to in section 259 fall into two categories: either any ditch or watercourse[79] which is so foul or in such a state as to be prejudicial to health or a nuisance, or any part of a watercourse (nor ordinarily navigated by vessels) which is so choked or silted up as to obstruct or impede the proper flow of water, thereby causing a nuisance or giving rise to conditions prejudicial to health. However, in this latter category, nothing is deemed to impose any liability on any person other than the person by whose act or default the nuisance arises or continues. It appears that, in so far as any natural obstruction occurs through silting, for example, the present powers will not be available, a conclusion reinforced by the proviso to section 259 referred to in the previous sentence.[80] If, on the other hand, an obstruction is a non-natural, artificial obstruction, a riparian owner may be obliged to remove it at common law.[81] Nevertheless, whatever the nature of the obstruction, if an order is made under section 28 of the Land Drainage Act 1991 but necessary works are not executed, the person in default there would not enjoy the protection of the proviso to section 259 just mentioned. Section 260 empowers parish councils to act in relation to ditches, etc., and a local authority (without prejudice to its power to act in relation to statutory nuisances) may exercise all of the parish council's powers under this section. Section 261 relates to boundary ditches and empowers a magistrates' court to make appropriate orders for cleansing, on acceptance of proceedings by one local authority against an adjoining local authority.

Land Drainage Works Governed by the Land Drainage Act 1991

Development control requirements

Reference was made previously to the likely need for planning permission under the Town and Country Planning Act 1990 in respect of works associated with

[75] subss.(3) and (4).
[76] *cf.* Chap. 10, "Statutory Nuisance".
[77] Environmental Protection Act 1990, s.80.
[78] *Ibid.* s.82.
[79] The section refers also to ponds, pools and gutters.
[80] *Neath RDC v. Williams* [1951] 1 K.B. 115.
[81] *Ibid. per* Lord Goddard at 123.

drainage operations on land.[82] Nevertheless, any "drainage body"[83] has permitted development rights under the Town and Country Planning General Development Order 1988[84] in respect of development[85] "in; on or under a watercourse or land of drainage works in connection with the improvement, maintenance or repair of the watercourse or works".[86] Rather more extensive permitted development rights operate in favour of NRA.[87]

Environmental and recreational duties

It is the duty of an internal drainage board, of each of the Ministers, and of the NRA in formulating or considering "*any* proposals relating to *any* functions of such a board" to further the conservation and enhancement of the environmental features listed in the legislation,[88] to have regard to the desirability of protecting and conserving buildings, sites and other features of historic or other interest and (finally) to take account of the effect of any proposals on the various environmental features.[89] The duty also extends to matters of public access to land,[90] and to proposals relating to the functions of the NRA and sewarage and water undertakers in so far as they are related to internal drainage board activities.[91]

The duties prescribed by section 61A(1) and (2) extend to the formulation or consideration of any proposals relating to the functions of a local authority under the Land Drainage Act 1991.[92]

Where (in England) the Nature Conservancy Council or (in Wales) the Countryside Council is of the opinion that an area of land is of special interest by reason of its flora, fauna or geological or physiographical features and may "at any time" be affected by the "works, operations or activities" of an internal drainage board or a local authority, that fact shall be notified to the board or local authority, as the case may be.[93] Significantly, the section makes no references to any requirement for prior notification of "sensitive" sites. The provision extends also to land in a National Park or in the Broads.[94]

A relevant Minister[95] under the Act is empowered to give directions to an internal drainage board where it is considered that works, operations or activities which are being, or are about to be carried out are "likely" to destroy or seriously

[82] See n.77, *supra*.
[83] As defined by s.72(1) of the Act.
[84] S.I. 1988 No. 1813.
[85] Town and Country Planning Act 1990, s.55.
[86] S.I. 1988 No. 1813, art.3, Sched. 2, Pt. 14.
[87] *Ibid*. Pt. 15.
[88] Land Drainage Act, s.61A, inserted by the Land Drainage Act 1994.
[89] *Ibid*. subs.(1).
[90] *Ibid*., subs.(2).
[91] *Ibid*. subs.(3)
[92] *Ibid*., s.61B.
[93] *Ibid*. s.61C.
[94] *Ibid*. subs.(2).
[95] *Ibid*. s.72(1).

damage various features which (in the Minister's opinion) are of national or international importance.[96]

The Ministers are empowered to approve (by order) Codes of Practice for the purpose of giving practical guidance[97] and to promote "desirable practices".[98] Contravention of a code does not of itself constitute a breach of sections 61A, B or C and does not give rise to any civil liability. However, each of the Ministers is under a duty "to take account" of any contravention or likely contravention in determining the manner of any exercise of powers under the Land Drainage Act in relation to any local authority or internal drainage board.[99]

General drainage powers

Except in relation to a main river, an internal drainage board or local authority is empowered to construct new works through the creation of any new watercourse or drainage work required for the "... drainage of any land".[1] These powers may be undertaken by agreement with the person whose land is affected, or by means of compulsory powers.[2] NRA consent will be required in so far as any of these drainage works will interfere with or affect another board and its drainage works.[3] Failure to comply with these requirements activates NRA default powers,[4] while any disagreement about matters concerning NRA consent are determined by the relevant Minister.[5]

Both internal drainage boards and local authorities have considerable powers of compulsory land acquisition for present purposes,[6] as well as powers to make byelaws.[7] Reference has been made already to the necessity for NRA consent in respect of local authority drainage works.[8] NRA will consult with any relevant internal drainage board prior to any decision. In the absence of any decision at the expiration of a period of two months, the application is deemed to have been granted. In the event of a dispute about the NRA decision for present purposes, that dispute will be resolved by the Minister responsible.[9]

Drainage of small areas

In some instances, the designation of an internal drainage district may not be practicable for the purpose of a relatively modest scheme of drainage works. To meet this situation, NRA or any local authority other than a district council may

[96] *Ibid.* s.61D.
[97] For the purpose of ss.61A and 61C (to internal drainage boards), and for the purpose of ss.61B and 61C (to local authorities).
[98] Land Drainage Act 1991, s.61E.
[99] *Ibid.* subs.(2).
[1] *Ibid.* s.14(2)(c).
[2] *Ibid.* s.62.
[3] *Ibid.* s.7(2).
[4] *Ibid.* subs.(4).
[5] *Ibid.* subs.(5).
[6] *Ibid.* s.62.
[7] *Ibid.* s.66.
[8] See n.31, *supra.*
[9] Land Drainage Act 1991, s.17.

be empowered by a scheme to enter land for the purpose of undertaking drainage works which appear, in the circumstances, to be desirable.[10] Any such scheme is subject to approval by the various appropriate procedures that apply. Facilities are provided for notification of the proposed scheme and for objections, which may be dealt with by means of a public inquiry.

Maintenance

Maintenance powers available to internal drainage boards and local authorities relate to existing works. Boards and authorities are empowered to "... cleanse, repair or otherwise maintain in a due state of efficiency any existing watercourse or drainage work".[11] However, it is stated elsewhere in the Act[12] that nothing in the Act "... shall affect any powers of an internal drainage board under any local Act so far as they existed immediately before the commencement of this Act". Clearly, any duty to maintain under such a Local Act would be enforceable against a board rather more easily than the enforcement of a mere power under the Act of 1991. A potentially significant remedy in the Act is to be found in section 14,[13] relating as it does to a failure in the exercise of any of the powers mentioned by the section, which also include the improvement of existing work. The remedy is in favour of any person who is injured by reason of an exercise of the section 14 powers by any internal drainage board or local authority; the responsible board or authority is liable to make "full compensation" to the injured person. In the event of a dispute, the amount of compensation is determined by the Lands Tribunal whose approach, not surprisingly perhaps, is based on a test of reasonable probability.[14]

Any use of maintenance powers is subject to certain protective provisions.[15] Of particular significance is the fact that nothing in the present Act, such as an exercise of maintenance powers, can prejudice or affect NRA fisheries functions under the Water Resources Act 1991 or the Salmon and Freshwater Fisheries Act 1975.[16]

Obstructions in watercourses

The erection of a variety of obstructions that would affect the flow of an ordinary watercourse cannot take place without the consent of the drainage board concerned.[17] That consent cannot be withheld unreasonably, and any failure to notify a determination within two months of the submission of an application or payment of any application fee is indicative of a deemed consent.[18] Any dispute

[10] *Ibid.* s.18.
[11] *Ibid.* s.14(2)(a).
[12] *Ibid.* s.67(8).
[13] *Ibid.* subs.(5).
[14] *Marine Industrial Transmissions v. Southern Water Authority* (1989) 29 R.V.R. 221.
[15] Land Drainage Act 1991, s.67.
[16] *Ibid.* subs.(5).
[17] *Ibid.* s.23(1).
[18] *Ibid.* subs.(3).

arising from the decision is subject to arbitration.[19] Normally, the appropriate internal drainage board will be responsible for decision-making here, but in so far as there is a watercourse situated outside an internal drainage district, responsibility lies with NRA.[20] Failure to comply with the prohibition on obstructions amounts to a nuisance in respect of which the drainage board can serve an abatement notice on any person with power to remove that obstruction.[21] Any failure to comply with an abatement notice, or contravention of such a notice, is an offence. The penalty, on summary conviction, is a fine and (if the contravention or failure is continued after conviction) a further fine for every day on which the contravention or failure is continued.[22] Without prejudice to any criminal proceedings, the drainage board is also empowered to take default action and to recover reasonably incurred costs.[23]

Maintenance of flow

If the proper flow of an ordinary watercourse is impeded by the condition of that watercourse, which is not attributable to subsidence due to mining operations, the relevant internal drainage board (or NRA if the watercourse is not in an internal drainage district) or local authority may serve a notice requiring that the condition be remedied.[24] The notice may be served on the person controlling the relevant part of the watercourse or any person whose act or default is attributable to the condition of the watercourse.[25] However, a notice requiring works on land not in the ownership of the person on whom the notice is served cannot be served without the consent of the owner or occupier unless it is not reasonably practicable, on reasonable inquiry, to ascertain their name and address.[26] The notice must indicate the nature of the works and the period allowed for their completion, as well as the availability of an appeal under section 27 and the period within which it must be brought.[27] Failure to undertake the works specified by the notice empowers the internal drainage board or local authority to act in default and to recover any reasonably incurred expenses.[28] Without prejudice to the power to serve a notice here, any failure to undertake works specified by a notice renders the person responsible liable, on summary conviction, to a fine.[29] In so far as a drainage board or local authority seeks to recover expenses through acting in default, it is not open to the defendant to raise any question which could not have been raised on a section 27 appeal.[30] Any expenses incurred by the

[19] *Ibid.* subs.(5).
[20] *Ibid.* subs.(8).
[21] *Ibid.* s.24(1), (2).
[22] *Ibid.* subs.(3).
[23] *Ibid.* subs.(4).
[24] *Ibid.* s.25(1), (2).
[25] *Ibid.* subs.(3).
[26] *Ibid.* subs.(4).
[27] *Ibid.* subs.(5).
[28] *Ibid.* subs.(6).
[29] *Ibid.*
[30] *Ibid.* subs.(7).

owner or occupier of the land under these provisions may be recovered by the one against the other: an adjustment between the parties is not prevented by the section.[31]

In so far as a local authority seeks to use the powers in section 25, it is obliged, before these powers are used, to notify the internal drainage board for the district in question, or NRA if the watercourse falls outside such a district.[32] If a local authority has powers beyond section 25 for securing an appropriate flow in a watercourse, such as the powers in sections 259–261 of the Public Health Act 1936,[33] no body is empowered to use the section 25 powers in relation to the subject watercourse except with the agreement of the local authority or if, after reasonable notice from an internal drainage board or (as the case may be) NRA, the local authority either fails to exercise its powers or exercises them improperly.[33a] Where the subject watercourse is under the jurisdiction of a navigation, harbour or conservancy authority which is exercising its powers, section 25 powers cannot be utilised except with the authority of any such authority or board of conservators.[34]

Where a section 25 notice is served, there is an appeal against that notice to the magistrates' court within 21 days' of service on any of a number of grounds.[35] The court is able to deal with the appeal if satisfied that any informality, defect or error in or in connection with a notice is not material.[36] Any order as the court thinks fit may be made with respect to the person responsible for any works, the contributions from others towards the works and the proportions of expenses to be recoverable.[37] However, in this context the court is obliged to have regard to the terms of any tenancy and the nature of the works required, as well as the degree of benefit to be derived by the different persons concerned.[38] Any person aggrieved by an order, determination or other decision of the magistrates' court is able to appeal to the Crown Court.[39] Where the decision of any internal drainage board, local authority or (as the case may be) NRA to serve a section 25 notice is varied or reversed on appeal, it is the duty of one of these bodies to give effect to the order of the court.[40]

Disposal of spoil from watercourses

Section 15 of the Land Drainage Act empowers any internal drainage board or local authority to appropriate and dispose of spoil removed in the course of works widening, deepening or dredging any ordinary watercourse. Furthermore, such

[31] *Ibid.* subs.(8).
[32] s.26(1).
[33] See nn.76–81, *supra.*
[33a] Land Drainage Act 1991, s.26(2).
[34] *Ibid.* subs.(3). *Cf.* s.266, Public Health Act 1936: see n.23, *supra.*
[35] Land Drainage Acts s.27(1). Procedure is by way of complaint for any order: s.27(2).
[36] *Ibid.* subs.(4).
[37] *Ibid.* subs.(6).
[38] *Ibid.* subs.(7).
[39] *Ibid.* subs.(8).
[40] *Ibid.* subs.(9).

spoil may be deposited on the banks of any such watercourse, or (within certain limits) on land adjoining.[41] These powers are subject to limits or potential limitations on local authority powers in the present context,[42] as well as further limitations in so far as the present powers can be used by a local authority only for works under a drainage scheme for small areas,[43] or only so far as may be necessary for the purpose of preventing flooding or mitigating any damage caused by flooding in its area.[44]

If injury is sustained by any person by reason of an exercise of the present powers of spoil deposit by an internal drainage board or a local authority, the board or local authority may, if it thinks fit, pay him such compensation as it may determine.[45] If the injury could have been avoided if the powers had been exercised with reasonable care, the machinery for compensation contained in section 14(5) and (6) will apply.[46]

Agreements between, on the one hand, internal drainage boards and local authorities and, on the other, district councils and the councils of the London boroughs are provided for to enable disposal of any spoil removed from subject works, as well as payment for such disposal.[47]

The spoil that is recovered in the course of drainage works is "industrial waste" for the purposes of Part II of the Environmental Protection Act.[48]

NRA Flood Defence and Land Drainage Functions

Division of functions

Previous sections of the present chapter have concentrated on the functions of internal drainage boards in relation to land drainage, along with accompanying functions of local authorities and NRA in the same broad area. Most of these functions are governed by the Land Drainage Act, whereas NRA flood defence and land drainage responsibilities are governed by Part IV[49] of the Water Resources Act 1991, along with a variety of other provisions, to be referred to below. The discharge of responsibilities by NRA and the regional and local flood defence committees was referred to at the beginning of the present chapter.[50] Environmental and recreational duties in similar terms to those set out in the Land

[41] *Ibid.* s.15(1), but only as long as no statutory nuisance is created: subs.(3).
[42] *Ibid.* ss.16 and 17. *Cf.* nn.30 and 31, *supra.*
[43] *Ibid.* s.18. *Cf.* nn.32 and 10, *supra.*
[44] *Ibid.* s.15(2).
[45] *Ibid.* subs.(4)(a).
[46] *Ibid.* subs.(4)(b): *cf.* nn.13 and 14, *supra.*
[47] *Ibid.* subs.(5).
[48] Controlled Waste Regulations 1992 (S.I. 1992 No. 588), Sched. 3, para. 5.
[49] ss.105–113.
[50] See nn.3–13, *supra.*

Drainage Act[51] relate to the discharge of NRA flood defence and land drainage functions under the Water Resources Act.[52]

NRA is obliged to arrange for all its functions relating to flood defence under the Water Resources and Land Drainage Acts to be carried out by regional flood defence committees: the purpose is to enable the carrying out of any flood defence function, other than an internal drainage function[53] so far as the execution of that function appears to NRA likely to affect materially its management of water for purposes other than flood defence.[54] No doubt any such direction may be exceptional in taking NRA beyond its normal supervisory relationship with the various committees. Whatever the background to any particular transaction in this context, it seems clear that the NRA environmental and recreational duties must be borne in mind to the extent that those duties are defined by the Act.

Main river functions

A critical distinction that characterises the Land Drainage Act provisions is the distinction between an "ordinary watercourse" and a "main river". It is the Water Resources Act provisions which govern the main river functions of NRA. The term "main river" is defined as:

> "... a watercourse shown as such on a main river map [including] any structure or appliance for controlling or regulating the flow of water into, in or out of a channel which—
>
> (a) is a structure or appliance situated in the channel or in any part of the banks of the channel; and (b) is not a structure or appliance vested in or controlled by an internal drainage board".[55]

The term "watercourse" is defined by the Water Resources Act to include "... all rivers, streams, ditches, drains, cuts, culverts, dykes, sluices, sewers and passages through which water flows ... except a public sewer".[56]

NRA is obliged to maintain for public inspection a main river map which is conclusive evidence for all purposes as to what is a "main river". Each map identifies the main rivers for the area of each regional flood defence committee.[57] To ensure that each main river map is properly up-to-date, facilities are provided for amendment of maps.[58] At the centre of the Water Resources Act provisions is section 107, which stipulates that the section has effect for conferring functions in

[51] See nn.88–99, *supra*.

[52] ss. 16 and 17. *Cf.* s.18, relating to codes of practice for these purposes, and general duties in ss.19 and 20.

[53] As defined by Water Resources Act, s.106(5).

[54] *Ibid.* subs.(3).

[55] *Ibid.* s.113(1).

[56] *Ibid.* ss.113(1) and 221(1). *Cf.* the similar terms in the Land Drainage Act, s.72(1).

[57] Water Resources Act, s.193.

[58] *Ibid.* s.194.

relation to main rivers on NRA which are functions of drainage boards in relation to other watercourses. Accordingly, NRA functions under section 107 are additional to NRA functions which are exercisable concurrently with an internal drainage board under the Land Drainaage Act.[59] This means, *inter alia*, that NRA can exercise powers under section 25 of the Land Drainage Act (to secure the maintenance of flow of a watercourse) in relation to a main river.[60]

Powers are provided by the Water Resources Act whereby a scheme may be prepared by NRA and submitted to the relevant Ministers[61] for confirmation, under which main river functions and any related property of an internal drainage board, or any other body having power to make or maintain works for the drainage of land, are transferred to NRA from a local authority, for example.[62] In so far as there is any dispute for this or other purposes about the status of drainage work and whether it relates to a "main river", that dispute will be referred to the appropriate Minister for decision although, if the parties agree, the matter may be referred to arbitration.[63] Similar arrangements for transfer of functions to NRA and other accessions of responsibilities for the purpose of improving the drainage of land are provided for in the Act.[64] In this case, such arrangements may be made with various navigation and conservancy authorities and are not necessarily limited to main rivers.

Structures in, over or under a main river

NRA approval is necessary if any person wishes to erect any structure in, over or under a watercourse which is part of a main river. NRA approval is associated with a need for compliance with plans and sections approved by it.[65] Similar consent requirements relate to any work of alteration or repair to the structures just described, in so far as the works would be likely to affect the flow of water or impede any drainage work,[66] as well as any altered or erected structure designed to contain or divert the floodwaters of any part of a main river.[67] Except in respect of these latter works, there is recognition in the Act[68] of the power to carry out emergency works, allied to the need to advise NRA as soon as practicable of the carrying out of the works and the circumstances in which they were carried out. NRA consent must not be withheld unreasonably, but in so far as consent be neither granted nor refused within a period of two months of an application being made or an application fee required to be paid (whichever is the later), a deemed consent exists.[69] Where a consent is granted in other circumstances, it may be

[59] *Ibid.* s.107(6).
[60] *Ibid.* subs.(3).
[61] As defined by s.108(9).
[62] *Ibid.* s.108. The procedures are to be found in Sched. 14.
[63] Land Drainage Act, s.73.
[64] Land Drainage Act, s.111.
[65] *Ibid.* s.109(1).
[66] *Ibid.* subs.(2).
[67] *Ibid.* subs.(3).
[68] *Ibid.* subs.(5).
[69] *Ibid.* s.110(2), (3).

subject to any reasonable conditions as to the time at which and the manner in which the work is to be carried out.[70] Any dispute about the question whether a consent has been withheld unreasonably may be determined by arbitration, if the parties agree, or otherwise by the Minister of Agriculture or (in Wales) the Secretary of State.[71]

Special agricultural schemes

If it appears to NRA that the interests of agriculture require the carrying out, improvement or maintenance of drainage works in connection with any watercourses in the area of any regional flood defence committee, a scheme for the purpose may be submitted to either of the Ministers by NRA.[72] Provision is also made for the levying of a special drainage charge in respect of so-called "chargeable land" within the subject area.[73] Any watercourse concerned is identified as a main river for the purposes of the Water Resources and Land Drainage Acts.[74] In practice, it may be difficult to distinguish between the appropriateness of such an agricultural scheme, compared with that of an internal drainage district designation, for present purposes.

General powers for flood defence and drainage works

In relation to main rivers NRA enjoys general powers[75] which, in some respects, are comparable with those available to internal drainage boards and local authorities in areas other than main rivers.[76] NRA is empowered to maintain existing drainage works,[77] to improve existing drainage works[78] and to construct new works.[79] Furthermore, NRA also has power to maintain, improve or construct drainage works for the purpose of defence against sea water or tidal water, both above and below the low-water mark, irrespective of whether any such works are conducted in relation to a main river.[80] Added to this is a power enabling NRA to carry out all such works and to do all such things in the sea or in any estuary as may, in its opinion, be necessary to secure an adequate outfall for a main river.[81] In undertaking any of the foregoing functions, NRA is authorised by the Act to enter a person's land only for the purpose of maintaining existing works. General powers of entry are prescribed elsewhere in the Act.[82] General drainage powers of NRA extend to works being undertaken for others at their

70 *Ibid.* subs.(2).
71 *Ibid.* subs.(4).
72 *Ibid.* s.137. *Cf.* Sched. 16.
73 *Ibid.* s.138.
74 *Ibid.* s.137(4).
75 *Ibid.* s.165.
76 Land Drainage Act, s.14(2).
77 As defined by s.165(1)(a).
78 As defined by s.165(1)(b).
79 As defined by s.165(1)(c).
80 *Ibid.* subs.(2).
81 *Ibid.* subs.(3).
82 *Ibid.* ss.169–173 and Sched. 20.

expense,[83] no matter what the situation of those works, and, in relation to main river works, agency arrangements, in which NRA functions may be undertaken on its behalf on agreed terms by any local authority or navigation authority.[84] Unlawful interference with NRA works in a number of defined respects is a criminal offence.[85]

Provision of flood warning systems

A flood warning system is any system whereby, for the purpose of providing warning of any danger of flooding, information with respect to rainfall, the level or flow of any inland water[86] or any other matters appearing to NRA to be relevant for the purpose, is obtained and transmitted, automatically or otherwise.[87] NRA has powers to provide and operate any such system, to provide, install and maintain apparatus required for such system and to carry out any engineering or building operations required.[88] It appears that caution is required on the part of NRA in exercising the authority to provide flood warning systems. The statutory authority for this purpose cannot authorise any act or omission which might be actionable (typically in tort), apart from any liability that may accrue because NRA exceeds its capacity.[89] Clearly liability in nuisance is one prime area that must be borne in mind in action associated with the provision, installation, operation and maintenance of flood defence systems, apart from any associated works that may be involved.

Disposal of spoil from flood defence works

Similar powers to those provided by the Land Drainage Act enable NRA (without making payment for it) to appropriate and dispose of any matter removed in the course of carrying out any works for the widening, deepening or dredging of any watercourse, and to deposit any matter so removed on the banks of the watercourse or (within certain limits) on adjoining land,[90] as long as a statutory nuisance for the purpose of Part III of the Environmental Protection Act 1990 is not created.[91] NRA is also empowered to agree with a district council or the council of a London borough for the disposal of matter removed under these powers, on such terms as may be agreed.[92]

[83] *Ibid.* s.165(4).
[84] *Ibid.* subs.(5).
[85] *Ibid.* s.176.
[86] As defined by s.148(5).
[87] *Ibid.*
[88] *Ibid.* s.166.
[89] *Ibid.* subs.(2).
[90] *Ibid.* s.167(1). *Cf.* n.48, *supra*, in relation to the status of spoil.
[91] *Ibid.* subs.(2).
[92] *Ibid.* subs.(3).

Anti-pollution works and powers

NRA has powers to undertake works where it appears that any poisonous, noxious or polluting matter or any solid waste is likely to enter, or to be or to have been present in, any controlled waters which are defined[93] to include relevant territorial waters, coastal waters, inland fresh waters and ground waters.[94] The range of works depends on the circumstances, but the Act refers both to preventative and to remedial measures.[95] NRA is able to recover expenses reasonably incurred in undertaking works, either from a person who has caused or knowingly permitted matter to be present at any place from which NRA considers it likely to enter any controlled waters, or from a person who has caused or knowingly permitted matter to be present in controlled waters.[96] Any such action by NRA is without prejudice to the range of other criminal or civil proceedings which may be available in the circumstances.[97]

Additional powers are available under the Act to deal with interception, treatment or disposal of foul water arising or flowing on land belonging to NRA or over or in which NRA has any necessary easement or rights, or to prevent pollution[98] in respect of the same land.[99] For these purposes, NRA is empowered to construct and maintain drains, sewers, watercourse, catchpits and other works.[1]

Powers to discharge water

Subject to a number of reservations, NRA is able, *inter alia*, to cause the water in any of its works to be discharged into any available watercourse where, for example, it is carrying out or about to carry out the construction, alteration, repair, cleaning or examination of any work belonging to or used by it for the purpose of carrying out any of its functions.[2] Among the reservations relevant to any exercise of this power is the need for NRA, if it is to avoid conviction for a summary offence, to take all necessary steps to secure that any water discharged is as free as may be reasonably practicable from mud and silt, solid, polluting, offensive or injurious substances, and any substances prejudicial to fish, spawn or spawning beds, or food of fish.[3] NRA is required to apply for consent for such discharges and to serve a copy of any such application on any person registered

[93] *Ibid.* s.104(1).
[94] *Ibid.* s.161.
[95] *Ibid.* subs.(1)(a), (b).
[96] *Ibid.* subs.(3).
[97] *Ibid.* subs.(5).
[98] As defined in s.159(6)(b).
[99] *Ibid.* s.162(1).
[1] *Ibid.*
[2] *Ibid.* s.163.
[3] *Ibid.* subs.(3).

with NRA and having premises within three miles of the discharge site.[4] Any disputes are referable to arbitration.[5] Contravention of requirements here renders NRA liable to conviction for a summary offence.[6]

Compensation for the exercise of works powers

The Act makes provision for compensation payments in respect of the exercise of certain of the powers referred to above, in sections 161–167.[7] Of particular significance for present purposes are provisions governing compensation for discharges for works purposes under section 163 and compensation in respect of flood defence and drainage works under sections 165 and 167.[8]

It is stated to be the duty of NRA to cause as little loss and damage as possible in the exercise of section 163 powers and to pay compensation for any loss caused or damage done in the exercise of those powers. For this purpose, any extra expenditure which it becomes reasonably necessary for (say) a water undertaker to incur for the purpose of properly carrying out any statutory functions and which is attributable to any discharge under section 163 is deemed to be a loss sustained by the undertaker and to have been caused in exercise of those powers. Disputes are subject to arbitration.[9] If, on the other hand, injury is sustained by any person by reason of an exercise of powers by NRA under section 165(1)–(3), NRA is liable to make full compensation to the injured party. Disputes are determined by the Lands Tribunal.[10] If injury is sustained by any person by reason of an exercise by NRA of its powers to deposit dredged spoil under section 167(1)(b), NRA may, if it thinks fit, pay such compensation as it may determine. However, if the injury could have been avoided by an exercise of the powers with reasonable care, the foregoing approach governing section 165(1)–(3) will apply.[11]

Protective provisions

A number of NRA works cannot be undertaken in so far as they would interfere with functions which are the responsibility of other agencies and undertakers.[12] If a particular function is included in the catalogue found in Schedule 22 of the Water Resources Act, NRA must seek the consent of the agency or undertaker before proceeding.

[4] *Ibid.* s.164. As to emergencies, see subs.(7).
[5] *Ibid.* subs.(6).
[6] *Ibid.* subs.(8).
[7] *Ibid.* s.177 (referring overall to ss.159 to 167) and Sched. 21.
[8] *Ibid.* Sched. 21, paras. 4 and 5, respectively.
[9] *Ibid.* para. 4.
[10] *Ibid.* para. 5(1), (2).
[11] *Ibid.* para. 5(3).
[12] *Ibid.* s.178 and Sched. 22.

Another protective provision operates without prejudice to the foregoing provisions in Schedule 22 and divides into two parts.[13] The first part[14] indicates that nothing in the Water Resources Act confers power on any person to do anything which interferes with, *inter alia*, works used for draining, preserving or improving any land under any statutory provision except with the consent of the person who uses them. Any consent (which may be subject to conditions) cannot be unreasonably withheld.[15] If NRA proposes (otherwise than with compulsory powers) to construct or alter inland waters in an internal drainage district and those waters do not form part of a main river, or to construct or alter any works on or in any such inland waters, NRA is obliged to consult the internal drainage board concerned.[16]

Savings for planning and existing drainage obligations

Subject to permitted development rights being available to NRA under the Town and Country Planning General Development Order,[17] it is generally the case that planning permission is required for NRA development. In other words, no deemed planning permission will normally arise in favour of NRA as a result of any other authorisation given, for example, by the Minister of Agriculture or Secretary of State for Wales.[18]

A further saving rising from the Water Resources Act indicates that nothing in its flood defence provisions operates to release a person from an obligation under section 21 of the Land Drainage Act 1991.[19] Such an obligation (enforceable by a drainage board under section 21) may arise by virtue of tenure, custom, prescription or otherwise. However, NRA flood defence responsibilities under the Act are equally not limited by the existence of some such obligation binding that other person.[20]

NRA land provisions

Where NRA is proposing, in connection with the discharge of its functions, to carry out any engineering or building operations, or to discharge water into any inland waters or underground strata, it is obliged to seek a compulsory works order from either of the Ministers.[21] Any such order granted secures any necessary compulsory powers and grants authority for the subject works.[22] Either of the Ministers is empowered to authorise compulsory purchase by NRA for the

[13] *Ibid.* s.179.
[14] *Ibid.* subs.(1). Disputes are referable to arbitration: subs.(4).
[15] *Ibid.* subs.(3).
[16] *Ibid.* subs.(2).
[17] See n.87, *supra.*
[18] Water Resources Act, s.183.
[19] *Ibid.* s.185.
[20] *Ibid.* subs.(2).
[21] *Ibid.* s.168 and Sched. 19.
[22] *Ibid.* subs.(2).

fulfilment of its functions.[23] The Act further restricts disposals of compulsorily acquired land, requiring authorisation from one of the Ministers responsible.[24] If it is certified by the Minister responsible that there has been an accretion of land in favour of NRA as a result of any drainage works, the statutory provisions governing NRA acquisition of land compulsorily or by agreement will apply.[25]

Byelaws

NRA is empowered to make byelaws for purposes connected with the carrying out of its functions.[26] Provision is made for NRA powers in this context[27] and associated procedural matters.[28] The Water Resources Act also deals with matters of enforcement and defines an ascending order of severity in penalties arising from failure to comply with particular categories of byelaw, as well as various default powers which are available to NRA.[29]

Coast Protection

Administration

Protection of land from sea is governed by the Coast Protection Act 1949. The Minister responsible is the Minister of Agriculture and, in Wales, the Secretary of State. Locally, the district council whose area abuts the sea is the coast protection authority for the purposes of the Act, its administration and enforcement. Distinguishing between the flood defence responsibilities of the regional flood defence committees and NRA and the coast protection responsibilities of a district council is not always easy. However, the provision of sea defence lies within the province of the regional flood defence committees, while measures to control coast erosion fall within the province of the coast protection authority and the Act of 1949.

Coast protection powers

A coast protection authority is empowered to undertake coast protection works considered necessary or expedient for the purpose of protection of land within

[23] *Ibid.* s.154.
[24] *Ibid.* s.157.
[25] *Ibid.* s.155.
[26] *Ibid.* s.210.
[27] *Ibid.* Sched. 25.
[28] *Ibid.* Sched. 26.
[29] *Ibid.* s.211.

the district.[30] Various contributions, as well as grant-aid, may be available for this work.[31] Any necessary land may be acquired compulsorily or by agreement for this purpose.[32] The range of works here is considerable.[33]

Works other than repair or maintenance

Coast protection works will require planning permission and will have to be notified, as a set of proposals, in the particular locality.[34] Any objections are referable to the minister responsible. A public local inquiry may be convened prior to any decision by the Minister on the proposals. If there is a need to purchase land compulsorily for the purpose of executing coast protection proposals, a works scheme will be sought.[35]

Maintenance and repair

A coast protection authority is empowered to maintain and repair coast protection works[36] and will usually be compelled to do so by the terms on which any grant is made, initially for the purpose of constructing the works. An expedited procedure is also provided by the Act.[37]

[30] Coast Protection Act 1949, s.4. Coast protection having significant environmental effects may require an environmental assessment: Town and Country Planning (Assessment of Environmental Effects) (Amendment) Regulations 1994 (S.I. 1994 No. 677).
[31] Coast Protection Act 1949, ss.4(2), 20 and 21.
[32] *Ibid.* ss.4(3) and 14.
[33] *Ibid.* s.49(1).
[34] *Ibid.* s.5(1).
[35] *Ibid.* s.8.
[36] *Ibid.* s.4.
[37] *Ibid.* s.5.

Chapter 4

WATER POLLUTION

Introduction

The present chapter interrelates with Chapters 2, 3 and 4, "Water Resources and Supply", "Sewage Effluent and Disposal", and "Land Drainage and Flood Defence", respectively. Civil and criminal enforcement of the law governing the protection of water quality is the essential focus of the chapter, indicating a number of relationships with the above chapters. The initial concern here is with the common law and the various areas of liability which may be relevant, particularly where (as an incidence of landed interests) conditions of adverse water quality cause loss, damage or injury to the plaintiff. A variety of aquatic quality standards govern not only potential common law liabilities but also regulatory matters provided for by statute. Accordingly, the chapter progresses to examine different categories of so-called "vulnerable waters", as well as a range of legal limits on a number of polluting introductions to the aquatic environment, all governed by E.C. law. In addition to E.C. legal requirements governing the aquatic environment, a number of international conventions also influence the picture and are covered in this chapter. The remainder of the chapter is devoted to the statutory framework, concentrated primarily in the Water Resources Act 1991, which governs the regulatory requirements applying to "controlled" waters, accounting for most of the aquatic environment up to the seaward limit of territorial waters. In addition, attention is given to maritime pollution, particularly by reference to its potential for harm to land-based facilities and interests.

The Common Law Position

The range of common law liabilities

The common law liabilities in respect of water pollution fall into five sometimes closely related categories, each of which is examined below in turn. Those categories are as follows:

(a) nuisance and riparian rights and liabilities;
(b) strict liability;
(c) breach of statutory duty;
(d) trespass; and
(e) negligence.

Nuisance, riparian rights and liabilities

> "A riparian owner has as an incident to property a natural and proprietary right not dependent on prescription, grant or acquiescence of the riparian owner above, but arising *jure nature* to have water in any normal channel which is known and defined on which his land abuts, or which passes through his land to flow to him in its natural state, both as regards quantity and quality, whether he has made use of it or not."[1]

The immediate relationship with the law of nuisance can be appreciated here, by reference to the attachment of a "natural and proprietary right" *jure nature*. Furthermore, the law of nuisance is based on the requirement of an unreasonable interference which may, but need not, arise from some negligent act or omission. Any such interference must also be continuous, a requirement which may aid the establishment of another, often difficult, prerequisite: causation.[2]

In one of the leading authorities—*Young v. Bankier Distillery Co.*[3]—it was said that "... every riparian owner is ... entitled to the water of his stream in its natural flow, without sensible alteration in its character or quality"[4] and (by another member of the House of Lords) that the "... lower owner is entitled to have the water transmitted to him with its natural qualities unimpaired ...".[5] If a riparian owner requires water in connection with his riparian use of the land (say) for domestic and agricultural purposes, this is characterised as an "ordinary" riparian use and may even exhaust the supply in question. On the other hand, the riparian owner may require water for some purpose unconnected with his riparian ownership. In these circumstances, the owner is entitled to take only so much of the available water as will not materially diminish its quantity and quality. Furthermore, in these circumstances the riparian owner is obliged to return the water to source materially similar both in quantity and quality.[6] Failure to comply with this obligation will give a plaintiff riparian owner downstream a cause of action without having to prove any loss, damage or injury.[7]

In the case of underground waters percolating through an aquifer that passes beneath land in the ownership of the plaintiff and the defendant, the Court of Appeal has held that the defendant will be strictly liable for any polluting activity that interferes with the plaintiff's "natural" right (as an incident of his ownership) to draw unpolluted water from that aquifer.[8] The essential principle has been expressed thus:

[1] Stuart-Smith J. in *Scott-Whitehead v. National Coal Board* (1985) 53 P. & C.R. 263, quoting *Halsbury's Laws*, Vol. 49, para. 392.
[2] *Sedleigh-Denfield v. O'Callaghan* [1940] A.C. 880.
[3] [1893] A.C. 691.
[4] *Per* Lord Macnaughton.
[5] *Per* Lord Shand.
[6] *Attwood v. Llay Main Collieries Ltd* [1926] Ch. 444.
[7] *Ibid.*
[8] *Cambridge Water Co. Ltd v. Eastern Counties Leatherwork PLC* [1993] Env. L.R. 287, C.A.

> "... although nobody has any property in the common [water] source, yet everybody has a right to appropriate it, and to appropriate it in its natural state, and no one of those who have a right to appropriate it has a right to contaminate that source so as to prevent his neighbour from having the full value of his right of appropriation."[9]

Two important matters flow from the above decision of the Court of Appeal in *Cambridge Water*, although it should be noted that an appeal to the House of Lords was pursued solely by reference to strict liability principles.[10] First, negligence has no relevance to the determination of liability on the facts of such cases. Secondly, the aforementioned "right" to receive unpolluted water appears to be a matter to be judged by reference to quality standards as prescribed by E.C. directives on water quality, at least to the extent of indicating what, for E.C. requirements, would be acceptable standards of "wholesomeness".

Proceedings in the present context may be met with two potentially significant arguments, either that the defendant has a statutory right to abstract water or that a prescriptive right to pollute applies. In the first case, the Water Resources Act[11] indicates that the holder of an abstraction licence is "... taken to have a right to abstract water to the extent authorised by the licence and in accordance with the provisions contained in it".[12] Reliance on such a defence therefore depends on the extent of the defendant's activity by reference to the limits of the licence. Alternatively, and for other purposes, the holder of the licence may of course assert that the terms of the licence modifies pre-existing riparian rights. The second case of prescriptive rights is a matter of proof by the defendant that such rights have been enjoyed continuously for a period of 20 years.[13] However, a particular point of difficulty arises in relation to the need to establish that the subject activity—typically a polluting activity—has not exceeded the levels that obtained at the commencement of the "period of prescription".[14] Closely connected with these matters is the matter of statutory control over licences for discharges to "controlled" waters under the Water Resources Act.[15] That statutory control may occur in one of two ways, either through a review by the National Rivers Authority (NRA hereafter) of a consent granted by it, or through a review which NRA is directed to undertake by the Secretary of State. By notice served on the holder of the consent, that consent may be revoked or its conditions modified, or (in the case of an unconditional consent) it may be subject to the addition of conditions. A direction from the Secretary of State may be given on various grounds, including the protection of public health or by reference to any representations or objections made. Subject to NRA liability to

[9] *Per* Lord Brett M.R. in *Ballard v. Tomlinson* [1881–85] All E.R. Rep. 688 at 691. This principle was followed by the Court of Appeal in *Cambridge Water, supra.*

[10] [1994] 2 W.L.R. 53, H.L.

[11] s.48.

[12] Water Resources Act, s.48(1): *cf* subs.(2) and Sched. 7, para. 2.

[13] *Crossley v. Lightowler* (1867) L.R.2 Ch. 478.

[14] *Blackburne v. Somers* (1880) L.R. Ireland 5 Ch. Div. 1 at 18.

[15] s.88 and Sched. 10.

pay compensation in some circumstances here, riparian rights may be defended without the necessity for litigation.[16]

Strict liability

It appears that strict liability principles from *Rylands v. Fletcher*[17] are applied in the present context of water pollution only with great difficulty. Blackburn J. defined the principle as follows:

> "... the person who, for his own purposes, brings on his land and keeps there anything likely to do mischief if it escapes, must keep it at his peril, and, if he does not do so, he is *prima facie* answerable for all the damage which is the natural consequence of its escape. He can excuse himself by showing that the escape was owing to the plaintiff's default, or, perhaps, that the escape was the consequence of *vis major*, or the act of God ..."[18]

The foregoing principle has been confused by the requirement that such strict liability should relate only to "non-natural" user of land.[19] However, while this has fuelled judicial confusion, the status of strict liability in civil law has been very marginal. One area of particular note concerns the escape of sewage from local authority facilities and now, principally, sewerage undertakers' premises. In *Smeaton v. Ilford Corporation*,[20] for example, Upjohn J. considered that the collection of "large volumes" of sewage on land is not a natural user of that land. Albeit *obiter*, the same judge doubted whether a local authority was exempt from strict liability "... on the ground that use of land for sewage collection purposes is such a use as is proper for the general use of the community".[21] A similar view was expressed by Harman J. in *Pride of Derby and Derbyshire Angling Association v. British Celanese*[22] at first instance, subsequently doubted by Denning L.J. in the Court of Appeal.[23] The potential, or otherwise, of strict liability at common law appears now to be determined by the opinion of the House of Lords in *Cambridge Water Co. v. Eastern Counties Leather Ltd.*[24] The case is set against a background of perchloroethene pollution of groundwater used for abstraction by the water company. The chemical had been brought on to the industrial premises of Eastern Counties Leather and used over many years for the treatment of leather. Use of the chemical had led to undetected spillages which, in turn, had percolated into the ground waters. The focus of the appeal was strict liability and the principle in *Rylands v. Fletcher.* As a result of the House of Lords opinion, the common law will now insist on foreseeability of harm or injury of the type

[16] Water Resources Act, Sched. 10, para. 6.
[17] (1866) L.R.1 Ex. 265.
[18] *Ibid.*
[19] *Rickards v. Lothian* [1913] A.C. 263.
[20] [1954] Ch. 450.
[21] *Ibid.* at 470, 471.
[22] [1952] 1 All E.R. 1326 at 1337.
[23] [1953] 1 All E.R. 179, affirming the first instance decision on other grounds.
[24] [1994] 2 W.L.R. 53.

complained of if strict liability is to be found. Having concluded the case on this basis, the members of the House of Lords found it unnecessary to attempt any redefinition of the concept of a natural or "ordinary" use which has for so long bedevilled any attempt to create an effective definition of strict liability in this country. Lord Goff, speaking for their Lordships, was content to conclude that the storage of chemicals in substantial quantities and their use in the manner employed by the company in the present proceedings could not fall within the natural user exception to which *Rylands v. Fletcher* has been subject. In more general terms, the House of Lords considered that controversial issues of strict environmental liability should be determined by Parliament rather than the courts. Despite the conclusion outlined above, there is some potential for strict liability, at least to the extent that a plaintiff can establish that the defendant owner or occupier of industrial premises reasonably foresaw harm or injury of the type complained of before the substance or material introduced to those premises left the control of the defendant. This latter requirement is a complicating factor, largely as a result of the House of Lords' view that, once the perchlorothene had reached the chalk aquifer beneath Eastern Counties' premises, it passed from the company's control for strict liability purposes. Whether the potential referred to is realised depends on difficult matters of proof based on the balance of probabilities, which are undoubtedly at odds with normal assumptions associated with strict liability and easily capable of confusion with scientific standards of proof which extend well beyond the 51 per cent. threshold of probabilities.

What is alleged to be an "escape" for present purposes may of course be authorised under the terms of a discharge consent issued by NRA under the Water Resources Act. Again, reference is made to the availability of powers of review in relation to consents, as well as the licensing powers themselves.[25] Both mechanisms are available for the purpose of protecting the aquatic environment in respect of anything likely to do mischief if it escapes.

It is provided by the Water Industry Act[26] that a sewerage undertaker shall carry out its functions in the present context so as not to create a nuisance. In *Smeaton*, this provision was sufficient to justify a dismissal of the action which was based on damage caused by overloaded, overflowing sewers.

Breach of statutory duty

Part III of the Water Resources Act, dealing with the control of pollution of water resources, indicates that, unless provision is made, nothing in this Part of the Act confers a right of civil action in respect of a range of defined contraventions that may occur in this statutory context. Similarly, nothing in Part III derogates from any right of action or other remedy, civil or criminal, in proceedings beyond this part of the Act.[27] In so far as Part III does contain duties which could form the basis of a civil action for breach of statutory duty, this

[25] See n.15, *supra*.
[26] s.117(6).
[27] s.100.

provision prevents any such action. Nevertheless, any other right of action that may arise (say) in nuisance would not be blocked. As far as breach of statutory duty is concerned, Part III contains very few duties of the sort that would attract tortious liability for breach. The general duty requiring the Secretary of State and NRA to exercise their powers for the achievement of statutory water quality objectives, for example, is insufficiently specific to admit of tortious enforcement. Elsewhere in Part III, NRA as the main enforcement agency is given various powers—and discretion—but is subject to very little in the way of mandatory and directly enforceable duties for present purposes.

Elsewhere in the Water Resources Act, NRA may be liable (subject to any contrary indication in the relevant section) for loss or damage caused by an escape of water from a pipe vested in it.[28] A similar provision imposes liability on a water undertaker under the Water Industry Act.[29] The potential for pollution arising from the activities of sewerage undertakers is considerable. However, matters of enforcement are concentrated in many cases on the administrative enforcement provisions in section 18 of the Water Industry Act. Consequently, the opportunity for actions in tort in the present context must necessarily be limited.

Trespass

In some respects, trespass may have significance in relation to matters of water pollution. Although trespass is actionable *per se*,[30] this advantage is probably outweighed by the requirement that the plaintiff should be able to establish some direct physical interference with land, arising from the defendant's unlawful act.[31] For example, it must be a matter of debate as to whether effluent deposited on the banks of a river is deposited sufficiently directly as a result of the flow of the river.[32] There is no doubt that matters of "directness" and intention (also a matter of significance in the proof of trespass) are far more difficult if polluting effluent is washed into and onto the plaintiff's land from the sea.[33] Even more difficult than that would be pursuit of an action in trespass where oil, discharged from a vessel off shore, catches fire and damages the plaintiff's land on the shoreline.

Negligence

Although a most important tort in general terms, the utility of negligence is probably limited in this and other areas of environmental control. Negligence raises the need to prove that a duty of care is owed by the defendant to the plaintiff, that there has been a breach of that duty by the defendant, and that that breach has given rise to foreseeable loss, damage or injury. Although negligence will remain an important cause of action in relation to accidents and occurrences

[28] Water Resources Act, s.208.
[29] s.209.
[30] *Jones v. Llanrwst UDC* [1911] 1 Ch. 393, *per* Parker J. at 402.
[31] *Smith v. Giddy* [1904] 2 K.B. 448 at 451.
[32] See n.30, *supra*.
[33] *Esso Petroleum Co. Ltd v. Southport Corporation* [1956] A.C. 218.

involving "private" parties, particular interest focuses on the extent to which, if at all, regulatory authorities may be liable in negligence in the discharge, or purported discharge, of their functions. It has been suggested, for example, that (in the context of Canadian federal approval for pesticides) a licensing agency may "... have been negligent in granting registration to a product before sufficient trial experiment has been conducted".[34] More directly in point is the decision of the High Court in *Scott-Whitehead v. National Coal Board*,[35] where it was held that a water authority was in breach of a duty of care in failing to warn the plaintiff farmer of the risks of dangerous levels of salinity in a river and advising that water be checked prior to use for irrigation. However, trends in the law of negligence suggest that regulatory authorities such as NRA will not owe a duty of care to licensees or would-be licensees except where (and probably exceptionally) there is some reliance to be found in the relationship between the parties.[36]

Remedies

Three categories of remedy are relevant to present concerns: the injunction, damages and "self-help" measures on the part of regulatory authorities such as NRA. In defence of "natural" riparian rights, a perpetual injunction may be appropriate. The effect of works undertaken by the defendant water company in *Clowes v. Staffordshire Potteries Waterworks Co.*,[37] for example, was to render the subject waters unsuitable for dyeing, primarily because the waters had become excessively muddy. In these circumstances, the court was able to grant a perpetual injunction to prevent fouling of the watercourse in question. Nevertheless, the court has a discretion and may, for example, suspend the injunction for (say) three months to allow compliance by the defendant and even then to permit the defendant to seek a further extension. In this way, matters of practicality and convenience can be taken account of, to allow measures to be taken to implement anti-pollution works.[38] It may be possible to obtain an injunction in these circumstances even if there is no proof of actual damage, as in the case of *Clowes*.[39]

Damages may be available in respect of an infringement of riparian rights where, for example, loss is suffered through a need to obtain some alternative supply of clean water for manufacturing purposes, or where that manufacturing capacity is damaged as a result of exposure to polluted water.[40] There is the possibility that such damages will be awarded in lieu of an injunction[41] or, perhaps, in addition to the injunction. Where damages are sought for the impact

[34] *Per* Nicholson J., *obiter*, in *Willis v. F.M.C. Machinery and Chemicals Ltd* (1976) 68 D.L.R. (3d) 127 at 157.
[35] (1985) 53 P. & C.R. 263.
[36] *Murphy v. Brentwood District Council* [1990] 2 All E.R. 908.
[37] (1872) 8 Ch. App. 125.
[38] *A.-G. v. Colney Hatch Lunatic Asylum* (1868) 4 Ch. App. 146.
[39] *Per* Parker J. in *Jones v. Llanwrst UDC* [1911] 1 Ch. 392 at 402. The court may order the defendant to indemnify the plaintiff against all damage arising from a suspension.
[40] For a wider view, see Buckley J. in *Earl of Harrington v. Derby Corporation* [1905] 1 Ch. 205.
[41] Chancery Amendment Act 1858, s.2.

of pollution on fishing rights, the court will inquire into the natural and probable consequences of the unlawful act alleged to have caused the pollution. In *Marquis of Granby v. Bakewell UDC*,[42] for example, fish were poisoned and, in assessing damages, the court took account of the loss of fish and fish food in the river, indicating the court's willingness to take account of limited environmental factors.

NRA has a very significant "self-help" measure in section 161 of the Water Resources Act 1991, a measure of particular value if it has the financial resources for an environmental clean-up. If it appears to NRA that any poisonous, noxious or polluting matter, or any solid waste matter, is likely to enter, or to be or to have been present in, any controlled waters, a range of works and operations can be carried out. These works (which are not restricted to any particular land such as landfill which is leaching toxic liquid, for example) extend to preventative action, action to remove and dispose of matter, as well as action to remedy or mitigate any pollution caused and even to restore the waters affected "... so far as it is reasonably practicable to do so ...". However, these operations or works may not impede or prevent any discharge to controlled waters authorised by NRA under Part III of the same Act. Expenses reasonably incurred in undertaking the works or operations may be recovered by NRA. Finally, and perhaps significantly, nothing comprehended by these powers derogates from the pursuit of any other civil or criminal remedy lying beyond section 161. NRA is also able, under section 162, to undertake anti-pollution works in relation to land in its ownership or in respect of which it has other rights or easements. These powers are without prejudice to those comprised in section 161.

Vulnerable Waters

E.C. directives

Community directives governing the aquatic environment may be categorised in two ways, according to whether they relate to matters of water quality or restrictions on polluting introductions to the aquatic environment. In some cases, particular Directives serve both purposes.

The aquatic quality directives

Directives falling into this category are as follows:

(a) Directive 75/440[42a] (quality of water abstracted for drinking);
(b) Directive 80/778[42b] (quality of water intended for human consumption);
(c) Directive 76/160[42c] (quality of water for bathing);

[42] (1923) 21 L.G.R. 329.
[42a] [1975] O.J. L194.
[42b] [1980] O.J. L229.
[42c] [1976] O.J. L31.

(d) Directive 78/659[42d] (quality of fresh waters for the protection and improvement of fish life); and
(e) Directive 79/923[42e] (quality of shellfish waters).

Directives restricting polluting introductions

Directives falling into this category are as follows:

(a) Directive 76/464[43] (dangerous substances discharged into the aquatic environment);
(b) Directive 78/176[43a] (prevention and progressive reduction of waste from the titanium dioxide industry); and
(c) Directive 91/676[43b] (prevention or reduction of the use and storage of certain fertilizers and manure on agricultural land for the purpose of protection from pollution by nitrates).

Directives satisfying both objectives

Two directives fall into this category, in their concern both for quality standards and restrictions on polluting introductions:

(a) Directive 91/271[43c] (urban waste water treatment); and
(b) Directive 80/68[43d] (ground water).

The former Directive is concerned with reductions in the introduction of, *inter alia*, domestic sewage and industrial waste water to fresh waters as well as estuarial and coastal waters. In addition, the Directive contains restrictions on the disposal of sewage sludge. Overall, therefore, Directive 91/271 is a significant complement to Directives 75/440, 78/659, 76/160 and 79/923, above. The second Directive that satisfies both objectives is the ground water Directive, controlling the introduction of dangerous substances to ground waters for the maintenance of quality, particularly in so far as there is an overall need to protect sources of drinking water.

Modes of restriction on polluting introductions

The urban waste water treatment Directive sets limit values for discharges to vulnerable waters and defines performance targets to be met by various forms of treatment in place at particular sewerage and other treatment plants. Lesser treatment requirements will apply in so-called "less sensitive" areas, as designated by NRA. NRA, in turn, is the regulatory authority charged with the task of

[42d] [1978] O.J. L222.
[42e] [1979] O.J. L281.
[43] [1976] O.J. L129.
[43a] [1978] O.J. L54.
[43b] [1991] O.J. L375.
[43c] [1991] O.J. L135.
[43d] [1980] L.J. L20.

authorising discharges to "controlled" waters,[43e] including discharges from sewerage and other treatment plants covered by the present directives.

The ground water Directive refers to so-called "List I" and "List II" substances and requires Member States to prevent the former being introduced to ground waters and to limit the latter's introduction for the purpose of avoiding adverse polluting effects on the waters. In relation to matters of prevention for the purpose of List I substances, any direct discharge is prohibited: a "direct discharge" is something other than a percolation through the ground. In the case of List II substances, authorisation is possible prior to any discharge, but subject to any necessary investigation. Responsibility for authorisation rests with NRA in relation to discharges to "controlled waters" (which include ground waters) and waste regulation authorities under Part II of the Environmental Protection Act, in so far as any deposit of "controlled waste" would fall within the terms of the Directive.

The dangerous substances Directive is also founded on "listed" substances. Particularly toxic substances are found in List I, with the less toxic substances comprised in List II. The Directive raises an obligation to prohibit List I substances in the aquatic environment and to seek a reduction of pollution by substances in List II. However, authorisation by a competent regulatory authority is required for the discharge of substances in both lists. In the case of List I substances, any application for authorisation will be processed through the integrated pollution control provisions of Part I of the Environmental Protection Act by Her Majesty's Inspectorate of Pollution. However, no authorisation may be granted if NRA certifies that its water quality objectives would not be achieved in relation to the waters in question. Alternatively, an authorisation granted may include conditions required by NRA for these purposes.[44] NRA, exercising its licensing functions in relation to discharges to controlled waters,[45] has responsibility in relation to those substances not included in the foregoing List I. A number of "daughter" directives relate to specific substances: mercury,[46] cadmium,[47] hexachlorocyclohexane,[48] pentachlorophenol[49] and DDT and the so-called "drins".[50]

The titanium dioxide Directive[51] creates a duty on the part of Member States to ensure that the wastes do not endanger human health or harm the environment. A variety of acts are subject to the requirement of an authorisation by a competent authority, including discharges. In this respect, NRA has responsibility under the Water Resources Act[52] to consider and determine applications for consent to make discharges to "controlled" waters.

[43e] Water Resources Act, Pt. III.
[44] Environmental Protection Act, s.28(3).
[45] Water Resources Act 1991, s.88 and Sched. 10.
[46] Directive 82/176: [1982] O.J. L81.
[47] Directive 83/513: [1983] O.J. L291.
[48] Directive 84/491: [1984] O.J. L274.
[49] Directive 86/280: [1986] O.J. L181.
[50] Directive 86/280: [1986] O.J. L181 and Directive 88/347: [1988] O.J. L158.
[51] Directive 78/176: [1978] O.J. L54.
[52] See n.45, *supra*.

The Directive on nitrate pollution from agriculture[53] requires each Member State to identify vulnerable areas that may be adversely affected by nitrates from agricultural sources. The Water Resources Act[54] makes provision for water protection zones and nitrate-sensitive areas. In both cases, the designation is a means by which certain relevant activities may be regulated, with or without payments of compensation.

The Control of Pollution

Controlled waters

Part III of the Water Resources Act deals with pollution control measures in relation to "controlled" waters, as defined by the Act.[55] The Act proceeds on the basis of a classification of waters, as follows:

(a) "relevant territorial waters";
(b) "coastal waters";
(c) "inland fresh waters"; and
(d) "ground waters".

Relevant territorial waters

There are waters that extend seaward for three miles from the baselines from which the breadth of the territorial sea adjacent to England and Wales is measured.[56] The Secretary of State may by order provide that any area of territorial sea (extending up to 12 miles by virtue of the Territorial Sea Act 1987) is to be treated as if it were an area of relevant territorial waters, usually in relation to estuaries which would otherwise fall outside designated controlled waters. These controlled waters mark the limit of NRA jurisdiction for a variety of purposes in Part III of the Act, except that NRA is obliged to enforce the law where a person "... causes or knowingly permits any trade effluent or sewage effluent to be discharged ... from land in England and Wales, through a pipe, into the sea outside the seaward limits of controlled waters" without an appropriate consent.[57]

Coastal waters

These are waters within the area extending landward from the baselines referred to previously, as far as the limit of the highest tide or, in the case of the waters of any "relevant river or watercourse", the fresh water limit of that river or

[53] Directive 91/676: [1991] O.J. L375.
[54] ss.93 and 94. *Cf.* nn.55–62, *infra.*
[55] Water Resources Act, s.104.
[56] s.104(1)(a).
[57] *Ibid.* s.85(3).

watercourse, together with the waters of any enclosed dock which adjoins waters within that area.[58] A "relevant river or watercourse" means any river or watercourse (including an underground river or watercourse and an artificial river or watercourse) which is neither a public sewer nor a a sewer or drain which drains into a public sewer. The "fresh water limit" is the limit as presently represented on the map deposited with NRA by the Secretary of State.[59] The present provision includes estuaries extending up to the fresh water limit of any river or watercourse, unless the Secretary of State, by order, has indicated that a particular watercourse is excluded.[60]

Inland fresh waters

The Act contains three different definitions of the term "inland waters", for the purpose of Part II (dealing with water resources management), Part VII (dealing with land and works powers) and Part VIII (dealing with information provision)[61]; section 148 (dealing with the payment of grants for flood warning systems)[62]; and the present Part III.[63] However, Part III refers to "inland fresh waters": the waters of any relevant lake or pond or of so much of any relevant river or watercourse as is above the fresh water limit. A lake or pond may include a reservoir of any description, while the reference to any "relevant lake or pond" means any lake or pond which (whether it is natural or artificial or above or below ground) discharges into a relevant river or watercourse or into another lake or pond which is itself a relevant lake or pond.[64] The need for the inland waters here to be above the fresh water limit is a matter that may be determined by reference to the map of the river or watercourse deposited with NRA.[65] Not surprisingly, for the purposes of Parts III, VII and VIII of the Act, the definition goes appreciably further, referring, for example, to "... any channel, creek, bay, estuary or arm of the sea".[66]

Lakes and ponds

It was noted previously that a lake or pond may include a reservoir of any description. However, lakes and ponds are to be regarded as "controlled waters" only incidentally, by reference to the inland fresh waters previously referred to. Even here, it should be noted that any lake or pond which does not discharge into a "relevant river or watercourse" or a "relevant lake or pond" may by an order of the Secretary of State be designated a "relevant lake or pond", bringing it back to

[58] *Ibid.* s.104(1)(b).
[59] *Ibid.* s.192.
[60] *Ibid.* s.104(4)(d).
[61] *Ibid.* s.221(1).
[62] *Ibid.* s.148(5).
[63] *Ibid.* s.104(1)(c).
[64] *Ibid.* subs.(3).
[65] See n.59, *supra.*
[66] Water Resources Act, s.221(1): *cf.* s.148(5) in very similar terms.

the categories of "controlled waters".[67] If such lakes or ponds remain outside the designation of "controlled waters", there are limited opportunities comparatively to deal with matters of enforcement following their pollution. Nevertheless, an offence is committed if trade or sewage effluent is discharged from a building or from any fixed plant into the waters of a lake or pond not comprising inland fresh waters.[68] Otherwise, statutory nuisance provisions may be resorted to, at least to the extent that "... any pond ... is so foul or in such a state as to be prejudicial to health or a nuisance ...",[69] in which case the conditions can be regarded as a statutory nuisance and therefore amenable to the measures and remedies provided for under Part III of the Environmental Protection Act 1990.

Ground waters

Inclusion of ground waters is crucial by reference to the requirements of E.C. Directive 80/68, referred to earlier in the present chapter. Controls operate in two principal areas, by reference to the licensing process under the jurisdiction of NRA and to criminal enforcement of pollution of "controlled waters".

Quality objectives

Water quality has been assessed, usually by reference to the purposes for which water is used. This is the case in relation to E.C. water directives, with a range of provision for standards that include requirements for drinking water and shellfish, to name but two. In general, it appears that requirements for and monitoring of water quality by reference to a range of possible uses brings a number of practical difficulties:

> "There are two broad approaches to water monitoring. One involves examining physical and chemical characteristics of water samples, particularly to identify the presence of pollutants. The other, biological monitoring, involves examining the flora and fauna of waterbodies. Current thinking recognises that the two approaches provide complementary information and one will often compensate for deficiencies in the other."[70]

The physical and chemical characteristics of water have formed the basis for a system of water classification hitherto. This system was based on a fourfold classification, extending downwards from "good quality" to "fair quality", "poor quality" and (finally) "bad quality". In broad terms, national policy hitherto has been aimed at the elimination of "class 4" waters and the steady reduction of "class 3" waters.

[67] Controlled Waters (Lakes and Ponds) Order 1989 (S.I. 1989 No. 1149). *Cf.* Water Resources Act, s.104(2)(b).
[68] *Ibid.* s.85(4).
[69] Public Health Act 1936, s.259.
[70] Royal Commission on Environmental Pollution, 16th Report, Cm. 1966 (1992), para. 4.5.

Classification of water quality

The Secretary of State is empowered by regulation to prescribe a system of classification, according to defined criteria, in relation to any description of controlled waters. Any such description may apply to some or all of the waters of a particular class or of two or more different classes. The criteria to be specified in regulations here will comprise:

(a) general requirements[71] as to the purposes for which the waters to which the classification is applied are to be suitable;
(b) specific requirements as to the substances that are to be present in or absent from water, and as to the concentration of substances which are or are required to be present in the water; and
(c) specific requirements as to other characteristics of those waters.[72]

The process of classification, operating as a prerequisite for the development of statutory water quality objectives, is the first part of a process that operates within a statutory framework. Compliance with E.C. legal requirements here demands something other than a purely voluntary, discretionary system, as seen in the days before the Water Act 1989 whose provisions in the present context are now consolidated in the Water Resources Act. Three issues arise in relation to the present provisions of section 82 dealing with classification. First, the enabling power for the purpose of making regulations is very widely drawn in a variety of respects, including a marked absence of any legal requirement to undertake consultation with any interested individuals or organisations. Secondly, there is no assumption that regulations should be made which prescribe classifications for all categories of controlled waters. Finally, the range of criteria is widely defined, allowing considerable freedom in the determination of any classification.

The first regulations to be made were the Surface Waters (Classification) Regulations 1989[73] prescribing a system for classifying the quality of inland waters, according to their suitability for abstraction by water undertakers for supply (after treatment) as drinking water. Classifications DW1, DW2 and DW3 reflect the mandatory values assigned by E.C. Directive 75/440.[74] These classifications are relevant to the setting of water quality objectives for rivers, lakes and other inland waters under the following provisions of the Water Resources Act, as well as determining water treatment requirements for the purpose of public supply under the Water Supply (Water Quality) Regulations 1989.[75]

A second set of regulations is the Surface Waters (Dangerous Substances) (Classification) Regulations 1989.[76] These Regulations determine approaches to

[71] Such as drinking water: Directive 75/440.
[72] Water Resources Act, s.82. Note the Surface Water (River Ecosystem) (Classification) Regulations 1994 (S.I. 1994 No. 1057), prescribing a system of classification for the general quality of inland fresh waters.
[73] S.I. 1989 No. 1148.
[74] See n.71, *supra*.
[75] S.I. 1989 No. 1147.
[76] S.I. 1989 No. 2286.

classification of inland waters, coastal waters and relevant territorial waters in terms of dangerous substances and their concentrations. As such, the Regulations are referable to quality objectives in a number of relevant E.C. directives. The Regulations modify section 83, on water quality objectives, to enable compliance with E.C. Directive 76/464 through removal of the Secretary of State's duty to give three months' notice prior to initial determination of water quality objectives by reference to dangerous substances.

The third set of regulations is the Bathing Water (Classification) Regulations 1991,[77] implementing the requirements of E.C. Directive 76/160. A classification BW1 is prescribed, applying to relevant territorial waters, coastal waters and inland waters which are bathing waters.[78] The regulations set the criteria for classification BW1, as well as imposing sampling requirements and defining quality standards. As in the previous set of regulations, the Secretary of State's obligation to give three months' notice prior to initial determination of water quality objectives does not apply here. Nevertheless, section 83 operates as if the Secretary of State is subject to a duty to apply classification BW1 to the waters covered by the provision.

The fourth set of regulations, the Surface Waters (Dangerous Substances) (Classification) Regulations 1992,[79] adds a classification DS3 to pre-existing classifications DS1 and DS2, introduced under the 1989 Regulations, referred to previously.[80] The same waters are covered, but additional substances and their prescribed concentrations are specified. Section 83 has effect as if the Secretary of State were subject to a duty to apply DS3 to the waters covered by the provision. Once again, the Secretary of State's duty to give three months' notice prior to initial determination of water quality objectives does not apply.

Statutory water quality objectives

Classifications *per se* have no status since they are instrumental, as between the Secretary of State and NRA, in the sestablishment of water quality objectives under the Water Resources Act.[81] Indeed, it is for the purpose of "maintaining and improving" the quality of controlled waters that the Secretary of State is empowered to serve a notice to NRA relating to the classification of waters, for the establishment of objectives for "any" waters. In general terms, it is arguable that water quality objectives would be characterised by "... requirements to safeguard specific uses of water ... requirements of relevant EC directives ... and ... possibly a general purpose classification scheme ..." providing general statements about the state of similar types of water at any one time.[82] Furthermore, it is also arguable that a statutory water quality objective should be capable of protecting certain uses such as "basic amenity", which would be

[77] S.I. 1991 No. 1597.

[78] As defined in art.1.2 of the Directive, including other waters which are used for bathing.

[79] S.I. 1992 No. 337.

[80] See n.76, *supra*.

[81] s.83.

[82] Royal Commission on Environmental Pollution, 16th Report, Cm. 1966 (1992), p.45.

designed to "... stop waters from becoming a nuisance and is a test of aesthetic acceptability".[83]

Whether for the purpose of establishing objectives or varying them, the Secretary of State is required to give public notice of his proposals and to allow at least three months for the making of any representations or objections. Any such notice is required to be copied to NRA and must be published by the Secretary of State in such manner as he considers appropriate for bringing it to the attention of those likely to be affected by it. Any such notice, as well as a notice served on NRA to the effect that objectives for any waters should remain unchanged, must be published by NRA in the register maintained for pollution control purposes.[84]

The present provisions in section 83 of the Act also provide for a review of water quality objectives by the Secretary of State. In the first place, the Secretary of State may initiate such a review five or more years following the establishment of objectives. Secondly, NRA may request a review having consulted with "... such water undertakers and other persons as it considers appropriate".[85] However, the Secretary of State must not exercise his power to establish objectives for any waters by varying the existing objectives for those waters except in consequence of such a review.[86]

The duty to achieve and maintain objectives

> "The importance of SWQOs [statutory water quality objectives] is that the Secretary of State and the regulatory authorities [NRA] are required to exercise their relevant pollution control powers (for example in setting discharge consents) so as to achieve the objectives, so far as practicable."

This is the description of the important duty to be found in section 84 of the Water Resources Act, as described in the 16th report by the Royal Commission on Environmental Pollution.[87] The Royal Commission goes on to say that NRA should use SWQOs as a means of gradually tightening discharge consents over a longer-term period until the desired improvements had been achieved.[88] Indeed, the statutory duty of the Secretary of State and NRA is to exercise powers under the water pollution provisions of the Act (except sections 82, 83, 104 and 192) in such a manner as ensures "so far as it is practicable" that the water quality objectives notified under section 83 are achieved "at all times". Any default or perceived default by NRA could activate the Secretary of State's powers to issue general or specific directions to NRA.[89]

Additionally, NRA is subject to a duty, for the purpose of carrying out its water pollution functions, to monitor the extent of pollution in controlled waters.[90]

[83] *Ibid.*
[84] Water Resources Act, s.190.
[85] *Ibid.* s.83(3).
[86] *Ibid.*
[87] See Royal Commission on Environmental Pollution, 16th Report, Cm. 1966 (1992), p.43.
[88] *Ibid.* at para. 4.48.
[89] Water Resources Act, s.5.
[90] *Ibid.* s.84(2).

The Licensing of Discharges

The giving, revocation and modification of consents

The process governing the licensing of discharges to controlled waters is under the jurisdiction of NRA whose functions are detailed in Schedule 10 to the Water Resources Act, with facilities for appeal defined by section 91 of the same Act.[91] Schedule 10 deals with applications for consents, reference of certain applications to the Secretary of State, the variation and revocation of consents and the alteration and imposition of conditions. In general terms, any discharge which may convey any poisonous, noxious or polluting matter into controlled waters requires a licence.

Applications for consent

NRA is obliged to publish a notice of any application in local newspapers and to send a copy to, *inter alia,* every local authority and water undertaker in whose area the discharge will occur. However, these publicity requirements may not apply if NRA proposes to grant a consent, considering that the discharges in question will have "no appreciable" effect on the receiving waters. In relation to what may be regarded as a controversial decision, it seems unlikely that a judicial review would be easily available here in relation to a matter of judgment and opinion on the part of NRA.

Independently of Schedule 10 is the requirement in section 190 of the Act that pollution control registers maintained by NRA should contain particulars of, *inter alia*, applications, consents and certificates granted by the Secretary of State under Schedule 10, paragraph 1(7). If the Secretary of State, on receiving an application, is satisfied that it would be contrary to the public interest or would prejudice to an unreasonable degree some private interest if information were disclosed about a trade secret, a certificate here may exempt an application, consent, sample or analysis of a sample from the above publicity requirements, as well as the above pollution control register requirements.[92]

Consideration and determination of applications

NRA is obliged to consider any written representations or objections submitted in respect of an application within a period of six weeks of the date of publication. The discretion of NRA is widely defined: it may (assuming that the foregoing publicity requirements have been satisfied) consider whether to give the consent applied for, either unconditionally or subject to conditions, or to refuse it. However, if within four months of the receipt of an application (or any longer period that may be agreed between the parties) no consent has been granted, it is

[91] *Ibid.* s.88(2). As to consents required by NRA, see s.99 and the Control of Pollution (Discharges by the National Rivers Authority) Regulations 1989 (S.I. 1989 No. 1157).

[92] Water Resources Act, Sched. 10, para. 1. *Cf.* detailed requirements in the Control of Pollution (Registers) Regulations 1989 (S.I. 1989 No. 1160).

deemed to have been refused. NRA may impose such conditions as it thinks fit on a grant of consent, including conditions about the place of discharge, characteristics of the discharge, sampling, metering, recording of effluent discharge and information provision to NRA.[93]

Where NRA proposes to grant a consent and objections or representations have been made, it is obliged to notify any such person making those objections or representations and not to give the consent until time has been allowed for replies.[94] If any representations or objections are made to the Secretary of State, he may direct NRA to refer the application to him, and may also facilitate a local inquiry or hearing. Following consideration of an application in these circumstances, the Secretary of State will be required to direct NRA to come to a decision in conformity with his directions to it.[95]

Provision is made for the giving of a consent in the absence of an application if it appears to NRA that a person has caused or permitted effluent or other matter to be discharged in contravention of certain provisions of the Act[96] and that similar contraventions are likely. However, NRA is obliged to publicise the consent in similar terms to those relating to publicity for applications and to consider any objections or representations made.[97]

Revocation of consents and alteration and imposition of conditions

From time to time, NRA is obliged to review consents granted and conditions imposed. Any such consent must specify a period of time during which no action shall be taken for revocation, modification of conditions or the imposition of conditions on an unconditional consent. If a notice is served by NRA for any of these purposes, it will specify a period during which any further notice of modification will not be served for any of these purposes. However, these safeguards will not necessarily apply to any consent granted in the absence of an application.[98] Beyond the foregoing restrictions, NRA may, as a result of any review, revoke a consent, modify conditions or impose conditions on an unconditional consent. NRA is empowered to revoke a consent if it appears that there has been no discharge in the preceding 12 months. The Secretary of State is empowered to direct NRA to revoke a consent, modify conditions or impose conditions on an unconditional consent in three circumstances: to enable compliance with an E.C. or international legal obligation, to react to any representations or objections made to him and (finally) to protect public health or flora and fauna dependent on an aquatic environment. In this latter area, NRA may be liable to pay compensation for any loss or damage sustained as a result of compliance with the direction. However, such compensation entitlement is

[93] Water Resources Act, Sched. 10, para. 2.

[94] *Ibid.* para. 3.

[95] *Ibid.* para. 4. *Cf.* Control of Pollution (Consents for Discharges) (Secretary of State Functions) Regulations 1989 (S.I. 1989 No. 1151).

[96] ss.85(3) and 86, dealt with below.

[97] Water Resources Act, Sched. 10, para. 5.

[98] *Ibid.* para. 7.

dependent on action that infringes the "period of grace" referred to above and incorporated in each consent, as well as being an indication that the direction is not given in consequence of a change of circumstances that could not reasonably have been foreseen initially or by reference to material information which was not reasonably available to NRA initially.[99]

Appeals

The appeal facility in the Act applies to action by NRA otherwise than in relation to requirements imposed by the Secretary of State by means of direction. Among others, the grounds of appeal immediately of interest relate to any refusal of consent, any conditional grant of consent, any revocation of consent, or any modification of conditions or imposition of conditions on what is otherwise an unconditional consent. Where, on an appeal, the Secretary of State considers that a decision of NRA should be modified or reversed, NRA will be obliged to comply with directions accordingly. However, compliance with any such direction is taken not to affect the legality or validity of anything done by reference to the NRA decision subject to modification or reversal.[1]

The acquisition of information

NRA is empowered to serve a notice on any person, requiring that person to furnish information "reasonably required" by NRA for the purpose of carrying out its water pollution functions under the Act. The requirement is enforceable by means of summary criminal proceedings.[2] This useful general power is one that may be seen to complement the existing power enabling NRA to impose conditions which no doubt would facilitate a rather more efficient flow of information, at least in the licensing context.

The categories of consent

Three categories of consent have been recognised[3]: numeric consents, non-numeric consents and descriptive consents. Numeric consents

> "... apply to significant discharges for which the consent specifies numeric limits for the flow and for concentrations of one—or more commonly several—constituents or determinands. These are the consents for which compliance is commonly monitored and assessed by regular or continuous sampling ...".

Non-numeric consents

[99] *Ibid.* para. 6.
[1] *Ibid.* s.91. *Cf.* the Control of Pollution (Consents for Discharges) (Secretary of State Functions) Regulations 1989 (S.I. 1989 No. 1151).
[2] Water Resources Act, s.202.
[3] National Rivers Authority, *Discharge consent and compliance policy* (Water Quality Series No. 1, 1990), p.10.

"... relate to a variety of significant discharges where—with or without numeric limits on flow—the conditions which substantially influence the acceptability of the discharge are not so readily expressed in terms of numeric limits on quality determinands. Such conditions often relate, for example, to the technical requirements which must be met by processes or facilities through which the effluent passes before discharge."

Descriptive consents are a sub-group of non-numeric consents and generally relate to small discharges of little or no environmental significance, from very small sewage works, for example.[4] Toxicity-based consents may be considered in relation to the present regulatory process. Such consents would allow controls over complex chemical discharges whose constituents could not be monitored and individually consented to. However, the strict legal framework for this or indeed any other consent requires close attention to the conditions that may be attached, to ensure that all critical elements of a discharge are caught. It is likely, for example, that any consent for a discharge from a sewage works which omits reference to ammonia would be flawed and, in relation to that substance, unenforceable.

NRA policy will be an important element in decision-making for present purposes. NRA policy on ground water,[5] for example, indicates that by reference to E.C. Directive 80/68 it will refuse to consent the discharge of List I substances (as previously described in this chapter) into ground water and will limit the entry of List II substances.[6]

Charging for consents

In certain specified circumstances, NRA is able to impose a charge in respect of its licensing of discharges to controlled waters. The precise circumstances are set out in the Water Resources Act[7]: normally any charge will be payable by the licence holder or any person making an application.[8] Any charging scheme prepared by NRA requires approval by the Secretary of State.[9]

The Pollution Offences

The range of offences

Section 85 of the Water Resources Act sets out a range of offences relating to the pollution of controlled waters. These offences are supplemented by a variety of offences under section 90, relating to deposits and vegetation in rivers. The

[4] *Ibid.*
[5] National Rivers Authority, *Policy and Practice for the Protection of Groundwater* (1992).
[6] *Ibid.* p.38: Policy F.4.
[7] s.131(1).
[8] Water Resources Act, s.131(2).
[9] *Ibid.* s.132.

section 85 offences are extended by facilities in section 86 for the prohibition of some discharges through a notice served by NRA or by means of regulations proscribing certain substances, concentrations of those substances or particular processes. Section 87 provides clarification in connection with a sewerage undertaker's liability in respect of discharges into and from public sewers. Elsewhere, provision is made in sections 88 and 89 for defences to the various prescribed offences.

The first offence

A person commits an offence if he causes or knowingly permits any poisonous, noxious or polluting matter, or any solid waste matter, to enter any controlled waters.[10] There is a significant difference between matter which is poisonous, noxious or polluting, on the one hand, and solid waste matter, on the other. None of these terms is defined in the legislation. However, discolouration *per se* is unlikely to justify enforcement measures under the present provisions.

"Poisonous", "polluting"

The word "polluting" is a matter of some difficulty under section 85(1) and under a broadly similar provision in section 4(1) of the Salmon and Freshwater Fisheries Act 1975. In two widely contrasting cases—*Schulmans Inc. v. National Rivers Authority*[11] and *National Rivers Authority v. Egger (U.K.)*[12]—the Divisional Court and Crown Court respectively were concerned with the impact on watercourses of fuel oil and construction site run-off. In *Schulmans*, the evidence suggested that the concentration of fuel oil in the watercourse was insufficient to be poisonous to the fish present in the waters for the purposes of the Act of 1975. The Crown Court in *Egger* was concerned only with charges under the Water Resources Act. The company was convicted and fined heavily on the basis of a view of "polluting matter" governed by whether the matter is *capable* of causing harm, to the extent that it *may* damage the *potential* usefulness of the watercourse. The fact that rainwater run-off gathers potentially harmful matter en route to a vulnerable watercourse may therefore be sufficient to ground a conviction under section 85. One clear distinction between the cases relates to the specific measure found in the Act of 1975, as opposed to the rather more general provision in the Water Resources Act. The former Act refers in section 4(1) to actions which ". . . cause the waters to be poisonous or injurious to fish or the spawning grounds". The close proximity of the words "poisonous" and "polluting" in section 85(1) indicates the justification for the wider meaning of the latter word. The test of "potential" referred to in *Egger* is clearly important in the development of strict liability. While E.C. standards in relevant directives may be particularly useful as a marker in the presentation of evidence, it is difficult to anticipate what may be encompassed in any reference to a river or watercourse's "potential usefulness".

[10] *Ibid.* s.85(1).

[11] [1992] Env. L.R. D1, D2.

[12] (1992) 209 ENDS Rep. 39.

"Solid waste matter"

A further term worthy of mention is "solid waste matter", a term sufficient to cover a situation in which the aquatic environment is adversely affected by almost any "garbage" or other litter: again, the term is not defined by the legislation.

"Causes"

The leading statement of principle on the offence of "causing" is to be found in the House of Lords speeches in *Alphacell Ltd v. Woodward.*[13] A defendant who "causes" pollution must be involved in an "active operation" (Lord Wilberforce), or in "positive activities" (Lord Pearson), or a "positive act" (Lord Cross), or an "active operation of plant" (Lord Salmon), or his "acts" must be referable to an "operation of the works" (Viscount Dilhorne). Accordingly, the law does not import any mental element into what is an offence of strict liability,[14] in contrast to the offence of knowingly permitting pollution, which is dealt with below. The word "cause" must receive its ordinary English meaning for present purposes, which means that not only should the defendant's intentional conduct be excluded from consideration but also any negligent conduct. In *Alphacell*, a breakdown in the defendant's systems in a factory led to the discharge of polluted water to a river. The absence of any negligence associated with the failure of pumps to a storage tank when those pumps became clogged with vegetation was immaterial to the court's confirmation of the defendant's conviction.

In *Southern Water Authority v. Pegrum*,[15] the defendant farmer was convicted when heavy rain caused a slurry lagoon to overflow, as a result of which a nearby stream was polluted. It was suggested here that an act of God, represented by a very heavy rainfall, was sufficient to break the chain of causation, an argument rejected by the court. The House of Lords in *Alphacell* had suggested that both an act of God and the intervening act of a trespasser would be sufficient to break the chain of causation. This latter defence was successful in *Impress (Worcester) Ltd v. Rees*,[16] where an unknown trespasser was found to have entered industrial premises and to have opened a valve, as a result of which a nearby stream was polluted by the contents of the tank. There is some evidence for suggesting that even the act of a third party lawfully on the defendant's premises may break the chain of causation, enabling that defendant to avoid conviction for "causing". In *Welsh Water Authority v. Williams Motors (Cwmru) Ltd*,[17] the court found no "positive act" in a chain of operations by the defendant garage owner that had caused the pollution when diesel fuel overflowed. Of particular significance were findings by the court that the company delivering the fuel allowed the storage

[13] [1972] 2 All E.R. 475.

[14] *F.J.H. Wrothwell Ltd v. Yorkshire Water Authority* [1984] Crim. L.R. 43.

[15] [1989] Crim. L.R. 442. *Cf. R. v. British Coal Corporation* (1993) 227 ENDS Rep. 44, relating to a break in the chain of causation following an overwhelming natural force of gravity.

[16] [1971] 2 All E.R. 357.

[17] *The Times*, December 5, 1988.

tank to overflow in circumstances where, contractually, the garage owner had no control over the delivery company.

It appears that a defendant's positive, active operation of a site requires a distinction to be drawn in which the offence of "causing" may not arise if there is a mere passive spectating. In circumstances not dissimilar to those in *Williams Motors*, the Court of Appeal in *Wychavon District Council v. National Rivers Authority*[18] held that a local authority exercising agency powers was not guilty of "causing" pollution, despite failure promptly to discover the source of the unlawful discharge and failure to clear the blockage that led to the discharge. This approach to strict liability was followed in *National Rivers Authority v. Welsh Development Agency*,[19] where the defendant was held not to be guilty of "causing" pollution, both for the purposes of the present offence and that comprised in section 4(1) of the Salmon and Freshwater Fisheries Act 1975. The river pollution in question was allegedly caused by one of the defendant's tenants. The court observed that it was the defendant that had designed, constructed and maintained the sewers through which the polluting effluent had reached the river. Nevertheless, in the court's view, these circumstances did not amount to a positive or deliberate act sufficient to attract criminal responsibility.

The more recent cases suggest a need for evidence of some active involvement in the operation of the site. However, this approach may suggest that immunity from strict liability arises if a site's operation continues without any active intervention that could be characterised as a "positive, deliberate act". Nevertheless, it has been suggested in some cases—the *Wychavon* case, for example—that prosecution for the offence of "knowingly permitting" may be rather more successful in these circumstances, despite suggestions in *Alphacell* that the onus of proof in cases where "causing" is charged should be reversed and placed on the defendant, in view of the evidential constraints of such cases.

"Knowingly permits"

A conviction for "knowingly permitting" pollution depends on proof of the defendant's failure to prevent the pollution known to him. Consequently, that failure of prevention must be accompanied by knowledge: the offence is designed to deal with the type of case in which a person knows that contaminated effluent is escaping over his land into controlled waters and does nothing at all to prevent it. It has been suggested[20] that inclusion of the word "knowingly" before "permits" is otiose. It may be argued that the need to establish knowledge as an important prerequisite to a conviction makes a prosecution for "causing" (accompanied by a possible reversal of the onus of proof) the more attractive option. Be that as it may, it has been seen already—in the *Wychavon* case, above—that a charge of "knowingly permitting" may be more successful on the particular facts. Those "particular" facts also appear to have arisen before the

[18] [1993] Env. L.R. 330. *Cf. National Rivers Authority v. Yorkshire Water Services Ltd*, *The Times*, November 24, 1993.

[19] [1993] Env. L.R. 407.

[20] *Per* Lord Salmon in *Alphacell*, n.13, *supra*.

court in *Price v. Cromack*.[21] In *Price*, effluent was introduced to land by the agreement of the owner, only for the effluent to escape into an adjoining river. Despite the positive act of the owner in entering the agreement and making his land available for receipt of the effluent, the court chose not to convict for "causing" but indicated that the facts were probably more amenable to a charge of "knowingly permitting".

The second offence

A person commits an offence if he causes or knowingly permits any matter, other than trade effluent or sewage effluent, to enter controlled waters following discharge from a drain or sewer in contravention of a statutory prohibition imposed under section 86.[22]

"A statutory prohibition"

This offence only arises where a statutory prohibition has been imposed so that there is no "automatic" offence where, for example, construction site run-off, or even rainwater run-off, occurs into controlled waters. The same approach, in which the offence depends on the prerequisite of a statutory prohibition, applies also to the fourth offence, described below.

The statutory prohibition is a flexible instrument available to NRA in a variety of circumstances which inform the operation of the two section 85 offences described above. The notice which NRA may use for the imposition of a statutory prohibition covers:

(a) the making or continuation of a discharge;
(b) the making or continuation of a discharge requiring observation of specified conditions;
(c) the discharge of prescribed substances or concentrations of those substances;
(d) any discharge deriving from a prescribed process or a prescribed process involving prescribed substances; or
(e) the use of substances in quantities beyond prescribed amounts.

Normally, the notice will have effect no earlier than a period of three months from the date when the notice is given by NRA. However, there are a number of qualifications to this general time limit. The minimum three-month period of notice does not apply where the subject discharge relates to prescribed substances, concentrations and processes, referred to above. In the same way, the minimum notice requirement does not apply where NRA is satisfied that there is an

[21] [1975] 2 All E.R. 113.
[22] Water Resources Act, s.85(2).

emergency requiring the prohibition to come into force at an earlier date. Notices here are not available in respect of discharges from a vessel. Where a notice has been served in respect of a discharge which has been made or which is continuing or which requires observation of specified conditions, and an application is made to NRA for a discharge consent, the notice is deemed not to expire until the result of the application becomes final.[23]

"Drain or sewer"

The terms have the meanings ascribed by the Water Industry Act 1991. Accordingly, a "drain" refers to a drain used for the drainage of one building or of any buildings or yards appurtenant to buildings within the same curtilage.

A sewer, on the other hand, is defined to include all sewers (and all drains not included in the above definition) which are used for the drainage of buildings and yards appurtenant to buildings.[24]

The third offence

A person commits an offence is he causes or knowingly permits any trade or sewage effluent to be discharged into controlled waters or from land in England and Wales, through a pipe, into the sea outside the seaward limits of controlled waters.[25]

"Trade or sewage effluent"

"Trade effluent" includes any effluent which is discharged from premises used for carrying on any trade or industry, excluding surface water and domestic sewage. "Sewage effluent", on the other hand, includes any effluent from the sewage disposal or sewerage works of a sewerage undertaker, excluding surface water. "Effluent" is defined to cover any liquid, including particles of matter and other substances in suspension in the liquid.[26]

The fourth offence

A person commits an offence if he causes or knowingly permits any trade or sewage effluent to be discharged, in contravention of a statutory prohibition, from a building or from any fixed plant onto or into any land, or into any waters of a lake or pond which are not inland fresh waters.[27]

[23] *Ibid.* s.86.
[24] Water Industry Act 1991, s.219(1).
[25] Water Resources Act, s.85(3).
[26] Water Resources Act, s.221(1). Contrast the definition of "trade effluent" in s.141(1) of the Water Industry Act 1991, relating to trade effluent licensing in connection with discharges to the public sewer.
[27] Water Resources Act, s.85(4).

Enforcement priorities for ground waters

NRA is concerned with, *inter alia*, ground water protection, and its policies take significant account of the facilities provided by sections 85 and 86 of the Water Resources Act. In the context of discharges to underground strata, it has been recognised that considerable value attaches to the licensing requirements and the system of statutory prohibitions described above. Their value is recognised in three areas. First, consent will always be required for the discharge of sewage and trade effluents directly to ground water. Secondly, sewage and trade effluents discharged to soakaway from fixed plant or a building may be controlled either by means of a statutory prohibition or by the issue of a consent, depending on the pollution potential of the effluent. Thirdly, surface run-off discharged directly to ground water, or via pipe to soakaway, may be controlled by means of a statutory prohibition. The facilities available in sections 85 and 86 may be of value also in relation to diffuse pollution prejudicial to ground waters.[28]

The fifth offence

A person commits an offence if he causes or knowingly permits any matter whatever to enter any inland fresh waters so as to tend (either directly or in combination with other matter which he or another person causes or permits to enter those waters) to impede the proper flow of the waters in a manner that leads or is likely to lead to a substantial aggravation of pollution due to other causes, or the consequences of such pollution.[29]

Penalties for the five offences

A person convicted for contravention of the requirements set out in section 85 or the conditions of any consent granted for discharge is liable to summary conviction or conviction on indictment.[30] In the case of any summary offence, the usual time limitation of six months for the commencement of summary proceedings is replaced with a longer period of 12 months.[31]

The sixth and seventh offences

A person commits an offence if, without the consent of NRA, he removes from any part of the bottom, channel or bed of any inland fresh waters a deposit accumulated by a dam, weir or sluice holding back those waters and does so by causing the deposit to be carried away in suspension in those waters without necessarily causing pollution. However, this prohibition and its criminal enforcement (described below) do not apply to the exercise of the various

[28] National Rivers Authority, *Policy and Practice for the Protection of Groundwater* (1992), pp.37, 38 and 45.
[29] Water Resources Act, s.85(5).
[30] *Ibid.* subs.(6), which sets out the penalties applicable.
[31] *Ibid.* s.101.

statutory powers relating to land drainage, flood prevention and navigation to be found principally in the Land Drainage and Water Resources Acts. A person commits the seventh offence if, again without NRA consent, he causes or permits a substantial amount of vegetation to be cut or uprooted in any inland fresh waters (or so near to any such waters as to fall into them) and fails to take all reasonable steps to remove that vegetation from the waters in question. A person guilty of either of these offences is liable to summary conviction.[32] Consents from NRA are granted subject to conditions.[33] An appeal is governed by Schedule 10 and may be available against a refusal or conditional grant of a consent.[34]

Defences to the first five offences

Where the entry of any matter into any waters or any discharge is in accordance with or is the result of any act or omission referable to some legal authority, a defence to proceedings in respect of the first five offences is available. The generic reference to "legal authority" is a reference to:

(a) a discharge licence under the predecessor provisions of Part II of the Control of Pollution Act;
(b) an authorisation granted in relation to integrated pollution control by Her Majesty's Inspectorate of Pollution under Part I of the Environmental Protection Act;
(c) a waste management or disposal licence granted, respectively, under Part II of the Environmental Protection Act or Part I of the Control of Pollution Act;
(d) a licence granted for dumping at sea under Part II of the Food and Environment Protection Act;
(e) discharges for works purposes under section 163 of the Water Resources Act or section 165 of the Water Industry Act;
(f) any local statutory provision or statutory order conferring power for the discharge of effluent to water; and
(g) any prescribed enactment.[35]

A range of additional defences is provided for, again in relation to the first five offences.[36] The first of these defences applies where any entry or discharge is caused or permitted in an emergency, to avoid danger to life or health, but only where reasonably practicable steps were taken to minimise the entry or discharge and to minimise the polluting effects, and where NRA is advised as soon as is reasonably practicable after the entry occurs. It appears that reliance on this defence will usually direct attention to the question whether an occurrence is beyond the defendant's control, in parallel with the defence of "reasonable

[32] *Ibid.* s.90. The prescribed penalty on summary conviction is to be found in subs.(3).
[33] *Ibid.* subs.(5).
[34] *Ibid.* s.91(1)(f).
[35] *Ibid.* s.88.
[36] *Ibid.* s.89.

excuse" found in many other statutory contexts.[37] In *NRA v. ICI Chemicals and Polymers*,[38] the court was dealing with a situation involving a factory explosion, as a result of which various chemicals were discharged. The court was not prepared to extend the operation of the section 89 defence to this situation, bearing in mind the wording of the provision itself. Apart from the reference to a need to avoid danger to life or health, it is clear that the defendant should also take reasonably practicable steps to minimise the extent of the entry or discharge and its polluting effects, and to advise NRA.

The four other defences found in section 89 cover a variety of situations. The first of these defences is available if a person is shown to have caused or permitted any discharge of trade or sewage effluent from a vessel. The second defence is available for a defendant who is able to show that a discharge has occurred by reason only of his permitting water from an abandoned mine to enter controlled waters. The third defence will not operate where there is evidence of an entry of any poisonous, noxious or polluting matter into any controlled waters. In these circumstances, a defendant will have a defence in respect of certain deposits of solid mine or quarry waste so that they fall into or are carried into inland fresh waters. One crucial element of this defence, however, is a requirement for NRA consent in respect of the deposit. Finally, a fourth defence relates to any highway authority or other person empowered to keep a drain open.[39] That defence is available where the defendant has caused or permitted a discharge from any such drain, unless that discharge is in contravention of a statutory prohibition.[40]

Discharges by sewerage undertakers

The application of the third and fourth offence under section 85 is subject to some adjustment under the Water Resources Act. An undertaker here is deemed to have "caused" the discharge for the purpose of these offences if any sewage effluent is discharged from the undertaker's works (even if he did not cause or knowingly permit that discharge) but was bound to receive at the works matter included in the discharge.[41] The reality of this provision is starkly illustrated in *NRA v. North West Water*,[42] where there was a discharge to sewer of certain toxic "red list" substances. However, the treatment of those substances by the sewerage undertaker provided no exemptions in respect of the undertaker's legal obligation to comply with a discharge consent granted by NRA in respect of nearby controlled waters.

An undertaker is not, however, guilty of an offence under section 85 by reason only of the fact that a discharge from a sewer or works contravenes conditions in a consent relating to the discharge. On the other hand:

[37] *NRA v. North West Water* (1992) 208 ENDS Rep. 40.
[38] (1992) 204 ENDS Rep. 37.
[39] By virtue of s.100 of the Highways Act 1980.
[40] See n.22, *supra*.
[41] Water Resources Act, s.87(1).
[42] (1992) 205 ENDS Rep. 39.

(a) the contravention must be attributable to a discharge which another person caused or permitted to be made into the sewer or works;
(b) the undertaker must not have been bound to receive the discharge or conditions for receipt were broken; and
(c) the undertaker could not reasonably have been expected to prevent the discharge into the sewer or works.[43]

In *NRA v. Yorkshire Water*,[44] it was argued by the company that it had not "caused or knowingly permitted" any discharge: the discharge, it was alleged, was triggered by an illegal discharge to sewer of a solvent that eventually led to a failure of the filters in the treatment works. The Crown Court rejected arguments by NRA based on the strict liability argument that the company was liable for "causing" the subject pollution, confirming the direct relevance of the facts to the provisions of section 87(2). Once again, the court's view of an "active operation" appears to require something more than a mere passive spectating.

More generally, a person is not guilty of any section 85 offence in relation to a discharge which he caused or permitted to be made into a sewer or works vested in a sewerage undertaker if that undertaker was bound to receive the discharge there unconditionally or subject to conditions that were observed.[45]

The Prevention and Control of Pollution

A number of provisions in Part III of the Act[46] are generally consistent with the precautionary principle of environmental and pollution control. The Secretary of State is empowered to impose measures enabling precautions to be taken against pollution through the medium of regulations and to designate areas known as water protection zones. The Minister of Agriculture, on the other hand, is empowered to designate nitrate-sensitive areas.

Regulations for pollution prevention

Regulations authorised by the Act[47] may seek to prohibit a person from having custody or control of any poisonous, noxious or polluting matter unless prescribed works, precautions "and other steps" are executed in order to prevent or control entry of such matter into controlled waters. The regulations may also seek to require a person already having custody or control or using poisonous, noxious or polluting matter to take necessary precautions or execute appropriate works for present purposes. Powers may be conferred on NRA to determine the circumstances in which a person may be required to carry out works, or to take precautions "or other steps". These powers provide the background to NRA

[43] Water Resources Act, s.87(2).
[44] (1992) 209 ENDS Rep. 39.
[45] Water Resources Act, s.87(3).
[46] *Ibid.* ss.92–97.
[47] *Ibid.* s.92.

enforcement because it may also have power under such regulations to serve a notice imposing prescribed requirements and specifying and describing the works, precautions or other steps to be taken. An appeal facility in respect of such notices may provide an appeal to the Secretary of State. Finally, it may be provided that contravention of the regulations is an offence whose punishment should not exceed the maxima found in section 85(6).[48] In exercising any of the powers that may be provided by such regulations, NRA may take account of any contravention or likely contravention of a code of good agricultural practice,[49] dealt with below.

The Regulations

The Control of Pollution (Silage, Slurry and Agricultural Fuel Oil) Regulations 1991[50] have been made under the above statutory powers. The prescribed conduct falls into the following categories:

(a) the making of silage;
(b) the storage of slurry; and
(c) the storage of fuel oil on farms.

These activities are subject to various restrictions, for example, silage must be made in a silo complying with standards in the regulations, slurry must be kept under custody or control in a storage system complying again with standards in the regulations and fuel oil must also be stored by reference to similarly prescribed measures. Contravention of these requirements is a criminal offence: there is also an appeal facility to the Secretary of State if NRA seeks to enforce certain areas of the regulations by notice.[51]

The requirements of the regulations and, in particular, the standards for the construction of storage facilities on farms represent important precautionary measures for the protection of ground waters. In particularly vulnerable locations, NRA will seek to discourage farm waste storage unless adequate measures can be agreed to minimise pollution.

Water protection zones

Water protection zones are provided for by the Water Resources Act[52] and allow controls, particularly in relation to almost any risk of pollution from point or diffuse sources. At the time of writing, only one application for the designation of

[48] See n.30, *supra.*
[49] Water Resources Act, s.97.
[50] S.I. 1991 No. 324.
[51] See NRA, *Policy and Practice for the Protection of Groundwater* (1992), p.47.
[52] s.93. *Cf.* s.96, dealing with licensing and appeal requirements where an order here requires NRA consent for particular purposes.

such a zone has been made to the Secretary of State. Where any such order is made, the area affected will be subject to defined restrictions or prohibitions on identified activities, probably of an industrial nature. The essential purpose, again, is the protection of controlled waters and the prevention or control of entry to such waters of poisonous, noxious or polluting matter, except nitrates used in connection with land for agricultural purposes.

An order under the present provisions must be made only following an application by NRA to the Secretary of State and in conformity with other provisions of the Act.[53] NRA is required to submit a draft order, to publicise a notice concerning the application in local newspapers and to serve a copy of the notice on every local authority and water undertaker in the subject locality. The notice will invite any objections to be made to the Secretary of State who may, in turn, convene a local inquiry into the matter. The Secretary of State is able to modify the draft order submitted by NRA, but he may require additional notices from NRA if he considers that any proposed modification is "likely adversely to affect any persons". Any order finally made may contain a variety of provisions, including circumstances in which prohibitions or restrictions will affect activities (including the nature of those activities), prohibitions or restrictions on activities which do not have NRA consent with or without conditions, and prescription of offences for failure to comply with prohibitions or restrictions.

Nitrate-sensitive areas

The protection of controlled waters and ground waters in particular is the essential purpose of nitrate-sensitive areas declared under and regulated by sections 94 and 95 of the Water Resources Act:

> "Nitrate is a significant diffuse source pollutant. In areas of low effective rainfall upon vulnerable aquifers it is difficult, if not impossible, to have intensive arable and livestock husbandry and avoid leaching from the soil to groundwater resulting in concentrations in excess of the drinking water limit for nitrate."[54]

The essential purpose, therefore, of a nitrate-sensitive area is to control the entry of nitrate to controlled waters in relation to activities referable to a use of land for agricultural purposes. A number of such areas have now been designated by the Minister of Agriculture. Either of the Ministers may give directions with respect to orders for designation, requiring action by NRA, for example. Such designations by statutory order enable that order to impose "requirements, prohibitions or restrictions". In addition, section 95 of the Act empowers the Minister for the purposes just listed to enter an agreement relating to the management of subject land.

[53] Sched. 11.
[54] See NRA, *Policy and Practice for the Protection of Groundwater* (1992), p.44.

The designation process

Initiative for the making of an order comes from NRA. The process is governed overall by Schedule 12 to the Act, which requires that no application should be made unless it appears to NRA that pollution is or is likely to be caused by nitrate entry to controlled waters through agricultural activity on land and that existing measures to deal with the situation are inadequate.

The content of an order

An order designating a nitrate-sensitive area may not only contain requirements, prohibitions or restrictions in relation to prescribed activities on agricultural land; it may provide for payment of amounts of money by the Minister in return for the performance of relevant obligations targeted at the reduction or limitation of nitrate generation. This financial provision marks out a significant difference between nitrate-sensitive areas and water protection zones. Furthermore, the use of the word "requirement" indicates that positive works may, for example, be required (say) for the engineering of facilities to secure substances prescribed for present purposes.[55]

Significantly, there is statutory authority for an order here to include provision for consent to be given in respect of otherwise proscribed activities. Indeed, contravention of any requirement, prohibition or restriction, as well as a condition attached to any consent, may be designated as an offence.[56] Various other matters may be provided for in an order, including definition of the circumstances in which the carrying on of any activity is required, prohibited or restricted, as well as circumstances in which there may be an obligation to repay amounts already paid under an order.[57] Regulations may further provide for various other matters, particularly in relation to the licensing of and consents for various activities, where such consents are obtainable from the Minister of Agriculture.[58] References to the Minister here are substituted by references to the Secretary of State for Wales where land is situated in Wales.[59]

Where the order contains so-called "mandatory" provisions requiring, prohibiting or restricting certain activities, specific procedures are called for.[60] These procedures require, *inter alia*, that the proposed order is publicised in a local newspaper or newspapers and that a notice of the proposed order is served on NRA as well as on every local authority and water undertaker whose area includes the whole or part of the relevant locality. Any objection to the proposed order may be addressed to the Minister or the Secretary of State for Wales, or both (as the case may be), who may convene a local inquiry prior to arrival at a decision on the order.

[55] Water Resources Act, s.94(3). *Cf.* n.53, *supra.*
[56] *Ibid.* subs.(4)(d). As to the maximum penalty, see s.85(6).
[57] *Ibid.* subs.(4).
[58] *Ibid.* s.96.
[59] *Ibid.* s.94(7).
[60] *Ibid.* Sched. 12, Pt. II.

Nitrate-sensitive area agreements

Beyond the "mandatory" orders referred to above, which may or may not include compensation provision, among other things, the Water Resources Act contains a facility permitting the Minister[61] to enter an agreement with the freehold owner of land or (with his consent) another person with some other interest in that land. Any such agreement may provide for the payment of compensation in return for the performance of defined obligations, referable to the protection of controlled waters from nitrates in a nitrate-sensitive area. If the agreement is so expressed, it will bind successors in title.[62]

Codes of good agricultural practice

Reference was made previously[63] to the status of codes of good agricultural practice for the purpose of regulations that may be made under section 92 of the Act. The Ministers[64] may by order approve a code of practice:

> "... for the purpose of—
> (a) giving practical guidance to persons engaged in agriculture with respect to activities that may affect controlled waters; and
> (b) promoting what appear to them to be desirable practices by such persons for avoiding or minimising the pollution of any such waters ..."[65]

However, contravention of a code does not of itself give rise to any criminal or civil liability, although NRA may take account of any actual or likely contravention in relation to an exercise of powers flowing from regulations made under section 92 (as seen above) and for the purpose of considering imposition of a statutory prohibition under section 86.[66] Any order for present purposes may not be made here without prior consultation with NRA.[67]

The information base for pollution prevention and control

Law enforcement is supported by various provisions to be found in Part VIII of the Act. To begin with, NRA is subject to a duty to furnish the Secretary of State or the Minister with such information as may reasonably be required in connection with, *inter alia*, the execution or proposed execution of its functions.[68]

[61] As defined by s.95(4).
[62] *Ibid*. s.95.
[63] See n.49, *supra*.
[64] The Minister of Agriculture and the Secretary of State for Wales acting singly or together: s.221(1).
[65] Water Resources Act, s.97(1).
[66] see n.23, *supra*.
[67] Water Resources Act, s.97(3).
[68] *Ibid*. s.196.

To reinforce this relationship, NRA may be subject to specific and general directions from the Secretary of State in respect of pollution control functions under Part III of the Act. The Act imposes a further duty on NRA where either of the Ministers (the Minister of Agriculture or the Secretary of State for Wales) requires advice and assistance for the purpose of undertaking their water pollution functions under the Act.[69] Complementary provisions impose a further duty on NRA to provide a water undertaker with information (which could relate to pollution occurrences, for example) which is reasonably requested. A reciprocal duty also applies to any water undertaker.[70]

Sampling

Sampling is a process that is precisely defined by the Act for the purpose of evidential requirements in particular. The Act[71] stipulates that the result of the analysis of any sample[72] taken on behalf of NRA under an exercise of powers is not admissible in any legal proceedings in respect of any effluent passing from any land or vessel unless three requirements are observed. Those requirements stipulate, first, that on taking the sample the occupier of the land (or the owner or master of the vessel) must be advised of an intention to have it analysed.[72a] Secondly, the sample must there and then be divided into three parts appropriately sealed and marked.[72b] Finally, one sample must be "delivered" to the occupier (or the owner or master of the vessel), one sample retained and the third sample submitted for analysis, for future comparison. If it is not reasonably practicable to comply with these requirements, the requirements are treated as having been complied with if compliance follows as soon as reasonably practicable after the sample is taken.

The present section is very precise in indicating that admissibility depends on compliance with the foregoing "tripartite" requirements in relation to "... the result of the analysis of any sample taken on behalf of the Authority in the exercise of any power conferred by ..." the Water Resources Act.[72c] Clearly, these requirements need not apply where NRA is sampling for the purpose of its own monitoring, although difficulties arise on any occasion when, in the course of that monitoring, it is found that unlawful pollution of controlled waters may have occurred. If proceedings before the court are to be instituted, it cannot be argued that the "tripartite" requirements apply only to a sample of effluent: the term "any sample" is unambiguously wide.[73] If a sample is not taken on behalf of NRA, then

[69] *Ibid.* s.202.

[70] *Ibid.* s.203.

[71] *Ibid.* s.209.

[72] Previously the Water Resources Act 1963 had referred to "effluent".

[72a] There is no requirement for advance notice of a sample: *Attorney General's Reference (No. 2 of 1994), The Times*, August 4, 1994, C.A.

[72b] *Ibid.* The reference to "there and then" suggests some immediacy in relation to the transaction.

[72c] As to the admissibility of readings from mobile water monitors, see *R. v. CPC (UK) Ltd, The Times*, August 4, 1994.

[73] *National Rivers Authority v. Harcros Timber and Building Supplies Ltd* [1993] 1 Env. L.R. 172, *per* Lloyd L.J. at 174.

of course the "tripartite" requirements will not apply, although the impact of evidence presented without this framework may be more limited. This must also be the case even if a sample without the "tripartite" requirements is to be found in the pollution register.

The pollution register provided for under section 190 of the Act and regulated in detail by the Control of Pollution (Registers) Regulations 1989[74] is required to indicate whether a sample has been taken by NRA and whether, in turn, the requirements above, in section 209(1) or (2), have been complied with. If a sample taken by any other person is included in the register, various other items of information (if they can be ascertained) must also be included: the date, time and place of the sample, as well as an analysis of the sample in particular.[75] Accordingly, it is possible for a distinction to be made between "mere" monitoring samples, those subject to the requirements of section 209 and those samples which are not taken on behalf of NRA. The quest for information under the Regulations in connection with these latter samples emphasises the possible frailty of such evidence, which may, for example, be vulnerable to the accusation of unlawful collection through trespass.

Section 209 refers only to "the analysis of any sample". The term "sample" itself is taken to refer to a ". . . test of any description" arising from a process where there is some physical isolation of that sample.[76] The width of this term may have the effect of bringing a wide variety of tests into the framework of "tripartite" sampling. However, some tests are simply incapable of being subjected to "sampling" in this way. In *Trent River Board v. Sir Thomas and Arthur Wardle*,[77] a bailiff took a sample of water from the defendant's pipe but did not comply with the tripartite sampling requirements. It was argued before the court that evidence should be allowed from a biologist on the effect on fish of exposure to the water in the sample. It was held by the Divisional Court that the justices were wrong to exclude the evidence. If an analysis had been made then, of course, the prosecuting authority would have had to comply with the tripartite requirements. However, it was open to the authority to prove its case in any way it chose and its method was not open to objection.

The pollution control register

This register is maintained by NRA by virtue of a duty defined by section 190 of the Act and by reference to detailed regulations, the Control of Pollution (Registers) Regulations 1989, referred to above.[78] The Act demands that a variety of information is comprised in the register, which must be maintained to enable inspection by the public at all reasonable times, free of charge. Copies of the register attract a charge.

The register is required to contain:

[74] S.I. 1989 No. 1160.
[75] *Ibid.* reg.7.
[76] Water Resources Act, s.221(1). *Cf.* nn.72b and c, *supra.*
[77] [1957] Crim. L.R. 196.
[78] See n.74, *supra.*

(a) particulars of notices of water quality objectives or other notices served under section 83 of the Water Resources Act[79];
(b) applications for discharge consents;
(c) consents granted and details of any conditions attached;
(d) certificates of confidentiality of information in respect of applications for discharge consents[80]; and
(e) sampling information and authorisations granted in the context of integrated pollution control under section 20 of the Environmental Protection Act.

Maritime Pollution

The range of regulation and control

Reference has been made to the status of United Kingdom territorial waters for the purposes of Part III of the Water Resources Act.[81] Additional statutory controls apply within and sometimes outside those territorial waters, often for the purpose of implementing various international conventions, such as the International Convention for the Prevention of Pollution from Ships.[82]

Requirements for the prevention of oil pollution

Ships registered in the United Kingdom wherever they are operating, and ships of other nationalities, when sailing in United Kingdom territorial waters, are prohibited from discharging oil and oily mixtures into any part of the sea.[83] Also prohibited is a discharge comprising chemicals and other substances which are likely to cause harm to the marine environment. Within United Kingdom territorial waters, foreign and United Kingdom tankers are prohibited from discharging oil, subject to various exceptions.[84] Elsewhere in this context, there are detailed requirements governing discharge monitoring and control, together with prescriptions for oil tank cleaning. Enforcement is by reference to a prescribed criminal offence, the financial penalty for which may contribute to the cost of clean-up for an unlawful spill or discharge.[85] The maintenance of standards, particularly in relation to the security of oil cargoes, is also enforceable through a system of improvement and prohibition notices referable to enforcement of standards and other requirements under various items of relevant legislation including the Prevention of Oil Pollution Act 1971.[86] Under this

[79] See n.81, *supra*.
[80] Water Resources Act, Sched. 10, para. 1(7): see n.92, *supra*.
[81] See nn.56–60, *supra*.
[82] Referred to as MARPOL.
[83] Merchant Shipping (Prevention of Oil Pollution) Order 1983 (S.I. 1983 No. 1106), as amended by, *inter alia*, S.I. 1992 No. 98.
[84] *Ibid.*
[85] *Ibid.*
[86] Merchant Shipping Act 1984.

Act,[87] there is an important reporting requirement binding on the owner or master of a vessel (in respect of oil or oily mixtures discharged or escaped from a vessel into a harbour in the United Kingdom) or the occupier of land (in respect of oil or oily mixtures that have escaped from the subject land). A report for these purposes must be made to the relevant harbour authority, which will probably provide, in prescribed cases, facilities for the reception and treatment of oil and oily mixtures.

Within the seaward limits of United Kingdom territorial waters and inland waters navigable by seagoing vessels, it is an offence for an occupier of land to discharge from that land any oil or oily mixture, an offence subject to limited defences.[88] The same Act[89] proscribes the discharge of oil or oily mixtures from any vessel into inland waters and other waters on the landward side of the limit of territorial waters which are navigable by seagoing vessels. A defence is available here if it can be established that there was no lack of reasonable care and that the discharge was remedied as soon as was practical following discovery of the spill.

The above defence also applies in respect of any proceedings for a further offence which is committed where certain oils are discharged into any part of the sea from pipelines or (otherwise than from a ship) as a result of operations for the exploration of the seabed and sub-soil or the exploration of their natural resources in an area designated under section 1 of the Continental Shelf Act 1964.[90]

Preventative measures in relation to oil and other pollution

A local sea fisheries committee is empowered to make byelaws for prohibiting or regulating the deposit or discharge of any solid or liquid substance detrimental to sea fish or sea-fishing.[91] Local Act powers may also be available. The Zetland County Council Act 1974 was in issue before the Court of Session in Scotland, in *Micosta S.A. v. Shetland Islands Council.*[92] Section 39 of the Act empowers the harbour authority to take all such action considered necessary and desirable for, *inter alia*, the provision, maintenance, operation and improvement of port and harbour facilities in the area. In this context, the court held that the harbour master as Sullom Voe oil terminal was empowered to give a direction to the master of a Greek tanker preventing the vessel from berthing when evidence came to light that the tanker had been causing pollution in the vicinity of the terminal.

In broader terms, the Merchant Shipping (Prevention of Oil Pollution) Regulations 1983[92a] empower the Secretary of State to prohibit the berthing of a vessel in a United Kingdom port or offshore terminal if satisfied that, by reference to non-compliance with prescribed requirements, there is an unreasonable threat

[87] s.11.
[88] Prevention of Oil Pollution Act 1971, s.2(1)(c)–(e).
[89] s.2(2A).
[90] Prevention of Oil Pollution Act 1971, s.3.
[91] Sea Fisheries Regulation Act 1966, s.5.
[92] (1984) 2 Ll. L.R. 525.
[92a] S.I. 1983 No. 1106.

to the marine environment. In some circumstances, detention of a vessel is possible if it is suspected that that vessel is operating in breach of prescribed requirements and standards.[93]

The Secretary of State under the Prevention of Oil Pollution Act 1971[94] is empowered to give directions as respects a ship or its cargo to the owner, master, salvor or any other person in possession of the vessel where:

(a) an accident has occurred to or in a ship;
(b) in the opinion of the Secretary of State, oil from the ship will or may cause pollution on a large scale in the United Kingdom or in the waters in or adjacent to the United Kingdom up to the seaward limits of territorial waters; and
(c) in the opinion of the Secretary of State, the use of the powers conferred is urgently needed.

Failure to comply with a direction here is an offence. If the Secretary of State considers that these powers are inadequate, he may, for the purpose of preventing or reducing oil pollution, or the risk of oil pollution, take (as respects a vessel or its cargo) any action of any kind whatsoever. That action could include the sinking or destruction of the vessel. However, this further power is subject to another provision in the Act,[95] which states that any person who suffers expense or damage as a result of, or by himself taking, action required by the Secretary of State's direction under section 12 shall be entitled to recover compensation from the Secretary of State. Such compensation is recoverable where the action was not reasonably necessary to prevent or reduce oil pollution or the risk of oil pollution, or the effect of the action was out of proportion to the expense involved. Disputed claims are dealt with by the High Court.

Civil liability for oil pollution damage

The Merchant Shipping (Oil Pollution) Act 1971 deals with the matter of civil liability for oil spills and implements (along with the more recent Merchant Shipping (Salvage and Pollution) Act 1994) the 1969 Convention on Civil Liability for Oil Pollution Damage. More particularly, the Convention and the Acts deal with civil liability for "clean-up", the measure of damages applicable and questions of jurisdiction.

Where, as a result of any occurrence taking place while a ship is carrying bunker or other oil, or a cargo of persistent oil in bulk, such oil is discharged or escapes, the owner is liable for any contamination damage in the United Kingdom, the cost of measures reasonably taken to prevent or reduce damage after escape, and any damage caused in the United Kingdom by measures taken

[93] Reg.33.
[94] s.12.
[95] s.13.

after discharge or escape.[96] No liability is incurred where it is proved that discharge or escape resulted from an act of war, hostilities, civil war, insurrection or an exceptional, inevitable and irresistible natural phenomenon, or was due wholly to the negligence or wrongful act of a government or other authority in exercising its functions of maintaining lights or other navigational aids for the maintenance of which it is responsible.[97] Whereas the first section of the Act imposes strict liability, the Act goes on to exempt the owner and his servants or agents from other types of legal liability (in negligence, for example) as a result of any discharge or escape and even though there is a defence available under section 2.[98] The court is able to impose a limit on the amount for which an owner may be liable, if a request is made for this purpose. However, this facility applies only where the owner is not at fault.[99] Compulsory insurance is required for liability in respect of pollution: movements of vessels may be restricted in those sea areas controlled by the United Kingdom unless such insurance is in force.

The foregoing regime is modified and extended as a result of the Merchant Shipping Act 1988.[1] Modification occurs in various respects:

(a) the statutory framework will relate to any oil capable of being described as hydrocarbon mineral oil;
(b) the cost of action to prevent or mitigate loss or damage and similar action in the face of any imminent risk of contamination may be recoverable;
(c) the statutory regime will cover tankers in ballast; and
(d) "damage" will extend to environmental impairment referable to a resultant loss of profits and reasonable costs of reinstatement undertaken or anticipated.

The Merchant Shipping Act 1974 implements the 1971 International Convention on the Establishment of an International Fund for Compensation for Oil Pollution Damage. The Act provides for the payment of contributions to the Fund by all persons who import or receive oil in excess of an annual metric tonnage.[2] A person injured by oil pollution damage in the United Kingdom is entitled to compensation from the Fund where any of the exceptions to liability on the part of the ship owner allowed by section 2 of the Act of 1971 (above) apply, or where the owner or guarantor liable for the damage cannot meet his obligations in full, or where the damage exceeds the financial limits set out by section 4 of the Act of 1971. As with the Act of 1971, disputed claims are dealt with by the courts of the United Kingdom.

International voluntary provision for compensation is represented by

[96] Merchant Shipping (Oil Pollution) Act 1971, s.1. Extended now by the Merchant Shipping (Salvage and Pollution) Act 1994 to apply to "any occurrence" as a result of which oil escapes or is discharged.

[97] *Ibid.* s.2.

[98] *Ibid.* s.3.

[99] *Ibid.* ss.4 and 5.

[1] Sched. 4.

[2] s.2.

TOVALOP (Tanker Owners' Voluntary Agreement concerning Liability for Oil Pollution) and CRISTAL (Contract regarding Interim Supplement to Tanker Liability for Oil Pollution). These provisions are based on strict liability against owners and charterers for the discharge (wherever it may occur in the world) of persistent oil from tankers, laden or unladen. The liability is backed by insurance and compensation is payable for the reasonable costs of preventing and cleaning up pollution.

Dumping at sea

It is unlawful to dump substances or articles in United Kingdom waters, or to dump substances or articles in the sea outside United Kingdom waters from a British ship, aircraft, hovercraft or marine structure, or to load substances or articles on to a ship, aircraft, hovercraft or marine structure in the United Kingdom or in United Kingdom waters for dumping in the sea, whether in United Kingdom waters or not, or to cause or permit substances or articles to be dumped or loaded as previously mentioned.[3] Substances are "dumped" if they are permanently deposited in the sea. The foregoing acts of dumping require a licence from the Minister of Agriculture. In determining any application for a licence, the Minister is obliged to have regard to the need to protect the marine environment and the living resources which it supports from any adverse consequences of dumping. Conditions may be imposed on a licence for the purpose of achieving such environmental protection.[4] Consideration can be given in the course of the determination of a licence application to the suitability of alternative forms of disposal. As a matter of enforcement, the Minister enjoys wide powers to require remedial action: otherwise (and subject to various defences) enforcement is by reference to a range of offences.[5] Licences granted are recorded in a public register.[6]

Miscellaneous protection for the marine environment

The foregoing Food and Environment Protection Act also seeks to regulate marine incineration, a process used to dispose of liquid industrial wastes whose composition make them less suitable for disposal by means of land-based incineration or treatment. Control again is by means of licensing by the Minister of Agriculture.[7]

The Deep Sea Mining (Temporary Provisions) Act 1981 governs the licensing of exploration and exploitation of mineral resources. In exercising his licensing function, the Secretary of State is obliged to have regard to the need to protect the marine environment. Any licence granted must contain conditions considered necessary or expedient to avoid or minimise harmful effects.[8]

[3] Food and Environment Protection Act 1985, s.5.
[4] *Ibid.* s.8.
[5] *Ibid.* s.9.
[6] *Ibid.* s.13.
[7] *Ibid.* s.6.
[8] Deep Sea Mining (Temporary Provisions) Act 1981, s.5(1), (2).

Exploration for and exploitation of oil and natural gas is also subject to a licensing regime. Any such licence incorporates model clauses contained in petroleum production regulations and include provisions about oil flows, working practices, interference with fishing and other matters that may relate to protection from pollution of the marine environment.

CHAPTER 5

LAND POLLUTION

Introduction

The present chapter covers the following areas:

(a) waste management;
(b) contaminated land;
(c) litter control;
(d) pesticides; and
(e) the environmental release of genetically modified organisms.

These areas are governed primarily by statute, dominated by the Environmental Protection Act 1990. At the outset, however, the common law is dealt with, with particular reference to some of the areas above governed by statute. Much of the common law framework focuses on waste management and contaminated land and (to a lesser degree) issues arising from the management and use of pesticides.

The Common Law

General principles

If an individual has suffered loss, damage or injury, he may have a remedy in the private law of tort. Where that individual's rights—or interests—are recognised by the common law of tort, there is the possibility of pursuing an action in any one or more of the following:

(a) trespass;
(b) negligence;
(c) nuisance (public or private);
(d) strict liability; and
(e) breach of statutory duty.

Each of the foregoing actions may be pursued successfully where the plaintiff complains of some invasion of "environmental" rights or interests. However, the law has distinguished very sharply between those rights and interests identifiable with the integrity of the person or his property and much broader "rights", relating to what is often referred to as the "natural environment". An early example of this issue is found in *Mayor of Bradford v. Pickles*,[1] where the House of Lords confirmed the view that interference with water flowing underground in undefined channels so that, for example, it does not reach the plaintiff's reservoir is not actionable.

If an action in tort is successful, the remedies available require examination. Essentially those remedies divide into two: damages and injunctions. In awarding damages, the court is concerned primarily with *restitutio in integrum* so that, if at all possible, the plaintiff is restored to the position that would have obtained in the absence of any tort. If pollution of the plaintiff's land has occurred, there are various possibilities open to the court. In general terms, there is the possibility of restoration of the land as well as compensation, reflecting the plaintiff's inability to use and enjoy his land. More specifically, the court will have to address the devaluation of the subject land, as well as the expense involved in eliminating—or mitigating—the source of the pollution.

An award of damages can be made in lieu of an injunction, usually where the plaintiff's loss is trifling, rendering injunctive relief an excessive response to the problem. Although the prohibitory injunction is the better-known variety of injunction in preventing the continuation of a nuisance, for example, the mandatory injunction is also a significant remedy, commanding a person to act according to law where the applicant has a private right arising out of a failure to perform some public duty. The interlocutory injunction seeks to preserve the status quo between the parties until trial of the issue dividing them. Such an injunction, which may be useful in environmental litigation, may be granted if it is seen that there is a serious question to be tried and the court considers that, on the balance of convenience, the injunction should be granted. Finally, the *quia timet* injunction may be relevant even if, as yet, there is no cause of action but there is a need to obviate loss, damage or injury that may arise. Not surprisingly, such injunctive relief is likely to be forthcoming only if that loss, damage or injury is anticipated as being significant and it is probable that the unlawful act will occur. The court must also be satisfied that damages will be inadequate. The court has a very wide discretion in deciding whether an injunction should be granted, a discretion that is particularly important where industrial pollution may suggest a need to close down an industrial process. In these circumstances, the court will look closely at other alternatives, such as suspension of the injunction or an award of damages.

Trespass

This tort does not require proof of fault and is actionable *per se*, without proof of damage. The cause of action is referable to the trespass itself, when land is subject to some unlawful, direct interference and not from that point when any damage is first manifested. There may of course be a lapse of time between these events.

[1] [1895] A.C. 587.

Any unlawful interference with the plaintiff's land must be direct, physical interference, so raising the question of how a particular trespass is occasioned. It is this requirement of "direct" interference that provides the biggest difficulty. A polluting emission into the waters of a defined river channel may lead to direct, polluting depositions on the plaintiff's riverside land,[2] whereas a coastal oil spill may lead to uncertain "indirect" deposition on the shoreline by virtue of the fluctuations in wind and tide.[3]

Negligence

The three fundamental prerequisites for liability in negligence are that the defendant must be shown to owe the plaintiff a duty of care, a breach of duty must be established, and the breach must give rise to foreseeable loss, damage or injury. Negligence is often a supplementary cause of action in environmental litigation, particularly where the tort is in partnership with nuisance. In this case, a polluting discharge or emission from an industrial process may adversely affect a neighbouring area of land sufficiently to be regarded as an unlawful—and unreasonable—interference with the plaintiff's land. However, that state of affairs may be said by the plaintiff to be referable to the defendant's negligent operation of his industrial process.

Merely because a licence, consent or permission has been granted by statute does not provide a defence to proceedings in negligence. Whatever the circumstances of an action in negligence, the availability of damages may be limited, particularly where damages for economic loss are being claimed.[4] The critical issue for present purposes is the essential objective of any legislation under which particular functions relating to environmental health are undertaken. The case of *Murphy*[5] related to alleged negligence on the part of a local authority in the discharge of its functions and responsibilities under the Building Act and Building Regulations 1991. As a result of the case, it is clear that economic loss is unlikely to be recoverable against the local authority in this and other similar circumstances. Given that this legislation was seen in law as being concerned with physical health and safety, it appears that only negligence of a local authority leading to adverse physical consequences for the plaintiff might attract damages.

There may be circumstances in which the court is willing to reverse the onus of proof, so that it is up to the defendant to explain the act or omission because "the thing speaks for itself"; *res ipsa loquitur.* This reversal of the onus of proof will not occur where any one of a number of persons might be at fault.[6] Furthermore, there is no reversal of the onus even where the defendant produces no explanation but the facts are equally consistent with negligence or no negligence.

[2] *Jones v. Llanwrst UDC* [1911] 1 Ch. 393.

[3] *Esso Petroleum Co. Ltd. v. Southport Corporation* [1956] A.C. 218.

[4] *Murphy v. Brentwood District Council* [1990] 3 W.L.R. 414.

[5] *Ibid. Cf.* Chap. 11, "Building Control", nn.15–24, *infra.*

[6] *Pritchard v. Clwyd County Council* [1993] P.I.Q.R. P21, C.A.

Nuisance

Of all the torts, nuisance is undoubtedly the most significant in defence of matters affecting the environment and environmental health. The essence of nuisance is an unlawful, unreasonable interference with the plaintiff's use and enjoyment of his land, as long as the land use itself is not particularly sensitive.

Whether or not an existing owner or occupier is legally liable for a nuisance, a previous owner or occupier may continue to be liable in respect of matters for which he was responsible and of which it can be said that he could reasonably have had notice.[7]

If, as is often the case, a nuisance arises from various sources, but any one source by itself is insufficient to amount to an actionable nuisance, each person responsible for each source will be responsible in law.

The law distinguishes between a private nuisance, affecting only the plaintiff, and a public nuisance. A public nuisance will affect a class of individuals adversely in a variety of respects. Typically, any such class will be affected in terms of their comfort, convenience and enjoyment of property rights as a result of some unlawful act or by virtue of a failure to undertake a duty in law. The breadth of public nuisance is potentially very wide and could encompass all sorts of acts or omissions with an impact on the environment or environmental health, even where such acts or omissions are not proscribed as such by statute or under the common law. A public nuisance is enforceable under the criminal law and may be subject to injunctive proceedings by the Attorney-General *ex officio* or *ex relatione* or by a local authority using powers under section 222 of the Local Government Act 1972.

Strict liability

The essence of strict liability is that fault is not a prerequisite in proceedings against the defendant. The principle is expressed thus in *Rylands v. Fletcher*[8]:

> "... the person who for his own purposes brings onto his lands and collects and keeps there anything likely to do mischief if it escapes, must keep it at his peril, and if he does not do so, is prima facie answerable for all the damage which is the natural consequence of its escape."[9]

Subsequently, in *Rickards v. Lothian*,[10] the strict liability principle was limited to any damage generated by a "non-natural" user of land.[11]

It appears that to establish strict liability there is also a requirement that harm or injury of the type complained of must be foreseeable at a time when the substance

[7] *Sedleigh-Denfield v. O'Callaghan* [1940] A.C. 880, H.L.
[8] (1866) L.R. 1 Ex. 265.
[9] *Ibid. per* Blackburn J. at 279.
[10] [1913] A.C. 263.
[11] As to the court's attitude to statutory undertakers' potential liability, see *Smeaton v. Ilford Corporation* [1954] Ch. 450 and Chap. 2, "Sewage and Effluent Disposal", nn.15 and 16, *supra*.

or material is still within the control of the defendant.[12] Furthermore, it now appears that in an industrial context the storage of chemicals in substantial quantities, for example, and their use on site for a manufacturing purpose will not amount to a natural user, so as to fall into this exception to strict liability under *Rylands v. Fletcher.*[13]

Breach of statutory duty

The tort of breach of statutory duty attracts an award of damages where the terms of a statute indicate that an identifiable class of persons is the beneficiary of the prescribed duty.[14] The incidence of statutory duties enforceable in this way through the law of tort is exceptional in the area of environmental health law. More usually, a variety of acts will be prohibited and subject to enforcement through the application of criminal sanctions.[15]

Waste Management

The Environmental Protection Act

Part II of the Act of 1990 and a number of E.C. directives shape the core of the law of waste management. The implementation and enforcement of the law is in the hands of a number of agencies. A very significant part of the system depends on a requirement for waste disposal authorities to form local authority waste disposal companies or otherwise to privatise the waste disposal function. Both devices characterise the emphasis of Part II of the Act on privatisation of important elements of the waste management function. The scope of that function and its regulation depends on the definition of a number of words and phrases, suggesting (as will be seen below) a wide range of control available to the regulatory agencies. At the heart of that statutory control is an important distinction between so-called "special" (hazardous) waste, controlled waste and wastes which are not regarded as "controlled" wastes. The starting point of control under Part II is the criminal enforcement of any unauthorised or harmful deposit, treatment or disposal of waste. Criminal enforcement extends to any person who is in control of waste at any one time, through the requirements of a statutory duty of care which is prescribed by a code of practice representing "best" practice in the management of waste from cradle to grave.

Various proscribed activities involving controlled waste as outlined previously may be undertaken under the terms of a waste management licence issued by a waste regulation authority. A normal prerequisite for such a licence is a valid planning permission. In turn, the authority is obliged to undertake close supervision of the licensed activity which is also subject to detailed requirements

[12] *Cambridge Water Co. v. Eastern Counties Leather PLC* [1994] 2 W.L.R. 53, H.L.
[13] *Ibid.*
[14] *Reffell v. Surrey County Council* [1964] 1 W.L.R. 358.
[15] See here the Health and Safety at Work Act 1974, ss.2–7, and contrast s.47.

on cessation so that any eventual abandonment of a landfill, for example, will also be subject to detailed management requirements. Equally detailed statutory requirements are to be found in connection with the collection, disposal or treatment of controlled waste.

Part II of the Act sets down a variety of requirements for enforcement at local level, in particular, but also through intervention from central government. Broader issues of accountability are dealt with through requirements for publicity, particularly in relation to matters of licensing and enforcement.

The Part II authorities and disposal companies

The Act identifies three categories of authority:

(a) the waste regulation authority;
(b) the waste disposal authority; and
(c) the waste collection authority.

The council of a non-metropolitan county will be a waste regulation authority, while in Greater London the function is undertaken by the London Waste Regulation Authority.[16] The council of a non-metropolitan county will also act as a waste disposal authority, along with defined London borough councils.[17] The district council in England and Wales outside Greater London, and (in Greater London) the London borough council, will act as a waste collection authority.[18]

Reference is made throughout Part II to the waste disposal contractor whose functions are central to the privatisation of many important functions under Part II. Any such contractor is defined as a company formed for all or any of the purposes of collecting, keeping, treating or disposal of waste by a waste disposal authority, or by other persons, or a partnership, or an individual.[19] Any company formed for this purpose is a company whose status is provided for by the Companies Act 1985. If a company has been formed for present purposes by a waste disposal authority, it may have been formed for the purposes of complying with requirements from the Secretary of State for the Environment to form such a company and to transfer to it that part of its undertaking which relates to the disposal, keeping, treatment or collection of waste.[20] Whether the company has been formed at the instigation and with the participation of the local authority or otherwise, that company's objects must equate with the requirements set out in

[16] Environmental Protection Act 1990, s.30(1)(a), defining other authorities also undertaking this function.
[17] *Ibid.* subs.(2), also defining other authorities charged with the function.
[18] *Ibid.* subs.(3), also defining other authorities charged with the function.
[19] *Ibid.* s.30(5).
[20] *Ibid.* s.32. *Cf.* Department of the Environment Circular 8/91.

section 30(5). Any company in which that local authority has an interest must be a so-called "arm's length company" through compliance with Part V of the Local Government and Housing Act 1989. Any company under a local authority's control will be a "subsidiary" for the purposes of the Companies Act in three situations. In the first place, a local authority could be in a position to control majority voting at general meetings of the shareholders. A second option is that an authority is empowered to appoint or remove a majority of the directors. A final option is that an intermediate company controlled by an authority controls the company in question.

In operational terms, a fundamental requirement is that any local authority in the foregoing circumstances avoids "undue discrimination" in determining the terms and conditions of any contract for the disposal, keeping or treatment of waste.[21] Clearly, a local authority would be accountable in law where terms and conditions for any disposal contract were so fixed that a company in which it had an interest gained a material advantage over another company not so connected with the local authority.

The definition of "waste"[22]

Central to the operation of Part II is the Act's definition of waste, which depends not only on the terms of the Act (shaped, in turn by E.C. law) but also on the development of common law perceptions of waste. At the time of writing, the law is in a considerable state of flux, largely by virtue of the requirement to comply with E.C. law. Consequently, a necessary starting point for present purposes is the law's position as determined by relevant directives, as interpreted by the courts.

E.C. Directives 75/442[22a] *and 91/156*[22b]

The earlier directive was supplemented by Directive 78/319 on toxic and dangerous waste, while the later directive is a newer framework directive on waste. The earlier directives defined "waste" as "... any substance or object which the holder disposes of or is required to dispose of pursuant to the provisions of national law in force".[23] This view of "waste" does not exclude substances and objects which are capable of economic utilisation: it cannot be presumed that any waste holder disposing of any substance or object intends to exclude all economic re-utilisation by others.[24]

Subsequently, an amendment to the definition of waste was put in place by Directive 91/156. The amendment represents a new approach to definition. Henceforth, "waste" is to mean any substance or object listed in Annex I of the

[21] *R. v. Avon County Council, ex p. Terry Adams Ltd., The Times*, January 20, 1994, C.A.
[22] See Department of the Environment Circular 14/92 (Welsh Office 30/92).
[22a] [1978] O.J. L194.
[22b] [1991] O.J. L78.
[23] Directives 75/442 and 78/319, art.1(a).
[24] Cases C–206, 207/88, *Vessoso and Zanetti*: [1990] 2 L.M.E.L.R. 133, E.C.J.

directive which the waste holder discards or intends or is required to discard. At the time of writing the government intends to substitute the section 75 definition of waste set out below (and that comprised in the Control of Pollution Act 1974). For the moment the Waste Management Licensing Regulations 1994[24a] incorporate the definition of "waste" from Directive 91/156, referring to any substance or object defined in detail which the producer or person in possession discards or intends or is required to discard.[24b]

Environmental Protection Act, s.75

The section 75 definition of waste provides only that:

> "waste . . . includes:
> (a) any substance which constitutes a scrap material or an effluent or other unwanted surplus substance arising from the application of any process; and
> (b) any substance or article which requires to be disposed of as being broken, worn out, contaminated or otherwise spoiled;
>
> but does not include a substance which is an explosive within the meaning of the Explosives Act 1875."[25]

Despite the perhaps limited nature of the definition compared with the newer definition now emerging from the Framework Directive and referred to previously, supplementary assistance is available in the same section, which indicates that anything discarded or otherwise dealt with as if it were waste is presumed to be waste unless the contrary is proved.[26] Supplementary assistance is available also from a number of cases which, although decided under previous legislation in the Control of Pollution Act 1974, still remain relevant to the question "what is 'waste'"?

The case law

A well-established starting point is the statement of Judge Chapman Q.C. in Bradford Crown Court in *Long v. Brooke*[27] that although one man's waste may be another man's valuable material, on its true construction the Act defines waste from the point of view of the person discarding the material. Even soil, as a substance capable of recycling, is open to the description of waste.[28] The presence of solvents on an industrial site for recycling purposes may nevertheless invite the conclusion that those solvents are "waste", according to the approach described previously.[29] In another industrial context it was observed by the court that, in the

[24a] S.I. 1994 No. 1056.
[24b] *Ibid.* reg.1(3). *Cf.* Department of the Environment Circular 11/94 (Welsh Office 26/94).
[25] Environmental Protection Act, s.75(2).
[26] *Ibid.* subs.(3).
[27] [1980] Crim. L.R. 109.
[28] *Charles Neil Ashcroft v. Michael McErlain Ltd.*, January 30, 1985 (unreported).
[29] *R. v. Rotherham MBC, ex p. Rankin* [1990] 1 P.L.R. 93.

first place, the nature of particular material must be considered at the time of its removal from a site where the status of that material on delivery at another site is in issue for present purposes. In this instance, the material had been discarded and had lain on the first site for many years. At this stage, and also on its arrival at the second site, the court had no doubt that the material was "waste". Any usefulness of that material as fill on the second site did not change its character, even if it was separated from other material prior to deposit on the second site. However, the court did speculate that different considerations might apply if material is recycled or reconstituted prior to deposit.[30] The fact that a price is paid by a collector of material to its originator may be relevant, but is not crucial, and should not distract attention from the essential view of that material on the part of the originator and disposer.[31]

Circular 14/92 guidance

Waste regulation authorities are recommended to consider a number of questions from the point of view of a person producing or discarding a substance, material or article when determining whether it is "waste". The questions are as follows:

"(a) is it what would ordinarily be described as waste;
(b) is it scrapmetal;
(c) is it an effluent or other unwanted surplus substances arising from the application of any process;
(d) is it being discarded or otherwise dealt with as if it were waste?"

If the answer to any of these questions is "yes", the Circular suggests that the substance, material or article should be regarded as "waste".[32]

Controlled waste

At the heart of most of the regulation by Part II of the Act of waste management is the requirement for "waste" to be "controlled waste". Again, reference should be made to the Waste Management Licensing Regulations and the accompanying circular from the Department of the Environment.[32a] The critical elements of Part II relating to the enforcement of unlawful deposition, the duty of care on any holder of waste and the licensing of waste management are based on an assumption that subject waste is "controlled waste".

Waste categories

The Act provides the outline for what is a complex, many-faceted definition of controlled waste, beginning with the statement that such waste means household,

[30] *Kent County Council v. Queenborough Rolling Mills* (1991) 89 L.G.R. 306.
[31] *Berridge Incinerators Ltd. v. Nottinghamshire County Council*, April 14, 1987 (unreported).
[32] Department of the Environment Circular 14/92 (Welsh Office 30/92), paras. 17 and 18.
[32a] See nn.24a and 24b, *supra*.

industrial and commercial waste.[33] The Act goes on to define each of these three categories, primarily by reference to the nature of the premises generating that waste.[34] The variability of definition is to be seen in Regulations that indicate that these categories individually may or may not fall within the term "controlled waste" for the purpose of particular provisions in Part II of the Act.[35] By way of illustration, the E.C. framework Directive 91/156 indicates that waste licensing requirements may not apply if waste disposal occurs at the point of production or where specific waste recovery and disposal processes operate. In these circumstances, it may be possible to introduce a registration requirement for relevant categories of waste and to exempt those categories (say) from the Act's requirements relating to the duty of care.[36]

Household waste Section 75, in its definition of household waste, refers to waste from:

(a) domesic property;
(b) a caravan which usually and for the time being is situated on a caravan site;
(c) a residential home;
(d) premises forming part of a university or school or other educational establishment; and
(e) premises forming part of a hospital or nursing home.

It should be noted, however that particular descriptions of waste are not prescribed as household waste, so that it is unlawful to treat, keep or dispose of those descriptions of waste within the curtilage of domestic property unless a waste management licence is in force for the purpose. Those descriptions include asbestos and clinical waste.[37] Although defined as being unlawful, it should also be noted that other elements of the management of such waste see its maintenance of the description "household waste", for example, where the duty on the collection authority to arrange for collection is concerned. Furthermore, the Act provides that in the case of this description of household waste, or any other household waste, collection is normally free of charge.[38] One of several exceptions relates to garden waste, while another relates to clinical waste.[39]

Industrial waste Section 75 refers to industrial waste as waste from;

[33] Environmental Protection Act, s.75(4).
[34] *Ibid.* subss.(5), (6) and (7).
[35] *Ibid.* subs.(8) and *cf.* the Controlled Waste Regulations 1992 (S.I. 1992 No. 588).
[36] Directive 91/156, art.4 and *cf.* the Controlled Waste (Amendment) Regulations 1993 (S.I. 1993 No. 566 and the Waste Management Licensing Regulations 1994 (S.I. 1994 No. 1056), regs.17 and 18 and Sched. 3).
[37] Controlled Waste Regulations 1992, reg.3(1).
[38] Environmental Protection Act, s.45(3).
[39] Controlled Waste Regulations 1992, reg.4 and Sched. 2.

(a) any factory;
(b) any premises used for the purpose of, or in connection with, the supply to the public of gas, water or electricity or the provision of sewerage services;
(c) any premises used for the purposes of, or in connection with, the provision to the public of transport services by land, water or air; and
(d) any premises used for the purposes of postal or telecommunication services.

By way of illustration, the Regulations[40] prescribe that for all purposes under Part II of the Act waste from works of construction or demolition (including waste arising from preparatory work) and septic tank sludge are to be treated as industrial waste. However, sewage sludge or septic tank sludge which is treated, kept or disposed of within the curtilage of a sewerage treatment plant as an integral part of the operation of these works is not regarded as industrial waste or, indeed, commercial waste.[41]

Commercial waste Commercial waste is stated by section 75 to refer to waste from premises used wholly or mainly for the purpose of a trade or business or the purposes of sport, recreation or entertainment, but excluding household waste, industrial waste, waste from any mine or quarry and waste from agricultural premises. It is also open to the Secretary of State to prescribe other categories of waste to be regarded as commercial waste. This power to make detailed provision by Regulations is increasingly important where, for example, E.C. requirements indicate that exemptions in respect of agricultural waste may no longer apply.

Litter

Part IV of the Act dealing with litter is described later in the present chapter but, for present purposes, the management of litter in several important respects is dependent on the provisions of Part II dealing more generally with waste management. Again, the Secretary of State is empowered by the Act to make Regulations for the purposes of the interlinking of the two Parts of the Act.[42] For this purpose, the Controlled Waste Regulations contain provisions described below.[43]

Litter and refuse collected by virtue of the statutory duty to keep land and highways clear of litter, by virtue of default powers following non-compliance with a litter abatement notice or by virtue of street litter control notices under sections 89(1), 92(9) and 93 respectively, is now regarded as household, industrial or commercial waste. Accordingly, such waste, as controlled waste, is subject to the widely defined management framework described below. Matters of collection and disposal are defined, as between the collection and disposal

[40] *Ibid.* reg.5(2).
[41] *Ibid.* reg.7(1).
[42] Environmental Protection Act, s.96.
[43] S.I. 1992 No. 588, reg.8. *Cf.* Circular 14/92, Annex 4.

authorities, together with the facility for the imposition of charges by these authorities. Furthermore, the Controlled Waste Regulations indicate the scope of collection and disposal authorities' statutory responsibilities in connection with waste collection under section 45.[44] That function and its attendant responsibilities are applied specifically where litter and refuse has been collected by a local authority from a highway maintainable at the public expense, or by a "principal litter authority"[45] from open land under its control and to which the public have access, or from land as a result of an exercise of default powers following non-compliance with a litter abatement notice.

Unlawful deposition, treatment or disposal of waste

The criminal enforcement of unlawful deposition, treatment or disposal of controlled waste focuses attention on the fact that only licensed activities of this sort are permitted. This is the essential framework of section 33, which prohibits four categories of activity.

Deposition

Section 33 first provides that a person shall not deposit controlled waste or knowingly cause or knowingly permit controlled waste to be deposited in or on any land unless a waste management licence authorising the deposit is in force and deposition is in accordance with it.[46] This element of section 33 therefore provides for criminal enforcement of the act of deposition, as well as conduct knowingly caused or knowingly permitted. But for the defences in subsection (7), the offence of deposition would give rise in part to a strict liability offence not requiring proof of knowledge. It is also arguable that the term "deposit" here assumes that waste may not have reached its last resting place. The force of the argument here is that the environmental objectives of the legislation can only be served by a facility for enforcement where waste is an intrusion into the amenity of an area or locality, even if that waste will be removed.[47] However, a competing view in favour of any deposit being associated with a last resting place for waste appears to be heavily dependent on the court's concern for the essential objectives of the waste-licensing system, albeit under the terms of the predecessor provisions of Part I of the Control of Pollution Act 1974.[48] Arguably, the former view, although based on the Act of 1974 as well, is to be preferred in terms of broader concerns about environmental enforcement. It seems likely that the terms of Part II of the Act are rather more amenable to this broader view, albeit in terms of practicalities; the question to be asked is how temporary is the deposition for the purposes of enforcement?

[44] *Ibid.*
[45] Environmental Protection Act, s.86(2), (3).
[46] *Ibid.* s.33(1)(a).
[47] *R. v. Metropolitan Stipendiary Magistrate, ex p. London Waste Regulation Authority* [1993] 3 All E.R. 113.
[48] *Leigh Land Reclamation v. Walsall Metropolitan Borough Council* [1991] J.P.L. 867.

Beyond the offence of deposition are the other offences of knowingly causing or knowingly permitting the deposition of controlled waste. To "cause" an unlawful deposition requires some positive, active operation on the part of the defendant, as opposed to a mere passive spectating.[49] By way of contrast, "knowingly" permitting an unlawful deposition involves failure to prevent such deposition where it is known to the defendant.[50] It may be that the evidential burden on the prosecution relating to the defendant's knowledge is such that reliance on the strict liability offence of unlawful deposition is the favoured option. In pursuing any prosecution for knowingly permitting the unlawful deposition of controlled waste, what is required is proof of knowledge of the subject deposit, rather than knowledge that the act of deposition was in contravention of any specific terms of a particular waste management licence.[51]

A further offence of unlawful deposition of uncontrolled waste is provided for by section 63(2). As to the penalties, see section 33(9).

Treatment, keeping or disposal

The second category of offences in section 33 relates to any person who treats, keeps or disposes of controlled waste, or any person who knowingly causes or knowingly permits such waste to be treated, kept or disposed of in or on any land or by means of any mobile plant (such as an incinerator) without complying with a waste management licence.[52] The Act refers to the treatment of waste in terms of its subjection to "any process", including any process by which the waste is made re-usable or substances are reclaimed from it.[53] The reference to the keeping of controlled waste, on the other hand, is not elucidated in the Act but it seems that, as a matter of fact and degree, some measure of permanence and continuity are likely prerequisites.

A third category of offences relates to any person who treats, keeps or disposes of controlled waste in a manner likely to cause pollution of the environment or harm to human health.[54] The significant difference between this category and the former category is that, in the latter category, a prosecution can be pursued despite the existence of a valid waste management licence in force.

Contravention of licence conditions

A fourth category of activity prohibited under section 33 is contravention of any condition of a valid waste management licence.[55] The Environmental Protection Act has rationalised what was a considerable problem under the terms of the predecessor legislation in Part I of the Control of Pollution Act 1974. Under that

[49] *Alphacell Ltd. v. Woodward* [1972] A.C. 824, H.L.
[50] For an insight into the potential of the offence of "knowingly permitting", see *Price v. Cromack* [1975] 1 W.L.R. 988.
[51] *Ashcroft v. Cambro Waste Products* [1981] 1 W.L.R. 1349.
[52] Environmental Protection Act, s.33(1)(b).
[53] *Ibid.* s.29(6).
[54] *Ibid.* s.33(1)(c).
[55] *Ibid.* s.33(6). *Cf.* the powers of enforcement under s.42(1), n.1, *infra.*

earlier legislation, enforcement of any such condition depended on there being some associated, unlawful act of deposition. Accordingly, it is now easier to enforce a variety of management requirements, such as a need for secure site fencing, for example.

The offences and defences

The four categories of offence described previously provide considerable coverage for enforcement purposes. The Act declares that contravention of any of the requirements in the first three categories and of any condition of a waste management licence (the fourth category, above) is an offence.[56] However, the Act provides for various defences where a person charged with any of the foregoing offences can prove:

(a) that he took all reasonable precautions and exercised all due diligence to avoid commission of the offence; or
(b) that he acted under instructions from his employer and neither knew nor had reason to suppose that the acts done by him constituted a contravention of any of the first three categories above; or
(c) that the acts alleged to constitute the contravention were done in an emergency in order to avoid danger to the public and that, as soon as reasonably practicable after they were done, particulars of them were furnished to the waste regulation authority in whose area the treatment or disposal of the waste took place.[57]

The first of the defences referring to reasonable precautions and due diligence connotes the relevance of objectively reasonable action, bearing in mind the defendant's perception of and action to accommodate requirements to avoid an infraction of the law. The defendant's position as the holder of waste for the time being may take account of a number of significant variables, including the nature and size of any business or other undertaking, any system for managing waste and any arrangements involving third parties. Against this background, it may be asked whether any of the circumstances giving rise to the prosecution were reasonably foreseeable and whether, in turn, reasonable care was taken. In some circumstances, it may not be reasonably foreseeable that a third party contractor, for example will interfere with well-organised arrangements on site for waste handling.[58]

The second defence requires the defendant to establish that he acted under instructions from his employer and neither knew nor had reason to suppose that the acts constituted a contravention of the first three categories set out above. In so far as an employee is prosecuted, the present defence is available except in a prosecution for breach of a condition of a waste management licence. The

[56] *Ibid.*
[57] *Ibid.* s.33(7).
[58] *Austin Rover Group v. H.M. Inspector of Factories* [1989] 3 W.L.R. 520, H.L. *Cf. Tesco Ltd. v. Nattrass* [1972] A.C. 153.

defence emphasises the importance on any site used for waste management of clear information being available to employees as well as other persons who may be on site. Such information, which may be subsumed as instructions, will usefully extend to matters such as safety, health and pertinent requirements of any waste management licence.

The third defence depends on a need to establish that the acts amounting to the alleged offence were undertaken in an emergency in order to avoid danger to the public and that, as soon as reasonably practicable after they were done, particulars were given to the appropriate waste regulation authority for the area concerned. A not dissimilar defence is to be found in the Water Resources Act 1991.[59] The court's attitude to the Water Resources Act defence depends very much on those matters which are within the defendant's control.[60] Only if an occurrence is beyond the defendant's control is the defence likely to be successful. The closest analogy is probably the defence of "reasonable excuse" arising in other areas of environmental health legislation. In other litigation under the Water Resources Act,[61] the court was not prepared to extend the defence to a situation involving a factory explosion. In the case of emergencies of this sort, the court will no doubt take account of any reasonably practicable steps that can and have been taken to minimise adverse polluting effects of any occurrence within the Act.

The offences contained in section 33 may be prosecuted summarily, or on indictment. If the waste in question is "special", hazardous waste, the penalty of imprisonment following trial on indictment has a more severe maximum term than that which can be imposed for offences involving other controlled wastes.[62]

The duty of care in relation to waste

The duty of care is an important innovation in the law of waste management, requiring a waste holder (as defined below):

(a) to take "reasonable" measures in that capacity to prevent contravention by any other person of the requirements just examined in section 33;
(b) to prevent an escape of waste from his control or the control of any other person; and
(c) on transfer of the waste, to secure that the transfer is to a person who is "authorised" (or authorised for transport purposes) and that a significant written description of the waste is also transferred, enabling others to avoid contravening of section 33 and to comply with the foregoing duty to prevent an escape of waste.[63]

A waste holder for present purposes is any person who imports, produces, carries, keeps, treats or disposes of controlled waste or (as a broker) has control of such

[59] s.89(1)(a).
[60] *NRA v. Northwest Water* (1992) 208 ENDS Rep. 40; 4 L.M.E.L.R. 131.
[61] *NRA v. ICI Chemicals and Polymers* (1992) 204 ENDS Rep. 37; 4 L.M.E.L.R. 131.
[62] Environmental Protection Act, s.33(8), (9).
[63] *Ibid.* s.34(1). *Cf.* Department of the Environment Circular 19/91 (Welsh Office 63/91).

waste.[64] The duty does not apply to an occupier of domestic property as respects household waste produced on that property.[65]

The duty of care, which operates by reference to a code of practice, referred to below, was introduced (supposedly) by reference to the absence, in the case of waste which is not "special" waste, of a fully documented "chain" linking the producer and disposer and any intermediaries. The essence of the duty of care, therefore, is that responsibility in law arises from a combination of a person's control as a holder of waste and the capacity in which that person holds the waste. One area of potential difficulty relates to waste brokers, whose status is now subject to statutory recognition. Of particular concern in practice is the role of brokers in the import of wastes. E.C. Directive 91/156 states that:

> "Establishments or undertakings . . . which arrange for the disposal or recovery of waste on behalf of others (dealers or brokers), where not subject to authorisation, shall be registered with the competent authorities."[66]

The Waste Management Licensing Regulations now provide for a detailed broker registration scheme.[66a] Enforcement would be by means of criminal sanctions for those who act as brokers or dealers without registering with a waste regulation authority. A key element in enforcement will be the requirement that waste producers use only registered brokers; failure here would again attract criminal sanctions. Conviction of certain relevant offences would act as a bar to registration as a broker.

Authorised persons

Reference was made previously to a responsibility to ensure that waste is transferred only to an "authorised" person. This is a further, significant part of the waste "chain" that characterises the duty of care. For this purpose, an "authorised person" is defined in six different ways and refers to, *inter alia*, a waste collection authority, the holder of a waste management licence or (under Part I of the Control of Pollution Act 1974) a waste disposal licence, and any person registered as a carrier of controlled waste under section 2 of the Control of Pollution (Amendment) Act 1989.[67]

Authorised transport purposes

Reference was also made previously to a responsibility to ensure that transfer of waste is to a person authorised for transport purposes.[68] In this case, the Act refers to three situations:

[64] *Ibid.*
[65] *Ibid.* s.34(2).
[66] art.12.
[66a] (S.I. 1994 No. 1056), art.20 and Sched. 5.
[67] Environmental Protection Act, s.34(3).
[68] *Ibid.* subs.(4).

(a) the transport of controlled waste within the same premises between different places in those premises;
(b) the transport to a place in Great Britain of controlled waste brought from outside Great Britain but not landed until it arrives at that place; and
(c) the transport by air or sea of controlled waste from a place in Great Britain to a place outside Great Britain.

Documentary evidence

Documentary evidence is fundamental to the integrity of the waste "chain" referred to previously. Accordingly, the Secretary of State is empowered to make Regulations for the purpose of imposing on any person subject to the duty of care requirements in connection with the making and retention of documents, as well as the furnishing of documents or copies of documents.[69] In the exercise of this power, the Secretary of State has made the Environmental Protection (Duty of Care) Regulations 1991.[70] The Regulations compel a transferee to secure the completion and signing of a transfer note simultaneously with the creation of the written description of waste as required in section 34(1)(c)(ii), described previously.[71] Also contained in the Regulations is a description of the information required for these purposes.[72] Both items—the written description and the transfer note—must be kept by the parties to the transaction for two years from the date of the transfer.[73] Although copies must be produced on demand, there is no explicit requirement for documentation such as the transfer note to be carried on any journey for the transportation of the waste in question.[74]

The code of practice

The Act provides that the Secretary of State is obliged to prepare and issue a code of practice containing practical guidance on the discharge of the duty of care. However, a prerequisite is that the Secretary of State first consults with those who appear to be representative of the interests concerned.[75] The Department of the Environment and the Welsh Office issued the first such code of practice in December 1991. It covers four requirements, relating to:

(a) the prevention of breaches of section 33;
(b) the prevention of the escape of waste;

[69] *Ibid.* subs.(5).
[70] S.I. 1991 No. 2839.
[71] *Ibid.* reg.2(1).
[72] *Ibid.* reg.2(2).
[73] *Ibid.* reg.3.
[74] *Ibid.* reg.4.
[75] Environmental Protection Act, s.34(7).

(c) the transfer of waste to authorised persons; and
(d) the sufficiency of waste description.

In relation to the duty to prevent breaches of section 33, the code of practice invites consideration of standards of reasonableness that might be expected if (say) a registered carrier[76] regularly collects special waste from each of two manufacturing companies, the same lorry visiting both sites. One company suspects irregular disposal, while the other is uncertain about treatment of the waste as it is handled by a broker, a consignee from the registered carrier. Once again, the code forces attention on the reasonableness of the parties' conduct according to their capacity as "waste holders" in the "chain". In the first case of irregular disposal suspected, it will be necessary to consider the nature of the evidence and what (if anything) the first company has done in the circumstances. In the second case, the code would no doubt prompt the question whether the circumstances suggest that there was a need to check some or all of the waste consigned.

The duty to prevent escapes of waste focuses necessarily on various factors such as the packing of waste or its repacking by a subsequent holder, the nature of the waste and its location (say) inside or outside a company's premises. Not surprisingly, the primary duty falls on a waste producer as far as packing to prevent an escape is concerned. Other critical questions will relate to the sufficiency of the packing in relation to the waste description and the location of the waste once packed (say) in containers.

The transfer of waste to authorised persons is likely to concern, at some point, the activities and status of a registered carrier under the Control of Pollution (Amendment) Act 1989, dealt with below. Most usually, there will be two alternatives; transfer to such a carrier, or transfer to a licensed waste manager. In both cases, the duty of care will impose a need for reasonable measures as the waste holder consigns the subject waste. A crucial question here relates to the likely assumptions that can be made in evaluating the reasonableness of the waste holder's conduct. It may be assumed, as far as the producer is concerned, that the matter will be treated in accordance with the relevant terms of any waste management licence. Nevertheless, any waste holder might reasonably demand to see the licence and, indeed, any licence apparently held by a registered waste carrier.

Where a description of wastes is concerned, there may be many variables which could be relevant for the central purpose of charting the progress of the waste from cradle to grave. The description may be a "full" or a "simple" description, according to the risk factors involved. Construction of the description may be by reference to the activity generating the waste or by reference to the physical or chemical characteristics of the substances in question. More generally, though, the code of practice forces consideration of the purposes for which an adequate description is required for discharge of the duty of care in

[76] As defined by the Control of Pollution (Amendment) Act 1989, dealt with below.

particular circumstances. In particular, the need for an adequate description of waste is driven by a number of factors, including the following:

(a) the avoidance of a breach of section 33;
(b) the prevention of escape of waste;
(c) the enabling of treatment or disposal by a licensed waste manager under the terms of the licence and its conditions;
(d) the permitting of identification of the quantity of the waste, its nature, hazards and intended disposition; and
(e) the enabling of information to pass down the "chain" prior to final disposal.

A code of practice is admissible in evidence before the court. Furthermore, if any provision in such a code appears to that court to be relevant to any question arising in the proceedings, it is to be taken into account in determining that question.[77]

Any person who fails to comply with the section 34 duty or with any requirement imposed by the Regulations authorised under subsection (5)[78] is guilty of an offence which is triable summarily, or on indictment.[79]

Waste carrier registration

Various references have been made to the transportation of waste and the integrity of the waste "chain" linking the waste producer and the disposer of waste. The problem of fly-tipping as well as a more general need for the management of waste transportation under Part II of the Environmental Protection Act emphasises the significance of the Control of Pollution (Amendment) Act 1989. At the time of its enactment, it was reported[80] that 90–95 per cent. of fly-tipped wastes came from the construction industry and that 15–20 per cent. contained some toxic elements. It was also pointed out[81] that fly-tipping is difficult to prosecute successfully unless the perpetrators are caught "red-handed", or the prosecuting authority is able to rely on some very good witnesses. Against this background, the Act of 1989 seeks to address the problem of effective enforcement through a requirement for the registration of controlled waste transporters.

The core of the Act of 1989 is the prescription of an offence for any person who is not a registered carrier of controlled waste, in the course of any business of his or otherwise with a view to profit, to transport any controlled waste to or from any place in Great Britain.[82] A number of exemptions from criminal liability are provided for, including the transportation of waste within the same premises.[83]

[77] Environmental Protection Act, s.34(10).
[78] See n.70, *supra*.
[79] Environmental Protection Act, s.34(6).
[80] *Toxic Waste*, House of Commons Environment Committee, Second Report, Session 1988–89.
[81] *Ibid*.
[82] Control of Pollution (Amendment) Act, s.1(1).
[83] *Ibid*. subs.(2).

Various defences are set out in the Act[84] including emergency action, defined[85] to include action to avoid, remove or reduce any serious danger to the public or serious risk of damage to the environment. Another significant defence relates to any situation in which a defendant neither knew nor had reasonable grounds for suspecting that waste was controlled waste and took reasonable steps to ascertain the nature of the waste.

The Act empowers the Secretary of State to make regulations for the purpose of enabling the establishment and operation of machinery for the registration of carriers with a registration authority. As a result, the Controlled Waste (Registration of Carriers and Seizure of Vehicles) Regulations 1991[86] have been made.

Exemptions from registration

While the Act provides generally for registration by waste regulation authorities,[87] the foregoing Regulations prescribe detailed requirements. The Regulations provide for a number of exemptions from registration. Those exempted include waste collection, disposal and regulation authorities, a producer of controlled waste (except where that waste is building or demolition waste) and any charity.[88] The exemption of any producer of controlled waste recognises the application of the duty of care in such a case, but without prejudice to the obligation of such a producer to pass the waste over to a registered carrier for transportation. The exemption, however, does not apply to building or demolition waste, presumably in recognition of the problem of fly-tipping, adverted to previously. "Building or demolition waste" is defined to extend from waste arising from works of construction or demolition to include works which are preparatory to such works.[89]

Restrictions on registration

A waste regulation authority is not authorised to refuse an application for registration except where, in relation to the application, there has been contravention of the requirements of the foregoing Regulations or the applicant or "another relevant person"[90] has been convicted of a prescribed offence[91] and, in the opinion of the authority, it is undesirable for the applicant to be authorised to transport controlled waste. If the question of the revocation of registration is before the authority, the matter will be processed by reference to a conviction for a prescribed offence and the opinion of the authority. Any authority, in determining whether it is desirable that any individual be allowed to transport or

[84] *Ibid.* subs.(4).
[85] *Ibid.* subs.(6).
[86] S.I. 1991 No. 1624. *Cf.* Circular 11/91 (Welsh Office 34/91).
[87] Control of Pollution (Amendment) Act, ss.2 and 9.
[88] S.I. 1991 No. 1624, reg.2.
[89] *Ibid.* reg.2(2).
[90] Such as an employee: Control of Pollution (Amendment) Act, s.3(5).
[91] S.I. 1991 No. 1624, Sched. 1.

to continue to transport controlled waste, is obliged to have regard to the question of whether that individual has been party to the carrying on of a business in a manner involving the commission of prescribed offences.[92]

Registration decisions

The Regulations prescribe detailed requirements in relation to applications for registration.[93] If an application for registration or renewal of registration is refused, the applicant must be notified and be furnished with reasons for the refusal.[94] An appeal to the Secretary of State is available in these circumstances; any notice of appeal must specify the grounds of appeal and be accompanied by various other prescribed information. The notice of appeal must also be served on the authority in question.[95] The notice of appeal must be given within 28 days of various prescribed dates, but most commonly within 28 days of receipt of a notice of refusal from the authority.[96] In some circumstances, a registration may remain in force pending the determination of an appeal.[97] If either party to the appeal requests it or the Secretary of State so decides, an appeal may be determined by means of a hearing.[98] Ultimately, the Secretary of State is obliged to notify the appellant of his decision in writing, such decision to be accompanied by reasons and (if a hearing has been held) a copy of the report concluded by the person conducting that hearing. In turn, all of these documents must also be sent to the registration authority.[99]

If an application for registration is accepted, or the authority is directed to register the applicant following an appeal, an appropriate entry must be made in a register of carriers by the authority. Provision is also made in the Regulations for the amendment of entries, changes of circumstances and registration of additional partners, the recording of any cessation of registration and the return of certificates.[1] All of these requirements are to be seen against the background of the Act's requirement that a registration authority should maintain a register of carriers to which the public should have access.[2] The duration of a registration is normally a period of three years from the date of registration.[3]

The duty to produce authority

The Act gives specific powers to any duly authorised officer of a waste regulation authority or a constable to intervene to stop and search for the purpose of

[92] Control of Pollution (Amendment) Act, s.3.
[93] S.I. 1991 No. 1624, reg.4.
[94] *Ibid.* reg.5.
[95] *Ibid.* reg.15. *Cf.* 4 of the Control of Pollution (Amendment) Act.
[96] S.I. 1991 No. 1624, reg.16.
[97] Control of Pollution (Amendment) Act, s.4(7).
[98] S.I. 1991 No. 1624, reg.17.
[99] *Ibid.* reg.18.
[1] *Ibid.* regs.6–8, 12 and 13.
[2] Control of Pollution (Amendment) Act, s.2.
[3] S.I. 1991 No. 1624, reg.11.

enforcing registration requirements. However, only a constable in uniform may stop a vehicle on any road for present purposes. The power to stop and search is triggered where it "reasonably appears" to any such officer or constable that a person is not a registered carrier of controlled waste.[4] A person may be required to produce his authority forthwith or by presenting it or sending it to the principal office of the waste regulation authority within seven days of any demand.[5] The present requirements are enforceable through the criminal law that provides for two offences[6]: the first offence arises where a person intentionally obstructs any authorised officer of the waste regulation authority or a constable in the exercise of his powers, and the second offence arises where a person fails to show reasonable excuse for failing to comply with any requirements imposed for present purposes. However, it is a defence to proceedings in the case of this second offence to show that the waste in question was not controlled waste and that the person did not transport that waste to or from a place in Great Britain.[7] Each of these offences is a summary offence.[8]

Supplementary powers of enforcement

Certain provisions to be found in the Environmental Protection Act[9] relating to powers of entry, powers for dealing with imminent pollution and powers to obtain information are referable to enforcement requirements under the present legislation.[10] Furthermore, restrictions on the flow of information under section 94 of the Control of Pollution Act do not apply to information flow between waste regulation authorities, the Secretary of State and other local authorities for the purpose of facilitating the exercise of their functions under the Act by waste regulation authorities.[11] Failure to comply with any requirement to provide information, without reasonable excuse, is a summary offence, as is the provision of false information either knowingly or recklessly.[12] Once again, the onus of proof in relation to reasonable excuse lies on the defence.[13]

Seizure and disposal of vehicles used illegally

The Act sets out the prerequisites for the seizure of any vehicle, under a warrant issued by a justice of the peace. There must be reasonable grounds for the justice of the peace to believe that an offence of unlawful deposition, etc., has been committed and that the vehicle in question was used in connection with the commission of the offence, that no proceedings for the offence have been

[4] Control of Pollution (Amendment) Act, s.5(1), (2).
[5] *Ibid.* subs.(3): *cf.* S.I. 1991 No. 1624, reg.14.
[6] Control of Pollution (Amendment) Act, s.5(4).
[7] *Ibid.* subs.(5).
[8] *Ibid.* subs.(7).
[9] Environmental Protection Act, ss.68(3), (4) and (5), 69–71.
[10] Control of Pollution (Amendment) Act, s.7(1).
[11] *Ibid.* subs.(2).
[12] *Ibid.* subs.(3).
[13] *Ibid.*

brought as yet and that the authority has failed to obtain information about who was used the vehicle at the time of the commission of the offence.[14] These powers therefore appear to rule out any seizure in anticipation of the commission of any offence.

Any duly authorised officer or constable may stop a vehicle specified in a warrant and seize the vehicle and its contents. However, as indicated previously, only a constable in uniform may stop a vehicle on a road while the seizure of any property by a duly authorised officer can only occur when accompanied by such a constable.[15]

Where property has been seized in present circumstances, various powers and responsibilities are imposed on the authority in respect of the safe custody, return and disposal of the property.[16] Regulations made under the Act provide detailed requirements in relation to the return of seized property, the disposal of such property and the application of proceeds of sale.[17]

The intentional obstruction of an authorised officer or a constable in the exercise of any power conferred by a warrant is a summary offence.[18]

Waste licensing

The regulatory framework for waste management (now described substantially in a recent Department of the Environment Circular)[18a] is tied to the waste management licence granted by a waste regulation authority. Such a licence, which will usually be subject to conditions, will authorise the treatment, keeping or disposal of any specified description of controlled waste in or on specified land. Equally, a waste management licence may operate similarly in relation to the treatment or disposal of controlled waste by means of mobile plant.[19] The reference here to "disposal" of waste includes disposal by way of deposit in or on land, and waste is "treated" when it is subjected to any process to make it re-usable or to enable reclamation of substances from it.[20] Crucially, therefore, recycling is clearly subject to the present regulatory regime. "Land" for present purposes includes land covered by waters where land is above the low-water mark of ordinary spring tides. Furthermore, any reference here to land on which controlled waste is treated, kept or deposited are taken to be references to the surface of the land, including any structure set into that surface.[21] Finally, the term "mobile plant" refers to plant (such as incineration plant) which is designed to move or to be moved, whether on roads or other land.[22]

[14] *Ibid.* s.6(1); *cf.* S.I. 1991 No. 1624, reg.20.
[15] Control of Pollution (Amendment) Act, s.6(2), (3).
[16] *Ibid.* subss.(5), (6). As to the removal of vehicles seized, see S.I. 1991 No. 1624, reg.21.
[17] S.I. 1991 No. 1624, regs.22–25.
[18] Control of Pollution (Amendment) Act, s.7(9).
[18a] Department of the Environment Circular 11/94 (Welsh Office 26/94).
[19] Environmental Protection Act, s.35(1). *Cf.* the Waste Management Licensing Regulations 1994 (S.I. 1994 No. 1056) and Department of the Environment Circular 11/94 (Welsh Office 26/94).
[20] Environmental Protection Act, s.29(6).
[21] *Ibid.* subs.(7).
[22] *Ibid.* subs.(9).

Licence holders

The Act distinguishes carefully between the treatment, keeping or disposal of waste in or on land and the treatment or disposal of waste by means of mobile plant. In the first case, a licence may be granted to the person in occupation of the land, while in the second case a licence may be granted to the person who operates the mobile plant.[23] The reference to occupation in the first case emphasises the choice of control rather than ownership as the necessary focal point for regulation through licensing. Possession here may not necessarily be exclusive possession, although the measure of control will no doubt be ascertainable from (say) the relationship between lessor and lessee. That relationship may be complex, as where lessor and lessee share occupation and divide control of the site for different purposes according to their respective interests.

Conditions

The Act confers a widely drawn power on a waste regulation authority for the imposition of conditions on a licence. Accordingly, any such authority may grant a licence on "... such terms and subject to such conditions as appear ... to be appropriate ...".[24] Those conditions may relate to the activities which the licence authorises and to the precautions to be taken and works to be carried out in connection with or in consequence of those activities. Accordingly, conditions may anticipate landfilling, for example, by requiring (say) that the receiving land be suitably engineered in order to prevent leaching once deposition is under way. Equally, conditions may seek to regulate matters once landfilling has ceased as where, for example, a requirement is imposed for aftercare management of the site and the venting of methane gas.[25] Technical requirements in these and many other similar cases are governed by waste management papers, published by the Department of the Environment.

Reference was made earlier[26] to the capacity in which a person may hold a waste management licence. It is against this background that the Act goes on to indicate that conditions may require a licence holder to carry out works or do other things, notwithstanding that he is not entitled to carry out the works or do the things in question. In these circumstances, the Act goes on to stipulate obligations to be recognised and performed by any person whose consent would be required, as an owner, for example. Any such person is obliged to give any necessary consent to an occupier in the typical case, so that the occupier is able to comply with any licence requirements.[27] The Act refers to the granting of any necessary rights in respect of "the land" without identifying this as the land on which the subject waste is treated, kept or disposed of, or the land on which any

[23] *Ibid.* s.35(2).
[24] *Ibid.* subs.(3).
[25] *Ibid.*
[26] See n.23, *supra.*
[27] Environmental Protection Act, s.35(4).

works will be executed. The Act's silence on this matter may suggest that either option may be appropriate if this power is resorted to by a waste regulation authority.

Across Europe, there is some disagreement about the mixing of wastes that go to landfill. The present statutory provisions relating to waste management licence conditions anticipate one set of circumstances in which both controlled waste and waste other than controlled waste may be treated, kept or disposed of. Any condition may relate to that waste which is not controlled waste by requiring, for example, that landfilling of the two waste types occurs only in a strictly engineered sequence.[28]

Central control of the licensing function

The Secretary of State is empowered (by section 35(6)) to make regulations indicating the conditions which are, or are not, to be included in any licence. This facility is particularly important for the purpose of implementing the requirements of E.C. law, for example, in relation to controls over the disposal of waste oils.[29] Any deposit or discharge which is harmful to the soil is prohibited, in which case it could normally be expected that an appropriate condition would appear in a relevant waste management licence. The facility is equally important in the protection of ground waters,[30] where, again, it would normally be expected that any detrimental substances would be subject to control by means of an appropriate condition in a licence.[31] This facility is further reinforced through powers also available to the Secretary of State where a licence application has been made to a waste regulation authority. The Secretary of State is empowered to give that authority directions as to the terms and conditions which are, or are not, to be included in the licence. The authority, in turn, is obliged to give effect to any such directions.[32] Any such authority is also required, in less mandatory terms, to have regard to any guidance issued by the Secretary of State in relation to the discharge of its licensing function.[33]

Planning control requirements

A waste management licence may be issued only where planning permission is in force in relation to the particular use of land for the treatment, keeping or disposal of waste or where an established use certificate is in force, governed in both cases by the Town and Country Planning Act 1990. This prerequisite to the grant of a waste management licence assumes that the process of treating, keeping or disposal of waste on land is (for the purposes of the law of development control) a

[28] *Ibid.* subs.(5).
[29] Directive 75/439: [1975] O.J. L194, as amended by Directive 87/101: [1987] O.J. L42. *Cf.* S.I. 1994 No. 1056, reg. 14.
[30] Directive 80/68: [1980] O.J. L20. *Cf.* the Waste Management Licensing Regulations 1994 (S.I. 1994 No. 1056), reg. 15 and Department of the Environment Circular 11/94, Annex 7.
[31] See particularly Circular 2/82 (Welsh Office 7/82), para. 11. *Cf.* n.30, *ibid.*
[32] Environmental Protection Act, s.35(7).
[33] *Ibid.* subs.(8).

use of land rather than an operational development. In some instances, planning permission for such use will not be required if it is pursued as a matter of "ancient right" since July 1, 1948,[34] where the Crown is occupier of the land in question or planning permission is granted by statutory order for the purposes of so-called "permitted development". The requirement, it should be noted, is for planning permission in force "... in relation to that use of land".[35] These words will not necessarily exclude a pre-existing planning permission granted originally for the purpose of permitting mineral extraction and culminating with a requirement for restoration of the land, for example.[36] The restoration requirements in such planning permission may not necessarily conform to later requirements when the site is to be landfilled prior to restoration. One possibility in these circumstances is that the parties agree to a revocation of earlier permission by means of an agreement under section 106 of the Town and Country Planning Act 1990 and its replacement with new and more appropriate planning permission as a prerequisite to the grant and issue of a waste management licence. The section 106 agreement may contain a covenant by the applicant to forego compensation for revocation, in return for the local planning authority's covenant to grant a new permission.

The discretionary licensing power

If an application for a licence has been duly made and satisfies all the formalities, that application may not be rejected if the waste regulation authority is satisfied that the applicant is a "fit and proper person" unless satisfied that rejection is necessary for any one of three reasons. The first of these reasons for rejection is the authority's satisfaction that anything other than rejection would not prevent serious detriment to the amenities of the locality.[37] However, this reason for rejection is not available where planning permission is in force in relation to the use to which the land will be put by virtue of the licence. A second reason for refusal is prevention of pollution of the environment, while a third reason relates to the prevention of harm to human health.[38] The width of the waste regulation authority's discretion here is to be seen through the meaning given by the Act[39] to the words "pollution of the environment" and "harm". The first set of words, referring to "pollution of the environment", is stated to mean pollution of the environment due to the release or escape (into any environmental medium) from the land on which controlled waste is treated, the land on which controlled waste is kept or the land in or on which controlled waste is deposited, and release or escape from fixed plant by means of which controlled waste is treated, kept or disposed of, in each case of substances or articles constituting or resulting from the waste, and capable (by reason of the quantity or concentration involved) of

[34] *Berridge Incinerators v. Nottinghamshire County Council*, April 14, 1987 (unreported). *Cf.* 31, *supra*.
[35] Environmental Protection Act, s.36(2).
[36] *R. v. Derbyshire County Council, ex p. N.E. Derbyshire District Council* (1979) 77 L.G.R. 389.
[37] Environmental Protection Act, s.36(3)(c).
[38] *Ibid.* subs.(3)(a) and (b).
[39] *Ibid.* s.29.

causing harm to man or any other living organisms supported by the environment.[40] The width of the authority's discretion as determined by matters of environmental impact is added to by the Act's view of "harm", both as it appears in the foregoing definition and as it appears in the second possible ground for the authority's rejection of a licence application. "Harm" is defined as meaning harm to the health of living organisms or other interference with the ecological systems of which they form part and, in the case of man, includes offence to any of his senses or harm to his property.[41] Effectively, it may be argued that almost any application is capable of rejection on the ground of pollution of the environment when set against the background of these statutory definitions.

If an authority proposes to issue a licence it is required first to refer that proposal to the National Rivers Authority and the Health and Safety Executive. However, the authority need only consider any representations from these two agencies within the period allowed for such representations.[42] If the National Rivers Authority requests that a licence not be issued or disagrees with any condition to be imposed on the proposed licence, either party may refer the dispute to the Secretary of State, whose decision is binding on those parties.[43] In practice, it is likely that arguments by the National Rivers Authority to the effect that a waste regulation authority's controls will be ineffective may not be sufficiently persuasive, particularly where (in effect) it is seeking total cessation of or prohibition of waste management on the subject site.[44]

Where the land in respect of which an authority proposes to issue a licence is notified already as a site of special scientific interest under section 28 of the Wildlife and Countryside Act 1981, the proposal must first be referred to the appropriate nature conservation body. In England, that body is the Nature Conservancy Council for England, while in Wales that body is the Countryside Council for Wales. Once again, the waste regulation authority is obliged to consider any representations about the proposal from the body in question within the time allotted for representations.[45] Any such site is, in any event, vulnerable to the extent that it may be disturbed, or even destroyed, if any appropriate planning permission is in force.

Reference is made below to the appeal facility available in respect of various licensing decisions under Part II of the Act. More immediately, the waste regulation authority's decision must be regarded as a deemed refusal unless a licence has been granted or notice of rejection been given.[46] It appears that, in the event of a decision to grant a licence, there is no necessary reason in law why notification of that decision should occur within the period of four months (or any longer period agreed between the parties) specified by the Act. The danger, though, is seen in the fact that a deemed refusal occurs if that period expires

[40] *Ibid.* subs.(3).
[41] *Ibid.* subs.(5).
[42] *Ibid.* s.36(4).
[43] *Ibid.* subs.(5).
[44] (1993) 224 ENDS Rep. 11.
[45] Environmental Protection Act, s.36(7).
[46] *Ibid.* subs.(9).

without any apparent response to the application, giving rise to an appeal to the Secretary of State.[47]

Fit and proper persons

A central feature of the licensing discretion is the fact that a waste regulation authority shall not reject an application if satisfied that the applicant is a fit and proper person unless rejection is required for any one of the three reasons (including pollution of the environment) referred to previously. Assessment of the question of whether an applicant is a "fit and proper person" is aided by reference to the terms of the advisory waste management papers, the provisions of section 74 of the Act, the Waste Management Licensing Regulations 1994[47a] and Department of the Environment Circular 11/94.

The necessary starting point under section 74 is the issue of whether the applicant is a fit and proper person by reference both to the activities that may be authorised by a licence and the fulfilment of its requirements.[48] The Act sets out three separate grounds as a basis for denying that an applicant is a "fit and proper person". The first ground arises where it appears that the applicant, or "another relevant person", has been convicted of a "relevant offence".[49] Nevertheless, the waste regulation authority may, if it considers it proper to do so in any particular case, treat a person as a fit and proper person despite the existence of a relevant conviction.[50] Regulations made under the section may prescribe various offences for present purposes. A variety of offences is now prescribed,[51] including the transportation of controlled waste without registered carrier status.[52] This ground is framed in general terms, so that it is not necessarily the case that any such conviction should relate to conduct in relation to any site for which a licence is now sought. The inclusion of a reference to "another relevant person" allows for an important linkage permitting consideration of a rather wider constituency of responsibility. This wider constituency is achieved by the inclusion of three sets of circumstances according to whether a licence holder was the employer of a convicted person, a director, manager, secretary or similar officer of a body corporate that was convicted, or a body corporate, a director, manager, secretary or similar officer of which was convicted.[53]

A second ground arises where it appears to the waste regulation authority that the management of the activities which are or are to be authorised by a licence are not or will not be in the hands of a technically competent person.[54] The primary "badge" of technical competence will normally be a relevant certificate of

[47] *Ibid.* s.43.
[47a] S.I. 1994 No. 1056.
[48] *Ibid.* s.74(2).
[49] *Ibid.* subs.(3)(a).
[50] *Ibid.* subs.(4).
[51] S.I. 1994 No. 1056, reg. 3.
[52] Control of Pollution (Amendment) Act 1989: see nn.80 *et seq.*, *supra.*
[53] Environmental Protection Act, s.74(7).
[54] *Ibid.* subs.(3)(b).

technical competence awarded by the Waste Management Industry Training and Advisory Board.[54a] The guidance seems to point to any technically competent person being in a position to control the day-to-day activities authorised by the licence and carried out at the licensed site. It would appear that the technical management of a facility does not necessarily have to rest with one person only. In what is characterised as a flexible system, it may be a matter for the applicant or licensee to demonstrate, to the satisfaction of the waste regulation authority, how the particular nature of the management structure and control mechanisms satisfy the requirements.

The third ground arises where it appears to the waste regulation authority that the person who holds or who is to hold the licence has not made and either has no intention of making or is in no position to make financial provision adequate to discharge the licence obligations.[55] At the time of writing, there is no doubt about the difficulties surrounding this particular ground. The best that may be achieved here is a general financial statement provided on a voluntary basis, as long as section 74 fails to require any proof of financial provision. Beyond such a general financial statement, persuasion may suggest the usefulness of a detailed financial statement, referable to licensed operations where a draft licence is available for perusal. That an applicant has sufficient finance may be reinforced through an audit certificate. It has been suggested previously by the Department of the Environment that attention be given to evidence of the three most recent (audited) sets of accounts. The alternative for the waste regulation authority might be to obtain an appropriate credit rating.

Licence modification

The modification of a waste management licence may be justified for a variety of reasons and, for this purpose, the Environmental Protection Act recognises that the initiative may come from either the waste regulation authority or the licensee.[56] In so far as the initiative comes from the authority, that authority must hold the opinion that the modification of conditions is desirable and is unlikely to require unreasonable expense on the part of the holder.[57] During the currency of a licence, the authority is obliged to modify licence conditions to the extent which, in its opinion, is required for the purpose of ensuring that the activities authorised do not cause pollution of the environment or harm to human health, or become seriously detrimental to local amenities.[58] As in the case of the initial licensing process described above, the Secretary of State is also empowered to direct the making of modifications for the purpose, for example, of complying with European Community legal requirements.[59] Whatever the nature of any proposed modification of conditions, the authority is obliged to carry out the

[54a] S.I. 1994 No. 1056, regs.4 and 5.
[55] *Ibid.* subs.(3)(c).
[56] *Ibid.* s.37(1).
[57] *Ibid.*
[58] *Ibid.* subs.(2).
[59] *Ibid.* subs.(3).

consultations previously described in relation to the main licensing process.[60] Furthermore, and once again reflecting the main licensing process previously described, any failure to respond by a waste regulation authority to an application for modification within the stipulated time limit of two months is a deemed refusal. Any such deemed refusal triggers a right of appeal to the Secretary of State, described below.[61]

Licence modification may be justified for a variety of reasons (as indicated previously), particularly where there are concerns about ground water. If no action is proposed for the protection of such waters by means of a water protection zone declared under the Water Resources Act 1991, modification of a waste management licence may be the necessary alternative. Waste regulation authorities are counselled to review licences for the disposal of so-called "List 1" substances for the purposes of the E.C. Directive on the protection of ground water against pollution caused by certain dangerous substances.[62] "List 1" substances are particularly toxic substances characterised by their persistence and bioaccumulation. If the National Rivers Authority advises that discharges from a landfill site are liable to affect ground water adversely, there may be an obligation, not legally enforceable unless the Secretary of State has issued a direction under section 37(3),[63] to review licence.[64] Earlier in any typical licensing process is a requirement on the waste regulation authority not to license the deposit of wastes containing "List 1" substances[65] where the concentrations and amounts would lead to a discharge of these substances into the ground water.[66]

Licence revocation and suspension

A waste regulation authority has various powers for the revocation or suspension of waste management licences.[67]

In the case of revocation, the authority may exercise its powers to secure either the entire revocation of a licence or the revocation of a part only of the licence.[68] If it appears to the authority that management is no longer in the hands of a technically competent person, so that the licence holder can no longer be regarded as a "fit and proper person", the authority may exercise its powers of partial revocation.[69] In two other sets of alternative circumstances, the authority may, if it thinks fit, exercise powers of total or partial revocation. The first set of circumstances arise where it appears to the authority that the licence holder has ceased to be a "fit and proper person" by reason of having been convicted of a

[60] *Ibid.* subs.(5). *Cf.* nn.42 and 43, *supra.*
[61] *Ibid.* subs.(6).
[62] Directive 80/68.
[63] See n.59, *supra.*
[64] Circular 20/90 (Welsh Office 34/90), paras. 3 and 4. *Cf.* S.I. 1994 No. 1056, reg.15 and Department of the Environment Circular 11/94, Annex 7.
[65] *Ibid.* App. 2.
[66] *Ibid.* para. 4.
[67] Environmental Protection Act, s.38.
[68] *Ibid.* subs.(3) and (4).
[69] *Ibid.* subs.(2).

relevant offence.[70] The second set of circumstances arise where it appears to the authority that continuation of authorised activities would cause pollution of the environment or harm to human health, or would be seriously detrimental to local amenity, and that pollution, harm or detriment cannot be avoided by a modification of conditions under the preceding section 37.[71] In the event of a partial revocation only, the waste regulation authority is able to identify licence requirements which will continue to be binding on the licence holder.[72]

The authority's powers of licence suspension are, again, total or partial according to circumstances. Those circumstances fall into two categories. In the first set of circumstances, it must appear to the authority that a licence holder has ceased to be a fit and proper person because management is no longer in the hands of a technically competent person. The second set of circumstance arise where it appears to the authority that serious pollution of the environment or serious harm to human health has resulted from, or is about to be caused by, licensed activities or an occurrence affecting those activities, so that those activities or that occurrence will cause serious pollution of the environment or serious harm to human health.[73] Control is extended here through the power of the Secretary of State to give directions to the authority to exercise its powers of suspension—or revocation—as stipulated.[74]

If a licence is suspended for any of the reasons just listed under section 38(6),[75] the Act confirms that licensed activities are not authorised (or that, alternatively, any activities specified by the authority have no effect.) This latter provision is of particular interest, to the extent that it appears to allow the exercise of powers of suspension by reference to activities which may not necessarily be referable to the licence. Nevertheless, the authority would be unable to specify activities which are not referable to the grounds for suspension found in subsection (6).[76] If a licence is suspended by reference to grounds in subsection (6), the authority enjoys further powers that are exercisable to deal with or avert the pollution or harm as it considers necessary. Such powers may be exercised either at the time of suspension or at any time when the licence is suspended.[77] The Act provides for criminal enforcement of these powers according to whether a person fails to comply with any requirement in relation to special waste or waste otherwise than special waste. In both cases, the Act provides for offences triable either summarily or on indictment, with differing penalties according to the type of waste involved. In both cases, there is a defence of reasonable excuse, indicating that the defendant had no control over circumstances as a result of which he was unable to comply with the requirements of the authority.[78]

[70] *Ibid.* s.74(6).
[71] *Ibid.* s.38(1).
[72] *Ibid.* subs.(5).
[73] *Ibid.* subs.(6).
[74] *Ibid.* subs.(7).
[75] See n.73, *supra*.
[76] Environmental Protection Act, s.38(8).
[77] *Ibid.* subs.(9).
[78] *Ibid.* subss.(10) and (11).

In the event of a revocation or suspension, or in the event of any requirement imposed during the suspension of a licence, that revocation, suspension or requirement must be conveyed by means of a notice served on the licence holder. The notice must advise the holder of the time at which the revocation, suspension or requirement takes effect and, in the case of a suspension, the date of cessation.[79]

The surrender of licences

An enduring problem under Part I of the Control of Pollution Act 1974 was the facility to abandon landfilling and similar activities licensed under that Act on a unilateral basis and without any monitoring of technical issues surrounding the environmental integrity of a site. This matter is addressed by Part II of the Environmental Protection Act, section 39 of which puts in place a number of prerequisites to be satisfied prior to surrender. In the case of a "site licence" (as opposed to a licence in respect of mobile plant), the Act is unequivocal in stipulating that a licence may be surrendered by its holder to the waste regulation authority granting it only if that authority accepts the surrender.[80] An application in the prescribed form must be made to the authority, accompanied by a fee.[81] On receipt of an application, the waste regulation authority is obliged to inspect the land to which the licence relates and may (if necessary) require further information—or evidence—to be furnished.[82]

The core of the Act's concern for the implications of any licence surrender is found in the duty of the authority to determine whether it is "likely or unlikely" that the condition of the land resulting from the treatment, keeping or disposal of waste (whether or not in pursuance of the licence) will cause pollution of the environment or harm to human health.[83] At the time of writing, it appears that the procedure running up to a surrender application will begin when the authority modifies the waste management licence to initiate a period of so-called "completion monitoring". This will be done, it would appear, when it is considered that a site's pollution control systems are no longer required. However, it seems likely that a good run of monitoring data will have to be made available by a licensee in relation to the active and post-closure phases of operation before any consideration can be given to completion monitoring. If eventually the waste regulation authority is satisfied that the condition of the land is unlikely to cause the pollution or harm previously referred to, there is a duty in law to accept a surrender application. However, before any proposed acceptance can be executed, the authority must refer the proposal to the National Rivers Authority and consider any representations from it made within a period of 21 days or a longer period (if agreed) from the date of receipt. If the National Rivers

[79] *Ibid.* subs.(12).

[80] *Ibid.* s.39(1). *Cf.* S.I. 1994 No. 1056, Sched. 1.

[81] *Ibid.* subs.(3). Schemes for fees are provided for by section 41.

[82] *Ibid.* s.39(4).

[83] *Ibid.* subss.(5), (6).

Authority requests that a surrender not be accepted, the difference between the two parties must be arbitrated by the Secretary of State.[84]

Of particular significance in the process of referring any surrender proposal to the National Rivers Authority is the opportunity given for consideration of its ground waters protection policy. Vulnerable ground waters are, of course, a particular concern for present purposes. The approach of NRA here is to identify "source protection zones", focusing on vulnerable areas of ground water as well as undesirable activities within, or within the near proximity of, such areas. A significant element in the policy is the list of dangerous substances found in E.C. Directive 80/68.

If a licence surrender is accepted, a certificate of completion will be issued to the applicant along with a notice of the waste regulation authority's determination. That determination will advise the applicant that the authority is satisfied in respect of the matters of pollution or harm referred to previously and that on issue of the certificate the licence ceases to have effect.[85] If, within a period of three months[86] from receipt of the surrender application, the authority has neither issued a certificate of completion nor notified rejection, the waste regulation authority is deemed to have rejected the application, giving rise to an appeal to the Secretary of State under section 43, described below.[87]

The transfer of licenses

The Act makes provision for the transfer of a waste management licence, even if that licence be partially suspended or revoked. The machinery for transfer is built on an application for that purpose made jointly to the waste regulation authority by the licence holder and the proposed transferee in a prescribed form and accompanied by a fee.[88] The essential issue for the authority in dealing with such an application is whether the proposed transferee is a "fit and proper person". If that transferee is considered to be a fit and proper person, the authority is obliged to effect the licence transfer.[89] If, within a period of two months (or such longer period as may be agreed between the parties) of receipt of an application, there is neither a transfer nor a notice of rejection of the application, it is deemed that the authority has refused an application, so generating an appeal to the Secretary of State under section 43, described below.[90]

The appeal facility

Reference has been made to a variety of circumstances in which an appeal to the Secretary of State is available in relation to the licensing process.[91] In each case, an

[84] *Ibid.* subs.(7).
[85] *Ibid.* subs.(9).
[86] Or such longer period as the parties may have agreed.
[87] Environmental Protection Act, s.39(10).
[88] *Ibid.* s.40(1)–(3). *Cf.* S.I. 1994 No. 1056, Sched. 2.
[89] *Ibid.* subs.(4). *Cf.* s.74 and nn.48–55, *supra*.
[90] *Ibid.* subs.(6).
[91] *Ibid.* s.43(1).

appeal to the Secretary of State may be pursued by an applicant, licence holder or former licence holder, as the case may be. In the case of a proposed licence transfer, an appeal against an adverse decision may be pursued by the proposed transferee.[92] Any matter arising from an appeal may be referred by the Secretary of State to a "person appointed", normally an inspector. Equally, the Secretary of State may direct that the appeal or any matter arising from it should be determined by such a person.[93] The appeal proceedings are conducted in writing, but this is subject to a request from a party or a decision of the Secretary of State that a hearing be made available. That hearing may be at the discretion of the person conducting the proceedings, and be heard in private, wholly or in part.[94]

In some cases, the pursuit of an appeal has the effect of rendering the decision appealed ineffective. These cases relate to the modification of conditions and the revocation of a licence.[95] However, the revocation or modification decision of the waste regulation authority will remain effective if any notice of revocation or modification includes a statement of the authority's opinion in support of continuing revocation or modification. That statement will indicate that continuing revocation or modification is necessary for the purpose of preventing or (where that is not practicable) minimising pollution of the environment or harm to human health.[96] By way of contrast, the pursuit of an appeal has no effect on the suspension of a licence. However, if the Secretary of State or any other person determining an appeal concludes that a waste regulation authority has acted unreasonably in suspending a licence or (as the case may be) in certifying that a revocation or modification should have effect despite the appeal on an application by a licence holder or former licence holder, the "disability" may be lifted. Furthermore, the licence holder or former licence holder may claim compensation in respect of any loss suffered in consequence of the "disability". Any dispute about entitlement to or the amount of compensation is determined by arbitration.[97]

False statements in the licensing process

An offence, triable summarily or on indictment, is provided for where a person makes any statement which he knows to be false in a material particular or where he makes a statement recklessly where, again, that statement is false in a material particular, in the course of the licensing process.[98] The "licensing process" for this purpose relates to any application for a licence, any modification of licence conditions and any transfer or surrender of a licence.[99]

[92] *Ibid.*
[93] *Ibid.*
[94] *Ibid.*
[95] *Ibid.* subs.(4).
[96] *Ibid.* subs.(6).
[97] *Ibid.* subs.(7).
[98] *Ibid.* s.44.
[99] *Ibid.*

The supervision of licensed activities

A significant characteristic of Part II of the Environmental Protection Act is the facility for a waste regulation authority to supervise activities covered by a waste management licence issued by that authority. Where such a licence is in force, it is the duty of the authority to take the steps needed to ensure two things. First, the authority may need to act to ensure that authorised activities do not cause pollution of the environment or harm to human health, or become seriously detrimental to local amenities affected by those activities. Secondly, the authority may need to act for the purpose of ensuring that licence conditions are complied with; a significant alternative to the criminal enforcement of licence conditions.[1]

If, during the subsistence of a licence, it appears to the authority that water pollution is likely to be caused by licensed activities, that authority is obliged to consult the National Rivers Authority in connection with the duty just described.[2] These anticipatory steps may be taken without any necessity for establishing cause and effect in any conclusive terms. Furthermore, work may be carried out on land by an authorised officer of the authority if it appears to be necessary due to an emergency. Not only may work be carried out on the land: it may also be carried out in relation to plant or equipment on the land to which the licence relates and even mobile plant (such as an incinerator) to which a licence relates.[3] However, any expenditure incurred here may be recovered from the licence holder or former licence holder where the licence has been surrendered. The licence holder or former licence holder may be able to avoid the authority's attempt to recover if it can be shown that there was no emergency requiring any work or that certain of the expenditure was unnecessary.[4]

Reference was made previously to the waste regulation authority's power to take steps to ensure compliance with licence conditions and the availability of criminal enforcement under section 33(6) of the Act. Without prejudice to this facility for criminal enforcement, the authority may require a licence holder to comply with any condition within a specific time. If the authority is of the opinion that the licence holder has not complied with any such condition within the time allowed, a range of very significant powers become available to it.[5] More particularly, the condition may be revoked in so far as it authorises the carrying out of the "offending" activity or activities identified by the authority, the licence may be revoked in its entirety, and (finally) the licence may be suspended in so far as it authorises the carrying out of the "offending" activity or activities identified by the authority.[6] The Secretary of State has a reserve power for present purposes, exercisable by direction, requiring a waste regulation authority to exercise its enforcement powers under the present section 42.

[1] *Ibid.* s.42(1). *Cf.* s.33(6), n.55, *supra.*
[2] *Ibid.* s.42(2).
[3] *Ibid.* subs.(3).
[4] *Ibid.* subs.(4).
[5] *Ibid.* subs.(5).
[6] *Ibid.* subs.(6). As to the mechanics of revocation or suspension here, see s.38.

Special waste

Controlled waste may be considered by the Secretary of State to be so dangerous or difficult to treat, keep or dispose of that special provision is required for dealing with it, involving its treatment, keeping or disposal.[7] At the time of writing, the Regulations in force are the Control of Pollution (Special Waste) Regulations 1980,[8] made under the Control of Pollution Act 1974. The European Community background to the regulations is to be found in Directive 78/319, to be replaced by Directive 91/689 on hazardous waste.[8a]

The transfrontier transportation of hazardous waste is governed by the Basel Convention on the Control of Transboundary Movement of Hazardous Wastes and their disposal.[9] This Convention provides a framework for states to control movements of hazardous waste so that, for example, in the case of export, responsibility is placed on a United Kingdom exporter to ensure that waste will be handled in an environmentally satisfactory manner in the receiving country. The Basel Convention is implemented in Member States of the European Community through the waste shipments regulation, directly applicable to each Member State.[10]

For the foreseeable future, the legal definition of hazardous waste will be referable to a new formula generated by Directive 91/689. The point of reference will be three Annexes, categorising hazardous waste types by nature or by reference to any activity by which they are generated informed, in turn, by any constituents or properties pointing to hazardous qualities.

The Special Waste Regulations

These Regulations are under review at the time of writing by reference to factors such as the definition of hazardous waste referred to above, as well as the directive's prescription against the mixing of different types of hazardous waste and the mixing of such waste with non-hazardous waste. Such factors will have to be taken account of in the waste management licensing process previously described. Equally, any waste management papers published by the Department of the Environment and containing guidance on matters such as the management and control of special hazardous waste will feature in decision-making. These waste management papers, in acting as a vehicle for best practice, should reflect also the approaches prescribed by the directives then in force. Such guidance may also reflect particular requirements in relation to the transfer and transportation of waste, indicating the relevance and significance of the duty of care in Part II of the Act.

Pending their replacement, the Special Waste Regulations[11] are constructed by

[7] *Ibid.* s.62.
[8] S.I. 1980 No. 1709, as amended.
[8a] [1991] O.J. L377.
[9] Cm. 984.
[10] reg.259/93: [1993] O.J. L30. *Cf.* the Transfrontier Shipment of Waste Regulations 1994 (S.I. 1994 No. 1137).
[11] See n.8, *supra*.

reference to six sections. An introductory section seeks, *inter alia*, to define special waste, presently by reference to impact on the human form but (eventually) by reference to environmental factors also. The second part of the Regulations relates to a fundamental feature of the law here: the need for consignment notes in a chain that will link (as appropriate) producers, carriers, importers, exporters and disposers. A further segment of the Regulations provides for special arrangements in the event of regular consignments of special waste. The Regulations require producers, carriers and disposers to maintain registers of consignment notes and those making deposits on land to maintain site records of the waste's location. The Secretary of State is given power to direct the holder of a disposal licence to accept and dispose of special waste at a specified location. Finally, the Regulations provide for matters of enforcement.[12] It is provided that an offence is committed, which is triable either summarily or on indictment, where the Regulations are not complied with. However, a defence is available if it can be established that the person charged took all reasonable precautions and exercised all due diligence to avoid commission of the offence by himself or by someone under his control. In the case of certain offences against the Regulations, it is a defence that the person charged was not reasonably able to comply with the Regulations by virtue of an emergency, but that all reasonable steps were taken to ensure that necessary copies of consignment notes were completed and furnished as soon as practicable after the event.

Waste collection

A waste collection authority will be one of the local authorities referred to earlier in the present chapter.[13] The Act sets out the statutory duties of any such authority.[14] Each authority is obliged to arrange for the collection of household waste in its area, free of charge. In so far as there are exceptions to the general immunity from charging, those exceptions are set out in the Controlled Waste Regulations 1992.[15] There is one exception to the duty to collect household waste and that relates to collection from a place so situated as to be (in the opinion of the authority) so isolated or inaccessible that the cost of collection would be unreasonably high, where the authority is in turn satisfied that adequate arrangements for disposal have been or can reasonably be expected to be made by the person in control of the waste. The authority is also under a duty to collect commercial waste[16] from premises, if requested to do so by an occupier of those premises.[17] By way of contrast, in the case of industrial waste,[18] a collection authority may, on a request for collection made by an occupier, collect that waste, but not before obtaining the consent of the waste disposal authority for the area.[19]

[12] S.I. 1980 No. 1709, reg.16.
[13] See n.18, *supra*. *Cf.* s.30(3).
[14] Environmental Protection Act, s.45(1).
[15] S.I. 1992 No. 588, reg.4, Sched. 2. *Cf.* the requirements set out in s.45(3).
[16] Environmental Protection Act, s.75(7).
[17] *Ibid.*
[18] *Ibid.* subs.(6).
[19] *Ibid.* s.45(2).

Any person requesting the collection of waste other than household waste is liable to pay a "reasonable charge" for collection and disposal. That charge is payable to the authority arranging collection of the waste.[20]

The emptying of privies and cesspools

Each collection authority is under a duty to make arrangements (without charge) for the emptying of privies serving one or more private dwellings, as considered appropriate. A duty to act also arises where a person controlling a cesspool serving only one or more private dwellings in its area requests the emptying of the cesspool. However, the duty is qualified, at least to the extent that such of the contents may be removed by the collection authority as it considers appropriate on payment (if the authority requires) of a "reasonable charge".[21] In the case of any other privy or cesspool in the authority's area, that authority may empty any of the contents on similar terms.[22]

Infrastructure for waste collection

The waste collection authority, may, if it wishes, construct, lay and maintain, even outside its area, pipes and associated works for waste collection. This power also extends to contributing to the cost of some other person's expenditure for the purpose of connecting with the local authority's own pipes.[23] Furthermore, an authority may contribute to another person's costs in providing or maintaining plant or equipment intended to deal with commercial or industrial waste prior to arrangements for collection already referred to.[24]

Ownership of waste

Where waste is collected under the powers and duties just described, that waste belongs to the waste collection authority and may be treated accordingly. However, the status of such waste is subject to section 48(1) which imposes a duty on the authority to deliver for disposal all waste so collected to such places as the waste disposal authority directs.[25]

Household waste receptacles

When the duty to arrange for collection of household waste arises, the collection authority may by notice served on an occupier require that occupier to place the waste for collection in receptacles of a kind and number specified.[26] Any such requirement must be "reasonable" but, subject to that, separate receptacles or

[20] *Ibid.* subs.(4).
[21] *Ibid.* subs.(5).
[22] *Ibid.* subss.(6), (12).
[23] *Ibid.* subs.(7).
[24] *Ibid.* subs.(8).
[25] *Ibid.* subs.(9).
[26] *Ibid.* s.46(1).

compartments of receptacles may be required for waste to be recycled and that which is not to be recycled.[27] The authority has a number of options in relation to the provision of receptacles, ranging from provision by the authority free of charge through to a requirement that they be provided by the occupier.[28] Considerable discretion also extends to the detailed specification of the management of the collection process, again through the notice served on the occupier and referred to above. However, in notifying its requirement about placing waste in receptacles, that requirement must not extend to a placing of receptacles on a highway or road unless the relevant highway or roads authority has consented and arrangements have been made as to the liability for any damage arising.[29]

Any failure, without reasonable excuse to comply with various requirements[30] is a summary offence.

If an occupier is required to provide any receptacles he may (within a period of 21 days[31]) appeal to a magistrates' court against any requirement, on the ground that the requirement is unreasonable or that the receptacles in which household waste is placed for collection from premises are adequate.[32] The meaning of the word "provide" was before the court in *East Hampshire District Council v. Roberts*,[33] albeit in relation to similar statutory wording found in the former Control of Pollution Act provision. In the event, the court placed heavy reliance on section 46 of the Environmental Protection Act in concluding that "provide" means "supply" but does not connote any requirement for payment. The learned Judge, Henry J., found that

> "... where the notice states that the household waste will only be collected by the Authority if placed in the receptacle to be provided by the council but that should a replacement receptacle ever be required the expense of that would be charged to the occupier, that is not a requirement upon the occupier to provide a receptacle ... because 'provide' ... does not have the meaning of paid for. 'Provide' there has the meaning of supply ..."

If an appeal is pursued, the requirement in question is of no effect pending determination of the appeal. The court dealing with the appeal has three options: to quash or modify the requirement or dismiss the appeal. Finally, any question of the reasonableness of a local authority's requirement may be entertained in the course of an appeal but not otherwise in any criminal proceedings for non-compliance with a requirement.[34]

[27] *Ibid.* subs.(2).
[28] *Ibid.* subs.(3).
[29] *Ibid.* subs.(5). As to the likely unlawful obstruction that may result, see *Wandsworth Corporation v. Baines* [1906] 1 K.B. 470.
[30] *Ibid.* s.46(1), (3)(c) or (d) or (4).
[31] *Ibid.* subs.(8).
[32] *Ibid.* subs.(7). As to appeal requirements, see s.73(1)–(5).
[33] [1982] C.O.D. 488.
[34] Environmental Protection Act, s.46(7).

Commercial and industrial waste receptacles

Where a person has requested the collection of commercial or industrial waste by the collection authority, that authority may accede to his request for a supply of receptacles in return for a "reasonable" charge which, in any event, may be waived in the case of a receptacle for commercial waste.[35] It may appear to the collection authority that failure to store commercial or industrial waste at premises is likely to cause a nuisance or be detrimental to the amenities of the locality. In these circumstances, the authority is empowered to require the occupier to provide at the premises receptacles of a reasonably suitable kind and number.[36] As in the case of household waste receptacles, in the case of receptacles for commercial and industrial waste there must also be no requirement that a receptacle be placed on the highway or a road unless arrangements have been made as to any liabilities that may arise.[37] Similar provision is made in respect of a summary offence for failure to comply with an authority's requirement[38] and in respect of an appeal against any such requirement,[39] although here a ground of appeal is that the waste is not likely to cause a nuisance or be detrimental to the amenities of the locality.[40]

Waste collection authority disposal duties

Reference was made earlier, in relation to the duties in law of a collection authority, to the additional duty to deliver for disposal all waste collected at a point directed by the waste disposal authority.[41] This additional duty will not apply to household or commercial waste in respect of which the authority has made arrangements for recycling. The exception relates to any arrangements made by the disposal authority with a waste disposal contractor whereby that contractor will recycle household or commercial waste. Such arrangements will justify an objection by the disposal authority to the collection authority's proposal for recycling.[42] In so far as arrangements are put in hand by the collection authority for recycling, the authority is obliged to have regard for its waste recycling plan, as provided for by section 49, described below.[43] These arrangements must be notified to the waste disposal authority as soon as is reasonably practicable.[44] In pursuing such recycling arrangements, the collection authority is empowered to provide plant and equipment for the sorting and baling of any waste which is retained.[45] However, if a collection authority is also a

35 *Ibid.* s.47(1).
36 *Ibid.* subss.(2), (3), (4).
37 *Ibid.* subs.(5).
38 *Ibid.* subs.(6).
39 *Ibid.* subss.(7), (8), (9). As to appeal requirements, see s.73(1)–(5).
40 *Ibid.* subs.(7)(b).
41 *Ibid.* s.48(1).
42 *Ibid.* subs.(2), (4), (5).
43 *Ibid.* subs.(2).
44 *Ibid.* subs.(3).
45 *Ibid.* subs.(6).

disposal authority, as in a metropolitan area, this facility does not apply, so that arrangements must be made with a waste disposal contractor for these purposes, although bottle banks and similar facilities can undoubtedly be provided by such authorities.[46] The plant and equipment used by the collection authority may be made available to other persons at a reasonable charge.[47]

Waste disposal

It was seen previously[48] that, principally, the functions of a waste disposal authority will be undertaken by the council of a non-metropolitan county and, in London, by a London borough council. Set out below are the statutory functions of the waste disposal authority. Also set out below is the statutory framework for the waste disposal plans of waste regulation authorities.

Waste disposal authority functions

Subject to transitional arrangements[49] following on the phased repeal of the Control of Pollution Act, it is the duty of each waste disposal authority to arrange for the disposal of controlled waste collected by the waste collection authorities and to arrange for places at which residents may deposit household waste and, in turn, the disposal of that waste. In either case any arrangements are to be made with waste disposal contractors.[50] Each category of arrangement is dealt with in turn.

In the case of arrangements for the disposal of collected controlled waste, the waste disposal authority is required:

- (a) to direct a collection authority in its area as to whom and the places at which waste is to be delivered;
- (b) to arrange for the provision (within or without its area) by waste disposal contractors of places at which waste may be treated or kept prior to removal for treatment or disposal;
- (c) to make available to waste disposal contractors (and therefore to own) plant and equipment for the purpose of keeping or transporting such waste;
- (d) to make available (and to hold) land to enable such contractors to treat, keep or dispose of waste on that land;
- (e) to contribute to the cost of providing and maintaining plant or equipment by producers of industrial and commercial waste where that plant and equipment is used to deal with the waste prior to collection; and

[46] *Ibid.* subs.(7).
[47] *Ibid.* subs.(8).
[48] See n.1, *supra.*
[49] Environmental Protection Act, s.77.
[50] *Ibid.* s.5(1). *Cf.* Pt. II of Sched. 2.

(f) to contribute to such producers' costs in providing or maintaining pipes or associated works provided by a waste collection authority for the purpose of facilitating waste disposal.[51]

The Act channels arrangements for fulfilment of the duty just described through waste disposal contractors as well as in the case of the duty concerning the provision of places where household waste may be deposited. In both cases, the waste disposal authority exercises (or may exercise) a supportive role as where, for example, plant, equipment or land may be made available to a waste disposal contractor.[52] Equally, the authority may again make available to contractors places where waste may be treated or kept prior to removal for treatment or disposal.[53]

Any arrangements made by an authority in connection with the second duty must secure that places made available are reasonably accessible to persons resident in an area and that they are available at "all reasonable times", free of charge.[54] Arrangements may include access to facilities by "other persons" who are not resident in the authority's area on such terms as to payment (if any) as that authority may determine.[55]

Waste disposal plans

Predecessor waste disposal plans were made under the Control of Pollution Act by the waste disposal authorities provided for under that Act. The new plans provided for under Part II of the Environmental Protection Act are substantially different to the former plans, although transitional arrangements are provided for. Accordingly, on the appointed day for plans,[56] any disposal plan approved under the Control of Pollution Act will be regarded as a disposal plan under section 50 of the Environmental Protection Act pending approval of a "section 50 plan", in accordance with the criteria under that section, set out below.

The new plan will be quite radically different to predecessor plans in identifying current and projected waste arising for the area of the waste regulation authority. The central planning function is to match such arisings with existing and planned facilities for treatment and disposal. Equally central is the statutory insistence that the waste disposal plan identify relevant authority policies for disposal and recycling of waste.[56a]

In approaching the plan-making process, the waste regulation authority is obliged, at the outset, to investigate arrangements for treating or disposing of controlled waste so as to prevent or minimise pollution of the environment or

[51] *Ibid.* subs.(4). *Cf.* Circular 8/91 (Welsh Office 24/91), Annex D.
[52] *cf.* s.51(5)(b), (c), in relation to the second duty.
[53] *Ibid.* subs.(5)(a).
[54] *Ibid.* subs.(2).
[55] *Ibid.* subs.(3)(b).
[56] *Ibid.* s.77(4).
[56a] Department of the Environment Circular 11/94, paras. 15–17.

harm to human health, and to decide how to relate the licensing process to such an objective. Thereafter, the authority is further obliged to prepare a statement—"the plan"—of the arrangements made and proposed to be made by waste disposal contractors for waste treatment or disposal. The longer-term elements of the process are seen in terms of an obligation to undertake further investigation to allow decisions to be made about changes to the plan.[57] In preparing the plan and considering longer-term modifications, the waste regulation authority is required to have regard to the likely cost of any arrangements or modifications, as well as any likely beneficial effects on the environment.[58] The preparatory process necessitates consultation with various bodies, including the National Rivers Authority and the relevant waste collection authority, and, prior to final determination of a plan or modification, the authority must take such steps which, in its opinion, will give adequate publicity to the plan or modification in its area and provide members of the public with opportunities to make representations to the authority. Any representations made must be considered and any "appropriate" changes made by the authority in the light of this public consultation.[59] This latter exercise in public participation is subject to one important measure of discretion on the part of the authority; the requirement to bring proposed plan modifications to the attention of the public and to consider their representations will not apply if the authority is of the opinion that no person will be prejudiced through non-application of public consultation.[60]

Despite foregoing requirements for consultation involving various bodies and the public at large, the Act obliges the waste regulation authority at any stage in making and modifying a plan to consider various matters in consultation with the waste collection authorities in the area and "any other persons". Those matters relate to any arrangements that can reasonably be expected to be made for waste recycling and plan provisions for that purpose.[61]

The waste regulation authority is subject to a duty to include in its plan information as to a number of matters listed by the Act. The seven matters listed may be modified by regulations made by the Secretary of State, who may also require that certain prescribed matters are also taken into account in plan preparation. Among the seven matters listed by the Act are the following:

(a) the policy of the authority in its waste management licensing capacity;
(b) the kinds and quantities of controlled waste expected to be disposed of in the area during the period covered by the plan; and
(c) the methods (and priorities relating to the deployment of those methods) by which the authority considers that controlled waste should be disposed of or treated during the plan period.[62]

[57] *Ibid.* s.50(1).
[58] *Ibid.* subs.(2).
[59] *Ibid.* subs.(5).
[60] *Ibid.* subs.(6).
[61] *Ibid.* subs.(7).
[62] *Ibid.* subs.(3). References here to "disposal" now include references to recovery of waste: S.I. 1994 No. 1056, Sched. 4, para. 9(8).

For this latter purpose, the waste regulation authority is obliged to have regard to the desirability of giving priority to recycling, but only in so far as that is a reasonably practicable option, taking account (say) of suitable market availability for recycled material.[63]

Before finally determining the content of a plan or any modification of it, the authority is obliged to forward a draft to the Secretary of State who will determine whether the foregoing requirements about information content have been complied with. To secure compliance with those requirements, the Secretary of State is empowered to serve an appropriate direction on the authority, which is bound to comply with it.[64] Indeed, whatever the duty under the present section 50, the Secretary enjoys widely defined powers enabling the giving of directions to enforce any of the various duties.[65]

Ultimately, when the content of a plan has finally been determined, including any modification, there are further procedural duties for the authority to comply with. In the first place, the authority is obliged to take those steps which, in its opinion, will give the plan (or modification) adequate publicity in its area. Additionally, the authority will send a copy of the plan or any modification to the Secretary of State.[66]

At the time of writing, proposals exist which would change the framework for waste planning if the projected Environment Protection Agency (EPA) is introduced.[67] A "National Statement of Waste Policies and Priorities" would be concluded across the country, taking account of a need for strategic guidance in respect of waste disposal planning and policy and produced by the Secretary of State from data generated by the new EPA. EPA would take account of advice from the local planning authorities. Regional planning guidance from the Secretary of State would be complementary to the National Statement. In turn, any local planning authority compiling a structure or unitary plan would be obliged to have regard to the National Statement and regional guidance. Finally, compilation of any waste local plan would necessitate regard for any structure plan and the National Statement.

Recycling

Although the matter of recycling has been referred to previously, there are particular provisions in Part II of the Act that relate specifically to recycling. Nevertheless, it is important to see recycling as one of several methods of waste treatment and disposal. Increasingly, E.C. policy on waste management is built on a crude hierarchy of waste minimisation first, recycling second and landfill third.[67a] This is a crude hierarchy for a variety of reasons, including the fact that

63 *Ibid.* subs.(4).
64 *Ibid.* subs.(9).
65 *Ibid.* subs.(11).
66 *Ibid.* subs.(10).
67 Department of the Environment, "The Environment Agency: Waste Disposal Planning: A Consultation Paper" (August 1992).
67a Government policy is summarised in Department of the Environment Circular 11/94, paras. 9–11.

infrastructure requirements may render larger-scale minimisation impracticable, while recycling, although appropriate for some materials, may not be appropriate for others. Furthermore, recycling will almost inevitably depend on the availability of appropriate markets for the recycled material. Nevertheless, the present section of the chapter seeks to address three matters either in isolation or, more likely, by reference to those issues already dealt with that necessitate an appreciation of the legal regulation of recycling. The first matter relates to the recycling plans of waste collection authorities, the second matter relates to what are often referred to generically as "recycling credits", while the final topic relates to recycling powers generally. For present purposes, these topics are dealt with in reverse order.

Recycling powers

Statutory powers are conferred on waste disposal and collection authorities and the Act contains a simple division between the two.[68]

In the case of a waste disposal authority, that authority may exercise powers falling into four categories[69]

(a) In the first place, the authority is empowered to make arrangements with waste disposal contractors for them to recycle waste which the disposal authority is otherwise duty-bound to dispose of by virtue of section 51(1) of the Act.[70]
(b) The second of four discretionary powers available allows the authority to arrange with a waste disposal contractor to use waste for the production of heat or electricity, or both.
(c) The third power is to buy or otherwise acquire waste with a view to its being recycled.
(d) Finally, a waste disposal authority may use, sell or otherwise dispose of waste—again despite the disposal duty under section 51(1)—or anything produced from such waste.[71]

Where a collection authority is concerned, such an authority has discretionary power enabling it to buy or otherwise acquire waste with a view to recycling it, and to use or dispose of (by sale or otherwise to another person) waste belonging to it or anything produced from that waste. Bearing in mind the recycling objective of section 55, the latter power could permit a waste collection authority to give away waste (say) to a voluntary recycling organisation operating in the community.

[68] Environmental Protection Act, s.55.
[69] *Ibid.* subs.(2).
[70] See n.50, *supra.*
[71] Environmental Protection Act, s.55(2).

Waste collection authorities' recycling plans

A set of provisions not unlike those relating to waste regulation authorities' waste disposal plans[72] governs collection authorities' waste recycling plans.[73] Each such collection authority is obliged to undertake (in respect of household and commercial waste arising in its area) an investigation of arrangements appropriate for dealing with the waste by separating, baling or otherwise packaging it for the purpose of recycling. Having decided what arrangements are needed for this purpose, the collection authority is then obliged to prepare a statement, referred to as "the plan", stipulating arrangements made or to be made by the authority and other persons for dealing with the waste by separation, baling or packaging.[74] In making any such plan (including any modification), the authority is obliged to have regard to the effect of any arrangements on local amenities, as well as any likely cost or saving.[75] Certain categories of information must be included in a plan, including the estimated costs or savings attributable to the methods of waste management included in that plan.[76] A draft copy of the plan is required to be sent to the Secretary of State. If it is found that any part of the plan does not comply with statutory requirements, directions may be given to ensure compliance by the authority.[77]

Following completion of the plan, or any modification, the collection authority is obliged to provide what, in its opinion, is "adequate publicity" for the plan in its area and forward copies to the waste regulation and waste disposal authorities for the area.[78] The plan, or any modification, must be made available for scrutiny by the public, free of charge.[79]

Waste recycling payments

The purpose of recycling credits

> "... is to make available to recyclers the savings in disposal and collection costs which result from recycling housing waste. Since there is no direct charge for collecting or disposing of household waste (with minor exceptions), there has been no proper financial incentive to avoid collection or disposal costs by recycling instead".[80]

Section 52 of the Act obliges waste disposal and waste collection authorities to pay recycling credits to each other. The credit flow from a waste disposal to a waste collection authority occurs where the latter authority recycles waste which

[72] *Ibid.* s.50: see nn.57 *et seq., supra.*
[73] *Ibid.* s.49.
[74] *Ibid.* subs.(1).
[75] *Ibid.* subs.(2).
[76] *Ibid.* subs.(3).
[77] *Ibid.* subs.(4).
[78] *Ibid.* subs.(5).
[79] *Ibid.* subs.(6).
[80] Circular 4/92 (Welsh Office 10/92), para. 10.

otherwise would have entered the household waste stream.[81] Credits may flow in the opposite direction if waste does not fall to be collected by virtue of a discharge of its functions by the waste disposal authority.[82] If, as in Wales, the collection and disposal function is vested in one authority, credits do not apply. Credits are payable to third parties, either by a disposal or a collection authority.[83]

There is no statutory definition of "recycling", although reference is made in the provisions governing the waste recycling plans of waste collection authorities[84] to acts preparatory to recycling, through the separation, baling or packaging of waste. Waste Management Paper No. 28[85] does deal with the nature of recycling by referring to the collection and separation of materials from waste and their subsequent processing to produce marketable products.

The calculation of the value of a waste disposal credit depends on a formula prescribed by regulations.[86] The amount payable by a disposal authority is the full sum saved for every tonne of recycled waste. The method of calculation for a disposal credit is based on the most expensive disposal route for the waste of each collection authority.

General enforcement of waste management

Part II of the Act contains a variety of provisions concentrating on enforcement of activities involving waste not already covered by the Act. The provisions fall into four categories, relating to:

(a) miscellaneous enforcement powers;
(b) central government supervision and enforcement;
(c) publicity; and
(d) civil liability for waste (apart from pure common law liabilities) which is deposited unlawfully.

Miscellaneous enforcement powers

Three areas of enforcement are comprehended here, involving:

(a) requirements for the removal of waste from land where such waste has been deposited unlawfully;
(b) prohibition on interference with waste sites and receptacles for waste; and
(c) the treatment of land which, through deposits of controlled waste causing the emission or discharge of noxious liquids, is causing or may cause pollution of the environment or harm to human health.[87]

[81] Environmental Protection Act, s.52(1).
[82] *Ibid.* subs.(2).
[83] *Ibid.* subss.(3) and (4).
[84] *Ibid.* s.49. *Cf.* n.74, *supra.*
[85] HMSO 1991.
[86] Environmental Protection (Waste Recycling Payments) Regulations 1992 (S.I. 1992 No. 462), as amended.
[87] Respectively, ss.59, 60 and 61, Environmental Protection Act.

The first of the provisions refers to the deposit of any controlled waste in or on any land in contravention of section 33(1).[88] In these circumstances, either the waste disposal or the collection authority may serve a notice on the occupier requiring action on one or both of the following: removal of the offending waste within a stipulated period of time or action to eliminate or reduce the consequences of the deposit of the waste.[89] Any such requirement gives rise to a right of appeal to the magistrates' court. The court must quash the requirement if satisfied that the occupier neither deposited nor knowingly caused nor knowingly permitted the deposit, or that there is a "material defect" in the notice. In any other case, the court is obliged to modify the authority's requirement or dismiss the appeal.[90] In relation to similar proceedings under the Control of Pollution Act 1974, it has been held that any "deposit" for present purposes need not necessarily be in any final resting place, such is the broader environmental purpose of the legislation.[91] Furthermore, merely because a notice carrying the "requirement" under section 59(1) is too vague does not mean that the notice contains a material defect where the court is dealing with an appeal. There is no reason why a notice here should specify the waste to which it applies. An enforcing authority cannot be expected to make an inventory of the waste required to be removed. A combination of photographic evidence supported by oral evidence may be sufficient in practice.[92] Any appeal has the effect of suspending a requirement.[93] A failure, without reasonable excuse, to comply with a requirement is a summary offence, with the additional possibility of imposition of a continuing fine for non-compliance if the failure continues after conviction.[94] Failure to fulfil a requirement empowers the enforcing authority to act in default and to recover any expenses reasonably incurred from the person on whom the requirement was imposed.[95] However, additional default powers are available to an enforcing authority where it appears that waste has been deposited in or on any land contrary to section 33(1). These powers are available where it appears that, in order to remove or prevent pollution of land, water or air or harm to human health, the waste should be removed forthwith, or other measures taken to eliminate or reduce the adverse consequences, or both; or there is no occupier of the land; or the occupier neither made nor knowingly permitted the deposit. If any of these situations applies, the authority is able to remove the waste or is able to take "other steps" to eliminate or reduce the consequences of the deposit. A further option is for the authority to remove the waste and to take steps to eliminate or reduce the consequences.[96] The authority is able to recover its costs from an occupier who is unable to show that they were unnecessarily

[88] See nn.46 *et seq.*, *supra.*
[89] Environmental Protection Act, s.59(1). Not in force at the time of writing.
[90] *Ibid.* subss.(2) and (3). As to appeal requirements, see s.73(1)–(5).
[91] *R. v. Berkshire County Council, ex p. Scott* [1993] Env. L.R. 417.
[92] *Ibid. per* Watkins L.J. at 425.
[93] Environmental Protection Act, s.59(4).
[94] *Ibid.* subs.(5).
[95] *Ibid.* subs.(6).
[96] *Ibid.* subs.(7).

incurred, or any other person. However, liability for costs is heavily qualified, to the extent that there are considerable disincentives to recovery for an enforcing authority.[97]

The second provision concerns interference with waste sites and receptacles for waste. The Act proscribes three categories of conduct unless there is a consent or other right authorising that conduct. It is unlawful, in the first place, for a person to sort over or disturb anything deposited at a place provided for the deposit of waste. In the second place, it is unlawful to sort over to disturb anything deposited in a receptacle for waste (public or private) and provided by any one of a variety of bodies, including waste collection authorities. Finally, it is unlawful to sort over or disturb the contents of any receptacle for waste on the highway provided for the purpose of household, commercial or industrial waste.[98] Contravention of any one of these prohibitions is a summary criminal offence.[99] A range of consents and "rights" is set out in the Act so that, for example, the waste collection authority may consent to the sorting through of waste receptacles provided on a site by the waste collection authority.[1]

The third provision covers any land not subject to a waste management licence. In the case of any such land in its area, a waste regulation authority is under a duty to inspect it from time to time to detect any conditions causing pollution of the environment or harm to human health.[2] The crucial evidence for the purpose of the powers in this section[3] is that there be a concentration or accumulation in, and emission or discharge from, land of noxious liquids or gases caused by deposits of controlled waste in the land.[4] Clearly contemplated, therefore, is the microbiological breakdown of waste which generates explosive methane. Although closed landfills are not specifically identified, nevertheless the noxious liquids that may leach and the noxious gases that may be emitted from such sites are clearly contemplated by the section. For enforcement purposes, the waste regulation authority is given wide-ranging powers to enter and inspect land. However, entry and inspection may be undertaken only in any one of three defined situations. In the first situation, there must be controlled waste deposited in or on subject land by virtue of a waste management licence or a waste disposal licence granted under the Control of Pollution Act. The second situation is one in which the authority has reason to believe that controlled waste has been deposited in the land at any time. Finally, there must be, or the authority must have reason to believe that there are, concentrations of noxious gases or noxious liquids. Each of these options will assume different levels of evidence in the possession of the authority.[5] The section also contemplates an ongoing responsibility of the authority to enter and inspect land whose condition triggers

[97] *Ibid.* subs.(8). Recovery from an occupier is limited to a case falling within subs.(7)(a).
[98] *Ibid.* s.60(1).
[99] *Ibid.* subs.(3).
[1] *Ibid.* subs.(2).
[2] *Ibid.* s.61(1). *Cf.* s.29.
[3] Not in force at the time of writing.
[4] Environmental Protection Act, s.61(2).
[5] *Ibid.* subs.(3).

its powers.[6] If the condition of the land is such that it appears to the authority that pollution of water is likely to be caused, the National Rivers Authority must be consulted in connection with any "reasonable" works (and any other measures) on the land or "adjacent" land by the authority for the purpose of avoiding such pollution.[7] The period for which an authority has responsibility for land under the present provisions runs from the time when the condition of the land first appeared to the authority until that authority is satisfied that no pollution of the environment or harm to human health will be caused by the land's condition.[8] The works referred to previously may be undertaken not only for the purpose of avoiding pollution but also for the purpose of avoiding "harm", a term very widely defined in section 29 of the Act.[9] The authority's duty to carry out these works on an inspection of land revealing the likelihood of pollution to the environment or harm to human health allows a recovery of the costs (except those incurred unreasonably) against the land's owner.[10] The generic reference here to the owner of "the land" probably refers to the site or any adjacent land on which works are undertaken. Cost recovery, however, is not available in respect of land in respect of which the surrender of a waste management licence has been accepted.[11] Any decision about cost recovery obliges the authority to have regard to any hardship to the owner of the land in question.[12]

Civil liability

Reference was made at the outset of this chapter to the question of common law liability.[13] Without prejudice to proceedings to establish any such liability, section 73(6) of the Act provides some ground rules that may prove to be useful for any individual or enforcing authority seeking to establish civil liability in circumstances where damage has been caused by the unlawful deposition of waste. Potentially this provision[14] has great utility in attracting civil liability for almost every unlawful deposition of waste extending to the unlawful keeping, treatment and disposal of waste, be it controlled or "uncontrolled" waste. More specifically, the Act stipulates that damage must be caused by waste deposited on or in land so that any person making the deposit (or knowingly causing or knowingly permitting the deposit) commits an offence against section 33(1) or 63(2). In order to establish civil liability, it is not necessary to point to a specific conviction. However, a defendant would be permitted to rely on certain defences. In the first place, the defendant may be able to establish that the damage was due wholly to the fault of the person who suffered it, or that the damage was

[6] *Ibid.* subs.(4).
[7] *Ibid.* subss.(5), (7).
[8] *Ibid.* subs.(6).
[9] *Ibid.* subs.(7).
[10] *Ibid.* subs.(8).
[11] *Ibid.* subs.(9).
[12] *Ibid.* subs.(10).
[13] See nn.1–15, *supra.*
[14] Environmental Protection Act, s.73(6); not in force at the time of writing but *cf.* the broadly similar provision in s.88 of the Control of Pollution Act 1974.

suffered by a person who voluntarily accepted the risk of the damage being caused. Furthermore, a defence may be built around any of the three defences found in section 33(7), namely that all reasonable precautions were taken and all due diligence exercised, that action was taken under instructions from an employer, and that contravention was referable to an emergency in order to avoid danger to the public.[15] Damage by waste includes the death of, or injury to, any person, including any disease and "any" impairment of physical or mental condition.[16] An action may be successful subject to a reduction of damages by virtue of the plaintiff's contributory negligence.[17] The provision of this statutory opportunity to establish civil liability for unlawful deposition may prove most useful to any enforcing authority seeking to recover its expenses in respect of clean-up.

Central government prescription, supervision and enforcement

Powers of supervision and enforcement by the Secretary of State are to be found throughout Part II of the Act. Two notable examples relate to directions to a waste regulation authority as to the terms and conditions on which a waste management licence may be granted,[18] and to guidance which may be given to a waste regulation authority in respect of its performance of functions under section 61 of the Act relating to land posing an adverse environmental threat through the leaching of noxious liquids or the emission of noxious gases.[19]

The present category of supervisory and enforcement powers relates to:

(a) the Secretary of State's power to require controlled waste to be accepted, treated, disposed of or delivered[20];
(b) the power of the Secretary of State to make regulations to extend Part II controls to waste from mines, quarries and agriculture[21]; and
(c) the Secretary of State's power to appoint inspectors, oversee their functions and powers, direct the acquisition of information and exercise default powers.

The power to require the acceptance, treatment, disposal or delivery of controlled waste is directed at the holder for the time being of any such waste. Any notice served for the purpose of conveying the requirements of the Secretary of State may, and of necessity will, stipulate delivery, etc., at specified places on specified terms.[22] Also by notice in writing, the Secretary of State may direct any person who is keeping controlled waste on land to deliver that waste to a specified person, again on specified terms, with a view to its being treated or disposed of by

[15] Environmental Protection Act, s.73(7).
[16] *Ibid.* subs.(8).
[17] *Ibid.* subss.(8), (9).
[18] *Ibid.* s.35(7).
[19] *Ibid.* s.61(11).
[20] *Ibid.* s.57.
[21] *Ibid.* s.63.
[22] *Ibid.*s.57(1). Not in force at the time of writing.

that other person.[23] Any direction here may require the person directed to deliver the waste to pay the person specified his reasonable costs of treating or disposing of the waste in question.[24] Failure to comply with a direction without reasonable excuse is a summary offence.[25]

The Secretary of State retains a residual power to make regulations for the purpose of bringing waste from any mine or quarry or from agricultural premises within the regulatory framework of Part II of the Act.[26] At the time of writing, it is unclear whether these categories of waste fall within the framework directive on waste (Directive 91/156) unconditionally. It seems likely, again at the time of writing, that the directive relates to "non-natural" farm and agricultural waste and, in the case of mines and quarries, non-mineral waste.

The final category of provisions dealing with central government direction of waste management under Part II relates to matters of supervision and enforcement. In the first place, the Secretary of State is obliged to keep under review the discharge by the waste regulation authorities of their functions. Inspectors may be appointed by the Secretary of State to assist in the discharge of his functions under Part II of the Act. A similar power is conferred on any waste regulation authority.[27] Inspectors have wide-ranging powers of entry, as well as powers to deal with a variety of circumstances encountered following entry to premises. Such powers are exercisable in relation to, *inter alia*, land in or on which controlled waste is being or has been deposited, treated or disposed of, and land in or on which controlled waste is (on reasonable grounds) believed to be being, or to have been deposited, treated, kept or disposed of, as well as land which is or is (on reasonable grounds) believed to be affected by the deposit, treatment, keeping or disposal of controlled waste on *other* land. The powers of entry available for inspectors are cumulative when set against the other powers of entry provided for more generally by other parts of the Act, under section 61, for example. Furthermore, important anticipatory powers are provided, so that an inspector may, for example, enter premises at any time if he forms the opinion that there is a significant risk of serious pollution of the environment or serious harm to human health. A range of summary offences is provided by the Act where, for example, a person fails, without reasonable excuse, to comply with any requirement authorised under the present provisions dealing with entry to premises.[28] An inspector is not liable in any civil or criminal proceedings for anything done in what is described as the "purported" performance of his functions if the court is satisfied that the act was done in good faith and that there were reasonable grounds for doing it.[29] Given the width of inspectors' powers of entry, the likelihood of any "informality" of the sort anticipated by this provision is remote. Although there are circumstances in which an inspector may compel

[23] *Ibid.* subs.(2).
[24] *Ibid.* subs.(4). *Cf.* the general scope of any direction in subs.(3).
[25] *Ibid.* subs.(5).
[26] *Ibid.* s.63(1).
[27] *Ibid.* s.68.
[28] *Ibid.* s.69.
[29] *Ibid.* s.68(4). Also applicable to the powers exercisable under s.70, n.22, *supra.*

production of documents, the Act does exempt documents protected by legal professional privilege, as well as documents that, in law, could be withheld in the face of an order for discovery through an action in the High Court.[30] Additional powers to seize any article or substance are conferred on an inspector where the item, found on premises for which there is authority to enter, is considered (in the circumstances) to be a cause of imminent danger of serious pollution of the environment or serious harm to human health. Any such article or substance may be seized and rendered harmless. A prerequisite to the use of this power is a requirement, if practicable, to take a sample. As soon as possible after seizure and the rendering harmless of the article or substance, the inspector is obliged to prepare a report detailing the circumstances of the seizure and other measures taken. Intentional obstruction of an inspector in the exercise of these powers is an offence triable summarily, or an indictment.[31] More generally, and for the purpose of discharging his functions under the Act in Part II, the Secretary of State may require a waste regulation authority to furnish information. In addition, both the Secretary of State and a waste regulation authority may require any person to furnish information for the purpose of discharging their respective functions under Part II of the Act. A failure, without reasonable excuse, to comply, or the provision of false or misleading information, is an offence triable summarily or on indictment.[32] The final supervisory power is the power of the Secretary of State to exercise default powers where he is satisfied that a waste regulation authority has failed to discharge its functions. Compliance will be sought by means of a default order. Failure by the authority to comply with the order leaves the Secretary of State with an option to enforce the order either through an application under Order 53 of the Rules of the Supreme Court for an order of mandamus or by requiring the function to be transferred to him.[33]

Publicity

Each waste regulation authority is obliged to maintain a public register containing particulars of a variety of matters, including:

(a) current or "recently current" licences granted by the authority;
(b) current or recently current applications for licences;
(c) applications for licence modification;
(d) notices effecting the revocation or suspension of licences;
(e) certificates of completion in relation to the surrender of licences;
(f) convictions of holders of licences granted by the authority in respect of any Part II offence;

[30] *Ibid.* s.69.
[31] *Ibid.* s.70.
[32] *Ibid.* s.71.
[33] *Ibid.* s.72.

(g) details of the use of any supervision powers under section 42[34] or the powers of intervention under section 61[35]; and
(h) appeals relating to decisions of the authority.

A licence is "recently" current for present purposes for a period of 12 months after it ceases to be in force, while an application is "recently" current if it relates to a licence which is current or recently current. It is not only the waste regulation authority which is obliged to maintain a public register: the waste collection authority is also required to maintain a public register, containing details of the treatment, keeping or disposal of controlled waste in its area.[36] If information to be included in any such public register is regarded by the Secretary of State as being contrary to the interests of national security by virtue of its inclusion, the Secretary of State may exercise powers under the Act to seek exclusion of the subject information.[37] Information may, on the other hand, be commercially confidential in relation to any individual or person and inclusion in a register prejudicial to an unreasonable degree to the commercial interests of that person or individual. In these circumstances, such information may not be included in a register without the consent of the individual or person concerned. Any determination of the status of information will be made initially by the authority, with an appeal to the Secretary of State.[38]

Each waste regulation authority is required to publish an annual report as a means of achieving greater public accountability. Not only is the report referable to the discharge of functions under Part II of the Act, but also to the terms of any European Community "instrument", such as the waste framework directive.[39]

Contaminated Land

The framework for treatment of contaminated land issues

It is only when the nature and scale of contamination problems is appreciated that the variety of legal reaction can be seen in perspective. Above all, land contamination is likely to be a hugely complicated problem, focusing on a number of equally complex variables, relating to:

(a) historic uses of a site;
(b) the likely mixture of polluting substances present on the site;
(c) the web of ownership and control over the site; and
(d) the identity of rights and interests of those who, in terms of proximity, are adversely affected as neighbours or otherwise.

[34] See n.1, *supra*.
[35] See nn.92–3, *supra*.
[36] Environmental Protection Act, s.64.
[37] *Ibid.* s.65.
[38] *Ibid.* s.66. *Cf.* S.I. 1994 No. 1056, regs.10 and 11.
[39] *Ibid.* s.67.

Against this background, the subject looks at:

(a) soil quality standards against which contamination may be recognised;
(b) the treatment of that contamination;
(c) common law liabilities arising from the condition of the land,
(d) statutory regulation of contamination problems,
(e) liabilities and responsibilities for clean-up as provided for by statute; and
(f) the law's approach to possible redevelopment of the land.

Reference is made briefly to the contemporary debates on European proposals for liability in the present context.

Soil quality standards

Problems with contaminated land, often derelict sites, are capable of producing irreversible changes in soil quality leading, in turn, to adverse effects on land use capabilities. Those adverse effects will be seen most often in the gradual accumulation of persistent chemicals from a range of sources inevitably associated with long-standing industrial processes, in many cases. The wider-ranging impacts from such land focus primarily on the threat to ground waters through the leaching of persistent contamination chemicals, found in or on the land.

The identification and definition of contamination is not a straightforward task. Different approaches to the task are possible. In an evolving area of environmental definition and control, the tendency in the United Kingdom is to regard land as being contaminated when it is found to contain hazardous substances likely to affect its proposed development: a "fitness for purpose" approach. Other approaches could comprise the incidence of toxic concentrations exceeding natural background levels (as in the Netherlands), or the recognition that land is contaminated when it presents a threat to human health, the welfare of natural resources such as ground waters or normal soil functions (as in Denmark and Germany). The emphasis of the approach in the United Kingdom is towards remediation of contaminated sites for the purpose of redevelopment, driven essentially by the "best practicable environmental option", through which an optimum solution must be found at a reasonable cost. Accordingly, there is no necessary assumption that land should be fit for all possible future uses.[40]

Guidelines on contamination levels are given by the Interdepartmental Committee on the Redevelopment of Contaminated Land.[41]

[40] Circular 21/87 (Welsh Office 22/87), "Development of Contaminated Land" (now superceded by PPG23: Planning and Pollution Control: *infra*, n.74).

[41] Department of the Environment, "Guidance on the assessment and redevelopment of contaminated land" (ICRCL 59/83, 2nd ed.).

Trigger concentrations

Guidance on the assessment and remediation of contaminated sites is based on so-called "trigger concentrations" for certain contaminants in the context of intended uses of the subject site. Trigger values divide into a "threshold" value and an "action" value.[42] Where all concentrations are below threshold values, no remedial action is needed for the proposed land use. Where some or all concentrations lie between threshold and action values, there is a need to consider whether remedial action is required for the proposed use or whether any planned use should be reconsidered. Thirdly, where some or all concentrations are equal to or exceed the action value, action of some kind, ranging from minor remedial treatment to changing entirely the intended site use, becomes inevitable.

Values and guidance

The Interdepartmental Committee has set a variety of values and continues to provide guidance and advice to local authorities and the Department of the Environment, which takes a continuing interest in the appropriateness of any methods chosen by local authorities and developers. Detailed guidance is available, for example, in relation to the restoration and aftercare of any site formerly used for metalliferous mining when it is proposed to use that site for pasture and grazing. Responsibility for deciding this intended afteruse lies with the applicant, the landowner and the minerals planning authority. Attention will concentrate on the impact of trace elements of the metals on plants and animals. If natural vegetation has developed into a close-knit sward, toxicity problems for grazing animals are probably absent, according to the Interdepartmental Committee, except on low pH soils, where lead may be a problem. Furthermore, if sewage sludge is to be applied, there will be a need to observe the requirements of the Sludge (Use in Agriculture) Regulations.[43]

Factors that are considered in identifying values include adverse impacts on human health as a result of direct ingestion and inhalation of soil, the consumption of contaminated plants and dermal exposure. Although, strangely, environmental hazards have not generally featured in the setting of values, photo-toxicity and chemical attack on building materials, together with fire and explosion hazards, have been taken into account. There remains a lot of progress to be made in setting action values for many contaminants. There are, at the time of writing, no values relating to the impact of contaminants on ground waters beyond the controls found in the E.C. Directive on ground waters, necessitating attention to ground waters vulnerable to dangerous substances.[44]

The trigger values referred to have no statutory force or administrative recognition in law. Nevertheless, it seems likely, at the time of writing, that the

[42] *Ibid.*
[43] S.I. 1989 No. 1263.
[44] Directive 80/68. *Cf.* Circular 4/82 (Welsh Office 2/82).

number of contaminants covered by trigger values will be extended. It is likely that guidance will concentrate on inorganic chemicals and compounds such as phosphorus, organic chemicals and compounds such as chlorinated solvents and pesticides, and organic and aromatic hydrocarbons such as petrol, toluene, diesel and benzene.

The identification of contamination

Brief reference has been made to the basis on which a decision may be made about whether a site is a contaminated site. Inextricably linked to such a question is the question of how contamination is identified in the first place. The starting point is probably site history.[45] Certain uses are likely to have been contaminative uses: sewage works and farms[46] and chemical works, for example.

The environmental impact of contamination

The hazards and environmental impacts of a contaminated site are various, affecting those who may work on the site, any occupiers or users of the land and buildings, the buildings themselves and water services.[47] Potentially, all environmental media may be adversely affected, whether through leaching to ground waters, through the emission of methane gas or through the inability to exploit the soil on site, to give three prominent examples. The fact of land contamination is a legally relevant "material" consideration

> "... to be taken into account at various stages of the planning process including the preparation of development plans and the determination of planning applications. The best way of minimising any associated risks is to ensure that areas of potentially contaminated sites are identified at the earliest stage of planning. The necessary investigations can then be carried out before the particular form of development is decided. This should then enable cost-effect solutions to be devised, so reducing the need for urgent and expensive emergency action."[48]

Registration of contaminative uses

The identification of sites subject to contaminative uses and their attendant environmental impact can be achieved through a registration of those sites. This is explicitly recognised by the Environmental Protection Act, under which the Secretary of State is empowered to specify such uses and the registration processes through regulations.[49] At the time of writing, it is unlikely that registration of contaminative uses will be pursued, for a variety of reasons. Among those reasons

[45] Circular 21/87, App. A. (now superceded: *supra*, n.40).
[46] Department of the Environment, ICRCL 23/79.
[47] Circular 21/87, para. 4 (now superceded).
[48] *Ibid.* para. 5 (now superceded).
[49] Environmental Protection Act, s.143.

is the apparent disadvantage of permanent registration despite completion of clean-up on the land, the disadvantage of basing registration on a limited category of contaminating activities eliminating many sites that are contaminated, and (finally) the apparent ambivalence of the proposed system to any proactive treatment of registered sites. The market's own adjustment of site values where contaminative uses have occurred may render increasingly attractive the expenditure necessary for remediation in anticipation of redevelopment.

The treatment of contamination

The expenditure necessary for remediation may fall on the private sector, or (as will be seen below in a review of the statutory powers available) on the public sector. For the private sector, in particular, the expense of remediation will represent a crucial variable in the redevelopment decision-making process, taking into account (no doubt) any grant-aid that may be available.[50] Other variables of importance will relate to the logistics of remediation, particularly in terms of determining whether work can be carried out *in situ* on the land or whether such work would necessitate activity off the site. The former possibility may in turn suggest greater costs in some cases, particularly if other redevelopment work is unable to proceed simultaneously.

Methods of treatment

The range of treatments available for the purpose of remediation is potentially enormous, depending on the conditions to be dealt with. Aerobic treatment involving microbiological degradation of mainly organic substances may be achieved *in situ* while, on the other hand, soil may have to be stripped from land and transported away for washing. Such soil may also require treatment with chemicals on or off site. The treatment of water which is contaminated probably necessitates attention on site, usually by air stripping, in which air is blown through the contaminated liquid.

Common law liabilities

Reference was made at the beginning of the present chapter to common law liabilities. In the present context, just a few words are added in order to stress the preventative framework within which a contaminated site may be managed—particularly for the purpose of remediation—in order to avoid (as far as possible) the liabilities that may be thrown up by the common law. At the time of writing, the issue of how liabilities should be defined in law for historic and other pollution is the subject of debate, particularly at E.C. level, as explained below. As presently constituted, following the decision in *Cambridge Water Co. v. Eastern Counties Weather*,[51] the law of strict liability appears to require that, in the case of

[50] Circular 21/87, paras. 22–27, listing grant-aid at the date of the Circular (August 17, 1987) (now superceded).

[51] See n.12, *supra*.

an unnatural user of land, any escape of what may be described generically as a "hazardous" substance from land must involve harm or injury of the type complained of being foreseeable at a time when the substance or material is still within the defendant's control. Evaluation of historic pollution is likely to be complex from the point of view of a purchaser or would-be purchaser of the site in question. The key concern may be the timeliness of any remedial intervention, if only to avoid a plaintiff's future argument, should litigation be joined, that the prerequisites for strict liability had been established. Much, therefore, depends on appropriate remediation for the purpose of retrieving (say) toxic chemicals that have leached, or continue to leach, into ground waters. The risk of such tactics from a perhaps negative standpoint is that any possible immunity from strict legal liability may be lost if it appears that control of the substance or material appears still to reside with the defendant for the purpose of the argument based on foreseeability of the harm or loss complained of. Also to be borne in mind for present purposes is the possible combination of liabilities in negligence and nuisance by reference to the standards of skill and care deployed in the process of remediation. Failure to comply with what the court considers to be objectively reasonable measures for these purposes could attract damages, as well as the possibility of an injunction, at least where the plaintiff neighbour can establish something other than economic loss.

Statutory regulation

Reference to statutory regulation requires specification of particular statutory powers that are suited to peculiar problems arising from sites which are found to be contaminated. The range of regulatory powers extends over the Environmental Protection Act, the Town and Country Planning Act 1990, the Public Health Act 1936 and the Water Resources Act 1991.

Environmental Protection Act powers

Two sets of powers are relevant: those dealing with statutory nuisances under Part III of the Act[52] and those dealing with the situation relating to land (which may be a closed landfill, for example) where a waste regulation authority becomes aware of conditions in which accumulations of noxious liquids and gases and resulting emissions may cause pollution of the environment or harm to human health.[53] The statutory nuisance provisions will tend in practice to be limited to rather minor difficulties thrown up by contaminated land. Despite the potential of the powers, particularly in the hands of the local authority, the scale of many land contamination problems would tend to suggest only a piecemeal role for statutory nuisance law. The exercise of enforcement powers, for example, may raise in the mind of the local authority the question of whether such a piecemeal approach is appropriate where the scale of the problem is such that only a large investment in remediation will begin to tackle the difficulties.

[52] See Chap. 10, "Statutory Nuisance", for a commentary on the law overall.
[53] See nn.92–93, *supra*.

Town and Country Planning Act powers

Where it appears to a local planning authority that the amenity of any part of its area (or an adjoining one) is adversely affected by the condition of land, a notice may be served on the owner and occupier requiring remedial measures to be taken in a period specified by the notice. A notice may be appealed to the magistrates' court on a variety of grounds, including authorisation of any relevant operations on the land by virtue of valid planning permission, and the fact that matters of amenity are not adversely affected by the condition of the land. Failure to comply with a notice within the stipulated period is a summary offence. The local authority may exercise default powers and recover any expenses reasonably incurred.[54]

The foregoing powers are quite widely drawn and apply to open or other land which is not necessarily derelict but is (say) an unkempt, badly managed scrap metal site. However, like the provisions governing statutory nuisances under Part III of the Environmental Protection Act, the present powers will tend to be used for the purpose of addressing relatively minor amenity problems. Even here, there may be discouragement, in so far as any notice served is vulnerable to an appeal to the magistrates' court.

Where the local authority chooses to resort to a notice under section 215, certain provisions of the Public Health Act 1936 will apply, if necessary.[55] Accordingly, the authority may be empowered to sell any materials removed from land, although the owner may reclaim the materials within a period of three days of removal.[56] Where an owner of land subject to a notice complains to the magistrates' court that the occupier has prevented the execution of works specified by the notice, the court may order execution of the works by that occupier.[57] Finally, where the local authority seeks to recover expenses against a person who, in law, is the "owner" of the subject land, and it appears that he is no more than an agent or trustees for some other person, the authority is able to recover from him only such total amount of money as he may have or have had in his hands as such an agent or trustee.[58]

Water Resources Act powers

Two provisions of particular significance here relate to powers available to the National Rivers Authority to take action for the purpose of undertaking anti-pollution works and operations and the status of certain codes of good agricultural practice for the purpose of protecting the aquatic environment.

The first of the provisions gives the National Rivers Authority responsibility for forming a judgment on the question of whether any poisonous, noxious or polluting matter, or any solid waste matter, is likely to enter, or to be or to have

[54] Town and Country Planning Act, ss.215–219.
[55] Town and Country Planning General Regulations 1976 (S.I. 1976 No. 1419), reg.17.
[56] Public Heath Act 1936, s.276.
[57] *Ibid.* s.289.
[58] *Ibid.* s.294.

been present in, any controlled waters. If any of these circumstances applies, NRA is empowered to carry out certain works and operations of a preventative nature, or of a remedial nature where any polluting matter has actually reached controlled waters.[59] Any such works or operations may not impede a discharge licence granted under the Act.[60] Any expenses reasonably incurred may be recovered by NRA from any person who caused or knowingly permitted the polluting matter to be in a position from which it was likely (in NRA's opinion) to enter controlled waters, or to be in the controlled waters, as the case may be.[61] There is no doubt that these powers are drawn in fairly wide terms, if only because they do not refer to any particular land over which they may be exercised. Furthermore, the powers are driven by an exercise of NRA's own expert judgment. However, the prospect of what may be considerable expenditure by NRA in undertaking preventative measures will always be seen as a disincentive, particularly when it is seen that recovery of reasonably incurred expenditure is from a person who "caused" or "knowingly permitted" the offending pollution or threatened pollution.

The second provision relates to the power of the Secretary of State for the Environment and the Minister of Agriculture to approve codes of good agricultural practice for the purpose of giving practical advice to those in agriculture about threats to controlled waters and for the purpose of promoting desirable practices for the avoidance or minimisation of water pollution.[62] A contravention of a code of practice does not of itself give rise to any criminal or civil liability. Nevertheless, the National Rivers Authority is obliged to take into account whether there has been or is likely to be any contravention in deciding when and how it should exercise two sets of powers under the Act. The first set of powers relates to the establishment and enforcement of a "relevant prohibition" under section 86, while the second set of powers relates to prohibition through breach of any Regulations made under section 92 concerning precautions against pollution. At the time of writing, work is progressing on a new code of practice for soil protection, which is likely to introduce numerical guidelines to protect soil against contamination by waste. The approach may, it is suggested, go beyond existing mandatory statutory limits relating to the application of sewage sludge to land under the Sludge (Use in Agriculture) Regulations 1989,[63] so introducing advisory limits for certain substances.[64]

The enforcing authorities

Beyond the range of powers set out above, it is clear that a number of statutory authorities have a responsibility for applying the requirements of the law. Apart from different local authority departments, other authorities involved are the

[59] Water Resources Act, s.161(1).
[60] *Ibid.* subs.(2).
[61] *Ibid.* subs.(3).
[62] *Ibid.* s.97(1).
[63] See n.34, *supra.*
[64] (1992) 215 ENDS Rep. 32.

National Rivers Authority, the waste regulation authorities, the Health and Safety Executive and Her Majesty's Inspectorate of Pollution.

Liabilities and responsibilities for clean-up

The range of common law liabilities referred to previously may depend on a wide range of variables. For example, a lessee of land may be liable for the consequences of land contamination on common law principles alone, apart from any terms of the lease under which he occupies the land for business purposes, for example. An issue of growing significance is the extent to which, if at all, a lending institution may be liable in respect of any adverse consequences arising from contaminated land. In the United States, admittedly for the purpose of the Comprehensive Environmental Response Compensation and Liability Act,[65] lender liability can arise through participation in the financial management of a facility to a degree indicating a capacity to influence a corporation's treatment of hazardous waste.[66]

Beyond the uncertainties of the common law, statutory regulation of liabilities and responsibilities appears to present a rather more definite picture. Nevertheless, identification of the person legally responsible for the costs of remedial works may still be beset by difficulties, for example, in defining for the purposes of the Water Resources Act 1991 whether a person has caused or knowingly permitted the polluting incident or threatened polluting incident.[67] If such a matter is seen as a formidable barrier to progress, the Act does stipulate that the content of the section—section 161—does not derogate from or prevent any right of action or other remedy in proceedings (at common law, for example) taken beyond the section.[68] Statutory aid for clean-up is also to be found in the Environmental Protection Act, examined earlier in this chapter.[69]

Specific and fairly detailed guidance on the identification of the person responsible is to be found in the legislation on statutory nuisance to be found in Part III of the Environmental Protection Act. While the Act commences with a definition of a "person responsible" for the purposes of Part III,[70] it goes on to indicate against whom an abatement notice should be served or against whom proceedings for a nuisance order should be commenced.[71]

Reference has been made previously to the potential difficulty of recovering any expenses reasonably incurred, under the Water Resources Act, for example, in respect of default powers exercised by the National Rivers Authority. In some instances, it may be appropriate for legislation to provide a facility for the imposition of a charge on premises as a means of recovery. Prior to the

[65] 42 U.S.C. ss.9601–9657 (1982 and West Supp 1988): so-called "Superfund" legislation.
[66] *U.S. v. Fleet Factors Corporation* 901 F. (2d.) 1550 (1990).
[67] See n.52, *supra.*
[68] Water Resources Act, s.161(5).
[69] Environmental Protection Act, s.73(6); see nn.5–8, *supra.*
[70] *Ibid.* s.79(7).
[71] *Ibid.* ss.80(2) and 82(4). *Cf.* Chap. 10, "Statutory Nuisance".

reformulation of the law on statutory nuisance, the law as it was set out in the Public Health Act provided a facility for the imposition of a charge on premises as a means of enabling a local authority to recover its expenses for acting in default following non-compliance with an abatement notice. This facility is now to be found in the amended Environmental Protection Act.[72]

The redevelopment of contaminated land

Planning policy may be prescriptive in seeking to set priorities and preferences for redevelopment. Such an approach will, in turn, feed into the development control process.[73] Guidance is available to local authorities and developers on the identification, assessment and development of contaminated land.[74] Reference to particular parts of Circular 21/87 (now superceded by PPG23 on Planning and Pollution Control) has been made already.[75] Reference has also been made to the advisory functions of the Interdepartmental Committee on the Redevelopment of Contaminated Land.[76] Two British Standards are also relevant for present purposes, along with an accompanying guidance from the British Standards Institution. BS5930 contains a code of practice on site investigations and is accompanied by guidance—referred to as DD175—for the assesment of contaminated land. BS1377 contains the standard methods for the testing of soils for civil enginering purposes.

Building control

Under the Building Regulations 1991, Approved Document "C" deals with site preparation and resistance to moisture and contains an important section on contaminants.[77] It is stressed that, in addition to solid and liquid contaminants arising out of a previous use, problems can arise due to gases. The Approved Document deals with the identification of contaminants, sites likely to contain contaminants and action to deal with such a problem, as well as alternative approaches. Gaseous contaminants receive considerable attention, stressing the significance for present purposes of radon and landfill gases, methane in particular.

The development of strict liability

At the time of writing, both the European Community and the Council of Europe have published, respectively, a Green Paper consultation document entitled "Remedying Environmental Damage[78] and a Convention on Civil

[72] Environmental Protection Act, ss.81A and 81B.
[73] Town and Country Planning Act 1990, s.54A.
[74] PPG23: Planning and Pollution Control (HMSO, 1994).
[75] See nn.31, 36, 38, 39 and 42, *supra*.
[76] See nn.32, 33 and 37, *supra*.
[77] S.I. 1991 No. 1620. *Cf.* Circular 13/92 (Welsh Office 29/92) and Chap. 11, "Building Control", nn.37–39, *infra*.
[78] COM(93)47 final, Brussels (1993).

Liability.[79] Both documents will be influential in developing perceptions of strict liability for waste and the role of complementary compensation schemes where liability may not be "fixed" for various reasons.

Litter, Rubbish and Refuse

The broad context of litter, rubbish and refuse

This part of the chapter relates to a disparate collection of statutory provisions whose concern is the regulation and control of litter, rubbish and refuse, primarily by the local authorities responsible under the various items of legislation. A major element in statutory control is the collection of provisions to be found in Part IV of the Environmental Protection Act, adding to an existing body of legislative control. However, Part IV and that existing body of legislation referred to below has to be seen against the background of Part II of the Act referred to earlier in the present chapter. Of particular significance is the set of provisions in Part II dealing with waste collection.[80] Equally significant are the facilities for enforcement to be found in Part II and, in particular, the offences of unlawful deposition of waste.[81] At the outset, though, a variety of miscellaneous provisions are dealt with.

Miscellaneous provisions

Reference has been made already to the Town and Country Planning Act powers[82] in relation to contaminated land. In that context, it was suggested that these powers would tend to be deployed by a planning authority for the purpose of dealing with relatively minor amenity problems. Indeed, the problem of a site which, by virtue of the presence of litter or refuse, is prejudicial to the amenity of an area is a far more likely purpose for which these powers may be used.

Closely allied in some respects to these Town and Country Planning Act powers are powers exercisable by a district or county council under the Public Health Act 1961.[83] If it appears to a local authority that there is on any land in the open air any rubbish[84] which is seriously detrimental to the amenities of the neighbourhood, that authority may take such steps as are considered necessary for the removal of that rubbish. Not less than 28 days prior to any such action, the authority is obliged to serve on the owner and occupier of the land a notice indicating the action proposed. Any person on whom the notice is served and any person with an interest in the land may, within 28 days of the notice being served, serve a counter-notice on the authority, stating that he will undertake the action

[79] Council of Europe, Strasbourg (1993).

[80] See nn.13–20, 23, 24, 26–34, *supra*.

[81] Environmental Protection Act, ss.33 and 63(2).

[82] Town and Country Planning Act 1990, ss.215–219: see n.45, *supra*.

[83] Public Health Act, s.34.

[84] Defined by subs.(5) to mean rubble, waste paper, crockery and metal and any other kind of refuse (including organic matter), but not waste accumulated for any business or deposited under a waste management licence.

in question, or appeal to the magistrates' court on the ground that the local authority was not justified in concluding that action should be taken or that the action proposed is unreasonable. In the case of a counter-notice, the authority should take no further action unless the person serving the counter-notice either fails within what the authority considers to be a reasonable period of time to begin to take the action referred to in the notice or, having commenced action to deal with the condition of the land, fails to make what the authority would regard as reasonable progress to complete any works. If an appeal is pursued, the local authority may take no further action until final determination of the appeal or any withdrawal of that appeal. In hearing the appeal, the magistrates' court may direct that no further action be taken by the local authority, or that prescribed action should be taken by the authority, or that the appeal should be dismissed.[85]

Similar powers are to be found in the Building Act 1984 in relation to rubbish or other material resulting from, or exposed by, the demolition or collapse of a building or structure lying on the site or on any adjoining land so that the site or land is in such a condition as to be seriously detrimental to the amenities of the neighbourhood. In these circumstances, the local authority is empowered, by notice, to require the owner of the site or land to act to remove the rubbish or material as necessary, in the interests of amenity. In the event of a failure to comply, the local authority may act in default. However, prior to any default action that may occur, the local authority is required to serve a notice on the owner or occupier indicating what the authority proposes to do. The recipient may serve a counter-notice indicating that he intends to act, or he may appeal to the magistrates' court on the ground that the authority's action is not justified. As with section 34 of the Public Health Act 1961, the authority must allow time for action.[86] "Rubbish" for this purpose could include chattels from a building.[87]

The unauthorised dumping on any land in the open air or otherwise forming part of the highway of a motor vehicle or parts dismantled from it on the land is an offence. This offence also extends to the abandonment of any other thing brought to the land for the purpose of abandoning it there. The burden of proof is effectively placed on the person who leaves any thing on land in such circumstances or for such a period as to indicate an intention to abandon: it is up to that person to show that that was not the intention.[88] Where a person is convicted here in respect of abandonment of a motor vehicle, the court, on an application by the authority concerned, may (apart from any other order against the defendant) order payment to that authority of any sum in respect of the vehicle, usually the cost of recovery.[89] Closely related is the power of a highway authority to require any person who has deposited anything constituting a nuisance on a highway to remove that thing, by virtue of a notice duly served. An order for removal and disposal may be made by the magistrates' court on

[85] Public Health Act, s.34.
[86] Building Act 1984, s.79.
[87] *McVittie v. Bolton Corporation* [1945] 1 K.B. 281. Notice in particular the reference in s.79 to "rubbish or other material".
[88] Refuse Disposal (Amenity) Act 1978. s.2.
[89] *Ibid.* s.5(3).

application for that purpose by the authority where the notice has not been complied with. The court may order removal and disposal by the authority, although emergency action may be taken without resort to the court where the object deposited is considered to be a danger to highway users. Disposal may be permitted by an order of the magistrates' court. The authority is able to recover expenses for action taken either against the person responsible for the deposit or any person who claims entitlement to the object deposited.[90]

The foregoing powers under the Public Health Act, the Town and Country Planning Act and the Building Act are concerned essentially with problems arising in relation to privately owned land: hence the reference to action against an owner or occupier. The emphasis in the Refuse Disposal (Amenity) Act and the Highways Act is somewhat wider, extending to include the highway or land forming part of the highway. These powers contrast, in turn, with the powers to be found in the Environmental Protection Act[91] where action may be taken to remove, or eliminate or reduce the impact of controlled waste deposited on land. The waste disposal or waste collection authority is empowered here to pursue remedial action against an occupier of the land in question. However, the Refuse Disposal (Amenity) Act does not permit a local authority to remove anything other than a motor vehicle if it appears that the object or objects in question is or are situated on land appearing to be "occupied", unless that person is first notified and fails to object to the proposed removal.[92]

Abandoned vehicles

The Refuse Disposal (Amenity) Act is concerned primarily with a regulatory framework for the removal of abandoned vehicles and their disposal. If it appears to a local authority (principally a district or London borough council) that a motor vehicle in their area is abandoned without lawful authority on "... any land in the open air or on any other land forming part of a highway", it is the duty of that authority to remove that vehicle.[93] The Act also deals with the disposal of vehicles and the recovery of expenses from their owners.[94] The provisions seek to balance the powers of removal and disposal with the integrity of the owners' rights of ownership. This is achieved essentially through a requirement that any powers are exercised only as reasonably necessary for the safe custody of any vehicle removed, except where the local authority is of the view that the condition of a vehicle is such that it ought to be destroyed and have affixed a notice for a prescribed period indicating that intention.

If the duty to remove does not apply, the local authority may still remove or

[90] Highways Act 1980, s.149. *Cf.* s.151, relating to the powers available to a highway authority where refuse falls from land on to the highway.

[91] Environmental Protection Act, s.59: see n.80, *supra.*

[92] Refuse Disposal (Amenity) Act, s.6(1), (2). *Cf.* ss.2 and 5(3): see nn.79 and 80, *supra.*

[93] *Ibid.* s.3. Contrast the Road Traffic Regulation Act 1984, ss.99–103, dealing with vehicles illegally, obstructively or dangerously parked.

[94] *Ibid.* ss.4 and 5.

arrange for the removal of a vehicle (to any place off or away from a road) where it has broken down or been left so that it appears to have been abandoned without lawful authority.[95] Charges for the removal, storage and disposal vehicles are prescribed by the Removal, Storage and Disposal of Vehicles (Prescribed Sums and Charges etc.) Regulations 1989.[96] A detailed prescription of requirements is also provided for in connection with the disposal of abandoned vehicles which are in their custody following the exercise of the "section 3 duty", described above. In no case may an authority dispose of a vehicle before the expiry of its current licence. If there is no licence, or it has expired, the vehicle may then be disposed of immediately in the case of a vehicle to which a notice has been affixed indicating an intention to dispose for destruction, and otherwise if, after compliance with prescribed steps, there is no trace of or response from the owner. The owner may claim the vehicle at any time prior to disposal but must pay a prescribed charge.[97]

Statutory nuisance

It is always the case that litter, rubbish and refuse may constitute a statutory nuisance, in which case the powers under Part III of the Environmental Protection may be deployed, either by a local authority or by an individual who is aggrieved.[98] Particular categories of statutory nuisance relevant for present purposes relate to premises which are in such a state as to be prejudicial to health or a nuisance and to any accumulation or deposit which is prejudicial to health or a nuisance.[99]

Litter

The statutory framework here is governed by the Litter Act 1983 and Part IV of the Environmental Protection Act 1990. The principal litter authorities undertaking the enforcement responsibilities are the county councils, district councils and London borough councils.[1] Parish and community councils are also regarded as litter authorities, but only for the purposes of the Litter Act 1983.

Litter Act 1983

The principal concern of this legislation is to provide for litterbins[2] and for litter strategies at county council level.[3] A litter authority may provide and maintain

[95] Removal and Disposal of Vehicles Regulations 1986 (S.I. 1986 No. 183), reg.5, exercisable subject to the Road Traffic Regulation Act 1984, ss.99 and 100.
[96] S.I. 1989 No. 744, as amended.
[97] Refuse Disposal (Amenity) Act, ss.4 and 5. *Cf.* the Removal and Disposal of Vehicles Regulations 1986 (S.I. 1986 No. 183), Pt. III.
[98] See Chap. 10, "Statutory Nuisance".
[99] Environmental Protection Act, s.79(1)(a) and (e).
[1] *Ibid.* s.86(2).
[2] Litter Act 1983, ss.5 and 6.
[3] *Ibid.* s.4: not in force at the time of writing.

receptacles for refuse or litter in any street or public place. What is a discretion is accompanied by a duty to arrange for the regular emptying and cleansing of any such litter bins provided not only by virtue of these powers but also by virtue of the powers found in section 185 of the Highways Act 1980. Regular emptying here has to be sufficiently frequent to ensure that no litter bin or its contents becomes a nuisance or gives reasonable ground for complaint.

Environmental Protection Act, Pt. IV

Part IV of the Act provides for the following matters:

(a) the offence of leaving litter[4];
(b) areas known as litter control areas[5];
(c) duties associated with freedom of land from litter[6];
(d) street litter[7]; (all of which ((a) to (e) may be extended to animal droppings: (S.I. 1991 No. 961)); and
(e) abandoned shopping trolleys.[8]

The offence of leaving litter The offence of leaving litter applies to any public open space, referred to by the Act as any place in the open air to which the public are entitled or permitted to have access without payment, including any covered place open to the air on at least one side and available for public use. The offence also applies to other places which are not public open spaces but comprise any place on land of a principal litter authority, any relevant highway maintainable at public expense and any place on relevant land of a designated educational institution, among others.[9]

The Act sets down a complex set of circumstances in which an offence is committed. The defendant's act should be shown to cause, or contribute to, or tend to lead to, the defacement of any place by litter. The act of the defendant must also be such as to show that he threw down, dropped or otherwise deposited in, into or from any place and left "anything whatsoever". However, if the depositing or leaving of litter is authorised by law or has the consent of the owner, occupier or other person or authority having control of the place in or into which the litter was deposited, no offence is committed.[10]

A fixed penalty scheme may be adopted by a litter authority where an authorised officer of that authority has reason to believe that the offence of leaving litter has been committed. The person whom the officer believes to have committed the offence may be given a notice in prescribed form[11] offering an

[4] Environmental Protection Act, ss.87 and 88.
[5] *Ibid.* s.90.
[6] *Ibid.* ss.89–92.
[7] *Ibid.* ss.93 and 94.
[8] *Ibid.* s.99.
[9] *Ibid.* ss.86, 87 and 98.
[10] *Ibid.* s.87.
[11] Litter (Fixed Penalty Notices) Order 1991 (S.I. 1991 No. 111).

opportunity to discharge any liability to conviction by payment of a fixed penalty.[12]

Litter control areas The Secretary of State is empowered to identify descriptions of land and a local authority may designate a litter control area. For this purpose, land may be described by reference to its ownership or occupation or by reference to activities carried out on the land. However, an area will not be designated unless the litter authority is of the opinion that, by reason of the presence of litter or refuse, the condition of the land is, and but for designation is likely to continue to be, such as to be detrimental to local amenities. Prior to any designation by an authority (a process that may not be delegated under section 101 of the Local Government Act 1972), those who appear to be affected must be notified and allowed to make representations which must then be taken into account in the decision-making process.[13]

Two important purposes for which a litter control area may be designated relate to the duty of the occupier of land within a litter control area to ensure that the land is, so far as is practicable, kept clear of litter and refuse[14] and to the power of a magistrates' court to act on a complaint made by any person that he is aggrieved by the defacement, by litter or refuse, of any relevant land within a litter control area.[15] Any order designating a litter control area must be entered on a public register maintained by each principal litter authority.[16]

The duty to keep land free of litter The Act creates two sets of duties: the first duty is to ensure that land is, so far as is practicable, kept clean, and extends to each local authority (as respects any relevant highway), the Secretary of State (as respects any trunk road) and each principal litter authority (as respects land open to the air under the authority's direct control to which the public are entitled or permitted to have access with or without payment), together with certain Crown authorities, designated statutory undertakers, the governing body of designated educational institutions and (in respect of land in a litter control area) occupiers of land.[17] The second duty extends to each local authority (as respects any highway for which it is responsible) and the Secretary of State (in respect of certain trunk roads and other highways).[18]

In determining compliance with these duties, it is necessary to have regard to the character and use of the land, highway or road, as well any measures "which are practicable in the circumstances". Special provision is made in relation to the duty as it relates to highways and roads, for a variety of purposes, one of which is for the avoidance of confusion between litter functions and functions which may, for example, relate instead to road safety.[19]

[12] £10 at the time of writing: s.88(6), (7).
[13] Environmental Protection Act, s.90. *Cf.* the Litter Control Areas Order 1991 (S.I. 1991 No. 1325).
[14] *Ibid.* s.89(1)(g).
[15] *Ibid.* s.91(1)(g).
[16] *Ibid.* s.95.
[17] *Ibid.* s.89(1).
[18] *Ibid.* subs.(2).
[19] *Ibid.* subss.(4)–(6).

A code of practice is provided for by the Act and is intended to facilitate practical guidance in relation to the discharge of the two duties referred to at the outset. Any person subject to one or other of the duties is required to "have regard" to the Code in force in the discharge of that duty.[20] The Code has a statutory and a non-statutory element. The first, statutory part operates by reference to four grades: "A" (no litter or refuse items); "B" (predominantly free of litter and refuse apart from small items); "C" (widespread distribution of litter or refuse with minor accumulations), and "D" (heavily littered with significant accumulations). Land is divided into 11 broad zones by the Code, taking account of land usage and traffic volume. It is a matter for the local authority or other agency to allocate geographical areas to particular zones and to publicise any such allocation. The Code also recommends that zoning of areas for present purposes be considered for inclusion in the public registers provided for by section 95 of the Act. Overall, the Code states that it is concerned with "output standards" rather than "input standards", which means that the concern is with how clean land is rather than the regularity of sweeping.

The Act permits a person to make a complaint to a magistrates' court on the grounds that he is aggrieved by the defacement, by litter or refuse, of various land, including any relevant highway, any relevant land of a designated educational institution and any relevant land in a litter control area.[21] The court may also respond to a complaint by any person on the ground that he is aggrieved by the lack of cleanliness of certain highways.[22] No complaint in either of these circumstances can be pursued by a principal litter authority. Any person who is regarded as a "person aggrieved" here will bring proceedings against any person under a duty to keep land clear of litter or refuse or a highway or road clear.[23] A complainant is required to give not less than five days' notice in writing of the intended complaint, together with details of the matter subject to complaint. If the complaint before the court is sustained, a litter abatement order may be made, requiring the defendant to clear away the litter or refuse or clean the highway, as the case may be. In two circumstances, the court will not make an order: where it is proved that there was compliance with the duty under section 89(1) or (2) or where the matter "appears" to have arisen from a local authority's compliance with directions from the highway authority specifying, for example, certain days when cleaning will not take place.[24] Failure to comply with a litter abatement order without reasonable excuse is a summary offence, subject to a continuing fine for each day of non-compliance.[25] Compliance with the section 89(1) and (2) duties will be a defence to these criminal proceedings.[26] The Code of Practice is admissible in criminal proceedings here and the court may take into account any

[20] *Ibid.* subs.(7)–(13). The present Code dates from November 1990.
[21] *Ibid.* s.91(1).
[22] *Ibid.* subs.(2).
[23] *Ibid.* s.89(1), (2), respectively.
[24] *Ibid.* s.91(7), (8).
[25] *Ibid.* subs.(9).
[26] *Ibid.* subs.(10).

relevant provision of the Code.[27] If, ultimately, the court is satisfied that there was cause for the complaint at the time of that complaint, which was brought on reasonable grounds, the court may require the defendant to pay a reasonable amount towards the complainant's costs, reflective of the fact that any prior remediation would deny a litter abatement order with no opportunity for costs.[28]

It was seen previously that a principal litter authority is not a "person aggrieved" for the purpose of a complaint under section 91. However, summary proceedings are available to such an authority under the Act, albeit in respect of a fairly limited number of situations. Those situations relate to relevant Crown land, any relevant land of a designated statutory undertaker, relevant land of a designated educational institution and (finally) any relevant land within a litter control area. If the authority (but not a county council) is satisfied that the land is defaced by litter or refuse, or that defacement is likely to recur, a litter abatement notice may be served.[29] That notice may require compliance with a so-called "requirement" or "prohibition", or both. A requirement relates to a need for the litter or refuse to be cleared within a specified period, while a prohibition seeks to ensure that the land is not permitted to become defaced by litter or refuse.[30] There is an appeal against the notice to the magistrates' court, and the appeal must be allowed if it is established that there was compliance with the duty under section 89(1).[31] Non-compliance with a notice without reasonable excuse is a summary offence, with a facility for a continuing fine. It is, however, a defence to establish compliance with the duty under section 89(1).[32] The Code of Practice is again admissible in evidence and any relevant provision can be taken into account.[33] Failure to comply with a requirement expressed in a notice empowers the authority to use its default powers. Accordingly, the authority may enter on the land, clear the litter and refuse and recover from the person in default the expenditure attributable to the exercise of default powers, except in so far as it can be shown that any of the expenditure was unnecessary.[34]

The duty referred to throughout the present area of litter control is a duty to act so far as it is "practicable" to act. This duty—found in two parts in section 89(1) and (2)—has been seen to be relevant for a variety of purposes, not the least of which being as a defence for the purpose of proceedings. What may be "practicable" has been open to interpretation in a number of cases from rather different contexts than the present.[35] There seems little doubt that variables of finance and risk factors are relevant for present purposes, with the statutory context of Part IV of the Act also suggesting locality as a further variable.

[27] *Ibid.* subs.(11).
[28] *Ibid.* subs.(12).
[29] *Ibid.* s.92(1).
[30] *Ibid.* subs.(2).
[31] *Ibid.* subss.(4), (5).
[32] *Ibid.* subss.(6), (7).
[33] *Ibid.* subs.(8).
[34] *Ibid.* subs.(9). This does not apply to Crown Land or relevant land of statutory undertakers: subs.(10).
[35] *e.g. Edwards v. National Coal Board* [1949] 1 K.B. 704.

Street litter A principal litter authority (but not a county council) is empowered to issue a street litter control notice aimed at the occupiers of premises with a view to the prevention of accumulation of litter and refuse in and around any street or open land adjacent to any street.[36] The Act is rather more specific, in indicating that there are quite distinct circumstances in which a notice may be served on an occupier or, if premises are unoccupied, on the owner of those premises. The premises in question must have a frontage on a street and be commercial or retail premises. The notice may be served in three alternative situations:

(a) first, a notice may be resorted to where there is recurrent defacement by litter or refuse of any land which is part of the street or open land adjacent to the street which is in the vicinity of the premises;
(b) secondly, a notice may be resorted to where the condition of any part of the premises which is open land in the vicinity of the frontage is and (in the absence of a notice) is likely to continue to be detrimental to the amenities of the locality by reason of the presence of litter or refuse;
(c) thirdly, a notice may be resorted to where activities on the premises produce quantities of litter or refuse of such a nature and in such amounts as are likely to cause the defacement of any part of the street or of open land adjacent to the street, which is in the vicinity of the premises.[37]

A street litter control notice will identify the premises and state the ground (described above) on which the notice is issued. The notice will also specify an area of open land which adjoins or is in the vicinity of the frontage of the premises on the street. Finally, the notice will specify, in relation to the area or any part of it, reasonable requirements as considered appropriate by the authority in the circumstances.[38] Requirements here could include the emptying of receptacles for litter or refuse.[39]

Any person to be served with a notice must be informed by the authority and given an opportunity to make representations which, in turn, must be taken into account by the authority.[40] An appeal against a notice eventually served goes to the magistrates' court, which may quash the notice or quash, vary or add to any requirement imposed.[41] If it appears to the authority that a person has failed or is failing to comply with a requirement of the notice, an application may be made to the magistrates' court for an order requiring compliance within a stipulated period of time.[42] A person who fails to comply with the court's order without reasonable excuse may be convicted of a summary offence.[43]

[36] Environmental Protection Act, s.93(1).
[37] *Ibid.* subs.(2).
[38] *Ibid.* subs.(3).
[39] *Ibid.* s.94(4). *Cf.* the Street Litter Notices Order 1992 (S.I. 1992 No. 1324).
[40] Environmental Protection Act, s.94(6).
[41] *Ibid.* subs.(7). Any variation or addition must be entered on the register: s.95(2).
[42] *Ibid.* s.94(8).
[43] *Ibid.* subs.(9).

Abandoned shopping and luggage trolleys A local authority may decide to adopt and apply the provisions to be found in Schedule 4 to the Environmental Protection Act relating to luggage trolleys and shopping trolleys, as defined by that Schedule.[44] At least three months must elapse from the passing of a resolution before the Schedule comes into force. The local authority (principally a district council and a London borough council) must publicise the passing of the resolution as well as the general effect of Schedule 4 in at least one newspaper circulating locally. However, a prerequisite to the resolution is a requirement that the local authority consult with those who appear to the authority to be affected by an application of Schedule 4. Thereafter, and following any such resolution, the authority is obliged "from time to time" to consult with those persons (or their representatives) who appear to be affected by the Schedule and its operation.[45]

Schedule 4 applies where any shopping or luggage trolley[46] is found by an authorised officer of the local authority on "... any land in the open air" where the trolley "... appears to him to be abandoned".[47] The Schedule will not apply, on the other hand, to a variety of other situations, where, for example, a trolley is found on land in which the trolley owner has a legal estate (say) as the owner of a supermarket. Elsewhere in Schedule 4 there are various powers for the retention, return and disposal of trolleys, as well as the imposition of charges by the local authority responsible.[48] These powers are exercisable only after an authority has lawfully seized and removed any trolleys through its other powers in the Schedule.[49]

The status of litter and refuse collected

In the exercise of functions under Part IV through which litter and refuse is collected, a question of possible significance concerns the status of such litter or waste. The Act empowers the Secretary of State to make regulations for the purpose of identifying this litter and waste as controlled waste, allowing appropriate elements of Part II of the Act to apply on the assumption that the litter and refuse had been collected by a waste collection authority.[50] The implementation of this provision, particularly through the Controlled Waste Regulations, was described previously in this chapter.[51]

[44] Environmental Protection Act, s.99.
[45] *Ibid.*
[46] *Ibid.* Sched. 4, para. 5.
[47] *Ibid.* para. 1(1).
[48] *Ibid.* paras. 3 and 4.
[49] *Ibid.* para. 2.
[50] *Ibid.* s.96. Note in particular the assumption in s.75 that waste is generated from "premises".
[51] See nn.42–45, *supra*.

Pesticides

The scope of regulation and control

Until the Food and Environment Protection Act 1985 was legislated, there was no formal statutory framework governing pesticides. There existed—and continues to exist—a considerable body of legislation which recognises the environmentally adverse character of many pesticides for the purpose of preventing or mitigating their impact on the three fundamental media of water, air and land. This division is also reflected in E.C. directives where, on the one hand, certain directives relate to pesticides specifically, and, on the other hand, a collection of various other directives relates to dangerous substances in water, for example, where certain pesticide substances appear in the categories of such substances.

E.C. law

The principal directives seek to impose restrictions on the use of pesticides[52] and to regulate their labelling[53] and to control maximum pesticide residue levels in relation to fruit and vegetables and various other food stuffs.[54] The first Directive—79/117—is implemented primarily through the Control of Pesticides Regulations,[55] made under the terms of the Food and Environment Protection Act. The second Directive—78/631—is implemented under the Control of Pesticides Regulations and the Classification, Packaging and Labelling of Dangerous Substances Regulations 1984.[56] The third set of directives on maximum residue levels are implemented primarily under Regulations made by virtue of the Food and Environment Protection Act 1985, the Pesticides (Maximum Residue Levels in Crops, Food and Feeding Stuffs) Regulations 1994.[57]

The objectives of primary, municipal legislation

The provisions of Part III of the Food and Environment Protection Act have effect to protect the health of human beings, creatures and plants, to safeguard the environment, to secure safe, efficient and humane methods of controlling pests and to make information about pesticides available to the public.[58] The Act's central feature is its concern for so-called "specific prohibitions", namely importation, sale, offer or exposure for sale or possession for the purposes of sale,

[52] Directive 79/117: [1979] O.J. L33, as amended.
[53] Directive 78/631: [1979] O.J. L259, as amended.
[54] Directives 76/895: [1976] O.J. L340, 86/362: [1986] L.J. L221, 86/363: [1986] O.J. L221, 90/642: [1990] O.J. L350 and 91/132: [1991] O.J. L66.
[55] S.I. 1986 No. 1510.
[56] S.I. 1984 No. 1244.
[57] S.I. 1994 No. 1985.
[58] Food and Environment Protection Act, s.16(1).

supply or offers to supply, storage, use and advertisement.[59] The legislation sets out an approvals system in respect of these prohibitions with arrangements for consents in respect of advertisement, sale, supply, storage and use of pesticides.

"Pesticide"

The term "pesticide" is defined to mean any substance, preparation or organism prepared or used for the destruction of any pest.[60] This rather negative terminology takes no account of the preventative uses of various chemicals, for example. As a result, the Act goes on to specify, *inter alia,* chemical and other substances, preparations and organisms prepared or used for regulating plant growth, providing protection against harmful creatures and rendering such creatures harmless. This part of the process of definition is particularly important in identifying the micro-organisms which are increasingly important products of the biotechnology industry.

Enforcement of statutory requirements

Apart from a variety of enforcement devices built into the Act, such as the seizure of "unlawful" pesticides, the Act relies also on a variety of criminal offences.[61] The offences fall into two categories. First, it is an offence for a person, without reasonable excuse, to contravene or cause or permit any other person to contravene any provision of the Regulations such as the Control of Pesticides Regulations, any condition of approval or any requirement of those Regulations, including any information requirement above pesticides.[62] Secondly, it is an offence, where information is to be required for the purposes of the Act, knowingly to furnish false information, to be reckless in relation to a material particular or intentionally to fail to disclose any material particular.[63]

The Act contains considerable powers of enforcement in conferring rights of entry, control and direction on those delegated the task of ensuring compliance. Either of the Ministers responsible for the Act's enforcement—the Secretary of State for the Environment and the Minister of Agriculture—may authorise certain local authority officers to enforce the provisions of the Act.[64] Of particular significance are two sets of enforcement powers. The first set specifies that an officer may be of the opinion that an offence from the first of the two categories above[65] is being committed. In this case, the officer may require by notice that any land, for example, is left undisturbed for as long as is reasonably necessary or

[59] *Ibid.* subs.(3).
[60] *Ibid.* subs.(15).
[61] *Ibid.* subs.(12).
[62] *Ibid.* subs.(12)(a).
[63] *Ibid.* subs.(12)(b).
[64] *Ibid.*
[65] *Ibid.* s.16(12)(a).

that any reasonable remedial or preventative measures are taken. In the case of the second set of enforcement powers, if it is the officer's opinion that there is a risk of one of the foregoing offences being committed, he may notify a requirement that the subject activity should not be undertaken until some remedial action is taken.

The Act provides for a defence of due diligence in respect of any offence charged under the Art. This defence may be of considerable significance in relation to the two offences just referred to. The enforcement powers referred to are notable by virtue of the fact that they are triggered by an opinion that a relevant offence is being committed or that there is a risk that it may be committed. Enforcement action could also result in considerable loss or other prejudice to a potential defendant who, unless there is a prosecution, has no legally recognised opportunity (such as an appeal) to establish that reasonable diligence was exercised.

The Control of Pesticides Regulations[66]

Detailed implementation of the Act's broad objectives is to be found in the Regulations that can be made under the Act. The present Regulations list a number of substances which are not subject to the statutory controls.[67] First, controls do not apply to organisms other than bacteria, fungi, viruses and mycoplasmas used for destroying or controlling pests. This means that pesticides developed with monoclonal antibodies, eliminating harmful insect pests without harm to the rest of the environment, are included. Secondly, the controls do not apply if a substance is already subject to control, for example, sheep dip solutions under the Medicines Act 1968. Thirdly, pesticides are excluded from controls if they are intended solely for export from the United Kingdom.

At the heart of the Regulations are provisions dealing with prohibitions, approvals and consents.[68] The prohibitions cover the advertising, sale, supply, storage and use of pesticides for which it is necessary to obtain either a "provisional" or a "full" approval, where advertising and sale are concerned, or an "approval", in relation to the remaining prohibitions. In addition to any such approval, it is necessary to obtain a consent and to comply with any conditions imposed, as well as any additional conditions which apply to aerial spraying. The Ministers' approvals fall into three categories. An experimental permit allows testing and development of a pesticide for the purpose of providing the Ministers with safety and other data. A provisional approval operates for a stipulated period and is intended to satisfy the Ministers' outstanding data requirements. Finally, a full approval operates for an unstipulated period. Each category of approval may authorise use, supply and storage of a pesticide while, in addition, any provisional or full approval may authorise the sale and advertisement of a subject pesticide. Even when an approval has been given, the Regulations reserve the power to

[66] S.I. 1986 No. 1510.
[67] *Ibid.* reg.3(1).
[68] *Ibid.* regs.4, 5 and 6, respectively.

impose conditions subsequently. However, it may be the case that there are very serious anxieties about an approved pesticide. In these circumstances, the Regulations permit the Ministers responsible to review, revoke or suspend an approval, and to amend conditions of approval at any time. The Regulations set out the "basic" conditions which apply to consents,[69] although any consent may be subject to further conditions.[70] There is no appeal facility by which decisions and conditions may be challenged. Judicial review may not be a practical remedy in many cases, although there may be occasional collateral challenges through criminal prosecutions. Accordingly, what remains is the prospect of voluntary reconsideration of decisions and conditions.

Wide powers for the seizure and disposal of pesticides are provided by the Regulations.[71] The Regulations refer to breaches of specified prohibitions or of a condition of approval or consent. In such cases, the Ministers have power to seize or dispose of a pesticide or to require that "some other" person shall dispose of it. Similar powers relate to "anything treated" with the subject pesticide. Furthermore, in relation to any such contravention, "some other person" may be directed to take "... such remedial action as appears to the Minister to be necessary as a result of the contravention".[72] If the contravention occurs in relation to any imported pesticide, the Ministers are empowered to require its removal from the United Kingdom.[73]

The Regulations make provision for public access to information about pesticides.[74] Where a provisional or full approval has been given, or where there has been an amendment of conditions, the Minister may, at the request of any person, facilitate the inspection of the relevant evaluation of the pesticide. However, if any such person satisfies the Ministers that the evaluation gives insufficient information, they may decide to make available the study reports or other data supplied in support of the application. The person supplied with this information is prohibited from making any commercial use of it and, without the Minister's written consent, shall not publish its contents.

The approval of pesticides

Unlike the legislation in some other countries, Part III of the Food and Environment Protection Act does not provide criteria for the approval of pesticides. The nearest that the Act gets to any explicit statutory criteria is in the provisions from section 16 of the Act cited previously.[75] Those words previously cited indicate the elements of "risk" and "adverse effects" in the broadest environmental terms. The absence of explicit statutory criteria for the approvals

[69] *Ibid.* Scheds. 1 to 4.
[70] *Ibid.* reg.6.
[71] *Ibid.* reg.7.
[72] *Ibid.*
[73] *Ibid.*
[74] *Ibid.* reg.8. *Cf.* Chap. 9, "Access to Environmental Health Information", n.24, *infra.*
[75] See n.47, *supra.*

process is matched by statutory silence on the matter of public participation in decision-making.

Having approved a pesticide, the Control of Pesticides Regulations anticipate a possible need for reconsideration of that approval. The Ministers responsible may review, revoke or suspend an approval, or amend any conditions that have been attached. Once again, there are no statutory criteria for the decision, a noticeable absence of any facility for a challenge to the decision and (again) no facility for public intervention to secure an exercise of the available powers. In these circumstances, there may be some difficulty in ensuring explicit statutory re-evaluation of some pesticides in the light of experience and scientific developments.

Consents and matters of competence

The Control of Pesticides Regulations deal with the important matter of levels of competence. In relation to the sale, supply, storage and use of pesticides, a duty to take all reasonable precautions is imposed, for example, in safeguarding the environment and human health. With regard to sale, supply and storage, any person "... shall be competent for the duties which he is called upon to perform".[76] This requirement is extended to include the need for a certificate of competence recognised by the Ministers in the case of agricultural pesticides which may (as an alternative) be sold, supplied or stored under the direct supervision of someone holding such a certificate.[77] Furthermore, it is the duty of employers to ensure that instructions and guidance are given to employees who are selling, supplying or storing subject pesticides so that they achieve recognised standards of competence.[78] As to use, it is stipulated that a pesticide shall not be used in the course of a business unless there has been adequate instruction and guidance in the safe, efficient and humane use of pesticides for a user who is also required to be "competent".[79] Furthermore, an approved agricultural pesticide cannot be used in commercial service unless the user has a certificate of competence recognised by the Ministers or unless he uses that pesticide under the direct and personal supervision of the holder of such a certificate.[80] Finally, there is an age limit governing the use of pesticides for agricultural use: no person born later than December 31, 1964 shall use such a pesticide without a recognised certificate of competence, although such a person may use this category of pesticide under the direct and personal supervision of a certificate holder.

Aerial and other spraying

The Control of Pesticides Regulations contain fairly detailed requirements in connection with aerial spraying. Apart from the requisite licences, there is a

[76] Control of Pesticides Regulations, Sched. 2(1)(b).
[77] *Ibid.* paras. (1) and (2).
[78] *Ibid.* para.(3).
[79] *Ibid.* Sched. 3(4).
[80] *Ibid.* para. (5).

requirement for prior consultation with certain individuals and organisations interested in or affected by spraying. There is also prohibition on spraying near certain sensitive areas and a requirement for ground markers to show the limits of operation.[81] The statutory requirements for consultation appear to crystallise common law standards of care. In *Tutton v. A.D. Walter Ltd.*,[82] the court held that a farmer owed a duty of care to local beekeepers in applying an insecticide. The bees' presence in the area of the crop was known, but the farmer failed to comply with published recommendations in favour of spraying when the flowers on the crop were dying down. The court held that there had been a breach of the duty of care and that there had been inadequate warning to the beekeepers of the spraying. The judge placed emphasis on the fact that for "basically safe sprays", "... the warning envisaged by the code of conduct was a 24-hour warning of spraying ... Dangerous spraying of the kind resorted to would require more notice ..."[83] The Regulations do incorporate a notice requirement of not less than 48 hours for the benefit of beekeepers,[84] but this applies only to aerial applications. Unless specific conditions are set in consents relating to the use of pesticides in sensitive areas, it seems likely that common law standards will continue to play an important role.

Enforcement powers

The Food and Environment Protection Act incorporates a variety of powers of entry for enforcing officers: for example, it is provided that an officer may enter land if he has reasonable grounds to believe that "any" pesticide is being or has been applied to or stored in it and that it is necessary to secure entry for the purposes of the Act. These widely drawn powers, which do not necessarily presuppose an unlawful use of pesticides, are supplemented by similar powers of entry to aircraft, vehicles and vessels, as well as a power to demand information.[85]

Where an officer is of the opinion that an offence is being or has been committed or that certain activities involve a risk that an offence will be committed against the Act, provision is made to deal with both sets of circumstances. In the former situation, the officer can notify the reasons for the opinion and direct that the subject land, vessel, etc., be left undisturbed or that "any reasonable remedial or preventative measures ... be taken".[86] In the latter situation, the Act confers similar powers except that any direction will require that the particular activities are not continued until the matter giving rise to the "risk" is remedied. These summary powers are drawn very widely, but it is noticeable that there are very limited opportunities for challenge to their exercise. In theory, facilities for judicial review would be available but, more realistically, the only point of challenge would arise in the course of any prosecution for an

[81] *Ibid.* Sched. 4.
[82] [1985] 3 W.L.R. 797.
[83] *Ibid.* at 810.
[84] Control of Pesticides Regulations, Sched. 4(2)(g).
[85] Food and Environment Protection Act, s.19 and Sched. 2.
[86] *Ibid.* s.19(5).

offence under Schedule 2, paragraph 10. Such a prosecution would relate, for example, to a failure "without reasonable excuse" to comply with an officer's requirements or directions. Entry to a dwelling requires a magistrates' warrant if a search is to be conducted.[87]

Offences

The Act defines various categories of offences. In the first place, it is an offence, without reasonable excuse, to contravene or cause or permit any other person to contravene any provision of the Regulations, any condition of approval or any requirement imposed by virtue of the Regulations. A second category of offences concerns the falsity of information. These categories are additional to the categories of offence already referred to. Whatever the offence with which a person be charged, the Act stipulates that it is a defence for the person charged to prove that he took all reasonable precautions and exercised all due diligence to avoid commission of the offence.[88] If either of the Ministers does anything in response to a failure by any person to comply with the Regulations made under section 16, any expenses reasonably incurred may be recovered from that person.[89]

Access to information

Release of information to the public is a facility that operates following the granting of a provisional approval, a full approval or an amendment of any conditions. Although the information which may be released is in the nature of an "evaluation", relevant "study reports" may be released, along with any other data submitted with an application, if the Ministers are satisfied that an evaluation gives insufficient information.[90] Any person supplied with this information is prohibited from making any commercial use of that information and, without written authorisation of the Ministers, cannot publish the contents of the evaluation or study reports.[91]

The Environmental Release of Genetically Modified Organisms

The nature of genetically modified organisms

Genetically modified organisms compromise those organisms that may be changed genetically through the introduction of new DNA (deoxyribonucleic acid) to their cell structure by means of recombinant DNA technology. The DNA may be synthesised, or may come from some other organism. Thereafter, later organisms will inherit the new genetic imprint. The newly introduced

[87] *Ibid.* Sched. 2(7).
[88] *Ibid.* s.22.
[89] *Ibid.* s.16(13A).
[90] Control of Pesticides Regulations, reg.8.
[91] *Ibid.*

organisms may have a variety of merits, for example, in enabling new strains of plant to be resistant to certain diseases. Biotechnology therefore adopts scientific and engineering principles for the purpose of enabling biological agents to generate new cell forms that may be applied to a wide variety of processes. It has been possible, for example, to create micro-organisms that react with PCBs, thus rendering them less toxic.

Having developed a new micro-organism through these complex technological processes, there may be a need to test the impact of a new development on the environment. Many introductions to the environment are likely to be entirely harmless, but others may have an adverse impact, particularly if a pathogenic organism is involved. Any regulatory system for the management—and containment—of such risks should recognise the variability of such risks and develop a regulatory response accordingly. Matters of environmental impact also involve concerns about the variety of purposes for which environmental release may be sought. Experimental release is one such purpose and marketing of the finished product is another.

Regulatory control

Regulatory control of environmental release is achieved through Part VI of the Environmental Protection Act 1990, reinforced by the Genetically Modified Organisms (Deliberate Release) Regulations 1992.[92] Prior to the introduction of this new legislation, the control of genetically modified organisms had focused on so-called "contained" work in the laboratory, governed by the Health and Safety at Work Act and the Genetic Manipulation Regulations 1989.[93] Following the enactment of two E.C. directives, one dealing with the contained use of genetically modified organisms[94] and the other dealing with the deliberate release of genetically modified organisms,[95] a framework was set for the foregoing municipal legislation, including new Regulations for contained use, enforced by the Health and Safety Executive.[96] While the contained use directive is aimed at the protection of human health and demands, *inter alia*, a prior risk assessment, the deliberate release directive targets not only deliberate release but also products entering the market and comprising genetically modified organisms.

Organisms subject to control

A genetically modified organism may be a single organism, such as a genetically modified tomato, or several organisms combined in a "product".[97] The legislation is concerned not with genetic modification that occurs naturally but

[92] S.I. 1992 No. 3280, as amended.
[93] S.I. 1989 No. 1810.
[94] Directive 90/219: [1990] O.J. L117.
[95] Directive 90/220: [1990] O.J. L117.
[96] S.I. 1992 No. 3217.
[97] "The Regulation and Control of the Deliberate Release of Genetically Modified Organisms" (Department of the Environment, 1993), p.11; Environmental Protection Act s.106.

with artificial modification. Consequently, a fusion of plant cells to form a new cell which can also be produced by "traditional breeding methods" is effectively exempt from regulation and control.[98]

The essential purpose of control

The Environmental Protection Act declares that Part VI of the Act has effect for the purpose of preventing or minimising any damage to the environment which may arise from the escape or release from human control of genetically modified organisms.[99]

The achievement of control

Part VI of the Act is wholly regulatory and does not address the matter of liability for damage, loss or injury caused by a deliberate release. The essential core of the regulatory regime is to be seen in a series of provisions, reinforced by the Regulations referred to earlier. Those provisions are built, first, on the prohibition of importation, acquisition, release and marketing of genetically modified organisms without a risk assessment relating to possible adverse environmental impact and the requirement to notify the Secretary of State of the proposed release.[1] The provisions of Part VI are built, secondly, on a requirement for a consent from the Secretary of State in respect of importation, acquisition, keeping, release or marketing of genetically modified organisms. However, the categories or types of genetically modified organisms subject to prohibitions are to be prescribed by Regulations. Following such prescription, other provisions in the Act relating to risk assessment and notification, referred to above, will not apply. In addition, a duty of care set out in the Act and described below will not apply in these circumstances.[2]

Part VI terminology

Beyond the types of organism subject to regulation and control and the nature in law of genetic modification, the Act seeks to define a number of other terms. Of particular significance are the following terms: "environment", "damage to the environment", "harm", "harmful", "harmless" and (where an organism is under a person's control) the circumstances in which that organism can be regarded as having been "released".[3]

"Environment" receives a wide definition, being regarded as consisting of "... land, air and water and any of those media".[4] "Damage to the environment", on the other hand,

[98] *Ibid.* p.13.
[99] Environmental Protection Act, s.106.
[1] *Ibid.* s.108. *Cf.* the risk assessment and notification requirements in respect of a proposed keeping of genetically modified organisms.
[2] *Ibid.* s.111.
[3] *Ibid.* s.107.
[4] *Ibid.* subs.(2).

> "... is caused by the presence in the environment of genetically modified organisms which have (or of a single such organism which has) escaped or been released from a person's control and are (or is) capable of causing harm to the living organisms supported by the environment".[5]

This definition lies at the heart of Part VI controls, having a central role to play in relation to

(a) risk assessment and notification requirements;
(b) the duties of care;
(c) the service of prohibition notices;
(d) the setting of conditions and limitations in consents;
(e) rights of entry and inspection for enforcement purposes;
(f) rights of the Secretary of State to secure information for the purpose of fulfilling his statutory responsibilities under Part VI;
(g) powers to deal with the cause or causes of imminent danger of damage to the environment; and
(h) powers to exclude certain information from the public registers available under Part VI.

"Damage to the environment" is defined by reference to a number of facts, the first of which is the requirement that genetically modified organisms should be present in the environment. This matter is clarified through an indication that the organism may be present in or on any human or other organism "or any other thing" which is itself present in the environment.[6] A second requirement is that there should have been an escape or release of organisms that have escaped or been released from a person's control. The Act provides a fairly detailed prescription of "control" for present purposes, as well as an indication of the circumstances in which an organism under a person's control is released.[7] Finally, and very significantly, the Act refers to the need for organisms (or any one organism) to be "capable" of causing harm to the living organisms supported by the environment. The Act regards an organism as being capable of causing harm whether being active by itself or in numbers or through the activity of descendants.[8]

"Harm" is taken by the Act to mean harm to the health of humans or other living organisms or other interference with the ecological systems of which they form part. Furthermore, where many organisms are in the environment, "harm" includes offence caused to any person's senses or harm to his property. The terms "harmful" and "harmless" refer, respectively, to organisms being capable or incapable of causing harm.[9] The Secretary of State may prescribe, through regulations, that certain types of harm may be disregarded in circumstances

[5] *Ibid.* subs.(3).
[6] *Ibid.* subs.(4).
[7] *Ibid.* subss.(9), (10).
[8] *Ibid.* subs.(5).
[9] *Ibid.* subss.(6), (7).

where, otherwise, harm would be a significant variable.[10] This facility is available to permit the use of genetically modified organisms (such as biopesticides and pollution clean-up agents) whose function is to act on the environment in a specific way, including the exertion of a negative effect on some other organisms supported by the environment, the result of which may be to confer other benefits.[11]

Risk assessment and notification

No person is able to import or acquire, release or market any genetically modified organism unless, in anticipation of release, an assessment of the risks of damage to the environment be undertaken and notice of intention be given to the Secretary of State. Although these requirements relate typically to low risk releases, nevertheless the Secretary of State retains powers to direct that an application for consent is made.[12]

Duties of care

While the foregoing risk assessment and notification requirements relate to importation, acquisition, release or marketing of genetically modified organisms, the Act extends the catalogue of activities to include the keeping of genetically modified organisms for the purpose of defining three sets of duties according to whether a person proposes to import or acquire subject organisms, to keep such organisms, or to release them to the environment.[13] However, the duties do not apply in some circumstances, for example, to the holder of a consent under the present Part VI, if any such consent covers any one or more of the foregoing activities. Among a variety of different duties according to the circumstances is the duty on a person who keeps genetically modified organisms to use best available techniques not entailing excessive cost for keeping those organisms under his control, and for preventing any damage to the environment being caused as a result of their continuing to be kept.

Consents

The Act stipulates that no person may import or acquire, release or market any genetically modified organisms except in accordance with a consent granted by the Secretary of State, and any conditions or limitations attached to such a consent.[14] Although the Secretary of State is empowered to prescribe those cases

[10] *Ibid.* subs.(8) and Genetically Modified Organisms (Deliberate Release) Regulations 1992 (S.I. 1992 No. 3280).
[11] *Ibid.*
[12] Environmental Protection Act, s.108.
[13] *Ibid.* s.109.
[14] *Ibid.* s.111.

requiring his consent, the Genetically Modified Organisms (Deliberate Release) Regulations indicate that, for the moment at least, all releases require consent.[15]

A single application may suffice to cover a number of releases. Each application must be accompanied by a risk assessment and other technical information.[16] Of particular significance here is an evaluation of impacts and risks relating to human health if release to the environment is permitted. Material information here is likely to target the biological make-up of the genetically modified organism and the characteristics of the "host" environment.

Human health hazards

The impact on human health of a release raises a large number of questions. An applicant company *qua* employer will be obliged to take account of statutory duties under the Health and Safety at Work Act 1974.[17] Other factors to be considered for the purpose of an application may include pathogenic hazards, the ability of a genetically modified organism to colonise and the size and distribution of local human populations. Monitoring and emergency plans will also be significant subjects in the compilation of technical information to accompany the application to the Secretary of State. Reference may also be made to any evidence from previous, similar releases to the environment, as well as information submitted for similar releases in other E.C. Member States in compliance with the requirements of Directive 90/220.

Advertisement of applications for consent

An applicant is required to advertise his application for consent to release. Despite prescription of advertising requirements,[18] it is likely that the scale and content of the publicity will be determined largely by the scale, complexity and area of the proposed release. Notification of an application made to the Secretary of State must be given to various agencies and individuals, including the owner of the site of the release if different from the applicant, the local authority for the area, the Nature Conservancy Council for England and the Countryside Council for Wales, the National Rivers Authority and the water undertaker for the area.[19]

Decisions

The Act and regulations stipulate that the Secretary of State is obliged to communicate a decision on the application within a period of 90 days from the date of receipt of the application.[20] The Act provides no facility for an appeal against adverse decisions of the Secretary of State.

[15] Genetically Modified Organisms (Deliberate Release) Regulations, reg.5(1). The only exception is an "approved product" defined by reg.2.

[16] *Ibid.* reg.6 and Sched. 1.

[17] Health and Safety at Work Act, ss.2 and 3.

[18] Genetically Modified Organisms (Deliberate Release) Regulations, reg.8.

[19] *Ibid.*

[20] *Ibid.* reg.15.

Decision-making and general responsibilities for implementation and enforcement of the Act lie with the Secretary of State for the Environment. Nevertheless, many functions may be delegated, to the Health and Safety Executive, for example,[21] and may be exercised jointly by the Secretary of State and the Minister of Agriculture.[22] Advice in connection with decision-making and the making of regulations comes from the Advisory Committee on Releases to the Environment, appointed under powers provided by the Act.[23]

Limitations and conditions

The Secretary of State enjoys a considerable discretion to include in a consent such limitations and conditions as he thinks fit. Every consent will contain certain implied general conditions. Such conditions are categorised according to whether a consent relates to importation or acquisition of genetically modified organisms, the keeping of such organisms, or the release or marketing of genetically modified organisms.[24] Any such general condition has effect, subject to any conditions that may be imposed under the Secretary of State's general discretion referred to above.[25] The same applies to a general condition implied into a consent for the keeping, releasing or marketing of genetically modified organisms. The condition set out by the Act reflects the novelty of so many aspects of the environmental impact and significance of genetically modified organisms. It is implied into every consent falling into this category that the holder of the consent will take all reasonable steps to keep himself abreast of developing techniques for the prevention of damage to the environment through pursuit of the activities authorised by the consent. Furthermore, if it appears that any better techniques are available than those required by any condition of the consent, the holder of the consent is obliged to notify the Secretary of State, who may then choose to exercise his powers to revoke, or vary the consent, its conditions or limitations.[26]

Access to information

The Secretary of State is required to maintain a public register for the purposes of Part VI of the Act.[27] That register will contain, *inter alia*, details of prohibition notices served by the Secretary of State's inspectors in respect of various unauthorised activities, described below, applications for consent and convictions for offences under Part VI of the Act.[28] In the case of applications the information required is as follows[29]:

[21] Environmental Protection Act, s.125.
[22] *Ibid.* s.126.
[23] *Ibid.* s.124.
[24] *Ibid.* s.112(3), (4), (5).
[25] *Ibid.* subs.(6).
[26] *Ibid.* subs.(7). As to revocation or variation, see s.111(10).
[27] *Ibid.* s.122.
[28] Genetically Modified Organisms (Deliberate Release) Regulations, reg.17.
[29] *Ibid.*

(a) the name and address of the applicant;
(b) a general description of the genetically modified organisms featuring in the application;
(c) the location for release;
(d) the purpose for which consent to release or market is required;
(e) the foreseen dates of release;
(f) methods and plans for monitoring and emergencies; and
(g) evaluation of environmental impact.

Environmental Information Regulations[30]

If information is not placed on the public register described above, it may be available by virtue of the Environmental Information Regulations unless there are reasons of confidentiality to restrict or prohibit disclosure.

Enforcement

To aid the Secretary of State in the fulfilment of his statutory functions under Part VI and enforcement in particular, if it appears that any person has so-called "relevant information", the Secretary of State can require that that information be furnished to him. The power to demand the information is widely defined, targeting not only any person who appears to be involved in the importation, acquisition, keeping, release or marketing of genetically modified organisms, but also any person about to become or any person who has been involved in these activities. "Relevant information" here is information concerning any aspects of these activities, including any damage to the environment which may be or have been caused by them.[31]

Prohibition notices

The Secretary of State has powers to act against any person if there is reason to believe that that person is proposing to import or acquire, release or market genetically modified organisms, or is keeping such organisms. If it is considered that any such activities would involve a risk of causing damage to the environment, the Secretary of State may serve a prohibition notice to prohibit any of the defined activities, which could include a prohibition on the person's continued keeping of such organism. The width of the powers is further emphasised by the Act's stipulation that a notice may even prohibit an activity which is otherwise authorised by a consent. If a person is prohibited from continuing to keep particular organisms, he is obliged to dispose of them as quickly and as safely as is practicable or as required by the notice itself.[32]

[30] S.I. 1992 No. 3240. *Cf.* Chap. 9, "Access to Environmental Health Information".
[31] Environmental Protection Act, s.116.
[32] *Ibid.* s.110.

Inspectors' powers

The Secretary of State is empowered to appoint suitably qualified inspectors as necessary, for the purpose of carrying Part VI of the Act into effect.[33] The powers of entry to and inspection of premises extend to any land but not domestic premises. The range of powers is available where there is reason to believe that a person is keeping or has kept any genetically modified organisms or that they have escaped or been released. Those powers are also available where there is reason to believe that there may be harmful genetically modified organisms or evidence of damage to the environment caused by them. The powers themselves variously include:

(a) the right to enter premises;
(b) the seizure of articles and substances found on premises;
(c) the sampling of articles and substances; and
(d) the seizure of records and other data.[34]

Where an inspector, lawfully exercising his power to enter premises, discovers anything that is or consists of a genetically modified organism in circumstances such that it is a cause of imminent danger of damage to the environment, action may be taken to render it harmless. If it is practicable to do so, the inspector is obliged to take a sample and give a portion to a responsible person at the premises.[35]

Offences

A variety of offences is provided for by the Act.[36] Many of the foregoing enforcement devices are subject to criminal enforcement: to contravene a prohibition notice, to fail to comply (without reasonable excuse) with an inspector's requirement following a lawful entry to premises, and to fail to comply (without reasonable excuse) with the Secretary of State's requirement for information.[37] Otherwise, the offences focus essentially on failures to comply with statutory requirements in connection with notification and risk assessment, failures to comply with the consent requirements and obstruction of inspectors. In what is a complex catalogue of offences, there is an equally complex menu of penalties and modes of trial.

If a person is charged with offences[38] in respect of contraventions of the duties of care (under section 109) or the conditions to which a consent is subject (under section 112) referable to the need to adopt the best available techniques not entailing excessive cost, the onus of proof is on the defendant to establish that

[33] *Ibid.* s.144.
[34] *Ibid.* s.115.
[35] *Ibid.* s.117.
[36] *Ibid.* s.118.
[37] *Ibid.* subs.(1)(f), (g) and (k), respectively.
[38] *Ibid.* subs.(1)(c) and (d).

there was no better available technique not entailing excessive cost than that which was in fact used to satisfy the duty requirement or the condition.[39]

Remedial measures

Where the court convicts a person for certain of the offences contained in the Act[40] and the offences relate to matters which it appears the defendant has power to remedy, there is jurisdiction to require specified remedial measures to be taken. Such measures may be required in addition to or instead of any punishment. Within the time permitted for execution of remedial measures, no further criminal proceedings can be taken against the defendant.[41]

If the commission of the offences just mentioned has caused harm which it is possible to remedy, the Secretary of State has power to arrange for any reasonable steps to be taken towards remedying that harm and to recover the costs associated with any such measures from the person convicted. However, these powers are not available if any steps are to be taken on, or will affect, land not in the occupation of the person convicted, unless any such person other than the offender gives permission.[42]

[39] *Ibid.* s.119.
[40] *Ibid.* s.118(1)(a)–(f)
[41] *Ibid.* s.120.
[42] *Ibid.* s.121.

Chapter 6

ATMOSPHERIC POLLUTION

The Position at Common Law

The range of liabilities

There is no doubt that, in theory at least, common law rules extend widely to cover the distribution of liabilities arising from atmospheric pollution. Those rules that are of particular significance include nuisance, strict liability and negligence. Of these areas, there is an important link between liability for nuisance and incidents of atmospheric pollution. Note also the potential importance of strict liability under *Rylands v. Fletcher*,[1] an area of the common law that has not developed to any significant extent under English law. Each of these three areas—nuisance, negligence and strict liability—is examined below, emphasising throughout the predominance of the law of nuisance.

Nuisance: public and private

Veale J., in *Halsey v. Esso Petroleum Co. Ltd*,[2] emphasised that nuisance is commonly regarded as a tort ". . . in respect of land".[3] The starting point, therefore, is a need for some unreasonable interference with the plaintiff's use and enjoyment of his land. This interference for present purposes would typically involve material injury to the plaintiff's land or his premises arising from smoke or other similar emissions to the atmosphere.[4] Pursuit of an action in nuisance requires proof of ". . . sensible injury to the value of the property".[5] In other words, the damage

> ". . . must be such as can be shown by a plain witness to a plain common juryman. The damage must also be substantial, and it must be, in my view, actual; that is to say, the Court has, in dealing with questions of this kind, no right to take into account contingent, prospective or remote damage."[6]

[1] (1866) L.R. 1. Ex. 265.
[2] [1961] 1 W.L.R. 683; [1961] 2 All E.R. 145.
[3] At 692.
[4] As to which see the facts of *Halsey*.
[5] *St. Helen's Smelting Co. v. Tipping* (1865) 11 H.L. Cas. 642 at 650.
[6] James L. J. in *Salvin v. North Brancepeth Coal Co.* (1874) 9 Ch. App. 705 at 708.

Damages have been awarded in the present context for a loss of amenity: more particularly in respect of offensive smells from a pig unit: *Bone v. Seale.*[7]

Whereas an action in private nuisance rests on some unreasonable interference with the plaintiff's use and enjoyment of his land, proceedings for public nuisance do not require the plaintiff to show an interest in land. The essence of a public nuisance is that the reasonable comfort and convenience of the life of a class of Her Majesty's subjects are materially affected by its impact.[8] In these circumstances (as in *Halsey*) the private plaintiff can sue as long as it can be proved that "special" damage has been suffered. Denning L.J., in *Att.-Gen. v. PYA Quarries Ltd*[9] declined to answer the question of how many people are necessary to make up "Her Majesty's subjects generally":

> "I prefer to look to the reason of the thing and to say that a public nuisance is a nuisance which is so widespread in its range or so indiscriminate in its effect that it would not be reasonable to expect one person to take proceedings on his own responsibility to put a stop to it, but that it should be taken on the responsibility of the community at large."

A public nuisance can be prosecuted as a common law offence[10] and may be subject to injunctive proceedings by the Attorney-General *ex officio* or *ex relatione*, or by a local authority using powers available under section 222 of the Local Government Act 1972. In the case of a private nuisance, a cause of action may arise even if the plaintiff is a mere licensee.[11] Equally critical to the cause of action are matters relating to the location and sensitivity of the subject land. As a matter of degree, if any already polluted area is subject to further and excessive pollution from smoke, for example, there may still be liability in nuisance.[12] However, it is doubtful whether a defence could be established in these circumstances, based on an argument that the plaintiff "came to" the pre-existing nuisance.[13] In determining whether there is an actionable nuisance, the court will take account of the characteristics of the area and even any appropriate planning permission that may be in force for the purpose of deciding any claim based on adverse interference with the plaintiff's use of his premises, as opposed to any property damage.[14]

If a nuisance arises from various sources but one source by itself is insufficient to found a cause of action in nuisance, each person responsible for the individual

[7] [1975] 1 W.L.R. 797; [1975] 1 All E.R. 787.

[8] *Att.-Gen. v. PYA Quarries Ltd* [1957] 2 Q.B. 169 at 184; *Att.-Gen. v. Keymer Brick and Tile Co. Ltd* (1903) 67 J.P. 434.

[9] *Ibid.*

[10] Triable summarily or on indictment: Criminal Law Act 1977, s.16(1).

[11] *Khorasandjian v. Bush* (1993) 25 H.L.R. 392, C.A., but contrast the older authority of *Malone v. Laskey* [1907] 2 K.B. 141.

[12] *Rushmer v. Polsue and Alfieri Ltd* [1906] 1 Ch. 234, C.A.; [1907] A.C. 121, H.L.

[13] *Bliss v. Hall* (1838) 4 Bing N.C. 183.

[14] See n.5, *supra* and *cf.* the decisions in *Halsey* and *Gillingham Borough Council v. Medway (Chatham Docks) Co. Ltd* [1992] Env. L.R. 98.

sources will be subject to liability.[15] If a nuisance arises in one Member State of the European Community but the damage occurs in another Member State of the Community, the plaintiff has the option to sue in either State.[16]

Defences to an action in nuisance

The defences can be grouped under five headings:

(a) statutory authority;
(b) 20 years' prescriptive rights;
(c) *volenti non fit injuria*;
(d) contributory negligence; and
(e) limitation of time.

Each defence is now dealt with in turn.

A defence of statutory authority will be available in respect of the inevitable consequences of construction and use of premises, for example, authorised by statute.[17] In *Allen v. Gulf Oil Refining Ltd*,[18] it was decided that noise, smell and vibration were the inevitable consequences of the establishment of an oil refinery under Private Act powers. However, if a discretion is given that allows a choice as to the siting of an oil refinery, for example, that discretion must be exercised so that a nuisance is avoided.[19] Similarly, what may appear to be statutory authority to construct an undertaking may be seen to extend to actual operation but not negligent operation. Comparisons with the law of compulsory purchase may be relevant in so far as a particular Act of Parliament may or may not contain provision for compensation. It may be argued that statutory authority most safely applies where statutory compensation is attracted to the "taking" in question. In other words, elimination of compensation entitlement may suggest a continuing opportunity to rely on private rights at common law. However, such a suggestion seems to have been refuted by the House of Lords in *Allen*. The status of an Act of Parliament here can be contrasted with the status of some other sort of licence, such as a planning permission. That licence does not eliminate the plaintiff's common law rights: its task is to provide a "badge", indicating suitability of the subject site for a particular type of development covered by the consent. However, if a planning consent is granted for the development of land, any question of an actionable nuisance falls to be determined by reference to a neighbourhood with that development and not by reference to that neighbourhood before the development.[20] As a consequence, certain activities

[15] *Blair v. Deakin* (1877) 57 L.T. 522.
[16] *Bier v. Mines de Potasse d'Alsace* [1977] 1 C.M.L.R. 284.
[17] *Allen v. Gulf Refining Ltd* [1981] 2 W.L.R. 118.
[18] *Ibid.*
[19] *Metropolitan Asylum Board v. Hill* (1881) 6 App. Cas. 193.
[20] *Gillingham BC v. Medway (Chatham) Dock Co. Ltd:* see n.14, *supra.*

may be rendered "innocent" where, before a grant of planning permission, they could have been the subject of an actionable nuisance.

The defence of 20 years' prescriptive use operates in relation to a private but not a public nuisance. However, the period of 20 years runs only from the point when the plaintiff becomes aware of the existence of the nuisance.[21]

Volenti non fit injuria may be available as a defence to proceedings in nuisance. However, there must be evidence to indicate that the plaintiff accepts the allegedly unreasonable interference and no evidence of negligence in the defendant's conduct.[22]

Contributory negligence is undoubtedly a misnomer in the present context. However, the term "fault" as it appears in section 1 of the Law Reform (Contributory Negligence) Act 1945 extends to include liability for a nuisance.

Limitation of time requirements for present purposes are defined by section 2 of the Limitation Act 1980. This section provides that the cause of action should accrue within a period of six years, except in a case of personal injuries.

Nuisance and negligence

The defendant's negligence may also be a critical factor in establishing an actionable nuisance where, for example, failure to take reasonable care permits a continuing relaxation of safeguards against atmospheric pollution. There is no doubt that fault on the defendant's part will be at the centre of any inquiry, along with the requirement of foreseeability.[23] Apart from such questions of foreseeability, the need for due diligence will often focus on standards of plant operation in the industrial sector. Such a focus for common law liability may permit concentration on the integrated operation of a plant that is now alleged to have "realised" its polluting potential. Furthermore, and assuming that the generation of atmospheric pollution is sufficiently material as an interference rather than simply manifesting personal sensitivity, there is every chance that common law proceedings here could operate below the "threshold" of statutory air quality limits arising from E.C. law. However, in an already heavily polluted area, it may require further assaults from even heavier or excessive pollution before an action is likely to be sustainable at common law.[24]

In an action for negligence, the onus is on the plaintiff to prove the negligence: the evidential onus is not on the defendant to disprove any negligence. However, the onus of proof on the plaintiff may be very difficult to discharge because, for example, an occurrence could not have been within his knowledge. On these occasions the evidential maxim *res ipsa loquitur* ("the thing speaks for itself") will apply and the plaintiff's evidence will be based solely on the occurrence or accident. In other words, the normal evidential requirement will be amended where the court is satisfied that there would have been no occurrence in the absence of negligence. Resort to *res ipsa loquitur* may be particularly useful on

[21] *Sturges v. Bridgman* (1879) 11 Ch.D. 852.

[22] *Kiddle v. City Business Properties Ltd* [1942] 1 K.B. 269.

[23] *The Wagonmound (No. 2)* [1967] 1 A.C. 617, *per* Lord Reid at 639.

[24] See n.12, *supra*.

those occasions when an explosion on factory premises has led in turn to atmospheric pollution and related damage in the locality.[25] However, if the defendant produces an explanation, even though it is equally consistent with negligence or no negligence, the onus of proof remains with the plaintiff.

Strict liability

It has been seen earlier that the basis of strict liability in tort is the rule in *Rylands v. Fletcher*[26]: the person who for his own purposes brings on to his lands and collects and keeps there anything likely to do mischief if it escapes must keep it at his peril, and, if he does not do so, is prima facie answerable for all the damage which is the natural consequence of its escape, at least to the extent that there is foreseeability of harm or injury of the type complained of.

It is at least possible that many polluting occurrences are capable of attracting claims based on nuisance, negligence and strict liability. However, the above strict liability principle has seen only a limited development in English law generally and its application to any so-called "environmental claim" is limited in so far as it is necessary to establish an escape from the defendant's land to other land not under his occupation as well as the pursuit of a "non-natural" user on the defendant's land.[27] However, the decision in *Rylands v. Fletcher* does indicate that strict liability could affect an independent contractor.

Cases not connected directly to atmospheric pollution show that many industrial uses have not always been characterised by the courts as being "non-natural" uses of subject land. Lord Moulton in *Richards v. Lothian*[28] considered that:

> "It is not every use to which land is put that brings into play that principle. It must be some special use bringing with it increased dangers to others, and must not merely be the ordinary use of the land or such a use as is proper for the general benefit of the community."

In *Read v. Lyons and Co. Ltd*,[29] Viscount Simon was also of the view that, to attract strict liability, there must be some special use of the subject land bringing with it increased dangers to others, as opposed to some ordinary use of land or, on the other hand, some use which is "proper" for the general benefit of the community.[30] Viscount Simon also took the view that the manufacture of munitions in wartime would not be a non-natural use of the subject land.[31]

[25] For an analogous situation, see *McDonald v. Associated Fuels* [1954] 3 D.L.R. (3d) 775.

[26] See n.1, *supra*.

[27] *Rickards v. Lothian* [1913] A.C. 263; *Cambridge Water Co. v. Eastern Counties Leather Ltd* [1994] 2 W.L.R. 53.

[28] *Ibid.* at 280.

[29] [1974] A.C. 156.

[30] *Ibid.* at 169–170.

[31] A rather different conclusion was arrived at in *Rainham Chemical Works Ltd v. Belvedere Fish Guano Co. Ltd* [1921] A.C. 465. The House of Lords in *Read v. Lyons* did not consider itself bound by that case.

Subsequently, there are many indications that, for the most part, industrial uses are not to be categorised as "non-natural" uses. However, more recently the House of Lords has concluded (*obiter*) that a storage of chemicals in substantial quantities and their use in a manner leading to escape could not fall within the natural user exception.[32] However, *Halsey v. Esso Petroleum Co. Ltd*[33] does suggest that there are some industrial processes which may be vulnerable to strict liability, if only because of their sensitive location in a residential area, for example. This was the case in *Halsey*, where the problems arose from smuts issuing from a boiler exhaust.

The emission of acid smuts in *Halsey* resulted in both strict liability and liability in nuisance, public and private. Strict liability related to damage to clothing on the plaintiff's land and damage to his car while it was parked on the public highway following escape of the noxious smuts. The liability for private nuisance arose from the damage to the clothes: material injury to the plaintiff's property resulting from the trade carried out by the defendants on neighbouring property. The impact of the noxious smuts on the plaintiff's car amounted to "special" damage for the purpose of liability in public nuisance. Finally, and apart from the findings of liability for noise from the site, the defendants were also liable for the smells generated. These smells, the court held, amounted to a private nuisance, notwithstanding any absence of proof of damage to the plaintiff's health. The court held that damage to health is not a prerequisite for any cause of action for nuisance involving smells.

It is clear that if *Rylands v. Fletcher* strict liability is to apply, it is necessary to reconcile a number of very important variables. These are well illustrated in the Canadian case of *Gertsen v. Municipality of Metropolitan Toronto*,[33a] where one local authority agreed with another to take the latter's refuse, including putrescible organic matter, for landfilling. Methane gas leached from the site into an adjoining residential area where, on one occasion, a fire broke out, requiring residents to park their cars in the street. Still later, officials of the local authority owning the landfill assured residents that the problem had been solved and that private garages could again be used. However, methane gas continued to leach and subsequently an explosion occurred in the plaintiff's garage, injuring him and destroying the garage and his car. It was held that a landfill project for the disposal of garbage in a heavily populated district was a non-natural user of the subject land. As a consequence, the local authority was strictly liable. Despite the local authority's statutory authority to acquire land for the purpose of landfilling, the project was not executed pursuant to that statutory authority. The generation and escape of methane could reasonably have been anticipated and amounted to a nuisance. However, to expect the local authority to excavate and remove the content of the landfill to abate the nuisance would be unreasonable, so that damages were awarded for interference with the beneficial use of the plaintiff's land. The local authority was also held to be liable in negligence in landfilling

[32] *Cambridge Water Co. v. Eastern Counties Leather PLC* [1994] 2 W.L.R. 53, *per* Lord Goff at 59.
[33] [1961] 2 All E.R. 145.
[33a] (1973) 41 D.L.R. (3d) 646.

putrescible organic matter when they knew or ought to have known that decomposition would generate methane and when they should have acted to prevent gas leaching and to warn residents. A defence of *volenti non fit injuria* was also unsuccessful by reference to the fact that the plaintiffs had received no information that a situation of escaping methane existed in their garage or on their land.

In concluding that the defendants were strictly liable, the judge emphasised the variables of "time, place and circumstances", not excluding purpose in evaluating possible liability.[34] Furthermore, it was stressed[35] that the ". . . distinction between natural and non-natural user is both relative and capable of adjustment to the changing patterns of social existence". On the evidence the judge concluded that the one local authority had held out a "carrot" to the "accepting" local authority. The judge concluded that the landfilling

> ". . . having regard to its location together with the known temporary and permanent problems caused by such a garbage-fill project, cannot be said to be supported by the 'overriding public welfare' theory . . . Applying the propositions of time, place and circumstances and not excluding purpose, I find that this was a non-natural user of the land . . .".[36]

Negligence, nuisance and strict liability

It is clear from the foregoing that negligence, nuisance and strict liability may all come together for the purpose of determining liabilities and their distribution in the event of atmospheric pollution subject to the scientific difficulties of proving causation. Industrial development in particular may be vulnerable to strict liability and not only in exceptional cases, as shown by an application of the variables of time, place and circumstances. It may be increasingly difficult to impose liability at common law in view of regulatory requirements which, *inter alia*, will require special attention to matters of location. This regulatory element, along with a number of others, would presumably address matters such as the organisational and operating requirements for industrial and similar plants, thereby reducing the likely incidence of actions for negligence and nuisance. Perhaps the most obvious example of the regulatory process "filtering out" likely common law liabilities emerges from local authority atmospheric pollution control under Part I of the Environmental Protection Act 1990.

Remedies

The task of the common law in providing remedies divides into two through the provision of damages and injunctions. The function of an award of damages is to put the plaintiff in a position he enjoyed before the commission of the tort. Part of the calculation may take into account any loss of use or enjoyment of subject land

[34] Lerner J. at 665.
[35] *Ibid.*
[36] *Ibid.* at 666.

as a result of the tortious conduct. Environmental damage in the abstract will not be compensated, for example, the loss of wildlife features. There are circumstances in which the court may award damages in lieu of an injunction.[37] Normally that power will apply to mere trifling loss, damage or injury.

The injunction in the law of tort is normally a prohibitory injunction, often granted in proceedings for nuisance. In *Halsey*, for example, an injunction was granted, *inter alia*, for the purpose of dealing with the smells generated from the defendant's site. The injunction is a remedy that the court will decide to grant by reference to a fairly wide discretion. In *Halsey*, for example, there was some reluctance on the part of the judge, Veale J., to grant an injunction, the effect of which would be to close the defendant's factory. Nevertheless, in granting an injunction in respect of the smells coming from that factory, Veale J. was prepared to suspend the remedy in order to allow the defendant an opportunity to introduce improvements.

Statutory Sources: The Clean Air Act 1993

The background to the law

The Clean Air Acts 1956–68 (now consolidated in the Clean Air Act 1993) represent a very significant contribution to environmental control of the atmosphere, in two main respects: the regulation of specific emissions and the introduction of smoke control areas. Part IV of the Control of Pollution Act 1974 (also consolidated in the Act of 1993) also contained some very important provisions governing matters like the sulphur content of fuel oil and the acquisition of information about atmospheric emissions. Much of the law in the present context is linked to E.C. law which, increasingly, prescribes limits for emissions to the atmosphere. A lot of the E.C. legal requirements are found in a variety of directives, to be translated into English law through regulations made under the Act of 1993, for example.

The Clean Air Act 1993

This legislation is concerned with the abatement of air pollution and was first introduced following the report of the Committee on Air Pollution.[38] The controls set down in the legislation in relation to atmospheric emissions will not apply in so far as any process is a prescribed process for the purposes of Part I of the Environmental Protection Act 1990 relating to integrated pollution control and local authority atmospheric pollution control.[39]

[37] Chancery Amendment Act 1858, s.2.
[38] Cmnd. 9322.
[39] Clean Air Act 1993, s.41.

Dark smoke

Section 1 of the Act of 1993 prohibits dark smoke being emitted from chimneys of buildings. The prohibition extends beyond industrial buildings to include dwelling-houses also. However, the prohibition does not extend to all smoke, or to gases or sulphurous fumes. The smoke must be as dark as or darker than shade 2 on the Ringelmann Chart. However, for the purposes of any proceedings under section 1, the court may be satisfied that smoke is or is not dark smoke notwithstanding that there has been no actual comparison with such a chart.[40]

The scope of section 1 of the Act of 1993 is extended by section 2 of the Act by making it an offence to emit dark smoke (subject to exceptions)[41] from any industrial or trade premises, otherwise than from a chimney. The offence of emitting dark smoke from industrial or trade premises now goes beyond the occupier to include any person who *causes or permits* the emission. The Secretary of State is empowered to exempt, by regulation, the emission of dark smoke in the open where the smoke is caused by the burning of any prescribed matter.[42] In *Sheffield City Council v. ADH Demolition*,[43] it was held that a demolition site is "premises" within the section and that the act of demolition is a "trade process". Consequently, demolition contractors who burn debris on a site generating dark smoke will be in breach of the section. Section 2(3) of the Act of 1993[44] stipulates that there shall be taken to be an emission of dark smoke from premises where material is burned on those premises and the circumstances are such that the burning would be likely to give rise to any emission of dark smoke, unless the occupier or any person who caused or permitted the burning shows that no dark smoke was emitted. This provision can be seen as an attempt to remove some of the evidential problems in the way of enforcement, along with the provision found in section 3 of the Act.

The offence prescribed by section 1 of the Act appears, in isolation, to be an offence of strict liability, in so far as ". . . dark smoke shall not be emitted from a chimney of any building . . .". However, the defences prescribed by section 1(4) refer to what may or may not be "practicable" or what may or may not be "reasonably foreseen", suggesting scope for evidence that would indicate that the offence may be rather less strict than at first appears. The term "practicable" is defined elsewhere in the Act[45] as meaning:

> "reasonably practicable having regard, amongst other things, to local conditions and circumstances, to the financial implications and to the current state of technical knowledge, and 'practicable means' includes the provision and maintenance of plant and its proper use."

[40] *Ibid.* s.3.
[41] See the Clean Air (Emission of Dark Smoke) (Exemption) Regulations 1969 (S.I. 1969 No. 1263). *Cf.* the Dark Smoke (Permitted Periods) Regulations 1958 (S.I. 1958 No. 498) and, in relation to vessels, S.I. 1958 No. 878.
[42] Clean Air Act, s.2(2).
[43] (1984) 82 L.G.R. 177.
[44] Inserted into the original Act of 1968 by the Control of Smoke Pollution Act 1989, s.2.
[45] Clean Air Act, s.64(1).

A similar conclusion seems to follow from the structure of the offence prescribed by section 2, in so far as ". . . dark smoke shall not be emitted from any industrial or trade premises . . .". The defence in section 2(4) refers to an "inadvertent" contravention in circumstances where all practicable steps had been taken to prevent or minimise the emission of dark smoke. However, section 2(1), in prohibiting emissions, makes the "occupier"[46] liable to conviction as well as any person who causes or permits the emission.

The offence is built on the requirement that a defendant occupier should "cause or permit" a subject emission.[47]

A person guilty of an offence under section 1 is liable on summary conviction to a fine not exceeding level 3 on the standard scale[48] in the case of emission of dark smoke from the chimney of a private dwelling, and a fine not exceeding level 5 on the standard scale in the case of an emission of dark smoke from any other chimney.[49]

The latter penalty also applies on conviction for the offence in section 44 of the Act relating to the emission of dark smoke from vessels in territorial waters.[50] Conviction attracts a fine not exceeding level 5 on the standard scale.[51]

Under sections 1 and 2, a local authority is empowered to institute proceedings for an offence even if the emission has come from a chimney or premises (as the case may be) outside their district, as long as the subject smoke affects their district.[52]

As an aspect of more general enforcement, an authorised officer of the local authority[53] is required to notify occupiers of infractions. Failure of such notification activates a defence in the relevant criminal proceedings.[54]

The foregoing provisions relating to the criminal enforcement of requirements in relation to dark smoke have to be seen in the context of Parts I and III of the Environmental Protection Act 1990 relating to integrated pollution control and local authority air pollution control (Part I) and statutory nuisances (Part III), respectively.[55] Both areas of the Act of 1990 will supersede the Clean Air Act provisions.[56]

Smoke from furnaces

Section 4 of the Clean Air Act prohibits the installation of new industrial furnaces unless they are capable, so far as practicable, of being operated without emitting

[46] *Ibid.* subs.(2).

[47] Contrast *Alphacell Ltd v. Woodward* [1972] A.C. 824 and *Price v. Cromack* [1975] 1 W.L.R. 988, both involving water pollution offences.

[48] Criminal Justice Act 1982, s.75.

[49] Clean Air Act, s.1(5).

[51] s.44(2).

[52] Clean Air Act, s.55.

[53] The district or London borough council.

[54] Clean Air Act, s.51: the period in question is to run to the end of four days next following the day of the offence.

[55] See, in particular, s.79.

[56] Clean Air Act, s.41.

smoke. Notice must be given to the local authority of any proposal to install such a furnace.[57] Failure to comply is a summary offence. An exception to the section 4 prohibition is in respect of domestic furnaces with a heating capacity of less than 55,000 Btu/hr. More generally, the local authority may give prior approval, in which case the furnace is deemed to comply with the requirements of section 4. There is no appeal against this decision, although the furnace can still be installed if it is smokeless. Once again, it is likely that the installation and use of furnaces and incinerators on land may well be comprised within a "process" and so be subject to regulation under Part I of the Environmental Protection Act 1990.

Grit and dust from furnaces

Section 5 of the Clean Air Act enables the Secretary of State to prescribe limits on the quantities of grit and dust which may be emitted from chimneys other than small domestic furnaces. Where such limits are prescribed, it is an offence to exceed the limit, subject to the defence that best practicable means have been used to minimise the emission.[58] The Clean Air (Emission of Grit and Dust from Furnaces) Regulations 1971[59] prescribe limits that are applicable to certain furnaces.

Certain categories of furnace must be provided with plant for arresting grit and dust (as approved by the local authority). Furthermore, it is a statutory requirement that that plant should be properly maintained and used. Exemptions may be provided by the Secretary of State in respect of new, non-domestic furnaces. The Secretary of State has made the Clean Air (Arrestment Plant) (Exemption) Regulations 1969 which exempt, *inter alia*, mobile furnaces providing a temporary source of heat during building operations.[60] By means of regulations, the Secretary of State may also substitute the burning capacity of any non-domestic furnace although, to date, no regulations have been made. The provisions governing arrestment plant apply also to any outdoor furnace.[61] An appeal lies to the Secretary of State in respect of any adverse decision of the local authority.[62] Failure to comply is an offence.[63]

The Act deals with the measurement of grit and dust emitted from furnaces. Section 10 of the Act empowers the Secretary of State to make regulations requiring the measurement and recording of grit and dust emitted from chimneys. A local authority may then, by notice in writing, require occupiers burning pulverised fuel or solid fuel at a rate of a ton or more per hour or using ovens subjecting solid fuel to the application of heat to comply with the Secretary of State's requirements. The Clean Air (Measurement of Grit and Dust from Furnaces) Regulations 1971[64] prescribe the requirements to be observed in

[57] *Ibid.* s.4(1), (4).
[58] *Ibid.* s.5(4).
[59] S.I. 1971 No. 162.
[60] S.I. 1969 No. 1262.
[61] Clean Air Act, ss.6–8 and 13.
[62] *Ibid.* s.9(2).
[63] *Ibid.* s.6(5).
[64] S.I. 1971 No. 161.

recording measurements of grit and dust from certain furnaces. The Act extends to a wide range of furnaces and applies also to fumes for the purpose of a local authority's power to direct, in individual cases, that an owner should measure the grit and dust emitted from a furnace. In the case of smaller furnaces, the local authority itself may undertake measurements if the owner so wishes. The authority may also be represented when measurements are made.

As an aid to enforcement in the present context, section 12 empowers a local authority to require information as to furnaces and ovens. Failure to comply with a local authority's request for information or the provision of false information is an offence.[65]

Section 13 applies to outdoor furnaces. For these purposes, sections 6–8 and sections 5–12 of the Act apply to such furnaces.

The height of chimneys for present purposes is governed by sections 14–16. The essential purpose of the provisions is to require a local authority to consider plans which can be rejected unless there is satisfaction that the height of the chimney will be sufficient to prevent, so far as practicable, the smoke, grit, dust or gases from becoming prejudicial to health or a nuisance,[66] having regard to the purpose of the chimney, the position and description of neighbouring buildings, the levels of neighbouring ground and any other circumstances. The Act stipulates that, where a new chimney is constructed or the capacity of the furnace or furnaces served by an existing chimney is increased, it will be an offence to use the chimney unless its height has been approved by the local authority. Exemptions from this provision are to be found in the Clean Air (Height of Chimneys) (Exemption) Regulations 1969.[67]

As with previous areas of the present legislation, careful account should be taken of Part I of the Environmental Protection Act 1990. In practice, it is increasingly likely that the industrial background to many emissions will be encompassed within a "process" subject to control under the provisions for integrated pollution control or local authority air pollution control.[68]

Smoke control areas

A local authority may, by an order confirmed by the Secretary of State, declare whole or part of its district to be a smoke control area in which, subject to exemptions and limitations, the emission of dark smoke will be an offence.[69] Schedule 2 provides (subject to restrictions to be found in Department of the Environmental Circular 9/93) for the payment of grants by local authorities, and Exchequer contributions towards the cost of any necessary conversion of appliances in private dwellings, churches, chapels and buildings used by charities, *inter alia*. Prior to 1968, declaration of a smoke control area by a local authority

[65] Clean Air Act, s.12(2).

[66] See s.79, Environmental Protection Act 1990.

[67] S.I. 1969 No. 411.

[68] See in particular s.41 of the Clean Air Act and also s.8(1), (2).

[69] Clean Air Act, s.20: on summary conviction, a fine not exceeding level 3 on the standard scale may be imposed.

was entirely a matter for that authority. Section 19 of the Act now empowers the Secretary of State, after consultation, to require an authority to prepare proposals for the making of an order. Failure by the authority to observe the requirement triggers the Secretary of State's default powers.[70]

If a local authority proposes to declare a smoke control area, Schedule 1 to the Act requires an order to be advertised before confirmation.

Once an operative order is in force, it acts to prohibit the emission of smoke from the chimney or any building in the area. The only defences available to the occupier are that the emission of smoke was not caused by fuel other than an "authorised fuel", or that a verbal or written warning had not been given by an authorised officer by virtue of section 16. An additional offence is to be found in section 23, whereby it is an offence to acquire or sell any solid fuel other than an "authorised" fuel, as defined by the Act and regulations made thereunder, for use in a smoke control area.

In so far as there is any overlap between the foregoing controls and premises whereon "processes" subject to authorisation under Part I of the Environmental Protection Act 1990 are undertaken, the latter controls will apply.[71] Such controls will relate either to a process which is subject to integrated pollution control or local authority air pollution control.

There is no doubt about the significant impact of smoke control through the Clean Air Act, although the emphasis of the law appears to be changing as a result of E.C. directives and, in particular, the Directive on smoke and sulphur dioxide.[72] The focus of influence from E.C. law here is on mandatory air quality standards. More particularly, the Air Quality Standards Regulations 1989[73] oblige the Secretary of State to ". . . take any appropriate measures" to ensure that concentrations of sulphur dioxide, for example, do not exceed limit values prescribed by the appropriate directives. Despite the complex processes associated with the creation and confirmation of smoke control areas, there is no doubt that the Secretary of State's power to direct a local authority to prepare proposals for such an area represent an important vehicle for realisation of concentrations in the atmosphere through observance of the limit values found in the relevant directives.

Miscellaneous matters

It was seen previously that the provisions governing the emission of dark smoke apply also to vessels and railway engines.[73a] Similar provision is made under section 42, requiring the owners of mine and quarry spoil banks to minimise smoke and fumes from those spoil banks.

Elsewhere in the Act, a local authority can grant exemption from enforcement

[70] *Ibid.* s.19.
[71] *Ibid.* s.41.
[72] Directive 80/779 [1980] O.J. L229.
[73] S.I. 1989 No. 317.
[73a] *Ibid.*

in respect of many of the requirements of the Acts (including statutory nuisance provisions of the Environmental Protection Act 1990) in the interest of research into, and investigation of, air pollution.[74] Section 46 requires a local authority to report to the responsible Minister any dark smoke outside a smoke control area, any smoke nuisance or any dark smoke from a vessel, where the premises or vessel concerned are Crown property. Thereupon the Minister is obliged to take suitable steps to remedy the matter.

Enforcement

The Act indicates that it is the duty of the local authority to enforce the provisions of the Act.[75] The local authority is the district council or, in London, the London borough council or the Common Council of the City of London.[76] However, nothing in the present provisions on enforcement extends to enforcement of the provisions of the Building Regulations made under the Building Act 1984.[77]

Entry to land may be demanded as of right, except in respect of a private dwelling, although in this case entry may be demanded as of right in connection with the adaptation of fire places. The general right of entry is subject to stringent requirements relating to entry via a justice's warrant. The right of entry is given to "any person authorised in that behalf by a local authority", suggesting a wide category of person, compared with the "authorised officer" referred to in section 287 of the Public Health Act 1936. The powers of entry are drawn widely in referring to "any land or vessel", although the "inspections, measurements and tests" on such land or vessel may suggest a restriction on such activities as they may relate (say) to neighbouring land. A local authority is obliged to pay "full" compensation to any person who sustains damage to rights of entry and inspection. Such powers are enforceable through provision for a summary offence of wilful obstruction.[78] However, if any person discloses information relating to any trade secret used in carrying on any particular undertaking, which has been given to or obtained by him under the Act or in connection with its enforcement, he is guilty of an offence and liable on summary conviction to a fine not exceeding level 5 on the standard scale. However, there are exceptions, where disclosure is made with the consent of the person carrying on the undertaking, in connection with enforcement of the Act, or for the purpose of legal proceedings arising from the Act or for the purpose of any report of such proceedings.[78a]

Various specific summary offences are provided for in sections 4(4), 8(2), 10(3), 12(2) and 43(4). Furthermore, conviction for certain offences[79] in circumstances where it is shown that the offence was substantially a repetition or continuation of an earlier offence for which there was a conviction can render

[74] Clean Air Act, s.45. The categories of exemption are set out in subs.(1).
[75] *Ibid.* s.55.
[76] *Ibid.* s.64.
[77] *Ibid.* s.55(1).
[78] *Ibid.* ss.56 and 57.
[78a] *Ibid.* s.49.
[79] *Ibid.* ss.10(3) and 43(4).

the defendant liable, on summary conviction, to a fine not exceeding level 5 on the standard scale or not exceeding £50 for every day on which the earlier offence was repeated or continued, within a stipulated time limit.[80]

Where the occupier of a building requires the consent of the building owner in order to ensure that a building's use complies with the Act or where (for a similar purpose) he considers that the whole or part of any costs should be borne by that owner, an application may be made to the county court which can make such order as it considers to be "just".[81]

Section 62 of the Act applies Part XII of the Public Health Act 1936 in relation to matters of local administration and machinery for enforcement. Furthermore, section 61 permits any two or more local authorities to combine for the purpose of declaring a smoke control area.

Air pollution control

Part IV of the Act contains a variety of provisions referable to air pollution control. Sections 31 and 32 are referable to E.C. Directives 75/716[81a] and 87/219[81b] on the sulphur content of gas oil. Using his powers to make regulations here, the Secretary of State is able to introduce specific E.C. requirements.[82]

Cable burning is prohibited under section 33: among other things such a process can produce very toxic PCBs (polychlorinated biphenyls). Normally, such cable burning will be permitted only under an authorisation granted through the integrated pollution control provisions of Part I of the Environmental Protection Act 1990.[83]

A group of sections in Part V of the Act empowers a local authority to require the occupiers of "any premises" in its area to furnish estimates or other information about emissions into the air from those premises.[84] There is an appeal against any such notice to the Secretary of State. The provisions also empower local authorities to record emissions themselves. In so far as entry to premises is concerned, section 56 requires authorisation from the local authority. The powers available are quite widely drawn, referring to emissions ". . . from any chimney, flue or other outlet".[85] However, the powers do not extend to private dwellings and premises subject to authorisation by Her Majesty's Inspectorate of Pollution under the integrated pollution control provisions of Part I of the Environmental Protection Act 1990. The local authority, in so far as it uses these facilities and powers in Part V of the Act, is able to arrange for publication of the information obtained, although there is no statutory specification of the form of any register to be maintained.

[80] *Ibid.* s.50.
[81] *Ibid.* s.54.
[81a] [1975] O.J. L307.
[81b] [1987] O.J. L91.
[82] The limit for sulphur content is now 0.3 per cent.: S.I. 1990 Nos. 1096 and 1097.
[83] See Chap. 7, "Integrated Pollution Control".
[84] ss.79–83.
[85] Control of Atmospheric Pollution (Research and Publicity) Regulations 1977 (S.I. 1977 No. 19).

The Air Quality Standards Regulations,[85a] as seen previously, oblige the Secretary of State to take any appropriate measures to ensure that concentrations of sulphur dioxide, for example, do not exceed limit values prescribed by the appropriate E.C. directives. These requirements must be seen in the light of the powers and functions of local authorities under the present group of sections in Part V. Of particular significance potentially is the power of the Secretary of State to direct a local authority to provide measuring equipment and to convey relevant information obtained to him.[86] The group of sections also have potential significance in the enforcement of Part I of the Environmental Protection Act 1990.

E.C. standards

Hitherto in the present chapter, considerable emphasis has been given to the matter of sulphur dioxide emissions to the atmosphere. Also of prime concern are nitrogen dioxide and lead in the atmosphere. Both pollutants are subject to E.C. directives,[87] and both pollutants, along with sulphur dioxide, are the subject of the Air Quality Standards Regulations.[88]

Along with sulphur dioxide, nitrogen dioxide is a major concern of the large combustion plant Directive,[89] whose implementation is seen in the integrated pollution control provisions of Part I of the Environmental Protection Act 1990. The Directive applies to plants with a thermal rated input of 50 MW or more, no matter what type of fuel is used. Member States are required to reduce progressively total annual emissions from existing combustion plants. The requirement is compliance with the emission ceilings and percentage reductions for sulphur dioxide and oxides of nitrogen found in Annex I and II to the Directive. Each Annex deals with phased reductions: Annex I dealing with SO_2 and Annex II, NO_x. Article 15 of the Directive refers to mean values taken from monthly averages. However, Her Majesty's Inspectorate of Pollution has considered that additional controls should be applied in relation to periods over which emission limits are averaged. In its second annual report,[90] the Inspectorate states that for

> ". . . inspection purposes the Inspectorate needs to assess operational performance more frequently, and for nitrogen oxides and particulate matter it will be looking for controls in addition to those contained in the Directive".[91]

[85a] See n.73, *supra*.
[86] Clean Air Act, s.39.
[87] Directives 85/203: [1985] O.J. L87 and 82/884: [1982] O.J. L378. *Cf.* Directives 89/369: [1989] O.J. L163 and 89/429: [1989] O.J. L203 on municipal waste incinerators.
[88] S.I. 1989 No. 317.
[89] Directive 88/609: [1988] O.J. L336.
[90] 1988–89.
[91] *Ibid.* p.7.

The broader framework Directive (Directive 84/360[92]) also provides a foundation for the integrated pollution control provisions of the Environmental Protection Act.

It has been seen that reaction in the United Kingdom to the problem of sulphur dioxide concentrations is by reference to E.C. legal requirements, of which the large combustion plant Directive is the most significant. Considerable interest here focuses on FGD (flue gas desulphurisation).[93] When SO_2 limits are examined, it becomes clear that FGD may be an attractive option in the quest for compliance with E.C. legal requirements. However, closer examination reveals that the matter cannot be seen in simple terms. FGD, for example, is known to accentuate carbon dioxide emissions as well as being a complex system to build. There are also potential cross-media pollution problems if there is no market or no sufficient market for FGD byproducts, such as sulphuric acid. It is well known that British coal tends to have a high sulphur content, so that there would be little hope in the electricity-generating industry that such coal could be used without FGD being built into power station plant. A possible alternative is gas. Use of gas generates very little, if any, SO_2 and very much less carbon dioxide compared with coal. However, in the time allowed for achievement of targets laid down in Directive 88/609 it is unlikely that compliance will occur only with resort to gas.

Directly related to E.C. standards in the present context are those provisions in Part I of the Environmental Protection Act relating to local authority air pollution control, the subject of the following section.

Local Authority Controls Under the Environmental Protection Act

Local authority functions

Air pollution control by local authorities operates also within the broader context of Part I of the Environmental Protection Act 1990. For present purposes, the Act of 1990 defines a local authority principally as a London borough council in Greater London, and a district council outside Greater London.[94] Pollution control here is not necessarily restricted to stationary sources: Part I of the Act refers to control over "processes" which are defined to mean ". . . any activities carried on . . . whether on premises or by means of mobile plant, which are capable of causing pollution of the environment".[95] Furthermore, control is based on specific emission limits for certain pollutants founded on lists contained in the framework Directive on air pollution. Hitherto, enforcement of the law in this area has focussed primarily on statutory nuisances and the various provisions of the Clean Air Act examined previously in this chapter. Implementation of Part

[92] [1984] O.J. L188.

[93] See, *e.g.* the Third Report of the House of Commons Select Committee on Energy (Session 1989–90).

[94] s.4(11). *Cf.* Circular 3/91 (Welsh Circular 19/91).

[95] s.1(5).

I provisions from the Act of 1990 is likely to result in reduced reliance on these other statutory controls in the present context.

The scope of control

Reference has been made already to the term "process", as defined by the Act of 1990. However, another set of terms[96] defining "the environment", "pollution of the environment" and "harm" indicate the potential width of local authority controls. The "environment" consists of:

> ". . . all or any of the following media, namely, the air, water and land and the medium of the air includes the air within buildings and the air within other natural or man-made structures above or below ground."

"Pollution of the environment" means:

> ". . . pollution of the environment due to the release (into any environmental medium) from any process of substances which are capable of causing harm to man or any other living organisms supported by the environment."

"Harm" means:

> ". . . harm to the health of living organisms or other interference with the ecological systems of which they form part and, in the case of man, includes offence caused to any of his senses or harm to his property . . ."

Prescribed processes

Against the background of the above definitions, the Environmental Protection (Prescribed Processes and Substances) Regulations 1991 (as amended) define those processes subject to local control.[97] Earlier reference to the term "process" refers to "activities" defined to mean ". . . industrial or commercial activities or activities of any other nature whatsoever (including, with or without other activities), the keeping of a substance".[98] The definition of "pollution of the environment" refers to the release into any environmental medium of substances from any process. The Act stipulates that a substance is "released" into any environmental medium whenever it is released directly into that medium and that "release" includes (in relation to air) ". . . any emission of the substance into the air".[99] The term "substance" is treated as including electricity or heat.[1]

[96] Defined by s.1(2), (3) and (4), respectively.
[97] S.I. 1991 No. 472 and *cf.* s.1(7). A definitive catalogue is to be found in "The Environmental Protection (Prescribed Processes and Substances) Regulations—A Consolidated Version", HMSO, August 1994.
[98] s.1(6).
[99] subs.(10).
[1] subs.(13).

An enabling power in section 2(1) empowers the Secretary of State to prescribe any description of process as a process for which any authorisation from the local authority is required by virtue of section 6. The Prescribed Processes and Substances Regulations[2] distinguish between so-called "Part A" and "Part B" processes, Part B processes being those subject to local control for present purposes.[3] Schedule 4 to the Regulations lists the substances which are most potentially harmful or polluting when emitted to the atmosphere. These substances and their management must comply with best available techniques not entailing excessive cost (BATNEEC) for the purpose of preventing their release to the atmosphere or (if this is not practicable) to minimise releases.[4] Some processes involving Schedule 4 substances are excluded from control as long as there are no offensive smells noticeable outside the subject premises; for example, where there are trivial emissions that cannot cause harm, such as the melting of metal in conjunction with jewellery-making.

The catalogue of processes in Schedule 1 is subject to rules contained in Schedule 2, the most important of which is that these rules do not override any specific provision in Schedule 1. The rules are aimed at assisting in circumstances where there are difficulties of interpretation across Schedule 1 in relation to Part A and Part B processes. For example, if a process comprises two or more "sub-processes" described in the same section of Schedule 1 and those processes are operated by the same person at the same location, this is to be treated as a single process, attracting one authorisation for the purpose of section 6. However, if one of these "sub-processes" comes under Part A, all will attract central control by Her Majesty's Inspectorate of Pollution under the regime for integrated pollution control.[5] On the other hand, three (Part B) hot blast cupolas operated by the same person at the same location would constitute one iron and steel process for the purpose of local authority air pollution control and require one authorisation, falling as they do within the same section of Schedule 1.[6] In cases of doubt, local authorities are encouraged to liaise with Her Majesty's Inspectorate.

The determination of applications

A local authority has a period of 12 months in which to arrive at a decision on an application for authorisation in relation to an existing process[7] and a period of 18 months in the case of existing small waste oil burners under 0.4 MW. These periods are substituted for the shorter (four-month) periods relating to most other cases.[8] The periods in each case start to run from the date of receipt of the application.

[2] See n.97, *supra*.
[3] S.I. 1991 No. 472, Sched. 1.
[4] s.7(2)(a)(i). Whether or not a prescribed substance, BATNEEC requirements will be applicable for rendering it harmless: *ibid.* subs.(2)(a)(ii).
[5] Secretary of State's guidance (GG1 (91)), p.6.
[6] *Ibid.*
[7] S.I. 1991 No. 507, Sched. 3, para. 14.
[8] *Ibid.* Sched. 1, para. 5.

Best available techniques not entailing excessive cost

Reference has been made previously to BATNEEC being the fundamental reference point for control, to prevent and minimise emissions of prescribed substances and to render harmless all releases. The application of legal requirements and the associated technical requirements are aided by the Secretary of State's process guidance notes.[9]

The relevant directives refer to "technology" rather than "techniques". The latter term, incorporated in the Environmental Protection Act, is intended to be rather wider and to contemplate not only the "hardware" associated with a process but also operational requirements. In essence, an authorisation, founded as it is on BATNEEC, should represent a complete statement on the technology and its operation of the subject process. Inevitably, this authorisation process will be subject to a range of variables, such as plant design, arrangement, size and peculiar characteristics of the site and the operation of the process. Nevertheless, statements of BATNEEC will be directly comparable in the case of similar processes. However, BATNEEC is but one of the objectives behind the authorisation process.[10]

Authorisation objectives

Apart from BATNEEC and its role in preventing or minimising emissions and rendering harmless all emissions, section 7(2) refers to three other objectives:

(a) compliance with directions from the Secretary of State for the purpose of conforming with requirements in E.C. and international law;
(b) compliance with limits or requirements and achievement of any quality standards or objectives prescribed by the Secretary of State; and
(c) compliance with any requirements for authorisations found in plans from the Secretary of State indicating, *inter alia*, limits for the total amount of any substance to be released into the United Kingdom environment.

BATNEEC: the critical elements

The term "technique" is referable to the process, including matters of concept and design, together with the operation of that process and its components and their inter-relationship with the process. Note also the relevance of staffing, training, work methods and supervision.[11] Any appropriate techniques have to be "available" to the process operator. Those techniques may not be generally in

[9] s.78(11) requires a local authority to have regard to any guidance for the application of s.7(1) and (2), in relation to the techniques and environmental options appropriate to any description of prescribed process.
[10] s.7(1), (2)
[11] s.7(10).

use: the important matter is that the techniques should be generally available, albeit from a sole, monopoly supplier. The techniques referred to must be the most effective techniques, hence the reference to "best" available techniques. However, to be the most effective techniques, there must be regard for the need for prevention, minimisation and neutralisation of atmospheric pollution.

The requirement that best available techniques should be those "not entailing excessive cost" represents a most important variable affecting conclusions about the first part of the formula, bearing in mind that achieving the best available techniques may be excessively costly or even pose a threat to environmental health when weighed against environmental benefits. More generally for present purposes, there is a presumption that best available techniques will be used. As far as existing processes are concerned, the Secretary of State's process guidance notes stipulate appropriate time scales over which processes should be upgraded or, in some cases, decommissioned.[12]

There is no one prescribed approach to the expression of BATNEEC. BATNEEC may be expressed in technological terms by reference to process requirements for certain "hardware" and its operation. Equally, the expression may be in terms of an emission standard. Brought together, BATNEEC here would no doubt be described as a "performance standard" with a variable concern for the encouragement of ever better techniques subject to the constraints referred to previously, namely the excessive cost or health risks attracted.

Applications and authorisations

Section 6 declares that a prescribed process shall not be undertaken ". . . except under an authorisation granted by the enforcing authority and in accordance with the conditions to which it is subject".[13] Detailed requirements here are to be found in the Environmental Protection (Applications, Appeals and Registers) Regulations 1991.[14] The Regulations stipulate five categories of information to be submitted with an application:

(a) operator details and process location;
(b) the process and its essential techniques for the purpose of preventing or minimising emissions and rendering harmless emission to air of all substances;
(c) source, nature and amount of emissions;
(d) proposals for monitoring, sampling and measuring emissions; and
(e) an environmental assessment of the impact of the emissions.

It is critically important that any such application identify the achievement of

[12] See in particular the guidance contained in arts.12 and 13 of Directive 84/360, the framework Directive on air pollution.
[13] s.6(1).
[14] S.I. 1991 No. 507.

objectives found in section 7(2) for the purpose of complying with the general condition found in section 7(4). The local authority is able to demand additional information and to impose a time limit for its submission.[15] The application must be submitted with the appropriate fee, as set by the Secretary of State's charging scheme.[16]

Advertisement and consultation

Part I of the Environmental Protection Act requires that applications are advertised and details entered on a register open to the public. Both the public and certain statutory consultees have an opportunity to comment on an application so that, in turn, their representations are taken into account by the local authority. If additional information is requested by the local authority, the foregoing requirements in relation to advertisement and consultation will not apply, although it is still open to the local authority on a voluntary basis to operate these facilities in this case. Nevertheless the local authority's request for additional information may be voluntarily communicated to members of the public and statutory consultees.

There are two statutory consultees, one of whom—the Health and Safety Executive—is to require all applications, with one small exception. The second statutory consultee represents the nature conservation interest and comprises the Nature Conservancy Council for England, the Countryside Council for Wales and the equivalent natural heritage body for Scotland. In the case of the nature conservation interest, consultation by the local authority is required if an emission to the atmosphere will affect a site of special scientific interest designated under Part II of the Wildlife and Countryside Act in any part of the local authority's area. The Secretary of State's process guidance notes contain useful guidance on circumstances in which the consultation requirement may be triggered.[17]

With two minor exceptions, there is a requirement to advertise all applications in one or more newspapers circulating in the area in which the process is intended to operate. The Regulations stipulate the range of information to be included in the advertisement and (most importantly) indicate that a period of 28 days is permitted (from the advertisement) for written representations to be made to the lcoal authority. This advertising requirement emphasises a further element of the coverage of Part I: its application to mobile plant, such as mobile incineration and roadstone coating plant. The responsible local authority for this purpose will be the local authority in whose area the operator has his principal place of business.[18] It is foreseen by the Secretary of State's guidance[19] that the subject local authority will undertake a co-ordinating role, so that other local authorities in whose area the mobile plant is operated will undertake inspection and monitoring functions.

[15] Sched. 1, para. 1(3), (4).
[16] s.8 and *cf.* the detailed charges set out in the Secretary of State's guidance (GG1 (April 1991)).
[17] GG3 (1991), p.6.
[18] s.4(3).
[19] At pp.10–11.

Authorisations

The Act[20] insists that an authorisation contains three possible categories of condition,[21] namely:

(a) any conditions considered appropriate for the purpose of fulfilling the objectives set out in section 7(2);
(b) any conditions required by virtue of a direction from the Secretary of State under section 7(3); and
(c) such other conditions (if any) appearing to be appropriate to the enforcing local authority.

However, no condition can be imposed whose sole aim is to secure the health of persons at work.[22] Furthermore, no condition can be attached to an authorisation for the purpose of regulating the final disposal by deposit in or on land of "controlled waste".[23] Nevertheless, the local enforcing authority is obliged to notify the waste regulation authority for the area in question.[24] The Radioactive Substances Act 1993, as amended, deals with the registration and licensing of accumulations of radioactive material. In so far as there is conflict between conditions imposed under the Act of 1993 and under Part I of the present legislation, the former takes precedence.[25]

Part I of the Environmental Protection Act does not prescribe any detailed content that should characterise an authorisation. Nevertheless, it has been seen already that there are certain conditions that must feature in an authorisation and the Secretary of State's guidance[26] does confirm the need for inclusion of certain "standard particulars", such as the purpose of the authorisation, a description of the process, general and specific conditions and so on.

In dealing with the specific and general conditions, the Secretary of State's guidance[27] considers that authorisations will be clearer for everyone (local authority, industry and the public) if conditions that are specific are grouped under four main headings:

(a) emission limits and controls;
(b) monitoring, sampling and measurement of emissions;
(c) operational controls (including materials handling and arrestment plant); and
(d) chimneys, vents and process exhausts.

In the case of the so-called "general" condition, which is implied under section

[20] s.7(1).
[21] *cf.* "Authorisation objectives", *supra*.
[22] See n.20, *supra*.
[23] s.28(1).
[24] *Ibid.*
[25] s.28(2).
[26] GG2, p.4.
[27] *Ibid.*

7(4) as the "residual" condition, local authorities are advised to include that condition in each authorisation. However, this general condition will relate to those parts of the subject process outside the terms of the specific conditions. The guidance from the Secretary of State[28] notes that detailed conditions will be "beneficial" in three particular ways:

> "They will:
> (a) make plain to the operator the standards of control he must achieve in carrying on his process:
> (b) often be more readily enforceable than the general condition, and
> (c) provide more comprehensive information to members of the public who wish to consult the public register.
>
> A detailed authorisation is also likely to command far greater public confidence. The main control parameters for any process, therefore, should be set down in specific conditions."

The Secretary of State's guidance[29] also sets down four criteria for the drafting of authorisation conditions, referring to enforceability, clarity for the benefit of industry and the public, relevance to air pollution control over the process and (finally) "workability". By way of illustration, consider the following requirements that may be found in an authorisation:

(a) measurement of emissions, but no indication of a method of measurement;
(b) the wearing of protective clothing on site;
(c) off-site monitoring of emissions for the purpose of complying with statutory air quality standards;
(d) upgrading of techniques presently used on the site where the process is located;
(e) the use of anything other than low sulphur coal in a combustion process.

Taking each of the foregoing in turn:

(a) A condition omitting the method of measurement would be vulnerable to attack on the ground of uncertainty, rendering the condition (and possibly the whole authorisation) unenforceable. Referring to planning conditions, Lord Denning has considered that: ". . . a planning condition is only void for uncertainty if it can be given no meaning or no sensible or ascertainable meaning, and not merely because it is ambiguous or leads to absurd results."[30]
(b) A requirement that protective clothing be worn on site is of doubtful relevance to the process of authorisation in the present context. Note the status of the Health and Safety Executive as a statutory consultee.

[28] *Ibid.* pp.4 and 5.
[29] *Ibid.* p.5.
[30] *Fawcett v. Buckinghamshire County Council* [1960] 3 All E.R. 503.

(c) Off-site monitoring of emissions seems to require some caution, if only to avoid a situation in which the local enforcing authority is vulnerable to attack on the ground of an unlawful attempt to "off-load" its statutory responsibilities for air quality monitoring.[31] If, however, the clear concern is to (say) monitor sulphur dioxide levels from the combustion process on the subject site by reference to the limit values in the Air Quality Standards Regulations, there can be little doubt about the legality of the requirement.

(d) If it is proposed to upgrade a subject process, section 11(1) enables an operator to notify the local authority of any relevant change proposed. The terms of the illustrative condition (a "requirement" to upgrade) may be rather too assertive, particularly in view of the fact that it may be very much in the operator's interests to advise the local authority of a change in the process. Accordingly, any such condition may be superfluous in many cases.

(e) A restriction on the use of anything other than low sulphur coal may be justified by the terms of section 7(8), albeit exceptionally. Such a condition will need to serve a well-defined purpose, such as a concern for concentrations of sulphur dioxide in the context of the limit values of the Air Quality Standards Regulations. It should be noted also that location of a process may be important in the decision-making process if, for example, there is a likelihood of a breach of limit values. Consequently, to overcome such a potential problem a condition about sulphur content may be appropriate.

Variation of authorisations The authorisation regime under Part I, influenced as it is by BATNEEC, in particular emphasises that it is not a "once and for all" licensing system. This is reflected in two crucial sections of the Act[32] which respectively, require an enforcing local authority to follow developments in technology and techniques for the reduction of environmental pollution, and to vary an authorisation if it is found that conditions in an authorisation do not comply with section 7 with its references to BATNEEC and other objectives.

Section 10 empowers the local authority to undertake variation, while section 11 permits an operator to initiate a change that can lead to formal variation of the authorisation. If the local authority serves a notice under section 10, the operator is obliged to advise that authority of his response to the varied authorisation. The onus is then on the authority to decide if what is proposed is a "substantial change"[33] in the subject process. Not surprisingly, such a change will be of a magnitude that justifies submission of a full application which, in turn, triggers the full public consultation machinery in this area of Part I of the Act. By way of illustration, a fundamental change in the materials being processed—or their quantity—might well give rise to evidence of a substantial change in process.[34]

[31] *Hall v. Shoreham UDC* [1964] 1 All E.R. 1.
[32] ss.4(9) and 10(1).
[33] As defined by s.10(7).
[34] *cf.* the examples at GG1 (1991), p.14.

At the centre of the section 11 procedure is the requirement for a "relevant change".[35] Typically, a relevant change is likely to involve a change in the manner of undertaking the process or in the substances (or their quantity) emitted to the atmosphere. The operator is well advised to advise the local authority in these circumstances, since he may well be found to be in breach of the authorisation and subject to enforcement proceedings. Having advised the local authority there are two options: to request a determination[36] or a specific variation.[37] Thereafter, the local authority may either refuse a variation or issue a notice for variation of the subject authorisation. Any refusal of variation or the imposition of conditions through a notice of variation are subject to appeal. The foregoing machinery will not apply to an expedited procedure through which the operator can request of the local authority that a specific alteration be made to a condition of an authorisation.[38] However, this is without prejudice to the power of the local authority to determine that the condition is not acceptable or that the change amounts to a "substantial change", so the more comprehensive procedures previously described will apply. Application may also be made by the holder of an authorisation for the variation of conditions in circumstances where he is not, or not yet, undertaking the prescribed process.[39]

Appeals

The operator of a prescribed process has a right of appeal to the Secretary of State in respect of refusal of an authorisation or a variation, revocation of an authorisation, grant of a conditional authorisation or (finally) variation, prohibition and enforcement notices.[40] Furthermore, the operator has a right of appeal, again to the Secretary of State, in respect of a decision that information shall be included in a public register under Part I on the ground that that information is not commercially confidential. Procedures for present purposes are to be found in the Environmental Protection (Applications, Appeals and Registers) Regulations 1991.[41]

The appeal is required to be in writing and accompanied by various supporting documents, including a copy of the authorisation, where appropriate.[42] In pursuing such an appeal, the operator is also obliged to include a statement of the grounds of his appeal, together with an indication of method of disposal of the appeal, either with written representations or a hearing.[43] Simultaneously, the appellant is obliged to copy these documents to the local authority in question.

[35] As defined by s.11(11).
[36] s. 11(2).
[37] subs.(6).
[38] *Ibid.*
[39] subs.(5).
[40] The enforcement process is dealt with below.
[41] S.I. (1991) No. 507, *Cf.* s.15.
[42] reg.9.
[43] *Ibid.*

Time limits

Although exceptionally the Secretary of State may extend the period, the Regulations[44] stipulate limits of time for appeals, according to five categories:

(a) in the case of a refusal or conditional grant of an authorisation or the refusal of a variation—within six months from the date of the decision;
(b) in the case of the deemed refusal of an authorisation—within six months from the date of the deemed refusal[45];
(c) in the case of the revocation of an authorisation—before the date on which the revocation takes effect[46];
(d) in the case of enforcement, prohibition and variation notices[47]—within two months of the notice; and
(e) the case of refusal to exclude information from a public register which is commercially confidential—within 21 days of a refusal.

Written representations or hearings

The parties must agree on determination of an appeal by written representations. The alternative is determination of the appeal through a hearing (which may be held in private), if either party so requests or the Secretary of State so decides.[48]

Having received notification of an appeal, the local authority is obliged, within 14 days, to notify the statutory consultees and those individuals who made representations in relation to an application for an authorisation or a variation.[49] Such a notification must stipulate that further representations can be made to the Secretary of State within 21 days and that previous representations will be forwarded unless the authority hears to the contrary. By way of contrast, if the appeal relates to an enforcement, prohibition or revocation notice, the local authority will be obliged to notify only those individuals considered to have a particular interest in the matter.

The procedures[50] stipulate particular time limits for the determination of the appeal. This mode of determining an appeal is particularly appropriate for those cases giving rise to commercially confidential information. If there appears to be undue delay, the Secretary of State is empowered to continue the appeal process through a hearing.

If the appeal is to be processed through a hearing, the procedures[51] require the Secretary of State to advise the parties of the date, time and venue for that hearing,

[44] reg.10.
[45] As determined by Sched. 1, para. 5(2).
[46] As determined by s.12(3).
[47] As to variation notices, see s.10(2).
[48] s.15(5).
[49] S.I. 1991 No. 507, reg.11.
[50] *Ibid.* reg.12.
[51] *Ibid.* reg.13.

at least 28 days in advance. Also to be notified are those who have previously made representations. Practice will be heavily reliant on approaches found in planning law and the contents of the Secretary of State's guidance constitute a code of practice for present purposes.[52] A critically important part of the process is the requirement for the appellant and the local authority to provide a full written statement of their cases to the Department of the Environment within six weeks of the appeal, or at least 21 days before the hearing. Subject to the rules of natural justice, no rigid pattern is prescribed for the hearing itself. Both here and in the case of a procedure involving written representations, the inspector may undertake a site visit to the subject process.

The Secretary of State may take account of new evidence or new issues of fact (not relating to government policy) which become available to him following completion of hearing or written representation procedures but before any final decision is taken on the appeal.[53] Any material new evidence will be put before the parties for comment. If either party requests it, the hearing can be re-opened, as is the case if it is considered necessary to undertake a proper investigation of that new evidence. Similar procedures as applied originally will apply to the re-opened hearing.[54]

The decision

A written report to the Secretary of State from the inspector containing conclusions and recommendations is required prior to the decision.[55] Thereafter, the Secretary of State is obliged to deliver a decision in writing. The Secretary of State's jurisdiction here is wide enough to enable him to deliver a decision on any aspect of an authorisation subject to appeal. For example, more stringent conditions could be imposed even if the appeal were directed at the deletion of one or other condition attached to the authorisation. A copy of the written decision and an appended copy of the inspector's report is forwarded to the appellant, the local authority (for inclusion in the public register provided for by section 20) and the statutory consultees. Copies will also be sent to those members of the public who made representations, along with those appearing at the hearing.[56]

Public registers

Provision is made in Part I of the Act for registers of relevant information to be kept by the local enforcing authority.[57] In turn, the Regulations oblige the local authority to maintain information in the register in respect of processes that have received its authorisation. The subject information comprises the following:

[52] (GG5 1991), paras. 20–27.
[53] *Ibid.* para. 28.
[54] *Ibid.*
[55] reg.13(8).
[56] reg.14.
[57] s.20 and regs.15 and 16.

(a) copies of applications;
(b) paragraph 1(3) notices[58];
(c) representations from statutory consultees;
(d) authorisations granted;
(e) variation, enforcement, prohibition and revocation notices, together with variation of condition notices, notices specifying action to comply with a variation notice and notices withdrawing prohibition notices;
(f) notices issued in connection with appeals;
(g) details of convictions under section 23;
(h) monitoring data from the local authority's monitoring, from a condition of an authorisation or by virtue of section 19(2)[59];
(i) stipulations concerning compliance with conditions in the case of commercially confidential data not on the register;
(j) environmental assessments by the local authority or Her Majesty's Inspectorate of Pollution relating to the environmental impact of the process on the locality; and
(k) general directions from the Secretary of State to the local enforcing authority.[60]

The register has to be available for public inspection at all reasonable times and to facilitate the copying of entries.[61] Whereas access to the register must be free of charge, the local authority can charge for copying. One of the prime functions of the register is to enable members of the public to make representations in respect of applications for authorisations and it is the local authority's duty to consider any representations so made within the stipulated time limit.[62]

Commercially confidential information

The local authority can withhold information from the register in so far as it is prejudicial to national security or commercially confidential.[63] The key issue here is that disclosure of the information in the latter case would unreasonably prejudice an individual commercial interest, for example, in terms of a perceived commercial advantage over a fellow manufacturer. It is the responsibility of the particular individual to prove that there is a good justification for exclusion of the subject information from the register. Factors that may well incline against exclusion could include availability of the information from other sources in the public domain and the supposed adverse impact on the manufacturer's reputation only.

[58] Requiring an applicant to furnish further information to the enforcing authority.
[59] The local authority is obliged to maintain this information on the register for a minimum of four years from the date of first recording on that register.
[60] reg.15.
[61] s.20(7).
[62] Sched. 1, para. 2(5).
[63] ss.21 and 22.

Charges

The local authority is empowered to impose charges in respect of its various functions under Part I of the Act. These functions relate to the determination of applications for authorisation and "substantial changes" in respect of each process. In addition, an annual subsistence charge is payable.[64]

Enforcement

Local authority inspectors have powers of entry to premises for the purpose of discharging their functions under Part I.[65] There are also considerable powers of seizure where any article or substance is found by an enforcing authority's inspector on premises that he is empowered to enter, in so far as there is reasonable cause to believe that the item is a cause of imminent danger or serious harm. The power extends to rendering the item harmless, by destruction or otherwise.[66] However, there is an important procedural requirement obliging the provision of samples, if practicable, to the person responsible at the premises prior to the article or substance being rendered harmless.[67] Thereafter, an inspector is obliged to prepare a written report on the seizure and action to render the item harmless.[68]

Provision is made for various relevant offences in section 23. The most severe penalties (on summary conviction a fine not exceeding £20,000; on conviction on indictment, a fine or imprisonment for a term not exceeding two years, or both) are reserved for three offences: contravention of a section 6 authorisation,[69] failure to comply with requirements or prohibitions in enforcement or prohibition notices, and (finally) failure to comply with a court's order to remedy the cause of an offence under section 26, whereby the court is empowered to order the cause of either of the above offences to be remedied. The court's power here can be exercised in addition to or instead of the imposition of any punishment.[70]

Section 24 of the Act allows the local enforcing authority to take proceedings in the High Court if proceedings for the offence of failing to comply with or contravening an enforcement or prohibition notice would be "ineffectual" in its opinion. Potentially, this is a very strong weapon, in so far as it presents the enforcing authority with an opportunity to seek an injunction in aid of enforcement. The reference in section 24 to an "ineffectual" remedy appears to extend the authority's powers beyond the position in relation to the parallel

[64] Local Enforcing Authorities Air Pollution Fees and Charges Scheme (England and Wales) 1991, operating from April 1, 1991.

[65] s.17.

[66] s.18.

[67] *Ibid.* subs.(2).

[68] *Ibid.* subs.(3).

[69] In any proceedings here for a failure to comply with the implied condition in the authorisation under s.7(4), the onus of proof is on the defendant to prove that there was no better available technique not entailing excessive cost: s.25(1).

[70] s.26(1).

powers in section 222 of the Local Government Act 1972. In *Stoke on Trent City Council v. B & Q (Retail) Ltd*,[71] the House of Lords was of the view that a local authority should try the effect of criminal proceedings before seeking the assistance of the civil courts, but can take the view that the defendants would not be deterred by a maximum fine.

The local enforcing authority may serve an enforcement notice if of the opinion that a person undertaking an authorised process is contravening a condition of the authorisation or is likely to contravene such a condition.[72] The Secretary of State's guidance[73] considers that such notices ". . . may be particularly useful to reinforce an existing condition. They may also be used to spell out a matter which is not covered by a specific condition in an authorisation". As in the case of variation and prohibition notices, there is no suspension of a notice pending the determination of an appeal.[74]

If the local enforcing authority is of the opinion that there is an imminent risk of serious pollution of the environment, even though there has been no breach of an authorisation, there is a duty to serve a prohibition notice on the person undertaking the subject process.[75] The Secretary of State's guidance notes state that these notices are exceptional means of dealing with immediate and serious risks; they are not an "everyday" enforcement tool.[76]

Revocation notices are characterised as an option of "last resort".[77] Although the notice is not restricted in its application, it is specifically referable to any situation in which a prescribed process subject to a valid authorisation has not been carried on or not for a period or 12 months.[78]

Enforcement and other general functions under Part I of the Act may be transferred to the national inspectorates.[79]

Sections 157 to 160 of the Environmental Protection Act relate to various miscellaneous enforcement matters. Section 157 permits proceedings against directors, managers, secretaries and other officers of a body corporate when, in proceedings against such a body corporate, it is proved that the offence was committed with the consent or connivance of, or was attributable to the neglect of, any such person. If the commission of a Part I offence is due to the act or default of some other person, that other person may be charged with and convicted of the offence, whether or not proceedings are taken against that other person.[80] Section 159 confers immunity on the Crown in respect of criminal prosecution. However, a local enforcing authority can make application to the High Court for a declaration that the Crown's act or omission in contravention of

[71] [1984] A.C. 754.
[72] s.13.
[73] GG1 (1991) p.23.
[74] s.15(9).
[75] s.14: notice the requirement of withdrawal under s.14(5).
[76] See, n.73, *supra*.
[77] *Ibid.* and *cf.* s.12.
[78] *Ibid.* subs.(2). *Cf.* s.8(8), permitting revocation where an annual subsistence charge has not been paid.
[79] s.4(4).
[80] s.158.

Part I, or any regulation or order made under Part I, is unlawful. Section 160 provides details of requirements for the service of notices and other documents.

Mobile Sources

Pollution sources in the United Kingdom

The use of road transport and the generation of electricity produce about 80 per cent. of the oxides of nitrogen, 60 per cent. of the sulphur dioxide and 55 per cent. of the carbon dioxide emitted to the atmosphere. Road transport is the largest generator of nitrogen oxides. Emission limit values are being made more rigorous by the E.C., particularly in relation to new vehicles.[80a] The problems of emissions from lorries and other heavy diesel vehicles have focused for a long time on smoke emissions. More recently, a directive[81] addressed gaseous emissions from heavy diesel vehicles. Associated problems of noise have been the subject of fairly long-standing E.C. regulation by directive.[82] One pollutant that is not presently subject to control is carbon dioxide.

In the case of the petrol engine, there is no doubt that the advent of lead-free petrol has represented one of the most significant changes in vehicle emissions.[83] Emissions from diesels produce:

- (a) nitrogen oxides;
- (b) hydrocarbons;
- (c) smoke;
- (d) particulate matter;
- (e) sulphur dioxide and sulphates; and
- (f) carbon dioxide and carbon monoxide.[84]

Reference has been made earlier[85] to air quality standards generated by the E.C. in the shape of air quality limit values for nitrogen dioxide, sulphur dioxide and suspended particulates, together with guide values for nitrogen dioxide and sulphur dioxide.

Guide and limit values

Guide values are described in a Department of the Environment Circular[86] where it is said that they:

> ". . . may be used as long term goals although they are not mandatory. They can be used in the setting of limits in specially designated zones but there is

[80a] See E.C. Directives 70/220: [1970] O.J. L76; 77/537: [1977] O.J. L220; 88/77: [1988] O.J. L36.
[81] Directive 88/77, *supra.*
[82] Directive 84/424: [1984] O.J. L238, amending Directive 70/157: [1970] O.J. L42.
[83] Directive 85/210: [1985] O.J. L96. *Cf.* the Lawther Report on lead and health (HMSO, 1980).
[84] Royal Commission on Environmental Pollution, Fifteenth Report, Cm 1631 (1991).
[85] See, nn.73 and 85, *supra.*
[86] Circular 11/81 (Welsh Office Circular 18/81), para. 27.

no requirement for action to be taken where they are exceeded unless zones are designated. The Directive [Directive 80/779 on air quality and smoke and sulphur dioxide emissions] asks that Member States should in the longer term endeavour to move towards these guide values; local authorities should note these objectives and, in those areas where pollution is already below the limit values, may wish to consider whether any further progress towards these guide values is desirable and economically feasible."

It is against this background that the Air Quality Standards Regulations 1989 require the Secretary of State to take ". . . any appropriate measures" to ensure that concentrations of sulphur dioxide, for example, do not exceed the limit values prescribed by the relevant Directive.

In *Budden v. BP and Shell Oil*,[87] the Court of Appeal struck out various claims arising from what was claimed to be the adverse impact on child health of exposure to vehicle emissions in the inner city. The fact that the petrol companies had complied with statutory regulations on the composition of petrol was decisive. However, Megaw L.J. went on to say that:

> ". . . this is not to say that the courts are bound to hold, where a limit has been prescribed in the interests of a safety by statute or statutory regulations, that one who keeps within these limits cannot be guilty of negligence at common law."[88]

The encouragement of local authorities to promote guide values as a result of E.C. legislation here may suggest some circumstances in which there may well be an enforceable duty of care to observe and implement emission limits below formally legislated limits.

A legal framework for vehicular emissions

The legal framework can be represented in two ways, according to whether specific areas of municipal law are concerned with the establishment of limits for emissions or with monitoring and measuring functions. However, there is also provision for legally enforceable requirements, for example, in the enforcement of relevant statutory nuisance provisions in Part III of the Environmental Protection Act 1990.[89] The local authority's own enforcement priorities may result in proceedings arising from evidence of lead in the atmosphere where, for example, ". . . any dust . . . or other effluvia [arises] on industrial, trade or business premises . . . being prejudicial to health or a nuisance . . ." and, as a statutory nuisance, leads to proceedings under section 80 of the Act of 1990.

The establishment and enforcement of limits for emissions is most clearly seen in section 30 of the Clean Air Act 1993, empowering the Secretary of State to make regulations relating to the composition and content of motor fuel.[90] A

[87] [1980] J.P.L. 586.
[88] *Ibid.*
[89] See Chap. 10, "Statutory Nuisance".
[90] The penalty for non-compliance is found in s.32.

similar situation is found in the Road Traffic Act 1972 and the regulation-making power of the Secretary of State, the reuslt of which is a series of Construction and Use Regulations.[91] Various E.C. directives provide the foundation for so-called "type approval" for road vehicles, stipulating, *inter alia*, the mode of construction that will enble certain prescribed emission limits to apply. Directive 91/441,[91a] for example, relates to cars and the requirement that all new models used or manufactured in the E.C. after July 1, 1992 should be fitted with three-way catalytic converters.

Monitoring and measuring functions most clearly arise from the Air Quality Standards Regulations 1989 and sections 34 and 35 of the Clean Air Act 1993. The latter provisions empower local authorities to investigate, research and publish information on air pollution.[92]

Ozone depletion

Chlorofluorocarbons (CFCs) have a propensity to destroy the ozone layer. To address this crucial environmental problem, the Vienna Convention for the Protection of the Ozone Layer and the Montreal Protocol to the Convention was concluded and is now implemented in the E.C. through E.C. Regulation 594/91,[92a] which is directly applicable in Member States and obliges CFC manufactures and others to respond to the limitations on importation, production and consumption. Directive 92/72, on the other hand, is concerned with a need to monitor and record photochemical ozone pollution in Member States by reference to criteria established by the World Health Organisation. The Directive is implemented by the Ozone Monitoring and Information Regulations 1994.[93] These Regulations require the Secretary of State to designate or establish measuring stations for measuring ozone concentrations and provide methods of measurement. In addition, the Secretary of State is obliged to advise the public when ozone concentration thresholds are exceeded.

Planning Considerations

Planning and other powers of pollution control

In practice, there are a number of crucial difficulties in the use of planning powers under the Town and Country Planning Act 1990 for pollution control in this and other contexts. First, there may not be sufficient technical expertise available in the planning authority for the purpose of dealing with pollution control

[91] See, e.g. the Road Vehicles (Construction and Use) (Amendment No. 2) Regulations 1990 (S.I. 1990 No. 1131), implementing recent emission requirements for petrol engines stipulated by E.C. directives.

[91a] [1991] O.J. L242.

[92] See nn.84 and 85, *supra*.

[92a] [1991] O.J. L67.

[93] S.I. 1994 No. 440.

problems. Secondly, consultation requirements in the case of planning control may not be sufficiently extensive or well informed. Finally, on those occasions when pollution issues are taken account of in planning decisions, there may be a concern for certain pollution issues but not others. This latter point is recognised by the Royal Commission on Environmental Pollution:[94]

> "Pollution is only one of the factors which need to be taken into account in planning decisions and in many situations there will be other factors which have to be given equal or higher priority. There may be pressures on a local authority to improve housing or local employment opportunities, or an authority may wish, for example, to put derelict land into use . . . Our concern is that pollution . . . is often dealt with inadequately, and sometimes forgotten altogether in the planning process. In part this stems from lack of guidance and advice . . . Such advice is not always sought . . . Consultation to establish the pollution implications of . . . planning proposals should be a regular practice."

The Royal Commission recommended the need for better pollution policies based on comprehensive scientific study to be embodied in structure plans and developed in the more detailed district and local plans. It was further recommended that there should be better consultation on pollution within the planning authority, as between the planning and environmental health departments and with the pollution control agencies, such as Her Majesty's Inspectorate of Pollution. Significant guidance is now to be found in PPG 23: "Planning and Pollution Control".[94a] The Royal Commission also observed[95] that:

> "In deciding applications for industrial development and especially for [prescribed processes under Part I of the Environmental Protection Act] local planning authorities sometimes impose planning conditions designed to control air pollution from the plant, even though separate legislation exists for that purpose. This practice is misguided. The [enforcing authority under Part I of the Environmental Protection Act is] legally responsible for controlling emissions from [prescribed processes] and it is wrong in principle that local authorities should attempt to assume this authority by the use of the planning laws. It is also confusing and potentially counterproductive in practice: conditions identical to those imposed by the pollution control authority serve no useful purpose in the short term but, because planning conditions cannot be updated,[96] could in the long term undermine the

[94] Fifth Report (1976), paras. 334–336.

[94a] HMSO, 1994.

[95] Para. 357.

[96] For an example of a situation in which pollution control requirements were fixed by Her Majesty's Inspectorate of Pollution and then imposed as a planning condition, see the case of *Ferro-Alloys and Metal Smelter* [1990] L.M.E.L.R. 176, a decision of Secretary of State for the Environment. *Cf. Gateshead MBC v. Secretary of State for the Environment and Northumbrian Water PLC* (1994), unreported, C.A.

pollution control authority's work in seeking progressive improvements in control . . . If the planning conditions are less stringent than the pollution control requirements then the developer is given an argument against those requirements. The pollution control requirements are likely to be set close to the best the plant can physically achieve: it is therefore unlikely that any more stringent requirements imposed as planning conditions could be regularly met. If the planning authority, using air quality guidelines, consider that an unacceptable amount of pollution is likely to be emitted from a proposed plant when the [enforcing authority's] requirements have been set their sanction should be the refusal of planning permission not the imposition of planning conditions designed to control emissions."

Development control powers

Air pollution issues are likely to impinge on the development control process (in its widest sense) in a variety of ways. Four matters merit comment:

(a) the development plan background;
(b) publicity for development proposals;
(c) environmental assessment requirements; and
(d) development control decision-making.

Development plan policies

There is little doubt that if a local planning authority, whether for the purpose of a structure plan or a local, district plan, proposes to include policies on pollution control generally or atmospheric pollution in particular under Part II of the Town and Country Planning Act 1990, great caution must be exercised by reference to the competing regulatory powers available. Assuming that any such policy is incorporated in a relevant development plan, that policy will be particularly influential at the point when the development control decision-making occurs, particularly by reference to section 54A of the Act of 1990.

Publicity for development proosals

Section 65 of the Town and Country Planning Act 1990 prescribes a broad framework for the purpose of publicity requirements for applications for planning permission. Failure to comply on the part of the applicant developer requires that the local planning authority shall not entertrain the application.[97] Specific requirements are set out in the Town and Country Planning General Development Order 1988[98] and, in particular, in article 11. The Order stipulates that certain categories of application for planning permission shall be publicised, to enable representations to be made to the local authority. The authority is then obliged to take account of any such representations in arriving at a decision on the

[97] s.65(2).
[98] S.I. 1988 No. 1813.

application.[99] The categories of so-called "unneighbourly" development in article 11 may well include development that is capable of generating atmospheric pollution, although this would probably be an unusual case, given the contents of the article.

Consultation is also a possible legal requirement prior to a decision being taken on an application for planning permission. The list of statutory consultees is set out in article 18 of the General Development Order. The Health and Safety Executive is one consultee, in respect of any development involving the processing of hazardous substances in certain, defined circumstances.

Environmental assessment requirements

Proposed development may attract the requirement for an environmental assessment by virtue of its position in Schedule 1 or 2 of the Town and Country Planning (Assessment of Environmental Effects) Regulations 1988,[1] or by virtue of the application of other similar environmental assessment regulations, usually applicable where there are no development control implications. In determining the application for planning permission, the local planning authority will be obliged to take account of the environmental assessment. Any proposed development falling within Schedule 1 attracts the need for a mandatory assessment, whereas development falling within Schedule 2 attracts an assessment only if the local planning authority, for example, considers that the development will have significant effects on the environment. An example of a Schedule 1 development would be the creation of an integrated chemical installation, while an example of a Schedule 2 development would be smelting plant for non-ferrous metals.

Development control decision-making

In determining an application for planning permission, the local planning authority is obliged to have regard to the provisions of the development plan, so far as material to the application, and to any other material considerations.[2] A material consideration must be relevant to planning and, as such, must relate to the use and development of the subject land.[3] Matters relating to atmospheric pollution may therefore be legally relevant considerations in the decision-making process.[4]

[99] s.71(1).
[1] S.I. 1988 No. 1199.
[2] Town and Country Planning Act 1990, s.70(2).
[3] *Stringer v. Minister of Housing and Local Government* [1971] 1 All E.R. 65 at 77.
[4] *RMC Management Services Ltd v. Secretary of State for the Environment* (1972) 222 E.G. 1593.

Chapter 7

INTEGRATED POLLUTION CONTROL

Multi-media Pollution Control

Multi-media pollution

The tradition of environmental regulation has been to use control and regulation techniques in relation to each of the fundamental environmental media of air, water and land. Each of these media has been regarded as separate entities. The Alkali etc. Works Regulation Act 1906 and the Health and Safety at Work Act 1974 regulated atmospheric emissions in the case of certain, so-called "scheduled" processes, usually in a range of industrial contexts. The system of regulation depended on enforcement of "best practicable means" for the purpose of minimising pollution of the atmosphere. However, the scheduled process will often have generated other forms of pollution through discharges to water and solid waste to land. These polluting processes will have been subject to regulation and control by the National Rivers Authority and the appropriate waste regulation authority. It will be seen in the body of the present chapter that under Part I of the Environmental Protection Act 1990 a new, integrated system of control and regulation supersedes this formerly disparate system in the case of certain prescribed industrial processes, so that all of the environmental media affected are considered together in the authorisation that will permit the process to operate.

The development of multi-media control

To a large extent, the development of multi-media control has emerged from E.C. environmental policy. A good example of this approach is to be found in Directive 87/217[1] which addresses asbestos pollution, its prevention and reduction.[1a] The directive defines an obligation to reduce asbestos pollution at source, as well as preventing such pollution so far as is "reasonably practicable". If asbestos is in use, there is a further obligation to employ "best available technology not entailing excessive costs". Significantly, the directive defines emission limit values in respect of discharges to water and in respect of emissions to the atmosphere. Very specific requirements apply to landfilling and, especially, the need to prevent asbestos fibre being released.

[1] [1987] O.J. L85.
[1a] E.C., Fourth Environmental Action Programme.

The 1976 report of the Royal Commission on Environmental Pollution, "Air Pollution Control: An Integrated Approach",[2] drew attention to the links between air, water and land pollution. In doing so, the Royal Commission recommended the creation of a unified pollution inspectorate whose aim would be the achievement of BPEO ("best practicable environmental option") for an industrial process, taking account of the total pollution generated and the technical possibilities for its reduction. Integrated pollution control goes well beyond the former statutory regime governing atmospheric pollution from "scheduled" processes under the Alkali etc. Works Regulation Act and the Health and Safety at Work Act and concern for one environmental medium only. The integrated pollution control (hereafter "IPC") provisions in Part I of the Environmental Protection Act owe much to E.C. environmental policy. The standards at the heart of IPC are based on the idea of "best available technology" and (apart from Directive 87/217) have received their strongest recognition from Directive 76/464[2a] (dangerous substances), Directive 84/360[2b] (framework directive on air pollution) and Directive 88/609[2c] (large combustion plants). As a result, the law has progressed from a concern for "best practicable means" (under the Acts of 1906 and 1974) to "best available techniques not entailing excessive cost" (under the Environmental Protection Act 1990).

The recommendations of the Royal Commission were strongly endorsed by a report on pollution control from the Cabinet Office Efficiency Unit in 1986.[3] The Unit reported that, for as long as the three environmental media were treated separately, there was a danger that the allocation of resources would not reflect an overall view of where the problems were most severe. The end result would be a haphazard disposal of pollutants unrelated to an overall assessment of the optimum solution for the environment as a whole.

The aims and objectives of IPC

The Department of the Environment's "Practical Guide to IPC"[4] sets out two objectives for IPC:

> "(a) to prevent or minimise the release of prescribed substances and to render harmless any such substances which are released;
> (b) to develop an approach to pollution control that considers discharges from industrial processes to all media in the context of the effect on the environment as a whole."

The aims of IPC are stated to be:

[2] Cmnd. 6371 (1976).
[2a] [1976] O.J. L129.
[2b] [1984] O.J. L188.
[2c] [1988] O.J. L336.
[3] Reported in *Integrated Pollution Control: A Practical Guide* (Department of the Environment/Welsh Office), p.5.
[4] *Ibid.*

"(a) to improve the efficiency and effectiveness of Her Majesty's Inspectorate of Pollution [the unified pollution inspectorate referred to by the report of the Royal Commission and now charged with implementing and enforcing IPC];
(b) to streamline and strengthen the regulatory system, clarifying the roles and responsibilities of Her Majesty's Inspectorate of Pollution, other regulatory authorities and the firms they regulate;
(c) to contain the burden on industry, in particular by providing for a 'one stop shop' on pollution control for the potentially most serious polluting processes;
(d) to maintain public confidence in the regulatory system by producing a clear and transparent system that is accessible and easy to understand and clear and simple in operation;
(e) to ensure that the system will respond flexibly, both to changing pollution abatement technology and to new knowledge on the effects of pollutants; and
(f) to provide the means to fulfil international obligations relating to environmental protection."

Competition between environmental media

The White Paper, "This Common Inheritance",[5] observes that:

> "Reducing disposal of waste to one medium may increase discharges of the same waste to another medium. As the Royal Commission on Environmental Pollution established, it is important to choose the method of waste disposal which causes the least overall damage to the environment. For example, flue gas desulphurisation involves a very substantial reduction in air pollution but some increased contamination of both land and water. On balance the overall impact on the environment of flue gas desulphurisation is considered to be much less damaging than the air pollution which would take place without it."[6]

Flue gas desulphurisation (hereafter FGD) is one response to the problem of sulphur dioxide pollution of the atmosphere. Along with nitrogen oxides, sulphur dioxide pollution is a central feature of the controls set out in E.C. Directive 88/609 on large combustion plants, which dominates the IPC framework in Part I of the Environmental Protection Act. However, the issue of sulphur dioxide emissions from industrial plants emphasises the difficulty and complexity of IPC controls, particularly by reference to the need to adhere to the "best practicable environmental option". Despite the White Paper's conclusion that FGD is much less damaging than the air pollution that would take place without it, it is instructive to consider the elements of such a difficult IPC assessment. FGD, for example, is known to accentuate carbon dioxide emissions

[5] Cm. 1200 (HMSO, 1990).
[6] *Ibid.* para. 10.6.

as well as being a complex system to build. There are also potential cross-media pollution problems if there is no market or no sufficient market for FGD byproducts, such as sulphuric acid. It is well known that British coal has a high sulphur content, so that there would be little hope in the electricity generating industry that such coal could be used without FGD being built into power station plant. An attractive alternative (perhaps) is gas. Use of gas generates very little, if any, sulphur dioxide and very much less carbon dioxide compared with coal. However, in the time allowed for achievement of targets laid down in Directive 88/609, it is unlikely that compliance will occur only with resort to gas.

Another problem that focuses on the assessment of cross-media impacts in the present context relates to the phasing out of the dumping of sewage sludge in the North Sea. Again, the best practicable environmental option is not necessarily clear cut.[7] The Ministry of Agriculture[8] has estimated that it would cost £50m to build an incineration plant capable of dealing with the present volume of sludge. Annual running costs would be £5.5m. The cost of dewatering and lorry transportation to landfill is estimated at £13m capital, plus £6m annual running costs. However, available landfill sites would soon run out, given especially the competition from domestic refuse. The cost of tankering sludge a distance of 50 km would be approximately £25m per annum. This latter option would relate to use of the sludge for agricultural purposes. Other options would include use of the sludge in land reclamation and pyrolysis of sludge with possible conversion of organic constituents to useful products.

IPC: the statutory framework

Part I of the Environmental Protection Act 1990 divides into a number of segments, summarised here and developed in detail throughout the remainder of the present chapter. The Part I provisions supersede the pre-existing regulatory framework under the Alkali etc. Works Regulation Act 1906 and the Health and Safety at Work Act 1974, relating to so-called "scheduled processes".

Prescribed processes and substances

The Secretary of State for the Environment is responsible for prescribing those processes and substances that will be subject to IPC, by regulation. The prescription of substances is an indication of their potential harm and polluting potential when exposed to the environment. As such, these substances attract particular requirements to ensure that there is no release to relevant environmental media or alternatively, if that is not possible, to ensure that the substance's impact is minimised or rendered harmless. The Secretary of State has made the Environmental Protection (Prescribed Processes and Substances)

[7] Ministry of Agriculture, Fisheries and Food, Report on the Disposal of Waste at Sea 1986 and 1987, HMSO, 1989, pp.53–58.

[8] *Ibid.* p.55.

Regulations 1991 for present purposes. Both Part I and the Regulations also cover a set of processes which are subject to local authority air pollution control only. This area of legal regulation was dealt with separately in Chapter 6.

Authorisation

At the centre of the law governing IPC is the requirement that no prescribed process shall be undertaken without an authorisation granted by Her Majesty's Inspectorate of Pollution. The application process overall is subject to detailed requirements, set out in the Environmental Protection (Applications, Appeals and Registers) Regulations 1991. The licensing discretion of Her Majesty's Inspectorate of Pollution is drawn quite widely: an authorisation may be granted conditionally or unconditionally, or may be refused. An application must be refused if it is concluded that a process cannot be undertaken in conformity with conditions to be attached. Powers of direction are given to the Secretary of State for the purpose of directing the grant or refusal of an authorisation.

Any conditions attached to an authorisation must accord with certain objectives set out in Part I of the Environmental Protection Act. Essentially, there are three objectives referable to conditions:

(a) that best available techniques not entailing excessive cost (hereafter BATNEEC) are used to prevent release or render harmless certain prescribed and other substances in so far as they would cause harm if released into the environment;
(b) that releases do not cause, or contribute to, the breach of any direction from the Secretary of State to implement any E.C. or international legal obligation for protection of the environment, any statutory environmental quality standards or objectives, or any other statutory limits or requirements; and
(c) that, in so far as any process is likely to give rise to a release to more than one environmental medium, the best practicable environmental option (hereafter BPEO) is achieved.

Conditions are required to recognise each of the above objectives and, in the event of any competition between more and less stringent requirements, the former will prevail. In practice, this means that BATNEEC is likely to be a baseline but without prejudice to more exacting requirements emerging through the attached conditions. Furthermore, and again without prejudice to the categories of condition specifically required by statute, HMIP is empowered to impose such other conditions as are considered appropriate in relation to any particular authorisation. Above all, though, is the implication of BATNEEC for the purposes of prevention or minimisation of releases, as described previously. This implied condition relating to BATNEEC relates primarily to detailed plant design and operation. In any proceedings by reference to the offence of failing to comply with implied BATNEEC conditions, the onus of proof is reversed, requiring the process operator to prove that BATNEEC was in use.

Public and specialist consultation

The Environmental Protection Act requires applications for authorisation to be advertised locally. Any representations received as a result of the advertisement are required to be considered by HMIP. Beyond any initial authorisation of a process, there is a similar publicity requirement subsequently on any occasion when the process operator is considering a substantial change in the subject process. Specialist consultation is represented by the presence of certain statutory consultees. The widening of the decision-making base through public consultation is seen also in the provision of public registers to which the public is given access. The registers contain information about IPC applications and authorisations, variation, monitoring and enforcement. The registers are maintained at HMIP regional offices. Some information referable to national security and commercial confidentiality may be excluded from the registers.

Variation of authorisations

Both the process operator and HMIP have facilities in the Act for initiating a variation procedure in relation to an authorisation. The recognition of the potential importance of variation comes from a need to appreciate that BATNEEC is a dynamic principle. BATNEEC implicitly includes (among other things) a recognition that techniques—and technology—are always developing. As a consequence, the variation procedure obliges both operator and HMIP, either separately or together, to initiate variation as a means of updating a pre-existing authorisation. In any event, there is a statutory requirement that conditions be reviewed every four years. There is a facility for the imposition of a condition obliging the process operator to advise HMIP of any change in the execution of a subject process. However, it is also possible for an authorisation to be constructed to permit immaterial changes to be undertaken without formal reference to HMIP. The same flexibility seems to be possible also in relation to processes that have to operate with frequent variation in modes of operation.

Enforcement

The core of IPC enforcement is seen in provision for enforcement notices (where it is considered that a process operator is in contravention of, or is likely to be in contravention of, conditions attached to the subject authorisation) and prohibition notices (where, even in the absence of any contravention of an authorisation, HMIP considers that there is an imminent risk of serious pollution). Further powers exist by which HMIP may formally revoke an authorisation. Furthermore, the Act makes provision for a wide variety of offences, including contravention of an authorisation granted under the Act. HMIP may also have resort to proceedings in the High Court if it is considered that prosecution in the magistrates' court for failure to comply with an enforcement or prohibition notice would be ineffectual. If, however, a penalty is being considered by the court for contravention of an authorisation or an enforcement or prohibition notice, consideration may be given to an order requiring the person convicted to take steps to remedy the situation giving rise to the offence, either instead of or in addition to the penalty in question. There are, in addition, default powers here, although the operator may be liable for the costs and expenses associated with the remedial measures. A general measure in the Act imposes liability on any corporate director, manager or similar officer where it is established that their consent, connivance or neglect led to the commission of the subject offence by the company. Criminal proceedings under Part I are not available against the Crown, although a High Court declaration that a breach of authorisation is unlawful is available. Otherwise, the Crown's IPC processes are subject to HMIP regulation.

Appeals

A variety of appeals is provided for by the Act, including an appeal against refusal of an application for authorisation. Appeals are to the Secretary of State for the Environment and are governed by the Environmental Protection (Applications, Appeals and Registers) Regulations 1991. If an appeal is pursued against revocation of an authorisation, that revocation is suspended, although the same is not true of appeals against other notices and conditions.

Cost recovery charging

Most functional costs associated with the implementation of IPC are recoverable by virtue of a charging scheme made under the Act. Cost recovery charging falls into two categories that attract charges for any application for authorisation, including any proposed substantial change to a process, and the annual subsistence of an authorisation. This latter annual subsistence charge endures for as long as the IPC authorisation continues in force.

Related regulatory functions

IPC as a multi-media environmental control system effectively supersedes other relevant regulatory controls, although the relationship between HMIP and the other regulatory agencies is not one of total exclusion of the latter. In so far as any application for an authorisation includes a proposal for discharges to controlled waters, the National Rivers Authority is consulted and may require HMIP to include specific conditions in a subject authorisation, usually as a means of reinforcing water quality objectives. If the National Rivers Authority certifies that the discharge will frustrate achievement of a quality objective, HMIP is prevented from granting the authorisation. Furthermore, NRA may require HMIP to vary conditions attached to an authorisation. The relationship between NRA and HMIP is informed by a memorandum of understanding for present purposes. In relation to waste management, HMIP is limited in so far as its regulatory functions go as far as the point when waste is finally disposed of: such disposal remains within the jurisdiction of the waste regulation authority. As a result, IPC controls focus on the generation and management of waste in prescribed processes. IPC controls do not extend to the keeping, use or disposal of radioactive substances, subject to the Radioactive Substances Act 1993 and (in the same way) do not extend to health and safety at work, subject to the Health and Safety at Work Act 1974. On the other hand, discharges of trade effluent to the public sewer is subject to IPC and is therefore outside the normal statutory framework for control, the Water Industry Act 1991. IPC control may also supersede controls under Part III of the Environmental Protection Act relating to statutory nuisances. The local authority is unable to issue summary proceedings under Part III if proceedings may be instituted under Part I: a judgment to be made by the Secretary of State. Finally, IPC controls do not depend on the existence of any appropriate planning permission, as is the case with waste management licensing under Part II of the Environmental Protection Act. Nevertheless, there exists a potential for duplication of controls under both regimes with all of the attendant dangers, particularly in so far as planning conditions are not amenable to flexible change.

At the time of writing the Department of the Environment has announced proposals for a new Environment Agency, to be constituted under an Environment and Countryside Act, in 1995.[8a] The aim is to develop a body that promotes sustainable development through high quality, integrated environmental protection, management and enhancement. In bringing together Her Majesty's Inspectorate of Pollution, the National Rivers Authority and the local waste regulation authorities, the Agency will develop and apply an integrated approach to the existing functions of these bodies. The Agency will be a non-departmental public body sponsored by the Department of the Environment. Many of the Agency's staff will operate at regional level.

Fundamental Criteria and Environmental Media for IPC

Statutory definitions

For the purpose of Part I, section 1 of the Environmental Protection Act sets out a variety of definitions of fundamental words and phrases. These words and phrases relate particularly to the operation of:

(a) section 3 (emission, etc., limits and quality objectives);
(b) section 4 (discharge and scope of functions under Part I);
(c) section 6 (IPC authorisations);
(d) section 7 (conditions of authorisation);
(e) section 14 (prohibition notices);

[8a] Department of the Environment News Release 576, October 13, 1994.

(f) section 17 (powers of inspectors); and
(g) section 18 (powers to deal with the causes of imminent danger of serious harm).

"The environment"

This term appears in two critical sections of Part I, sections 3 and 7. The term is defined so that it

> "... consists of all, or any, of the following media, namely, the air, water and land; and the medium of air includes the air within buildings and the air within other natural or man-made structures above or below ground".[9]

The width of the definition is significant in two immediate respects under Part I. First, under section 3, the Secretary of State may make plans for, *inter alia*, "... establishing limits for the total amount, or the total amount in any period, of any substance which may be released into the *environment* in, or in any area within, the United Kingdom ...".[10] Secondly, section 7 (which deals with conditions attached to authorisations) requires that the conditions achieve particular objectives, including that of ensuring that:

> "... the best available techniques not entailing excessive cost will be used for minimising the pollution which may be caused to the *environment* taken as a whole by the releases having regard to the best practicable environmental option available as respects the substances which may be released into more than one environmental medium".[11]

Section 1 also defines the term "pollution of the environment"[12] but is dependent for its definition on five other terms: "release", "medium", "process", "substance" and "harm". The respective definitions of these terms are dealt with first, before we return to an examination of the Act's definition of "pollution of the environment".

"Harm"

This term is defined as meaning "... harm to the health of living organisms or other interference with the ecological systems of which they form part and, in the case of man, includes offence caused to any of his senses or harm to his property", and "harmless" has a corresponding meaning.[13] This definition is particularly significant in giving a very wide dimension to the term "pollution of the environment".

[9] s.1(2).
[10] s.3(5)(a).
[11] s.7(7).
[12] s.1(3).
[13] subs.(4).

"Process"

A "process" means "... any activities carried on in Great Britain, whether on premises or by means of mobile plant, which are capable of causing pollution of the environment" and "prescribed process" means "a process prescribed under section 2(1) ...".[14] The critical element of this definition is the requirement that any subject process is capable of causing pollution of the environment. As to the meaning of the term "process", some caution is required:

> "'Process' is a word of very wide general meaning and must take colour from its context. When used in the context of defining a factory it is natural to think of the word 'process' in the context of the operations carried on within the factory ... [In relation to the Factories Act 1961 and the Asbestos Regulations 1969] ... the word 'process' is ... used in the ... broader sense of including any activity of a more than minimal duration ... There has to be some degree of continuity and repetition of a series of acts."[15]

In view of Lord Griffiths' emphasis on the need for caution in interpreting the term "process" according to its specific statutory context, it is perhaps significant that the term here merely refers to "... any activities", suggesting the widest possible meaning. In *Sheffield City Council v. ADH Demolition*,[16] it was held that a demolition site was "premises" and that the act of demolition was a "trade process" for the purpose of the Clean Air Act.

"Release"

Part I of the Act stipulates that a substance is "released" into any environmental medium whenever it is released directly into that medium whether it is released into it within or outside Great Britain. Furthermore, "release" is stated to include:

> "(a) in relation to air, any emission of the substance into the air;
> (b) in relation to water, any entry (including any discharge) of the substance into water;
> (c) in relation to land, any deposit, keeping or disposal of the substance in or on land ...".[17]

The foregoing references to "water" and "land" are to be construed by reference to subsections (11) and (12), which deal (respectively) with the medium of release and ground waters.

Medium of release The Act[18] sets out the criteria for determining into

[14] subs.(5): *cf.* the Environmental Protection (Prescribed Processes and Substances) Regulations 1991 (S.I. 1991 No. 472) (as amended).
[15] *Per* Lord Griffiths in *Nurse v. Morganite Crucible Ltd* [1989] 1 All E.R. 113 at 116.
[16] (1984) 82 L.G.R. 177.
[17] s.1(10).
[18] subs.(11).

what medium a substance is released. Accordingly, any release into the sea or the surface of the seabed, any river, watercourse, lake, loch or pond (whether natural or artificial or above or below ground) or reservoir, or the surface of the riverbed or of other land supporting such waters or ground waters, is a release into water. Any release into any other land covered by water (or the water covering that land), or the land beneath the surface of the seabed or of other land supporting waters of any river, watercourse, lake, loch or pond or reservoir, is to be regarded as a release into land. Finally, any release into a sewer is treated as a release into water, although a sewer and its contents are disregarded in determining whether there is pollution of the environment at any time. The reference to ground waters here is a reference to any waters contained in underground strata or in a well, borehole or similar work sunk into underground strata, or any excavation into underground strata where the level of water in the excavation depends wholly or mainly on water entering it from the strata.[19]

"Substance"

The term "substance" is defined to include electricity or heat.[20] Otherwise, the range of meaning is necessarily very wide and clearly extends to substances natural and artificial in any state.

"Activities"

This term is defined to mean "... industrial or commercial activities or activities of any other nature whatsoever (including, with or without other activities, the keeping of a substance) ...".[21] The reference to the keeping or storage of substances arises from a need to avoid confusion over the scope of the term "activities". In *Hillil Property and Investment Co. Ltd v. Naraine Pharmacy Ltd*,[22] the Court of Appeal was confronted by the question of whether use of shop premises by contractors as a temporary dumping ground for spoil was an "activity" of the tenants for the purposes of section 23(2) of the Landlord and Tenant Act 1954. It was held by the court that an "activity" for present purposes, though it might be something that was not strictly a "trade, profession or employment", must nevertheless be something that was correlative to the conceptions involved in those words. Accordingly, an "activity" connoted some general use by the persons occupying the premises in question and not some particular—as it were, casual—operation such as had been carried out by the contractors in using the subject premises as a dumping ground for spoil.

[19] subs.(12). *Cf.* s.104(1)(d), Water Resources Act 1991.
[20] subs.(13).
[21] subs.(6).
[22] (1979) 39 P. & C.R. 67.

"Pollution of the environment"

The Act here refers to "... pollution of the environment due to the release (into any environmental medium) from any process of substances which are capable of causing harm to man or any other living organisms supported by the environment".[23] The critical issue arising from this definition is the reference, not to any need for actual harm, but to the capacity to cause harm to man or any other living organisms supported by the environment.

Prescribed Processes and Substances

The prescribed processes

Section 2 of the Environmental Protection Act empowers the making of Regulations by the Secretary of State to enable the identification of those descriptions of processes requiring authorisation under section 6 of the Act. Reference was made earlier in this chapter to the requirement that any "process" for present purposes must be one that is capable of causing pollution of the environment[24] and as such it must involve an activity of more than minimal duration with a degree of continuity and repetition of a series of acts.[25] The Regulations may be widely drawn according to the enabling powers in the Act.[26] The Secretary of State is empowered to use the regulations for the purpose of describing a process by reference to its characteristics or the area or other circumstances in which the process is carried on, or even by reference to those persons who will operate the process.[27] A fundamental power allows the Secretary of State to designate certain processes as being subject to central control, by Her Majesty's Inspectorate of Pollution, with others being subject to local authority control. Local authority control relates to air pollution control and is dealt with separately in Chapter 6. The Regulations that have been made under these powers are the Environmental Protection (Prescribed Processes and Substances) Regulations 1991.[28] At the heart of these Regulations is a division between Part A processes (subject to central IPC control through Her Majesty's Inspectorate of Pollution) and Part B processes (subject to local authority air pollution control).[29]

[23] s.1(3).
[24] See n.14, *supra*.
[25] See n.15, *supra*.
[26] s.2(1)–(4).
[27] *Ibid*. s.2(2). *Cf*. subs.(3), which provides further flexibility in the prescription of processes.
[28] S.I. 1991 No. 472, as amended. *Cf*. "The Environmental Protection (Prescribed Processes and Substances) Regulations—A Consolidated Version", HMSO, August 1994.
[29] *Ibid*. Sched. 1. *Cf*. reg.5.

Excepted processes

The Environmental Protection (Prescribed Processes and Substances) Regulations (hereafter the 1991 Regulations) contain a number of exceptions from Part A or Part B processes. The first exception can be described as a *de minimis* exception, in so far as a process will not be a Part A process because there is no release or a very insignificant release of prescribed substances into each of the three environmental media of air, water and land.[30] The exemption here does not apply to any process described in the 1991 Regulations if that process may give rise to an offensive smell noticeable outside the premises where the process is carried on. The prescribed substances are defined elsewhere in the 1991 Regulations.[31] In the case of releases into the air the prescribed substances include oxides of sulphur, nitrogen and carbon[32]; in the case of releases into water, the prescribed substances include mercury, cadmium and aldrin[33]; and (finally) in the case of releases into land, the prescribed substances include organic solvents, halogens and pesticides.[34] A second exception indicates that a process will not be a Part B process because there is nothing more than a trivial release of the substances in Schedule 4, such as oxides of sulphur, nitrogen and carbon.[35] The list of exceptions also includes the running on or within an aircraft, locomotive, ship, etc., of an engine used for its propulsion[36] as well as any process carried on as a domestic activity in connection with a private dwelling.[37]

Description of the processes

The subject processes are confined under six Chapters in Schedule 1, as follows:

(a) the production of fuel and power and associated processes (Chapter 1);
(b) metal production and processing (Chapter 2);
(c) mineral industries (Chapter 3);
(d) the chemical industry (Chapter 4);
(e) waste disposal and recycling (Chapter 5); and
(f) other industries (Chapter 6).

"Other industries" are categorised as follows:

(a) paper and pulp manufacturing processes;
(b) di-isocyanate processes;
(c) tar and bitumen processes;
(d) processes involving uranium;

[30] *Ibid.* reg.4(1).
[31] *Ibid.* reg.6 and Scheds. 4, 5 and 6.
[32] *Ibid.* Sched. 4.
[33] *Ibid.* Sched. 5.
[34] *Ibid.* Sched. 6.
[35] *Ibid.* reg.4(2).
[36] *Ibid.* reg.4(4).
[37] *Ibid.* reg.4(5).

(e) coating processes and printing;
(f) the manufacture of dyestuffs, printing ink and coating materials;
(g) timber processes;
(h) processes involving rubber; and
(i) the treatment and processing of animal or vegetable matter.

By way of illustration, reference is made to two of the above categories: metal productions and processing and mineral industries. In the first category, specific reference is made to iron and steel processing and production and, in the second, to glass manufacture and production.

Iron and steel processing and production The 1991 Regulations in Schedule 1 define processing and production in the present context to include, for the purpose of Part A:

> "(f) Making, melting or refining iron, steel or any ferro-alloy in any furnace other than a furnace described in Part B of this section.
> (g) Any process for the refining or making of iron, steel or any ferro-alloy in which air or oxygen or both are used unless related to a process described in Part B of this section . . ."

Glass manufacture and production The 1991 Regulations in Schedule 1 stipulate, as a Part A process: "The manufacture of glass frit[38] or enamel frit and its use in any process where that process is related to its manufacture . . . ."

Interpretation of the Schedule 1 process descriptions

The rules of interpretation are found in Schedule 2, but are subject to any specific provision to be found in Schedule 1. A central issue in Schedule 2 is the definition of a "process". That term is normally referable to any of the operations carried out by a person at the same location as part of the subject process. However, this rule will not apply in relation to any two or more processes described in different sections of Schedule 1, which therefore require distinct authorisation.[39] If one process at a particular location includes two or more processes to be found in the same section of Schedule 1, those processes are to be treated as a requiring authorisation as a single process. If the processes involved are described both in Part A and Part B of the same section, they are all to be regarded as part of a Part A process, attracting central control by Her Majesty's Inspectorate of Pollution.[40]

The foregoing requirements for the interpretation of Schedule 1 are illustrated in HMIP's "Practical Guide to IPC"[41]:

"Three hot blast cupolas operated by the same person (*i.e.* the authorisation

[38] A calcined mixture of sand and fluxes for the purpose of glass-making.
[39] Sched. 2, para. 2.
[40] *Ibid.* para. 3.
[41] *Integrated Pollution Control: A Practical Guide, op. cit.* pp.3 and 4.

holder) at the same location would constitute one iron and steel process for local authority air pollution control and require one authorisation."

"Three hot blast cupolas and an iron and steel refining operation operated by the same person (*i.e.* the authorisation holder) at the same location would constitute one iron and steel process for HMIP IPC control and require one authorisation. If the cupolas and the iron and steel refining operation were operated by separate persons at the same location, they would each require a separate authorisation."

"One glass manufacturing operation and one coating operation[42] operated by the same person (*i.e.* the authorisation holder) at the same location would constitute two processes and require two authorisations. Depending on whether the operations fell in Part A or Part B . . . the processes could
(i) both fall to local authority air pollution control;
(ii) both fall to HMIP IPC control; or
(iii) be split between the two control regimes."

A process that comes within two or more Schedule 1 descriptions is to be regarded as falling only within the description that fits it most aptly, subject to special rules governing any process that falls within descriptions in different sections of chapter 4 governing processes in the chemical industry.[43]

If, by reason of the use at different times of different fuels or different materials, or the disposal at different times of different wastes, processes of different descriptions are carried out with the same plant or machinery, and those processes include one or more Part A processes and one or more other processes, the other processes are to be regarded as being within the descriptions of the Part A processes.[44] On the other hand, if, by reference to the sort of use or disposal just referred to, processes of different descriptions are undertaken with the same plant or machinery and the processes include one or more Part B processes and one or more other processes (but no Part A processes), all of those processes shall be regarded as falling within the descriptions of Part B processes.[45]

Previous references to related processes in relation to Part A iron and steel processes and glass manufacturing are references to separate processes undertaken by the same person at the same location.[46]

The prescribed substances

Reference has been made already to the prescribed substances for the purposes of IPC.[47] The prescribed substances are those with the greatest potential for harm or

[42] Coating processes are detailed in Chap. 6 of Sched. 1.
[43] Sched. 2, para. 4.
[44] *Ibid.* para. 7(1).
[45] *Ibid.* para. 7(2).
[46] *Ibid.* para. 9.
[47] See n.31, *supra.*

pollution if released into the environment. Accordingly, these substances attract the controls through which BATNEEC is required to prevent release to environmental media or, if prevention is not practicable, to minimise release. BATNEEC is equally applicable for the purpose of rendering harmless those substances that could cause harm if released into any environmental medium. The relevant substances were described in outline previously.[48] The identification of particular substances for this purpose has come principally from relevant E.C. directives. At the time of writing, it is the collection of directives on air and water that have provided the more influential background to the prescription of substances for the purpose of IPC.

Directive 84/360[48a]

This directive relates to the control of air pollution from industrial plants as categorised, and requires any Member State to take measures necessary to ensure that such plants operate only after prior authorisation by a competent authority where specific requirements are taken account of at the design stage. Accordingly, a competent authority must satisfy itself of four matters:

(a) that preventative measures are in place in relation to air pollution by reference to best available technology not entailing excessive cost;
(b) that there will be no significant air pollution with particular reference to substances defined in an Annex[49];
(c) that there will be no excess of relevant emission limit values; and
(d) that account will be taken of relevant air quality limit values.

Directive 88/609

The large combustion plants directive is concerned with existing plant (for the purpose of requiring any Member State to compile a programme that complies with emission limits and percentage reductions in relation to sulphur dioxide and oxides of nitrogen set out in the Annexes[50]) and new plant (requiring construction and operating licences to comply with emission limits defined in the Annexes[51] in relation to sulphur dioxide, oxides of nitrogen and dust).

Directive 76/464[51a]

The directive relates to aquatic pollution from the discharge of dangerous substances into inland, territorial, coastal and ground waters. Any Member State is required to undertake appropriate steps for the following purposes: the elimination of pollution in the subject waters by reference to a catalogue of

[48] See nn.32, 33, 34, *supra*.
[48a] [1984] O.J. L188.
[49] Annex II.
[50] Annexes I and II.
[51] Annexes III to VII.
[51a] [1976] O.J. L129.

dangerous substances defined by the Annex[52]; and the reduction of pollution by reference to other dangerous substances elsewhere in the Annex.[53]

Prescribed substances under these directives

Annex II to Directive 84/360 includes sulphur dioxide, oxides of nitrogen, hydrocarbons, heavy metals, chlorine, asbestos and fluorine, among others.[54] Annexes I and II of Directive 88/609 refer to sulphur dioxide and oxides of nitrogen,[55] while Annexes III–VII relate to sulphur dioxide, oxides of nitrogen and dust.[56] List I in Directive 76/464—the "black" list—comprises those substances with defined toxicity, persistence or bio-accumulation.[57] List II of the directive—the "grey" list—is characterised by substances found in the black list but awaiting a definition of limit values, together with substances that have an adverse impact on the aquatic environment, albeit localised.[58] Subsequently, Directive 86/280[58a] has defined limit values and quality objectives for certain categories of substance defined as dangerous and included in List 1 to Directive 76/464 for the purpose of a subject discharge from relevant industrial plant: carbon tetrachloride, DDT and pentachlorophenol.

Prescribed substances and releases into land

It has been seen already that Schedules 4, 5 and 6 to the 1991 Regulations contain lists of prescribed substances relating to releases to air, water and land. Reference has also been made to the source of prescription in certain E.C. directives relating to releases to air and water. Among the prescribed substances in Schedule 6 (release into land) are polychlorinated dibenzoparadioxins (PCDDs) and polychlorinated dibenzofurans (PCDFs): a group of 210 closely related chemicals. The group of chemicals is better known by the generic term "dioxins". Of those 210 chemicals, 17 are toxic.

Standards, objectives and requirements for processes and substances

Section 3 of the Environmental Protection Act authorises the Secretary of State to make Regulations for the purpose of establishing standards, objectives or requirements in relation to particular prescribed processes or particular substances. This most important power is the vehicle for national implementation of many important E.C. requirements for the sort referred to above. Once in

[52] List I.
[53] List II.
[54] See n.49, *supra.*
[55] See n.50, *supra.*
[56] See n.51, *supra.*
[57] See n.52, *supra.*
[58] See n.53, *supra.*
[58a] [1986] O.J. L181.

place, any E.C. or international requirements will influence integrated pollution control in a variety of ways. Undoubtedly, one of the most significant areas of implementation is in relation to the imposition of conditions through the medium of authorisations, dealt with later in the present chapter.

Two categories of regulation are provided for by section 3. The first category found in subsection (2) covers standard limits (for the release of substances into any environmental medium from prescribed processes), in relation to matters such as substance concentrations. Two other categories relate to prescribed standard requirements for measurement, analysis or release of substances subject to prescribed limits and (in relation to any prescribed process) prescribed standards or requirements in relation to any aspect of the process. A second category found in subsection (4) permits the establishment (for any environmental medium) of quality objectives or standards in relation to any substances which may be released into that or any other medium from any process.

The present section also empowers the Secretary of State to make plans for a variety of purposes, again to enable translation of broad policy requirements into enforceable targets, particularly through the conditions applicable to IPC authorisations. Plans can be made to limit the amount of any substance that can be released into the environment, to establish quotas for similar purposes and to secure a progressive improvement in quality objectives and standards, among other things. One of the most significant plans to have been made relates to emissions reductions from large combustion plants of sulphur dioxide and oxides of nitrogen, by reference to annual targets.

The Authorisation of Processes

Basic requirements

The Act[59] indicates that no person "... shall carry on a prescribed process ... except under an authorisation granted by the enforcing authority and in accordance with the conditions to which it is subject". The detailed requirements relating to applications are to be found in Schedule 1 to the Environmental Protection Act and in the Environmental Protection (Applications, Appeals and Registers) Regulations 1991.[60] Any application for an authorisation must be accompanied by a fee, as described below.[61] Having considered the application, HMIP, or (in the event of the application being called in by the Secretary of State) the Secretary of State, "... shall either grant the authorisation subject to the conditions required or authorised to be imposed by section 7 ... or refuse the application".[62] The Act refers to any application "duly" made, indicating a need for compliance with various statutory formalities, dealt with below. Once

[59] s.6(1).
[60] S.I. 1991 No. 507.
[61] Environmental Protection Act, s.6(2).
[62] *Ibid.* s.6(3).

granted, an authorisation is open to review by HMIP from time to time and at least every four years.[63]

Applications for authorisation

Any application to HMIP must be advertised and accompanied by a fee. An application must be in writing and contain certain categories of information,[64] as follows:

(a) information identifying the applicant;
(b) (where a process is not to be undertaken with mobile plant) the name of the local authority in whose area the process will be undertaken and other information identifying the location of the premises;
(c) (where the process will be undertaken with mobile plant) the name of the local authority in whose area the applicant has his principal place of business as well as the address of that business;
(d) a description of the prescribed process;
(e) a list of prescribed substances (and any other substances which might cause harm if released into any environmental medium) which will be used in connection with, or which will result from, the carrying on of that process;
(f) a description of the techniques to be used for preventing the release into any environmental medium of such substances, for reducing the release of such substances to a minimum and for rendering harmless any such substances which are released;
(g) details of any proposed release of such substances into any environmental medium and an assessment of the environmental consequences;
(h) proposals for monitoring any release of such substances, the environmental consequences of any such release and the use of any techniques described in accordance with (f), above;
(i) the matters on which the applicant relies to establish that the objectives contained in section 7(2)[65] (including the objectives in section 7(7))[66] will be achieved and that he will be able to comply with the general condition implied by section 7(4)[67]; and

[63] *Ibid.* s.6(6).
[64] S.I. 1991 No. 507, reg.2.
[65] These objectives relate to the use of BATNEEC for the prevention of release of prescribed substances or for rendering harmless any other substances which might cause harm if released into any environmental medium; compliance with directions from the Secretary of State for the purpose of implementing obligations under E.C. or international laws on environmental protection; compliance with limits or requirements and achievement of quality standards or quality objectives prescribed by the Secretary of State; and compliance with requirements applicable to an authorisation specified by or under a plan made by the Secretary of State under s.3(5).
[66] Relating to releases to more than one environmental medium where the objective is to minimise pollution by reference to BATNEEC but having regard to the best practicable environmental option in relation to the substances to be released.
[67] Requiring the use of BATNEEC.

(j) any additional information which the applicant wishes the enforcing authority to take into account in considering the application.

HMIP may, by notice in writing to the applicant, require further information within a specified period for the purpose of determining the application made.[68] Any refusal to provide this further information justifies a refusal by HMIP to proceed with the application.

HMIP is obliged to maintain a register of applications in accordance with the requirements of the Environmental Protection (Applications, Appeals and Registers) Regulations,[69] a duty which is subject to sections 21 and 22 relating to exclusions from registers of information affecting national security and certain confidential information. In so far as any information (not just information about an application) is excluded from a register by virtue of section 22 relating to confidential information, a statement must be entered in the register indicating the existence of information of that description.[70] Any information on a register which ought to have been excluded from that register by virtue of section 21 or 22 may be subject to directions from the Secretary of State requiring its exclusion.[71]

A register may be kept in any form by HMIP.[72] HMIP is obliged to make any register available at all reasonable times for inspection by the public, free of charge and to provide facilities to the public for the taking of copies on payment of a reasonable charge.[73] These provisions represent a partial response to E.C. Directive 90/313[73a] relating to freedom of access to environmental information. The directive compels public authorities to facilitate the provision of information on the environment to any natural or legal person at his request, even though he may be without any specific interest in the matter.[74]

Fees and charges

Reference is made below to the operation of a charging scheme under Part I of the Act. For present purposes, however, the Act stipulates[75] that any application for an authorisation to HMIP shall be made in accordance with Part I of Schedule 1 to the Act and shall be accompanied by a prescribed fee. Only if an application is "duly" made by reference to these requirements is HMIP competent to entertain the application and move to a determination of it.[76]

The prescribed fee is set by the HMIP Integrated Pollution Control Fees and

[68] Sched. 1(3), (4).
[69] *Ibid.*
[70] s.20(5).
[71] subs.(6).
[72] subs.(8).
[73] subs.(7).
[73a] [1990] O.J. L158.
[74] See generally Chap. 9, "Access to Environmental Health Information".
[75] s.6(2).
[76] subs.(3).

Charges Scheme (England and Wales) 1991. This scheme, examined further, below, sets out three categories of charges covering an *application* fee, a *subsistence charge* payable annually for the holding of each IPC authorisation, and a *substantial variation fee*. The scheme identifies the application fee payable, subject to a variety of detailed exceptions.

Section 4(4)–(8) of the Act empowers the Secretary of State to transfer any individual Part B process or category of process from local authority to HMIP control. Where this exceptional power is used, the application fee payable to HMIP is at the rate payable under the local authority charge scheme.

If the planning, commissioning and development of a major installation is likely to be spread over a number of years, a staged application procedure may be negotiated with HMIP. If this is the case and information relating to the application, and the application itself, are to be submitted at different stages throughout the programme, the standard application fee is replaced with a fee calculated by reference to the actual time and cost generated in consideration of the components making up the application.

"Call-ins" and inquiries

Once an application for authorisation has been duly made, the Secretary of State may direct HMIP to submit that application to him for determination.[77]

Equally, the Secretary of State may direct that a particular class of application should be submitted to him for determination.[78] HMIP is obliged to advise the applicant of a transmission of the application: thereafter, the Secretary of State may either convene a local inquiry into the application or afford the applicant and HMIP an opportunity of appearing before and being heard by one of his inspectors.[79] However, any request from the applicant or HMIP that one or other of these powers is exercised must be made in writing within a period of 21 days beginning with the day on which the applicant was informed of the transmission of the application.[80]

Any local inquiry that is convened for present purposes is subject to the requirements of the Local Government Act 1972.[81] These requirements extend to the issue of a summons to attend to give evidence or produce documents, failure being punishable summarily, the payment of the costs of the inquiry by HMIP or a party to the inquiry, and the power of the Secretary of State to make orders as to costs. Having come to a decision on the application, the Secretary of State is obliged to give HMIP such direction as he thinks fit on the issue of whether the application should be granted and, if so, the conditions to be attached.[82]

[77] Sched. 1, para. 3(1).
[78] *Ibid. Cf.* reg.4.
[79] *Ibid.* paras. 2 and 3.
[80] Environmental Protection (Applications, Appeals and Registers) Regulations 1991, reg.8.
[81] subss.(2)–(5).
[82] Sched. 1, para. 3(5).

Advertisement of applications

A further formality in relation to applications is the need to advertise in one or more newspapers circulating in the locality where the prescribed process will be undertaken.[83] The advertisement must be published within a period of 28 days beginning 14 days after the day on which the application for authorisation is made.[84] That advertisement must include:

(a) the name of the applicant;
(b) the address of the premises where the process will be undertaken;
(c) a brief description of the process;
(d) the location of any register that will contain details of the application; and
(e) an explanation that any person may submit representations in writing within a period of 28 days beginning with the date of the advertisement and giving HMIP's address.[85]

These requirements do not apply to any application relating to the use of mobile plant.[86]

Consultation

Schedule 1 to the Act and the Environmental Protection (Applications, Appeals and Registers) Regulations prescribe the extent to which consultation is required in connection with the process of authorisation. While the Regulations prescribe those to be consulted, provision is also made for the Secretary of State to direct that certain persons are to be consulted.[87]

Those to be consulted listed by the Regulations,[88] excluding Scotland, are as follows:

(a) the Health and Safety Executive (in all cases);
(b) the Minister of Agriculture, Fisheries and Food (in the case of all processes designated for HMIP control);
(c) the Secretary of State for Wales (in the case of all processes designated for HMIP control in Wales);
(d) the National Rivers Authority (in the case of all prescribed processes designated for HMIP control and to be undertaken in England and Wales and which may result in the release of any substance to controlled waters for the purposes of Chapters I to III of Part III of the Water Resources Act 1991);

[83] S.I. 1991 No. 507, reg.5(1).
[84] *Ibid.* reg.5(2).
[85] *Ibid.* reg.5(3).
[86] *Ibid.* reg.5(4).
[87] *Ibid.* Sched. 1, para. 2(1).
[88] S.I. 1991 No. 507, reg.4.

(e) the sewerage undertaker (in the case of all prescribed processes designated for HMIP control which may involve the release of any substance into a sewer vested in the undertaker);
(f) the Nature Conservancy Council for England or the Countryside Council for Wales (in the case of all prescribed processes designated for HMIP control which may involve a release of any substance which may affect a site of special scientific interest within the Council's area); and
(g) the harbour authority (in the case of all prescribed processes designated for HMIP control which may involve a release of any substance into a harbour managed by the harbour authority.

The consultation requirement in aid of the nature conservation interest is potentially very wide, in so far as any substance "may" affect a site of special scientific interest. However, it should be noted that, initially at least, the judgment is one to be made by HMIP.

Schedule 1 to the Act refers to a time limit within which HMIP is obliged to notify consultees of the application.[89] By virtue of the Regulations,[90] the period for notification is a period of 14 days from the date when HMIP receives the application for authorisation. Thereafter, Schedule 1 requires HMIP to consider any representations from those consulted in arriving at a decision.[91] Furthermore, any representations made by any other persons within the period permitted are also to be considered by HMIP in the course of the decision-making process.[92] The period allowed for the making of representations is 28 days from the date when notice of the application is given in the case of those prescribed or directed to be consulted, and 28 days in the case of other persons, the period in this case running from the date when the making of the application was advertised.[93]

Conditions of authorisation

Having considered an application for authorisation, HMIP is empowered either to grant authorisation subject to the conditions required or authorised to be imposed by section 7 of the Act, or to refuse the application. HMIP is unable to grant an application unless it is considered that the applicant will be able to carry on the process so as to comply with the conditions which would be included in the authorisation.

Any authorisation is required to include up to four sets of conditions:

(a) such conditions as HMIP considers appropriate;
(b) a "general" condition;
(c) conditions specified in any direction from the Secretary of State; and
(d) such other conditions (if any) as appear to HMIP to be appropriate.[94]

[89] para. 2(1).
[90] reg.4(2).
[91] para. 2(3).
[92] para. 2(5).
[93] para. 2(6).
[94] s.7(1).

However, conditions cannot be imposed solely for the purpose of securing the health of persons at work.[95] Each of the above categories is now dealt with in turn, starting with the so-called "general" condition which is in fact an implied condition. The only situation in which this implied condition will not operate is where any aspect of a process is regulated by one of the conditions from categories just referred to.[96]

The implied condition is referable to every authorisation and obliges the person carrying on the process to use BATNEEC, for two purposes: to prevent the release of substances prescribed for any environmental medium into that medium or (where that is not practicable by such means) to reduce the release of such substances to a minimum and to render harmless any such substances which are so released, and, secondly (in the case of other substances which might cause harm if released into any environmental medium), to render such substances harmless.[97] Reference is made to the operation of BATNEEC later in the present chapter but, for the moment, it will be seen that one apparently major variable is the word "practicable". Whether a particular approach to the operation of a process is practicable may be answered, so it would appear, by reference to the techniques available or the cost involved. Ultimately, the most difficult question to answer is whether, in the circumstances of a particular process, an approach is practicable even though there are available the necessary techniques that do not involve excessive cost.

The second category of condition is that relating to those conditions considered appropriate by HMIP for the purpose of the objectives set by section 7(2) when taken with the general, implied condition dealt with previously. There are four objectives to be found in subsection (2), the first of which repeats the framework from subsection (4), set out immediately above. Accordingly, BATNEEC is once again seen as operating for two purposes: to prevent the release of prescribed substances for a prescribed medium into that medium or (if not practicable by reference to BATNEEC) to reduce any release to a minimum and to render harmless any such substances and, in the case of substances that are not so prescribed, to render those substances harmless in so far as they might cause harm if released into any environmental medium. The second objective to be found in subsection (2) refers to a need to comply with any direction from the Secretary of State given for the purpose of implementing E.C. or international legal requirements relating to environmental protection. Resort to such default powers must be by reference to the need to implement requirements imposed externally in relation to environmental protection. Nevertheless, the present provision may well be useful (say) in so far as HMIP would attempt to impose a condition in ignorance of accepted interpretations of limit values for atmospheric emissions, for example, unlikely though this may be in practice. The third objective in subsection (2) may be closely related to the second objective, in so far as it refers to a need for compliance with any limits or requirements and

[95] *Ibid.*
[96] *Ibid.* subs.(6).
[97] *Ibid.* subs.(4).

achievement of any quality standards or quality objectives prescribed by the Secretary of State, under the water resources legislation,[98] for example. The fourth objective refers to a need for compliance with any requirements applicable to the grant of authorisations as specified by or under a plan made by the Secretary of State under section 3(5) of the Environmental Protection Act, reference to which was made earlier in the present chapter.[99] In so far as there is likely to be a release of substances into more than one environmental medium, there is a further objective[1] of ensuring that BATNEEC will be used for minimising the pollution which may be caused to the environment taken as a whole by the releases, having regard to the best practical environmental option available in relation to those substances. Typically, any calculation for this purpose would look at the comparative merits of (say) incinerating or landfilling waste generated from a subject process.

The foregoing requirement in relation to BATNEEC, having regard to the best practicable environmental option, is one which may also focus attention on the amount or composition of any substance produced by or utilised in the process in any period of its operation. Perhaps significantly, HMIP may impose a condition limiting the throughput of certain substances. Limitations on high sulphur coal generating excessive quantities of sulphur dioxide is but one example.[2] This is clearly a very significant power: whether its use is to be exceptional remains to be seen.

The Secretary of State is given fairly broad powers to issue directions which operate generally, except in relation to the general, implied condition already referred to.[3] The Secretary of State may give HMIP directions as to the conditions which are, or are not, to be included in all authorisations, in authorisations of any specific description or in any particular authorisation. Any failure by HMIP to comply with basic legal limits on conditions available in the authorisation process is an obvious and necessary venue for the deployment of these powers. The foregoing legal limits apply again to the final set of conditions available to HMIP, in so far as any other conditions appear to HMIP to be appropriate. Such limits in administrative law terms relate to a need to comply with requirements of relevancy and to avoid any use of conditions for improper purposes. In broader terms, conditions must be enforceable, clear, relevant and workable.[4]

98 Water Resources Act 1991, Pt. III.

99 Standards, objectives and requirements for processes and substances: *cf.* s.3.

1 s.7(7).

2 subs.(8).

3 subs.(3). *Cf.* the need to comply with guidance: subs.(11).

4 As to the application of administrative law principles in the closely connected area of local authority air pollution control under Pt. I, see the section on "Authorisations" in Chap. 6 "Atmospheric Pollution Control".

Decision-making

Except where an application has been referred to the Secretary of State, as described previously, HMIP is required to determine an application for authorisation within four months of the date of receipt of the application, or within any longer period as may be agreed with the applicant.[5] A failure by HMIP to determine an application within these time limits entitles the applicant to notify HMIP to the effect that the failure is regarded as a deemed refusal of the application for authorisation.[6] If any duly determined application is decided in favour of an authorisation, details of that authorisation are to be entered on the public register maintained by HMIP.[7]

Appeals

Appeals under Part I of the Act are governed by section 15 and the Environmental Protection (Applications, Appeals and Registers) Regulations.[8] The scope of the appeal facility is wide and extends beyond an adverse decision on an application for authorisation (either through a refusal or a conditional grant of authorisation) to include refusal of a variation of an authorisation or a revocation of an authorisation, as well as an appeal against any variation, enforcement or prohibition notice.[9] Any such appeal is to the Secretary of State for the Environment. However, the Secretary of State may refer any matter involved in the appeal to an inspector or may even direct that such an inspector decide the appeal on his behalf. Whether the appeal function is being exercised by the Secretary of State or an inspector, either party may demand that the proceedings start or (as the case may be) continue as a hearing which the Secretary of State or the inspector may determine should be held, wholly or partly, in private.[10] In so far as the appeal relates to an adverse decision on an application for authorisation, a refusal of variation or its revocation, the Secretary of State or inspector may affirm the decision, direct the grant of an authorisation or its variation, quash all or any of the conditions attached to an authorisation or direct that any revocation decision be quashed, according to the basis of the appeal. Furthermore, in all of the foregoing cases where simple affirmation is not in issue, directions may be given in relation to any conditions to be attached to the authorisation.[11] In the case of an appeal against a variation, enforcement or prohibition notice, the notice may be quashed or affirmed, either in its original form or subject to such modifications as the Secretary of State thinks fit.[12] The bringing of an appeal against one of these notices does not have the effect of suspending the notice.[13] By

[5] Sched. 1, para. 5(1). *Cf.* para. 5(3).
[6] *Ibid.* para. 5(2).
[7] s.20(1)(b).
[8] regs. 9, 10 and 11.
[9] s.15(1), (2). As to variation, enforcement and prohibition notices, see (respectively) ss.10, 13 and 14.
[10] *Ibid.* s.15(5).
[11] *Ibid.* subs.(6).
[12] *Ibid.* subs.(7).
[13] *Ibid.* subs.(9).

contrast, any appeal against revocation will not affect the operation of the authorisation, pending determination of the appeal.[14]

Notice of appeal and time limits

The Environmental Protection (Applications, Appeals and Registers) Regulations provide for written notice of appeal to be given to the Secretary of State in the case of appeals under section 15 (dealt with above) and section 22(5), relating to determinations by HMIP of the question whether information is commercially confidential for the purpose of the public registers under Part I of the Act.[15] A variety of documents must accompany the notice of appeal, copied also to HMIP. The time limit for appeals depends on the category of an appeal, as determined by the Regulations.[16] The notice of appeal is required to be given within six months of the date of an adverse decision on an application for an authorisation, or the date of a deemed refusal, as described previously. A similar limit of time applies to a decision refusing variation of an authorisation. In the case of a revocation, a notice of appeal should be given before the date when the revocation takes effect while, in the case of appeals against a variation, enforcement or prohibition notice, a notice of appeal is required to be given before the expiry of two months beginning with the date of the subject notice. Failure to comply with the foregoing requirements as to time limits may be regarded in many cases, but not necessarily all, as a failure to comply with a mandatory procedural requirement. Lord Hailsham has said in the House of Lords[17] that:

> "... what the courts have to decide ... is the legal consequence of non-compliance on the rights of the subject viewed in the light of a concrete statement of facts and a continuing chain of events. It may be that what the courts are faced with is not so much a stark choice of alternatives but a spectrum of possibilities in which one compartment or description fades gradually into another ... [T]hough language like 'mandatory', 'directory', 'void', 'voidable' ... may be helpful in argument, it may be misleading in effect if relied on to show that the courts, in deciding the consequences of a defect in the exercise of power, are necessarily bound to fit the facts of a particular case and a developing chain of events into rigid legal categories ..."

The processing of third party representations

HMIP has certain duties relating to the promotion of public participation in the event of an appeal. The Regulations give HMIP a wide discretion in deciding who should receive written notice of the appeal within 14 days of its own receipt

[14] *Ibid.* subs.(8).
[15] reg.9(1). *Cf.* reg.15(j), relating to entries on the register of any notice of appeal, and the notification of the Secretary of State's decision on the appeal.
[16] reg.10.
[17] *London and Clydeside Estates Ltd v. Aberdeen District Council* [1980] 1 W.L.R. 182, at 189.

of a copy of the notice of appeal.[18] More specifically, HMIP can give a written notice to "... any person who appears to [HMIP] to have a particular interest in the subject-matter of the appeal insofar as it relates to the revocation of an authorisation or a variation, enforcement and prohibition notice."[19] In any other case, HMIP is obliged to give written notice of an appeal to any person who made representations to HMIP in connection with a grant or variation of an authorisation, and to any person in the list of statutory consultees in regulation 4 required to be consulted in connection with applications generally, as well as applications for variation.[20] The notice to be served on third parties by HMIP must contain certain prescribed information, such as a description of the application or the authorisation to which the appeal relates.[21]

The processing of appeals and decisions

Appeals can be processed under Part I either by means of written representations or by means of a hearing. In both cases, detailed prescriptions are found in the Regulations, together with detailed requirements relating to notification of a decision by the Secretary of State.[22]

Written representations

HMIP has a period of 28 days in which to furnish written representations to the Secretary of State, this period running from the date when HMIP receives a copy of the statement of the grounds of appeal and the appellant's choice of disposal of the appeal through written representations rather than a hearing. Within 17 days of those representations, the appellant may submit further representations by way of reply. Both parties are required to copy their representations to each other on submission to the Secretary of State. In the case of representations from a third party, the Secretary of State is required to copy these to the appellant and HMIP, giving them a period of not less than 14 days in which to make a response. In addition, a particular case may justify the Secretary of State setting later time limits than those stipulated as well as requiring additional exchanges between the parties involved.[23]

Hearings

The appellant and HMIP must receive at least 28 days' notice from the Secretary of State of the date, time and venue for a hearing, subject only to any shorter period that the parties may agree. In so far as any hearing is to be held wholly or partly in public, the Secretary of State is required to publish a notice identifying

[18] reg.11(1).
[19] *Ibid.* reg.11(1)(a).
[20] *Ibid.* reg.11(1)(b). *Cf.* reg.11(3), requiring HMIP to forward a copy of any representation made by the third party, its date and the name of that third party, to the Secretary of State.
[21] *Ibid.*, reg. 11(2).
[22] regs.12, 13 and 14.
[23] reg.12.

the date, time and venue for the inquiry at least 21 days before the holding of that inquiry, serving a copy of that notice on third parties making representations, as well as those third parties required to be notified of the appeal.[24]

At the hearing, the inspector is bound by the rules of natural justice and is required by the Regulations[25] to give a hearing to the appellant, HMIP and any third party who is entitled to be notified of the appeal. However, this requirement is without prejudice to the inspector's freedom to permit any other person to be heard: indeed, the Regulations declare that any such permission from the inspector shall not be unreasonably withheld.[26] Following the close of the hearing, the inspector is required to report in writing to the Secretary of State, including his conclusions and recommendations or his reasons for not making recommendations.[27]

Notifications of decision

The Secretary of State is obliged to notify the appellant in writing of his decision on the appeal and to furnish a copy of the inspector's report. Simultaneously, the Secretary of State is required to copy this documentation to HMIP and to third parties required to be notified of the appeal, as well as any third parties who made representations to the Secretary of State or who made representations in relation to the appeal at the hearing.[28] The public register maintained by HMIP is required to include (apart from details of the notice of appeal) any written notification of the Secretary of State's decision, together with any report accompanying that notification.[29]

Variation of authorisations

At the heart of integrated pollution control in Part I of the Act is the assumption that techniques relating to the various processes will undergo development and change. This assumption underpins BATNEEC and, in turn, gives rise to a set of provisions, in sections 10 and 11 of the Act, facilitating the variation of IPC authorisations. A variation may be instigated by HMIP (section 10) or in response to an application from the holder of an authorisation (section 11). The provisions governing variation and particularly those under section 10 have to be seen against the Act's requirement that HMIP undertakes periodic reviews of authorisations not less than once every four years.[30] The word "vary" for present purposes in relation to subsisting conditions or other provisions of an authorisation means "...adding to them or varying or rescinding any of them ...".[31]

[24] reg.13(1), (2).
[25] reg.13(6).
[26] reg.13(7).
[27] reg.13(8).
[28] reg.14.
[29] reg.15(j).
[30] s.6(6).
[31] s.10(8).

Variation by HMIP

At any time, HMIP is empowered to vary an authorisation and is subject to a requirement to vary in so far as it appears that section 7 (governing conditions) requires conditions to be imposed which are different to the subsisting conditions.[32] In so far as HMIP takes the initiative under these provisions, it is obliged to serve on the holder of the authorisation a variation notice specifying the variations decided on and specifying a date or dates when the variation will take effect. Furthermore, a notice will require the holder, within a specified time limit, to notify HMIP of action to comply with the varied authorisation, and to pay a prescribed fee.[33]

The action required to comply with the variation may amount to a "substantial change" in the execution of the process in the opinion of HMIP. Subject to any directions given to HMIP by the Secretary of State generally or in particular cases, a "substantial change" is defined by the Act[34] as a "... substantial change in the substances released from the processor in the amount or any other characteristic of any substance so released ...". One crucial area of importance where the meaning of the word "substantial" is of central interest arises in relation to E.C. Directive 86/280 on limit values and quality objectives for discharges of DDT, carbon tetrachloride and pentachlorophenol, mentioned earlier in the present chapter when reference was made to prescribed substances under various directives. The directive refers to "new plant" as comprising any new industrial plant which has become operational or its handling capacity increased beyond a prescribed limit. Nowhere in the directive is there a definition of the word "substantially". However, the Secretary of State has advised that "substantially ... should be interpreted as an overall increase of 20 per cent. or more in the handling capacity of the particular substance".[35] The Secretary of State also possesses wide powers for the purpose of directing HMIP to exercise or not to exercise powers granted by section 11.[36]

Where HMIP forms the view that a variation will involve a substantial change, it must notify the action required of the holder to those individuals and organisations to be consulted, according to the categories and requirements described previously in this chapter.[37] The holder is obliged to advertise the action proposed in two or more newspapers circulating in the locality.[38] Representations from anyone consulted must be considered by HMIP in its decision-making, as well as representations from others, in so far as they are submitted within the stipulated time limit, normally 28 days from the date of the notification or advertisement, as the case may be.[39]

[32] *Ibid.* subs.(1).
[33] *Ibid.* subs.(3), (4).
[34] *Ibid.* subs.(7).
[35] Circular 7/89, Department of the Environment, (Welsh Office Circular 16/89), para. 22.
[36] s.10(6).
[37] Sched. 1, para. 6.
[38] Environmental Protection (Applications, Appeals and Registers) Regulations 1991, reg.5(1)(b).
[39] See n.37, *supra*.

Variation at the request of an authorisation holder

Section 11 contains a number of possibilities which may depend on the existence of a so-called "relevant change" or a "substantial change". A relevant change in a prescribed process ". . . is a change in the manner of carrying on the process which is capable of altering the substance released from the process or of affecting the amount of any other characteristic of any substance so released".[40] Note the contrast with the definition of a substantial change as seen above,[41] referring to the substances released from a process. Accordingly, some substantial changes may exclude relevant changes although, inevitably, all substantial changes are "relevant".

The first of the possibilities referred to arises where a person undertaking a prescribed process by virtue of an authorisation wishes to complete a relevant change in that process. Closely related is the situation in which a person undertaking a prescribed process by virtue of an authorisation wishes to complete a relevant change and it appears to him that the change attracts a need for variation of conditions. Finally, if the holder of an authorisation is not proposing a relevant change in the subject process, a relatively uncomplicated application can be made to HMIP for variation of conditions, in so far as there is no operation of a prescribed process or any change is not a "relevant" change by reference to the definition above.[42] Also relatively uncomplicated is the procedure in the second situation described above. What is required here is an application for variation of the subject conditions.[43] Far more complicated is the procedure in the first of the possibilities listed above. Initially, HMIP is required to make a determination on four matters:

(a) whether any change would involve a breach of condition;
(b) whether (if no breach is involved) HMIP would be likely to vary the conditions as a result of the change;
(c) whether (if a breach is involved) HMIP would vary the conditions to enable the change requested; and
(d) whether any substantial change in the execution of the process will occur.[44]

HMIP is required to notify the holder of its determination in respect of these matters. If a determination indicates that a change leads to or would require a variation of conditions, the holder may proceed to apply for the necessary variation.[45] Section 15 does not include a right of appeal in respect of the

[40] s.11(11).
[41] See n.34, *supra*.
[42] s.11(5). *Cf.* the attendant procedures in relation to the notices referred to in s.11: Environmental Protection (Applications, Appeals and Registers) Regulations 1991, reg.3.
[43] *Ibid.* s.11(6).
[44] *Ibid.* subs.(2).
[45] *Ibid.* subs.(3).

foregoing HMIP determinations. If, on the other hand, the determination from HMIP indicates that an anticipated change would be a substantial change leading to or requiring a variation of conditions, the holder may (again) imitate the variation procedure.[46] Similar requirements to those described above relate to advertisement and consultation for the purpose of dealing with such a substantial change.[47]

Transfers

To avoid any gaps in the system of IPC control, section 9 permits the transfer of an authorisation granted under section 6 but only in respect of the "carrying on" of the process in question. The reference to "carrying on" is sufficiently wide to avoid a situation in which there are doubts about the discharge of responsibilities under an authorisation. What is open to transfer is the control, direction and ongoing responsibility for a process.[48] The transferee is obliged to notify HMIP in writing of the transfer not later than 21 days beginning with the date of the transfer. Non-compliance with this requirement is an offence.[49] Thereafter, the authorisation operates as if granted to the transferee under section 6 and subject to the same conditions, with effect from the date of the transfer.[50] The construction of the section is perhaps puzzling, bearing in mind the preoccupation of the section 6 authorisation procedures with the applicant's capacity to undertake the process for the purpose of complying with relevant conditions.[51] There is clearly no direct power in section 9 that would permit HMIP to veto a transfer. Accordingly, it would appear that the options available to HMIP relate to revocation, together with the other sanctions to be found in prohibition and enforcement notices, dealt with below.

Revocations

Section 12 provides for revocation of an authorisation ". . . at any time . . ." by HMIP, after a notice in writing to the holder of the authorisation or where HMIP has ". . . reason to believe that a prescribed process for which an authorisation is in force has not been carried on or not for a period of 12 months".[52] That period of 12 months must run to the date of the notice served under this section. As with the foregoing provision on transfers, the critical issue in the present provision on revocations is the reference to a process which has not been "carried on", again suggesting a need for evidence of active control and direction subject to the authorisation holder's ongoing responsibility for the subject process.[53] HMIP is

[46] *Ibid.* subs.(4).
[47] Sched. 1, para. 7.
[48] *Lewis v. Graham* (1888) 22 Q.B.D. 1, *per* Fry L.J. at 5; *Theophile v. Solicitor-General* [1950] 1 All E.R. 405, *per* Lord Porter at 411.
[49] s.23(1).
[50] s.9(3).
[51] s.6(4).
[52] s.12(1), (2).
[53] See n.48, *supra.*

obliged to place on the public register all particulars of any revocation it has effected.[54]

Best Available Techniques not Entailing Excessive Cost and Best Practicable Environmental Option

BATNEEC

It has been seen previously in the present chapter that BATNEEC is at the centre of the IPC authorisation requirements. This sees BATNEEC as a bench-mark for the prevention of a release to environmental media or (if prevention is not practicable) for the minimisation of release. Equally, BATNEEC is applicable to render harmless those substances that could cause harm if they are released into any of the environmental media. Each process is to be regarded individually and BATNEEC for that purpose will be constructed from the guidance notes compiled by Her Majesty's Chief Inspector of Pollution as one of the objectives of any authorisation and in respect of which conditions will apply.

The meaning of "best available techniques"

"Techniques" are referable to the process, including matters of concept and design, together with the operation of the process and its components, and their inter-relationship with that process. Also of relevance here are matters of staffing training, work methods and supervision. More particularly, the Act[55] stipulates that references to BATNEEC include (in addition to references to technical means and technology) references to the number, qualifications, training and supervision of persons employed in the process and the design, construction, layout and maintenance of the buildings in which it is carried out.

The need for techniques to be "available" means that any appropriate techniques have to be available. The Department of the Environment's "Guide to IPC"[56] points to the inclusion of a technique ". . . which has been developed (or proven) at a scale which allows its implementation in the relevant industrial context with the necessary business confidence".[57] Any technique may not be generally in use: the important matter is that the technique should be generally available, even if the source is a sole, monopoly supplier.

"Best" available technique indicates that it must be the most effective technique, taking account of the need for prevention, minimisation and neutralisation of pollution. However, more than one technique may achieve the label "best", indicating similar performance in the task of prevention, minimisation and neutralisation.

[54] s.20(1)(d) and Environmental Protection (Applications, Appeals and Registers) Regulations 1991, reg.15(i).
[55] s.7(10).
[56] See n.3, *supra.*
[57] *Ibid.* p.16.

The meaning of "not entailing excessive cost"

This element of the formula is a most important variable for present purposes, affecting conclusions about the first part of the formula, bearing in mind that achievement of "best available techniques" may be excessively costly when weighed against environmental benefits. However, while this view may be particularly pertinent in the context of new processes, other considerations may affect existing processes. More particularly, the situation of existing plants requiring progressive upgrading or (perhaps) decommissioning is likely to be influenced by the technical profile of the plant, its rate of utilisation and length of remaining life, the nature and volume of polluting emissions generated and (finally) the desirability of avoiding excessive costs in view of the economic circumstances of undertakings in the relevant industrial category.[58]

BATNEEC as a performance standard

Reference has been made to the dynamic character of BATNEEC, as seen through facilities in Part I of the Act for variation. BATNEEC is most obviously represented as a technological statement, particularly through the foregoing interpretation of "techniques". However, there is no reason why BATNEEC should not be seen as the core of the equation which realises emission standards for a process. As such, BATNEEC is a performance standard for the process. Overall, though, whatever emphasis is given, BATNEEC is ideally a complete statement of the technology (in its widest sense) for a process that it sufficiently flexible that it allows recognition of and response to newer, more efficient technology, as well as the operator's freedom to select the best, most appropriate techniques.

To assist BATNEEC in these foregoing tasks, the HMIP process guidance notes will:

(a) justify IPC requirements for a process and identify subject substances;
(b) define the standards HMIP believe can be achieved by techniques considered appropriate to the particular industrial context;
(c) describe any technique or range of techniques necessary to achieve the defined standards; and
(d) provide guidance on what amounts to a substantial change.

Throughout, a concern is likely to be for consistency for a system of regulation by authorisation for processes falling within categories, where those processes are of the same or a similar kind.

[58] *Ibid.* p.17.

BPEO

The inter-relationship between BATNEEC and BPEO was seen previously in relation to the operation of section 7 of the Act, where releases to more than one environmental medium are concerned. Consequently, the task of minimising pollution of the environment as a whole is addressed by BATNEEC but by reference to BPEO in relation to the substances in question. This probably requires a "tracking back" from identification of the particular substances and the "appropriate" BPEO to the definition of an appropriate BATNEEC for the process in question. Because BPEO will have a considerable influence on BATNEEC here, a lot depends on the variables and factors that will shape BPEO. The Royal Commission on Environmental Pollution in its 1988 report on BEPO[59] saw it as

> "... the outcome of a systematic consultative and decision-making procedure which emphasises the protection and conservation of the environment across land, air and water. The BPEO procedure establishes, for a given set of objectives, the option that provides the most benefit or least damage to the environment as a whole, at acceptable cost, in the long term as well as in the short term".[60]

Two matters require immediate attention in relation to the all-important options: the scope of those options and their initial evaluation. For any option to be "practicable", it needs to be consistent with contemporary technical knowledge while at the same time being financially feasible. Any attempt to derogate from BPEO must not be motivated by irrelevant social or political reasons.[61]

Enforcement

Inspection powers

HMIP and (in the case of local authority air pollution control) the local authorities are empowered to appoint inspectors under section 16 of the Act. Immunity from liability in civil or criminal proceedings is given to an inspector in respect of anything done "... in the purported performance of his functions ..." under sections 17 or 18[62] "... if the court is satisfied that the act was done in good faith and that there were reasonable grounds for doing it".[63] The significance of

[59] Cm. 310, (1988).
[60] *Ibid.* para. 2.1.
[61] *Ibid.* para. 2, generally.
[62] s.17 gives various powers, including entry to and examination of premises; section 18 relates to powers to deal with the cause of any imminent danger of serious harm.
[63] s.16(7).

this subsection is seen in its reference to the "purported" performance of functions by inspectors. Subject to the need for the court to be satisfied on the above issues, it seems that some informality in the performance may be forgiven in law. However, the provision does refer to personal liability and leaves open the question whether the enforcing authority is to be bound in law by the subject acts or omissions of the inspector, by example. More broadly, the present section empowers the Secretary of State to appoint a chief inspector for England and Wales.[64]

Specific powers

The prerequisite for an exercise of his powers by an inspector is the production (if required) of his authority, as long as those powers are being used "... for the purposes of the discharge of the functions of the enforcing authority".[65] Failure to fulfil this requirement may not necessarily render the inspector liable in trespass, for example, in so far as the terms of section 16(7), examined above, are satisfied. Section 17 is not confined to the exercise of powers in relation to "premises". However, in so far as they are so exercisable, they apply to premises on which a prescribed process is, or is believed (on reasonable grounds) to be, carried on, as well as premises on which a prescribed process has been carried on, but where their condition is believed (on reasonable grounds) to be such as to give rise to a risk of serious pollution of the environment.[66]

Inspectors' powers fall into 12 categories. There is a considerable and often significant overlap between the different categories, each of which is now examined in turn.

The first power to be listed in subsection (3) enables an inspector at any reasonable time (or, in a situation in which in his opinion there is an immediate risk of serious pollution of the environment, at any time) to enter premises which he has reason to believe it is necessary for him to enter.[67] These powers may also be exercised by any person authorised for the purpose in writing by the Secretary of State,[68] subject only to any regulations which may stipulate the procedures to be followed in connection with the taking, and the dealing with, of any samples.[69]

The second power builds on the first and allows the inspector to take with him any person duly authorised by the chief inspector and, if the inspector has reasonable cause to apprehend any serious obstruction in the execution of his duty, a constable. In addition, an inspector may take with him any equipment or materials required for any purpose for which the power of entry is being exercised.[70] These powers may also be exercised by any person authorised for the purpose in writing by the Secretary of State,[71] subject only to any regulations

[64] *Ibid.* subs.(3). *Cf.* subs.(4) on the question of delegation of functions by the Chief Inspector.
[65] s.17(1).
[66] *Ibid.* subs.(2).
[67] *Ibid.* subs.(3)(a).
[68] *Ibid.* subs.(9).
[69] *Ibid.* subs.(4).
[70] *Ibid.* subs.(3)(b).
[71] *Ibid.* subs.(9).

which may stipulate the procedures to be followed in connection with the taking, and the dealing with, of any samples.[72]

The third power permits an inspector to make such examination and investigation as may, in any circumstances, be necessary.[73] The wording of this power clearly anticipates action which may not necessarily centre on "premises". Once again, these powers may also be exercised by any person authorised for the purpose in writing by the Secretary of State,[74] subject only to any regulations which may stipulate the procedures to be followed in connection with the taking, and the dealing with, of any samples.[75]

The fourth power relates again to "premises" which the inspector is empowered to enter. Here, the inspector may direct that those premises, or any part of them, or anything in them, shall be left undisturbed (whether generally or in particular respects) for so long as is reasonably necessary for the purpose of any examination or investigation of the sort referred to in the previous power available to an inspector.[76]

The fifth power allows an inspector to take such measurements and photographs and make such recordings as he considers necessary for the purpose of the investigation or examination previously referred to.[77] Again, these powers may be exercised by any person authorised for the purpose in writing by the Secretary of Stae,[78] subject only to any regulations which may stipulate the procedures to be followed in connection with the taking, and the dealing with, of any samples.[79]

The sixth power permits an inspector to take samples of any articles or substances found in or on any premises which he has power to enter, and of the air, water or land in, on or in the vicinity of the premises.[80] These powers may be exercised by any person authorised for the purpose in writing by the Secretary of State,[81] subject only to any regulations which may stipulate the procedures to be followed in connection with the taking, and the dealing with, of any samples.[82] Significantly, the term "vicinity" is left undefined by the Act, leaving the matter as one of fact and degree for the inspector in question. However, it is suggested that the vicinity may be relative, involving far greater distances in the case of atmospheric emissions compared with (say) the generation of solid wastes from a prescribed process.

The seventh power refers to any articles or substance found in or on any premises which an inspector is empowered to enter. If those articles or that substance appears to the inspector to have caused or to be likely to cause pollution

[72] *Ibid.* subs.(4).
[73] *Ibid.* subs.(3)(c).
[74] *Ibid.* subs.(9).
[75] *Ibid.* subs.(4).
[76] *Ibid.* subs.(3)(d).
[77] *Ibid.* subs.(3)(e).
[78] *Ibid.* subs.(9).
[79] *Ibid.* subs.(4).
[80] *Ibid.* subs.(3)(f).
[81] *Ibid.* subs.(9).
[82] *Ibid.* subs.(4).

of the environment, the inspector may cause it to be dismantled or subjected to any process or test, but not to damage or destroy it unless this is necessary.[83] However, before taking such action, the inspector is obliged to consult those persons who appear to him to be appropriate for the purpose of ascertaining what dangers, if any, there may be in so acting.[84]

The eighth power is directly related to the previous power, in so far as the inspector is able to take possession of the article or substance and detain it so for as long as is necessary for all or any of a number of purposes.[85] Those purposes allow the inspector to examine the article or substance and do anything with it as described in relation to the previous power, to ensure that it is not tampered with before completion of an examination and to ensure that it is available for use as evidence in any proceedings for an offence under section 23 or any other proceedings relating to a variation notice, an enforcement notice or a prohibition notice. In so far as the inspector takes possession of an article or substance found on any premises, he is obliged to leave there, either with a responsible person or, if that is impracticable, fixed in a conspicuous position, a notice giving particulars of the article or substance sufficient to identify it and stating that it has been taken possession of by reference to these powers. Furthermore, if it is practical, the inspector is obliged to take a sample and give a responsible person on the premises a portion of the sample, clearly labelled.[86]

The ninth power enables an inspector to require any person whom he has reasonable cause to believe to be able to give any information relevant to any examination or investigation under the third power to answer (in the absence of persons other than a person nominated to be present and any persons whom the inspector may allow to be present) such questions as the inspector thinks fit to ask and to sign a declaration of the truth of his answers.[87] However, no answer given by a person here is admissible in evidence in England and Wales against that person in any proceedings.[88]

The tenth power allows an inspector to require the production of, or, where the information is recorded in computerised form, the furnishing of extracts from, any records which are required to be kept under the present Part I of the Act or which it is necessary for him to see for the purposes of an examination or investigation in relation to the third set of powers and to inspect and take copies of, or of any entry in, the records.[89]

The eleventh power empowers the inspector to require any person to afford him such facilities and assistance with respect to any matters or things within that person's control, or in relation to which that person has responsibilities, as are necessary to enable him to exercise any of the powers in section 17.[90]

[83] *Ibid.* subs.(3)(g).
[84] *Ibid.* subs.(6).
[85] *Ibid.* subs.(3)(h).
[86] *Ibid.* subs.(7). *Cf.* subs.(4).
[87] *Ibid.* subs.(3)(i).
[88] *Ibid.* subs.(8).
[89] *Ibid.* subs.(3)(j).
[90] *Ibid.* subs.(3)(k).

Finally, the Secretary of State may confer further powers on inspectors by regulation, for the purpose of section 17(1).[91]

The power of examination and investigation The third of the powers examined above is particularly significant in terms of the potential width of its application. It can be seen that this wide power is referable to the fourth, fifth, ninth and tenth powers conferred on inspectors by section 17(3).

Legal professional privilege

In so far as the foregoing provisions require the production of documentation, the section cannot be used to compel the production of any document that any individual would be entitled to withhold on grounds of legal professional privilege in response to an order for discovery made by the High Court.[92] Ideally, an attendance note should be prepared in relation to all transactions—meetings in particular—affecting lawyers' clients and detailing meetings, and a variety of other transactions. Some such transactions and the documentation generated may attract legal professional privilege, although that privilege would not extend to transactions between other professionals and their clients. To attract legal professional privilege for present purposes, the broad intention of the relevant communication must be the obtaining of legal advice by the client,[93] as opposed to communications between the parties to litigation or their legal advisers.[94] A document carrying the "without prejudice" label may prevent something being given in evidence, but not necessarily on the ground of legal professional privilege.[95]

Criminal enforcement of inspection powers

Section 23 of the Act identifies three situations that could attract criminal liability for present purposes. First, the defendant may, without reasonable excuse, have failed to comply with any requirement imposed under section 17.[96] Secondly, it may be alleged (in relation to any of the powers of inspection detailed by section 17(3)) that the defendant prevented any other person from appearing before or from answering any questions to which an inspector required an answer.[97] Thirdly, the defendant may have intentionally obstructed an inspector in the exercise or performance of his powers or duties.[98]

[91] *Ibid.* subs.(3)(1).
[92] *Ibid.* subs.(10).
[93] *Balabel v. Air India* [1988] 1 Ch. 317, C.A.
[94] *Parry v. News Group Newspapers Ltd, The Times*, November 22, 1990.
[95] *Ibid. per* Dillon L.J.
[96] s.23(1)(d).
[97] *Ibid.* subs.(1)(e).
[98] *Ibid.* subs.(1)(f).

Imminent danger of serious harm

Separate provision is made by section 18 for discovery (on any premises he has power to enter) by an inspector of any article or substance which he has reasonable cause to believe is a cause of imminent danger of serious harm, according to the circumstances in which it is found. On making any such discovery, the inspector is empowered to seize the article or substance and cause it to be rendered harmless, whether by destruction or otherwise.[99] However, in the case of any article forming a part of a batch of similar articles or any substance so discovered, before rendering the item harmless the inspector is obliged, if it is practicable so to do, to take a sample and give a suitably marked portion to a responsible person on the premises in question.[1] As soon as may be after an article or substance has been seized and rendered harmless, the inspector is required to prepare and sign a written report detailing the circumstances in which the article or substance was dealt with. A signed copy of the report must then be given to a responsible person at the subject premises and (unless that person is the owner of the article or substance) also serve a copy on the owner of those premises. If, after reasonable injury, the name and address of the owner cannot be ascertained, a copy of the report may be served on the owner by delivery to the "responsible person" previously referred to.[2] Any intentional obstruction of the inspector in the exercise or performance of his powers or duties is a criminal offence.[3]

Prohibition notices

The provisions on prohibition notices are widely defined[4] and permit enforcement action by HMIP, even if there is no suggestion of any infraction of a particular authorisation. If HMIP is of the opinion that continuation or continuation in a particular manner of a prescribed process under an authorisation involves an imminent risk of pollution of the environment, a prohibition notice must be served on the person carrying out the process.[5] Service of the prohibition notice can take place even if there is no contravention of any condition of authorisation, and the notice may relate to matters affecting any part of the process, whether or not that part of the process is subject to conditions.[6] The prohibition notice must mandatorily identify:

(a) the opinion formed by HMIP;
(b) the risks involved; and
(c) the steps to be taken to remove the risk and the period permitted for that purpose.

[99] s.18(1).
[1] *Ibid.* subs.(2).
[2] *Ibid.* subs.(3).
[3] s.23(1)(f). *Cf.* subs.(1)(h) and (k).
[4] s.14.
[5] *Ibid.* subs.(1).
[6] *Ibid.* subs.(2).

The notice also must direct that the authorisation shall, until the notice is withdrawn, wholly or to the extent specified in the notice, cease to have effect to authorise the carrying on of the process.[7] The Secretary of State is empowered to give directions to HMIP determining whether HMIP should perform its functions in relation to any aspect of the foregoing requirements relating to prohibition notices, and specifying any matters to be included in a notice that HMIP is directed to serve.[8] More generally, HMIP is able to notify a person served with a prohibition notice that the notice is withdrawn because there is satisfaction that steps required by the notice have been taken.[9]

Appeals, criminal enforcement and information access

Any person on whom a prohibition notice is served may appeal against that notice to the Secretary of State.[10] In pursuing that appeal, notice of the appeal must be given before the expiry date of the subject notice.[11] Criminal enforcement in support of the prohibition notice centres on the offence of failing to comply with or contravening any requirement or prohibition imposed by a prohibition notice.[12] As to information access, the public register to be maintained by HMIP must contain all particulars of any prohibition notice issued, as well as all particulars of any notice withdrawing a prohibition notice.[13]

Enforcement notices

Where HMIP is of the opinion that a person carrying on an authorised process is contravening any condition of the authorisation, or is likely to contravene any such condition, an enforcement notice may be served on that person.[14] That notice must state HMIP's opinion, the matters constituting the contravention or the matters making it likely that contravention will arise, and the period within which the requisite steps to deal with the situation should be taken.[15] As with prohibition notices, the Secretary of State may direct HMIP as to whether the present powers should be exercised and as to the steps that are required to be taken.[16] The foregoing items that are required to be contained in an enforcement notice are (as with a prohibition notice) mandatory requirements. Any omission of such requirements from a notice will render that notice a nullity and thus legally unenforceable *ab initio*.[17] However, the court would reject any application for a declaration of nullity here where it is obvious that an appeal under section

[7] *Ibid.* subs.(3).
[8] *Ibid.* subs.(4).
[9] *Ibid.* subs.(5).
[10] s.15(2).
[11] Environmental Protection (Applications, Appeals and Registers) Regulations 1991, reg.10(1)(d).
[12] s.23(1)(c).
[13] S.I. 1991 No. 507, reg.15(e)(f).
[14] s.13(1).
[15] *Ibid.* subs.(2).
[16] *Ibid.* subs.(3).
[17] *Miller-Mead v. Minister of Housing and Local Government* [1963] 1 All E.R. 459, *per* Upjohn L.J.

15(2) is the clear requirement.[18] An enforcement notice cannot be a nullity merely because the facts allegedly support the notice's allegation of an actual or likely contravention of a condition attached to the subject authorisation.[19]

Appeals, criminal enforcement and information access

Any person on whom an enforcement notice is served may appeal against the notice to the Secretary of State.[20] In pursuing that appeal, notice of the appeal must be given before the expiry of a period of two months beginning with the date of the subject notice.[21] The Secretary of State, in determining such an appeal, may either quash or affirm the subject enforcement notice. However, if the notice is affirmed, it may be affirmed either in its original form or with such modifications as the Secretary of State thinks fit[22] but these powers available on appeal will only permit immaterial variations. As a consequence, any purported notice that is a nullity cannot be so modified. Criminal enforcement in support of the enforcement notice centres on the offence of failing to comply with or contravening any requirements or prohibitions imposed by an enforcement notice.[23] As to information access, the public register to be maintained by HMIP must contain all particulars of any enforcement notice issued.[24]

Offences

A variety of offences is contained in section 23. In terms of their practical significance, the offences can most conveniently be categorised in three parts:

(a) the offence of contravening an authorisation under section 6[25];
(b) the offence of failing to comply with or contravening any requirement or prohibition imposed by an enforcement or a prohibition notice[26]; and
(c) other offences.[27]

Contravention of an authorisation

The essence of this offence is that the defendant has carried on a prescribed process without an authorisation from HMIP and by reference to the particular conditions. The rather bland wording of the offence tends to suggest that it is an

[18] *Square Meals Frozen Foods Ltd v. Dunstable Borough Council* [1974] 1 All E.R. 441, *per* Lord Denning M.R. at 446.
[19] *Jeary v. Chailey RDC* (1973) 26 P. & C.R. 280.
[20] s.15(2).
[21] See n.12, *supra*.
[22] s.15(7).
[23] See n.13, supra.
[24] reg.15(e).
[25] s.23(1)(a).
[26] *Ibid.* subs.(1)(c).
[27] *Ibid.* subs.(1)(b), (d)–(1).

offence of strict liability. The presence of words "knowingly" or "knowingly caused", for example, would have indicated an offence other than one of strict liability in which the prosecution would have been obliged to prove the presence of *mens rea* on the part of the defendant. In one set of circumstances, it appears that the onus of proof passes to the defendant. These circumstances are set out in section 25 and stipulate that, in any proceedings for the present offence consisting of a failure to comply with the general condition implied into every authorisation by section 7(4), it is up to the defendant to prove that there was no better available technique not entailing excessive cost than was in fact used to satisfy the condition. Because the reversal of the onus of proof is so limited, it clearly does not extend to any allegations relating to the specific conditions of authorisations attracting BATNEEC. A further aid to enforcement is found in section 25,[28] which also stipulates that, in so far as an entry is required to be made by virtue of section 7 in any record as to the observance of any condition and that entry has not been made, that fact is admissible as evidence that that condition has not been observed.

If the defendant is convicted of the present offence in respect of any matters which the court considers to be within his powers to remedy, the court may, in addition to or instead of imposing any punishment order, order him (within a time to be stipulated by the court) to take the necessary remedial steps.[29] Facilities are also available to extend or further extend the time available for remedial measures on an application to the court prior to expiration of the extended or further extended period.[30] In so far as matters continue during the period set for remedial measures, no offence is committed.[31] The foregoing reference to "necessary remedial steps", although not contained in the Act, probably refer to a limit on the court's jurisdiction. That limit probably restricts those steps to action referable to the specific non-compliance with the particular condition or conditions in issue.

If the defendant is convicted of the present offence and actual harm is thereby caused which it is possible to remedy, the chief inspector is empowered to arrange reasonable remedial measures in respect of that harm and to recover the cost from the convicted defendant.[32] However, these "default" powers can only be exercised with the written consent of the Secretary of State and any other person whose land may be affected by the remedial measures.[33]

Conviction for the present offence means that the defendant is liable, on summary conviction, to a fine not exceeding £20,000 and, on indictment, to a fine or to imprisonment for a term not exceeding two years, or to both.[34]

[28] subs.(2).
[29] s.26(1). Failure to comply is an offence: s.23(1)(I). As to the penalty applicable, see s.23(2).
[30] *Ibid.* subs.(2).
[31] *Ibid.* subs.(3).
[32] s.27(1).
[33] *Ibid.* subs.(2).
[34] s.23(2).

Breach of prohibition and enforcement notice requirements

This offence[35] divides into two parts, comprising:

(a) a failure to comply with any requirements or prohibition imposed by an enforcement or prohibition notice; or
(b) a contravention of any such requirement or prohibition.

Criminal enforcement in the present context may not be without difficulty when it is borne in mind that both enforcement and prohibition notices may be used even if there is no actual breach or contravention of an authorisation or condition attached to an authorisation. Notice, for example, that a prohibition may be served even though there is no contravention of any condition and that the notice may relate to matters affecting any part of the process, whether or not that part of the process is subject to conditions.[36] Notice also that an enforcement notice may be served if HMIP is of the opinion that a person carrying on an authorised process is likely to contravene a condition of the authorisation. Again, in the case of the prohibition notice, it seems that enforcement action is available to HMIP if it is considered that continuation or continuation in a particular manner of a prescribed process under an authorisation involves an imminent risk of pollution of the environment. No doubt considerable attention will be paid to the relationship between the subject requirements or prohibitions and the perceived risks, for example, in relation to those activities whether or not subject to conditions and whatever their location in relation to the process overall. The possibilities for difficulty and controversy in this context may well focus criticism on HMIP based on what may seem to be undue reliance on enforcement techniques for matters that should properly be the subject of authorisation and conditions under sections 6 and 7 or, eventually, variation. The system of enforcement here may have a valuable check on any undue extension of this area of enforcement through the presence of statutory powers of direction available to the Secretary of State.[37]

Where HMIP is of the opinion that criminal proceedings here would afford an "ineffectual" remedy, proceedings may be taken in the High Court for the purpose of securing compliance with the notice.[38] There may be a variety of circumstances justifying recourse to the High Court, usually by way of an application for an injunction, for example, there may be a very imminent risk of pollution despite service of a prohibition notice or the scale of the penalties available in respect of the section 23(1)(c) offence may be regarded as ineffective as a matter of deterrence. Those penalties are the same as the penalties applicable

[35] subs.(1)(c).
[36] See n.37, *infra*.
[37] s.13(3) and 14(4): See nn.9 and 17, *supra*.
[38] s.24. *Cf. Stoke on Trent City Council v. B & O (Retail) Ltd* [1984] A.C. 754.

to the section 23(1)(a) offence.[39] In the same way, the power of the court to order the cause of an offence to be remedied[40] and of the chief inspector to remedy harm[41] apply equally to the present offence.

Other offences

The remaining section 23 offences are set out individually, below.[42] In each case, the appropriate penalty is categorised at the end of the commentary on these remaining offences.

The first group of offences relates to:

(a) failure to give the notice as required by section 9(2) (notification to HMIP of a transfer of authorisation)[43];
(b) failure, without reasonable excuse, to comply with any requirement imposed by a notice under section 19(2) (power of the Secretary of State and the chief inspector to require any person to furnish information reasonably considered to be necessary for the discharge of functions)[44];
(c) the making of a statement which the defendant knows to be false or misleading in a material particular, or the reckless making of a statement which is false or misleading in a material particular, where the statement is made in purported compliance with a requirement to furnish any information by virtue of Part I of the Act, or for the purpose of obtaining the grant of an authorisation to himself or any other person, or the variation of an authorisation[45];
(d) the making, intentionally, of a false entry in any record required to be kept under section 7 by virtue of a relevant condition[46]; and
(e) the forgery or use by the defendant, with intent to deceive, of a document issued or authorised to be issued by virtue of a condition, or required for any such purpose, or to make or have in his possession a document so closely resembling any such document as to be likely to deceive.[47]

In each of these cases, the offence attracts, on summary condition, a fine not exceeding the statutory maximum and, on indictment, a fine or imprisonment for a term not exceeding two years, or both.[48]

The second group of offences relates to:

[39] See n.35, *supra*.
[40] See nn.30 to 32, *supra*.
[41] See nn.33 and 34, *supra*.
[42] The exception is the offence of failing to comply with an order of the court under s.26. See n.30, *supra*. As to prosecution, see s.23(5).
[43] s.23(1)(b).
[44] subs.(1)(g).
[45] subs.(1)(h).
[46] subs.(1)(i).
[47] subs.(1)(j).
[48] subs.(3).

(a) failure, without reasonable excuse, to comply with any requirement under section 17 relating to inspectors' powers[49];
(b) prevent any other person from appearing before or from answering any question to which an inspector may require an answer by virtue of section 17(3)[50];
(c) obstructing intentionally an inspector in the exercise or performance of his powers or duties[51]; and
(d) pretending, falsely, to be an inspector.[52] The penalty for these offences in aid of the inspection process attracts a fine not exceeding the statutory maximum on summary conviction.[53]

Access to Information

The power to obtain information

In order to enable the Secretary of State and the chief inspector to undertake their respective functions under Part I of the Act, section 19[54] empowers them to require any person to provide information which HMIP reasonably considers that it needs for this purpose. For similar purposes, the Secretary of State may also by notice require HMIP to furnish similar information, including information enabling the Secretary of State to discharge any E.C. or other international legal obligation.[55]

Public registers

Sections 20 to 22 of the Act contain facilities for the establishment of public registers of information relevant to integrated pollution and, in some cases, the exclusion of selected information from those registers. IPC information in respect of relevant processes is held at the respective HMIP regional headquarters. An index to the register as a whole is maintained at HMIP headquarters in London. In turn, local authorities comprising district, London and metropolitan borough councils hold information about IPC process in their respective areas.

E.C. Directive 90/313 on freedom of access to information on the environment contains an obligation compelling public authorities to provide access to information relating to the environment for the benefit of any natural or legal person, no matter what his standing. It may be doubtful whether present provisions, through the above sections of the Act, really represent compliance with the requirements of the Directive without reference also to the Environmental Information Regulations 1992.

[49] subs.(1)(d). See n.97, *supra*.
[50] subs.(1)(e). See n.94, *supra*.
[51] subs.(1)(f). See n.99, *supra*.
[52] subs.(1)(k).
[53] subs.(4).
[54] subs.(2).
[55] *Ibid.* subss.(1), (3). As to the criminal enforcement of the s.19 requirements, see nn.45–47, *supra*.

Section 20 of the Act prescribes a duty through which HMIP will be obliged to maintain a register containing certain categories of information described in fairly broad terms by the section[56] but set out in rather more detail under the Environmental Protection (Applications, Appeals and Registers) Regulations.[57]

Contents of the register

Any register maintained under the Act is required to contain the following information:

(a) all particulars of any application for an authorisation;
(b) all particulars of any notice to an applicant demanding further information submitted in response;
(c) all particulars of any representations made by any person required to be consulted by virtue of Schedule 1[58];
(d) all particulars of any authorisation granted;
(e) all particulars of any variation notice, enforcement notice or prohibition notice issued;
(f) all particulars of any notice issued withdrawing a prohibition notice;
(g) all particulars of any notification given to the holder of an authorisation in connection with substantial changes and variation;
(h) all particulars of any application for the variation of the conditions of an authorisation made by the holder of that authorisation;
(i) all particulars of any revocation of an authorisation effected by HMIP;
(j) all particulars of any notice of appeal against a decision of HMIP, the documents relating to the appeal, any written notification of the Secretary of State's determination of the appeal and any report accompanying such a written notification;
(k) details of any conviction of any person for an offence under section 23(1) which relates to the carrying on of a prescribed process under an authorisation granted by HMIP, including the name of the offender, the date of conviction, the penalty imposed and the name of the court;
(l) all particulars of any monitoring information relating to the carrying on of a prescribed process under an authorisation granted by HMIP, obtained by HMIP as a result of its own monitoring or furnished to it by virtue of a condition or as a result of the use of the powers in section 19(2)[59];
(m) (in a case where monitoring information is omitted from the register as commercially confidential information) a statement by HMIP, based on the monitoring information from time to time obtained by or furnished to them, indicating whether or not there has been compliance with any relevant condition of the authorisation;

[56] subs.(1).
[57] reg.15.
[58] Paras. 2, 6 and 7. *Cf.* nn.88 and 89, *supra*.
[59] See n.53, *supra*.

(n) all particulars of any report published by HMIP relating to an assessment of the environmental consequences of the carrying on of a prescribed process in the locality of premises where the prescribed process is carried on under an authorisation;
(o) all particulars of any direction[60] given to HMIP by the Secretary of State under Part I.

The Environmental Protection (Applications, Appeals and Registers) Regulations stipulate that nothing relating to the content of the public register requires HMIP to keep in such a register monitoring information which is four years or more old or information which has been superseded by later information four years after that later information was entered in the register.[61] However, apart from the content, the Act declares[62] that the register may be kept in any form, including (presumably) computerised form. Whatever the form of the register, it is the duty of HMIP[63] to secure that registers are available, at all reasonable times, for inspection by the public free of charge and to afford facilities for obtaining copies of entries on payment of a reasonable charge. Furthermore, the chief inspector is obliged to provide the National Rivers Authority with relevant particulars from HMIP registers to enable the NRA to maintain its duties in connection with public registers under the Water Resources Act 1991.[64]

The exclusion of information

The possibility of an exclusion of information about IPC from the public registers arises either because the subject information relates to matters of national security or because the information is commercially confidential. Apart from the fact that the Secretary of State may give directions for the purpose of requiring an exclusion from registers of information because it falls outside the statutory categories referred to above, he may also use directions for the purpose of excluding information by virtue of its categorisation as information which is commercially confidential or relevant to matters of national security.[65]

Exclusion on the ground of national security The Act requires that no information shall be included in a register if and so long as, in the opinion of the Secretary of State, inclusion would be "... contrary to the interests of national security".[66] For the purpose of securing exclusion or at least its consideration, the Secretary of State may direct HMIP that information or certain categories of information should be excluded or that specified descriptions of information should be referred to him for decision.[67] Until any such decision is made on the

[60] The exception is a direction from the Secretary of State under s.21(2).
[61] reg.17.
[62] s.20(8).
[63] *Ibid.* subs.(7).
[64] *Ibid.* subs.(9).
[65] *Ibid.* subs.(6).
[66] s.21(1).
[67] *Ibid.* subs.(2).

status of the particular information, it should be excluded.[68] It appears that any determination by the Secretary of State for present purposes is conclusive. The Environmental Protection (Applications, Appeals and Registers) Regulations contain measures cutting down the consultation and advertising requirements normally applicable to the operation of Part I of the Act.[69] In relation to consultation requirements, sewerage undertakers, the nature conservancy bodies and harbour authorities, where appropriate, are excluded from consultation on any occasion when the Secretary of State gives directions as described above or when he receives a notice from an individual suggesting that information may be covered by the present provisions requiring exclusion from the register.[70] In this latter situation, the individual is obliged to advise HMIP of his notification to the Secretary of State and, thereafter, no information may be included in the register until the Secretary of State has made a decision on the matter.[71] In the same way that consultation requirements are cut down for the two purposes in section 21,[72] so too are the normal advertising requirements, so that there can be no advertisement of the information which is to be excluded from the register.[73] In so far as HMIP excludes information from the register as a result of any directions from the Secretary of State, this fact must also be advised to him.[74]

Exclusion on the ground of commercial confidentiality This second ground of possible exclusion rests on an interpretation of the term "commercial confidentiality" by HMIP, or (on appeal) the Secretary of State. The Department of the Environment's "Practical Guide to IPC"[75] indicates that the Guide's principles should apply in considering any claim based on commercial confidentiality:

> "The guiding principle is that information should be freely available to the public ... The availability of this information will aid confidence in the system and facilitate public participation ... it will enable the public to ascertain that adequate pollution control measures are in force. It will also expose any failure to comply with the terms of an authorisation and bring into the open HMIP's action ... There will, however, be circumstances where the disclosure of information would prejudice to an unreasonable degree a person's commercial interests ... Any operator who seeks to have information kept from the public register for reasons of commercial confidentiality should demonstrate that disclosure ... would negate or significantly diminish a commercial advantage. This might, for instance,

[68] *Ibid.*
[69] reg.7(1), (2). As to other procedural requirements, see reg.7(5), (6).
[70] As to the remaining (statutory) agencies that are still open to consultation, see reg.4(a)–(e).
[71] s.21(4).
[72] subss.(2) and (4).
[73] S.I. 1991 No. 507, reg.7(4).
[74] s.21(3).
[75] See *Integrated Pollution Control, op. cit.* pp.31 and 32.

relate to preserving the secret of a new process technology, or of a particular raw material or catalyst, or some other specific feature which if made public might seriously affect a legitimate commercial advantage. Such cases are most likely to arise in relation to the information contained in applications for authorisation or for variations which involve a substantial change, where HMIP will need detailed information about the process. The onus is on the applicant to provide a clear justification for each item he wishes to be kept from the register. It will not be sufficient to say, for example, that the raw material to be used in the process is a trade secret and that consequently no details of the process must be made publicly available. The amount of information excluded from the register should be kept to the minimum necessary to safeguard the applicant's commercial advantage. It will not normally be appropriate to withhold information from the register in response to a general claim that disclosure might damage the reputation of the operator and hence his commercial competitiveness. HMIP will also take into account whether the information at issue could be obtained or inferred from other publicly accessible sources. Where information is withheld from the register, this should be limited to the minimum necessary to safeguard commercial confidentiality."

This extract from the Guide has to be set against the Act's reference to that information which is commercially confidential from the point of view of the individual in question. It is so commercially confidential "... if its being contained in the register would prejudice to an unreasonable degree the commercial interests of that individual or person".[76] The Act refers to information relating to the affairs of any individual or business and the fact that no such information should be included in the register without the consent of the individual carrying on the business if and so long as the information is commercially confidential, and is not required to be entered on the register in the public interest[77] unless HMIP or (on appeal) the Secretary of State has decided that the information is not commercially confidential.[78] HMIP may have obtained particular information for present purposes in two ways, either by virtue of an application for an authorisation or a similar transaction,[79] or in other circumstances.[80]

If the information comes to HMIP in the first of these circumstances and the applicant seeks exclusion from the register on the ground of commercial confidentiality, HMIP must arrive at a decision on the matter.[81] Any decision must be made within 14 days of the application: any failure here is a deemed decision that the information is confidential. If there is a decision that the

[76] s.22(11).
[77] By virtue of s.22(7), the Secretary of State may require, by direction, inclusion of information which is commercially confidential, in the public interest.
[78] s.22(1).
[79] Listed in s.22(2).
[80] s.22(4).
[81] *Ibid.*

information is not commercially confidential, entry in the register cannot occur until 21 days from notification of the decision to the applicant. There is an appeal to the Secretary of State from this decision: if an appeal is pursued, no information shall be entered on the register until a final determination or withdrawal of the appeal.[82]

Where the information comes to HMIP in any other way, so that HMIP considers that it might be commercially confidential, it is obliged to notify the person to whom or whose business it relates, indicating that the information is required to be included in the register. That individual must be given a reasonable opportunity to object and make representations. Having taken those representations into account, HMIP is obliged to make a decision on the information. The foregoing procedures about the timing of any entry and the facilities for an appeal also apply in these circumstances.[83] Similarly these procedures, along with the appeal facility, apply in so far as information excluded from the register is deemed to lose its commercial confidentiality after a period of four years from a decision to exclude it and the individual in question applies to continue the exclusion.

If an application is made to HMIP to exclude information, or if an objection is made to the inclusion of information in other circumstances, the same restrictions relating to consultation and advertising as apply to the operation of section 21 apply in relation to the present provisions.[84]

The Charging Scheme

The Act seeks to recognise the "polluter pays principle" through a system of fees and charges for authorisations by HMIP. The system is based on cost recovery charging whose advantages were rehearsed in a Consultation Paper, "Cost Recovery Charging for Integrated Pollution Control".[85] Apart from recognition of the "polluter pays principle", cost recovery charging enables the cost of the regulatory function to be borne directly by those undertaking the subject process, rather than the taxpayer, and makes industry aware of the costs associated with polluting discharges and emissions. On the other hand, there is no "incentive" for industry to reduce charges which may, in turn, run counter to government policy to reduce the burdens on industry which have little control over HMIP's costs. Furthermore, such charging requirements may tend to impair HMIP's valuable advisory role to industry. Finally, industry may feel aggrieved by reference to the fact that some HMIP work serves wider governmental or public objectives.[86]

The Act requires the Secretary of State, in framing a scheme, so far as practicable, to "... secure that the fees and charges payable ... are sufficient, taking one financial year with another, to cover the relevant expenditure

[82] s.22(5). *Cf.* s.15 (appeals).
[83] *Ibid.*
[84] See nn.70–74, *supra.*
[85] Department of the Environment/Welsh Office (1989).
[86] *Ibid.* p.5.

attributable to authorisations".[87] The "relevant expenditure attributable to authorisations" is defined as the expenditure incurred by HMIP in exercising their functions, together with the expenditure incurred by the National Rivers Authority in exercising its functions in relation to any authorisation which may involve the release of any substance to water.[88] Such situations are estimated to account for about one in six authorisations.[89] Payment of the fee in respect of any application for an authorisation or in respect of a variation is a mandatory requirement: non-payment permits HMIP to refuse to consider the application.[90]

The initial charging scheme made by the Secretary of State was the HMIP Integrated Pollution Control Fees and Charges Scheme 1991.[91] There are three categories of charge:

(a) an appliance fee;
(b) a subsistence charge payable annually for the holding of each IPC authorisation, to cover the ongoing costs of inspection, monitoring and enforcement; and
(c) a substantial variation fee, to cover the costs of considering an application for subsequent substantial variation of an authorisation.

There is an important ratio between (on the one hand) fees and charges and (on the other) the number of defined "components" comprised within the process.[92] On the other hand, some major installations may involve planning, development and commissioning stretching over a number of years. In these circumstances, and by prior arrangement with HMIP, an applicant may use a staged application procedure by which the application and supporting information will be submitted in batches at agreed stages. Such an arrangement will attract a charge based on HMIP's actual time and costs, rather than any standard fee. Finally, HMIP is able to revoke an authorisation if it appears that the holder has failed to pay the annual subsistence charge.[93]

IPC and other Regulatory Requirements

The possibility of an overlap between the authorisation of process under Part I of the Environmental Protection Act and other closely connected areas of regulatory control is recognised to a certain extent by the legislation. The main focus of that recognition is section 28 of the Environmental Protection Act, although it has been seen elsewhere in the present chapter that a condition cannot be imposed solely for the purpose of securing the health of persons at work.[94]

[87] s.8(6).
[88] s.8(7).
[89] Consultation Paper, *op. cit.* p.40.
[90] s.6(2) and 11(9).
[91] Consultation Paper, *op. cit.* pp.39–41.
[92] *Ibid.* App. 1.
[93] s.8(8).
[94] See n.95, *supra.*

In so far as HMIP is concerned, for the purpose of an authorisation, with a final disposal by deposit in or on land of controlled waste, no condition can be attached for this purpose or, indeed, in relation to any such disposal.[95] Nevertheless, this fact must be advised to the relevant waste regulation authority[96] but it is still open to the Secretary of State to remove control if satisfied that adequate control is available beyond Part II of the Act.[97] On those occasions when there is direct competition between Part I requirements and controls over the deposit and accumulation of radioactive waste by virtue of the Radioactive Substances Act, the latter regulatory regime will apply.[98]

In the case of any competition between IPC authorisation and the controls over discharges to controlled waters by virtue of the Water Resources Act 1991, IPC control will predominate. Nevertheless, no authorisation can be granted by HMIP as long as the National Rivers Authority certify that a discharge will result in or contribute to a failure to achieve a current water quality objective.[99] In so far as the National Rivers Authority considers it appropriate that particular conditions should appear in an authorisation. HMIP will be obliged to include those conditions in that authorisation.[1] HMIP must also use the power of variation if the National Rivers Authority, by notice in writing, requires that particular conditions of an authorisation are varied.[2] Closely related for these purposes are the statutory requirements in relation to the discharge of trade effluent to sewer: such a discharge is equated with a discharge to water, and thus subject to IPC control under Part I of the Act. Section 79 governs the relationship between the control of statutory nuisances and IPC control. There are some categories at statutory nuisance where a local authority may not pursue summary proceedings without the consent of the Secretary of State if proceedings might be pursued under Part I IPC controls. The difficulties here focus on whether IPC proceedings "might" be undertaken: a considerable matter of speculation in practice. However, the control exerted by the Secretary of State relates only to limits on summary proceedings for a statutory nuisance, not ruling out other local authority action short of such proceedings. In one area, planning control under the Town and Country Planning Act 1990, there is no formal statutory link with IPC control. However, in areas like atmospheric pollution control, it is often recognised that a lack of flexibility in relation to planning conditions provides a clear advantage in seeking regulation through other control. This is certainly the case with IPC where, among other things, variation of conditions is readily and flexibly available for the purpose of allowing regulatory requirements to follow changes in technology, for example.

[95] s.28(1).
[96] *Ibid.*
[97] s.33(4)(c).
[98] s.28(2).
[99] *Ibid.* subs.(3).
[1] *Ibid. Cf.* the memorandum of co-operation between HMIP and the NRA (and HSE): "Practical Guide", pp.45–55.
[2] Environmental Protection Act, s.28.

Chapter 8

NOISE POLLUTION

Noise as a Pollutant

The Royal Commission on Environmental Pollution, in its Tenth Report,[1] recognised that, because noise has virtually no lasting effects on the physical environment or on wildlife, it stands apart from most other environmental problems. It was also recognised that a study of noise presents problems of nature and scale unlike those of most pollutants, emphasised by the considerable problems in any objective measurement of noise.

The impact of noise on the human ear is described as a variation in air pressure through vibration, as detected by that ear. The route from source to ear is via waves whose frequency per second is defined in Hertz while amplitude of the pressure wave—manifested as loudness—is defined in decibels: dB. In turn, decibels are manifested in a logarithmic scale, allowing ranges of loudness to be referred to numerically, for easier "translation". Colloquially, the scale was referred to in these terms by Veale J. in *Halsey v. Esso Petroleum Co. Ltd*:

> "The scale of decibels from nought to 120 can be divided into colloquial descriptions of noise by the use of words: faint, moderate, loud, and so on. Between 40 and 60 decibels the noise is moderate, and between 60 and 80 it is loud. Between 80 and 100 it is very loud, and from 100 to 120 it is deafening."[2]

A two-stage process characterises the measurement and evaluation of noise as a pollutant. Beyond the physical measuring process, there is a process of determining impact on the human ear. Accordingly, any modern instrument for noise measurement will be set to mimic the characteristics of human hearing. This setting is referred to as the "A-weighting", so that calibration is by reference to dB(A). In the case of continuous noise, reference must be made to its impact on the human ear, taking account of the variables of loudness and frequency and their variation within a defined time scale. Some of the critical terminology is summarised in the report of the Noise Review Working party,[3] as follows:

[1] Cmnd. 9149 (1984), paras. 2.5 and 6.16.
[2] [1961] 1 W.L.R. 683 at 697.
[3] Department of the Environment, 1990. *Cf.* The Control of Noise (Measurement and Registers) Regulations 1976 (S.I. 1976 No. 37).

(a) LA10: The "A-weighted" noise level exceeded for 10 per cent. of the specified measurement period. It gives an indication of the upper limit of fluctuating noise such as that from road traffic.
(b) LA90,T: The "A-weighted" noise level exceeded for 90 per cent. of the specified measurement period (T). Often used to give an indication of background noise level.
(c) LAeq,T: The sound level of a steady sound having the same energy as a fluctuating sound over a specified measuring period (T). Used to describe many types of noise.

Impact noise demands different treatment, bearing in mind particularly the very limited period during which the human ear would be subject to high intensity impact. More generally, it should be noted that there is a "C-weighting" for loud sounds, a variation of the "A-weighting" mentioned previously.[4]

British Standard BS4142 relates to industrial noise measurement and prescribes the assessment process for determining the likely incidence of complaints from those living close to sources of noise from industry: "Experience suggests that in general an increase in the noise level of 5dB(A) is likely to give rise to some complaints and a 10dB(A) increase is very likely to do so. This is consistent with BS4142 assessments."[5] In the same context, it should be noted that an employer is obliged to make noise assessments.[6] More specifically, the employer is obliged to make such an assessment when there is the likelihood of an employee being exposed to an unacceptable noise level, to identify the employees so exposed, to provide the employee with information about the noise in question, and to review the position when changes are made.[7]

Reference is made later in the present chapter to noise in the context of development control under the Town and Country Planning Act 1990. More generally, Department of the Environment Circular 10/73, "Planning and Noise",[8] in recognising, *inter alia*, the importance of development control in avoiding new noise problems, also made (until superceded by PPG24: "Planning and Noise"[8a]) continual references to limits that may be drawn below 70dB.

Common Law and Statute

Noise pollution is subject to a variety of legal controls. Much of the present chapter will be taken up with statutory control, together with an outline of the

[4] *Ibid.* p.4.
[5] *Ibid.* p.6.
[6] Noise at Work Regulations 1989 (S.I. 1989 No. 1790). *Cf.* E.C. Directive 86/188: [1986] O.J. L137.
[7] *Ibid.* reg.4.
[8] Welsh Office Circular 16/73.
[8a] Department of the Environment, September 1994.

common law position and its relationship with certain points of statutory control. While in the context of statutory control, outline reference is made to noise as a statutory nuisance under Part III of the Environmental Protection Act 1990. The principal treatment of this subject is in Chapter 10, "Statutory Nuisance". The main emphasis of the present chapter is on "neighbourhood" noise, comprising the control of noise on construction sites, the control of noise in streets and noise abatement zones (under Part III of the Control of Pollution Act 1974) and the control of audible intruder alarms under the Noise and Statutory Nuisance Act 1993. Incidental reference is made to grant-aid for noise insulation, development control under the Town and Country Planning Act, requirements under the Building Regulations 1991, Codes of Practice under the Control of Pollution Act, "transportation" noise and noise generated by manufactured goods and equipment. Entertainment noise as governed by the licensing powers in the Local Government (Miscellaneous Provisions) Act 1982 and the Private Places of Entertainment (Licensing) Act 1967 is referred to in Chapter 14, "Miscellaneous Controls".

Significance of the common law

In cases of noise, it is common law nuisance that has primary significance in relation to any attempt to control what must be established as an unreasonable interference with the use and enjoyment of the plaintiff's land. Such control will undoubtedly occur through injunctive relief, although an award of damages may attempt a distribution of the attendant liabilities. Because it is unlikely that physical damage to property is an incidence of a noise nuisance, the location of the plaintiff's land will be a significant variable in determining liability at common law.[9] Other variables which may be of significance relate to matters of community benefit that may accrue from the defendant's activities,[10] as well as the objective reasonableness of the defendant's operation set against criteria for liability in negligence.[11]

The common law and statutory nuisance

A fundamental requisite for enforcement of liability for statutory nuisance under Part III of the Environmental Protection Act is the existence of a common law nuisance.[12] Part III permits a local authority or a person aggrieved by a statutory nuisance to take summary proceedings. In the first case, an abatement notice can be served and enforced through criminal proceedings by the local authority, with an appeal to the magistrates' court against the abatement notice. In the case of proceedings by a person aggrieved by a statutory nuisance, a complaint is available to the magistrates' court that there is, or will be a recurrence of, a noise nuisance.

Beyond this common ground where statutory control under Part III of the Act

[9] *St Helen's Smelting Co. v. Tipping* (1865) 11 H.L. Cas. 642.
[10] *Harrison v. Southwark and Vauxhall Water Co.* [1891] 2 Ch. 409.
[11] *Andreae v. Selfridge and Co. Ltd* [1938] Ch. 1.
[12] *National Coal Board v. Thorne* [1976] 1 W.L.R. 543.

of 1990 relies on the common law, there are few, if any, significant points of overlap. The Act defines in various ways the "person responsible" for a statutory nuisance and against whom various proceedings may be taken.[13] That person may be the person "responsible for the nuisance", the owner of subject premises (where a nuisance arises from any defect of a structural character) or the owner or occupier of the subject premises (where the "person responsible" cannot be found).[14] Clearly, therefore, there may be occasions when proceedings will be taken against someone who is not, in common law parlance, the tortfeasor.[15]

There is no obvious correlation between the defences available in the case of statutory nuisance and common law defences. Part III refers to defences of reasonable excuse and best practicable means. However, in *A. Lambert Flat Management Ltd v. Lomas*,[16] it was held to be no defence to proceedings in statutory nuisance that tenants knew of noisy lifts before taking up their lease.

It has been suggested that, at common law, a private nuisance requires some element of repetition or continuance.[17] Part III, by contrast, admits of the possibility that isolated noise nuisances can be subject to proceedings.

Although the point is not entirely without doubt, Part III may be based on a requirement that a statutory noise nuisance emanate from "premises", at least to the extent that additions to Part III arising from the Noise and Statutory Nuisance Act 1993 and relating to statutory noise nuisances in streets do not apply. Arguably, a statutory nuisance "exists, or is likely to recur" (to quote the words of section 80(1)) on premises, no matter where the actions which cause the nuisance occur.[18] In the face of any such lingering doubts about the scope of statutory nuisance, a broader common law approach has much to commend it. In *Halsey*,[19] for example, although the facts may now be amenable to the new statutory nuisance provisions governing noise in streets introduced by the Noise and Statutory Nuisance Act 1993, the court found that an actionable nuisance arose from the noise of the company's tankers using the road outside the plaintiff's house.

Compliance with any of the statutory controls on noise under Part III of the Control of Pollution Act, in relation to the control of construction site noise, for example, will not necessarily provide a defence in proceedings for common law nuisance. Indeed, the Court of Appeal has stressed that the powers of the court are in no way restricted by the statutory controls. The Court of Appeal has been prepared to confirm an injunction in respect of noisy building work without reference to a notice served by the local authority under section 60 of the Control of Pollution Act.[20]

[13] Environmental Protection Act, ss.80(2) and 82(4).
[14] *Ibid.*
[15] *A. Lambert Flat Management Ltd v. Lomas* [1981] 1 W.L.R. 898, *per* Ackner L.J.
[16] *Ibid.*
[17] *A.-G. v. P.Y.A. Quarries* [1957] 2 Q.B. 169.
[18] In *London Borough of Tower Hamlets v. Manzoni* 148 J.P. 123; [1984] J.P.L. 437. The point was not raised in the court.
[19] See n.2, *supra*.
[20] *Lloyds Bank PLC v. Guardian Assurance PLC*, 1986 (unreported). *Cf. Macleod-Johnstone-Hart v. Aga Khan Foundation*, 1981, C.A. (unreported).

Control of Pollution Act, Part III

Construction site noise

Sections 60 and 61 of the Act of 1974 "... are designed to give more effective control over the transient noise problems posed by construction and other works making it unnecessary to use the ..." powers to deal with statutory noise nuisance under Part III of the Environmental Protection Act[21]:

> "One of the most important features of these sections is the opportunity they give for local authorities and those responsible for construction works to settle any questions about noise before work starts. Although an approach for a formal consent under section 61 cannot be made until the building regulations approval stage (where this applies), this should not preclude earlier informal consultation ... The provisions of sections 60 and 61 apply to a very wide range of construction and other works. Many minor works will not produce significant noise and it would therefore be desirable to concentrate resources on those works which are potentially likely to cause the most noise nuisance. The code of practice for noise control on construction and demolition sites prepared by the British Standards Institution ... gives guidance on the technical areas of predicting, estimating and measuring noise levels ..."[22]

Section 60 powers

A local authority—principally a district council or the council of a London borough—may serve a notice imposing requirements as to the way in which works are to be carried out on a construction site if it appears that works within the section are being or going to be carried out on "any premises".[23] The works covered by the section include the erection, construction, alteration, repair or maintenance of buildings, structures or roads, demolition work and (whether or not comprised in these categories) "any work of engineering construction".[24] "Premises" includes land.[25] A notice may specify any plant or machinery which may or may not be used, hours of working and noise emission levels from the premises, and may provide for any change of circumstances.[26] However, in acting under this section, an authority is obliged to have regard to four matters:

[21] Department of the Environment Circular 2/76 (Welsh Office Circular 3/76), App. 1, para. 8.
[22] *Ibid.* paras. 24, 27 and 28.
[23] Control of Pollution Act, s.60(2). A s.60 notice is limited to works being undertaken at the time when the notice is issued. Accordingly, such a notice will not extend to works on the site which are uncontemplated and for which a fresh notice would be required; *Walter Lilly & Co. Ltd v. Westminster City Council, The Times*, March 1, 1994.
[24] *Ibid.* subs.(1). A "work of engineering construction" is defined by s.73(1).
[25] *Ibid.* s.105(1).
[26] *Ibid.* s.60(3).

(a) the relevant provisions of any code of practice[27] made under section 71;
(b) the need to ensure that best practicable means[28] are employed to minimise noise;
(c) the desirability of any specification referring to alternative plant or machinery; and
(d) the need to protect any persons in the locality from the effects of noise.[29]

The notice must stipulate the time for compliance with its requirements and any contravention (without reasonable excuse) is an offence punishable on summary conviction. The local authority is obliged to serve the notice on the person who appears to be carrying out, or going to carry out, the subject works and on such other persons appearing to be responsible for or to have control over execution of the works "as the local authority thinks fit".[30] Circular 2/76, already referred to, indicates that unless those responsible for the works indicate otherwise, it will normally be appropriate, when serving notice before work starts, to serve the notice on the promoter of the project (or one of his agents) but once work has begun, to serve the notice on the main contractor.[31] Within 21 days of service of the notice, the person served may appeal to the magistrates' court,[32] under the terms of the Control of Noise (Appeals) Regulations 1975,[33] dealt with below.

Section 61 licensing powers

Section 61 powers are used very little. "Contractors have been reluctant to seek prior consent for construction site noise perhaps because the industry believes that local authorities would wish to be too restrictive in what they will allow.[34] Any person wishing to carry out works covered by the previous section 60 may apply for a consent under section 61.[35] Having considered the application, if the local authority would not be minded to act under section 60, then that authority is obliged to give consent under section 61.[36] If building regulation approval is required for the subject works, a section 61 application must be made at the same time as that application, or later.[37] The local authority must have regard to the considerations set out in section 60(4)[38] and may impose conditions on a consent, limit or qualify that consent to take account of any change of circumstances, or even limit the duration of the consent; any person who knowingly carries out

[27] Control of Noise (Code of Practice for Construction and Open Sites) Order 1987 (S.I. 1987 No. 1730).
[28] As defined by s.72 of the Control of Pollution Act.
[29] *Ibid.* s.60(4).
[30] *Ibid.* subs.(5).
[31] para. 31.
[32] Control of Pollution Act, s.60(7).
[33] S.I. 1975 No. 2116.
[34] Noise Review Working Party report (1990), p.3.
[35] Control of Pollution Act 1974, s.61(1).
[36] *Ibid.* subs.(4).
[37] *Ibid.* subs.(2).
[38] See n.29, *supra*.

works or permits works to be carried out in contravention of any conditions commits an offence which is triable summarily.[39] Failure by the local authority to give a consent within a time limit of 28 days or the grant of consent within that period but subject to any condition, limit or qualification gives rise to an appeal to magistrates' court.[40] In any proceedings for an offence under section 60(8) in respect of a failure, without reasonable excuse, to comply with a notice under section 60 it is a defence that subject works were carried out in accordance with a consent under section 61.[41] However, any consent granted under section 61 must contain a statement that that consent does not "of itself" constitute any ground of defence in proceedings (by a person "aggrieved" by a statutory nuisance) under section 82 of the Environmental Protection Act.[42] If a consent under section 61 is in respect of works carried out by someone other than the applicant, it is the duty of that applicant to take "all reasonable steps" to bring the consent to the notice of that other person: failure to comply is a summary offence.[43]

Noise in streets

Section 62 of the Control of Pollution Act prohibits the operation (subject to some exceptions defined by the section) of a loudspeaker in a street between the hours of nine in the evening and eight the following morning. The prohibition extends at any other time in so far as a loudspeaker is deployed in a street for the purpose of advertising any entertainment, trade or business. Contravention is an offence punishable in summary proceedings.[44] The Secretary of State may, by order, amend the foregoing time limits.[45]

The Noise and Statutory Nuisance Act 1993[46] provides an adoptive provision through which local authorities may license the operation of a loudspeaker which otherwise would be in contravention of section 62.[47] The Act also specifies time limits for the adoption of Schedule 2 by a local authority, as well as accompanying publicity measures.[48] Upon adoption of Schedule 2, a local authority is empowered to consent to the operation in its area of a loudspeaker which otherwise would be in contravention of section 62, although a consent "shall not be given" to the operation of a loudspeaker in connection with "any election or for the purposes of advertising any entertainment, trade or business".[49] A consent may be granted "subject to such conditions as the local authority considers appropriate".[50] If the authority determines to grant consent, it "may cause" a

[39] Control of Pollution Act, s.61(5).
[40] *Ibid.* subs.(7).
[41] *Ibid.* subs.(8).
[42] *Ibid.* subs.(9).
[43] *Ibid.* subs.(10).
[44] *Ibid.* s.62(1).
[45] *Ibid.* subss.(1A) and (1B).
[46] s.8 and Sched. 2.
[47] Control of Pollution Act, s.62(3A).
[48] Noise and Statutory Nuisance Act, s.8(2), (3), (4).
[49] *Ibid.* Sched. 2, para. 1.
[50] *Ibid.* Sched. 2, para. 2.

notice giving details of that consent to be published in a local newspaper circulating in the area.[51]

Beyond these adoptive licensing provisions, there are various exemptions listed in section 62, and subsection (2) in particular. Car stereos are comprehended,[52] but only to the extent that they do not give "reasonable cause for annoyance" in their operation. To the extent that a car stereo does give rise to such annoyance, there would not be exemption from the criminal penalties for non-compliance with section 62(1) in relation to "any entertainment". Note also the Road Vehicles (Construction and Use) Regulations 1986,[53] stipulating that no motor vehicle may be used on a road in such manner as to cause any excessive noise which could be avoided by the exercise of reasonable care on the part of the driver.

"Street" is defined by the Environmental Protection Act[54] and means a highway and any other road, footway, square or court that is for the time being open to the public. An open space beneath a building may, in appropriate circumstances, be described as a "square" and where members of the public regularly go there for the purpose of attending a Sunday market, it may be regarded as a "street", being in the nature of a square open to the public.[55] Despite the absence of any reference to a thoroughfare in the Environmental Protection Act definition, that definition is consistent with the common law through the reference to the facility being "open to the public".[56]

Noise abatement zones

Sections 63 to 67 deal with the establishment and operation of noise abatement zones. The essential purpose of zones has been described by the Department of the Environment, as follows[57]:

> "[Zones have] . . . the purpose of preventing deterioration in environmental noise levels and achieving reductions in noise levels wherever practicable . . . Noise abatement zones will be areas designated . . . within which it will be possible to control noise from classified premises by establishing the current noise levels and using these as reference levels for control of noise from the premises in the future . . . The . . . powers are self-contained and can be used as such to deal with specific noise problems. They can also be used as a more general tool of planning to maintain or to improve environmental standards. The control of noise which can be exercised in the zone will be limited to control of noise from individual premises of the classes specified in the Noise

[51] *Ibid.* Sched. 2, para. 6.
[52] Control of Pollution Act, s.62(2)(d).
[53] S.I. 1986 No. 1078, reg.97.
[54] s.79(7).
[55] *Tower Hamlets LBC v. Creitzman* (1985) 83 L.G.R. 72.
[56] *cf.* Highways Act 1980, s.329.
[57] Circular 2/76, App. 2. *Cf.* n.21, *supra.*

> Abatement Order . . . It is not intended that a standard maximum noise level should be set for a zone . . . The form of a zone once designated is not immutable . . . Where planning permission for extensive new industrial development is sought, particularly if areas of mixed residential and industrial properties will result, consideration should be given to the need for a noise abatement zone in that area. The zones could be especially effective when used in conjunction with powers . . . to create general improvement areas . . . and . . . to control local traffic in the interests of amenity."

Zone designation

Section 63 empowers a local authority—principally a district council or London borough council[58]—to designate all or part of its area as a noise abatement zone. Any such order must specify the classes of premises to which it applies:

> "It is intended that only those selected classes of premises for which control is practicable and where control may afford some benefit should be subject to control. To control all premises in an area will not normally be a practicable undertaking . . . Similar noise levels should not be expected from all premises in a class."[59]

For illustrative purposes, the broad classes to be resorted to for present purposes are listed as follows[60]:

(a) industrial premises;
(b) commercial premises;
(c) places of entertainment or assembly;
(d) agricultural premises;
(e) transport installations; and
(f) public utility installations.

Not included here are domestic premises, more suitably dealt with under the Part III statutory nuisance provisions of the Environmental Protection Act. Classes of premises that will be subject to control may be designated, even if there are no buildings of the class designated in the zone at present. This will provide for the control of noise from new developments in the area. In classifying premises, it is important that long-term needs are considered as well as the short-term ones."[61]

The procedures for making an order and bringing it into operation are

[58] Control of Pollution Act 1974, s.73.
[59] Department of the Environment Circular 2/76, App. 2, paras. 2.3 and 2.4.
[60] *Ibid.* para. 2.5.
[61] *Ibid.* para. 2.8.

specified by a Schedule to the Control of Pollution Act. The local authority concerned is obliged to serve a notice on every owner, lessee and occupier of any of the premises in the area and of a class to which the order will relate and to publish a notice in prescribed newspapers before making an order. That notice must indicate the intention to make an order and its general effect, the location at which a copy of the order may be inspected and the limit of time within which "any person who willl be affected by the order" may object in writing to the local authority. Any such objection made but not withdrawn must be considered before an order can be made, unless it is considered that compliance with this requirement is unnecessary by virtue of the nature of the premises when the order comes into force or by virtue of the nature of the interests of the persons who have made objections not withdrawn.[62]

Although section 57 of the Act imposes a duty on a local authority to cause its area to be inspected from time to time to decide how to exercise powers relating to noise abatement, this is not a condition precedent to any exercise of the present powers under section 63.[63] A local authority here is not necessarily expected to duplicate efforts already made by officers, for example, to acquaint themselves with the characteristics of an area which may be subject to an order.

Bearing in mind the apparent purpose of noise abatement zones, such as a means of "rationalising" noise generation from a number of competing sources in a defined area, it seems clear that a local authority must maintain that purpose as an essential priority if its order under section 63 is not to be susceptible to judicial review under R.S.C., Ord. 53. An attempt to use an order as means of controlling noise from one category of (say) industrial premises in a zone might be seen as perversely unreasonable.[64]

Registration of noise levels

Having designated a noise abatement zone, a local authority is obliged to measure the level of noise emanating from premises within the zone in so far as they fall into any class included in the order. The methods of measurement relevant for present purposes are prescribed by the Control of Noise (Measurement and Registers) Regulations 1976.[65] A record of all measurements (including the method of measurement used and the points at which measurement were taken) must be maintained in such form as the local authority considers appropriate.[66] A notice must be served by the local authority on the owner and occupier of the subject premises, indicating the noise measurement recorded in the register. Any such person may appeal to the Secretary of State within 28 days of the date of service. Otherwise, the measurement may not be challenged in any other proceedings under Part III, suggesting that any other challenge to the merits of a

[62] Control of Pollution Act, Sched. 1, paras. 1–3.
[63] *Morganite Special Carbons Ltd v. Secretary of State for the Environment* (1980) 256 E.G. 1105.
[64] *Ibid.* citing *Associated Provincial Picture House Ltd v. Wednesday Corporation* [1948] 1 K.B. 223.
[65] S.I. 1976 No. 37. *Cf.* Circular 2/76, App. 2, para. 3.
[66] *Ibid.* reg.6.

measurement is ruled out, but without prejudice to any challenge to the legality of such a process through judicial review under R.S.C., Ord. 53. The noise level register is to be maintained open to public inspection by each local authority responsible.[67]

Noise in excess of registered levels Only with the consent of a local authority can noise levels exceed those registered in the noise level register. The local authority has a widely defined jurisdiction to determine conditions that should attach if consent is to be given, for example, in relation to certain periods of time when noise levels may be increased. An appeal lies to the Secretary of State in respect of any failure to determine an application within the statutory time limit or in respect of "the local authority's decision on the application". The Department of the Environment has declared[68] that there are two instances where

> ". . . the bias should be towards giving consent for higher noise levels where these are unavoidable:
> (i) when there has been a return to full working capacity since the measurements entered in the noise level register were made . . .
> (ii) where relocation of noisy processes to less noise-sensitive areas will give a net benefit to the public."

The Department also declares[69] that, in considering an application to exceed registered noise levels, the following factors may be taken into account:

> "(i) the purpose for which the noise abatement zone has been designated;
> (ii) the implications, especially the financial implications, for the applicant;
> (iii) the broader consequences of giving or withholding consent . . . for example . . . employment prospects in the area;
> (iv) the period for which consent to exceed the registered noise level is sought . . ."

The emission of noise in excess of registered levels or in excess of levels consented to is an offence triable summarily. If, in convicting a person for any such offence, the magistrates' court is satisfied that the offence is likely to recur, that court may make an order requiring the execution of any works necessary to prevent continuation or recurrence. Any person who, without reasonable excuse because, for example, circumstances are beyond his control, fails to comply with such an order commits an offence, triable summarily. Execution of the order in default may be the responsibility of the local authority but only after the local authority has had an opportunity of being heard before the court. Finally, the consent that may be granted by the local authority is no defence, of itself, to summary proceedings for a statutory nuisance under section 82 of the

[67] Control of Pollution Act, s.64. *Cf.* the Control of Noise (Measurement and Registers) Regulations 1976 (S.I. 1976 No. 37).
[68] Circular 2/76, App. 2, para. 4.5.
[69] *Ibid.*

Environmental Protection Act: the consent itself must contain a statement to this effect.[70]

Noise reduction notices

Where it appears to a local authority in the context of a noise abatement zone that the level of noise emanating from premises is not acceptable, having regard to the designating order, and that a reduction of level is practicable at reasonable cost and would afford a public benefit, that authority may serve a noise reduction notice. The notice (served on "the person responsible") will require a reduction to the level specified in the order and require the person responsible to prevent any subsequent increase without the consent of the local authority, taking any steps specified for the purpose. A minimum limit of six months is allowed within which the requirements of the notice must be complied with. A noise reduction notice may be flexible in its requirements, for example, in requiring different levels of reduction at different times of the day. Whatever its requirements, they must be entered in the noise level register. Contravention of a noise reduction notice without reasonable excuse is an offence triable summarily, although in proceedings relating to noise caused in the course of a trade or business there is a further defence available: that of best practicable means. Within three months of the date of service of a noise reduction notice, the person served may appeal against that notice to the magistrates' court. A noise reduction notice will take effect whether or not consent has been granted under section 65, authorising a level of noise higher than that specified in the notice.[71]

New and modified buildings in noise abatement zones

The power to control noise levels emitted from new and modified buildings in noise abatement zones under section 67 "... is an adjunct to existing planning powers ... where liaison with planning authorities is desirable".[72] The local authority is empowered—either on its own initiative or on an application by the owner or occupier or a person negotiating to acquire an interest in the premises—to determine an acceptable noise level from premises. Those premises may comprise a building going to be constructed and to which a noise abatement order will apply or any premises that will, as a result of any works, become premises to which a noise abatement order will apply. Any noise emission level resulting from a determination will be entered on the noise level register. That determination must be notified by the authority to the party or parties involved and an appeal lies to the Secretary of State within three months of the date of notification. The same appeal facility arises in default of a determination by the local authority. If a building or other premises become subject to a noise abatement order but no level of noise is determined for present purposes, the

[70] Control of Pollution Act, s.65.

[71] *Ibid.* s.66. As to possible uses of noise reduction notices, see Department of the Environment Circular 2/76, App. 2, para. 4.6.2.

[72] *Ibid.* para. 4.7.1.

noise reduction provisions of section 66 will apply. However, these provisions are modified, particularly in so far as it need only appear to the local authority that noise levels emanating from premises subject to a noise abatement order are not acceptable, by reference to the purposes of the order.[73] The Department of the Environment describes the matter thus[74]: "... where a determination is not made before the building comes into use the local authorities will, in these circumstances, have the right to specify noise abatement works going beyond 'best practicable means'."

Noise from plant or machinery

Regulations may be made by the Secretary of State which require the use of silencing devices on plant or machinery and limit noise levels from plant or machinery as used on construction sites and in factories. The power to make regulations may take account of local circumstances in different localities. The Secretary of State is obliged to consult persons appearing to him to represent producers and users of plant and machinery, to ensure that any requirements are not impracticable and do not involve unreasonable expense. Enforcement is by means of summary offences of contravening or causing or permitting others to contravene the regulations.[75]

Supplementary provision

Part III of the Control of Pollution Act makes supplementary provision in respect of the foregoing areas of noise regulation and control, as follows:

(a) supplementary sections of Part III provide for execution of works by a local authority[76];
(b) appeals to the Secretary of State and magistrates' court[77];
(c) codes of practice for minimising noise[78];
(d) best practicable means"[79]; and
(e) penalties for the various Part III offences.[80]

As to rights of entry and inspection, see sections 91 and 92. Power to obtain information and restrictions on its disclosure are contained in sections 93 and 94, respectively.

[73] Control of Pollution Act, s.67.
[74] Department of the Environment Circular 2/76, para. 4.7.1.
[75] Control of Pollution Act, s.68.
[76] *Ibid.* s.69.
[77] *Ibid.* s.70.
[78] *Ibid.* s.71.
[79] *Ibid.* s.72.
[80] *Ibid.* s.74.

Execution of works by a local authority

In certain circumstances, failure to execute works required of a person by virtue of a noise reduction notice[81] or an order of the magistrates requiring works to ensure no continuation or recurrence of noise in excess of the registered level,[82] following conviction for the subject offence, allows the local authority to undertake those works in default. Both in these circumstances and in circumstances where the local authority executes works on the direction of the magistrates' court,[83] that local authority is able to recover from the person in default the expenditure incurred, except so much of the expenditure as that person shows was unnecessary in the circumstances.[84] In proceedings to recover any amount due, the person in default is unable to raise any matter that could have been raised in any appeal against the subject order or notice.

The present facility omits reference to a power to impose a charge on the subject premises. That more extensive facility is to be found in connection with certain powers to be found in the Public Health Act 1936[85] and Part III of the Environmental Protection Act, relating to statutory nuisance.[86]

Appeals to the Secretary of State and magistrates' court

The Secretary of State has made the Control of Noise (Appeals) Regulations 1975.[87] Part II of the regulations relate to appeals to the magistrates' court where the procedure is by way of a complaint for an order. Appeals to the magistrates' court relate to decisions on the control of noise on construction sites,[88] decisions on applications for prior consent for work on construction sites[89] and noise reduction notices.[90] Appeals to the Secretary of State are dealt with in Part III of the regulations and relate to decisions to record particular noise limits in a noise level register,[91] decisions of a local authority in respect of an application to exceed a limit found in the noise level register[92] and decisions of a local authority to register a noise emission limit in respect of a new or modified building in a noise abatement zone.[93]

Part II of the Regulations stipulates the grounds for an appeal, as well as the powers of the court in dealing with that appeal. In so far as a ground of appeal refers to some informality, defect or error in, or in connection with, the subject

[81] *Ibid.* s.66.
[82] *Ibid.* s.65(6).
[83] *Ibid.* s.65(7).
[84] As to the identity of the "person in default", see s.69(3).
[85] s.291.
[86] ss.81A and 81B.
[87] S.I. 1975 No. 2116.
[88] Control of Pollution Act, s.60(7): *cf.* s.85 in connection with further appeals to the Crown Court.
[89] *Ibid.* s.61(7).
[90] *Ibid.* s.66(7).
[91] *Ibid.* s.64(3).
[92] *Ibid.* s.65(4).
[93] *Ibid.* s.67(3).

consent or notice (as the case may be), the court may dismiss the appeal if satisfied that the informality, defect or error was not a material one. In the case of an appeal to the Secretary of State, a notice of that appeal must be furnished stating the grounds of appeal. Within seven days of that notice (or such longer period as may be allowed by the Secretary of State), other prescribed documentation must be submitted by the appellant. Otherwise, Part III of the Regulations stipulates the powers of the Secretary of State in deciding the appeal.

In the case of a section 60 notice relating to the control of noise on a construction site and a noise reduction notice under section 66 subject to appeal, any such notice may be suspended under Part IV of the Regulations until the appeal is abandoned or decided by the court if the noise identified by the notice is caused in the course of the performance of a duty in law imposed on the appellant, or if compliance with that notice would involve "any person" in expenditure on the execution of works prior to the hearing of the appeal. However, no suspension will occur if, in the opinion of the local authority, the noise is injurious to health or is likely to be of limited duration, so that suspension would render the notice of no practical effect, or that expenditure to comply with the notice before an appeal decision would not be disproportionate to the public benefit to be expected in that period from compliance. If the notice is not to be suspended, it should contain a statement that it will have effect, notwithstanding any appeal to a magistrates' court not yet decided. Otherwise, and apart from the foregoing provisions, any notice under Part III of the Act is not suspended by reason of an appeal being brought to a magistrates' court or the Secretary of State.[94]

Codes of practice for minimising noise

The Secretary of State is empowered, by statutory order, to prepare, approve and issue codes of practice for the purpose of providing guidance on appropriate methods of minimising noise. A number of codes of practice have been approved and may be taken into account in proceedings relating to noise nuisance and similar problems.[95] One such code of practice is the Control of Noise (Code of Practice from Audible Intruder Alarms) Order 1981[96]; an area of noise control now subject to a formal statutory framework by virtue of the Noise and Statutory Nuisance Act 1993, dealt with below. Part III of the Control of Pollution Act specifically requires a local authority to have regard to the relevant provisions of any code of practice issued under section 71 in deciding whether to serve a notice under section 60 relating to the control of noise from construction sites.[97]

[94] Control of Noise (Appeals) Regulations 1975, reg.10.
[95] Control of Pollution Act, s.71.
[96] S.I. 1981 No. 1829.
[97] See, in particular, S.I. 1987 No. 1730.

"Best practicable means"

Apart from a requirement to have regard to any code of practice in determining whether or not to serve a notice under section 60, a local authority is also obliged to have regard to other matters, including a need to ensure that "best practicable means" are employed to minimise noise.[98] The use of best practicable means is also a defence to proceedings for failure to comply with a noise reduction notice where it can be established that noise was caused in the course of a trade or business.[99] For present purposes, the word "practicable" means "reasonably practicable" having regard *inter alia* to local conditions and circumstances, to the current state of technical knowledge and to the financial implications. The means to be employed include the design, installation, maintenance and manner and periods of operation of plant and machinery, as well as the design, construction and maintenance of buildings and acoustic structures. The test of best practicable means applies only in so far as it is compatible with any duty imposed by law and with safety and safe working conditions, as well as the exigencies of any emergency or unforeseeable circumstances. Any construction of the phrase "best practicable means" must have regard to any relevant code of practice.[1]

Noise and Statutory Nuisance Act 1993: Audible Intruder Alarms

Adoptive provisions

Section 9 and Schedule 3 to the Act introduce adoptive provisions by which a local authority (comprising a district council in England and Wales and a district or islands council in Scotland) may resolve that the detailed provisions in Schedule 3 relating to audible intruder alarms should apply to its area. An authority may resolve that the provision of Schedule 3 will apply only after consulting the chief officer of police. Following such a resolution, the provisions of Schedule 3 come into force in the area on a specified date, with the exception of paragraph 4, relating to the operation of alarms on or after a *second* "appointed day", the aforementioned date being the *first* "appointed day". Thereafter, on a second appointed day being specified, paragraph 4 will come into force and paragraphs 2 and 3 (governing the operation of alarms before the second appointed day) cease to have effect in the area. Relative time limits in relation to

[98] Control of Pollution Act, s.60(4).
[99] *Ibid.* s.66(9).
[1] *Ibid.* s.72.

the initial resolution of the local authority are defined by section 9.[2] Apart from a requirement to observe certain minimum periods in declaring the first and second appointed days, the local authority is also obliged to give local publicity to the resolution passed[3] and explain the effect of Schedule 3 by reference to each of the appointed days.[4]

Installation of new alarms[5]

A person who installs an audible intruder alarm on or in any premises shall ensure that the alarm complies with requirements, to be prescribed under regulations to be made by the Secretary of State, and that the local authority is notified within 48 hours of the installation. A person who contravenes either of these requirements without reasonable excuse commits an offence punishable with a fine on summary conviction. The penalty is a fine not exceeding level 5 on the standard scale[6] for a failure to comply with prescribed requirements. In any other case, such as a failure to notify the identity and other details of key holders as required by paragraph 5 or the local authority as required by paragraph 1(1)(b), the limit is a fine not exceeding level 2 on the standard scale. Reasonable excuse will operate as a defence where the evidence suggests that the defendant has no control over the circumstances surrounding the alleged offence.[7]

Operation of alarms before, on or after the second appointed day[8]

Criminal enforcement of requirements here is similar to that applicable under paragraph 1 with one exception, in the reference to "level" 4 in paragraph 3(2)(a). Paragraph 2 (unlike paragraph 1) refers to the obligation of a person who is *the occupier of any premises* when (on or after the first appointed day) an audible intruder alarm is installed on or in the premises. Any such occupier shall not permit an alarm to be operated except in compliance with the requirements of *paragraph 5*, set out below. The same obligation applies to a person who, on or after the first appointed day, becomes the occupier of premises where an alarm has been installed, as well as the occupier (under paragraph 4) of any premises where an alarm is operated on or after the second appointed day.

[2] Noise and Statutory Nuisance Act, s.9(3), (4).
[3] *Ibid.* subs.(5).
[4] *Ibid.* subs.(6).
[5] *Ibid.* Sched. 3, para. 1.
[6] Criminal Justice Act 1982, s.37, as amended.
[7] *Wellingborough Borough Council v. Gordon* [1993] Env. L.R. 218; [1991] J.P.L. 874. *Cf. Saddleworth UDC v. Aggregate and Sand* (1970) 114 S.J. 931, indicating that a lack of finance is not reasonable excuse.
[8] Sched. 3, paras. 2, 3 and 4.

Paragraph 5 requirements

The requirements are satisfied:

(a) if an alarm complies with prescribed requirements (explained previously);
(b) if the police have been notified in writing of the names, addresses and telephone numbers of the current key holders; and
(c) if the local authority has been informed of the address of the police station to which the notification previously described has been given.

The facility to prescribe requirements is in contrast to rather more specific requirements, to be found in the London Local Authorities (Miscellaneous Provisions) Act 1991, and section 23 of that Act in particular. This legislation for London includes a specific requirement for alarms to have a 20-minute cut-off device.

Entry to premises[9]

A duly authorised officer of a local authority may enter premises (but not by force) and turn off an alarm where the intruder alarm is operating audibly more than one hour after activation and is such as to give persons living or working in the vicinity of the premises "reasonable cause for annoyance".[10] Any such officer may apply for a warrant to authorise entry to the subect premises (if need be, by force) but a justice of the peace must be satisfied that:

(a) an intruder alarm is operating audibly more than one hour following activiation;
(b) the operation of the alarm is such as to give persons working or living in the vicinity of the premises "reasonable cause for annoyance";
(c) the officer has taken steps to obtain access with the assistance of current key holders whose identity has been advised to the police along with other information as required by paragraph 5; and
(d) the officer has been unable to obtain access to the premises without the use of force.

Prior to an application for a warrant, the local authority officer is obliged to leave a notice at the premises indicating that the audible operation of the alarm is such as to give reasonable cause for annoyance and that an application is to be made for a warrant to authorise entry.[11] Any entry to premises here may be effected only when accompanied by a constable.[12] Arguably, the need to establish a "reasonable cause for annoyance" is a more onerous requirement compared with the wording of the London Local Authorities (Miscellaneous Provisions) Act 1991 where it

[9] Sched. 3, paras. 6–10.
[10] *Ibid.* para. 6.
[11] *Ibid.* para. 7(1), (2).
[12] *Ibid.* para. 7(3).

must be shown to the satisfaction of a justice of the peace that "... the operation of [an] audible intruder alarm is causing annoyance".

The occupation of premises[13]

The Act does not contain a definition of "occupation" but rather an indication of the incidence of occupation where premises are in fact unoccupied or where premises are being erected, constructed, altered, improved, maintained, cleaned or repaired.

Miscellaneous Noise Regulation and Control

Planning control and noise

Development control powers available under the Town and Country Planning Act 1990 represent an important anticipatory method of noise control prior to the act of development. The fact that noise and other environmental factors are contemplated increasingly in development plans means that they play an increasingly significant role in shaping relevant development control decisions.[14] Equally, there is no doubt that noise emission can be a legally relevant and material consideration for development control decision-making purposes,[15] for example, a local planning authority could not exclude the likelihood of noise being emitted from one flat, in a proposed conversion of houses to flats, so as to cause disturbance to the occupier of another flat in its decision-making on an application for planning permission.[16]

The Department of the Environment's Planning Policy Guidance (PPG24)[17] contains various indications of the preferred approaches.[18] In some instances, noise emission will undoutedly be in issue for the purpose of environmental assessment, in so far as such an assessment is required as a mandatory prerequisite for development or is required because, as a matter of discretion, the proposed development will have a significant effect on the environment.[19]

[13] *Ibid.* para. 13.
[14] Town and Country Planning Act 1990, s.54A.
[15] *London Borough of Newham v. Secretary of State for the Environment and East London Housing Association Ltd* [1986] J.P.L. 607.
[16] *Ibid.*
[17] Department of the Environment, September 1994.
[18] *Ibid.* paras. 10–21 and Annexes.
[19] Town and Country Planning (Assessment of Environmental Effects) Regulations 1988 (S.I. 1988 No. 1199). *Cf.* PPG24, para. 22.

Noise insulation grants

The Secretary of State for the Environment is empowered to make regulations—the Noise Insulation Regulations[20]—which impose a duty or confer a power on responsible authorities (essentially highway authorities but subject to possible agency arrangements with other local authorities) to insulate buildings against noise caused by construction or use of public works or to make grants in respect of the cost of such insulation.[21] The Regulations focus on two fundamental provisions, in regulations 3 and 4. In the first of these regulations, where the use of a highway to which the regulation applies causes or is expected to cause noise at a level not less than the specified level,[22] a highway authority is obliged to carry out works or make a grant in respect of the cost of carrying out insulation work in or to an "eligible building". This obligation relates to a highway[23] and a highway for which an additional carriageway has been or is to be constructed which (in either case) was or will be open to public traffic after October 16, 1972. In the second of the regulations, there is a discretion for the highway authority to undertake work or make a grant in respect of an eligible building in similar circumstances to those found in regulation 3 but subject to some differences relating, for example, to "altered highways". The foregoing provisions are supplemented by a further discretionary power applicable in so far as regulations 3 and 4 do not apply but where prescribed highway works will, in the opinion of the highway authority, seriously affect (possibly for a substantial period of time) the enjoyment of an eligible building adjacent to any to any site where those works are being or will be carried out. In these circumstances, the highway authority may also carry out or make a grant in respect of the carrying out of insulation work in or to the building.[24]

The facility for execution of insulation works or payment of grants applies to dwellings and other buildings used for residential purposes: so-called "eligible buildings".

Building control

Building work carried out after June 1, 1992 is governed by the Building Regulations 1991 made under the Building Act 1984.[25] Technical requirements in the present context are to be found in Approved Document E on resistance to the passage of sound. Where there is to be a material change of the use of a whole building so that it will be used as a dwelling where previously it was not so used, the building work must be carried out to ensure compliance with stipulated elements of Part E to Schedule 1 of the Building Regulations.[26] The same

[20] S.I. 1975 No. 1763, as amended by S.I. 1988 No. 2000.
[21] Land Compensation Act 1973, s.20. *Cf.* PPG 24, Annex 6.
[22] L10 (18–hour) of 68dB(A).
[23] As defined by s.329(1) of the Highways Act 1980.
[24] Noise Insulation Regulations, reg.5.
[25] *cf.* Chap. 11, "Building Control".
[26] Building Regulations 1991, reg.6(1).

requirement applies if the building contains a flat where, previously, it did not. However, compliance does not require anything to be done except for the purpose of securing "reasonable" standards of health and safety for persons in or about a subject building (and others who may be affected by buildings, or matters connected with buildings).[27] Part E of Schedule 1 stipulates three sets of requirements relating to air-borne sound in relation to walls, air-borne sound in relation to floors and stairs and impact sound, also in relation to floors and stairs.

The foregoing requirements stress the importance of measures for noise insulation, particularly where flat conversions are concerned. However, while the Building Regulations specifically require prior notification before foundation excavations or drains and sewers subject to the Regulations are covered up,[28] a similar requirement does not apply to works for the installation of noise insulation.

E.C. controls: household appliances and lawnmowers

E.C. Directive 84/538,[28a] as amended, relates to the permissible sound pressure or power level of lawnmowers, while Directive 86/594[28b] relates to the permissible levels of air-borne noise from household appliances. Both Directives are implemented by reference to section 2(2) of the European Communities Act 1972 through regulations referred to below. Directive 86/594 is implemented through the Household Appliances (Noise Emission) Regulations 1990,[29] while Directive 84/538 is implemented through the Lawnmowers (Harmonisation of Noise Emission Standards) Regulations 1992.[30] Among other things, these latter Regulations prohibit the supply of lawnmowers (as defined by the Regulations) for the first time in the Community unless sound power levels comply with prescribed levels. The Regulations are enforced by reference to a prescribed offence of contravening or failing to comply with requirements without reasonable excuse.

Road vehicle noise

The control of road vehicle noise is based on a sometimes complex pattern of E.C. and municipal legislation, falling broadly into three categories. Those categories relate to construction and use requirements, E.C. requirements, particularly in relation to the control of noise from four-wheeled vehicles, motorcycles and tractors, and road traffic regulation.

[27] *Ibid.* reg.8.
[28] *Ibid.* reg.14.
[28a] [1984] O.J. L188.
[28b] [1986] O.J. L344.
[29] S.I. 1990 No. 161.
[30] S.I. 1992 No. 168.

Construction and use requirements

A wide variety of construction and use requirements relating to motor vehicles are prescribed by regulation. In particular, it is prescribed that no motor vehicle shall be used on a road in such manner as to cause any excessive noise which could have been avoided by the exercise of reasonable care on the part of the driver.[31]

E.C. requirements

E.C. Directive 70/157[31a] (as amended) determines permissible sound levels and describes requirements for exhaust systems in respect of motor vehicles and thus seeks to ensure that Member States' requirements do not introduce trade barriers as well as compliance with environmental limits. Implementation is by means of construction and use regulations referred to above and through vehicle type approval regulations. Similar purposes lie behind Directive 78/1015[31b] (as amended) on permissible sound levels for motorcycles implemented also through various Construction and Use Regulations.[32] Prevention of trade barriers is the justification for Directive 74/151[32a] (as amended) relating to tractors, one of whose purposes is to deal with noise emissions from such vehicles, also implemented through construction and use regulations.

Road traffic regulation

The Road Traffic Regulation Act 1984 makes general provision for traffic regulation both within and outside London.[33] A local authority is empowered to make a traffic regulation order if it appears to be expedient for a variety of purposes, including a need to preserve or improve the amenities of an area through which a road runs.[34] There is no doubt that one of the Act's essential objects is environmental protection and improvement.[35] Accordingly, an order requiring lorries of a certain size to be fitted with air brake silencers before they can be allowed to drive on certain urban routes is lawful.[36]

Aircraft noise

The principal legislation governing aircraft noise is the Civil Aviation Act 1982, section 76 of which stipulates that no action can lie in respect of trespass or nuisance "by reason only of the flight of an aircraft over any property at a height

[31] Road Vehicles (Construction and Use) Regulations 1986 (S.I. 1986 No. 1078), reg.97, made under the Road Traffic Act 1972, s.40, as consolidated by the Road Traffic Act 1988, s.41.

[31a] [1970] O.J. L42.

[31b] [1978] O.J. L349.

[32] *cf.* the Motor Cycle Noise Act 1976, as yet not in force.

[32a] [1974] O.J. L84.

[33] Road Traffic Regulation Act 1984, ss.1–5, 6.

[34] *Ibid.* s.1(1)(f): *cf.* s.2(4).

[35] *R. v. London Boroughs Transport Committee, ex p. Freight Transport Association Ltd* [1991] 1 W.L.R. 828.

[36] *Ibid.*

above the ground which, having regard to wind, weather and all the circumstances . . . is reasonable, or the ordinary incidents of such flight" so long as the Rules of the Air and Air Traffic Control Regulations[36a] and normal aviation practice have been observed. Closely related is section 77, which allows for an air navigation order to provide for the regulation of conditions under which noise and vibration may be caused by aircraft on aerodromes. Again, no action in nuisance is available "by reason only" of the noise and vibration caused by aircraft on an aerodrome[37] by virtue of an air navigation order, as long as its provisions are duly complied with. These provisions were introduced in the 1920s when air transportation was in its infancy and they continue to extend to cover both commercial and private, recreational flying. As such, the immunity from action is extensive, extending as it does to ground-running and taxiing. Section 76 does not exclude proceedings for a statutory nuisance under Part III of the Environmental Protection Act, although it should be noted that Part III does not in any event extend to noise caused by aircraft, other than model aircraft.[38]

The regulation of aircraft noise and vibration

The Secretary of State for Transport is empowered, in relation to airports designated for the purpose under section 80 of the Act of 1982, to prescribe noise abatement measures for aircraft taking off and landing.[39] Such measures are the responsibility of the aircraft's operator and relate to the limitation or mitigation of the effect of noise and vibration associated with take-off and landing.[40] The Secretary of State is also empowered to make noise insulation grant schemes if it appears that buildings near a designated aerodrome[41] require protection from noise and vibration attributable to the use of the aerodrome. Presently only Heathrow and Gatwick airports are designated for the purposes of noise abatement measures and noise insulation grant schemes. Stansted is designated only for the purpose of grant schemes.

Consultation on aerodrome management

The Civil Aviation Act 1982 allows the Secretary of State to designate certain aerodromes in which case any person responsible for their management is obliged to provide for the users, any local authority in whose area an aerodrome or part thereof is situated or whose area is in the neighbourhood, and any other organisation representing the interests of persons concerned with the locality in which an aerodrome is situated, "adequate facilities" for consultation on matters of aerodrome management and administration affecting their interests.[42] At

[36a] S.I. 1991 No. 2437.
[37] As defined by the Civil Aviation Act 1982, s.105.
[38] Environmental Protection Act 1990, s.79(1), (9) and (6).
[39] Civil Aviation Act 1982, s.78.
[40] *Ibid.* subs.(1).
[41] *Ibid.* s.80.
[42] *Ibid.* s.35.

present, designation covers national and regional airports and certain other aerodromes, nearly 50 in all. This facility for consultation is one of the few opportunities available to local authorities to influence the matter of aerodrome management and the matter of aircraft noise. Local authority concerns in relation to development control are likely to remain in so far as an aerodrome continues to operate with deemed planning permission, having been established before the Town and Country Planning Act 1947 probably with some measure of intensification (amounting perhaps to a material change of use requiring planning permission).

Environmental considerations

The licensing or re-licensing application in respect of an aerodrome requires consideration of environmental factors by the Civil Aviation Authority (CAA).[43] Furthermore, where noise vibration, *inter alia*, is attributable to aircraft employed in civil aviation, the Secretary of State is empowered to issue directions to CAA to act to deal with the problem, in so far as powers are available to meet that problem.[44]

E.C. requirements

E.C. directives set noise emission limits for subsonic aircraft as agreed by the International Civil Aviation Organisation.[45] Certain categories of aircraft must not be operated in Member States' territory without appropriate certification. Because the International Civil Aviation Organisation requirements are applied to British aircraft, the statutory orders implementing the Directive formally state the emission standards derived from the Organisation.

"Product" noise

So-called "product noise" refers to E.C. requirements relating to lawnmowers and various household appliances examined previously. Community requirements governing household appliances seek to ensure that uniform criteria for noise emissions apply to manufactured appliances for the avoidance of trade barriers between Member States.[46] Noise emission levels are also determined for lawnmowers, again by reference to an objective referable to an avoidance of trade barriers.[47]

[43] *Ibid.* s.5.
[44] *Ibid.* s.6.
[45] Directive 80/51: [1980] O.J. L18, as amended.
[46] Directive 86/594: [1986] O.J. L344. *Cf.* the Household Appliances (Noise Emission) Regulations 1990 (S.I. 1990 No. 161).
[47] Directive 84/538: [1984] O.J. L300, as amended. *Cf.* the Lawnmowers (Harmonisation of Noise Emission Standards) Regulations 1992 (S.I. 1992 No. 168).

Construction plant noise

Emission levels and methods of noise measurement in respect of construction plant are also subject to regulation under E.C. legal requirements.[48]

Measurement, Definition and Enforcement

E.C. requirements

Certainty of definition through measurement is fundamental to enforcement. Accordingly, most of the E.C. directives referred to previously identify noise measurement methods as well as limits on noise emissions.[49] The directives may seek to obtain objectives, however, which make noise emission limits superfluous, for example, because the essential task is to provide information that will raise public awareness.[50]

Approaches in municipal law

In the absence of criteria for measurement, the task of enforcement is necessarily more subjective and therefore far less likely to persuade the court in confirming enforcement measures. Failure to indicate the point from which noise emissions are measured will usually render attendant statutory enforcement impotent.[51] Appeal proceedings governed by the Control of Noise (Appeals) Regulations,[52] for example, may allow the magistrates' court to quash statutory notices for uncertainty.[53] Successful challenge may also be available where a notice fails to specify the precise steps necessary to secure compliance with noise reduction requirements.[54]

The courts' occasional concern for the mechanics of noise measurement is also seen in *W.T. Lamb Properties Ltd v. Secretary of State for the Environment*,[55] where it was held that, in determining whether premises were being used as a "light industrial building" for the purposes of the now repealed Town and Country Planning (Use Classes) Order 1972, it had to be considered whether the noise would be detrimental to *any* residential area. The fact that the noise from the premises could not be measured separately because the residential area was adjacent to an airport was held to be irrelevant. This approach contrasts significantly with the court's attitude to noise issues, particularly in their

[48] Directive 86/662: [1986] O.J. L384 as amended. *Cf.* the Construction Plant and Equipment (Harmonisation of Noise Emission Standards) Regulations 1988 (S.I. 1988 No. 361) (as amended).

[49] Note in particular Directives 70/157: [1970] O.J. L42, 78/1015: [1978] O.J. L349, 74/151: [1974] O.J. L84, 79/113: [1979] O.J. L33 and 84/538: [1984] O.J. L300.

[50] See Directive 86/594: [1986] O.J. L344.

[51] *R. v. Fenny Stratford JJ., ex p. Watney Mann (Midlands) Ltd* [1976] 1 W.L.R. 1011.

[52] S.I. 1975 No. 2116.

[53] *Ibid.* reg.4(2), (6).

[54] *Metallic Protectives Ltd v. Secretary of State for the Environment* [1976] J.P.L. 166.

[55] *The Times*, November 11, 1982.

treatment at public local inquiries. There has been a well-defined acceptance of an inspector's own judgment about the intrusion of noise in particular localities.[56] Noise pollution must be regarded cumulatively in any particular locality, even though this may give rise to peculiar problems, for example, where noise from two flats amounts to a nuisance but where noise from one separate unit would *not* be regarded as a nuisance.

[56] *Kentucky Fried Chicken (G.B.) Ltd v. Secretary of State for the Environment* (1978) 245 E.G. 839.

CHAPTER 9

ACCESS TO ENVIRONMENTAL HEALTH INFORMATION

Introduction

Across the often disparate areas that go to make up environmental health, it may be of importance to identify the circumstances in which information is available, from what source, for what purpose and to whom. The present chapter is not concerned with the reliability of scientific and other information that forms the basis of a decision to legislate, particularly in a national, municipal context or a European Community context. Rather, the chapter is concerned with an identification of the legal status of information relevant to environmental health. This matter of legal status is concerned at the outset with general information availability, particularly on those occasions when statute obliges an administrative agency to bring environmental information into the public domain, or to require others to do so. In the same way, the law will in many cases require the administrative agency or an individual to obtain or convey prescribed information, usually as part of a regulatory process.

Beyond the matter of general information availability and the power to obtain or convey information is the need for the law to define (as precisely as possible) what is comprised in the term "information", again for the purpose of some regulatory function in most cases. Equally the law must be concerned to ensure that there is an information base which is as reliable as possible, for enforcement purposes, for example. Accordingly, a statute may stipulate that evidence collected in a certain manner is to be regarded as conclusive for particular enforcement purposes, for example.

Much of the foregoing stresses the availability of information either in the public domain or for the regulatory benefit of an administrative agency. However, the law does often qualify this information availability, usually where there is some question of confidentiality. More generally, however, many Acts of Parliament anticipate the possibility that additional information-gathering facilities may be necessary, whether or not subject to the foregoing restrictions. In these circumstances, the statute will provide the Minister responsible with enabling powers to make and seek approval for facilitating subordinate legislation.

Whenever statute seeks to manage the information process in all its different facets, criminal enforcement is often a necessary complement. It is usually the case that minor, summary offences are provided for, such as the giving of false information.

The law divides environmental information access into two broad categories, comprising requirements governing information access either by virtue of the Environmental Information Regulations 1992[1] or otherwise. The Regulations (which are dealt with in the present chapter) impose certain minimum requirements for access and disclosure in the case of environmental information they cover. However, the Regulations, which implement European Community requirements,[2] also impose similar minimum requirements on other areas where statute requires access and disclosure.

Different areas of environmental health law throw up different approaches to the matter of access to and management of information. The older legislation typically creates "closed" systems of licensing and enforcement, with little or no room for "public ownership" of information beyond the two immediate parties, the administrative agency and the person subject to regulation or enforcement, as the case may be. More recent legislation is characterised by a far more "open" system, in which public awareness is encouraged, usually through the provision of facilities such as public registers of applications, decisions and enforcement action. This matter of public awareness and public accountability is extended in some cases by a requirement, either in the legislation itself or through the terms of a condition attached to a licence, that records and information are monitored, usually on the site from which a particular operation is being mounted.

Reference was made earlier to the Environmental Information Regulations. These important Regulations cover a very wide range of environmental information held by public agencies and other agencies under their control. As indicated previously, there are certain minimum requirements to be observed in response to any request for disclosure of such information.

The Management of Information Availability

General information availability

Almost inevitably, it is primary legislation that forces recognition of general information availability, usually for the benefit of the public at large. The Water Industry Act 1991 and the Water Resources Act 1991 contain some particularly significant instances of requirements to force environmental information into the public domain.

The Water Industry Act empowers the Secretary of State to arrange for the publication of information in connection with the carrying out of a company's appointment under the Act as a sewerage or water undertaker. However, any such publication must appear to the Secretary of State to be in the public interest. The Director-General of Water Services is also empowered to publish

[1] S.I. 1992 No. 3240.
[2] Directive 313/90: [1990] O.J. L158.

information and advice to any customer or potential customer of a company holding an appointment as a sewerage or water undertaker. Both the Secretary of State and the Director-General are obliged, so far as is practicable, to exclude any matters which may seriously and prejudicially affect the interests of any individual and to exclude any comparable information in so far as it is similarly considered to affect any incorporated or unincorporated body.[3]

Restrictions may operate differently, to the extent that public consultation may be limited to those appearing to be affected by a particular proposal, such as a proposal by the Secretary of State to establish or vary water quality objectives.[4] By way of contrast, the nature of the exercise, such as the Secretary of State's duty to publish the annual report of the National Rivers Authority (NRA), will normally indicate unrestricted publication.[5] The same unrestricted publication is to be seen in connection with NRA's duty to collate and publish information from which assessments can be made of actual and prospective demand for water, as well as actual and prospective water resources.[6]

Directly related to the foregoing is the issue of the availability of specific environmental information. This issue is addressed later in the present chapter, when open licensing and enforcement systems are examined. In these contexts, the special functions and status of public registers is examined.

The power to obtain and the duty to convey information

The power and duty here described are provided for in a number of enactments and supporting Regulations. Of considerable significance are the following enactments:

(a) the Public Health (Control of Disease) Act 1984;
(b) the Environmental Protection Act 1990;
(c) the Water Industry Act;
(d) the Water Resources Act; and
(e) the Clean Air Act 1993.

A number of other provisions are worthy of note initially in the present context.

The Control of Pollution Act 1974 provides that local authorities in particular may require, by notice, "any person" to furnish to any such authority information reasonably considered to be necessary for the purpose of functions referable to the Act, such as noise control in noise abatement zones.[7] Whatever the enactment under which a local authority is authorised to perform a function, that authority is able, by notice appropriately served, to demand information in relation to "any land" and, more particularly, the nature of interests in land.[8] There may be

[3] Water Industry Act 1991, s.201.
[4] Water Resources Act 1991, s.83.
[5] *Ibid.* s.187.
[6] *Ibid.* s.188.
[7] Control of Pollution Act 1974, s.93. *Cf.* s.91, dealing with rights of entry.
[8] Local Government (Miscellaneous Provisions) Act 1976, s.16.

circumstances in which the urgent nature of action to be taken in an emergency may leave the Act silent in relation to the acquisition of information. A very significant example of such an approach relates to the making of emergency orders where, *inter alia*, it is considered by the "designating authority" that there exists a situation which is likely to create a hazard to human health through human consumption of food.[9] A drainage board in an internal drainage district is empowered to require, again by notice, information about the occupier of any hereditament in respect of which a drainage rate is levied.[10] More generally, in the context of land drainage, the Ministers responsible under the Act are empowered to convene statutory inquiries into any matter arising under the legislation.[11] This is but one of many examples of statutory inquiries scattered throughout many enactments. The typical public local inquiry is a device, first and foremost, for the gathering of information (usually in the context of a statutory function affected or potentially attected by government policy) for the purpose of the resolution of a dispute.

The Public Health (Control of Disease) Act 1984

The Act, which is concerned with notifiable diseases and measures to deal with those diseases,[12] provides information-gathering facilities reflective of the seriousness and urgency of the local authority's statutory functions. The emphasis of those information-gathering facilities is reminiscent of the widely drawn powers referred to previously, under Part I of the Food and Environment Protection Act.[13] Of particular note under the Act of 1984 is:

(a) the requirement for a registered medical practitioner to certify to the local authority any notifiable diseases or food poisoning[14];
(b) the facility enabling a local authority to direct that additional diseases are notifiable[15];
(c) the power of a local authority to require information to be provided by an occupier of premises where a person suffering from a notifiable disease or food poisoning is or has been for remedial purposes[16]; and
(d) the prohibition or discontinuation of work, or certain types of work, on premises affected, by order of the local authority.[17]

However, it is significant that there is provided a statutory safeguard in respect of these widely drawn powers for information-gathering. The safeguard is expressed in terms of a requirement that a local authority should make "full" compensation

[9] Food and Environmental Protection Act 1985, s.1.
[10] Land Drainage Act 1991, s.53.
[11] *Ibid.* s.69.
[12] *cf.* Chap. 14, "Miscellaneous Controls".
[13] See n.9, *supra.*
[14] Public Health (Control of Disease) Act, s.11.
[15] *Ibid.* s.16.
[16] *Ibid.* s.18.
[17] *Ibid.* ss.20 and 28.

to any person who has sustained damage by reason of an exercise of its powers, always assuming that the individual himself is not at fault.[18]

The Environmental Protection Act 1990

The authorisation or licensing process under many Acts of Parliament, including the present Act, contains a power conferred on the licensing agency to seek additional information considered necessary before a decision can be made on an application. A typical example relates to the Part I authorisation requirements in respect of integrated control.[19] The enforcement machinery in Part I of the Act includes an array of powers given to inspectors appointed under the Act, including a variety of powers to retrieve information from premises.[20] Enhanced powers are conferred on inspectors where there is reasonable cause to believe that an article or substance is a cause of imminent danger or serious harm.[21] Such powers again include the power to take samples, a matter referred to elsewhere in the present chapter. The Act contains similar powers of entry for inspectors operating under Part II provisions relating to waste management.[22] An important element of central government control of waste regulation authorities is seen elsewhere in Part II, which allows the Secretary of State, in the discharge of his statutory functions, to require an authority to provide information about the discharge of its functions.[23] Furthermore, either the Secretary of State or the authority may by notice require any person to furnish information reasonably considered to be needed for the discharge of this information-gathering function. Failure to comply with such a request without reasonable excuse is an offence triable summarily or on indictment.[24]

A broadly defined information-gathering function is found in the Part III provisions relating statutory nuisance, dealt with elsewhere in this book. Part III of the Act opens with a reference to the duty of the local authority to cause its area to be inspected from time to time to detect any statutory nuisances which ought to be dealt with under its summary powers.[25] Furthermore, the local authority is under a duty to take such steps as are reasonably practicable to investigate any complaints of a statutory nuisance made by a person living in its area.[26]

Part VI of the Act, dealing with the regulation and control of genetically modified organisms in the environment, again relies on extensive powers of enforcement. The Secretary of State has widely drawn powers to seek and obtain information from those who appear to be involved in, or about to be involved in, various activities that may be subject to control under the Act.[27]

[18] *Ibid.* s.57.
[19] Environmental Protection Act, s.6 and Sched. 1, para. 1(3).
[20] *Ibid.* s.17.
[21] *Ibid.* s.19.
[22] *Ibid.* s.69.
[23] *Ibid.* s.71.
[24] *Ibid.* subss.(2), (3).
[25] *Ibid.* s.79(1).
[26] *Ibid.*
[27] *Ibid.* s.116.

The Water Industry Act 1991

In the case of companies holding appointments under this Act as water and sewerage undertakers, the Act requires the Director-General to collect information on various matters, including the level of overall performance.[28] Standards of performance are set down in the Act and further elucidated in accompanying regulations.[29] The requirement for collection of information is supplemented by a power, again conferred on the Director, to direct an undertaker to give certain other detailed information about performance standards. Whatever the type of information collected, the Director-General is also required to arrange for its publication at stipulated intervals.[30]

The particular statutory duties affecting any water undertaker inevitably involve a need to be aware of water quality standards and wholesomeness. The prescription of approaches to information collection, by sampling in particular, is set down in regulations. Among other things, such regulations stipulate the approach to sampling in technical terms through the specification of matters like the determination of sampling points and the frequency of sampling.[31] Elsewhere, there are equally detailed prescriptions concerning the collection and analysis of samples.[32] The observation of so-called "appropriate requirements" will be of considerable significance for a variety of purposes, not least of which will be enforcement. The local authority's functions in relation to private water supplies means that the foregoing requirements relating to water undertakers apply in very similar terms.[33]

The Act duly reflects the local authority's functions in relation to water quality. Indeed, the Act requires any such local authority to take all steps considered to be appropriate to keep itself informed about the wholesomeness and sufficiency of water supplies, including of course private water supplies.[34] In turn, the local authority is empowered to elicit, by notice, any information required in connection with the exercise of its powers and duties in connection with water quality under the Act.[35]

In addition to the information requirements of local authorities, the Act makes copious provision for similar requirements affecting the Secretary of State, the Director-General and undertakers themselves. In the first place, any company holding an appointment as an undertaker under the Act is required to furnish information to the Secretary of State in connection with the discharge of its functions and responsibilities, as well as the discharge of the Secretary of State's own statutory responsibilities. A demand may even be made for information

[28] *Ibid.* ss.38A and 95A.
[29] *Ibid.* ss.38 and 95. *Cf., e.g.* S.I. 1989 No. 1159.
[30] *Ibid.* ss.38A and 95A.
[31] Water Supply (Water Quality) Regulations 1989 (S.I. 1989 No. 1147), regs.11 and 13.
[32] *Ibid.* reg.21. *Cf.* Circular 20/82 (Welsh Office Circular 33/82).
[33] Private Supply Regulations 1991 (S.I. 1991 No. 2790), regs.13, 16 and 19.
[34] Water Industry Act, s.77.
[35] *Ibid.* s.84. The powers and duties are to be found in ss.77–82.

which is not in the possession of the undertaker.[36] It may appear to the Secretary of State or the Director-General, on the other hand, that an undertaker may be contravening, or may have contravened, conditions of appointment, or certain other statutory or other requirements enforceable under the Act. This duty to provide information for enforcement purposes is itself subject to criminal enforcement.[37] Finally, where a sewer, drain, pipe or similar facility is situated on land, the owner or occupier of that land is obliged to respond to a request for information from a sewerage undertaker. However, the sewer, drain, pipe or other similar facility must be used or intended to be used for the purpose of discharging trade effluent into a sewer belonging to the undertaker. Essentially, the duty to supply information relates to plans and other associated information. Again, failure to comply is a criminal offence and a person may be convicted in summary proceedings without the benefit of any defence based on reasonable excuse.[38]

Water Resources Act 1991

The power to obtain and the duty to convey information under the Act is characterised by an important network of obligations, falling into three categories. In the first category, there are certain reciprocal duties as between NRA and the water undertakers. A second category relates to NRA's general information obligations to the Secretary of State and the Minister of Agriculture. Finally, there is an obligation to supply NRA and the National Environment Research Council with certain types of information where a person proposes to undertake defined activities.

In the fact category, there are two provisions, the first of which[39] imposes on NRA a duty to provide a water undertaker with information in its possession, reasonably required for the purpose of discharging its statutory functions. In the same terms, an obligation binds any water undertaker to provide NRA with information in its possession. This duty is not directly enforceable before the court but is enforceable by means of enforcement orders made by the Secretary of State under section 18 of the Water Industry Act. Also in this first category is the statutory duty, again imposed on NRA, requiring the provision of information in its possession reasonably required by a water undertaker, for two purposes. The first purpose relates to the quality of controlled or other waters, while the second purpose relates to any incident in which any poisonous, noxious or polluting matter or any solid waste matter has entered controlled or other waters. Again, as a reciprocal duty, any water undertaker is bound by the same obligation. As in the previous instance, so too this reciprocal duty is enforceable under the provisions of section 18 of the Water Industry Act.[40]

The second category relates to NRA's general information obligation to the

[36] *Ibid.* s.202.
[37] *Ibid.* s.203.
[38] *Ibid.* s.204.
[39] Water Resources Act, s.197.
[40] *Ibid.* s.203.

Secretary of State and (in some instances) the Minister of Agriculture only. In the first place, NRA is subject to a duty, owed either to the Secretary of State or the Minister of Agriculture, to furnish information in relation to its property, the execution of its functions and its responsibilities generally. To this extent, NRA is obliged to provide such information as may be reasonably required, even if that information is not in its possession. The request is conveyed by means of a direction from the Secretary of State or the Minister. Included in the obligation here is a requirement that NRA shall permit an inspection of subject information comprised in accounts or other records.[41] Additionally, the Secretary of State or the Minister may require advice and assistance from NRA. In this case, the duty arises only if it appears appropriate that the information should be provided for the purpose of facilitating the discharge of statutory functions relating to water pollution. However, the provision of information is not limited, since the Secretary of State, the Minister of Agriculture or NRA may serve notice on "any person", requiring that person to furnish information reasonably required for the purpose of discharging pollution control functions under the Act. Any person who fails to comply with the requirements of any such notice without reasonable excuse is guilty of a summary offence.[42]

The third category again imposes an obligation to furnish information, by reference to the pursuit of any one of a number of different activities. In the first place, any person who proposes to construct or extend a boring to search for or abstract minerals is required to give NRA notice of the intention prior to any construction or extension. Failure to comply is a criminal offence triable summarily, or on indictment, but without the benefit of any defence based on reasonable excuse.[43] NRA is also empowered to give directions to any person who is abstracting water from a source of supply, requiring information about that abstraction. Failure to comply is an offence triable summarily, but without the benefit of any defence of reasonable excuse. However, representations may be made to the Secretary of State as a result of which any directions may be revoked or modified.[44] Finally, any person proposing to sink a well or borehole intended to reach a depth of 50 feet or more for the purpose of searching for or abstracting water is required to give prior notice to the Natural Environment Research Council. Additional information must also be made available to the Council. Failure to comply is a summary offence.[45]

The Clean Air Act 1993

Parts II and V of the Act contain some of the more coherent provisions relating to powers for the purpose of obtaining and conveying information. These provisions focus on the occupiers of buildings where furnaces and other

[41] *Ibid.* s.196.
[42] *Ibid.* s.202.
[43] *Ibid.* s.199.
[44] *Ibid.* s.201.
[45] *Ibid.* s.198.

appliances are responsible for emissions to the atmosphere, the local authorities responsible for enforcement and the Secretary of State.

Under Part II, where a furnace of a prescribed burning capacity is concerned, the occupier of the building containing the furnace may be required by the local authority, *inter alia*, to make and record measurements from time to time of the grit, fumes and dust emitted, and to notify the authority of the results.[46] Significantly, an occupier obliged to furnish the above information is also obliged to permit the local authority to be represented during the taking and recording of measurements. Failure to comply with these requirements is a summary offence of strict liability. The foregoing provision is supplemented in the case of certain other furnaces through a facility by which the occupier may require the local authority to undertake the making and recording of measurements.[47] To enable a local authority to perform functions "properly" under the foregoing provisions, the Act further empowers the authority to require an occupier to furnish information about any furnace, as well as information about fuel or waste burned in that furnace. Again, failure to comply with the authority's requirements here is a summary offence.[48]

Turning to Part V of the Act, a local authority is able to arrange for the investigation of problems of air pollution and publication of the resulting information.[49] In so far as a local authority arranges for the publication of such information, it must ensure that it is presented in such a way that no information relating to a trade secret is disclosed, except with the consent of a person authorised to permit disclosure. Significantly, a breach of this local authority duty is actionable in tort.[50] Although the provisions just described are discretionary, they may be of crucial importance where (say) the local authority would wish to publish information on dust and grit emissions from foundry operations in the district, for example. Publication could be undertaken both under the present provision or by virtue of section 12, described above.[51] The facilities to enable local authority collection of information about the emission of pollutants and other substances into the air are further added to by Part V of the Act.[52] In the first place, a notice under section 36 may be issued requiring an occupier of premises to provide an estimate or other information about emissions, although normally not emissions subject to control under Part I of the Environmental Protection Act. Failure to comply with a notice is a summary offence.[53] A section 36 notice is subject to appeal to the Secretary of State.[54] The second facility provided relates to entry to premises for the purpose of measuring or recording emissions, either by

[46] Clean Air Act, s.10, and the Clean Air (Measurement of Grit and Dust from Furnaces) Regulations 1971 (S.I. 1971 No. 161).
[47] Clean Air Act, s.11.
[48] *Ibid.* s.12.
[49] *Ibid.* s.34.
[50] *Ibid.* subss.(2) and (3).
[51] See n.48, *supra*. *Cf.* Circulars 7/76 (Welsh Office 9/76) and 2/77 (Welsh Office 6/77).
[52] Clean Air Act, s.35. *Cf.* the Control of Atmospheric Pollution (Research and Publicity) Regulations 1977 (S.I. 1977 No. 19) and Circular 2/77 (Welsh Office 6/77).
[53] Clean Air Act, s.36(8).
[54] *Ibid.* s.37.

agreement or by virtue of entry to premises as of right under section 56 of the Act. However, the power available to the local authority may not be exercised if, within stipulated time limits, an occupier gives notice to the local authority requiring service of a section 36 notice, previously described. The third facility provided for is one which depends on arrangements with an occupier, whereby that occupier measures and records emissions on behalf of the local authority.[55] Finally, in Part V the Secretary of State may, by direction, require that a local authority facilitate the measuring and recording of air pollution for transmission to him. However, prior to giving such a direction, the Secretary of State is obliged to consult with the local authority concerned, albeit in return for the capital costs involved.[56] Potentially, this provision is of considerable significance for the purpose of air pollution monitoring in compliance with E.C. Directive requirements.[57]

A complementary but more widely drawn provision in Part VII of the Act empowers a local authority, by notice, to seek information that it considers to be reasonably necessary for the purpose of any function under the Act relating to the control of certain forms of air pollution under Part IV, or the acquisition of information about air pollution under Part V. Failure, without reasonable excuse, to comply with a notice is a summary offence.[58]

Information definition

There comes a point in the implementation and enforcement of environmental health legislation when rather more specific requirements have to be observed if information is to be used effectively for these purposes. Consequently, it is necessary, as a starting point, to define what is or what is not "information" for the purposes of implementation and enforcement. Two important pieces of legislation indicate only what the term "information" includes. Accordingly, for the purposes of these Acts,[59] "information" includes anything contained in any records, accounts, estimates or returns.

The process of information definition precedes the process—such as sampling—by which information is collected, analysed and arranged so that it is at least adequate for the purpose of the enforcement process in particular. The matter of sampling is dealt with under the following heading, "Environmental information reliability". In the meantime, the task of information definition commences with the law's recognition of, for example, powers of entry, search and seizure, as seen already. The Environmental Protection Act, for example, allows inspectors acting under Part I to gain entry to premises for the purpose of measuring, photographing and sampling.[60] It may be necessary to obtain a

[55] *Ibid.* s.35.
[56] *Ibid.* s.39.
[57] Air Quality Standards Regulations 1989 (S.I. 1989 No. 317). *Cf.* Chap. 6, "Atmospheric Pollution".
[58] Clean Air Act, s.58. *Cf.* s.59, on the availability of local inquiries.
[59] Water Industry Act, s.219, and Water Resources Act, s.221.
[60] Environment Protection Act, s.17.

warrant for entry from a justice of the peace.[61] An inspector operating under the Food Safety Act 1990 may "at all reasonable times" inspect any food intended for human consumption which has been sold or offered or exposed for sale, or is in the possession of, or has been deposited with, or consigned to, any person for the purpose of sale or preparation for sale.[62] This form of words in the food safety legislation indicates the potential scope of information definition powers, driven in the first instance by the judgment and experience of the environmental health or other enforcing officer concerned. However, it is almost inevitable that a final judgment will have to be made on whether to proceed. This is clearly very critical if articles (such as food) have been detained in the possession of a local authority or other agency by virtue of statutory powers.[63]

Environmental information reliability

The reliability of environmental information is an issue that falls into a number of often inter-related categories. Legislation may be specific in referring to presumptions of conclusiveness of evidence for the purposes of enforcement. In dealing with trade effluent, the Water Industry Act 1991 indicates that any meter or apparatus provided in connection with trade effluent licensing for the purpose of measuring, recovering or determining the volume, rate of discharge, nature or composition of trade effluent discharged is presumed in any proceedings to register accurately unless the contrary is shown.[64] Furthermore, the same Act indicates that if a person furnishes information under the Act knowing that that information is false in a material particular, or is reckless in that connection, he is guilty of an offence which is triable summarily, or on indictment.[65] The Water Resources Act contains an offence in precisely similar terms.[66]

Legislation relevant to environmental health will often, as of necessity, refer to the important matter of sampling and the status of samples in law. The Environmental Protection Act empowers inspectors operating under Part I of the Act to take samples of "any articles or substances" found in or on any premises which they are empowered to enter, and ". . . of the air, water or land in, on, or in the vicinity of, the premises".[67] The procedure to be followed in the taking, and dealing with, of samples is to be prescribed by regulations to be made by the Secretary of State.[68] If, in the exercise of other related powers, an inspector takes possession of any article or substance found on premises,[69] he is obliged, *inter alia*, to take a sample (if that is practicable) and give a person at the premises a portion of the sample sufficient to identify it.[70]

[61] Control of Pollution Act 1974, s.91.
[62] Food Safety Act 1990, s.9. *Cf.* Chap. 13, "Food Safety".
[63] *Ibid.* s.9(4) in particular.
[64] Water Industry Act, s.136.
[65] *Ibid.* s.207.
[66] Water Resources Act, s.206.
[67] Environmental Protection Act, s.17(3)(f).
[68] *Ibid.* subs.(4).
[69] *Ibid.* subs.(3)(g), (h).
[70] *Ibid.* subs.(7).

Sampling is only one approach to enforcement under provisions relating to integrated pollution control and local authority air pollution control from whence the above powers are drawn. Under the Water Resources Act, there is a far more explicit recognition of the requirements to be observed if evidence from samples is to be truly reliable for enforcement purposes. Not only is there an explicit recognition of requirements to be observed for enforcement purposes; the sampling provisions refer to "any sample".[71] The Act provides that the result of the analysis of any sample taken on behalf of NRA is not admissible in any legal proceedings in relation to any effluent passing from any land or vessel unless the person who takes the sample complies with a threefold procedure.[72]

The threefold procedure requires, first, that on taking the sample the occupier of the land is notified of the intention to have the sample analysed. Secondly, the sample must be divided into three parts there and then and placed in sealed, marked containers. Finally, one part must be delivered to the occupier, one part retained and the other part submitted for future analysis so allowing for future comparison.

The Water Resources Act recognises that it may not be reasonably practicable for a person taking a sample to comply with the foregoing requirements. In these circumstances, the requirements are treated as having been complied with if in fact they are complied with as soon as reasonably practicable after the sample was taken.[73]

These Water Resources Act provisions are further reinforced by regulations, the Control of Pollution (Registers) Regulations 1989.[74] A register maintained by NRA must contain certain prescribed particulars in connection with samples taken by it, must indicate in relation to each sample taken whether the foregoing provisions of section 209 have been complied with, and must contain, in the case of a sample or its analysis emanating otherwise than from NRA, details of the date and time when the sample was taken, the location and the result of analysis.[75] If NRA or any other person chooses to take legal proceedings against a person by reference to a sample, an entry in the register must be made within prescribed time limits following final determination of the proceedings.[76]

Despite the foregoing statutory framework it is clear that, on occasions, the court will be obliged to clarify statutory uncertainties. There may, for example, be a lack of clarity on the matter of timing when a sample is processed.[76a] Equally there may be uncertainty about whether particular sampling techniques comply with statutory requirements.[76b]

[71] Water Resources Act, s.209. *Cf. National Rivers Authority v. Harcross Timber and Building Supplies* [1992] Env.L.R. D6.

[72] *Ibid.* subs.(1).

[73] *Ibid.* subs.(2).

[74] S.I. 1989 No. 1160.

[75] *Ibid.* reg.7(1), (2).

[76] *Ibid.* reg.7(4).

[76a] *Attorney-General's Reference (No. 2 of 1994), The Times*, August 4, 1994.

[76b] *R. v. CPC (UK) Ltd, The Times*, August 4, 1994.

The restricted disclosure of information

Environmental health legislation contains many different types of restriction on the disclosure of information. There may be a concern to ensure an exclusion from an application for consent to release a genetically modified organism of repetitious information contained in a previous application, for example.[77] On the other hand, there may be matters of real sensitivity to be considered, so that any certificate indicating the incidence of notifiable disease must be transmitted to the proper officer of the local authority in such a manner that the contents cannot be read during that transmission.[78]

More generally, primary or secondary legislation will often indicate that information obtained by virtue of the exercise of a relevant statutory function must not be disclosed except for certain very specific purposes. Such a restoration is usually enforceable by means of criminal sanctions. Particularly significant restrictions on information disclosure relate to matters of commercial confidentiality, trade secrets and even national security.

An often significant example of restriction on disclosure is to be found in the Food Safety Act 1990 where the sampling of foodstuffs is concerned. Information relating to an individual business may not be disclosed without the previous consent in writing of the person carrying out that business. The only exceptions to the obligation of confidentiality, breach of which is an offence, arise where a Minister issues directions necessary for the purposes of the Act or the purpose of complying with any European Community obligation, or where disclosure is necessary for the purposes of any proceedings for an offence against an order made under the Act, or any report of those proceedings.[79] The Act clarifies the circumstances in which disclosure is necessary for the purposes of the Act by including:

(a) the purpose of securing that food complies with food safety requirements; or
(b) in the interests of public health; or
(c) for the purpose of protecting or promoting the interests of consumers.[80]

Matters of trade secrets or commercial confidentiality frequently feature in the legislation, although it may not always be a foregone conclusion that commercial confidentiality can be relied upon as a means of restricting public access to particular information. The Environmental Protection Act stipulates that, in the case of authorisations under Part I of the Act, commercially confidential information may not be entered on a public register without the consent of an individual or business to which the information relates. However, it is for the enforcing authority to determine whether the information for which

[77] Genetially Modified Organisms (Deliberate Release) Regulations 1992 (S.I. 1992 No. 3280), reg.7.
[78] Public Health (Infectious Diseases) Regulations 1988 (S.I. 1988 No. 1546), reg.12.
[79] Food Safety Act, s.25(3).
[80] *Ibid.* subs.(4).

confidentiality is claimed is information which, if included in a register, would prejudice to an unreasonable degree the commercial interests of the individual or person in question.[81] A person who has been given or has obtained information by virtue of the Control of Pollution Act commits a summary offence if he discloses that information and it relates to any trade secret used in carrying out a particular undertaking. Although there is no statutory definition of a "trade secret" here, there are some familiar exemptions from criminal liability, including any disclosure in the performance of a duty or any disclosure by virtue of the consent in writing of the person having a right of disclosure.[82] This form of restriction is replicated in very similar terms by the Clean Air Act 1993.[83] However, the Clean Air Act also restricts the publication of information by a local authority relating to the problems of air pollution where that information contains trade secrets details, unless consent has been given by a person authorised to make disclosure. Unusually, the Act goes on to say that breach of the duty not to disclose information containing details of a trade secret is actionable in civil proceedings.[84] On some occasions, the purposes for which disclosure may be made are itemised in considerable detail, referring, for example, to:

(a) the execution of statutory functions;
(b) the enforcement of regulatory functions;
(c) compliance with European Community obligations; and
(d) the investigation of criminal offences or for the pursuit of any civil or criminal proceedings.[85]

However, the general rule may be that disclosure is not permitted in respect of information given in compliance with statutory requirements or where the information relates to a secret manufacturing process or a trade secret.[86]

The water legislation contains some fairly standard, uniform provisions on information restriction. Typically, it is declared that no disclosure shall occur where information has been obtained "... by virtue of any of the provisions of this Act", and relates to the affairs of any individual or to any particular business. However, the restriction is subject to two types of qualification. The first application is chronological, indicating that the restriction lasts during the lifetime of the individual or so long as the business in question is carried on. Unless these conditions are satisfied, the consent of the individual or person carrying on the business is required before any disclosure can occur.[87] The second qualification allows disclosure in a variety of situations where, for example,

[81] Environmental Protection Act, s.22(1), (11). *Cf.* the Environmental Protection (Applications, Appeals and Registers) Regulations 1991 (S.I. 1991 No. 507), reg.7. *Cf.* s.21, relating to restrictions on the disclosure of information relating to national security.

[82] Control of Pollution Act, s.94.

[83] Clean Air Act, s.49.

[84] *Ibid.* s.34(2), (3).

[85] Construction Products Regulations 1991 (S.I. 1991 No. 1620), reg.25.

[86] *Ibid.*

[87] Water Resources Act 1991, s.204(1). *Cf.* Sched. 24. Similar provisions are to be found in the Fire Precautions Act 1971, s.21.

disclosure is made for the purpose of facilitating the performance of functions by NRA or a local authority under the Act.[88]

Enabling powers in relation to information

Some environmental health legislation makes provision to empower the responsible Minister or Secretary of State to make regulations which may relate to information management, either generally or more specifically. Particular examples of enabling powers in relation to information management generally are to be found in the Water Industry Act,[89] the Water Resources Act[90] and the Public Health (Control of Disease) Act 1984.[91] A very much more specific power may be directed at the acquisition of information about substances and materials which are, or are believed to be, environmentally detrimental, for example.[92]

Information enforcement offences

Reference has been made already to the frequent resort—in primary and secondary environmental health legislation—to various criminal offences that support different information requirements, usually as part of an enforcement process. In general terms, there are three categories of offence to be identified. The first category relates to a failure to respond to a notice or other requirement to provide particular information. The second category deals with a failure to provide information in any situation where there is no prior notification of a requirement by an enforcing authority but where the obligation to furnish information arises automatically by virtue of the Act or related secondary legislation. The third category covers circumstances in which a person furnishes false or misleading information.

Most of the so-called information offences identified previously are triable summarily. However, the perceived seriousness of the criminal act or omission may exceptionally justify an offence triable either way, summarily or on indictment.[93] Most offences relating to the enforcement of information requirements do not admit of particular defences, although, exceptionally, some offences do offer reliance on reasonable excuse, presumably to reflect a possibility that the required information-giving power is not available to the defendant. While most offences are offences of strict liability, it is almost inevitably the case that a person may be convicted of giving false information only where he knows that a statement was false in a material particular or was reckless in the same regard.[94]

[88] *Ibid.* subs.(2). *Cf.* the Water Industry Act 1991, s.206, and the Land Drainage Act 1991, s.70. As to the protection of confidential information about underground waters, see the Water Resources Act, s.205.

[89] s.213.

[90] s.219.

[91] s.13.

[92] Environmental Protection Act, s.142.

[93] See, *e.g.* the Environmental Protection Act, s.71.

[94] See, *e.g.* the Control of Pollution Act, s.93(3).

By necessity, the statutory power to obtain or acquire information will be linked to the performance or fulfilment of functions under the legislation in question. Accordingly, the court may be unable to convict a defendant for failure to furnish information without hearing evidence that would link that defendant to a particular offence under the Act, for example.[95]

Information Access

Closed licensing systems

As indicated at the beginning of this chapter, older regulatory legislation typically creates "closed" systems of licensing, regulation and enforcement with little or no room for "public ownership" of information beyond the two immediate parties: the administrative agency and the person subject to regulatory requirements. The incidence of "closed" systems in which environmental health information has not normally been shared with the public at large through rights of access is a characteristic of most relevant legislation up to the early 1980s. The principal examples are the Pet Animals Act 1951, the Rag Flock and Other Filling Materials Act 1951, the Animal Boarding Establishments Act 1963, the Scrap Metal Dealers Act 1964, the Riding Establishments Act 1964, the Breeding of Dogs Act 1973, the Control of Pollution Act 1974, Part III,[96] and the Local Government (Miscellaneous Provisions) Act.[97] Notable exceptions to this early trend are to be found in the Caravan Sites and Control of Development Act 1960, containing an open licensing system, with registers of licences granted being open to the public,[98] and the Control of Pollution Act 1974, containing provisions in Part III for the maintenance by local authorities of noise level registers, again open to the public, in noise abatement zones.[99]

The Environmental Information Regulations[1]

In so far as the foregoing regulatory legislation requires information to be made available to any person, the Environmental Information Regulations will apply to information held by a local authority or any other administrative agency for present purposes.[2] These Regulations would apply, as explained later in this chapter, where any statutory provision requires information to be made available "to any person", in which case provision must be made to expedite disclosure or to explain a refusal of disclosure and to charge only a reasonable sum for any disclosure.[3]

[95] *J.B. & M. Motor Haulage Ltd v. London Waste Regulation Authority*, *The Times*, November 28, 1990.
[96] s.61, dealing with the licensing of noise on construction sites.
[97] ss.14 and 15, dealing with the licensing of acupuncture, tattooing, ear-piercing and electrolysis.
[98] s.25.
[99] s.64.
[1] S.I. 1992 No. 3240.
[2] *Ibid.* reg.5.
[3] *Ibid.*

Closed enforcement systems

A "closed" enforcement system is one in which there is no prior or general public notice of action to be taken. Perhaps not surprisingly, a system of this sort will be found in circumstances where it is necessary to expedite action for the protection of health in the community. Even if particular statutory powers are exercisable without specific information being made available to an individual or group of individuals, it may be the case that the legislation would provide for other, perhaps more general, community notification of threats to the public health. A closed enforcement system—short of "final" criminal enforcement—will usually require that prescribed action is taken. That prescribed action may be required by virtue of an emergency order or notice made under Part I of the Food and Environment Protection Act 1985, Parts I and II of the Prevention of Damage by Pests Act 1949 and the Public Health (Control of Disease) Act 1984, to give but three examples of "closed" systems. Even between these examples, there are striking variations of approach. The emergency order under Part I of the Act of 1985, referable to any existing or threatened contamination of food or food sources, is likely to be a broad-ranging restriction, relating (say) to a restriction on the movement of sheep from a particular area because of radioactive contamination of pastures. On the other hand, Parts I and II of the Act of 1949, relating to measures to deal with infestation by rats and mice and the infestation of food, empower the responsible local authority to serve a notice on the owner or occupier of the subject land and empower the responsible Minister to give "... such directions ... as he thinks expedient", respectively. Following the notice or the direction, as the case may be, there is facility for an appeal to the magistrates' court. In the case of the third example, taken from the Public Health (Control of Disease) Act, Regulations made under the Act permit wide-ranging action, again in defence of the public health. The Public Health (Infections Diseases) Regulations,[4] for example, empower a local authority, on receipt of a report of food poisoning, to require, *inter alia,* that a person discontinue any occupation connected with food until notified that any risk of causing infection has been removed.[5]

Open licensing systems

Open licensing systems are characterised by relatively free availability of relevant information in the public domain. Information may be freely available, because (in relation to a regulatory decision, for example) it is incorporated in a public register, because (for example, in relation to an application for a licence or consent) the law requires publicity as a fundamental prerequisite to any application or because (for example, in relation to the approval of certain relatively sensitive substances, their use and marketing) the law permits access usually on a restricted basis.

[4] S.I. 1988 No. 1546.
[5] *Ibid.* reg.9(2) and Sched. 4, para. 1(2)(a).

Widespread provision is made for public registers of information relating to matters of environmental health under the Caravan Sites and Control of Development Act 1960,[6] the Control of Pollution Act 1974,[7] the Reservoirs Act 1975,[8] the Building Act 1984,[9] the Control of Pollution (Amendment) Act 1989,[10] the Environmental Protection Act,[11] the Water Industry Act,[12] the Water Resources Act[13] and the Land Drainage Act.[14] Closely allied to such public registers which, typically, will contain information on matters such as applications submitted and decisions made, as well as sampling results, are other "quasi-registers". These "quasi-registers" will contain categories of significant information whose generation is primarily the responsibility of NRA, the sewerage undertakers and the water undertakers. Included here are maps of waterworks[15] sewer maps,[16] maps of fresh water limits[17] and main river maps.[18]

The open nature of a regulatory process is to be seen far earlier, where publicity is a prerequisite to consideration of an application or other proposal under the governing legislation. Two very clear instances again arise from the Water Industry and Water Resources Acts. Under the first Act, any proposal for the fluoridation of water submitted by the district health authority requires that public consultation shall have been undertaken as a prerequisite to any decision on the matter.[19] The Water Resources Act contains two very significant instances of publicity requirements in relation to particular categories of application: first, any application for water abstraction requires publicity[20] and, secondly, any application for a licence to discharge to controlled waters requires public notification before any decision can be made by NRA.[21] The responsibility for publicity in the first case lies with the applicant, whereas in the second case the responsibility lies with NRA. Its responsibilities are quite extensive, and include a requirement for publicity in appropriate local newspapers, as well as a requirement for notification of various interested agencies, including local authorities.[22] However, the publicity requirement may be waived if NRA is of the opinion that the proposed discharges will have no appreciable effect on the receiving waters.[23]

[6] s.25, site licences.
[7] s.84, noise level registers.
[8] s.2, proposals for reservoir construction.
[9] s.56, various building control notices.
[10] ss.2 and 3, registration of carriers of controlled waste.
[11] ss.20–22, 64–66 and 112 and 123, in particular.
[12] s.196, trade effluent registers.
[13] ss.189 and 190.
[14] s.52.
[15] Water Industry Act, s.198; Water Resources Act, s.195.
[16] Water Industry Act, ss.199 and 200.
[17] Water Resources Act, s.192.
[18] *Ibid.* s.193.
[19] Water Industry Act, s.89.
[20] Water Resources Act, s.37.
[21] *Ibid.* Sched. 10.
[22] *Ibid.* para. 1(4).
[23] *Ibid.* para. 1(5).

In limited cases, the law may permit access to information, usually where (as seen previously) the information relates to trade secrets, for example, and therefore may be excluded from any public register that includes details of applications. A striking example relates to a provisional or full approval in respect of a pesticide. In these circumstances, the Ministers responsible may accede to a person's request and make available to him (subject to any conditions they may determine) an evaluation of the pesticide.[24]

The statutory template for the "open" systems described above usually sees a straightforward division between the primary legislation, which insists on the public availability of registered information generally, and the secondary legislation, which will usually prescribe how registers are to be kept, the precise categories of detailed information to be maintained and (perhaps) any qualifications to access not dealt with in the primary legislation.[25] In some instances, the enabling legislation can be very general, leaving the secondary legislation to prescribe a number of important, detailed matters.[26]

Open enforcement and performance-monitoring systems

Statutory information requirements in relation to enforcement and performance monitoring in many areas of environmental health fall into three broad categories; information availability may relate to anticipatory enforcement, enforcement "after the event" and "indirect" enforcement. The essence of information availability in anticipation of enforcement is that notification and publicity are prerequisites, which must occur before any action by the administrative agency in question. Information in aid of enforcement after the event may serve a number of purposes, as will be seen below, not the least of which is public recognition through publicity of infractions of the law. The third category of information availability emphasises the indirect contribution of information availability to the enforcement process.

Anticipatory enforcement

Whether what is intended is straightforward enforcement of statutory requirements or merely an adjustment of the terms for enforcement, statutory provision may be made for prior notification. For example, a local authority is empowered to prohibit caravans on commons and, copies of the prohibition order must be displayed on the land affected.[27] On the other hand, and again by way of example, any proposal to relax requirements enforceable under the Building Regulations is subject to a prerequisite of public advertisement.[28] The law may set the background for requirements which may eventually be

[24] Control of Pesticides Regulations 1986 (S.I. 1986 No. 1510), reg.8.
[25] See in particular the Control of Pollution (Registers) Regulations 1989 (S.I. 1989 No. 1160).
[26] See n.24, *supra*. *Cf.* the Food and Environment Protection Act 1985, s.16(2)(j).
[27] Caravan Sites and Control of Development Act 1960, s.23.
[28] Building Act 1984, s.10.

enforceable, as, for example, where a local authority may be required to maintain and compile public registers of information relating to contingency plans in respect of radiation emergencies.[29] The onus of responsibility for the supply of the required information will necessarily be spelt out in appropriate detail.[30]

Information may also be required from specifically identified persons for other purposes in the present context, as where those subject to the duty of care in waste management under Part II of the Environmental Protection Act are required to keep copies of waste and transfer notes and to furnish copies to the waste regulation authority if required.[31] The requirement to furnish copies does not appear to extend to any obligation to carry any consignment note in the course of transporting waste so as to be available immediately on demand.

In the same way as a local authority is required to display a prohibition order on common land where caravans are prohibited, so too a local authority may be required to provide notification of other types of finely targeted law enforcement. The Environmental Protection Act provisions on law enforcement, for example, allow a local authority to make designation orders for the establishment of litter control areas. However, a prerequisite is that those considered to be affected must be notified and given an opportunity to make representations.[32]

Although the majority of the present section on "open" systems is taken up with enforcement, there are other isolated provisions in the Water Industry Act that require water and sewerage undertakers to provide information to customers about overall performance, failures in respect of which may lead to enforcement of standards under that legislation.[33]

Enforcement after the event

Information concerning enforcement after the event may arise in a variety of different ways. There may, for example, be a requirement whereby a local authority is to notify certain individuals or organisations of the removal of abandoned motor vehicles.[34] In some instances, public information availability may be both anticipatory and prospective, as with the case of the maintenance of certain public records by water undertakers for the purposes of the Water Industry Act. These records relate to action taken—or required to be taken—by a water undertaker in relation to enforcement of the statutory domestic water supply duty.[35] A local authority is obliged to maintain a public register of dogs seized, including a record of the date and time of seizure.[36] Similarly, a local

[29] Public Information for Radiation Emergencies Regulations 1992 (S.I. 1992 No. 2997), regs.3 and 4.
[30] *Ibid.* reg.3.
[31] Environmental Protection (Duty of Care) Regulations 1991 (S.I. 1991 No. 2839), reg.4.
[32] Environmental Protection Act, s.90(6).
[33] Water Industry Act, ss.39A and 96A.
[34] Removal and Disposal of Vehicles Regulations 1986 (S.I. 1986 No. 183), reg.15.
[35] Water Supply (Water Quality) Regulations 1989 (S.I. 1989 No. 1147), regs.29–31.
[36] Environmental Protection (Stray Dogs) Regulations 1992 (S.I. 1992 No. 288).

authority is required to maintain a public register of litter control orders and litter control notices for the purposes of section 93 of the Environmental Protection Act.[37]

Perhaps the most prominent facility for enforcement information after the event is to be found in the provisions of the Environment and Safety Information Act 1988. This Act requires certain authorities to maintain public registers and to enter on those registers details of various enforcement devices resorted to under four Acts of Parliament. The authorities in question are:

(a) any fire authority (in connection with prohibition orders served on occupiers under section 10 of the Fire Precautions Act 1971);
(b) any enforcing authority (for the purpose of improvement and prohibition notices under the Health and Safety at Work Act 1974);
(c) any local authority (for the purpose of notices under section 10 of the Safety and Sports Grounds Act 1975); and
(d) "the responsible authority", normally the Minister of Agriculture (for the purposes of notices enforcing aspects of the law on pesticides under Part III of the Food and Environment Protection Act 1985).

Whatever the enforcement device registered here, the notice or order registered must be maintained on the register for a period of not less than three years. In the event of any withdrawal or amendment of a notice, there is a parallel requirement for "similar" withdrawal or amendment in respect of the register entry. Special time limits apply in the event of an appeal affecting the notice.[38] Particular protection is given in respect of information relating to a trade secret or a secret manufacturing process.[39]

Information availability and "indirect" enforcement

Information to be made available by statute may indirectly facilitate enforcement of environmental health requirements, usually because the objective of enforcement is not spelt out explicitly. Registers of contaminative uses under the Environmental Act could conceivably indicate the incidence of historical contaminative use sufficiently recent and proximate to suggest the statutory enforcement powers for site clean-up might be used against the present owner.[40] On the other hand, the Water Industry Act makes provision for the preparation of customer service committee reports for submission to the Director-General of Water Services who, in turn, may seek to enforce statutory requirements against particular water undertakers.[41] The pollution control registers under the Water Resources Act, referred to previously, require entry of information that may include evidence from samples taken, which (in turn) may of course be used in

[37] Environmental Protection Act, s.95.
[38] Environment and Safety Information Act, ss.2 and 3.
[39] *Ibid.* s.4.
[40] Environmental Protection Act, s.143.
[41] Water Industry Act, s.194.

the cause of enforcement by NRA.[42] Under the same Act, there are reciprocal obligations relating to the provision of information as between NRA and water undertakers in connection with water flow. Such information, again, would be available to NRA for enforcement purposes.[43]

On-site records and information management

A number of statutory provisions approach the matter of environmental monitoring by requiring that records are maintained (possibly on site) and available for scrutiny by the enforcing agency. In general, there are three possibilities. The statute in question may insist that records of information be maintained on site, or that data be collected and transferred to the enforcing agency, or that data be managed in some other way, perhaps in compliance with specific conditions in a licence.

On-site maintenance of information

Very few areas of environmental health legislation require on-site maintenance of information. The Control of Pollution (Special Waste) Regulations 1980[44] require that a producer or disposer of special, hazardous waste maintain consignment and other notes in a register on site, but not a carrier, although this does not necessarily mean that a carrier is obliged to have a note in his possession on a journey with subject waste.[45] Similarly, the Scrap Metal Dealers Act 1964 requires that every scrap metal dealer should maintain a record of scrap metal received and processed at each place occupied as a scrap metal store.[46]

The collection and transfer of information

The Reservoirs Act 1975 obliges any undertaker responsible for those reservoirs covered by the Act to maintain instruments on site for the recording of water level and similar information.[47] For similar enforcement purposes, the Transfrontier Shipment of Hazardous Waste Regulations 1988[48] required the retention of consignment and similar documents but not necessarily at any particular site, such were the transactions covered by the Regulations. To enable the enforcing agency to ensure compliance with overall legal requirements, the Sludge (Use in Agriculture) Regulations 1989[49] require any sludge producer to prepare and maintain a register containing prescribed particulars but not

[42] Water Resources Act, s.190.
[43] *Ibid.* s.197.
[44] S.I. 1980 No. 1709.
[45] *Ibid.* regs.13 and 14.
[46] Scrap Metal Dealers Act, s.2.
[47] Reservoirs Act, s.11. *Cf.* the Reservoirs Act 1975 (Registers, Reports and Records) Regulations 1985 (S.I. 1985 No. 177), reg.5 and Sched. 2.
[48] S.I. 1988 No. 1562, reg.10, in particular. See now the Transfrontier Shipment of Waste Regulations 1994 (S.I. 1994 No. 1137) and E.C. Regulation 259/93: [1993] O.J. L30.
[49] S.I. 1989 No. 1263, regs.6 and 7.

necessarily on any of its operational sites. The same lack of specificity is found in the Rag Flock and Other Filling Materials Act 1951, which merely requires the occupier of registered premises to keep records of filling materials stored at or processed through "registered premises": even those records do not have to be physically maintained at those premises.[50] The need to ensure that recorded data is available, albeit not at any particular set of premises, may be part of a larger network of environmental health control, as in the case of the duty of care in relation to waste management under Part II of the Environmental Protection Act. In that case, the transferor and transferee of controlled waste are obliged to keep a written description of the waste, together with transfer notes and copies thereof for a period of at least two years.[51]

The Clear Air Act 1993 specifically requires that an occupier of a building containing a furnace measure grit, dust and fumes emitted from that furnace. Thereafter, the data must be forwarded to the local authority.[52] An owner or occupier of land may wish to undertake information gathering that has wider significance than just his own undertaking. In these circumstances, there may be an obligation to advise the enforcing agency and to indicate where the records are to be kept. This is the case where a person wishes to install any gauge for measuring and recording the flow, level or volume of inland waters. This intention must be communicated to NRA, together with details of the whereabouts of the records kept.[53]

Data on matters of environmental health may be managed in various other ways, particularly where a condition attached to a licence stipulates particular requirements. Whether such a regulatory condition may require more than is stipulated already, either in primary or secondary legislation, may be problematic. Arguably, most environmental legislation is likely to be drafted in sufficiently wide terms to enable more stringent information requirements to apply, for example, by enabling the enforcing agency itself to organise data collection on the premises subject to control.

The Environmental Information Regulations

Background to the Regulations

The Environmental Information Regulations[54] seek to implement E.C. Directive 90/313,[54a] whose objective is to ensure freedom of access to, and dissemination of, information on the environment held by public authorities, and to set the terms and conditions on the availability of such information. The many

[50] s.14.
[51] Environmental Protection (Duty of Care) Regulations 1991 (S.I. 1991 No. 2839), reg.3.
[52] Clean Air Act, s.10, and the Clean Air (Measurement of Grit and Dust from Furnaces) Regulations 1971 (S.I. 1971 No. 161).
[53] Water Resources Act 1991, s.200.
[54] S.I. 1992 No. 3240.
[54a] [1990] O.J. L158.

provisions examined earlier in the present chapter contain a variety of approaches to the extent to which information may be available in relation to matters concerning environmental health. In so far as any such statutory provision—or rule of law—seeks to impose a restriction or prohibition on disclosure, the present Regulations effectively replace that restriction or prohibition with a more liberal disclosure requirement.[55] If, on the other hand, a pre-existing statutory requirement seeks to enable disclosure of information over and above that required under the present Regulations, that more generous requirement will prevail.[56]

Existing rights to information

Where, apart from the present Regulations, information is required to be made available to any person, arrangements must be made to ensure that that information request is responded to by reference to certain minimum standards. Accordingly:

(a) every request must be responded to as soon as possible;
(b) no request should be responded to later than two months after being made;
(c) any refusal of information should be made in writing with a statement of reasons; and
(d) no more than a "reasonable" charge should be made for provision of the information requested.[57]

The requirement to provide information on the environment

The central obligation under the Regulations requires "a relevant person" who holds any information covered to make that information available to every person who requests it.[58] "Relevant persons" are defined elsewhere in the Regulations.[59]

"Relevant persons" The Regulations divide this expression into two. Falling within the first category are all Ministers of the Crown, government departments, local authorities and other persons carrying out functions of public administration at a national, regional or local level whose functional responsibilities relate to the environment. The second category includes any body with public responsibilities for the environment outside the previous category, but which is nevertheless under the "control" of any body or individual in that first category.[60]

The second category just described is inevitably the more difficult to clarify, bearing in mind that although "control" (typically) will arise from a statutory

[55] S.I. 1992 No. 3240, reg.3(7).
[56] *Ibid.* reg.2(1)(c).
[57] *Ibid.* reg.5.
[58] *Ibid.* reg.3(1).
[59] *Ibid.* reg.2(3).
[60] *Ibid.*

relationship, it may arise (say) by contract or even by virtue of some unilateral transaction sufficiently recognised in law. Not surprisingly (given a clear statutory status), a body like NRA is included here, along with a water undertaker, bearing in mind the statutory control functions available in respect of a body that has very clear public responsibilties for the environment. The crucial issue here is whether any controlled body has "public" responsibilities for the environment. A company in government ownership, for example, may undertake environmental tasks for the government, even though those tasks are not at all referable to public responsibilities, which, no doubt, would remain with the relevant Ministry.

"Information relating to the environment" Information relates to the environment for present purposes if, and only if, it relates to any one of three categories.[61] The first category refers to the state of any water or air, the state of any flora or fauna, the state of any soil or the state of any natural site or other land. The second category relates to any activities or measures (including activities giving rise to noise or any other nuisance) which adversely affect anything in the first category or are likely adversely to affect anything in that category. The third category relates to any activities or administrative or other measures (including any environmental management programmes) designed to protect any of the environmental media mentioned in the first category.

Apart from the fundamental requirement that information relate to the environment, any information subject to the access arrangements described below must be held by a relevant person in an accessible form. "Information" for these purposes includes anything contained in any records. In turn, "records" are defined to include registers, reports and returns, as well as computer records and other records kept otherwise than in a document.[62] Even if information is not obtained as a result of a body's environmental responsibilities, it is assumed that it is governed by the present Regulations. Furthermore, the Regulations cover information collected before they came into force on December 31, 1992.[63] The Directive is marginally more specific than the Regulations, in identifying information format, referring to "... any available information in written, visual, aural or data-base form ...".[64] The Department of the Environment guidance adds that what is not included is "... non-existent information that could be created by manipulating existing information ... [and] does not include information destroyed in accordance with established office procedures".[65]

It appears that there are very few, if any, geographical limits on the information covered by the Regulations.[66] For the purposes of environmental health, it appears again that a potentially enormous field of information may be covered. When, for example, it is borne in mind that atmospheric media necessarily

[61] *Ibid.* reg.2(3)(a) and (b).
[62] *Ibid.* reg.2(1) and (4).
[63] "Guidance on the Implementation of the Environmental Information Regulations", (Department of the Environment, 1992), p.6.
[64] Directive 90/313, art.2(a).
[65] "Guidance on the Implementation of the Environmental Information Regulations", *op. cit.*
[66] *Ibid.* p.7.

include the air within buildings and other structures, it may be appreciated just how widely drawn the Regulations are. More broadly, though, the inter-relationship between humans and their environment necessarily leads to the presumption that, even indirectly, much information relating to matters of environmental health can be presumed to be covered by the Environmental Information Regulations.

The matrix of information actually or potentially covered for the purpose of the obligations under the Regulations must also take account of the "activities or measures" previously referred to. "Activities or measures" may cut both ways, either as beneficial activities or measures or as deleterious activities or measures. Whatever the impact of the information, it is clear that by no means all of it will exist as objectively determined fact. In these circumstances, the advice to the person responsible for generating information is that a disclaimer be issued as to the accuracy of the information.[67]

Information generation in practice

The directive indicates that information relating to the environment should be made available to any natural or legal person at his request and without any requirement for the proof of an interest. It is also indicated by the directive that Member States be obliged to define the practical arrangements under which information is "effectively" made available.[68] The Regulations themselves stipulate that the obligation to make information available shall not require it to be made available "... except in such form, and at such times and places, as may be reasonable".[69] In broad terms, there is considerable merit in any body or agency subject to an obligation of information disclosure under the Regulations to provide to the public at large general environmental information held as well as information about the arrangements in place to manage the process of access and disclosure. Reference was made previously in this chapter to general information availability, as well as the various statutory facilities providing powers to obtain and the duty to convey information. Both these facilities could usefully be considered for this purpose. However, one of the most visible sources of information is the public register as required under a variety of legislation already referred to. Regulation 3(5) just referred to requires, *inter alia*, that information about the environment may be made available in such form "... as may be reasonable". These words suggest a large measure of discretion in favour of the body obliged to make information available, whether from a public register or otherwise. It may be the case that sampling data, for example, exists in technical form on a public register. The difficulty here is in determining whether it is reasonable to expect the body obliged to release the information to provide a non-technical "translation" of the data, particularly in favour of an applicant without the resources to generate such a "translation". Despite the initial

[67] *Ibid.* p.8.
[68] *Ibid.* p.8. *Cf.* art.3(1) of Directive 90/313.
[69] Environmental Information Regulations, reg.3(5).

attraction of such an argument, it may be suggested that, apart from the risks of voluntarily accepting an interpretative role, all that the Regulations require is a generation of the information held by the body dealing with an application for disclosure. Nevertheless, there may be other occasions where, in dealing with disparate records and other related information, a deal of collation and editing is required. In this case, it could be seen to be both unreasonable—and impracticable—to require that such tasks be undertaken by an applicant.

Procedural limitations

Any body or agency covered by the Regulations is obliged to arrange that any request is responded to as soon as possible, that no request is responded to more than two months after being made and that, in the event of a refusal, that that refusal is in writing accompanied by reasons.[70]

Charges

The Regulations[71] allow any body or agency affected to impose a charge on an applicant in respect of the costs "reasonably attributable" to the supply of information. Furthermore, it is open to that body or agency to make the supply of any information conditional on the payment of a charge. However, it must be borne in mind that where public registers are concerned, there is no charge levied in respect of inspection, although a reasonable charge may be made for the provision of copies. If information concerning the environment is not found in a public register, it may not be unreasonable to require payment of a charge for any supply of that information. That charge will no doubt be reflective of the resources deployed to make the information available to the applicant.

Refusal of access

Reference was made previously to the unavailability of information relating to any judicial or legislative functions. Equally, the body or agency to which an application is made may refuse that application if the request is manifestly unreasonable or is formulated in too general a manner.[72] Otherwise, the Regulations also stipulate circumstances in which information relating to the environment may be treated as confidential and circumstances in which such information must be treated as being confidential.[73] Whatever the circumstances, if there is a refusal of access, nevertheless the body or agency in question must supply any related information which is capable of being separated from that which is incapable of disclosure.[74]

[70] *Ibid.* reg.3(2).
[71] *Ibid.* reg.3(4).
[72] *Ibid.* reg.3(3).
[73] *Ibid.* reg.4(2) and (3).
[74] *Ibid.* reg.4(4).

Discretionary refusals

The Regulations list five sets of circumstances in which a judgment can be made by a body or agency covered by the Regulations on the matter of whether particular information should be treated as being confidential. In some instances useful reference can be made to those situations dealt with previously,[75] in which the law prescribes a number of legitimate restrictions on the disclosure of information, particularly where the "vehicle" for that information is the public register. The fact that the present Regulations stipulate that some information is "capable of being treated as confidential"[76] confirms that reference must be made to any pre-existing state of affairs. Thus, for example, if by statute information is subject to scrutiny by a body or other agency with statutory environmental health responsibilities, it may be able to determine that a case for exclusion from a public register has been made out on (say) the ground of commercial confidentiality. A good illustration here is to be found in Part I of the Environmental Protection Act. Part I provides that it is for the enforcing authority to determine whether particular information would, if included in a public register, prejudice to an unreasonable degree the commercial interests of the individual seeking to sustain the claim for confidentiality.[77]

The first discretionary ground for refusal is that the information relate to matters affecting international relations, national defence or public security. This ground will no doubt be an exceptional ground for disclosure. Nevertheless, certain types of documentation are clearly comprehended in requiring a refusal of disclosure, classified documents in particular. It should be noticed from earlier in the present chapter that, again, there are familiar issues of public and national security that are required to be excluded from public registers under various Acts.[78]

The second discretionary ground refers to information relating to, or to anything which is or has been the subject-matter of, any legal or other proceedings, whether actual or prospective. "Legal or other proceedings" are defined to include any disciplinary proceedings, the proceedings at any local or other public inquiry and proceedings at any hearing provided for under a statutory provision to allow the parties to make representations or objections.[79] Some information will be caught, as a matter of discretion, by this category. Among many other matters of considerable difficulty will be the determination of whether to disclose information presently or prospectively associated with appeal proceedings culminating in a decision of the Secretary of State and with enforcement proceedings (say) by a local authority in relation to a matter of environmental health requirements.

The third discretionary ground concerns information relating to the

[75] See nn.77 to 88, *supra*.
[76] Environmental Information Regulations, reg.4(2).
[77] See n.81, *supra*.
[78] *e.g.* Environmental Protection Act, s.21: *cf.* n.81, *supra*.
[79] Environmental Information Regulations, reg.4(5).

confidential deliberations of any relevant person,[80] or to the contents of any internal communications of a body corporate or other undertaking or organisation. Of the many possible issues of disclosure contemplated here, one in particular may be fairly common and relates to the process of policy-making where normally, no doubt, papers prepared as part of that process would remain outside the categories of disclosure. Nevertheless, a possible example of a willingness to disclose could arise where there is a policy in favour of public participation, although even here there would probably be limits on the scope of such disclosure. The present matter has to be seen—at least in the case of local government—against the background of a further area of entitlement to information, provided for by the Local Government (Access to Information) Act 1985. Entitlement here is referable to an individual's right to attend meetings, so releasing for scrutiny papers—and background papers—in respect of council, committee and sub-committee meetings. Despite a number of exceptions and exemptions, there is no doubt that the present Regulations represent a significant addition to rights of access, at least as far as information relating to the environment is concerned.[81]

A fourth discretionary ground relates to information contained in a document or other record which is still in the course of completion. A number of problems remain here from the rather bland wording of the Regulations. In the first place, it is difficult in many instances to determine whether a "cohort" of information is complete for present purposes. Ultimately, this matter must be matter of judgment for the body or agency with the task of deciding on disclosure. One critical variable concerns information reliability and the need for caution in considering release of, as yet, incomplete information. If, as a matter of discretion, such incomplete information is released, no doubt an appropriate caution or qualification would be added. If, on the other hand, a body or agency subject to the Regulations is engaged in a programme of sampling or analysis, there would be some difficulty in refusing access to data collected by reference to the present ground. Nevertheless, there is a necessity here for recognition of the practicalities, which may mean periodic release of analyses, samples or other related information. Even here, though, careful consideration needs to be given to the format to be adopted for disclosure.

The final discretionary ground deals with information relating to matters to which any commercial or industrial confidentiality attaches, or affecting any intellectual property. Reference has been made already to those occasions when disclosure will not be possible by virtue of existing statutory restrictions. For present purposes, where there is a discretion available, a balanced "reasonable" view is required on the question of whether disclosure should be permitted. There is little doubt that any argument in favour of non-disclosure by virtue of possible damage to a business reputation could not be sustained. Earlier in the present chapter, it was seen that various statutory provisions allow an appeal, usually to the Secretary of State, on the issue of the status of information as

[80] As defined previously: *ibid.* reg.2(3). *Cf.* n.60, *supra.*

[81] Local Government Act 1972, s.100A(3) and Sched. 12A.

commercially confidential information. Clearly, such a facility may be very relevant for present purposes, indicating an equally clear need for delay in arriving at a decision for the purpose of the present Regulations.

Mandatory refusal

In four situations, information relating to the environment must be treated as being confidential. Accordingly, any application for disclosure must be refused, although, as ever, there is a requirement for reasons for any such refusal.

The first ground for mandatory refusal is very general in nature, relating to any information whose disclosure is prohibited or may be prohibited by statute or by virtue of any agreement. Accordingly, if contravention of any such statutory provision, rule of law or other agreement would arise on disclosure of information which falls within the categories listed previously in the section on discretionary refusal, there is justification for a mandatory refusal of disclosure. By way of an example, the Control of Pollution Act 1974 contains an offence, triable summarily, where a person discloses information relating to a trade secret obtained by virtue of the Act.[82]

The second ground refers to personal information held in records concerning an individual who has not consented to disclosure. However, as indicated previously, if a pre-existing statutory requirement seeks to enable disclosure of information over and above any requirements under the present Regulations, that disclosure requirement will prevail.[83] Reference was also made to the statutory requirement whereby a local authority should maintain a public register of dogs seized, including a record of the date and time of seizure as well as the name and address of the owner: a notable example under the Environmental Protection Act of a statutory exception to restrictions on disclosure of personal information.[84]

The third ground relates to information voluntarily disclosed. This ground relates to information held by a "relevant person" and supplied by a person who was not, and could not be subject to, an obligation of disclosure, information not supplied so as to allow disclosure except under the present Regulations, and information supplied without any consent to disclosure. The third element just mentioned is potentially the most controversial component of this third mandatory ground but is justified by reference to a need not to discourage the free, voluntary flow of environmental information. Present restrictions on disclosure will not normally apply where particular information is clearly required, usually as part of an open licensing system, referred to earlier. Accordingly, an application for a licence will necessarily be founded on information that must be part of the public domain. Equally, but more specifically, in the case of a provisional or full approval for a pesticide, the

[82] s.94(1). Note that this offence differs from those listed earlier in the chapter under the heading "Information enforcement offences" in dealing with enforcement against those purporting to act for the enforcing authority.

[83] See n.56, *supra*: Environmental Information Regulations, reg.2(1)(c).

[84] See n.36, *supra*.

Ministers responsible may accede to a person's request and make available to him (subject to any conditions they may determine) an evaluation of the pesticide.[85]

The final mandatory ground refers to any favourable response to an application for disclosure which would, in the circumstances, increase the likelihood of damage to the environment. Clear examples of prejudicial information here focus on nature conservation and (in particular) the identification of sensitive sites.

Challenges to adverse decisions

Reference was made earlier to the facility for a refusal of an application, expressly by reference to a conclusion that a request is manifestly unreasonable or that a request is formulated in too general a manner.[86] Remedies that may be available through a challenge to an adverse decision fall into two clear categories: remedies provided by law and extra-legal remedies. Where legal remedies are concerned, a first reference must be to a statement in the Regulations that (without prejudice to any remedies apart from the present provisions) the obligation to make information available is a duty owed to the person who has requested the information.[87] Such an obligation would, no doubt, be enforceable under R.S.C., Ord. 53, in proceedings for an order of mandamus. However, any such proceedings would necessarily depend on the identification of a sufficiently specific duty on the local authority or other agency to make the subject information available to the applicant. The other possibility is that there exists other statutory provision by virtue of which an alleged failure or refusal to supply information contrary to the terms of the Regulations is a ground of appeal, usually to the Secretary of State. Extra-legal remedies focus attention on the possibility of seeking a reconsideration of a decision or pursuing a complaint (in the case of a local authority) through a councillor. Finally, any one of the Ombudsmen may accept a complaint where there appears to be injustice in consequence of maladministration following an alleged failure to comply with the Regulations.

[85] See n.24, *supra*.
[86] Environmental Information Regulations, reg.3(3).
[87] *Ibid.* reg.3(6).

CHAPTER 10

STATUTORY NUISANCE

The Statutory Background

Successive Acts of Parliament have dealt with statutory nuisance through an expedited system of enforcement, the initiative for which has been in the hands of the local authority or a private individual aggrieved by the circumstances giving rise to the statutory nuisance. For many years, the essential focal point for legislative definition was the Public Health Act 1936 and, since 1990, the Environmental Protection Act. Until the arrival of the Environmental Protection Act on the statute book there were various piecemeal additions to the law governing statutory nuisances to be found in the Clean Air Acts 1956–68 and in Part III of the Control of Pollution Act 1974, dealing with atmospheric and noise nuisances, respectively. The new law to be found in the Act of 1990 owed more to the Part III provisions on statutory noise nuisances in the Control of Pollution Act than the Public Health Act provisions, in several important respects.

Although the law governing statutory nuisance is now largely unified in Part III of the Environmental Protection Act, that law is amended in some respects by the Noise and Statutory Nuisance Act 1993. There also remain outside the Environmental Protection Act a limited number of situations defined as statutory nuisances by the Public Health Act 1936 and referable to the procedures and other requirements of the Act of 1990.[1]

The Environmental Protection Act, Part III

Statutory nuisance

The Environmental Protection Act lists a number of situations which, in law, amount to statutory nuisance. It is the duty of a responsible local authority (principally a London borough council and a district council[2]) to cause its area to be inspected from time to time to detect any statutory nuisance which ought to be dealt with in summary proceedings[3] and, so far as is reasonably practicable,

[1] s.141 (any well, tank, cistern or water butt used for a domestic supply of water liable to contamination may be a statutory nuisance), s.259 (any pond, pool, ditch, gutter or watercourse may be in such a condition as to be a statutory nuisance); s.268 (any tent, van, shed or similar structure used for human habitation may be a statutory nuisance).

[2] Environmental Protection Act, s.79(7).

[3] *Ibid.* s.80.

investigate any complaint in respect of a statutory nuisance made by a person living in its area.[4]

The categories of statutory nuisance

Eight categories of statutory nuisance are found in the Act. Each category is dealt with in turn. Identification of a statutory nuisance will trigger the various processes in Part III of the Act through which a remedy may be sought either by an individual aggrieved by the alleged statutory nuisance or at the instance of the local authority in whose area the statutory nuisance occurs.

Premises in such a state has to be prejudicial to health or a nuisance[5]

This is the first and broadest category of statutory nuisance where the assumption is that it is "premises" that are prejudicial to health or a nuisance. "Premises" are defined as including land and any vessel apart from one powered by steam-reciprocating machinery.[6] There is little doubt, therefore, about the inclusion of a houseboat, for example. In *West Mersea Urban District Council v. Frazer,*[7] for example, it was held that, for the purposes of the Water Act 1945, a houseboat moored on mudflats and connected to a water main by means of a flexible pipe was "premises", given the degree of permanency. The Act also defined premises as including land and that, according to the judge, Lord Goddard C.J., "... means some form of property used as domestic premises ..." with some degree of permanency.[8] Sewers, on the other hand, have been held not to be premises, although the reasoning behind this conclusion is not convincing. In *Fulham Vestry v. London County Council,*[9] the court was dealing with the Public Health (London) Act 1891, which stipulated that if any watercourse or drain is so foul or in such a state as to be a nuisance or injurious to health, it is a nuisance to be dealt with summarily under the Act. The court held that the provision did not extend to public sewers, so that the justices had no jurisdiction to make a summary order. Day J. said:

> "The words used are particularly applicable to nuisances arising from what I may call private sources. What are contemplated are nuisances arising from the acts of owners of property, as distinguished from anything which may be caused by the construction of great public works, which are entrusted to the County Council."[10]

There appears now to be no compelling reason why there should be exclusion of

[4] *Ibid.* s.79(1). As to the Secretary of State's default powers, see Sched. 3, para. 4.
[5] *Ibid.* subs.(1)(a).
[6] *Ibid.* subss.(7) and (12).
[7] [1950] 2 K.B. 119.
[8] *Ibid.* at 123–124.
[9] [1897] 2 Q.B. 76.
[10] *Ibid.* at 78–79. *Cf. R. v. Parlby* (1889) 22 Q.B.D. 520.

statutory nuisances from premises in respect of which a local authority or, indeed, any other public authority carries out a public duty.[11]

Premises and land in their "natural" state may be regarded as "premises" for present purposes. In one case, though, the weathering of rock led to erosion so that rocks fell down a slope on the land in question. In the absence of any "artificial" intervention on the land (say) through quarrying or mining, the site of the rocks could not be regarded as "premises in such a state as to be a nuisance".[12] That land in its natural state would be open to description in law as premises in such a state as to be a nuisance may be exceptional. In *Noble v. Harrison*[13] an overhanging branch of a beech tree growing on the defendant's land—Buckingham Park, Old Shoreham—broke and fell on the plaintiff's vehicle, damaging it. The mere fact of the branch overhanging the highway did not render the land a nuisance. A different view might be taken where, for example, a defendant is in breach of a duty to take reasonable precautions to avert a danger of which he is aware in relation to the natural state of the land in question.[14] In all of these cases, the critical variable is likely to be found in the answer to the question whether the premises constitute a nuisance at common law.[15]

It is doubtful whether a street may be "premises" for present purposes, primarily by reference to a later category of statutory nuisance where noise is emitted from or caused by a vehicle, machinery or equipment in a street.[16]

The term "prejudicial to health" is defined to mean "... injurious, or likely to cause injury, to health".[17] The term "nuisance" is not defined by the Act and is dependent on the common law meaning of a public or private nuisance. Accordingly, a statutory nuisance will not exist where the acts complained of affect only the personal comfort of those occupying the premises where the so-called "nuisance" took place.[18] Where, for example, a landlord of a flat, in respect of which the rent is in arrear, makes no application for possession but removes the front door and windows so interfering (by means of harassment) with the personal comfort of the tenants, there can be no statutory nuisance. Although a statutory nuisance must in some sense be injurious to health, there must be evidence of circumstances "prejudicial to health" or a nuisance at common law. It seems likely, therefore, that the law would draw a distinction between, on the one hand, circumstances adversely affecting health and, on the other hand, circumstances threatening physical injury.[19] Adverse physical conditions in houses affected by condensation appear to fall within the phrase

[11] *R. v. Epping JJ., ex p. Burlinson* [1948] K.B. 79.
[12] *Pontardawe RDC v. Moore-Gwyn* [1929] 1 Ch. 656.
[13] [1926] 2 K.B. 332.
[14] *Leakey v. National Trust* [1980] 2 W.L.R. 65.
[15] *National Coal Board v. Thorne* [1976] 1 W.L.R. 543.
[16] Environmental Protection Act, s.79(1)(ga).
[17] *Ibid.* s.79(7).
[18] *Betts v. Penge UDC* [1942] 2 K.B. 154.
[19] *Coventry City Council v. McNally* [1973] 3 W.L.R. 87.

"prejudicial to health".[20] Similarly, where premises are not adequately insulated against noise generated, for example, by a nearby railway, there may be adequate evidence of conditions which are prejudicial to health.[21]

Smoke emitted from premises so as to be prejudicial to health or a nuisance[22]

Smoke as a statutory nuisance is dealt with under the Environmental Protection Act rather than the Clean Air Act. "Smoke" is defined to include soot, ash, grit and gritty particles emitted in smoke[23]: precisely the same terms as the definition appearing in the Clean Air Act 1993. There is a potential overlap between the present category of statutory nuisance and other categories referring to the emission of fumes and gases and dust, steam, smell or other effluvia arising on industrial, trade or business premises and being prejudicial to health or a nuisance, dealt with below.

The present provisions relating to smoke as a statutory nuisance do not apply to premises occupied on behalf of the Crown for naval, military or air force purposes, or for the purposes of the Ministry of Defence, or occupied by or for the purposes of a visiting force as defined by the Visiting Forces Act 1952.[24] Furthermore, the present statutory nuisance provisions do not apply to emissions of smoke in four specific situations listed by the Act. First, there is no statutory nuisance where smoke is emitted from the chimney of a private dwelling in a smoke control area declared under Part III of the Clean Air Act 1993.[25] Secondly, there is no statutory nuisance where dark smoke is emitted from the chimney of a building or a chimney serving the furnace of a boiler or industrial plant attached to a building or for the time being fixed to or installed on any land. The definition of "dark smoke" is taken from the Clean Air Act,[26] which refers to shade 2 on the Ringelmann Chart, even though a court may be satisfied that smoke is or is not "dark smoke" notwithstanding absence of any comparison in relation to the Ringelmann Chart.[27] Thirdly, there is no statutory nuisance where smoke is emitted from a railway locomotive steam engine.[28] Finally, there is no statutory nuisance where dark smoke is emitted otherwise than is described above in the second situation, from industrial or trade premises.[29]

If proceedings for smoke emitted from premises so as to be prejudicial to health or a nuisance might be instituted under Part I of the Environmental Protection

[20] *Greater London Council v. Tower Hamlets London Borough Council* (1983) 15 H.L.R. 57. *Cf.* s.189 of the Housing Act 1985, as amended, and Chap. 12, "Housing".

[21] *London Borough of Southwark v. Ince* (1989) 21 H.L.R. 504.

[22] Environmental Protection Act, s.79(1)(b).

[23] *Ibid.* subs.(7).

[24] *Ibid.* subs.(2).

[25] As to an offence of emitting smoke in these circumstances, see s.20 of the Clean Air Act.

[26] *Ibid.* s.3.

[27] *Ibid.* As to enforcement of requirements relating to dark smoke emissions, see Part I of the Clean Air Act, applying s.1.

[28] As to enforcement of requirements relating to emission of dark smoke in this case, see s.43 of the Clean Air Act, applying s.1.

[29] As to enforcement of requirements here, see s.2 of the Clean Air Act.

Act, a local authority is unable to institute summary proceedings without the consent of the Secretary of States.[30] It will often be a difficult matter of speculation whether Part I proceedings "might" be taken. Assuming that such proceedings might be taken, it appears that the present safeguard against an overlap of Parts I and III of the Act extends back to any summary proceedings that might be instituted by a local authority under section 80 and not just proceedings for enforcement that could lead to a summary conviction under the section.

Fumes or gases emitted from premises so as to be prejudicial to health or a nuisance[31]

As in the previous category of statutory nuisance, the present category is carefully defined in terms of its relationship both with Part I controls under the Act and local authority air pollution control in particular, as well as the other categories of statutory nuisance. "Fumes" are defined to mean any air-borne solid matter smaller than dust, while "gas" is stated to include vapour and moisture precipitated from vapour.[32] A very significant limitation of this category of statutory nuisance is that it does not apply to premises other than private dwellings.[33] It is likely that emissions in this category will be caught by the following category of statutory nuisance in the case of commercial or industrial premises, or be subject to local authority air pollution control under Part I of the Act.

Any dust, steam, smell or other effluvia arising on industrial, trade or business premises and being prejudicial to health or a nuisance[34]

"Dust" does not include dust emitted from a chimney as an ingredient of smoke which may be dealt with as a statutory nuisance under an earlier part of section 79.[35] The present statutory nuisance does not apply to steam emitted from a railway locomotive engine.[36] A further limitation is to be found in the fact that a local authority may not, without the consent of the Secretary of State, institute summary proceedings here if proceedings might be instituted under Part I of the Act relating (say) to local authority air pollution control.[37]

The present statutory nuisance dealing with dust, steam, smell or other effluvia[38] is the only category of statutory nuisance exclusively referable to "industrial, trade or business premises". A similar formulation of this statutory nuisance was considered—as section 92(1)(a) of the Public Health Act—in

[30] Environmental Protection Act, s.79(10).
[31] *Ibid.* subs.(1)(c).
[32] *Ibid.* subs.(7).
[33] *Ibid.* subs.(4).
[34] *Ibid.* subs.(1)(d).
[35] *Ibid.* subs.(1)(b): *cf.* subs.(7).
[36] *Ibid.* subs.(5).
[37] *Ibid.* subs.(10): *cf.* n.30, *supra.*
[38] As to the meaning of "effluvia", see *Malton Board of Health v. Malton Manure Co.* (1879) 4 Ex.D. 302.

Wivenhoe Port v. Colchester Borough Council,[39] where dust from the handling of soya meal being unloaded from a coaster was alleged to be a statutory nuisance.

Butler J. observed:

> "To be within the spirit of the Act a nuisance to be a statutory nuisance has to be one interfering materially with the personal comfort of the residents, in the sense that it materially affects their wellbeing although it might not be prejudicial to their health. Thus, dust falling on motor cars might cause inconvenience to their owners; it might even diminish the value of their motor cars; but it will not be a statutory nuisance. In the same way, dust falling on gardens or trees, or on stock held in a shop will not be a statutory nuisance. But dust in eyes or hair, even if not shown to be prejudicial to health, will be so as an interference with personal comfort."

The transition through which statutory nuisances are now provided for in an Environmental Protection Act rather than a Public Health Act may cast doubts on the views quoted from the learned judge. Such limited views would undoubtedly cut down quite severely the enforcement of statutory nuisances as elements of wider environmental standards in the community at large.

Any accumulation or deposit which is prejudicial to health or a nuisance[40]

This statutory nuisance reflects directly the predecessor provision in the Public Health Act.[41] It appears that this category of statutory nuisance depends on there being "... an accumulation of something which produces a threat to health in the sense of a threat of disease, vermin or the like".[42] Accordingly, it has been held that there is no statutory nuisance where there is an accumulation of inert matter such as building materials, scrap iron, broken glass and tin cans, merely because that matter may cause physical injury to persons coming on to the land and walking on it.[43] If, on the other hand, such an accumulation attracts vermin, for example, there may be created conditions that are prejudicial to health or even a nuisance.[44]

A number of older cases provide some guidance on matters of interpretation for present purposes. A pile of garden manure giving off smells and collecting a great number of flies has been held to be a nuisance.[45] Even sheep droppings on a pavement have been held to be a nuisance for the purposes of the Nuisances Removal Act 1855.[46] In *Smith v. Waghorn*,[47] it was held that a stableman who

[39] [1985] J.P.L. 396, affirming [1985] J.P.L. 175.

[40] Environmental Protection Act, s.79(1)(e).

[41] Public Health Act 1936, s.92(1)(c).

[42] *Coventry City Council v. Cartwright* [1975] 1 W.L.R. 845.

[43] *Cf.* local authority controls over accumulations of rubbish under the Public Health Act 1961, s.34, noted in Chap. 14, "Miscellaneous Controls".

[44] Note local authority controls under the Prevention of Damage by Pests Act 1949, noted in Chap. 14, "Miscellaneous Controls".

[45] *Bland v. Yates* (1914) 58 S.J. 612.

[46] *Draper v. Sperring* (1861) 10 C.B. (N.S.) 113.

[47] (1863) 27 J.P. 744.

accumulated dung so that neighbouring inhabitants had to shut their windows had been rightly convicted under a Local Act which imposed a penalty on offensive matter being kept so as to be a nuisance. An accumulation of seaweed in a harbour has been held to be a nuisance,[48] as has an accumulation of cinders emitting an offensive smell.[49]

Any animal kept in such a place or manner as to be prejudicial to health or a nuisance[50]

This category of statutory nuisance may well overlap with local byelaws, although rather more comprehensive facilities for the enforcement of statutory nuisances may discourage resort to byelaws. Such byelaws, provided for under section 235 of the Local Government Act 1972, may provide that "... no person shall keep within any premises any noisy animal which shall be or cause a serious nuisance to residents of the neighbourhood".[51]

The court's view of the predecessor provision—section 92(1)(b) of the Public Health Act 1936—was that an animal could not come within the Act merely because it was noisy[52] although this was subsequently doubted.[53] If cats stray because of the defective state of premises and create a nuisance, there may be a statutory nuisance for the purposes of the Environmental Protection Act.[54] Accordingly, any attempt to challenge enforcement action is likely to be unsuccessful since the present category of statutory nuisance is concerned with the condition of premises in which animals are kept: the defective premises themselves represent the nuisance for present purposes.[55]

Noise emitted from premises so as to be prejudicial to health or a nuisance[56]

Noise is defined to include vibration for present purposes.[57] As with other categories of statutory nuisance, it appears that noise may fall into the present category either because it is prejudicial to health or because it is a nuisance in the sense of interfering unduly with the comfort or convenience of neighbouring occupiers. It is a requirement of the present category that noise be emitted from "premises". In a case decided by reference to the noise nuisance provisions in sections 58 and 59 of the Control of Pollution Act 1974 (now repealed), it was held that the term "premises" did not cover noise made in streets or public places.[58] Subject to the next category of statutory nuisance, relating to noise emitted from or caused by a vehicle, machinery or equipment in a street, the term

[48] *Margate Pier and Harbour Co. v. Margate Town Council* (1869) 33 J.P. 437.
[49] *Bishop Auckland Local Board v. Bishop Auckland Iron and Steel Co.* (1882) 10 Q.B.D. 138.
[50] Environmental Protection Act 1990, s.79(1)(f).
[51] As to enforcement requirements, see *Phillips v. Crawford* (1984) 82 L.G.R. 199.
[52] *Galer v. Morrissey* [1955] 1 All E.R. 380.
[53] *Coventry City Council v. Cartwright* [1975] 1 W.L.R. 846.
[54] *R. v. Walden-Jones, ex p. Coton* [1963] Crim. L.R. 839.
[55] *Ibid.*
[56] Environmental Protection Act, s.79(1)(g).
[57] *Ibid.* subs.(7).
[58] (1984) 148 J.P. 123: [1984] J.P.L. 437.

"premises" is now defined to include land.[59] Despite this extension of the term, it may still be arguable whether noise made by a person or group of persons at large in a public place could be said to be "emitted from land". An important exception indicates that the present category of statutory nuisance does not apply to aircraft noise, other than model aircraft noise.[60] A further exception is that the present category does not apply to premises occupied on behalf of the Crown for naval, military or air force purposes or for the purposes of the Ministry of Defence, or occupied by or for the purposes of a visiting force, as defined by the Visiting Forces Act 1952.[61] Noise which affects premises, although emanating elsewhere, can make the premises affected themselves a statutory nuisance if the noise is such as to be injurious to health.[62]

Noise emitted from or caused by a vehicle, machinery or equipment in a street[63]

This category of statutory nuisance, introduced into the Act by the Noise and Statutory Nuisance Act 1993,[64] does not extend to noise made by traffic, by any naval, military or air force of the Crown or by a visiting force, by a political demonstration, or by a demonstration supporting or opposing a cause or campaign. The Public Order Act 1986[65] seeks to regulate public processions in any "public place". This latter expression defined by the Act[66] refers to "any highway", as well as any place to which at the material time the public or any section of the public has access, on payment or otherwise, as of right or by virtue of express or implied permission.

Hitherto, Part III of the Environmental Protection Act has defined the "person responsible" for a statutory nuisance as "... the person to whose act default or sufferance the nuisance is attributable".[67] This definition is extended to take account of the present category of statutory noise nuisances in the street. However, both in relation to any vehicle, and any machinery or equipment, the "person responsible" for a statutory noise nuisance is stated to include the person in whose name the vehicle is for the time being registered and any other person who is for the time being the driver and (where machinery or equipment is concerned) any person who is for the time being the operator thereof.[68]

The term "street" is now defined by the Environmental Protection Act[69] to mean a highway and any other road, footway, square or court that is for the time being open to the public. It has been held that an open space beneath a building

[59] Environmental Protection Act, s.79(7).
[60] *Ibid.* subs.(8).
[61] *Ibid.* subs.(2).
[62] *Southwark London Borough Council v. Ince* (1989) 153 J.P. 597.
[63] Environmental Protection Act, s.79(1)(ga).
[64] s.2.
[65] ss.11–16.
[66] Public Order Act, s.16.
[67] Environmental Protection Act, s.79(7).
[68] *Ibid.* as inserted by the Noise and Statutory Nuisance Act 1993, s.2(4).
[69] *Ibid.*

could, in appropriate circumstances, be described as a "square" and, when members of the public regularly go there for the purpose of attending a Sunday market, it may be regarded as a "street", being in the nature of a square open to the public.[70]

Any other matter declared by any enactment to be a statutory nuisance[71]

Included under this miscellaneous category are the following situations, involving:

(a) storage containers for water used for domestic purposes so constructed or kept as to render the water liable to contamination and to be prejudicial to health[72];
(b) any foul watercourse or a choked or silted watercourse which is prejudicial to health or a nuisance[73]; and
(c) any tent, shed or similar structure used for habitation which is so overcrowded or so deficient in sanitary accommodation as to be a nuisance or prejudicial to health.[74]

Unfenced mines and quarries may be a statutory nuisance for present purposes.[75]

The duty to inspect

Local authorities with responsibilities under Part III of the Act are subject to a duty to cause their areas to be inspected from time to time to detect statutory nuisances which ought to be dealt with under summary procedures described below.[76] Procedures are set out in the Act in the event of default, which may lead to a direction from the Secretary of State enforceable by mandamus, or an order transferring the function to himself.[77] In these circumstances it appears that the foregoing administrative remedies are exclusive, to the extent that they appear to exclude resort to "judicial" remedies before the court.[78]

The scope of a local authority's obligations to inspect its area is allied to its broader duties of enforcement under the Act and, when the authority's area includes part of the seashore, that is also taken to include the territorial sea lying seawards from that part of the shore.[79] Accordingly, any references in Part III to

[70] *Tower Hamlets London Borough Council v. Creitzman* (1985) 83 L.G.R. 72.
[71] Environmental Protection Act, s.79(1)(h).
[72] Public Health Act 1936, s.141.
[73] *Ibid.* s.259.
[74] *Ibid.* s.268(2).
[75] Mines and Quarries Act 1954, s.151.
[76] Environmental Protection Act, s.80.
[77] *Ibid.* Sched. 3, para. 4.
[78] *Pasmore v. Oswaldtwistle Urban District Council* [1898] A.C. 387.
[79] Environmental Protection Act, s.79(11).

"premises" and the "occupiers of premises" is taken to include a vessel and the master of a vessel, respectively.

Summary Proceedings for Statutory Nuisances

The Environmental Protection Act deals with summary proceedings in two parts, referring to local authorities' powers as well as the powers available to individuals who may be aggrieved by statutory nuisances.[80] Each of these two categories is examined in turn, taking account of the extension of the provisions of Part III to deal with noise that is prejudicial to health or a nuisance and which is emitted from or caused by a vehicle, machinery or equipment in a street.[81]

Summary proceedings by the local authority

If a local authority is satisfied that a statutory nuisance exists, or is likely to occur or recur, that authority is under a mandatory duty to serve an abatement notice imposing all or any of the following requirements:

(a) requiring abatement of the subject nuisance or prohibiting or restricting its occurrence or recurrence;
(b) requiring the execution of works;
(c) requiring the taking of such other steps as may be necessary for any of these purposes; and
(d) specifying the time or times within which the requirements of the notice are to be complied with.[82]

Significantly, this facility to serve an abatement notice extends not only to statutory nuisances that have occurred but also to such nuisances as are anticipated by the local authority.

The abatement notice

Although the responsible local authority appears to be subject to a mandatory duty to serve an abatement notice, as described above, it is by no means the case that statutory nuisance abatement necessarily takes precedence over other remedies such as those relating to unfit housing, as provided for by the Housing Act 1985.[83] If, following service of a notice, it is complied with promptly and correctly, but the nuisance re-occurs some considerable time later, the court may conclude that there is an entirely "new" statutory nuisance rather than failure to comply with the original notice.[84] Service of an abatement notice through the

[80] *Ibid.* ss.80, 81 and 82, respectively.
[81] *Ibid.* s.79(1)(ga), accompanied by amendments inserted by the Noise and Statutory Nuisance Act 1993.
[82] Environmental Protection Act, s.80(1).
[83] *Nottingham Corporation v. Newton* [1974] 1 W.L.R. 923.
[84] *Battersea Borough Council v. Goerg* (1906) 71 J.P. 11; *Greenwich Borough Council v. London County Council* (1912) 76 J.P. 267.

letter-box of the occupier of the subject premises is sufficient for present purposes.[85]

The Act beyond section 80(1) provides no guidance on the form of the abatement notice, although it must include a statement advising the person served of the availability of the right of appeal and the time limit for that appeal.[86] Despite a lack of prescription, it would appear that an abatement notice should identify unequivocally the statutory nuisance alleged and any measures required of the person on whom it is served.[87] An abatement notice will often prescribe works to be undertaken, although difficulties may be encountered if a local authority seeks to be too prescriptive in identifying how specific operations are to be undertaken. At the other end of the scale, it may be sufficient simply to require cessation of certain activities. In one instance, it was indicated by an abatement notice that the person served was keeping pigs in such a way as to create a statutory nuisance; not only did the abatement notice require cessation of the nuisance, it also required cessation of use of the premises for pig-keeping. The court concluded that the notice was effective and enforceable and could not be attacked on the ground that it required cessation of pig-keeping without indicating alternative methods of abating the statutory nuisance.[88]

Problems may arise in relation to party walls where an abatement notice is contemplated. In the absence of evidence to the contrary, such walls are deemed to be owned by the owners on either side, the wall being divided down the middle.[89] In such cases, it is often the practice to serve an abatement notice on each owner, specifying the works to be undertaken by each owner to abate the nuisance in question. The alternative approach, where each owner is served with a requirement that he undertake the whole of the work, is less satisfactory since, normally, a party wall is not jointly owned. Some guidance is available in the Act for present purposes, to the extent that, normally an abatement notice be served on the person responsible for the nuisance.[90]

However, if the nuisance arises from any defect of a structural character, the notice will be served on the owner of the premises. Alternatively, if a person responsible for a nuisance cannot be found or the nuisance has not yet occurred, the notice will be served either on the owner or the occupier.[91] If the local authority acts in default, the court may be asked to apportion the expenses.[92]

The person on whom the notice is served The foregoing provisions of the Environmental Protection Act take as their starting point "the person responsible" for a statutory nuisance, as defined elsewhere in the legislation. If

[85] *Lambeth London Borough Council v. Mullings* (1990) R.V.R. 259; *Cf.* Local Government Act 1972, s.233(1), (9).
[86] Environmental Protection Act, Sched. 3, para. 6. *Cf.* s.80(3).
[87] *Salford Corporation v. McNally* [1976] A.C. 379. *Cf. Network Housing Association Ltd v. Westminster City Council, The Times,* November 8, 1994.
[88] *McGillivray v. Stephenson* [1950] 1 All E.R. 942.
[89] Law of Property Act 1925, s.38.
[90] Environmental Protection Act, s.80(2).
[91] *Ibid.*
[92] *Ibid.* s.81(4).

more than one person is responsible, summary proceedings will apply to each, whether or not what any one of them is responsible for would by itself amount to a nuisance.[93] One immediate problem relates to an abatement notice served on a landlord either as the person responsible or because the nuisance arises from any defect of a structural character. If that landlord is prevented by an occupier from completing the works required, a complaint may be made to the magistrates' court which is able to order that occupier to permit the works in question.[94] There may be other circumstances, however, where the landlord (or even some other person served with an abatement notice) may require access to other land, in which case an access order may be sought from the court.[95]

The "person responsible" for a statutory nuisance is defined as that person to whose act, default or sufferance the nuisance is attributable.[96] The person to whose act the nuisance is attributable is the "wrongdoer" and therefore obliged to abate the nuisance, no matter what his status and despite the fact that he may unable to prevent continuation of the nuisance.[97] In these circumstances, the default powers of the local authority may provide the only practical remedy.[98] The fact that the person served with the abatement notice has a right in law to undertake the act in question is not necessarily conclusive.[99] An "act" for present purposes may be one of giving orders, as where, for example, the superintendent of a religious association giving shelter to the destitute in a chapel was held to be the "person responsible" through orders given to a caretaker.[1] To the extent that there is a breach of obligation, a person may be responsible for a statutory nuisance by default, either by virtue of contract or statute. The terms of a landlord–tenant relationship, for example, may indicate the nature of a default (say) in relation to disrepair. Only in relation to structural disrepair is the Act able to offer guidance about the person on whom a notice is to be served.[2] Taking account of this statutory guidance it appears that, normally, any matter not amounting to structural disrepair requires that an abatement notice is served on the tenant *qua* occupier. If the tenant has covenanted to do the repairs, he is liable to the exclusion of all others, and this is even if the nuisance existed when the tenancy began.[3] In the absence of a contractual obligation to repair, a landlord may be liable if he has reserved the right to carry out necessary repairs.[4] It may be implied that a landlord has reserved a right to enter premises to do repairs in the

[93] *Ibid.* ss.79(7) and 81(1): *Cf.* ss.80A and 81(1A), relating to a statutory nuisance under s.79(1)(ga) and requirements for service of an abatement notice where the person responsible may or may not be identifiable.

[94] Public Health Act 1936, s.289.

[95] Access to Neighbouring Land Act 1992.

[96] Environmental Protection Act, s.79(7).

[97] *Thompson v. Gibson* (1841) 7 M. & W. 456.

[98] Environmental Protection Act, s.81(3).

[99] *Riddell v. Spear* (1879) 43 J.P. 317.

[1] *R. v. Mead, ex p. Gates* (1895) 59 J.P. 150.

[2] Environmental Protection Act, s.80(2)(b).

[3] *Gwinnell v. Eamer* (1875) L.R. 10 C.P. 658.

[4] *Heape v. Ind Coope and Allsop Ltd* [1940] 2 K.B. 476.

case of a weekly tenancy.[5] In the absence of a contractual obligation to repair, a landlord will be liable if the nuisance exists at the time of the letting.[6] A landlord will also be liable if he lets premises for a specific purpose which gives rise to a nuisance.[7] Statutory provision is made for repairing obligations in the case of short leases for dwelling-houses.[8]

The foregoing commentary can only provide general guidance on the matter of who should be served with an abatement notice. On those occasions, when there appears to be a dispute about liability in relation to what is claimed to be a public sewer, for example, the court may not be able to enter an inquiry as to responsibility. Such a case might arise where a pipe is blocked by sewage, in circumstances where a person now served with an abatement notice claims a legal right to discharge into what is claimed to be a public sewer which, in turn, is raised as an issue before the court. The matter was approached thus in *Wincanton RDC v. Parsons*[9]:

> "If in such proceedings the local authority *bona fide* dispute their obligation to repair, the justices cannot inquire into the question upon whom the obligation lies, and, if satisfied that but for the defendant's discharge of sewage into the pipe the nuisance would not have arisen, are bound I think to deal with him as the person by whose act the nuisance was caused."[10]

If a number of premises share a drain, for example, but it appears to a local authority that the subject nuisance has arisen in one set of premises alone, the authority may serve an abatement notice on the owner of those premises if he is considered to be responsible for the nuisance. There is no necessity for the authority to seek out all the owners affected by a particular nuisance.[11]

The third term to be found in the meaning of the term "person responsible" refers to "sufferance", indicating, *inter alia*, that a person may be served with an abatement notice if he allows a statutory nuisance to arise or continue, consistent with the position at common law.[12] Accordingly, an occupier of land will be taken to have continued a nuisance if, with knowledge or presumed knowledge of its existence, he fails to take reasonable measures to bring it to an end with ample time so to do. Adoption of a nuisance occurs if the occupier makes use of any erection or artificial structure in the foregoing circumstances. Presumed knowledge for present purposes may be a matter of some difficulty. In *Leanse v. Egerton*,[13] a window in a house was broken in the course of an air raid on a Friday

[5] *Mint v. Good* [1951] 1 K.B. 517.
[6] *Todd v. Flight* (1860) 9 C.B. (N.S.) 377.
[7] *Harris v. James* (1876) 45 L.J.Q.B. 545.
[8] Landlord and Tenant Act 1985, s.11.
[9] [1905] 2 K.B. 34.
[10] *Ibid. per.* Kennedy J. at 38.
[11] *Nathan v. Rouse* [1905] 1 K.B. 527.
[12] *Sedleigh-Denfield v. O'Callaghan* [1940] A.C. 880.
[13] [1943] K.B. 323.

night. The plaintiff was injured by the broken glass on the following Tuesday. Although the house was uninhabited and there was found to be no actual knowledge on the part of the owner about the physical state of the premises, nevertheless it was held that the owner had presumed knowledge. Such a conclusion appears to be justified by the reference to the broad responsibilities of ownership allied to the likelihood of injury or damage occasioned by land or premises which constitute a statutory nuisance. Whether such reasoning may be extended to an occupier is rather more problematic although, arguably, knowledge or presumed knowledge of physical conditions may be sufficient to justify a conclusion that an occupier is a "person responsible" through sufferance.

It appears that the court has given a wide interpretation to the word "sufferance". It has been decided, for example, that the owner of a market was a person by whose sufferance a nuisance arose when sheep droppings caused a nuisance when the owner allowed the sheep to be penned in a street.[14] On some occasions, the court appears to confuse the words "default" and "sufferance", as in a case where a nuisance had arisen on land adjoining a river by flooding through a breach in the floodbank thereon. The owner was obliged to abate the nuisance, notwithstanding that, apart from the statutory provisions governing statutory nuisances, there was no obligation by contract or otherwise to maintain or repair the floodbank.[15] The court rejected any idea that liability to abate the nuisance depended upon an obligation to prevent the subject nuisance. Such an approach is an important reflection of the policy of the Act in seeking to deal with statutory nuisances effectively and flexibly, without reference to difficult issues of precise legal responsibility. Furtherance of this policy of the Act is to be seen in the *Wincanton* case, examined above,[16] and the *Rhymney Iron Co.* case, examined below. For the moment, though, the present case of flooding appears to have been decided by reference to a broad interpretation of the word "default", rather than through reliance on the term "sufferance". Arguably, both words may be apt to connote failure to execute an obligation which may not necessarily be founded in law.

Although now less of a problem than hitherto, a local authority may have some difficulty in identifying the person responsible for a statutory nuisance. If the person cannot be found, an abatement notice may be served on the owner or occupier of the subject premises.[17] A potentially important question centres on what action is expected of the enforcing local authority before it can claim that the person responsible "cannot be found". It appears that such a person cannot be found if he cannot be identified without considerable investigation. Coleridge J. said:

> "I do not think that the opening of a drain for the execution of the works which the statute enables the local authority to do is a condition precedent

[14] *Draper v. Sperring* (1861) 30 L.J.M.C. 225.
[15] *Clayton v. Sale UDC* [1926] 1 K.B. 415.
[16] *Wincanton RDC v. Parsons* [1905] 2 K.B. 34.
[17] Environmental Protection Act, s.80(2)(c).

to inability to find [the person responsible]. The object of the Act is to give power to cause the abatement of nuisances with as much dispatch as possible in the public interest, leaving the liability which is not concluded by the service of the notice to be determined when the magistrates are called upon to confirm or refuse the order . . . I am of opinion that it is sufficient to satisfy the meaning of the words 'cannot be found' if on inspection the cause of the nuisance cannot be found."[18]

Intimation notices

A local authority may serve an "intimation notice" before serving the formal statutory abatement notice. Such an intimation notice will advise the recipient of the requirements for abatement of a statutory nuisance. The fact that the intimation notice lacks legal formality means that, in turn, any compliance is purely voluntary. Any such voluntary act may bar recovery of expenses incurred as between landlord and tenant, for example.[19] An agreement between such parties may provide for reimbursement of "outgoings", a term that has been interpreted to exclude voluntary payments under an intimation notice.[20] If an intimation notice is served and complied with under compulsion, that fact may allow recovery by the plaintiff against the local authority where it is clear that there is no voluntary compliance by that plaintiff in respect of a responsibility that in fact and in law rested with that authority.[21] Channell J. observed:

> "In my opinion the case comes clearly within the class of cases in which the law implies a promise to pay. This is a well-recognised principle, and seems to me to apply clearly to cases of this sort, where a local authority, being liable to do certain work, say in effect to a private person that he must do it, meaning, that the private person is legally liable to do it . . . the law says that, as in these circumstances the local authority are putting pressure on the individual, a promise will be implied on the part of the local authority to reimburse the private person the cost he has incurred in doing the work for which the local authority were really legally liable."[22]

The same Judge placed great stress on the presence—or absence—of protest as the crucial variable determining the legal position of the person in receipt of an intimation notice. Reliance on such an arguably tenuous matter probably emphasises the doubtful merit of intimation notices. If the court has to deliberate on the status and effect in law of an intimation notice, it is far better to rely, it is

[18] *Rhymney Iron Co. v. Gelligaer District Council* [1917] 1 K.B. 589 at 597.
[19] *Harris v. Hickman* [1904] 1 K.B. 563.
[20] *Ibid.* following *Valpy v. St. Leonard's Wharf Co.* (1903) 1 L.G.R. 305, distinguishing *Andrew v. St. Olave's Board of Works* [1898] 1 Q.B. 755.
[21] *Wilson's Music and General Printing Co. v. Finsbury Borough Council* [1908] 1 K.B. 563.
[22] *Ibid.* at 566–567.

submitted, on the strict legalities. For example, recovery of expenses by a plaintiff against a public authority in the wake of an intimation notice might be far more satisfactorily achieved through reference to any legal responsibilities of the authority erroneously imposed by a notice on the plaintiff.[23] The same conclusion should be possible through service of an abatement notice.[24]

Time for compliance

An abatement notice must prescribe a reasonable period of time for compliance.[25] Such a statement must be seen in the context of the wide range of circumstances that may give rise to statutory nuisances. In some circumstances, an extremely short period of time for compliance may be regarded as being reasonable.[26] In other circumstances, involving (say) the prohibition of the recurrence of a noise nuisance, a much longer or even an "open-ended" requirement could be regarded as being reasonable.[27] A notice that requires that road-breaking equipment should not be used until fitted with effective noise dampeners without a stated date for compliance comes into effect at midnight following the date of service.[28]

Appeal

The Act provides that the person served with an abatement notice may appeal to the magistrates' court against that notice within a period of 21 days from the date of service. An appeal may be based on any one or more of nine grounds specified by the Statutory Nuisance (Appeals) Regulations 1990.[29] The grounds of appeal are as follows:

(a) that the notice is not justified by section 80;
(b) that there has been some informality, defect or error in, or in connection with the notice;
(c) that the authority has unreasonably refused to accept compliance with alternative requirements or that the requirements of the notice are otherwise unreasonable in character or extent or are unnecessary;
(d) that in respect of certain types of statutory nuisance[30] that best practicable means had been used to prevent or counteract the effects of the nuisance;
(e) that the notice should have been served on some other person;
(f) that the time specified for compliance was not reasonably sufficient for the purpose;

[23] *Silles v. Fulham Borough Council* [1903] 1 K.B. 829.
[24] *Sedleigh-Denfield v. O'Callaghan, supra.*
[25] *Bristol Corporation v. Sinnott* [1918] 1 Ch. 52.
[26] *Strathclyde Regional Council v. Tudhope* [1983] J.P.L. 536.
[27] *R. v. Birmingham JJ., ex p. Guppy* (1988) 152 J.P. 159.
[28] *Rhymney Iron Co.* case, *supra.*
[29] S.I. 1990 No. 2276, as amended by S.I. 1990 No. 2483. Proceedings are subject to the Magistrates' Courts Act 1980.
[30] Environmental Protection Act, s.79(1)(a), (b), (d), (e), (f) or (g).

(g) that, in the case of noise emitted from premises, requirements are more onerous than those presently in force under other notices in force under the Control of Pollution Act 1974[31]; and
(h) that the notice might lawfully have been served on some person in addition to the appellant.[32]

The court may dismiss an appeal based on some informality, defect or error if satisfied that it was not material.[33] If the ground of appeal refers to someone who should have been served instead of the appellant, or additionally to him, that appellant is obliged to serve a copy of his notice of appeal on any other person having an estate or interest in the premises in question.[34]

On appeal, the court may quash the notice, vary the notice in favour of the appellant in such manner as it thinks fit or dismiss the appeal.[35] On hearing the appeal, the court may make such order as it thinks fit in connection with a person who is to undertake any work, and in connection with the contribution to be made to that work by any person, or the apportionment of any expenses to be borne by the authority as between the appellant and any other person.[36] Significantly for these purposes, the court is obliged as between an owner and occupier, to have regard to any contractual or statutory terms of a tenancy, as well as the nature of the works required. Furthermore, the court is obliged to be satisfied that a copy of the notice of appeal has been served on a person before imposing any of the foregoing requirements on such a person.[37]

In some circumstances, an abatement notice will be suspended until an appeal has been abandoned or decided by the court. However, if the nuisance is injurious to health or is likely to be of limited duration, or any expenditure incurred in compliance with the notice would not be disproportionate to any anticipated public benefit, and the notice states the existence of these circumstances, no suspension occurs. Where expenditure is incurred in securing compliance or (where noise is emitted from premises) there is performance of a duty imposed by law, suspension will occur.[38] In proceedings on appeal in respect of an alleged noise nuisance under the pre-existing provisions of the Control of Pollution Act it was held that the facts must be assessed by the court at the date of the hearing and not at the date of service of the abatement notice.[38a]

[31] ss.60, 61, 65, 66 and 67.
[32] Statutory Nuisance (Appeals) Regulations, reg.2(2).
[33] *Ibid.* reg.2(3).
[34] *Ibid.* reg.2(4).
[35] *Ibid.* reg.2(5). An appeal lies to the Crown Court: Environmental Protection Act, Sched. 3, para. 3.
[36] Statutory Nuisance (Appeals) Regulations, reg.2(6).
[37] *Ibid.* reg.2(7).
[38] *Ibid.* reg.3.
[38a] *Johnsons News of London v. Ealing London Borough Council* (1989) 154 J.P. 33.

Contravention of or failure to comply with a notice

Failure to comply with an abatement notice without reasonable excuse is an offence. "Reasonable excuse" has been argued as a defence in proceedings relating to statutory nuisance under the former Public Health Act provisions in *Saddleworth UDC v. Aggregate and Sand.*[39] The argument was that an expert had advised that certain works be undertaken but the fact that funds were exhausted prior to completion attracted the defence of reasonable excuse. The Divisional Court rejected the argument that a lack of finance was a reasonable excuse. Furthermore, the court considered that the reliance on independent advice was capable of being a defence only with great difficulty where the adviser's recommendations had not been implemented. It is important also to distinguish between what may be considered to be a reasonable excuse and a matter that may be regarded in terms only of mitigation. For example, a birthday celebration was not a reasonable excuse for a noise nuisance in one case.[40] A notice was served on the respondent in 1985 but the birthday celebration occurred three years later, in 1988. A variety of matters were found to be under the respondent's control and, although they may have been factors going to mitigation, they did not amount to a reasonable excuse. Accordingly, reasonable excuse may operate as a defence where matters are effectively beyond the control of the defendant.

In considering whether there is contravention of or failure to comply with an abatement notice where, for example, it is alleged that noise amounting to a nuisance has occurred or recurred, the prosecution is not necessarily required to establish that a particular occupier of property has actually suffered interference with reasonable enjoyment of his property.[41] There is no prerequisite as to the evidence to be offered to the magistrates.[42] A noise nuisance may be established on other evidence, such as expert evidence, if there is absence of admissible evidence from an occupier. An environmental health officer may introduce evidence based on decibel levels without a need necessarily to call the occupier in question. However, if the magistrates are not satisfied beyond reasonable doubt after hearing evidence from the environmental health officer, there is justification for dismissal of the information. In the event of a conviction, there are differential penalties, with more severe penalties applicable if a person commits the offence of contravening or failing to comply with a notice without reasonable excuse on industrial, trade or business premises.[43] Such premises are defined as premises used for any industrial, trade or business purposes or premises not so used on which matter is burnt in connection with any industrial, trade or business process.[44] Furthermore, premises are regarded as being used for industrial purposes where

[39] (1970) S.J. 931.
[40] *Wellingborough Borough Council v. Gordon* [1993] Env.L.R. 218.
[41] *Cooke v. Adatia* (1989) 153 J.P. 129.
[42] *Ibid.*
[43] Environmental Protection Act, s.80(5), (6).
[44] *Ibid.* s.79(7).

they are used for the purpose of any treatment or process as well as being used for manufacturing purposes.[45]

Where proceedings are taken in respect of contravention of or failure to comply with an abatement notice, certain additional defences are provided where the statutory nuisance comprises noise emitted from premises so as to be prejudicial to health or a nuisance, or noise emitted from or caused by a vehicle, machinery or equipment in a street.[46] The additional defences recognise that a person may well have a consent for the generation of noise in particular circumstances, thus avoiding a need to take enforcement action under Part III of the Environmental Protection Act.[47] Accordingly, a defence is available if any of the following measures are in place by virtue of the provisions of the Control of Pollution Act 1974 relating to construction sites, noise reduction notices and noise limits in respect of new buildings.[48]

Best practicable means

If criminal proceedings are taken in respect of a person's contravention of or failure to comply with an abatement notice, it is a defence to prove that the best practicable means were used to prevent, or to counteract the effects of, the nuisance.[49] However, the Act stipulates that this defence is not available in a variety of circumstances. First, the defence is not available if the nuisance falls into one of five categories of statutory nuisance described previously.[50] However, in so far as the nuisance arose on industrial, trade or business premises, the defence will be available.[51] Furthermore, the defence is not available in respect of noise that is prejudicial to health or a nuisance and which is emitted from or caused by a vehicle, machinery or equipment unless it is being used for industrial, trade or business purposes.[52] Secondly, the defence is not available in respect of a nuisance where smoke is emitted from premises, so as to be prejudicial to health or a nuisance, unless the smoke is emitted from a chimney.[53] Finally, the defence is not available in the case of a nuisance where fumes or gases are emitted from premises so as to be prejudicial to health or a nuisance in respect of any other matter declared by any enactment to be a statutory nuisance.[54]

The defence of best practicable means is potentially widely available in relation to industrial, trade or business premises, particularly in view of its status as a ground of appeal against an abatement notice.[55] The fact that the defence is not available in respect of fumes or gases emitted from premises so as to be prejudicial

[45] *Ibid.*
[46] *Ibid.* subs.(1)(g), 1(ga).
[47] *Ibid.* s.80(9).
[48] Control of Pollution Act 1974, ss.60, 61, 65, 66, and 67: *cf.* Chap. 8, "Noise Pollution".
[49] Environmental Protection Act, s.80(7).
[50] See nn.5, 34, 40, 50 and 56, *supra.*
[51] Environmental Protection Act, s.80(8)(a).
[52] *Ibid.* subs.(8), as amended by the Noise and Statutory Nuisance Act 1993, s.3(4).
[53] *Ibid.* subs.(8)(b), referring to s.79(1)(b).
[54] *Ibid.* subs.(8)(c), referring to s.79(1)(c) and (h), respectively.
[55] See n.32, *supra.*

to health or a nuisance indicates what may be a greater incidence of hazards in these circumstances, requiring stricter controls. Although the consent of the Secretary of State is required before the institution of summary proceedings by a local authority in respect of statutory nuisances defined by section 79(1)(b), (d) or (e),[56] if proceedings might be instituted under Part I of the Environmental Protection Act 1990 it is noticeable that this restriction does not operate in respect of fumes or gases emitted from premises under section 79(1)(c).

The meaning of "best practicable means" The Environmental Protection Act requires that "best practicable means" is interpreted by reference to four factors.[57] The first factor refers to the word "practicable" as meaning reasonably practicable having regard to *inter alia*, local conditions and circumstances and the current state of technical knowledge, as well as the financial implications. The second factor relates to the means to be employed, which may include the design, installation, maintenance and manner and periods of operation of plant and machinery, as well as the design, construction and maintenance of buildings and "structures". The third factor indicates that the test of best practicable means is to apply only so far as compatible with any duty imposed by law. Finally, the Act indicates that the test is to apply only so far as compatible with safety and safe working conditions and with the exigencies of any emergency or unforeseeable circumstances.[58] If a code of practice has been approved under section 71 of the Control of Pollution Act 1974 in connection with noise minimisation, regard may be had to that code in determining best practicable means.

In relative terms, it is not enough that precautions ordinarily adopted in the trade are in place: what is required are the best available means in order to secure the measures necessary by law.[59] The defence was in issue in *Wivenhoe Port v. Colchester Borough Council*,[60] where the claim was made that adoption of vacuum machinery for the avoidance of dust nuisance would render the industrial operation uneconomic. The court stressed that, while profitability is a relevant factor for present purposes, the onus of proof lies on the defendant. The mere incidence of increased expenditure or lack of profitability is not, *per se*, sufficient to establish the defence of best practicable means. The onus on the defendant is to show that, on the balance of probabilities, reasonable, practicable means have been adopted to prevent or counter the effect of noise, for example, emanating from the subject premises. In one instance, an application was made for planning permission to build noise-reducing structures following service of an abatement notice. No reply was forthcoming from the defendant when, subsequently, there

[56] See nn.22, 34 and 40, *supra*.
[57] Environmental Protection Act, s.79(7).
[58] (1984) 148 J.P. 123: [1984] J.P.L. 437.
[59] *Scholefield v. Schunk* (1855) 19 J.P. 84, a case decided by reference to similar provisions in the Factories Act 1844.
[60] [1985] J.P.L. 175, affirmed [1985] J.P.L. 396.

was a request for further information made by the local authority. In these circumstances, it was held that the defence was not available.[61]

Abatement notices in respect of noise in streets

Special provision is made in section 80 of the Environmental Protection Act for abatement notices in relation to noise in streets as defined by section 79(1)(ga).[62] An abatement notice in this context is available only where the subject statutory nuisance has not yet occurred, or arises from noise emitted from or caused by an unattended vehicle or unattended machinery or equipment.[63] Any other situation will continue to be governed by abatement notices as defined and analysed previously. The law in the present context is largely preoccupied with the circumstances in which the person responsible cannot be found and the notice is fixed to the vehicle, machinery or equipment. Otherwise, an abatement notice should be served on the person responsible for the vehicle, where that person can be found. The alternative chosen by a local authority suggests a discretion exercisable where, despite discovery of the person responsible, service may not be satisfactorily achieved for a variety of reasons, such as resistance on the part of the person to be served. Nevertheless, if the person responsible can be found within an hour of the notices being fixed to the vehicle, machinery or equipment, the local authority is obliged to serve a copy of the notice on that person.[64]

No form of notice is prescribed and no form may be prescribed: regulations for this purpose are not provided for. Nevertheless, the notice must include a statement advising the recipient of the right of appeal referred to previously.[65]

Enforcement

Where more than one person is responsible for a statutory nuisance, action may be taken against each person, regardless of whether or not the matter for which each is responsible would, taken in isolation, constitute a statutory nuisance.[66] Identification of a "person responsible" is necessarily the starting point for enforcement processes under the Act.[67] Separate provision is made by the Act for the purposes of determining service of an abatement notice where more than one person is responsible for a statutory nuisance arising from noise that is prejudicial to health or a nuisance and emitted from or caused by a vehicle, machinery or equipment in a street.[68] In these circumstances, it is now provided that an abatement notice may be served on anyone of the persons responsible for the

[61] *Chapman v. Gosberton Farm Produce Co. Ltd* [1992] C.O.D. 486.
[62] Environmental Protection Act, s.80A, as inserted by s.3(6) of the Noise and Statutory Nuisance Act 1993.
[63] *Ibid.* s.80A(1).
[64] *Ibid.* subs.(3).
[65] *Ibid.* Sched. 3, para. 6 and *cf.* nn.29–38, *supra.*
[67] *Ibid.* s.80(2)(a) and *cf.* n.93, *supra.*
[68] *Ibid.* s.79(1)(ga).

statutory nuisance.[69] If the statutory nuisance is attributable to noise emitted from or caused by an unattended vehicle or unattended machinery or equipment for which more than one person is responsible, the local authority has a discretion in identifying the person responsible.[70]

A local authority is empowered to act in respect of a statutory nuisance wholly or partly caused by some act or default occurring outside its area as if the occurrence was within its area. However, this is without prejudice to the requirement for any appeal to be dealt with by a magistrates' court having jurisdiction in the area where, it is alleged, the act or default occurred.[71] In principle, there seems to be no objection to statutory nuisance proceedings being involved where a local authority itself is the defendant.[72]

If an abatement notice has not been complied with, a local authority may abate the nuisance and do whatever may be necessary in execution of the notice whether or not criminal proceedings have been pursued under section 80(4) of the Act.[73] In abating or preventing the recurrence of a statutory nuisance here, the local authority may recover any expenses reasonably incurred from the person by whose act or default the nuisance was caused. If that person is the owner of premises, recovery will be against that person. Furthermore, the court may apportion the expenses between persons "... in such manner as the court considers fair and reasonable".[74] In some circumstances, it may be possible to exclude a power of apportionment in a lease.[75]

An amendment to the Environmental Protection Act[76] re-introduces the old Public Health Act facility for the imposition of a charge on premises as a means by which a local authority may recover its expenses for action in default following non-compliance with an abatement notice. Additionally, a facility for payment by instalments is made available where expenses are a charge on the subject property.[77] If expenses are recoverable from the owner of the premises, a notice initiates the process of recovery by charge. In the event of a change of ownership, a fresh notice would be appropriate. There is no time limit in respect of a demand or, indeed, on the number of demands that may be made.[78] In order that the powers of the section can apply, liability for repayment of expenses can only fall on the owner for the time being of the subject premises, so that liability "runs with the land". In these circumstances, there is no defence and certainly no ground of appeal that some other person such as a tenant under a tenancy agreement is liable. If that is the case, the matter is one that arises between the owner and a tenant or, indeed, any other party who may be involved. The

[69] *Ibid.* s.81(1A).
[70] *Ibid.* ss.80A and 81(1B).
[71] *Ibid.* 81(2).
[72] Public Health Act 1936, s.141.
[73] *Ibid.* s.259.
[74] *Ibid.* subs.(4).
[75] *Monro v. Lord Burghclere* [1918] 1 K.B. 291.
[76] ss.81A and 81B, introduced by the Noise and Statutory Nuisance Act 1993, s.10.
[77] *Ibid.* s.81B.
[78] *Dennerley v. Prestwich UDC* [1930] 1 K.B. 334. *Cf.* s.81A(3).

Environmental Protection Act[79] requires that any notice initiating recovery of expenses shall be served not only on the owner but also on every other person who, to the knowledge of the local authority, has an interest in the premises capable of being affected by the charge. This requirement of "knowledge" does not appear to impose an onerous obligation and it seems unlikely, for example, that a local authority would necessarily know of the presence of a weekly tenant. Equally, it is probably the case that such a minor interest is unlikely to be ". . . capable of being affected by the charge".[80] Otherwise, the present provision stipulates no time limit for service of a notice. The amount of any expenses specified in a notice and the accrued interest is a charge on the premises in question.[81] However, there are time limits before which a charge will not be enforceable.[82] It might have been expected that a charge should run from the date of completion of works rather than from a date referable to service of the notice under section 81A. Any charge is imposed on the property rather than any particular interest in it.[83] However, it seems unlikely that any such charge would adversely affect or override a covenant restricting use of the land charged for the benefit of an adjoining owner.[84] Such a conclusion rests on the straightforward proposition that what is amenable to a charge for present purposes are the premises of the owner in default.

Charges for the recovery of expenses now provided for under the Environmental Protection Act are registrable on the local land charges register. Charges take effect when registered as if they were created by a deed of charge by way of a legal mortgage but without prejudice to matters of priority.[85] Both the Environmental Protection Act[86] and the Law of Property Act 1925[87] stipulate powers available to a local authority for present purposes, including a power of sale, which may be in priority to earlier mortgages.[88] If such a "monetary" charge is to be enforced by sale, a substantive registration should be sought at the outset so that there can be no doubt about exercise of that power of sale by the local authority as proprietor of the subject charge. Failure to register in certain circumstances may not affect enforceability of the charge but will affect compensation.[89] In the absence of any document of charge, reference should be made to the Land Registry with a fully authenticated copy of the council's resolution, with a view to dispensation from statutory requirements on production of the charge certificate. Any claims to priority, for example, should be clearly articulated in these circumstances.

[79] s.81A(3).
[80] *Ibid.*
[81] *Ibid.* subs.(4).
[82] *Ibid.*
[83] *Tottenham Local Board of Health v. Rowell* (1880) 15 Ch.D. 378.
[84] *Guardians of Tendring Union v. Dowton* [1891] 2 Ch. 265.
[85] Local Land Charges Act 1975, s.7.
[86] s.81A(8).
[87] s.101.
[88] *Paddington Borough Council v. Finucane* [1928] Ch. 567.
[89] Local Land Charges Act 1975, s.10.

Finally, in the present context, caution is required on the part of a local authority seeking to recover expenses. It is likely that the law will insist that any expenses be reasonably incurred, suggesting a need for practical measures in favour of competitive tendering and timely execution of any necessary work.

Summary proceedings by persons aggrieved

The Environmental Protection Act repeats in broadly similar terms provisions which extend summary proceedings to individuals aggrieved by statutory nuisances. The Act of 1980 allows any person aggrieved by a statutory nuisance to complain to a magistrates' court directly. On a complaint, the court may require abatement of the nuisance or prohibition of its recurrence and may also impose a fine. Criminal enforcement occurs where there is failure to comply with any requirement or prohibition found in an order of the court, but subject to the defence of reasonable excuse seen previously in the enforcement facilities available to local authorities taking summary action. Also available in relation to summary proceedings by an individual is the defence of best practicable means, but not in the case of proceedings affecting all statutory nuisances.[90]

Magistrates' power to act on a complaint

Although summary proceedings were available under the now repealed provisions of section 59 of the Control of Pollution Act 1974, the present facility in section 82 extends far more widely and is not limited to an occupier of premises. A person whose health or that of his family is adversely affected clearly falls within the provisions of the present section.[91] In fact, there are probably very few restrictions on the categories of "persons aggrieved". One helpful approach for present purposes is to notice the terms on which particular statutory nuisances are defined and to take account of the following words of Lord Fraser in *Inland Revenue Commissioners v. National Federation of Self-Employed and Small Businesses Ltd*:

> "The correct approach in such a case is . . . to look at the statute under which the duty arises, and to see whether it gives any express or implied right to persons in the position of the applicant to complain of the alleged unlawful act or omission."[92]

In *Birmingham District Council v. McMahon*,[93] it was held that a council tenant in a block of flats who complained of a statutory nuisance affecting the block in general, but not his flat, was not a "person aggrieved". This decision suggests the importance of considering one further factor in relation to the categories of

[90] Environmental Protection Act, s.82.
[91] *Sandwell Metropolitan Borough Council v. Bujok* [1990] 3 All E.R. 385.
[92] [1981] 2 W.L.R. 722, H.L.
[93] (1987) 151 J.P. 709.

statutory nuisance, concerning the requirement for any such statutory nuisance to be "prejudicial to health or nuisance".

Proceedings against local authorities

Reference has been made earlier to authority for the proposition that proceedings may be taken against a local authority.[94] The powers in section 82 and its predecessor in the Public Health Act 1936 were used and continue to be used extensively against local authorities in housing cases. Such action is usually taken by reference to attempts to require a landlord to carry out repairs or to remedy defects resulting in problems such as excessive condensation or inadequate sound insulation. The fact that a local authority tenant may be able to enforce covenants in the tenancy agreement by virtue of section 11 of the Landlord and Tenant Act 1985 will not necessarily preclude statutory nuisance proceedings.[94a] In one case,[95] the House of Lords was told that the authority in question had been served with no less than 632 summonses under the former section 99 of the Public Health Act 1936 over a period of two years since June 1988.

Civil or criminal proceedings

Where proceedings were taken under the former section 99 of the Public Health Act 1936, it was always possible that a fine would be available in addition to a nuisance order. Because these proceedings were initiated by information and summons rather than by complaint, they were characterised as being criminal rather than civil. The format of section 82 now refers to proceedings by way of complaint, thus confusing the true nature of such proceedings. Nevertheless, there is under subsection (2) a power to permit the magistrates' court to impose a fine as well as making an order for the abatement of the statutory nuisance or prohibiting its recurrence. Given the criminal character of the proceedings, legal aid may be available.[96] The court also has jurisdiction to make a compensation order under section 35 of the Powers of Criminal Courts Act 1973.[96a]

Matters to be identified in a section 82 complaint

In the case of summary proceedings under section 99 of the Public Health Act 1936, the law's expectation was that the detail behind the information would be comparable with the detail to be found in any abatement notice, referable to the defendant's capacity in relation to the proceedings and also in relation to the remedial steps required to address the statutory nuisance.[97] However, the court

[94] See n.72, *supra*.
[94a] *R. v. Highbury Corner Magistrates' Court, ex p. Edwards* [1994] Env.L.R. 214.
[95] See *Bujok*'s case, *supra*.
[96] *R. v. Inner London Crown Court, ex p. Bentham* [1989] 1 W.L.R. 408: note that s.28(5) of the Legal Aid Act 1974 was in issue here. The successor provision—s.21(1) of the Legal Aid Act 1988—would probably have yielded the same conclusion.
[96a] *Botross v. Hammersmith and Fulham London Borough Council, The Times*, November 7, 1994.
[97] *Warner v. Lambeth London Borough Council* (1984) 15 H.L.R. 42.

has taken the view previously, again in relation to proceedings under section 99 of the Public Health Act 1936, that a failure to give "proper" particulars did not necessarily vitiate the information such as to oblige the justices to dismiss it.[98] The court confirmed the discretion of the justices to amend or modify the information within certain limits. On the facts, the court concluded that the local authority was able to ascertain what was alleged. Having allowed an amendment to the schedule of works—in favour of the local authority—the justices offered an adjournment, which the authority refused.[99] It seems likely that these prescriptions would apply equally to summary proceedings under section 82.

The nuisance order

The facility provided by section 82 is narrower than that provided by section 80, to the extent that summary proceedings by an individual can only relate to a statutory nuisance that exists. In these proceedings, the magistrates' court is empowered to make a nuisance order for either or both of two purposes in circumstances where the statutory nuisance exists or, although abated, is likely to recur on the same premises: the magistrates' court may make an order for the purpose of requiring the defendant to abate the nuisance within a period of time specified by the order and to execute any works necessary for the purpose, and it may also make an order prohibiting recurrence of the nuisance requiring the defendant, again within a period of time to be specified by the order, to execute works necessary to prevent a recurrence. Additionally, the court may impose a fine not exceeding level 5 on the standard scale as defined by section 17 of the Criminal Justice Act 1991.[1]

Once satisfied about the existence of a statutory nuisance, the magistrates' court is subject to a duty to make an order for abatement of the nuisance, although the terms of that order allow an apparently wide discretion which may take account of impending slum clearance, for example.[2] A critical issue for the court at the outset is the "material date" at which the statutory nuisance exists or is considered likely to recur: the court is obliged to consider this matter at the date when the complaint is heard.[3] Assuming that the magistrates' court is satisfied that a statutory nuisance exists, there is considerable discretion available for the purpose of specifying the steps (if any) to be taken for the purpose of abatement.[4] Where the court requires works for abatement of the statutory nuisance, they must be prescribed with particularity.[5]

If the statutory nuisance comprises noise that is prejudicial to health or a nuisance emitted from or caused by a vehicle, machinery or equipment in a street,

[98] *Blackpool Borough Council v. Johnstone* [1992] C.O.D. 464.

[99] *Ibid.*

[1] Environmental Protection Act, s.82(2).

[2] *Nottingham Corporation v. Newton* [1974] 1 W.L.R. 923.

[3] *Coventry City Council v. Doyle* [1975] 1 W.L.R. 845.

[4] *McGillivray v. Stephenson* [1950] 1 All E.R. 942.

[5] *R. v. Fenny Stratford JJ., ex p. Watney Mann (Midlands) Ltd*, [1976] 1 W.L.R. 1101; *Millard v. Wastall* [1898] 1 Q.B. 342.

the magistrates' court is required to make an order if satisfied that that statutory nuisance exists or (if abated) is likely to recur in the same street.[6]

The object of proceedings for an order

Normally, proceedings by an individual aggrieved by a statutory nuisance will be brought against the person responsible for the nuisance, as in the case of summary proceedings by a local authority under section 80. The pattern found in section 80 is also followed in the case of a nuisance arising from any defect of a structural character and in any case where the person responsible for a nuisance cannot be found where, respectively, proceedings must be brought against the owner of the premises or the owner or occupier.[7] If a statutory nuisance is caused by noise emitted from or caused by an unattended vehicle or unattended machinery or equipment, proceedings must be undertaken against the person responsible for the vehicle, machinery or equipment.[8]

If more than one person is responsible for a statutory nuisance, the provisions of section 82 will apply to each person even if what any one of them is responsible for it not of itself a nuisance. Once again, special provision is made in respect of a statutory nuisance caused by noise emitted from or caused by an unattended vehicle or unattended machinery or equipment in a street for which more than one person is responsible, to the extent that any person actually responsible for the vehicle, equipment or machinery will be subject to proceedings. If, on the other hand, more than one person is responsible for a statutory nuisance caused by noise emitted from or caused by a vehicle, machinery or equipment in a street which is prejudicial to health or a nuisance, even if that for which an individual is responsible is not by itself a nuisance, proceedings will be against each person responsible for the nuisance who can be found.[9]

Premises which are unfit for human habitation Where the magistrates court is satisfied that an alleged nuisance exists and, in the court's opinion, is such as to render the premises unfit for human habitation,[10] proceedings under section 82 may prohibit use of these premises for human habitation until they are rendered fit for that purpose to the satisfaction of the court.[11] Ostensibly, the powers available here are rather more restricted than those under the Housing Act 1985, Part VI, though in practice a number of variables will govern the question of whether a local authority will take the initiative using the Housing Act powers rather than act under section 80. Failure (for whatever reason) to act under either of these sets of powers may provoke summary proceedings by an individual. In turn, this may lead the court to use its powers to direct the local

[6] Environmental Protection Act, s.82(2), as amended by the Noise and Statutory Nuisance Act 1993, s.5(2).
[7] *Ibid.* s.82(4).
[8] *Ibid.* subs.(4)(d).
[9] *Ibid.* subss.(5), (5A) and (5B).
[10] Housing Act 1985, s.604. *Cf.* Chap. 12, "Housing".
[11] Environmental Protection Act, s.82(3).

authority to act in default where the person responsible or the owner or occupier cannot be found.[12]

Notice of intended summary proceedings

The predecessor provisions—section 99 of the Public Health Act 1936—imposed no requirement on a person aggrieved by a statutory nuisance to provide prior notice of intended summary proceedings.[13] The matter is now specifically addressed by section 82 of the Environmental Protection Act.[14] Prior to the institution of the proceedings by the person aggrieved against "any person", a notice must be served giving at least 21 days' notice of the intention to bring proceedings.[15]

Enforcement

Reference has been made already to local authority enforcement of its own summary action in respect of statutory nuisances. In the present context of an individual's summary proceedings, any person who, without reasonable excuse,[16] contravenes an order of the court under section 82(2) is guilty of a summary offence. This offence is punishable with a fine, together with a continuing fine for each day on which the offence continues after conviction.[17] As previously indicated, the magistrates' court is empowered to impose a fine at the time that an order is made in proceedings under section 82.[18] The fine referred to above on contravention of the order may be an additional fine: both fines must not exceed level 5 on the standard scale.[19]

As in the case of proceedings under section 80, there is a defence of best practicable means available in present summary proceedings by an individual.[20] The defence also extends to a statutory nuisance arising under section 79(ga),[21] but only where the noise is emitted from or caused by a vehicle, machinery or equipment being used for industrial, trade or business purposes.[22] However, the defence is not available in a variety of cases of statutory nuisance mirrored in the case of section 80,[23] but with the additional case of a nuisance which is such as to render premises unfit for human habitation, which is a potentially important aid to summary proceedings for statutory nuisance where there are adverse housing conditions.[24]

[12] *Ibid.* subs.(13).
[13] *Sandwell Metropolitan Council v. Bujok, supra.*
[14] subss.(6) and (7).
[15] *Ibid.* The period is three days in the case of a noise nuisance.
[16] See nn.39 and 40, *supra.*
[17] Environmental Protection Act, s.82(8).
[18] See n.90, *supra.*
[19] Criminal Justice Act 1991, s.17.
[20] See, nn.49–61, *supra.*
[21] See, n.63, *supra.*
[22] Noise and Statutory Nuisance Act 1993, s.5(7).
[23] See, nn.51–54, *supra.*
[24] Environmental Protection Act, s.82(10)(d).

If the court convicts the defendant under section 82, it may require the local authority to do anything which the person convicted was required to do. However, before these default powers can be used, the local authority in whose area the nuisance has occurred must be given an opportunity of being heard.[25]

The matter of costs were not addressed by the equivalent provisions relating to summary proceedings in the Public Health Act 1936. The present Act does address costs, so that any complainant will obtain his costs if it is established that the subject nuisance existed at the date of complaint, even if by the date of the hearing it had been remedied or otherwise abated. The Act does tie the entitlement to costs firmly to the "alleged nuisance" so that the complainant's expectations here will be frustrated unless he is able, by proof, to sustain the case founded on the proceedings originally notified.[26]

The Act makes provision for a second set of default powers beyond those already referred to[27] and referable to a situation where it appears to the magistrates' court that neither the person responsible for the nuisance nor the owner or occupier of the premises can be found. Once again, after giving the local authority an opportunity of being heard, the court may direct the authority to do anything which the court would have ordered the person responsible or the owner or occupier to do.[28] This default power is referable also to the person responsible for any subject vehicle, machinery or equipment for the purposes of the statutory nuisance provided for in section 79(1)(ga).[29]

Powers of entry are widely prescribed by the Act and cover not only entry for the purpose of taking "any" action or executing "any" work authorised or required under Part III of the Act but also entry for the purpose of ascertaining whether or not a statutory nuisance exists.[30] Entry to residential premises cannot be demanded as of right. 24 hours' notice must be given to the occupier of intended entry for the purposes of the Act, except in the case of an emergency.[31] A Justices' warrant may be available to allow entry to premises by an authorised officer of the local authority. However, that warrant may only be available if the Justices are satisfied about certain matters on the basis of sworn information in writing. Accordingly, it must be shown that

(a) admission to premises has been refused; or
(b) refusal is apprehended; or
(c) the premises are unoccupied; or
(d) the occupier is temporarily absent; or
(e) the case is one of emergency; or
(f) an application for admission would defeat the object of the entry.

[25] *Ibid.* subs.(11).
[26] *Ibid.* subs.(12).
[27] See n.22, *supra.*
[28] Environmental Protection Act, s.82(1), (3).
[29] Noise and Statutory Nuisance Act 1993, s.5(8).
[30] Environmental Protection Act, Sched. 3, para. 2(1). Normally, entry may be at any reasonable time on production of authority, if necessary.
[31] *Ibid.* para. 2(2).

In any of these cases, it must also be established to the satisfaction of the Justices that there is a reasonable ground for entry for the purpose for which entry is required.[32] Whether entry is effected as of right or otherwise, any authorised person who undertakes entry may take with him another person or any necessary equipment and may carry out such inspections, measurements and tests as he considers necessary for the discharge of the local authority's functions under Part III of the Act.[33] However, on leaving the premises, the person authorised who entered is obliged to leave the premises as effectively secured against trespassers as he found them.[34] In three circumstances above, entry may be effected in an emergency: in one case, those circumstances would provide an entitlement to enter premises as of right.[35] In two other circumstances, residential premises may be entered as of right and, again, entry may be by virtue of a Justices' warrant.[36] For any of these purposes, a reference to an "emergency" is a reference to a case where the person requiring entry has reasonable cause to believe that circumstances exist which are likely to endanger life or health and that immediate entry is necessary to verify the existence of those circumstances, or to ascertain their cause, and to effect a remedy.[37] Any person who wilfully obstructs a person in the exercise of the foregoing powers of entry is guilty of a summary offence.[38] On the other hand, if a person in exercising these powers of entry discloses any information relating to any trade secret obtained in the exercise of the powers, that person is also guilty of a summary offence. The only exceptions to criminal liability here arise where disclosure was shown to be made in the performance of the person's duty or where disclosure is shown to have been made with the consent of the person having the right to disclose the subject information.[39] More generally, the Act also provides protection from personal liability for members, officers and authorised persons acting under Part III.[40]

[32] *Ibid.* para. 2(3).
[33] *Ibid.* para. 2(4).
[34] *Ibid.* para. 2(5).
[35] *Ibid.* para. 2(1).
[36] *Ibid.* para. 2(2) and (3) respectively.
[37] *Ibid.* para. 2(7).
[38] *Ibid.* para. 3(1).
[39] *Ibid.* para. 3(2).
[40] *Ibid.* para. 5.

Chapter 11

BUILDING CONTROL

The System in Outline

The term "building control" refers primarily to a process through which legal control can be exerted for the purpose of preventing injury to and ensuring the health of those who, as occupiers or otherwise, may be affected by built structures as defined by the legislation. The main legislative framework for present purposes comprises the Building Act 1984 and the Fire Precautions Act 1971, supported by the Building Regulations 1991. Supplementary issues relate to the influence of the common law, particularly in relation to the issue of distributing liability in negligence if the system of control by local authorities breaks down, as well as the operation of a body of statutory provisions, to be found mainly in the Building Act, relating to a variety of miscellaneous controls over buildings.

The present chapter is in three main parts, dealing with:

(a) Parts I and II of the Building Act, the Building Regulations and the building control system generally;
(b) the related fire precautions legislation; and
(c) the miscellaneous controls over buildings to be found in Part III of the Building Act.

Much of the present framework for building control was anticipated in a White Paper, "The Future of Building Control in England and Wales",[1] which declared that while the present system

> ". . . produces safe buildings in which fire and serious structural failure is rare . . . there are persistent criticisms on other counts—in particular, that the system is more cumbersome and bureaucratic than it need be; and that the present detailed form of the Regulations is inflexible for many purposes, inhibits innovation, and imposes unnecessary costs. The prime concern must always be the preservation of public health and safety, but subject to that overriding requirement that there is scope for change to meet these points".[2]

It was against this background that a review of the building control system was

[1] Cmnd. 8179 (1981).
[2] *Ibid.* p.4.

launched and led, ultimately, to the Building Act 1984 and the Building Regulations 1985–1991. The White Paper declared that the framework for that review would be "... maximum self-regulation; minimum government interference; total self-financing; and simplicity in operation".[3] By way of conclusion, the White Paper anticipated that its proposed major changes would bring about significant improvements in the control of building operations:

> "They will increase the clarity of the Regulations and make them more readily usable; they will give the construction industry and building professions a new freedom to regulate their own affairs; they will enable local authorities to simplify their procedures; and they will reduce the commitment of public resources, both locally and nationally, to this function. At the same time, they will preserve the high standards of safety in buildings we have come to enjoy in this country, and they will enable control standards more easily to keep abreast of new developments in building techniques and materials."[4]

Statutory Building Control

The Building Act and building control

As the primary statutory framework for building control, the Building Act is essentially an enabling Act for the generation of the all-important regulations governing most aspects of the building process. As well as being an enabling Act, the Act of 1984 is also a consolidating Act and brought together various important provisions that had not come into force when incorporated originally in the Housing and Building Control Act 1984. These provisions relate to the private supervision and certification of building work covered by the Act, breaking the monopoly of control by local authorities. This new, alternative regime for control came into force on November 11, 1985, along with the Building Regulations 1985, which are now superseded (with amendments) by the Building Regulations 1991.

The power to make building regulations

It is the Secretary of State for the Environment who is empowered to make building regulations, for any one or more of the following purposes:

(a) securing the health, safety, welfare and convenience of persons in or about buildings and of others who may be affected by buildings or matters connected with buildings;

[3] *Ibid.*
[4] *Ibid.* p.16.

(b) furthering the conservation of fuel and power; and
(c) preventing waste, undue consumption, misuse or contamination of water.

Such regulations must, however, be made with respect to ". . . design and construction of buildings and the provision of services, fittings and equipment in or in connection with buildings."[5] The present building regulations are the Building Regulations 1991,[6] as amended. The 1985 and 1991 Regulations differ quite significantly from previous sets of building regulations, in that there is an absence of the detailed regulation that characterised building control prior to 1985. The present system of control rests on the Secretary of State's power to approve documents containing practical guidance for an application of building regulation requirements.[7] It was this detailed practical guidance that formerly characterised the building regulations in force prior to 1985. Evidence, but not conclusive evidence, of compliance or non-compliance with or contravention of the building regulations may be taken from evidence of compliance or non-compliance with the approved documents.[8] The Building (Prescribed Fees) Regulations 1985,[8a] as amended, govern the charging of fees for most building control functions.

Basic requirements of building control

Any person undertaking work falling within the Building Regulations 1991 is obliged to submit plans to the responsible local authority, normally the district council. In so far as the plans comply with the Building Regulations and are not otherwise defective, the local authority is obliged to approve those plans, subject to a variety of situations (examined later in the present chapter) in which plans have to be disapproved.[9] On the other hand, in a number of situations, the local authority may reject plans, as a matter of discretion.[10] Furthermore, the local authority can declare that a deposit of plans is of no effect if the applicant for approval fails to proceed with the subject works within a period of three years of deposit.[11] In so far as plans suggest that building works are to be undertaken with "short-lived" materials, it is open to the local authority to stipulate a period of time at the expiration of which the building should be removed, and to impose conditions relevant to the use of the materials in question.[12]

[5] s.1(1) and Sched. 1.
[6] S.I. 1991 No. 2768. As to the application of the Building Regulations and the Building Act in Inner London, see the Building (Inner London) Regulations 1985 (S.I. 1985 No. 1936), as amended.
[7] s.6.
[8] s.7.
[8a] S.I. 1985 No. 1576. In respect of work in respect of which plans were deposited, a building notice given or an initial notice given before October 1, 1994, S.I. 1985 No. 1576 (as amended) applies. In respect of the foregoing transactions occurring after this date the fee levels prescribed by the Building (Prescribed Fees) Regulations 1994 (S.I. 1994 No. 2020) will apply.
[9] s.16.
[10] ss.27 and 28.
[11] s.32.
[12] s.19.

Basic requirements of procedure and enforcement

The local authority is required to notify its decision within five weeks (or any extended period agreed between the parties, not exceeding two months).[13] Any dispute between the local authority and developer concerning alleged defects in plans or alleged contravention of the regulations may be referred to and decided by a magistrates' court if the parties have not opted to allow the Secretary of State to determine the matter. If the matter is referred to the Secretary of State, he has the power to state a case for the opinion of the High Court on a matter of law.[14]

If construction proceeds in contravention of the Building Regulations, the local authority is empowered to require the developer to pull down or alter the works. Failure to comply may trigger the local authority's default powers which may in turn attract compensation to the authority, but only in respect of action taken within 12 months of completion of the works. Such default powers and their exercise may be without prejudice to an application by the Attorney-General or the local authority for an injunction in those circumstances.

A local authority may form the view that operation of a regulation is unreasonable. In these circumstances, the Secretary of State, in consultation with the local authority, may dispense with or relax the requirement.[15] Even in respect of existing works, relaxation may be available,[16] unless prior to any application the local authority had decided to exercise the power to pull down or alter the works.

Fire precautions

The power to make building regulations includes a facility to regulate matters affecting fire precautions in building subject to these regulations. Accordingly, the requirements of the Building Regulations will be triggered where "building work" (as defined by regulation 3(1)) takes place, an expression that includes the erection or extension of a building and its material alteration. While the Building Regulations are aimed at fire precautions and, in particular, means of escape in the event of fire for "new" buildings or those subject to material alteration or change of use, the Fire Precautions Act 1971 sets out a scheme for the designation of certain categories of use of premises attracting the requirement of a fire certificate, dealing with means of escape and other fire precautions.[17]

The general duty

The Building Act imposes a general duty on the responsible local authorities "to carry this Act into execution in their areas" subject to, *inter alia*, the application of the Act to other authorities.[18] The principal authorities for this purpose are the

[13] s.16(12).
[14] s.30: a case must be stated if the High Court so directs.
[15] s.8.
[16] Sched. 2.
[17] Fire Precautions Act 1971, s.1.
[18] Building Act, s.91.

district councils and the London boroughs.[19] Default powers available to the Secretary of State for present purposes refer to a local authority's failure to discharge "functions" under the Act.[20] More particularly, the Act states that the Secretary of State may make a default order if satisfied that there has been a failure to discharge functions ". . . in a case in which they ought to have discharged them". The order will require removal of the default in the manner specified. Failure to comply with the order allows the Secretary of State to seek an order of mandamus against the local authority in question or, alternatively, to transfer (by order) such of the functions of the local authority as may be specified in the order.[21]

The Building Regulations

The Building Act provides for a variety of situations arising from implementation and enforcement of the Building Regulations and these are dealt with, in turn, below. Of prime importance is the control of building work and the operation of the Building Regulations.

The control of building work

Whether the requirements of the Building Regulations apply is an often complex inquiry. However, at the outset a fundamental question, touched on previously, is whether a person intends to undertake "building work" because this triggers the operation of the Regulations. More particularly, it demands[22] that building work is carried out so that it complies with Schedule 1 requirements (described below) and that, in securing any such compliance, there is no failure to comply with any other such requirement. Furthermore, following the completion of building work, any building extended or subject to a material alteration, any building in which a controlled service or fitting is provided, extended or materially altered, and any controlled service or fitting, must comply with Schedule 1 requirements or (in the absence of compliance) be no more unsatisfactory in relation to the requirement than before the work was executed. A "material alteration" here means work or any part of work executed, resulting in a building or a controlled service or fitting not complying with a relevant requirement (relating to structure, means of escape, internal and external fire spread, access and facilities for fire service and access and facilities for disabled people) where previously it did or, in a building or controlled service or fitting which before the work commenced did not comply with a relevant requirement, being more unsatisfactory in relation to such a requirement.[23] A "controlled

[19] *Ibid.* s.126.
[20] *Ibid.* s.116.
[21] *Ibid.*
[22] Building Regulations 1991, reg.4. As to the definition of a "building" for present purposes, see the Building Act, s.121.
[23] *Ibid.* reg.3(2).

service or fitting" is one to which the requirements relating to hygiene, drainage and waste disposal and heat-producing appliances in Schedule 1 apply.[24]

The Building Act provides that any regulations may provide for circumstances in which buildings or parts of buildings, *inter alia*, and the purposes for which or the manner and circumstances in which buildings or parts of buildings change in such a way as to constitute a "material change of use".[25] The Building Regulations 1991 provide that whether it is the whole or just part of a building which is subject to a material change of use, the work involved must be carried out to ensure compliance with relevant parts of Schedule 1, mentioned previously.[26] Schedule 1 to the Regulations set out requirements relating to:

(a) structure;
(b) fire safety;
(c) site preparation and resistance to moisture;
(d) toxic substances;
(e) resistance to the passage of sound;
(f) ventilation;
(g) hygiene;
(h) drainage and waste disposal;
(i) heat-producing appliances;
(j) stairs, ramps and guards;
(k) conservation of fuel and power;
(l) access facilities for disabled people; and
(m) glazing materials and protection.

Although the Regulations contain a detailed definition of the term "material change of use", including specification of buildings used either as a dwelling or a flat where previously not so used, that defintion is probably more restricted than the "equivalent" definition for the purposes of the Town and Country Planning Act 1990.[27] In general, therefore, it may be the case that planning permission could be required by virtue of the Act of 1990 where building control requirements are not triggered for present purposes.

Building work required to comply with Schedule 1 requirements must be carried out with "proper materials" which are "appropriate for the circumstances in which they are used", and "in a workmanlike manner". Accordingly, materials should be of a suitable nature and quality in relation to the purposes and conditions of their use, adequately mixed or prepared and applied, used or fixed so as to perform adequately the functions for which they are intended.[28] "Proper materials" include materials marked in accordance with the Construction products Directive,[28a] or which conform with an appropriate technical

[24] *Ibid.* reg.2(1).
[25] Sched. 1, para. 8(1)(e).
[26] Building Regulations, reg.6.
[27] See the Town and Country Planning Act 1990 and case law thereon.
[28] Approved documents, Building Regulations 1985. *Cf.* reg.7, 1991 Regulations.
[28a] O.J. L40/12.

specification, harmonised standard, British Standard, British Board of Agrément Certificate or any alternative national technical specification of an E.C. Member State. The Directive is implemented by the Construction Products Regulations 1991,[29] whose provisions are enforced by the weights and measures authorities.

Most of the Schedule 1 requirements do not require anything to be done except for the purpose of securing "reasonable standards" of health and safety for persons in or about buildings as well as others who may be affected by buildings.[30] The two exceptions here concern requirements for the conservation of fuel and power and access and facilities for disabled people.

Exemptions from the Regulations

The Building Act provides for a variety of exemptions from the operation of the Building Regulations, in respect of certain categories of building and (in particular) educational buildings and the buildings of statutory undertakers.[31] In addition, the Regulations may exempt certain bodies from procedural requirements.[32] The exempt bodies for this purpose comprise a local authority (defined to include principally a district council and a London borough council) and a county council, as well as any prescribed (public) body ". . . that acts under an enactment for public purposes and not for its own profit".[33]

Exempt buildings and work are defined by the Building Regulations.[34] The exemption extends from the erection of buildings and extensions to the execution of work on or in connection with such buildings or extensions, as long as the subject building or extension remains exempt following the works.

The public bodies referred to above may supervise the work carried out on their own buildings if approved for this purpose by the Secretary of State.[35] A "public body's notice" may be served on the local authority for present purposes: any such local authority should have been advised by the Secretary of State of that body's approval. The arrangements are broadly similar to those applicable to approved inspectors regulated under the Building (Approved Inspectors etc.) Regulations 1985,[36] except that there are no similar requirements in respect of matters of insurance and independence.

Approved documents

The Secretary of State is empowered by the Building Act to approve and issue any document which in his opinion gives suitable practical guidance about the application of the Building Regulations. In the exercise of his powers here under

[29] S.I. 1991 No. 1620. *Cf.* Department of the Environmental Circular 13/92 (Welsh Office Circular 29/92).
[30] Building Regulations, reg.8.
[31] Building Act, ss.3 and 4.
[32] *Ibid.* s.5.
[33] *Ibid.* subs.(1).
[34] reg.9 and Sched. 2.
[35] Building Act, s.54 and Sched. 4.
[36] S.I. 1985 No. 1066, as amended by S.I. 1992 No. 740.

section 6 of the Act, the Secretary of State has published a range of approved documents covering each of the technical requirements found in Schedule 1 to the Regulations.[37] The matter of materials and workmanship was referred to previously[38] and is the subject of a specific provision—regulation 9—in the Building Regulations 1991 as well as being the subject of a specific Approved Document. That Approved Document provides guidance on approaches to compliance with requirements relating to materials and workmanship. Compliance may be demonstrated in a variety of ways, for example, by following an appropriate British Standard or by the use of a product with a British Board of Agrément Certificate. Following such a standard or using a certified product may go beyond the Building Regulations' requirements. The Secretary of State has agreed aspects of performance for present purposes so that Agrément Certificates covering a wide range of products may confirm direct compliance with the Building Regulations in some cases, or a contribution to compliance in others. In these circumstances, the listing of products in regularly published supplements to the approved documents should indicate that a product or system covered by a certificate, and properly used in accordance with the certification, meets the relevant requirements.

Failure to comply with an approved document does not of itself render a person liable to any civil or criminal proceedings. However, if in any such proceedings it is alleged that there has been a contravention of building regulations, failure to comply with an approved document may be relied upon as tending to establish liability, while proof of compliance may be relied upon as tending to negate liability.[39]

Relaxation of building regulations

The Secretary of State retains a power to dispense with or relax any requirement found in building regulations if, on an application for a direction, he considers that operation of that requirement would be unreasonable in relation to the particular case to which the application relates.[40] However, the Building Regulations 1991 provide that this power is now exercisable by the local authority. Where a local authority arrives at a decision and notifies an applicant that there can be no dispensation from or relaxation of the particular requirement in the Regulations, that notification must contain information about the availability of an appeal under section 39(1) and (3) of the Building Act.[41]

In so far as the Secretary of State retains a power to deal with applications for a direction relaxing or dispensing with application of building regulations, those applications may be in prescribed form, although no such prescription applies at

[37] The approved documents are listed in Annex A to the Building Regulations 1991.

[38] See n.28, *supra*.

[39] Building Act, s.7.

[40] *Ibid*. s.8(1): the Secretary of State is also obliged to consult the local authority.

[41] Building Regulations, reg.10(1), (2). *Cf* s.8(4) of the Act, under which building regulations may provide for a public body to dispense with or relax particular requirements in some circumstances, relating to its own operations.

present. Where a local authority transmits the application for relaxation or dispensation, that authority is obliged to notify the applicant.[42] Specific requirements governing applications for relaxation or dispensation apply in respect of work carried out before any such application.[43]

Bearing in mind that a direction may be given by the Secretary of State, a local authority or some other public body, certain procedural requirements apply before a direction may be given. Not less than 21 days before the direction is given, local publicity in a newspaper circulating in the area where the site of the work is situated is required. That notice must indicate the situation and nature of the work, as well as the requirement to be dispensed with or relaxed. Furthermore, the newspaper publicity must invite representations in relation to any perceived impact of a direction on public health or safety.[44] A condition of the entertainment of an application may be that the applicant pay or undertake to pay the cost of publication here. However, there is no requirement for this publicity where it appears to the Secretary of State, local authority or public body that the impact of the direction will be limited (again in relation to public health or safety) to premises adjoining the site of the work. In these circumstances he (or it) is obliged to notify the owner and occupier of the adjoining premises. Whatever the context of the works, no publicity requirements here apply to work affecting only the internal part of a building. However, if publicity has occurred in the circumstances described above, any direction is dependent on consideration being given to any representations that are forthcoming. If the local authority with responsibility for deciding an application for a direction decides against a direction and an appeal is pursued under section 39 to the Secretary of State, he is entitled to receive copies of any representations received.[45]

Various consultative processes may be relevant in the present context. First of all, on a general basis, the Secretary of State is obliged to appoint a Building Regulations Advisory Committee to advise him on the exercise of his power to make building regulations ". . . and on other subjects connected with building regulations". The Act goes on to require that the Secretary of State "shall" consult the Advisory Committee and ". . . such other bodies as appear to him to be representative of the interests concerned" before making any building regulations containing substantive requirements.[46] The second consultative requirement arises where the power to relax or dispense with a requirement is exercisable by a local authority,[47] or a public body proposing to exercise its similar powers[48] in connection with requirements relating to structural fire precautions, the provision of means of escape from buildings in case of fire and (in connection with such provision) measures to ensure that any such facility can be used safely

[42] Building Act, s.9.

[43] *Ibid.* and Sched. 2.

[44] The publicity requirement may be delegated by the Secretary of State to a local authority, but not some other "public body": *ibid.* s.10(4).

[45] *Ibid.* s.10.

[46] *Ibid.* s.14.

[47] *Ibid.* s.8(2).

[48] *Ibid.* s.8(4).

and effectively at all material times. In so far as the local authority or public body is not the fire authority, they are obliged to consult the fire authority before exercising the power in relation to any premises or proposed premises.[49]

Appeals in respect of matters of dispensation or relaxation A refusal of an application by a local authority gives rise to an appeal to the Secretary of State, a notice of appeal in writing being required within one month of the date of the local authority's notification of refusal. A deemed refusal for this purpose arises if, within a period of two months of an application or such extended period as may be agreed between the parties, there is no notification forthcoming from the local authority.[50] When in force, a further provision of the Building Act facilitates (at the discretion of the Secretary of State) an opportunity for the appellant and the local authority to appear before and be heard by a person appointed by the Secretary of State.[51]

Building matter: type approval and type relaxation The term "building matter" receives a very wide definition in the Act, referring as it does to ". . . any building or other matter whatsoever to which building regulations are in any circumstances applicable".[52] The Secretary of State is empowered to grant relaxations in relation to a particular type of building matter. The Secretary of State is enabled to grant "general" or "class" relaxations in relation to any type of building matter following consultations with relevant representative bodies, either unconditionally or subject to conditions. This process may be undertaken either of the Secretary of State's own accord or on an application made for a relaxation.[53] Failure to comply with a condition previously referred to or to permit some other person to fail to comply with such a condition is an offence triable summarily, supplemented by daily fines for each day of default.[54]

In contrast to type relaxation, the Act also provides for type approval. The Secretary of State is enabled to approve by certificate particular types of building matter as complying with particular parts of the Building Regulations, either of his own volition or following an application submitted to him. The powers available are very flexible, for example, in allowing general or particular certification.[55] In turn, these powers may be delegated to "a person or body".[56] These provisions are yet to be brought into force, but it has been suggested that the power relating to type approval

> ". . . may be useful for enabling some new product or system of construction intended for general use to be formally assessed for building regulation

[49] *Ibid.* s.15.
[50] *Ibid.* s.39. As to detailed procedures, see subs.(3)–(6).
[51] *Ibid.* s.43.
[52] *Ibid.* s.11(8).
[53] *Ibid.* s.11. As to an early consideration of type relaxtion for cavity wall insulation, see Circular 84/75 (Welsh Office Circular 153/75), Circular 105/75 (Welsh Office Circular 185/75), etc.
[54] *Ibid.* subs.(6).
[55] *Ibid.* s.12.
[56] *Ibid.* s.13.

purposes. If desired, the approval could be made to apply for a limited period only. If the matter in question, although complying with some building regulation requirements, did not comply with others but was nevertheless acceptable, a type relaxation could be issued in conjunction with the type approval".[57]

Plans and notices under the Building Regulations

The process and requirements associated with the approval of plans is governed again by the Building Act and the Building Regulations. At the core of the process is the jurisdiction of the local authority to pass or reject supported by detailed requirements in the Regulations governing the service of building notices on the local authority in anticipation of the commencement of building work, together with supervision of the work as it continues to the point of completion, as confirmed by the authority.

The intention to carry out building work

Any person who intends to carry out building work[58] is obliged to give the local authority a building notice or to submit "full plans".[59] A building notice will state the name and address of the person intending to carry out the work and will have attached his signature or be signed on his behalf. Among other things, a notice will also contain a description of the proposed building work or material change of use, as well as the location of the building and its use or intended use.[60] Full plans must contain a description of the proposed building work or material change of use, together with various other details[61] and any other plans necessary to show that the work would comply with the Regulations.[62] A person is obliged to submit full plans if what is intended is building work in respect of a building put or intended to be put to a use designated for the purposes of the Fire Precautions Act 1971, as described below.[63] If a building notice has been given, a person carrying out building work or executing a material change of use is obliged, within a period of time specified, to provide such plans as are necessary for the purpose of discharging functions for the purpose of the Building Regulations.[64] However, subject to one exception,[65] neither a building notice nor accompanying plans (including plans submitted at a later time) are treated for the

[57] Circular 127/74 (Welsh Office Circular 194/74), para. 30.
[58] As defined by the Building Regulations 1991, reg.3.
[59] *Ibid.* reg.11.
[60] *Ibid.* reg.12.
[61] *Ibid.* paras. (1)–(4).
[62] *Ibid.* reg.13.
[63] *Ibid.* reg.11(2).
[64] *Ibid.* reg.12(5).
[65] *Ibid.* reg.11(5), referring to ss.219–225 of the Highways Act 1980 concerning the advance payments code.

purpose of section 16 of the Building Act (described below) as having been "deposited" in accordance with the Building Regulations.[66]

The duty to consider plans

The local authority's duty to consider plans is triggered where plans of any proposed work are "deposited" with that authority in accordance with the Building Regulations. The duty of the local authority is to pass the plans (assuming that there is no other provision of the Act expressly requiring or authorising rejection) unless those plans are defective or they show that the work proposed would contravene any of the building regulations. In the face of any such defect or contravention, the local authority has two options: either to reject the plans or to pass them, subject to conditions. However, this latter option is available only if a request for this purpose is made by the person submitting the plans, or that person has consented to such an approach. The conditions relevant here are, on the one hand, a specification by the local authority of modifications to the deposited plans and, on the other, that further plans be deposited. In relation to decisions generally, the local authority is obliged to notify the person depositing plans of the fact that they have been passed or rejected, within five weeks of deposit or such longer period (not exceeding two months) as may be agreed. Any dispute on the question of whether plans for proposed work are in conformity with building regulations or whether there is a prohibition on the rejection of plans by an approved inspector (under section 16(9)) is referable to the Secretary of State.[67]

Statutory justification for plan rejection

A variety of statutory provisions provide authority for a rejection of plans by the local authority. Plans must be rejected:

(a) if it is proposed to erect a building over a sewer, unless the authority, subject to any directions from the sewerage undertaker, considers that consent can properly be given[68];
(b) unless satisfactory provision is made for drainage[69];
(c) unless satisfactory provision is made for water supply[70];
(d) (in the case of public buildings) unless satisfactory means of ingress and egress are available[71];
(e) (in the case of plans for buildings other than residences, shops and offices) unless the local authority is satisfied that the height of the chimneys is adequate[72]; and

[66] *Ibid.* reg.12(6). *Cf.* Building Act, s.124.
[67] Building Act, s.16.
[68] *Ibid.* s.18.
[69] *Ibid.* s.21.
[70] *Ibid.* s.25.
[71] *Ibid.* s.24.
[72] Clean Air Act 1993, s.16.

(f) (in the case of industrial buildings) unless those buildings conform to the standards of insulation against loss of heat as prescribed by regulation.[73]

The statutory framework governing local authority action in relation to building plans is tightly defined. In some circumstances, this may confront the local authority with a dilemma. Nevertheless, some matter that is extraneous to the present statutory powers may not be used as a basis for refusal of an approval. Even if there appears to be exceptional evidence of a malicious rejection of plans, there will be no action for damages against the local authority, although proceedings by way of judicial review may be available under R.S.C., Ord. 53, for an order of mandamus.[74] In other circumstances, mandamus was refused where a local authority had refused approval for plans indicating that the building would interfere with the highway.[75] The validity of this conclusion must be in doubt even though execution of the plans here would produce unlawfulness. In these circumstances, it is suggested that, following implementation, the element of unlawfulness is treated by reference to any other powers that appear to be relevant for that purpose.

Building over a sewer, drain or disposal main

A building or an extension to a building shown on deposited plans may not be erected over a sewer, drain or disposal main without the consent of the authority. However, the authority may grant consent if satisfied (with or without the attachment of conditions) that compliance with specified requirements would be appropriate. Disputes are subject to adjudication by the magistrates' court. Because sewers, and public sewers in particular, are vested in the sewerage undertaker, the undertaker has wide powers to require the local authority to comply with any reasonable requirements not only in relation to sewers but also in relation to the undertaker's drains and disposal mains.[76] Where any such sewer, drain or disposal main is damaged in these circumstances, the sewerage undertaker's ownership of the facility will provide the basis for a remedy of damages and/or injunction.[77]

Satsifactory provision for drainage

The local authority is obliged to reject plans deposited unless satisfactory provision is made in those plans for drainage or unless that authority is satisfied that the requirement may be waived. The local authority may not insist on communication with a sewer:

[73] Thermal Insulation (Industrial Buildings) Regulations 1972 (S.I. 1972 No. 87).
[74] *Davis v. Bromley Corporation* [1908] 1 K.B. 170.
[75] *R. v. West Hartlepool Corporation, ex p. Richardson* (1901) 18 T.L.R. 1.
[76] Building Act, s.18. As to the duty to notify an undertaker, see subs.(2).
[77] *Cleckheaton UDC v. Firth* (1898) 62 J.P. 536: on the facts, there was found to be legal authority for the defendant's actions.

(a) if the nearest sewer is 100 feet or more away from the building, unless the authority pays the cost relating to that part beyond the 100 feet;
(b) if the levels make the requirement not reasonably practicable; or
(c) if the owner has no right to lay a drain through the intervening land.

The critical element of the present provision refers to the need for deposited plans to show that "... satisfactory provision will be made for the drainage of the building". In *Chesterton RDC v. Thompson*,[78] it was held that these words refer to the drains of the particular building and not to the system of drainage. Accordingly, a local authority, in considering whether to approve or reject deposited plans, is not able to take account of matters beyond the drains of the particular building. Whether provision for drainage may properly be dispensed with or whether drainage provisions ought to be accepted by the local authority, as being satisfactory are questions to be determined by the magistrates' court.[79]

The foregoing powers in section 21 of the Act are extended to the extent that, in appropriate cases, the local authority may require that two or more buildings be drained in combination. The extended power is limited to buildings only and is available only in advance of the approval of deposited plans, unless there is an agreement to forgo this requirement. A significant prerequisite for the exercise of these powers is the existence of a sewer, public or private.[80]

Satisfactory provision for water supply

Where plans deposited with a local authority relate to building work for a house, those plans must be rejected unless there is satisfactory provision of a supply of wholesome water for the occupants. Failure of such a supply obligation permits the local authority to notify the owner prohibiting his occupation of the house or prohibiting him from permitting others to occupy the premises until the authority has certified that a supply of wholesome water is available. Significantly, therefore, the present powers extend to occupied houses.[81] Guidance on the wholesomeness of water in the present context of "sufficiency for domestic purposes" is to be found in the Water Supply (Water Quality) Regulations 1989.[82] As to the nature of "domestic purposes", it has been observed that:

> "... water supplied for domestic purposes would mean water supplied to satisfy the needs, or perform or help in performing services, which, according to the ordinary habits of civilised life, are commonly satisfied and performed in people's homes, as distinguished from those needs and services which are satisfied or performed outside those homes, and are not connected with, nor incident to the occupation of them."[83]

[78] [1947] 1 K.B. 300.
[79] Building Act, s.21.
[80] *Ibid.* s.22.
[81] *Ibid.* s.25.
[82] S.I. 1989 No. 1147, reg.3.
[83] *Per* Lord Atkinson in *Metropolitan Water Board v. Avery* [1914] A.C. 118 at 126, 127.

Disputes or other questions arising under the present provision are determined by the magistrates' court.

Satisfactory means of ingress and egress in relation to public buildings

Where plans are deposited with a local authority and they relate to a variety of public buildings, including theatres and other places of public resort such as restaurants, shops and warehouses, those plans must be rejected unless they show that the building, or any extension, has satisfactory means of ingress or egress according to the purpose for which the building or the extension will be used. In exercising this function, the local authority is obliged to consult with the fire authority. Any question arising in the present context is referable to the magistrates' court for determination. However, the present provision will not apply where building regulation requirements apply in connection with means of escape in case of fire (as in Schedule 1, Part B of the Building Regulations 1991), or such requirements are dispensed with by virtue of section 8 of the Building Act. In the same way that the present provision would not apply in the above circumstances, there will also be exclusion of any Local Act operative in its place.[84]

A central issue on those occasions when this provision is operative concerns the matter of whether the public have resort to public premises. While there is no public resort to a genuinely private establishment, the same may not be true of a club which is ostensibly private but which is indiscriminate in its membership policy.[85]

Where plans deposited with a local authority relate to use of a building as a residence or residences, a shop or shops or an office or offices and include provision of a chimney to carry away smoke, grit, dust or gases, the plans must be rejected unless the authority is satisfied that chimney height is sufficient to prevent (so far as practicable) the emissions being prejudicial to health or a nuisance, taking account of a range of stated environmental considerations. Rejection gives rise to an appeal to the Secretary of State.[86]

Consultation with the fire authority

Plans deposited with a local authority indicating that a building is to be erected, extended or to be subject to structural alteration in accordance with building regulations may attract a requirement for that local authority to consult with the fire authority. Such consultation is required before plans can be passed, where the first use is either a "designated use" under the Fire Precautions Act[87] or as a dwelling characterised by the fact that, *inter alia*, living accommodation is provided two or more floors above the ground floor. Similar requirements apply

[84] Building Act, s.24.
[85] *Panama (Piccadilly) Ltd v. Newberry* [1962] 1 W.L.R. 610.
[86] Clean Air Act, s.16.
[87] s.43(1). *Cf.* n.17, *supra.*

if what is proposed is a change of use in respect of which plans are deposited with the local authority.

The use of short-lived materials

Where plans deposited with a local authority indicate that it is proposed to construct a building of short-lived materials, that authority has a discretion to reject the plans even if they are generally in accord with building regulations. Alternatively, the local authority may fix a period at the end of which the building must be removed and, in passing such plans, impose conditions relevant to use of the subject materials.

Notification of a decision must be given within five weeks, or such longer period as may be agreed (not exceeding two months). Disputes and questions arising here are referable to the magistrates' court. Building regulations may indicate that the present provision applies to any materials identified in those regulations that are, in the absence of special care, liable to rapid deterioration or are otherwise unsuitable for the construction of permanent buildings.[88]

Departure from and lapse of plans

Where plans have been deposited and passed, the local authority responsible will require additional plans to be deposited in respect of any proposed departure or deviation. Whether a change represents a departure or deviation is a question of fact and degree. It may be presumed that any informality surrounding a determination of the question whether there is a departure or a deviation will not be binding in law on the local authority, particularly in view of the delegation requirements of the Local Government Act 1972.[89] Where there is a deposit of plans in relation to a departure or deviation, section 16 of the Building Act will apply, as it does in respect of the original deposit.[90]

Commencement, compliance and completion

If work to which a plan relates is not commenced within three years of the date of deposit, the local authority may declare the plan to be of no effect.[91] Building work must not be commenced within this three-year limit unless the local authority has been notified of intended commencement and at least two days have elapsed since the end of the day on which the notice was given. Similar notification requirements (substituting a period of one day) apply to various types of work, including the covering up of foundations and drains and sewers. The

[88] Building Act, s.19, to be replaced by s.20 on a date to be appointed. As to the power of a local authority to sample materials, see the Building Regulations 1991, reg.17.

[89] s.101. *Cf. Western Fish Products Ltd v. Penrith District Council* (1979) 77 L.G.R. 185 and *Camden London Borough Council v. Secretary of State for the Environment* (1993) 67 P. & C.R. 59.

[90] Building Act, s.31 *Cf.* n.67, *supra.*

[91] *Ibid.* s.32.

local authority must also be notified if it is intended that a building should be occupied before it or any part of the building is completed. Contravention of these requirements permits the local authority to serve a notice on the person carrying out the building work who must, within a reasonable time, cut into, lay open or pull down so much of the work as prevents an appreciation of whether the Building Regulations have been complied with.[92] Finally, satisfaction of various detailed requirements will empower the local authority to give a completion certificate which is evidence (but not conclusive evidence) that the relevant requirements specified in the certificate have been complied with.[93]

Tests for conformity with building regulations

Any local authority with building control functions is empowered to require or carry out tests to ascertain conformity with building regulations. The authority is empowered to require any person by whom or on whose behalf work is (or is proposed to be) or was done to carry out tests, or may itself carry out such tests. The costs are met by the person responsible, although the local authority may, as a matter of discretion, bear some or all of the costs involved. Disputes and questions arising here are referable to the magistrates' court.[94]

Enforcement and issues of liability

The Building Act is enforced through criminal sanctions, as well as a range of administrative powers, including default powers. In addition, the Act stipulates circumstances in which the local authority may be liable for breach of certain statutory duties in building regulations, and liable for compensation as a result of damage sustained by reason of the exercise of powers under the Act: each of these elements is dealt with here, in turn. It should also be noted that there are powers of entry and powers for the execution of works in sections 95–102.

Contravention of building regulations

If a person contravenes any provision in building regulations (other than a provision designated as one to which the present provision does not apply), he is liable on summary conviction to a fine, as well as a continuing fine for each day on which the default continues following conviction.[95] However it is not *per se* unlawful to start work on plans not yet approved. Proceedings for this (or any other offence created by the Building Act) may not be taken by anyone other than a party aggrieved or a local authority whose function it is to enforce the statutory requirements, without the written consent of the Attorney-General.[96]

[92] Building Regulations 1991, reg.14.
[93] *Ibid.* reg.15.
[94] Building Act, s.33.
[95] Building Act, s.35. Offences against building regulations can be committed even though work on a building has not been completed: *Sunley Homes Ltd v. Borg* [1970] 1 Q.B. 115.
[96] *Ibid.* s.113.

In the case of the daily penalty for a continuing offence, the court may fix a reasonable period from the date of conviction for the defendant to comply with any directions from the court so that any daily penalty is thereafter recoverable from the expiration of that period.[97] Identification of continuing offences in the present context is not without its difficulty. In the old case of *Morant v. Taylor*,[98] a local Act provided that if buildings were erected otherwise than in accordance with a local authority's requirements, the authority could make a complaint to a local magistrate, who could thereupon order demolition of the building. It was held that, therefore, the complaint had to be made within six months of completion of the building. Construction of a building contrary to byelaws was an offence under another provision, but it could not be said that failing to demolish the building after construction was a continuing offence.

More recently, in *Torridge District Council v. Turner*,[99] it was held that the offence under section 35 is not a continuing offence. Referring to the earlier decision in *Hertsmere Borough Council v. Alan Dunn Building Contractors Ltd*[1] Woolf L.J. in the Divisional Court emphasised the importance of that decision in distinguishing between those parts of building regulations that create "do" requirements and other provisions. These "do" provisions do not create continuing offences. Consequently, Schedule 1A1(1),[2] requiring that the building ". . . shall be constructed. . ." so that the combined dead, imposed and wind loads are sustained and transmitted by it to the ground, is referable to a "do" provision, to secure compliance with the Building Act.[3]

In more general terms, it is notable that there is no provision in the Building Act whereby an offence committed by a company is proved to have been committed with the consent or connivance of, or to have been attributable to any neglect on the part of, a director, manager, secretary or other similar officer so that that person also may be proceeded against. Accordingly, in *Fuller v. Nicholas*,[4] it was held that a director of a company which owned a building on which structural alterations have been carried out is not necessarily liable for failure to comply with building regulations.

It is not open to a defendant to argue that he should avoid conviction for failure to comply with building regulations because refusal of access to the site means that practical completion stage is never reached.[5] Building works, unless very confined in scope,

> ". . . are not to be regarded as an indivisible whole for the purpose of the [Building] Regulations. A part or parts of building works may be regarded as having been carried out when the builder purports to have completed them.

[97] *Ibid.* s.114.
[98] (1876) 1 Ex.D. 188.
[99] *The Times*, November 27, 1991.
[1] (1985) 84 L.G.R. 214.
[2] Building Regulations 1991 (S.I. 1991 No. 2768).
[3] *Cf.* s.2 of the Building Act by which building regulations may impose continuing requirements.
[4] *The Times*, April 18, 1984.
[5] *Antino v. Epping Forest District Council* 53 Build.L.R. 56.

This will no doubt be the case in respect of every part of the works when practical completion stage is reached. But the builder will also purport to have carried out any part of the works when that part is complete and the builder is proved to have no intention of remedying such defects in that part as contravenes the Regulations".[6]

Removal or alteration of offending work

A local authority may require an owner to pull down or alter work carried out in contravention of building regulations, provided that a notice to this effect is given within 12 months of completion of the works. If the notice is ignored, the authority may pull down or remove or alter the works, charging the cost to the person on whom the notice was served. The authority serving the so-called "section 36 notice" for present purposes bears the burden of showing that the offending work does not comply; thereafter, the appellant against the notice bears the burden of showing that the regulations have been complied with.[7] The facility described here does not affect the right of the local authority, the Attorney-General or any other person to apply for an injunction for the removal or alteration of any work on the ground that it contravenes any regulation or any provision of the Building Act.[8]

A person on whom a section 36 notice has been served is able to obtain a report from a suitably qualified person concerning the work to whch the notice relates. If the authority withdraws the section 36 notice as a result of consideration of the report, that authority may meet the expenses associated with the obtaining of the report.[9]

A person who is aggrieved by a section 36 notice may appeal to the magistrates' court. The court may confirm the notice or direct the local authority to secure its withdrawal. However, the court's jurisdiction is necessarily constrained by the terms of section 36 so that, on an appeal here, the court can only ask itself the question "were the building regulations contravened on the facts?" Only where this question is addressed and dealt with will the court be in a position to order withdrawal of the section 36 notice, for example.[10] However, the court may direct withdrawal of the notice if the purposes of section 36 have been "substantially achieved". Where a report has been submitted to the local authority under section 37, the court may include the expenses incurred in obtaining the report in any order as to costs.[11] A further appeal to the Crown Court (under section 41) is available in respect of the magistrates' court's order, determination or decision for present purposes. The procedure in an appeal to the magistrates' court is by way of a complaint for an order.[12]

[6] *Ibid. per* French J. at 60.
[7] *Rickards v. Kerrier District Council* (1987) 15 J.P. 625.
[8] Building Act, s.36.
[9] *Ibid.* s.37.
[10] *Lord Mayor and Citizens of the City of Westminster v. Evans*, 1992 (unreported).
[11] Building Act, s.40.
[12] *Ibid.* s.103.

Civil liabilities

Breach of a duty imposed by building regulations may be actionable in civil proceedings unless the regulations provide otherwise, so far as the breach causes "damage", defined to include the death of, or injury to, any person (including any disease and any impairment of a person's physical or mental condition). The regulations may prescribe defences to any such actions. As yet this provision is not in force.[13] When the provision is brought into force, it will not prejudice any right of action at common law: it is an additional action and, furthermore, is not limited to local authorities and their officers. It is against this background that interest focuses on any common law liabilities, particularly in relation to local authority supervision and enforcement of building regulations. The existence of a duty of care and availability of damages in negligence was before the House of Lords in *Murphy v. Brentwood District Council.*[14]

Negligence liability The House of Lords, in *Governors of the Peabody Donation Fund v. Sir Lindsay Parkinson and Co.,*[15] had said that whether or not a duty of care of particular scope was incumbent on a defendant is subject to the consideration of whether it is just and reasonable that the duty should extend so far. The purpose of the powers relating to the building regulations is discussed by Lord Keith who said that they are

> ". . . not to safeguard building developers against economic loss resulting from their failure to comply with approved plans. It is, in my opinion, to safeguard the occupiers of houses built in the local authority's area, and also members of the public generally against dangers to their health which may arise from defective drainage installation. The provisions are a public health measure".[16]

The leading authority is now the statement of principle in *Murphy*. *Murphy* shows that the previous leading authority—*Anns v. Merton London Borough Council*[17]—was wrongly decided except in relation to the distinction between policy and operational decisions as a pointer to possible liability (or immunity from liability) in negligence. Not only did the House of Lords depart from its earlier position expressed in *Anns*, it also overruled the Court of Appeal decision in *Dutton v. Bognor Regis UDC.*[18] The result is that the law of negligence in this area has been reshaped quite considerably.

The facts in *Murphy* indicate that the local authority employed an independent contractor to advise on the adequacy of a raft to be used to support the foundations of the subject house. The local authority was advised that the raft was

[13] *Ibid.* s.38.
[14] [1990] 3 W.L.R. 414. As to questions of limitation in any actions that may arise here, see the Limitation Act 1980, ss.14A, and 14B and 28A.
[15] [1984] 3 All E.R. 529.
[16] *Ibid.* at 534.
[17] [1977] 2 W.L.R. 1024.
[18] [1972] 1 Q.B. 373.

adequate, whereupon approval was given by the authority under the building regulations then in force. Subsequently when the structure of the house failed, the plaintiff decided to sell and sought damages arising from the consequent losses.

The critical question for the House of Lords in *Murphy* was whether the avoidance of economic loss falls within the scope of any duty owed to the plaintiff by the local authority. The duty, it was considered, related to a restricted obligation to take reasonable care to prevent injury and ensure health and safety under the statute, and does not extend to the avoidance of pure economic loss. If the duty did so extend, it would open an exceedingly wide field of claims. The House of Lords left open any view on the possibility that the local authority might owe a duty to those who suffer injury through any failure to take reasonable care to secure compliance with building regulations.[19] It was speculated by Lord Keith that such a duty could not extend beyond injury to person or health and (possibly) damage to property other than the defective building itself. Lord Keith was unaware of any claim against a local authority based on injury to person or health as a result of a breach of any duty of care to secure compliance with building regulations. Such an example occurs in *Clarke and Clarke v. Shire of Gisborne*,[20] where dampness in the subject dwelling exacerbated arthritis following the local authority's failure to supervise the initial building.

The members of the House of Lords in *Murphy* concluded that a duty of care of a scope sufficient to make the local authority liable for economic loss can be based only on evidence of reliance by the building owner on the local authority for present purposes, along the lines of *Hedley Byrne and Co. Ltd v. Heller and Partners*.[21] However, the House of Lords' view is that there is nothing in the ordinary relationship of local authority and defective building purchaser that is capable of giving rise to such a duty. The approval of plans or building inspection in the performance of the local authority's functions and any subsequent purchase cannot in themselves introduce reliance.

The following general propositions emerge from *Murphy*:

(1) A local authority's duty of care in applying and enforcing building regulations does not extend to safeguarding building owners against economic loss, as where (for example) the defective dwelling is sold at a loss.
(2) The Building Act does not presently create any statutory rights in favour of the building owner against the local authority.
(3) Any duty of the local authority in the present context must relate to the supervision of the building process for the purpose of preventing injury and ensuring safety to health.
(4) There is the possibility that the local authority owes an enforceable duty of care to persons who suffer injury as a result of any failure to secure compliance with building regulations.

[19] *cf.* Building Act, s.38.
[20] [1984] V.R. 971.
[21] [1964] A.C. 465.

(5) In a the case of economic loss, a duty of care of a scope sufficient to make the local authority liable for such loss can be based only on the principle of reliance.
(6) Despite the principle of reliance, there is nothing in the ordinary relationship between the local authority and the defective building owner capable of giving rise to such a duty. The approval of plans or building inspection in discharge of the local authority's functions and any subsequent purchase cannot in themselves introduce reliance.

The decision in *Peabody*[22] foreshadows some of the developments that have emerged from *Murphy*. The decisions in *Investors in Industry Commercial Properties Ltd v. South Bedfordshire District Council*[23] and *Richardson v. West Lindsey District Council*[24] also represent a seachange in the law, culminating with the conclusions of the House of Lords in *Murphy*, emphasising that it is incumbent on the building owner to ensure that construction is in accordance with building regulations. In these and other cases, the courts have sought to develop distinctions between the original building owner (often the developer) and any future occupier, as well as those who do or do not rely on professional advisers such as architects. The variable duties imposed on local authorities now appear to have vanished in view of the conclusions in *Murphy*, pointing to an exclusion of any duty to safeguard against economic losses. Whether such variable duties emerge will depend on the appearance of cases where the plaintiff suffers something other than economic loss.

Statutory compensation for damage

Section 106 of the Building Act requires a local authority to make full compensation to a person who has sustained damage by reason of an exercise by that authority of any of their powers under the Act. Such entitlement assumes that the person in question has not himself been in default. This provision is aimed at making compensation available as a result of a lawful exercise of a power under the Building Act where the act would have been actionable but for that statutory power. Any negligent exercise of a statutory power will not give rise to a claim for compensation. Subject to the position in *Murphy*, previously described, the remedy in these circumstances is a common law action in tort.

Appeals

Reference has been make previously to the facility for an appeal in respect of an adverse decision in relation to relaxation of, or dispensation with, building regulations.[25] Reference was made also to the facility for an appeal in respect of a section 36 notice.[26] While there is provision for and appeal to the Crown Court

[22] See n.15, *supra*.
[23] [1986] 1 All E.R. 787.
[24] [1990] 1 All E.R. 296.
[25] See n.50, *supra*.
[26] See n.11, *supra*.

in respect of an order, determination or other decision of the magistrates' court under Part I dealing with building regulations,[27] certain decisions of the Secretary of State give rise to an appeal on a point of law to the High Court. The decisions cover appeal decisions, references and applications for directions under sections 8, 16, 19, 39 and 50. At any stage, it is open to the Secretary of State to state a case for the opinion of the High Court on any question of law. The Secretary of State also has a discretion (when the section comes into force) to enable the local authority and the appellant to be heard by an inspector, by virtue of section 43.[28] Prior to the Health and Safety at Work Act 1974 most such appeals were within the jurisdiction of the magistrates' court. Bearing in mind the technicality of issues involved, there is clear merit in the transfer of jurisdiction now provided for.

Application of building regulations to the Crown

The substantive provisions of building regulations and certain other relevant enactments are applicable to Crown buildings, at least when the relevant provision of the Building Act is brought into force.[29]

Until the provision is in force, building regulations will continue not to apply to Crown property.[30] The present provision of the Building Act gives the Crown powers of dispensation and relaxation analogous to those possessed by a local authority or the Secretary of State.[31]

Supervision of Building Work otherwise than by Local Authorities

The alternative system

An approved inspector may at the option of a person intending to carry out building work supervise that work instead of the local authority. The system is described in detail by the Building (Approved Inspectors etc.) Regulations 1985,[32] as are arrangements for supervision by approved public bodies of their own work, and the certification of plans deposited with a local authority.

Approved inspectors

An "approved inspector" is a person who has been approved by the Secretary of State or a person designated by him for the purpose. Approval may be given on application by a body corporate or any other person. In certain circumstances approval must be withdrawn, while in other cases it may be withdrawn as a matter

[27] Building Act, s.41.
[28] *Ibid.* s.42.
[29] *Ibid.* s.44.
[30] *Cooper v. Hawkins* [1904] 2 K.B. 165.
[31] Building Act, s.44(5).
[32] S.I. 1985 No. 1066, as amended.

of discretion.[33] Matters of approval and designation are normally notified to local authorities. An approved inspector may delegate work to another person, except the power to issue a plans certificate under section 50 of the Act, or a final certificate under section 51. Despite delegation, responsibility at law for acts of the delegate remains with the approved inspector.[34]

The work of the approved inspector falls into three categories:

(a) the inspection of plans;
(b) the supervision of work; and
(c) the giving of certificates and other notices.

Failure to undertake any of these tasks may attract liability in law for breach of contract, work being undertaken in return for a fee payment; breach of statutory duty under building regulations, and negligence. However, it would appear that the same constraints on liability for negligence affecting the local authority and discussed above would apply also to the position of the approved inspector.

The initial notice

An approved inspector and a person intending to carry out building work (hereafter "the developer") may serve an "initial notice" on the local authority. If that notice is accepted, the approved inspector has a statutory duty to undertake prescribed functions in relation to supervision of the building work. The notice is required to be in the prescribed form, accompanied by prescribed plans and accompanied also by evidence (again in prescribed form) that an approved insurance scheme applies to the work or that prescribed insurance cover relating to the work has been or will be provided.

A local authority's rejection of an initial notice can be based only on prescribed grounds. If those grounds exist then rejection is mandatory: the notice of rejection must clearly indicate the grounds in question. For example, proposals for the provision of drainage may be unsatisfactory if the exact position for connection to a sewer is regarded as being crucial but is not indicated in the plans. The local authority's jurisdiction is based on section 16 of the Act, as previously described.[35] If the authority has not rejected an initial notice within 10 working days of receipt, it is deemed to have accepted the notice. The initial notice comes into force when it is accepted by the local authority and remains in force until, *inter alia*, it is cancelled by another notice given either by the approved inspector or the developer under section 52.[36]

While the initial notice is in force, the local authority's enforcement powers

[33] *Ibid.* reg.6.
[34] Building Act, s.49.
[35] See n.67, *supra.*
[36] Building Act, s.47. As to grounds for rejection, see the Building (Approved Inspectors etc.) Regulations 1985, Sched. 3.

are not exercisable. Furthermore, for the purpose of various provisions, the giving of the initial notice is to be treated as the deposit of plans, the accompanying plans are treated as the deposited plans and the acceptance or rejection of the notice is to be treated as the passing or rejection of deposited plans, while the cancellation of an initial notice is treated as a declaration under section 33 of the Act that the deposit of plans is to be of no effect. Parallel provisions apply to fire precaution requirements.

Plans certificates

On a request from the developer, an approved inspector is obliged to give a plans certificate to the developer and local authority, assuming that those plans are in compliance: any dispute is referable to the Secretary of State. If a plans certificate is to be rejected, grounds to justify such a rejection are found in the Building (Approved Inspectors etc.) Regulations.[37] These grounds relate to deficiencies in information and lack of relevant declarations. Any rejection must occur within 10 working days of receipt: failure to comply is deemed to be acceptance. The work to which the certificate relates must be work for which an initial notice given by the same approved inspector is in force, except where there is a combined initial notice and plans certificate. The plans certificate may be rescinded if work has not started within three years of acceptance by the local authority.[38]

There may be circumstances in which an initial notice is cancelled and building work is carried out in accordance with the certified plans, under the local authority's supervision. If this is the case, the local authority is unable to give a section 36 notice and may not prosecute under section 35 for contravention of building regulations.[39]

Final certificates

Provided that detailed requirements have been completed to the satisfaction of the approved inspector,[40] he is required to give a final certificate in respect of completed work. The certificate must be given both to the developer and the local authority. The local authority's power of rejection—similar in terms to the grounds for rejecting a plans certificate—could be based, for example, on a failure of an undertaking to consult the fire authority. Following acceptance of the final certificate, the initial notice ceases to apply. Nevertheless, section 48 continues to apply, so that the local authority may not serve a section 36 notice or prosecute for contravention of building regulations under section 35.[41]

Both the Building Act and the Building (Approved Inspectors etc.) Regulations in principle permit an approved inspector to discharge his functions by random sampling for the purpose of compiling the final certificate. The fact

[37] Sched. 4.
[38] Building Act, s.50.
[39] Building (Approved Inspectors etc.) Regulations, reg.14.
[40] *Ibid.* reg.10.
[41] Building Act, s.51.

that a defect escapes detection cannot, of itself, constitute a proper basis for concluding beyond reasonable doubt that any statement that relevant functions have been performed for the purpose of regulation 10 is false.[42]

Cancellation of an initial notice

In some circumstances, an initial notice may be cancelled. If an approved inspector considers that building work is in contravention of building regulations, he is required to notify that contravention to the developer. Failure by the developer to rectify the contravention within three months obliges the approved inspector to cancel the initial notice. In the event of disagreement on the matter of alleged contravention, there is the possibility of a second approved inspector taking responsibility under a second initial notice. In any first-mentioned situation, however, the local authority must also be advised of the contravention. Other circumstances may justify cancellation: ill-health, for example. If there has been no cancellation, it is an offence for the developer to take no action to cancel. Failure to start the building work within three years of the acceptance of the initial notice permits the local authority to cancel the notice.[43]

Consequences of cessation of an initial notice

Suspension of the local authority's powers of enforcement continues only so long as there is no cancellation of an initial notice. The Building Act prescribes a variety of consequences in the event of cessation, particularly where plans certificates and final certificates are given prior to that date.[44]

Supervision of their own work by public bodies

If a public body approved by the Secretary of State proposes to carry out building work and that body considers that its own servants and agents can undertake adequate supervision of that work, it may certify its own work in particular cases. However, it is required that that public body should first give the local authority a "public body's notice". The scheme here is broadly similar to that in relation to that governing approved inspectors, although requirements about independence and insurance do not apply[45]

Appeals

There is a right of appeal to the magistrates' court against a local authority's rejection of an initial notice, a plans certificate or a final certificate given by an

[42] *NHBC Buiding Services v. Sandwell Borough Council* (1990) 50 B.L.R. 101.
[43] Building Act, s.52.
[44] *Ibid.* s.53.
[45] *Ibid.* s.54.

approved inspector or a public body. The court has the power to confirm a rejection or give a direction to the authority to accept the notice or certificate. There is a further appeal available to the Crown Court if a person is aggrieved by a determination, confirmation, direction or other decision of the magistrates' court.[46]

Registers

Each local authority is required to maintain registers of information about notices, certificates and insurance cover, to be made available to the public at all reasonable hours. The primary purpose of facilitating such information is to inform any future owner or injured party. The time scale for the recording of initial notices and public bodies' notices is limited, since they need appear on the register only for so long as they are in force. A record of a final certificate may bring the prospect of immunity from liability for the local authority in the event of damage, loss or injury accruing from a contravention of building regulations.[47]

Offences

It is an offence to give a notice or certificate which the person giving it knows to contain a false or misleading statement, or to give a notice or certificate recklessly where it contains a false or misleading statement.[48] In *NHBC Building Services v. Sandwell Borough Council*,[49] the court held that the facts found did not establish that there had been recklessness on the part of the appellant, an approved inspector, because the local authority site inspectors did not suggest that the final certificate was given in circumstances where there was an apparent risk that it was false, or that no thought was given to the risk of its falsity.

Fire Precautions

The Fire Precautions Act 1971

The Act strengthens and rationalises the law governing fire precautions in places of public entertainment and resort and in certain kinds of residential premises. Control is based on a requirement that a fire certificate specifying means of escape from fire, and fire-fighting and fire alarm systems, be obtained from the fire authority in respect of classes of premises designated by the Secretary of State for the Environment.

[46] *Ibid.* s.55.
[47] *Ibid.* s.56.
[48] *Ibid.* s.57.
[49] See n.42, *supra*.

Premises subject to the Act

The fire authority's certificate is required in respect of any premises put to a "designated" use. That process of designation by order of the Secretary of State is constrained by expressly defined classes of use, namely:

(a) use as, or for any purpose involving the provision of, sleeping accommodation;
(b) use as, or as part of, an institution providing treatment or care;
(c) use for the purposes of entertainment, recreation or instruction or for the purposes of any club, society or assocation;
(d) use for any purpose involving access to the premises by members of the public, whether on payment or otherwise; and
(e) use as a place of work.[50]

Under these powers the following orders have been made: the Fire Precautions (Hotels and Boarding Houses) Order 1972[51] and the Fire Precautions (Factories, Offices, Shops and Railway Premises) Order 1989.[52]

The only general exemption from the requirement for a fire certificate relates to premises consisting of or comprised in a house which is occupied as a single private dwelling.[53] This reference to a "private dwelling" is a reference to the dwelling of a private person: a company is incapable of such use.[54]

The Act stipulates that if premises consisting of part of a building are put to a designated use, any other part of the building which is occupied "together with" those premises "in connection with that use of them" shall be treated under the Act as forming part of the premises put to that use.[55] It should be noted that a "building" for the purposes of the Act "includes any temporary or movable building and also includes any permanent structure and a temporary structure other than a movable one".[56] The term "structure" is not defined in the Act. However it has been said that a "structure"

> ". . . is anything which is constructed, [involving] the notion of something which is put together, consisting of a number of different things which are so put together or built together, constructed as to make one whole which is then called a structure".[57]

In certain circumstances, the fire authority may impose a requirement for a compulsory fire certificate for the use of certain premises as a dwelling. Such a requirement will be contained in a notice served by the fire authority on the

[50] Fire Precautions Act, s.1.
[51] S.I. 1972 No. 238.
[52] S.I. 1989 No. 76.
[53] Fire Precautions Act 1971, s.2.
[54] *G.E. Stevens (High Wycombe) Ltd v. High Wycombe Corporation* [1962] 2 Q.B. 547.
[55] Fire Precautions Act, s.1(8).
[56] *Ibid.* s.43(1).
[57] *Per* Humphreys J. in *Hobday v. Nichol* [1944] 1 All E.R. 302.

owner or the occupier, or the person having overall management of the building. The premises in question must either have living accommodation which is, *inter alia*, two or more floors above the ground floor or be used for the keeping of explosive or highly flammable materials.[58] There is an appeal, on restricted grounds, to the magistrates' court in respect of a notice served by the fire authority under section 3 of the Act.[59]

Fire certificates

The process of certification attracts a wide range of requirements focusing on:

(a) application requirements;
(b) inspection;
(c) disclosure of information;
(d) the substance of the fire certificate;
(e) charging for certification; and
(f) the implications arising from changes to and alteration of premises.

Rights of appeal in the present context are also dealt with.

Fire certificate applications

The prescribed form of an application to the fire authority is laid down in regulations.[60] Pending a decision on the application, an occupier is subject to certain duties:

(a) to secure that means of escape in case of fire provided in the premises can be safely and effectively used at all times;
(b) to secure that means for fighting fire provided in the premises are maintained in efficient working order; and
(c) to secure that any persons employed to work in the premises receive instruction or training in what to do in the event of fire.[61]

The fire authority is obliged to advise the applicant of the foregoing duties, although it is the occupier who is subject to them and on whom any prohibition may be served for the purposes of section 10.

The fire authority is empowered to demand from the applicant additional information, including plans. However, if plans are not forthcoming in the prescribed period, the fire authority may regard the application as having been withdrawn.[62] Assuming that the authority considers that an application has been

[58] Fire Precautions Act, s.3. *Cf.* s.36.
[59] *Ibid.* s.4.
[60] Fire Precautions (Application for Certificate) Regulations 1989 (S.I. 1989 No. 77); Fire Precautions Act, s.5.
[61] Fire Precautions Act, s.5(2A).
[62] *Ibid.* subs.(2).

duly made, it is subject to a duty to carry out an inspection of the building.[63] According to the authority's view of the seriousness of fire risk, it may grant exemption from the requirement for a certificate in respect of the particular use of the premises. However, any such exemption is not available in respect of a hotel or boarding house, by virtue of the order affecting these premises.[64]

The fire certificate

Where the fire authority has undertaken an inspection of the premises subject to the application and is satisfied that means of escape from fire and related fire precautions are such as may reasonably be required in the circumstances, there is a mandatory duty to issue a fire certificate.[65] The certificate will list a number of matters, covering:

(a) the use or uses of the premises;
(b) the means of escape in case of fire;
(c) the means for ensuring that the means of escape can be safely and effectively used at all material times;
(d) the type, number and location of firefighting equipment available for use in the premises; and
(e) the type, number and location of fire alarms.[66]

Having inspected the premises in question, the fire authority may not be satisfied about these matters. If this is the case, that authority may serve a notice indicating to the applicant the steps required to remedy the situation and the time scale for such action. If a certificate is not then issued, or not issued within any extended period agreed with the authority, or by the court where there has been an appeal, there is a deemed refusal of the certificate and the premises may not be used for the purpose in question.[67]

In addition to the above "mandatory" matters to be included in a fire certificate, there are also various discretionary matters. These matters include the number of people who may be in the premises at any one time and requirements that means of escape are properly maintained and kept free of any obstruction.[68]

There is a prerequisite that all mandatory requirements are kept in accordance with the specification. In the case of the discretionary requirements, there is a need for them always to be observed.[69] Although it is the occupier of the premises

[63] *Ibid.* subs.(3).
[64] See, n.46, *supra*, and *cf.* ss.1(3) and 5A. As to the withdrawal of exemptions, see s.5B. As to change of conditions affecting exempted premises, see s.8A.
[65] Fire Precautions Act, s.5(3).
[66] *Ibid.* s.6(1).
[67] *Ibid.* ss.5(4) and 9(1)(a). As to the duty of the fire authority to consult with the relevant local authority for the purpose of s.5(4), see s.17 of the Act.
[68] *Ibid.* s.6(2).
[69] *Ibid.* subs.(4).

who is required to observe the foregoing requirements and other obligations in a fire certificate, the fire authority may also impose requirements on others. As a result, particular requirements or other obligations may be imposed on other individuals as well as, or instead of, the occupier. If the fire authority so wish, it may (after appropriate consultations) impose requirements in the fire certificate on other parts of a building in separate occupation.[70]

Reasonable fees may be charged by a fire authority for the issue of a fire certificate, the amendment of a certificate and for the issue of a new certificate as an alternative to amendment. However, the fee does not include any cost of inspection.[71]

Change of conditions affecting adequacy of a fire certificate

A proposal to undertake a material extension of or a material structural alteration to premises, or a proposal to undertake a material alteration to the internal arrangements of a set of premises (including furniture or equipment provided), must be notified in advance to the fire authority. Failure to comply is an offence. What is "material" for present purposes is a matter of fact, although it seems clear that even minor alterations which may affect means of escape, for example, will be caught by the notification requirement. The fire authority may take the view that precautions will be inadequate by reference to the alterations proposed. This fact will be notified to the occupier (who is the person responsible for initial notification under these provisions) and thereafter the fire authority will issue a new or amend the "old" fire certificate.[72]

Requirements affecting exempt premises

Reference was made previously to the matter of exemption from fire precautions requirements.[73] Whether premises are subject to exemption under section 1(3) or 5A of the Act, it is a requirement that those premises be provided with such means of escape in case of fire and such means for fighting fire as may reasonably be required in the circumstances of the case. Failure to comply with the duty enforced through an improvement notice here is an offence.[74] For the purpose of compliance with this duty, the Secretary of State is empowered to issue codes of practice.[75] Failure to comply with such a code of practice will not of itself render an individual liable to any criminal or civil proceedings. However, in any such proceedings, failure to observe the code may be relied on as tending to negate liability.[76]

[70] *Ibid.* subs.(5).
[71] *Ibid.* s.8B.
[72] *Ibid.* s.8. As to the duty to consult with the local authority, see s.17 of the Act.
[73] See n.159, *supra.*
[74] Fire Precautions Act, s.9A. *Cf.* the Housing Act 1985, ss.365 and 368 for detailed requirements in this context.
[75] *Ibid.* s.9B.
[76] *Ibid.* s.9C.

The duty under section 9A is enforceable by means of an improvement notice served by a fire authority which is of the opinion that this duty has been contravened.[77] The occupier of the premises on whom the notice may be served has a right of appeal to the magistrates' court.[78] The offence of failing to comply with an improvement notice is triable summarily, or on indictment.[79] Although the Act simply states that it is an offence for a "a person" to contravene "any requirement" imposed by an improvement notice, the notice must require the occupier (on whom it is served) to take steps to remedy the contravention. Accordingly, prosecutions are more likely to focus on that occupier's overall obligation to comply.

Excessive risk in case of fire

Where a fire authority is of the opinion that the risk to persons in premises in the event of fire will be so serious that use of those premises should be prohibited or restricted, that authority may serve a prohibition notice on the occupier. The element of risk here includes anything affecting escape from the premises in the event of fire. Although the notice may be primarily restrictive, nevertheless it may include directions about the steps to be taken to remedy the situation identified in the notice. The notice will take effect immediately it is served if the authority considers that the risk of serious personal injury is, or may be, imminent. In any other case, the notice will indicate that the notice takes effect at the end of a period specified.[80] There is an appeal against a prohibition notice to the magistrates' court. Unless the court so directs, that appeal will not have the effect of suspending the notice.[81]

Enforcement of the Fire Precautions Act

It is the duty of each fire authority to enforce within its area the provisions of the Act as well as the accompanying regulations and for these purposes to appoint inspectors. Where the inspection of premises is concerned, each fire authority is obliged to act in accordance with any guidance that may be given to them by the Secretary of State. In the case of specified premises used as a place of work, a fire authority may agree that certain specified functions be enforced by the Health and Safety Executive.[82]

[77] *Ibid.* s.9D.
[78] *Ibid.* s.9E.
[79] *Ibid.* s.9F.
[80] *Ibid.* s.10. A notice may be served also in respect of a dwelling covered by s.3 see n.53, *supra*, as well as in respect of premises whose use (designated or not) falls into any of the classes mentioned in s.1(2) but not premises exempt under s.2.
[81] *Ibid.* s.10B. As to a defence here, see s.10B(2).
[82] *Ibid.* s.18.

Powers of inspection and disclosure of information

An inspector is empowered to do anything necessary to carry the Fire Precautions Act into effect, including entry to premises "to inspect the whole or any part thereof and anything therein" and inquiries about the status of premises, as well as powers to require production of a fire certificate.[83]

An inspector may not disclose information obtained while on any premises for the purpose of executing duties under the Act unless that disclosure is necessary for the performance of duties, for the purpose of legal proceedings and for the purpose of an enforcing authority (as defined by the Health and Safety at Work Act 1974) discharging functions and responsibilities within its statutory jurisdiction.[84]

The appeals process

In the context of the enforcement process, the availability of an appeal and the impact of the result of any such appeal are significant factors. There is an appeal to the magistrates' court in a number of situations arising from decisions or other action of a fire authority, including a refusal to issue a fire certificate and any requirement in a direction given in connection with proposed alterations.[85] The court has a considerable power to make "such order as it thinks fit".[86] Reference has been made to the appeal facility in relation to prohibition notices.[87] Unlike the situation where an appeal is taken against a prohibition notice, an appeal in respect of a requirement contained in a fire certificate does not demand recognition and implementation of the requirement pending disposal of the appeal.[88] In the case of an appeal against the refusal of a fire authority to issue a certificate for premises, or the cancellation or amendment of a certificate as a result of section 8(7) or (9), no offence is committed for the purposes of section 7 where the premises are employed for a designated use or are used as a dwelling between the relevant date and the final disposal of the appeal.[89]

A further appeal from the decision of the magistrates' court is available under the Act, to the Crown Court. For the purpose of any such appeal, it is stated by the Act "for the avoidance of doubt" that both the fire authority and the local authority are "persons aggrieved".[90]

[83] *Ibid.* ss.19 and 20.
[84] *Ibid.* s.21.
[85] *Ibid.* s.9(1).
[86] *Ibid.*
[87] See nn.75 and 76, *supra*.
[88] Fire Precautions Act, s.9(4).
[89] *Ibid.* s.9(3).
[90] *Ibid.* s.27.

Offences

The offences referred to previously are to be seen in the context of a larger collection of offences in the Fire Precautions Act. Those offences fall into six broad categories.[91] If an offence is committed by a body corporate with the consent or connivance, or by the neglect, of any director, manager, secretary or other similar officer (or any person purporting to act in that capacity), that person will also be guilty of the subject offence.[92] If it is proved that an offence was caused by the act or default of some other person, that person may be charged, jointly or separately with the offence and will be liable to the same penalty.[93] Whatever the nature of the criminal proceedings under the Act, it is a defence for the person charged to prove that he took all reasonable precautions and exercised all due diligence to avoid commission of the offence in question.[94]

Civil liability

The Act states that, unless indicated otherwise, the statute is not to be construed as giving rise to a right to civil proceedings except for proceedings for the recovery of a fine. Any action at common law independent of the Act is not caught by this restriction, whereas proceedings for breach of statutory duty in tort would be caught.[95]

The modification of agreements and leases

On an application to the county court, that court may order that the terms and conditions of an agreement or lease shall be set aside or modified if considered just and equitable, for the purpose of undertaking compliance with fire precaution requirements initiated by the fire authority.[96]

The Fire Precautions Act and other legislation

Although certain premises are covered by Local Acts in connection with means of escape in case of fire and other fire precaution requirements, any such local provision lapses in so far as these matters are subject to a fire certificate under the

[91] *Ibid.* ss.17(1), (3), (3A), (4) and (6), 8(2), (3) and (7), 10B(1) and (2), 19(6), 21(1), 22(1).

[92] *Ibid.* s.23(1). An employee in charge of a shop during the general manager's absence on holiday was not a "manager" for present purposes: *R. v. Boal* [1992] 2 W.L.R. 890.

[93] *Ibid.* s.24.

[94] *Ibid.* s.25.

[95] *Ibid.* s.27A.

[96] *Ibid.* s.28.

Act of 1971 or subject to regulations made under section 12 by the Secretary of State.[97]

If premises are subject to regulatory licensing and the terms of any such licence overlap with fire precaution requirements under the Act of 1971, those licence terms (with some exceptions[98]) are suspended in so far as those matters could be dealt with by a fire certificate.[99]

Any person who fails to do anything in relation to premises in contravention of a Local Act is not treated as being in legal contravention of the Act if failure is attributable to the fact that any remedy would contravene the Fire Precautions Act.[1]

The building regulations

Where building regulations applied to a building at the time of initial construction or alteration, in connection with means of escape in case of fire requiring plans to be deposited with the local authority, a fire authority is unable to require execution of works for structural or other alteration in a notice of steps to be taken. However, this restriction will not apply if the fire authority considers that means of escape in the event of fire are inadequate by reason of circumstances, usually where the local authority has not required that the matter be addressed through a deposit of plans.[2]

Crown premises

The provisions of the Fire Precautions Act apply to Crown premises. However, the issue of fire certificates and enforcement generally are in the hands of fire inspectors from the Fire Service Inspectorates of the Home Office or the Scottish Office. Any building partially occupied by the Crown and partially in private occupation will therefore see a division of responsibility as between the fire inspectors and the appropriate fire authority. In general terms, there is a distinction between premises occupied by the Crown not subject to the "coercive" enforcement provisions of the Act and premises owned but not occupied by the Crown which are generally subject to coercive enforcement provisions.[3]

[97] *Ibid.* s.30(2).
[98] *Ibid.* Sched. 2, para. 7.
[99] *Ibid.* s.31(1).
[1] *Ibid.* s.32.
[2] *Ibid.* s.13.
[3] *Ibid.* s.40.

Miscellaneous Controls

Defective premises

There are two areas of significance here: the power of a local authority to act under section 76 of the Building Act, and the provisions of the Defective Premises Act 1972. Section 76 empowers a local authority (principally a district council or London borough) to require the remedying of defective premises, while the Act of 1972 provides for a statutory duty to build dwellings properly.

Defective premises control under the Building Act

Where premises appear to a local authority to be in such a defective state as to be prejudicial to health or a nuisance, and unreasonable delay in remedying the condition would be occasioned through the use of the statutory nuisance procedures of the Environmental Protection Act, Pt. III, the authority may serve on the person (on whom it could have served an abatement notice under section 80 of the Act of 1990) an alternative notice. That alternative notice will state that the local authority intends to remedy the defective state of the premises and identify the defects intended to be remedied. Where this power is used (and it may be used notwithstanding that the local authority might have proceeded under Part IX of the Housing Act 1985 by means of a repairs notice), the authority may be unable to recover its expenses if a magistrates' court considers that adoption of the section 76 procedure was not justified.[4] The person on whom the section 76 notice is served may remedy the defects himself if he serves the appropriate counter-notice and effects, or at least commences, the relevant works within a period of time considered by the local authority to be reasonable.[5]

Where a section 76 notice is served, there is no facility for an appeal. Furthermore, the Building Act makes no provision for any non-compliance with the section 76 notice. Section 99 of the Act relating to matters of content and enforcement of notices served under any provision of the Act does not apply to notices in the present context.

The Defective Premises Act 1972

The Act relates to any person who takes on work for or in connection with a building, whether involving its erection, conversion or enlargement, for the purpose of ". . . the provision of a dwelling". Any such person is subject to a duty to see that the work taken on is done ". . . in a workmanlike or, as the case may be, professional manner, with proper materials and so that as regards that work the dwelling will be fit for habitation when completed".[6] Discharge of this duty is deemed to occur where a person takes on the above work on terms that it is to be done in accordance with instructions given by or on behalf of another person

[4] As to an appeal against such a determination, see s.86.
[5] As to local authority officers' powers of entry for present purposes, see ss.95 and 96.
[6] Defective Premises Act, s.1.

requiring the work and the work is done properly in accordance with those instructions.[7] Local authorities and developers arranging for others to undertake work in respect of dwellings are, however, regarded in law as undertaking the work themselves.[8] The period of limitation is calculated by reference to the time when the dwelling is completed.[9]

No action for breach of statutory duty is available on the part of a person having or acquiring an interest in the dwelling in certain circumstances, more particularly where the dwelling and its first sale or letting is included in a scheme approved by the Secretary of State.[10]

If a dwelling is disposed of following commencement of the Act on January 1, 1974, that disposal does not negate any duty of care owed in respect of works of construction, repair, maintenance, demolition or other work on or in relation to the subject premises. The beneficiaries of such a duty are those who might reasonably be expected to be affected by the defects in the state of the premises created by the doing of the work.[11] Accordingly, the duty of care operates to protect those who might otherwise be subject to *caveat emptor*.

Dangerous, ruinous and dilapidated buildings

A range of provisions in the Building Act—sections 77–83—provide for buildings that fall within the above description as well as measures relating to demolition. If a structure or building (or any part thereof) is in a dangerous condition, the local authority is empowered to apply to the magistrates' court. The court may order the owner to undertake remedial work or, if he so chooses, to demolish the building or structure and to remove any resulting rubbish. In the event of any default by the owner, the local authority—again principally a district council or London borough—may execute the order itself in any manner it thinks fit and at the owner's expense. Additionally, the owner may be liable to a fine on summary conviction.[12] However, if it appears to the local authority that immediate action is necessary, it may take such steps as may be necessary to remove the danger, recovering its costs from the owner through the magistrates' court. However, if it is reasonably practicable, the local authority is required to give prior notice to the owner and occupier. If this set of powers is used by the local authority, the magistrates' court may, in the course of proceedings for the recovery of expenses, inquire whether proceedings under section 77 (above) might reasonably have been taken. Emergency action under section 78 may be taken by a "proper officer" of the local authority, namely an officer actually appointed for the purpose under powers of delegation.[13]

[7] *Ibid.* subs.(2).
[8] *Ibid.* subs.(4).
[9] *Ibid.* subs.(5).
[10] *Ibid.* s.2. Note the approval of NHBC schemes here.
[11] *Ibid.* s.3.
[12] Building Act, s.77. *Cf.* ss.283–288 of the Housing Act 1985, relating to obstructive buildings, described in Chap. 12, "Housing".
[13] *Ibid.* s.78.

A local authority may also deal with a ruinous building or structure. If it appears to the local authority that a building or structure is, by reason of its ruinous or dilapidated condition, seriously detrimental to the amenities of the neighbourhood, the authority may by notice require the owner to execute works of repair or restoration or (if he so chooses) demolish the building or structure and remove any rubbish or other material which is the product of the demolition. In the event of default, the local authority may undertake the necessary works and recover its expenses, as well as removing rubbish or other material from the land in question, in the interests of amenity. Any notice served here must comply with requirements in the Act for the content and enforcement of notices (section 99) and may be subject to appeal to the magistrates' court but, in relation to section 99, subject to some modifications.[14] Failure to comply with a local authority's requirements is an offence punishable on summary conviction with provision for continuing fines also.[15]

The Building Act also makes provision to ensure that, if demolition of the whole or part of a building occurs, a local authority is empowered to require that proper steps be taken for the purpose of shoring-up and weatherproofing adjacent buildings, removing materials and other rubbish, disconnecting and sealing drains, removing drains and other pipes and generally making good the surface of the ground. The local authority's requirements must be made within a stipulated period of time, although the person intending to undertake the demolition is first required to give notice of an intention to demolish. Any notice served by the local authority is subject to appeal to the magistrates' court.[16] Various permitted development rights in respect of demolition under the Town and Country Planning General Development Order 1988[17] do not affect the position and are not affected by the requirement to notify intended demolition to the local authority.

The protection of buildings

If it appears to a local authority—principally a district council or London borough—that a building (or structure) is not effectively secured against unauthorised entry or is likely to become a danger to public health, the authority may undertake works in connection with the building for the purpose of preventing unauthorised entry or for the purpose of preventing the building becoming a danger to public health. Prior to any action, the authority is required to serve a notice on each owner or occupier indicating the nature of its intentions. However, these powers are available only in respect of any unoccupied building or any building whose occupier appears to be temporarily absent.[18] An appeal is available in respect of a notice served here, the appeal being to the county court,[19]

[14] *Ibid.* s.79. *Cf.* ss.215–219, Town and Country Planning Act 1990.
[15] *Ibid.* s.99(2).
[16] *Ibid.* ss.80–83.
[17] S.I. 1988 No. 1813, as amended.
[18] Local Government (Miscellaneous Provisions) Act 1982, s.29.
[19] *Ibid.* s.31.

although there is an emergency procedure which will not require a notice if action is required "immediately" and the owner or occupier are not immediately identifiable.[20]

[20] *Ibid.* s.29(8).

CHAPTER 12

HOUSING

The Maintenance and Improvement of Physical Standards

The present chapter concentrates on a variety of statutory prescriptions to be found primarily in the Housing Act 1985 (as amended by the Local Government and Housing Act 1989), aimed at maintaining basic standards in the physical environment of housing and enhancing those standards where possible, usually through devices such as the scheme of grant-aid which is made available. The statutory framework divides into eight areas which form the body of the chapter, covering:

(a) the housing fitness standard[1];
(b) repair powers[2];
(c) clearance[3];
(d) multiple occupation[4];
(e) area renewal[5];
(f) grant-aid[6];
(g) over-crowding[7]; and
(h) common lodging houses.[8]

The Housing Fitness Standard

The housing fitness standard is the necessary starting point for most issues relating to environmental health and housing as represented by the topics previously listed. The Housing Act 1985[9] lists a number of criteria to be satisfied if any premises are to be categorised as fit for human habitation. Any local authority may form an opinion, however, that premises are unfit for human habitation, a

[1] Housing Act 1986, Pt. XVIII.
[2] *Ibid.* Pt. VI.
[3] *Ibid.* Pt. IX.
[4] *Ibid.* Pt. XI.
[5] Local Government and Housing Act, Pt. VII.
[6] *Ibid.* Pt. VIII.
[7] Housing Act, Pt. X.
[8] *Ibid.* Pt. XII.
[9] s.604.

conclusion based on the fact that those premises fail to meet one or more of the requirements listed by the Act with the consequence that they are not reasonably suitable for occupation.

A dwelling-house (or house in multiple occupation) is fit for human habitation unless, in the opinion of the local housing authority, it fails to meet one or more of the following standards and is thus not reasonably suitable for occupation. The standards concern the following matters:

(a) structural stability;
(b) freedom from serious disrepair;
(c) freedom from dampness prejudicial to the health of any occupants;
(d) adequate provision for lighting, heating and ventilation;
(e) adequate supplies of piped, wholesome water;
(f) satisfactory facilities for the preparation and cooking of food, including a sink with a satisfactory supply of hot and cold water;
(g) a suitably located fixed bath or shower and hand-basin, each provided with a satisfactory supply of hot and cold water, for the exclusive use of any occupants; and
(h) an effective system for the draining of foul, waste and surface water.[10]

Whether or not a dwelling-house which is a flat satisfies the foregoing requirements, it will be regarded as being unfit for human habitation if, in the opinion of the local authority, the building or a part of the building outside the flat fails to meet one or more of five requirements, meaning that the flat is not reasonably suitable for occupation.[11] Those five requirements are that the building or part of it:

(a) is structurally stable;
(b) is free from serious disrepair;
(c) is free from dampness;
(d) has adequate provision for ventilation; and
(e) has an effective system for the draining of foul, waste and surface water.[12]

This provision extends to a flat in multiple occupation.[13]

The necessary starting point in any determination of fitness is the effect of the conditions in question, which emphasises the requirement that the dwelling-house be "reasonably suitable for occupation". It has been observed, for example, that ". . . the standard of repair required . . . is naturally . . . a humble standard. It is only required that the place must be decently fit for human beings to live in".[14] It has also been observed[15] that unfitness may be referable not only to structural and

[10] *Ibid.* subs.(1), (3).
[11] *Ibid.* subs.(2).
[12] *Ibid.*
[13] *Ibid.* subs.(4).
[14] *Jones v. Green* [1925] 1 K.B. 659, *per* Salter J. at 668.
[15] *Hall v. Manchester Corporation* [1914–15] All E.R. 372.

other defects in a building, but also to other reasons, such as want of ventilation. Whatever the circumstances, "... the standard to be applied would seem to be that of the ordinary reasonable man".[16] Furthermore, judgments here are matters for the "judicial" discretion of the individual local authority.[17] An application of the statutory criteria must relate to the condition of the premises which will usually rule out consideration of the utilisation of those premises. One member of the court was able to conclude that "... by modern standards, the house was in winter, when, of course ... condensation was worst, virtually unfit for human habitation".[18] Such a conclusion may be supportable if the evidence available shows something other than an extraordinary use of the dwelling-house in question, referable in this type of case, no doubt, to the absence of adequate provision for ventilation.

Guidance on the fitness standard

A circular from the Department of the Environment[19] sets out Guidance Notes on the fitness standard.[20] These Guidance Notes are aimed at assisting local authorities in determining whether or not a dwelling-house is fit for human habitation. The Circular further stresses the importance of an objective interpretation of the standard, to ensure an accurate assessment of housing conditions and trends, the just administration of compulsory housing powers, and fair and equal access to mandatory grants under the house renovation grant scheme.[21]

In dealing with the matter of "fitness for human habitation", the Guidance Notes stress that discomfort, inconvenience and inefficiency may be relevant factors in making a judgment, although the primary concern is with safeguarding the health and safety of any occupants. The extent of any such risk will be governed by the nature of any defects present in the dwelling-house. The Guidance Notes refer to matters of use, already referred to, and go on to emphasise that premises must be reasonably suitable for occupation, so that there may be circumstances in which they could be unfit (say) for disabled occupation. A local authority should take each of the statutory requirements in turn for the purpose of applying the key test of reasonable suitability for occupation. For this purpose, the Guidance Notes recommend a thorough inspection of the dwelling-house internally and externally.

Freedom from serious disrepair focuses attention on whether there has been subsequent deterioration of elements and fixtures that go to make up a building in question. The safety of occupants may be threatened by deterioration of (say) the roof. Internally serious disrepair may be seriously threatening if, for example, a

[16] *Ibid. per* Lord Parker at 381.
[17] *Ibid.*
[18] *Quick v. Taff Ely District Council* [1985] 3 All E.R. 321, *per* Dillon L.J. at 323. *Cf.* n.28, *infra.*
[19] Circular 6/90.
[20] *Ibid.* Annex A.
[21] *Ibid. Cf.* "Monitoring the New Housing Fitness Standard" (Department of the Environment/HMSO, 1993).

stairway is in a state of near collapse. Accordingly, a local authority is advised to have regard to, *inter alia*, the extent to which, by virtue of disrepair, the fabric is liable to fail or dislodge, so becoming a real threat to the safety of the occupants. A further example of internal failure may show that a persistently leaking pipe is causing serious dampness, prejudicial to the health of the occupants. In practice, it has been shown that disrepair is the stumbling block for most dwellings, followed by dampness.[22]

Structural stability requirements seek "... to avoid safety hazards of a catastrophic nature such as death and injury due to collapse ...".[23] In a domestic building, typically, structural instability may be caused by deterioration of building materials. The local authority is advised to have regard to the various building regulations,[24] *inter alia*, although failure to meet requirements here is not regarded *per se* as being indicative of unfitness. Furthermore:

> "In deciding whether a dwelling-house is or is not unfit, the authority should consider whether the dwelling-house or building is currently able to withstand the combined dead, imposed and wind loads to which it is likely to be subjected in the ordinary course of events and when used for the purposes for which it is intended, and normal ground movement of the sub-soil caused by swelling, shrinkage or freezing and is free from ongoing movement and the probability of movement which constitutes a threat to any occupants."[25]

In arriving at a determination, a local authority is further advised to have regard to the structural adequacy and bearing of floors, stairs, ceilings and balconies, and the distortion, integrity and movement of foundations and footings, *inter alia*.[26]

The statutory requirement for dampness is that there should be freedom from dampness prejudicial to the health of any occupants. The Guidance Notes stress that wet surfaces caused by condensation or rising or penetrating damp, *inter alia*, are associated with ill health. Furthermore, the Guidance Notes point out that dampness can also be prejudicial to health, while the presence of excess moisture can lead, in addition, to instability and disrepair through decay of building materials. Once again, as in the case of the treatment of structural instability, regard may be had to a variety of standards such as those in the Building Regulations 1991.[27] The Guidance Notes point to the fact that the extent, location, frequency and persistence of any dampness, of whatever cause, will be particularly important in determining whether conditions are prejudicial to health. Dampness in the often controversial area of condensation should only, the

[22] *Ibid.*

[23] Circular 6/90, Annex A.

[24] *Ibid.*: see, in particular, the Building Regulations 1991 (S.I. 1991 No. 2768), Sched. 1, Part A, Approved Document A, and Circular 13/92 (Welsh Office Circular 29/92).

[25] Circular 6/90, Annex A.

[26] *Ibid.*

[27] Building Regulations 1991. See, in particular, Sched. 1, Part C, Approved Document C, and Circular 13/92 (Welsh Office Circular 29/92).

Guidance Notes declare, be considered as constituting unfitness if it is persistent and primarily attributable to the design, construction, modification, standard of amenities or state of repair of the dwelling.[28]

The adequate provision of ventilation, often a matter to be considered in the context of condensation problems, is also isolated specifically in the fitness standard. The Guidance Notes provide an explicit reminder of the fact that ventilation is essential for the removal of pollutants directly or indirectly injurious to health. Assessment of the severity and extent of defects may be by reference to standards, again to be found in the Building Regulations[29] and other sources, such as the appropriate British Standard,[30] although, again, failure to meet these standards would not, *per se*, constitute grounds of unfitness. In reaching a determination for present purposes, the local authority is advised to have regard to various matters, including the size and location of the openable parts of windows and doors, the size and location of louvres or other ventilators and the efficiency of any mechanical ventilation.[31]

The remaining elements of the fitness standard relate to:

(a) adequate provision of heating;
(b) the adequate provision of lighting;
(c) an adequate piped supply of wholesome water;
(d) satisfactory facilities for the preparation and cooking of food (including a sink with a satisfactory supply of hot and cold water);
(e) a suitably located water closet, wash-basin and bath or shower; and
(f) an effective system for the draining of foul, waste and surface water.

In dealing with the adequacy of heating, the Guidance Notes provide, again, detailed prescriptions drawing on the Building Regulations[32] and various British Standards.[33] The matter of adequate lighting requires consideration, again against a background of British Standards. In particular, the question is whether a dwelling-house has provision for sufficient natural lighting in habitable rooms to enable normal activities of a household to be carried out safely and conveniently without use of artificial light during normal daytime conditions.[34] Minimum standards for an adequate supply of wholesome water are set by regulation,[35] although standards may be drawn from other sources.[36] Despite an argument that a supply of water remains and may easily be restored, it may be the case that

[28] *Cf.* dicta in the case of *Quick, supra.*

[29] Building Regulations 1991. See, in particular, Sched. 1, Part F, Approved Document F, and Circular 13/92 (Welsh Office Circular 29/92).

[30] BS5250.

[31] Circular 6/90, Annex A.

[32] Building Regulations 1991. See, in particular, Sched. 1, Part J, Approved Document J, and Circular 13/92 (Welsh Office Circular 29/92).

[33] BS5449, on domestic central heating, for example.

[34] BS8206, on lighting for buildings, for example.

[35] Water Supply (Water Quality) Regulations 1989 (S.I. 1989 No. 1147), as amended by S.I. 1991 No. 1837. *Cf.* the Private Water Supplies Regulations 1991 (S.I. 1991 No. 2790).

[36] See, in particular, BS6700.

disconnection could render a dwelling unfit.[37] The Guidance Notes relating to facilities for the preparation and cooking of food again stress a large number of detailed prescriptions, based primarily on relevant British Standards.[38] The requirements for water closets, wash-basins and baths or showers refer again to a number of detailed prescriptions that spread across the Building Regulations,[39] British Standards[40] and the Department of the Environment's Design Bulletin.[41] The final requirement, relating to the provision of an effective system for the draining of foul, waste and surface water, naturally focuses on standards referable to an "effective" system. Those standards necessarily take account of both health hazards and problems of (say) dampness that may adversely affect the fabric and materials that go to make up the building. In arriving at a determination, the Guidance Notes advise that the following matters are taken into account:

(a) the coverage and capacity of the system;
(b) the system's susceptibility to blockage or leakage;
(c) facilities for the clearance of blockages;
(d) ventilation of the system; and
(e) measures to prevent foul air entering the dwelling.

Local authorities are advised to take account of the Building Regulations[42] and certain British Standards.[43]

Repair Powers

The core of Part VI of the Housing Act 1985 is a collection of provisions governing the service and enforcement of repair notices. The two principal provisions relate to any house, or house in multiple occupation, which is either unfit for human habitation or in such a state of disrepair that, although not unfit for human habitation, substantial repairs are necessary to bring it up to a reasonable standard. As to complementary powers which may be available, see Chapter 10 "Statutory Nuisance".

Repair powers and unfit houses

If a local housing authority is satisfied that a house (or a house in multiple occupation) is unfit for human habitation, that authority is normally subject to a mandatory duty to serve a repair notice on the person having control of that

[37] Disconnection obliges an undertaker to notify the local authority: Water Industry Act 1991, s.63.
[38] See, *e.g.* BS6172, on the installation of domestic gas cooking appliances.
[39] Building Regulations 1991. See, in particular, Sched. 1. Part G, Approved Document G, and Circular 13/92 (Welsh Office Circular 29/92).
[40] BS6465.
[41] Design Bulletin 24 (1972).
[42] Building Regulations 1991. See, in particular, Sched. 1, Part H, Approved Document H, and Circular 13/92 (Welsh Office Circular 29/92).
[43] *e.g.* BS8301, dealing with building drainage.

house, or house in multiple occupation, if satisfied that such a notice is the most satisfactory course of action in accordance with the Code of Guidance issued under section 604A for dealing with unfit premises.[44] Provision is also made by the Act for a repair notice to be served in the same way in respect of a dwelling-house in multiple occupation as a flat.[45]

The duty placed on the local authority, as a mandatory duty, is probably not enforceable by mandamus in proceedings for judicial review before the High Court under R.S.C., Ord. 53. Such a conclusion is based on the fact that a good deal of the present provision is based on the subjective judgment of the local authority. No doubt the most to be expected from such proceedings would be an order of mandamus requiring consideration or a reconsideration by the local authority in question.[46] Express exemption from what is probably only an ostensible duty is to be found elsewhere. The local authority is not obliged to serve a repair notice if it is satisfied that a group repair scheme including the house in question will be prepared within a period of 12 months.[47] However, if nevertheless the authority decide to serve a repair notice, that notice may relate only to those matters not contemplated by the group repair scheme.[48] More generally, the notice will be served on the person having control of the house. Such a person is entitled to receive the rack-rent of the premises.[49] In the case of a house in multiple occupation, the notice may be served on the person managing the house.[50] When the authority has served a repair notice on the person in control, it must also, as a mandatory requirement, serve a copy of the notice on any other person having an interest in the house, whether as freeholder, mortgagee or lessee.[51] If the housing authority is itself in control of a house for present purposes, a repair notice is not available, although the position would be different if the local authority had an interest in the house without being in control.[52]

A repair notice must require execution of the specified works within a reasonable time, defined as being no earlier than seven days from the operative date of the notice. Furthermore, the notice may specify not only works of repair but also additionally, or in the alternative, works of improvement.[53]

The decision to serve a repair notice

In broad terms, the Housing Act demands that a local housing authority shall at least once in each year consider housing conditions in its district with a view to determining what action to take in performance of its functions under the present

[44] Housing Act 1985, s.189(1).
[45] *Ibid.* subs.(1A).
[46] *R. v. Kerrier District Council, ex p. Guppy (Bridport) Ltd* (1977) 75 L.G.R. 129.
[47] Housing Act, s.190A.
[48] *Ibid.* subs.(1).
[49] *Ibid.* s.207.
[50] *Ibid.* s.189(1B).
[51] *Ibid.* subs.(3).
[52] *R. v. Cardiff City Council, ex p. Cross* (1981) 1 H.L.R. 54, affirmed (1982) 6 H.L.R. 6.
[53] Housing Act, s.189(2).

Part VI.[54] Any action that may be taken can only relate to a dwelling-house, or a house in multiple occupation. Whether premises fall into either of these categories is a question of law and fact, although other definitions elsewhere in the Act may, at best, be of marginal significance for present purposes. Although the court has referred to the need for a "judicial" exercise of the local authority's discretion in the present context[55] it appears that the law does not necessarily expect an in-depth analysis of data except to the extent prescribed by the requirement in section 189(1) that a local housing authority should have regard to the Code of Guidance issued by the Secretary of State under section 604A of the Act.[56]

Code of Guidance for dealing with unfit premises

Circular 6/90[57] sets out guidance for local authorities in relation to a number of Housing Act actions, including the service of repair notices. The Circular stresses that, having identified unfit premises by whatever means, an authority must consider the most satisfactory course of action to deal with them: renovation, closure or demolition, whether or not as part of a clearance area.[58] The Circular continues:

> "Authorities should therefore take into account a wider range of issues than just the cost of any works required to bring the premises up to the fitness standard. Both the costs and the longer term social implications of alternative courses of action should be considered. Account should also be taken of the impact of the alternatives available on other dwellings in the immediate vicinity ... Where possible authorities should make their decisions within the context of area strategies ... [A]uthorities should normally be able to show that they have not considered the unfit premises in isolation. They should, therefore, assess the effect of the various courses of action in the context in the areas in which the premises are situated... There may be certain circumstances in which a full survey and assessment would not be appropriate, for example in the case of completely isolated rural premises or a detached house in large grounds where the decision will be based simply on an appraisal of the various courses of action available for those premises."[59]

In deciding whether to serve a repair notice, the local housing authority is advised to:

(a) consider the physical condition of the premises;
(b) consider the life expectancy of those premises if repaired;

[54] *Ibid.* s.605.
[55] *Hall v. Manchester Corporation, supra.*
[56] *Bacon v. Grimsby Corporation* [1950] 1 K.B. 272.
[57] Annex F.
[58] *Ibid.* para. 4.
[59] *Ibid.* paras. 4 to 6.

(c) undertake an appraisal of the relative costs of renovation in relation to the other alternative courses of action;
(d) take into account proposals for the areas in which the premises are situated;
(e) take into account the condition of neighbouring properties;
(f) take into account the suitability of the premises for inclusion in a group repair scheme;
(g) consider local need for the particular type of premises;
(h) consider the wishes of the owner and occupants of the premises; and
(i) consider the local environment:
"... for example, the balance between residential and industrial premises, the suitability of the area for continued residential use and the effect which repair of the premises would have on the overall appearance of the immediate locality."[60]

Repair powers affecting fit houses in a state of disrepair

If a local housing authority is satisfied that a dwelling-house is in such a state of disrepair as to require substantial repairs to bring it up to a reasonable standard, having regard to its age, character and locality, the authority has a discretionary power which may lead to the service of a repair notice. Unlike the powers in section 189, there is no requirement that the dwelling-house be unfit for human habitation, and the powers are discretionary. The same characteristics also apply to accompanying powers where the authority may serve a repair notice on being satisfied about the state of disrepair of the dwelling-house, on a representation by an occupying tenant, as well as the fact that the condition of the dwelling-house is such as to interfere materially with personal comfort of that occupying tenant.[61]

The present powers extend, like the powers in section 189, to include houses and flats in multiple occupation and the provisions of section 190 also attract similar limits in relation to the earliest reasonable day on which works under the notice may commence.[62] If a notice is served in respect of a dwelling-house or flat,[63] it can be served only where there is an "occupying tenant" or the dwelling-house or building falls within a renewal area as provided for by Part VII of the Local Government and Housing Act 1989.[64] For present purposes, an "occupying tenant" is someone other than an owner-occupier who is entitled to occupy or actually occupies the house as a lessee, or is a statutory tenant, or occupies the house as a residence under a restricted contract, or is a "protected occupier" under the Rent (Agriculture) Act 1976, or is a licensee under an assured agricultural occupancy.[65]

As in the case of section 189 powers, a repair notice is normally served on the

[60] *Ibid.* para. 18.
[61] Housing Act, s.190.
[62] *Ibid.* subs.(2).
[63] But note a house in multiple occupation.
[64] Housing Act, s.190(1B). *Cf.* the following section of this chapter on area renewal.
[65] *Ibid.* s.207.

person having control of the dwelling-house in question, although in the case of a house in multiple occupation there is again an opportunity to serve the notice on a person managing that house.[66] Both sets of powers indicate that, if no appeal is brought, on the expiry of 21 days from the date of service of the notice, the notice becomes operative. Furthermore, the notice is regarded as being final and conclusive as to matters which could have been raised on appeal.[67] The notice under section 190 is not required to indicate completion of works to any particular standard, although, implicitly, the requirements should address the matter of "substantial repairs" to bring the house to a (relatively) reasonable standard. This is in contrast to the section 189 powers, which demand that a repair notice shall state the authority's opinion that the works specified will render the dwelling-house fit.[68]

A repair notice under section190 does not have to comply with high standards of particularity. The onus on the local authority has been described thus:

> "... the local authority must show the owner with reasonable precision what he has to do, but to dot every 'i' and cross every 't' would, I think, be impracticable and would, no doubt, result in an impossibly heavy burden upon local authorities and enormous expense in the surveying costs which they would be obliged to incur in preparing schedules of this sort."[69]

Furthermore: "... a reasonable test is that the schedule should be of sufficient particularity to enable the owner to obtain a costing for the work from a reasonable builder."[70]

The decision to serve a repair notice

The Code of Guidance referred to previously and provided for under section 604A is not applicable to the decision whether to resort to a repair notice under the present power contained in section 190. However, the important variables of "age, character and locality" will play a central role in the local authority's decision. The second possibility, arising from the representation of an occupying tenant, is that the condition of the dwelling-house is such that it interferes materially with the personal comfort of the occupying tenant. Historically this state of affairs had often been recognised—from *Betts v. Penge Urban District Council*[71]—as giving rise to a statutory nuisance that could be dealt with under the relevant provisions of the now repealed Public Health Act 1936. That remedy was denied by the Court in *National Coal Board v. Thorne*,[72] where the court insisted that the fundamental prerequisite for action under the Act of 1936

[66] *Ibid.* s.190(1C). *Cf.* the power in s.190(3), allowing service on others with an interest in the house.
[67] *Ibid.* ss.189(4) and 190(4).
[68] *Ibid.* s.189(2)(b).
[69] *per* Oliver L.J. in *Church of our Lady of Hal v. Camden London Borough Council* (1980) 255 E.G. 308 at 318.
[70] *Ibid.* at 319.
[71] [1942] 2 K.B. 154.
[72] [1976] 1 W.L.R. 543.

was—and still is under the reformulation of the law in Part III of the Environmental Protection Act 1990—a common law nuisance.

There is no doubt that the local authority, and any court on appeal, has a wide discretion in relation to the framing of and any deliberation on a repair notice under section 190. Indeed, so long as the matters that drive the notice are relevant and are referable to the serious, cumulative decay of a property, there is no limit to what may be covered by a section 190 repair notice.[73] "Reasonable expense", representing the ratio between the cost of repair and the final value of the repaired property, is a relevant consideration for the local authority, but not an overriding consideration, even though in practice it may be the local authority's principal concern.[74] The fact that these are so-called "policy" considerations may allow the court, on appeal, to overstress the reasonable expense criteria.[74a] There may be perfectly legitimate consideration of the fact that, without the attention of a section 190 repair notice, the dwelling-house will quickly become unfit for human habitation. The financial means of the owner may be a very significant variable and may serve to elevate the test of reasonable expense to very influential proportions. Nevertheless, the court may be willing to lift the "veil of incorporation" in order to reveal artificial devices such as the "one-house company".[75]

The dwelling-house as the object of the repair notice

A fundamental common denominator of the powers found in sections 189 and 190 is that both sets of powers are exercisable in relation to a "dwelling-house". While the Housing Act indicates what the term may include, there is no comprehensive definition in the legislation.[76] Perhaps the most useful guidance is to be found in the words of Lord Denning.

> "... a 'house' in the Act means a building which is constructed or adapted for use as, or for the purposes of, a dwelling. It need not actually be dwelt in, but it must be constructed or adapted for use as a dwelling, or for the purposes of a dwelling."[77]

Elsewhere it has been stressed that a house must be capable of being identified as a separate structure.[78] In another instance,[79] planning permission for use of premises as an office had been obtained. Thereafter certain alterations occurred so that the premises could no longer be conveniently used as a dwelling and no part had subsequently been so used. It was held that the relevant Minister was able to

[73] As to the variables which may affect a local authority's approach, see *Branchett v. Beaney, Coster and Swale Borough Council* (1992) 24 H.L.R. 348.

[74] *Kenny v. Kingston upon Thames Royal London Borough Council* (1985) 17 H.L.R. 344, C.A.

[74a] *Ibid.*

[75] *Hillbank Properties Ltd v. Hackney London Borough Council* [1978] Q.B. 998, C.A.

[76] Housing Act, s.207.

[77] *Ashbridge Investments Ltd v. Minister of Housing and Local Government* [1965] 1 W.L.R. 1320, at 1324.

[78] *Critchell v. Lambeth Borough Council* [1957] 3 W.L.R. 108.

[79] *Howard v. Minister of Housing and Local Government* (1967) 65 L.G.R. 257.

conclude that the premises were a house. Stephenson J. observed: "... he was entitled, and indeed bound, to consider ... its past history and the practicability of its being reconstructed and used again as a dwelling in the future."[80]

Repair notice appeals

Within a period of 21 days after service of a repair notice, a person aggrieved by that notice may appeal to the county court.[81] A "person aggrieved" is probably indicative of someone who has a material interest in the subject dwelling-house, evidenced by the categories of those who must receive a copy notice under both sections 189 and 190.[82] Any definition of the term "person aggrieved" relies heavily on the statutory context of that term. It has been said that the term includes "... a person who has a genuine grievance because an order has been made which prejudicially affects his interests".[83] The court's jurisdiction on appeal is remarkably wide, to the extent that it can make such order as it thinks fit either confirming, quashing or varying a notice.[84] Where an appeal is brought, there are specific time limits for the purpose of determining when the notice becomes operative.[85]

Grounds of appeal

The appellant is able to advance, as a ground of appeal, an argument that some other person should, as owner of the dwelling-house, the house in multiple occupation or part of the building concerned, execute any works or pay the whole or part of any cost of execution.[86] If the appellant chooses this approach, he is obliged to serve a copy of the notice of appeal on each person referred to, and the court's jurisdiction is amended for the purpose of reflecting any such successful ground.[87] Indeed, the court is required to take into account the relative interests in the dwelling-house, the parties' relative responsibilities for the state of the dwelling-house and the relative degree of benefit to be derived from the execution of any works.[88] If someone other than the appellant is required to execute works specified in the repairs notice, where that person is owner of the premises, he will be regarded as the person in control of the premises for the purpose of the remaining provisions of Part VI of the Act.[89]

A further ground of appeal in the case of a section 189 repair notice is that making a closing order[90] or a demolition order[91] is the most satisfactory course of

[80] *Ibid.* at 263.
[81] Housing Act, s.191(1).
[82] *Ibid.* and subs.(3), respectively.
[83] *Per* Lord Denning in *Att.-Gen. (Gambia) v. Pierre Sarr N'Jie* [1961] A.C. 517.
[84] Housing Act, s.191(2).
[85] *Ibid.* subs.(4).
[86] *Ibid.* subs.(1A).
[87] *Ibid.* subs.(3A).
[88] *Ibid.* subs.(3B).
[89] *Ibid.* subs.(3C).
[90] *Ibid.* s.264.
[91] *Ibid.* s.265.

action, taking account of the Code of Guidance.[92] If an appeal is allowed on either of these two grounds, the appellant or the local housing authority may require the Judge to include a finding to that effect in his judgment.[93]

Appeal or judicial review

Despite an argument that so-called "public law issues" may be challenged only through proceedings for judicial review in the High Court,[94] it appears that this principle divides into two. Accordingly, any attempt to assert a right *ab initio* will be required for High Court proceedings for judicial review,[95] whereas anyone seeking to defend proceedings associated with a repair note, for example, may be able to raise a matter of legality or *vires* here in the county court, since the local authority seeks to interfere directly with the right of the appellant in relation to the subject dwelling-house.[96]

Enforcement

The local housing authority is given power to act in default where there is failure to comply with the lawful requirements of a repair notice.[97] This contrasts with the facility whereby the authority may by agreement adopt agency powers from the person in control of the dwelling-house, so executing (at the controller's expense) the works required by virtue of the notice.[98] The housing authority's default powers indicate that if a repair notice is not complied with, the authority may themselves do the work required by the notice. However, the authority is obliged to exercise a genuine discretion here having properly considered the merits of the individual case.[99] For present purposes, the Act sets out a detailed prescription indicating the circumstances in which compliance can be assumed to have occurred.[1] However, even before expiry of the period of compliance, if it appears to the local housing authority that reasonable progress is not being made towards compliance, that authority may itself intervene for the purpose of undertaking the works required by the repair notice.[2]

If as a result of a local authority's action under the latter provision there is a demand made for recovery of expenses, a ground of appeal is that, at the time of the authority's notice of intention to enter to execute the works, reasonable progress was being made towards compliance with the repair notice.[3] This is part

[92] *Ibid.* s.191(1B).
[93] *Ibid.* s.191(3).
[94] R.S.C., Ord. 53; *Cocks v. Thanet District Council* [1983] A.C. 286, H.L.
[95] *Cocks, supra.*
[96] *Wandsworth London Borough Council v. Winder* [1985] A.C. 461, H.L.
[97] Housing Act, s.193 and Sched. 10.
[98] *Ibid.* s.191A.
[99] *Elliott v. Brighton Borough Council* (1980) 79 L.G.R. 506.
[1] Housing Act, s.193(2).
[2] *Ibid.* subs.(2A).
[3] Sched. 10, para. 6(1A).

of a group of provisions relating to recovery of the authority's expenses reasonably incurred through action in default where there has been a requirement to comply with various notices under the Act, including repair notices under sections 189 and 190. Any expenses are recoverable from the person "primarily responsible", a reference in the case of sections 189 and 190 to the person having control of the dwelling-house or part of the building to which the notice relates. The appeal facility referred to previously is available to a person aggrieved by the local authority's demand or by any order of that authority in relation to the expenses concerned. However, any matter that could have been raised on appeal against the repair notice may not be raised on an appeal in the present context.[4] A difficult situation is one in which the person aggrieved is unable to raise a challenge to the local authority's execution of works in default on appeal against the repair notice. To meet the difficulty, the court is willing to entertain the issue in the present appeal provisions relating to local authority demands for the payment of expenses.[5]

If local housing authority is about to enter premises[6] under the powers available in section 193, there is a mandatory requirement that notice in writing be given to the person in control of the premises and, if the authority thinks fit, to the owner of the premises.[7] Any occupier may be required, by an order of a magistrate's court, to permit the owner or person having control of the premises to carry into effect a repair notice or works in default where a notice of intended action has been served. The same obligation may bind an occupier, owner or person having control of the premises in respect of similar action by the local authority. Failure to comply with an order is a summary offence subject to a continuing fine for each day of failure to comply.[8] If the default of one owner of premises subject to a repair notice is seen on an application to the magistrate's court to be prejudicial to another owner making the application, the court may empower this applicant owner to enter to execute the required works forthwith. A prerequisite, however, is that notice of any such application be given to the local housing authority.[9]

Powers of entry are given to the local housing authority and the Secretary of State: any authorised person may gain entry at any reasonable time on giving seven days' notice to the occupier and (if known) the owner, for the purpose of survey and examination. However, it must appear to the authority that survey or examination is necessary in order to determine whether repair powers should be exercised in relation to the premises. Alternatively, survey and examination may

[4] *Ibid.* para. 6.
[5] *Elliott, supra.*
[6] "Premises", are defined to include a dwelling-house or part of a building: Housing Act, s.207.
[7] *Ibid.* s.194.
[8] *Ibid.* s.195.
[9] *Ibid.* s.196.

be directed at a situation in which a repair notice has already been served.[10] A specific offence of intentional obstruction of a person authorised to enter premises is provided for,[11] as is an offence by any person having control who intentionally fails to comply with a repair notice.[12]

Slum Clearance

The range of powers

Part IX of the Housing Act deals with a large range of situations relating to the demolition and closing of unfit premises.[13] The various provisions concern not only the use of demolition and closing orders in relation to individual premises but also the wider process of declaring and implementing clearance areas comprising a number of premises.

The closing of unfit premises

If a local housing authority is satisfied that a dwelling-house or house in multiple occupation is unfit for human habitation and that, by reference to the Code of Guidance,[14] action involving the making of a closing order is the most satisfactory course of action, such a closing order can be made by the authority.[15] A closing order prohibits the use of the premises in question for any purpose not approved by the local housing authority.[16] Just as the authority is required to determine the most satisfactory course of action in relation to a dwelling-house or a house in multiple occupation, so too the authority is required to have regard to the Code of Guidance in identifying the most satisfactory course of action in relation to a building containing one or more flats where some or all of those flats are unfit for human habitation.[17] In this latter case, the local authority is free to determine whether the whole or just part of the building should be closed.[18]

The decision to make a closing order

Whether a local housing authority makes a closing order depends again, as in the case of the repair notice option dealt with previously, on consideration of the Code of Guidance.[19] The Code indicates,[20] *inter alia*, that an authority should:

[10] *Ibid.* s.197.
[11] *Ibid.* s.198.
[12] *Ibid.* s.198A.
[13] The exercise of Pt. IX powers is subject to s.605, requiring a periodic inspection of its district by a local housing authority.
[14] *Jones v. Green* [1925] 1 K.B. 659, *per* Salter J. at 668.
[15] *Ibid.* s.264(1).
[16] *Ibid.* s.267(2).
[17] *Ibid.* s.264(2), (3).
[18] *Ibid.* subs.(2).
[19] *Ibid.* s.604A. *Cf.* nn.57–60, *supra*.
[20] Paras. 19 and 20.

(a) appraise the relative costs of closure;
(b) consider the premises' status as a listed building;
(c) take account of the position of the premises in relation to neighbouring buildings;
(d) consider local need for the particular type of premises;
(e) consider the wishes of the occupants;
(f) consider potential alternative uses;
(g) take account of any conservation area status and conservation proposals for the area in which the premises are situated;
(h) consider the effect of closure on the cohesion and well-being of the local community; and
(i) consider the availability of local accommodation for rehousing.

The demolition of unfit premises

If a local housing authority is satisfied that a dwelling-house which is not a flat, or a house (but not a flat) in multiple occupation is unfit for human habitation and that, by reference to the Code of Guidance, action involving demolition is the most satisfactory course of action, a demolition order may be made.[21] A demolition order requires the vacation of premises within a time limit measured from the operative date of the order, and the demolition of the premises within six weeks after the end of that period measured from the operative date or by reference to various other dates according to circumstances derived by the Act.[22] The Act prescribes the same approach where a building contains one or more flats and the local authority is satisfied that some or all of those flats are unfit for human habitation.[23]

The decision to make a demolition order

Whether a local housing authority makes a demolition order will be governed, again, by the Code of Guidance already referred to.[24] The Code indicates,[25] *inter alia*, that an authority should:

(a) consider the physical condition of the premises and their relationship with neighbouring buildings;
(b) appraise the relative costs of demolition;
(c) consider local need for the type of premises;
(d) take account of any proposals, such as clearance for the area overall;

[21] Housing Act, s.265. By virtue of s.304, the local authority is not able to make a demolition order in respect of a "listed building", *i.e.* a building of special architectural or historic interest: *ibid.* s.303. *Cf.* s.300, under which a local housing authority may purchase a dwelling capable of providing accommodation adequate for the time being, even though it should be subject to a demolition or closing order. Management powers are provided by s.302.
[22] *Ibid.* s.267.
[23] *Ibid.* subs.(2).
[24] *Ibid.* s.604A. *Cf.* nn.57–60, *supra.*
[25] Paras. 21 and 22.

(e) take account of the availability of local accommodation for rehousing;
(f) consider the wishes of the owner and occupants;
(g) consider the prospective use of the cleared site; and
(h) consider the local environment.

The operation of demolition and closing orders

The Housing Act prescribes that a local housing authority should not withhold its approval of a demolition or closing order unreasonably. Any person aggrieved by the withholding of approval may appeal to the county court within 21 days of the refusal.[26]

A copy of any demolition or closing order made by the local authority must be served on the person who is the owner of the premises (including a building containing flats) and on every mortgagee whom it is reasonably practicable to ascertain.[27] The order which is not subject to appeal becomes operative at the end of a period of 21 days from the date of service of the order and is final and conclusive as to the matters which could have been raised on appeal.[28] These words would suggest that, while matters of fact and degree going to the merits of an order are beyond challenge, challenge by way of judicial review may not be precluded, for example, in relation to the definition in law of some fundamental prerequisite, such as "premises".[29]

Appeals

A person aggrieved by an order may appeal to the county court within 21 days of the service of the order, subject to one restriction affecting a person in occupation of the subject premises by virtue of a lease or agreement with an unexpired term of three years or less.[30] As in the case of appeals against a repair notice, the court has a widely drawn jurisdiction to make such order, either confirming, quashing or varying an order as it thinks fit.[31] If an appeal is brought, the order is not operative except after certain prescribed time limits, for example, the period in which a person may bring an appeal to the Court of Appeal but (say) chooses not to.[32]

In the case of a closing order, it is a ground of appeal that either a repair notice under section 189 or a demolition order would be the most satisfactory course of action. Equally, in the case of a demolition order, it is a ground of appeal that either a repair notice under section 189 or a closing order would be the most satisfactory course of action. The court's determination here shall have regard to the Code of Guidance previously referred to.[33] If the court allows an appeal on

[26] Housing Act, s.267(3).
[27] *Ibid.* s.268.
[28] *Ibid.* subs.(2).
[29] *Pearlman v. Keepers and Governors of Harrow School* [1979] Q.B. 56, C.A.
[30] Housing Act, s.269(1), (2).
[31] *Ibid.* subs.(3).
[32] *Ibid.* subs.(6).
[33] *Ibid.* subs.(2A).

either of these two grounds, the judge shall, if requested to do so by the appellant or the local housing authority, include in his judgment a finding to that effect.[34]

The demolition order

Where a demolition order is operative, the local housing authority is obliged to serve on any occupier a notice stating the effect of the order, identifing the date by which the building is to be vacated and requiring that occupier to vacate the building before the date set for vacation or before the expiration of a period of 28 days from the date of service, whichever is the later. If the occupier fails to comply, the owner of the premises or the local housing authority may apply to the county court for vacant possession. The local authority is able to recover its expenses incurred in taking these measures, the amount being recoverable from the owner, or any of the owners, by action. The process of seeking possession here is not affected by Rent Act provisions. Finally, any person knowing of any operative demolition order who, after the date for vacation, enters into occupation or permits another to enter occupation commits a summary offence.[35]

When the order is operative, the owner is obliged to demolish the premises by razing them to the ground within the limit of time specified by the order. Nevertheless, the local authority itself must act in default here if the owner fails to comply with the order and is entitled to sell the materials.[36] The authority must give credit for the sale of materials in computing its expenses which are recoverable from the owner of the premises.[37] If necessary, the authority may use its powers to ensure that the premises are cleansed of vermin prior to demolition but only after serving a notice in writing on the owner for this purpose.[38]

There may be circumstances in which the local authority receives from the owner, or some other person, proposals for reconstruction, enlargement or improvement of the premises, or of buildings including those premises, for housing purposes. If the authority is satisfied that such action will produce one or more premises which are fit for human habitation, the demolition order may be extended and, on completion of the measures, revoked.[39] There are also circumstances where an owner, or some other person with an interest in the premises, may submit proposals to use those premises for a purpose other than human habitation, in which case the local authority may substitute a closing order for the demolition order.[40]

Obstructive buildings

An "obstructive building" is defined by the Housing Act as a building which, by virtue only of its contact with or proximity to other buildings, is dangerous or

34 *Ibid.* subs.(3A).
35 *Ibid.* s.270.
36 *Ibid.* s.271.
37 *Ibid.* s.272.
38 *Ibid.* s.273.
39 *Ibid.* s.274.
40 *Ibid.* s.275.

injurious to health.[41] The local authority is empowered to serve on every owner of a building which appears to be an obstructive building notice of a "time and place" meeting where the question of an order for demolition will be considered by that authority. At this meeting, every owner is entitled to be heard. If, having taken the matter into consideration, the authority is satisfied that the building is an obstructive building, there is a mandatory obligation to make an obstructive building order requiring demolition of the building, or part of it, as well as vacation of that building within two months of the operative date of the order.[42] There is a right of appeal against the order to the county court, exercisable within 21 days of service of the order.[43] The Housing Act also provides facilities for recovery of possession, in broadly similar terms to those set out in section 270.[44] Facilities are also provided by the Act through which a purchase notice may be served on the authority by the owner or owners of the building, within certain time limits. Although the Act provides that the authority "shall" accept the offer represented in the purchase notice, there is also recognition that, if the offer is not accepted, the owner or owners shall complete the required demolition, subject only to default powers of the local authority.[45]

Clearance areas

The provisions of the Housing Act here are referable to the treatment of unfitness, *inter alia*, where it is considered necessary by the local housing authority to clear an area so that it is cleared of "all" buildings. This "collective" treatment of unfitness contrasts with the individual treatment of such a condition, dealt with previously in the present chapter. Although clearance is not as much in evidence now as it was in the 1950s and 1960s, nevertheless it is still a potentially important option for the local housing authority in dealing with adverse housing conditions. In using this option, it will be seen that the local authority is obliged to undertake widespread consultation with those who may be affected. Furthermore, compulsory purchase of unfit dwellings previously has tended to generate local controversy and delay by virtue of the fact that compensation was not payable at market value. This limitation is now abolished.[46]

Clearance area declarations

In very broad terms, the local authority is obliged to declare a clearance area before going on to acquire the target properties in that area by compulsory

[41] *Ibid.* s.283(1). *Cf.* Chap. 11, "Building Control" and the section dealing with dangerous, ruinous and dilapidated buildings. *Cf.* Chap. 10, "Statutory Nuisance", dealing with buildings which may be dangerous or injurious otherwise than for the reasons set out in s.283(1).

[42] *Ibid.* s.284.

[43] *Ibid.* s.285.

[44] *Ibid.* s.286. *Cf.* n.35, *supra.*

[45] *Ibid.* s.287. *Cf.* s.288, relating to recovery of local authority expenses here.

[46] Local Government and Housing Act 1989, Sched. 9. *Cf.* Circular 6/90 (Department of the Environment), paras. 60 and 74.

purchase. The authority is obliged to declare a clearance area if satisfied that the buildings in the area (dwelling-houses,[47] houses in multiple occupation or buildings containing one or more flats) are unfit for human habitation or are, by virtue of bad arrangement or by virtue of the narrowness or bad arrangement of the streets, dangerous or injurious to the health of the inhabitants of the area. A further prerequisite is that any other buildings in the area be, for the same reasons, also dangerous or injurious to the health of the inhabitants of the area. However, before the authority proceeds to adopt the clearance option, it must be of the view that demolition is the most satisfactory method of dealing with the conditions.[48] That judgment requires the authority to take into account the Code of Guidance referred to previously.[49]

The decision to make a declaration

The Code of Guidance[50] requires the local housing authority to

> "... consider the desirability of clearance in the context of proposals for the wider neighbourhood of which the premises form part, and be satisfied that clearance is the most satisfactory course of action having regard to a number of factors."[51]

Those factors concern:

(a) the physical condition of the premises;
(b) the degree of concentration of unfit premises in the area;
(c) the density of buildings and the surrounding street pattern;
(d) the outcome of economic appraisal of alternative courses of action;
(e) the overall availability of housing accommodation;
(f) the proportion of fit premises and other, non-residential premises in sound condition;
(g) the need to acquire land surrounding or adjoining the proposed clearance area;
(h) the existence of listed buildings of special architectural or historic interest;
(i) the result of statutory consultations;
(j) rehousing arrangements;
(k) the need for "added" land and its possible acquisition by agreement;
(l) the impact of clearance on commercial premises; and
(m) the suitability of any proposed afteruse or uses.[52]

Many of these factors may be influential at the point when the Secretary of State is

[47] As to the meaning of the term "dwelling-house", see nn.76 to 80, *supra*.
[48] Housing Act, s.289(2).
[49] *Ibid.* s.604A.
[50] Circular 6/90, para. 16.
[51] *Ibid.*
[52] *Ibid.*

invited by the local housing authority to consider confirmation of any necessary compulsory purchase order, dealt with below.

Local consultation is an important element in the decision-making process. The local authority is obliged to consult with those likely to be directly affected by a clearance area declaration. A notice of the authority's intention to declare a clearance area must be given to every person with an interest in any building in the area in question. Typically, such notification would be given to a freeholder, leaseholder and mortgagee. Furthermore, the authority is obliged to inform occupants of the buildings affected by means of explanatory leaflets, for example. Notice of intention must also be advertised in a minimum of two newspapers circulating in the area. Any notices placed or information given here must invite representations to the authority within a period of at least 28 days. Thereafter, the local authority is obliged to take account of any representations made before arriving at a final decision on declaration.[53]

In addition to the foregoing considerations, the local housing authority must be satisfied that suitable alternative accommodation is available in advance of any displacement and that its resources are sufficient to carry any resolution into effect.[54] It seems unlikely that the authority would be obliged to consider very detailed data for present purposes.[55] Furthermore, the law is likely to regard the foregoing consultative exercise as being prima facie exhaustive of a right to be heard on the part of those who appear to be adversely affected by any clearance declaration.

Acquisition and demolition by the local authority

Following declaration, the authority is obliged to proceed to secure clearance of the area in question by securing by its own devices or otherwise, demolition of the subject buildings.[56] Two options—acquisition by agreement or acquisition under compulsion—are available to the authority. In the event of opposition, the authority will have little option but to pursue acquisition through a compulsory purchase order to be confirmed by the Secretary of State. However, if the Secretary of State is to be persuaded to confirm the order, five matters will have to be addressed, according to the Department of the Environment.[57] These matters concern:

(a) the justification for the declaration, taking account of the Code of Guidance and any economic assessment;
(b) the unfitness of the buildings in the clearance area;
(c) the justification for acquisition of so-called "added land" (addressed below);

[53] Housing Act, s.289(2A)–(2F).
[54] *Ibid.* subs.(4).
[55] *Goddard v. Minister of Housing and Local Government* [1958] 1 W.L.R. 1151.
[56] Housing Act, s.290(1).
[57] Circular 6/90, para. 59.

(d) proposals for rehousing and relocating commercial and industrial premises affected by clearance; and
(e) the proposed afteruse of the cleared site.

In addition, it is stated to be necessary for local authorities promoting clearance compulsory purchase orders to demonstrate that they have fully considered the economic aspect of clearance and responded to any objections put forward on this ground.

Added land

Despite a clear identification of land containing, *inter alia*, dwelling-houses which are unfit for human habitation, the Housing Act nevertheless empowers the local housing authority to purchase certain other categories of so-called "added land". Added land is either land surrounded by a clearance area or adjoining land. In either case, the authority must be able to provide evidential justification for the inclusion of such land in any scheme of purchase on the ground that inclusion is "reasonably necessary" to achieve certain objectives.[58]

The expedition of demolition

The policy of the Act is to ensure that, following the purchase of subject land by the local housing authority, every building on the land is demolished as "soon as may be", either through demolition by the authority or through disposal subject to a covenant that the buildings in question are demolished "forthwith".[59] It is quite clear, therefore, that once a clearance area has been declared, the local authority has only a limited jurisdiction to postpone demolition. Although property due for demolition may be used for short-term accommodation following purchase, it cannot be used to provide lawfully sub-standard accommodation.[60]

Despite submission of a compulsory purchase order by a local housing authority to the Secretary of State for confirmation, those proceedings may be discontinued. Discontinuation will occur if the Secretary of State is satisfied that the parties can secure demolition and that the local authority can secure clearance of the area without need to resort to compulsory acquisition of their land.[61]

Options for redevelopment

Any person, whether not a person with an interest in land, may submit to the local housing authority proposals for redevelopment of the land which may then be

[58] Housing Act, s.290(2), (3). *Cf. Coleen Properties Ltd v. Minister of Housing and Local Government* [1971] 3 W.L.R. 433, C.A.
[59] *Ibid.* s.291(1).
[60] *R. v. Birmingham City Council, ex p. Sale* (1983) 9 H.L.R. 33. Short-term use of such property of a standard "adequate for the time being" is provided for by s.301 of the Housing Act. As to general management powers, see s.302.
[61] Housing Act, s.292.

approved by the authority. On approval, the local authority is obliged to prescribe a time scale for completion of the several parts of the redevelopment. In these circumstances, the local authority will take no action by way of declaring a clearance area affecting the subject land, in the same way that the authority will take no action relating to the demolition, closing or purchase of unfit premises. However, these powers available to the authority may not be exercised where a demolition order becomes operative or where a compulsory purchase order for the clearance of land has been confirmed by the Secretary of State.[62] If a local housing authority gives notice of satisfaction in respect of such proposed redevelopment, it may certify, for the purpose of the Rent Act, that possession is required from a tenant to facilitate redevelopment, but only in so far as alternative accommodation is available for that tenant.[63]

The owner of a dwelling-house, house in multiple occupation or building containing one or more flats is able to submit to a local housing authority proposals for works of improvement or structural alteration. If, after consideration, the authority certifies that the dwelling-house, etc., is fit for human habitation after completion of the works, that authority may not act under the Act's clearance provisions to secure demolition. Equally, the authority may take no action in connection with demolition, closing or purchase of unfit premises. As with the foregoing provisions relating to an owner's proposals for redevelopment, the present provisions do not apply where a demolition order is operative or where a clearance compulsory purchase order has been confirmed by the Secretary of State.[64]

Where, in either of the above situations involving an owner's proposal for redevelopment or an owner's proposals for improvements and alterations, the local housing authority is seised of the matter, that authority may transmit the proposals to the Secretary of State who may treat them as objections to a relevant compulsory purchase order. If, instead of determining the application, the authority transmits the matter to the Secretary of State, his decision may be to exclude the dwelling-house, etc., or land (as the case may be) from the compulsory purchase order, in which case the authority will be obliged to come to its own determination in any event.[65]

Enforcement

The magistrates' court has jurisdiction to order certain persons to permit to be done "all things requisite" on premises for carrying into effect the present provisions of the Act governing slum clearance. Non-compliance is a summary offence, subject to a continuing fine.[66] The magistrates' court may also act on the application of an owner of premises subject to a demolition order or an obstructive building order if it is satisfied that default in compliance will prejudice

[62] *Ibid.* s.308.
[63] *Ibid.* s.309.
[64] *Ibid.* s.310.
[65] *Ibid.* s.311.
[66] *Ibid.* s.315.

the interests of the applicant owner. Notice of such an application must be given to the local housing authority.

There may be circumstances in which premises are, or are likely to become, dangerous or injurious to health or unfit for human habitation,[67] so prejudicing the interests of a person entitled to any interest in land used wholly or in part as a site for a dwelling-house or a house in multiple occupation, or both. On the other hand, the circumstances may suggest that such an applicant should be entrusted with the carrying out of a scheme of improvement or reconstruction (including a scheme under sections 308 and 310)[68] approved by the local housing authority. If either of these sets of circumstances is established to the satisfaction of the court,[69] an order can be made empowering the applicant to enter the land forthwith in order to undertake the necessary works within a period of time prescribed.[70]

Finally, the Housing Act makes provision for powers of entry so that a person authorised by the local housing authority (or the Secretary of State) may enter premises at any reasonable time on giving seven days' notice of intention to the occupier, and (if known) the owner, for a variety of purposes relevant to slum clearance.[71] It is a summary offence intentionally to obstruct an officer of the local authority (or of the Secretary of State) or any person authorised to enter premises for the purposes of the present Part IV in the performance of anything required or authorised.[72]

Overcrowding, Multiple Occupation and Common Lodging Houses

Three areas of control

Overcrowding, houses in multiple occupation and common lodging houses are dealt with together in the middle of the present chapter by virtue of their close relationship in practice. However, at the time of writing, it appears likely that the law governing common lodging houses in Part XII of the Housing Act will be repealed. The intention is that matters affecting common lodging houses will be dealt with under the Housing Act provisions governing houses in multiple occupation.

Overcrowding

Part X of the Act governs overcrowding in any "dwelling", defined to mean "... premises used or suitable for use as a separate dwelling".[73] Separate provision is

[67] *Ibid.* s.316.
[68] see nn.62 and 64, *supra.*
[69] The High Court or the county court, where these courts, respectively, have jurisdiction.
[70] Housing Act, s.318.
[71] *Ibid.* s.319.
[72] *Ibid.*
[73] *Ibid.* s.343.

made under Part XI of the Act in connection with overcrowding in a house in multiple occupation, dealt with below. The critical starting point for present purposes is the identification of what may be a "separate dwelling" and, more particularly, whether overcrowding occurs in premises used, or suitable for use, as a separate dwelling. In what is essentially a matter of fact and degree, it is necessary to identify two factors: whether premises are sufficiently discrete to be used independently, and whether user is by virtue of a personal right, in each case against a background of the circumstances overall.[74]

Measuring overcrowding

Provision is made by the Act for two approaches to the measurement of overcrowding: the so-called "room" and "space" standards. The two standards are not part of a cumulative requirement: overcrowding may occur where either standard is contravened. In the first place, the Act regards a dwelling as being overcrowded if the number of persons sleeping in that separate dwelling is such that two persons of opposite sexes who are not living together as husband and wife must sleep in the same room. For this purpose, children under the age of 10 are left out of account. It is also the case that a room is available as sleeping accommodation if it is of a type normally used in the locality as a bedroom or as a living room.[75]

If overcrowding is not found by reference to the room standard, the space standard may be applied by reference to a determination of permitted numbers of persons in relation to the available rooms which may be used as sleeping accommodation. There are two approaches to the space standard. The first approach indicates, for example, that if in the separate dwelling there are available three rooms, the permitted number of persons will be five. Where adoption of this first approach does not indicate overcrowding, resort can be made to a second approach, based on the aggregate size of the available rooms. For example, a room larger than 110 square feet should "sleep" two persons.[76]

Exception

The Housing Act provides for exceptions in respect of the legal limits to overcrowding in certain circumstances. An occupier[77] but no other person is able to apply to the local housing authority for a licence to authorise a number of persons in excess of the permitted number to sleep in the dwelling. If a licence is granted allowing the space standard to be exceeded, it must appear to the local authority that there are exceptional circumstances, such as a seasonal increase in population.[78]

Among the offences to be found in Part X of the Act is an offence by the

[74] *Goodrich v. Paisner* [1957] A.C. 65, H.L.
[75] Housing Act, s.325.
[76] *Ibid.* s.326.
[77] The facility extends also to an intending occupier.
[78] Housing Act, s.330.

occupier of causing or permitting overcrowding.[79] However, that occupier is not guilty of the offence where there is local authority authorisation, as described previously, and is similarly not guilty of the offence when the occupier has applied to the local authority for "suitable alternative accommodation".[80] Where a child has attained the age of one or 10 (so qualifying as a half or whole unit for the purposes of calculation of numbers),[81] or where a member of the occupier's family not living in the dwelling is in fact sleeping there temporarily, the law again provides for exceptions.[82]

The overcrowding offences

The Act provides for a variety of offences, one of which was described previously. Other offences are summarised here. First, a landlord is guilty of a summary offence where a rent book or similar document fails to summarise the provisions of Part X and to identify the permitted number of persons in respect of the dwelling.[83] A related summary offence is provided for where a duly authorised officer of the local housing authority requires for inspection any rent book or similar document relating to a house and any such document in the occupier's control is not produced.[84]

Two critical offences are provided for which affect the landlord in the present context. The first offence arises where a landlord causes or permits a dwelling to be overcrowded.[85] This offence is deemed to occur in a variety of detailed circumstances set out in the Act as where, for example, the landlord has reasonable cause to believe that the dwelling would become overcrowded in circumstances rendering the occupier guilty of an offence where, subject to some exceptions, it comes to his knowledge that a dwelling is overcrowded[86] and there is a failure on his part to notify the local housing authority.[87] An offence by an occupier arises on failure by that occupier to respond to a notice from the local authority demanding a written statement of the number, ages and sex of the persons sleeping in the dwelling.[88] If a dwelling is overcrowded, so rendering the occupier guilty of an offence, the local authority may serve a written abatement notice on that occupier requiring cessation of the overcrowding within 14 days of the notice.[89] If within three months of the end of the foregoing period of 14 days the notice has not been complied with, the local authority may apply to the county court requiring an order for possession in favour of the landlord.[90]

[79] *Ibid.* s.327.
[80] *Ibid.* s.342.
[81] *Ibid.* s.328.
[82] *Ibid.* s.329.
[83] *Ibid.* s.332.
[84] *Ibid.* s.336.
[85] *Ibid.* s.331.
[86] *Ibid.* subs.(2).
[87] *Ibid.* s.333.
[88] *Ibid.* s.335.
[89] *Ibid.* s.338.
[90] *Ibid.* subs.(2).

Powers of entry are available to any duly authorised person acting on behalf of the local housing authority.[91] These powers are enforceable by means of an offence of obstruction.[92] The prosecution of offences is a task assigned to the local housing authority. In the case of a prosecution of the authority, that prosecution by any other person would require the consent of the Attorney-General.[93]

Houses in multiple occupation

The law regulating houses in multiple occupation is to be found in Part XI of the Housing Act 1985.[94] In this area of regulation, the Act, in section 605, also requires a local housing authority to consider, at least once per year, housing conditions in its district, for the purpose of determining what action to take in performance of the Part XI functions.

"House in multiple occupation"

This expression is defined by the Act to mean a house which is occupied by persons who do not form a single household. This definition extends to include any parts of a building which, otherwise, would not be regarded as a house, although constructed or adapted to be occupied by a single household, thus allowing flats in particular to be considered as houses in multiple occupation.[95] The term "house" has been dealt with previously.[96] The reference to occupation as a separate dwelling may give rise to difficulties of fact and degree. In this connection, the court has adverted to the "awkward" situations that Parliament must have had in mind, indicating that even where a landlord shares a living room it may still be possible to find a separate dwelling within a dwelling-house.[97]

Registration

A local housing authority is able to introduce in its district a registration scheme for houses in multiple occupation.[98] A potentially important element of the law in this context is the power of the local authority to introduce control provisions to a registration scheme, failure to comply with which is an offence. In particular, control provisions may prevent multiple occupation unless a house is registered and the number of households or persons in occupation do not exceed the number registered. Equally, control provisions may prohibit persons from taking up residence in a house.[99] Various adverse decisions of the local housing authority

[91] *Ibid.* s.340.
[92] *Ibid.* s.341.
[93] *Ibid.* s.339.
[94] As to non-Housing Act legislation that may be relevant, see Circular 12/93, paras. 4.14 *et seq.*
[95] *Ibid.* s.345.
[96] See, nn.76–80, *supra.*
[97] *Goodrich v. Paisner* [1957] A.C. 65, H.L. *Cf. London Borough of Hackney v. Ezedinma* [1981] 3 All E.R. 438, dealing additionally with what may constitute "occupation".
[98] Housing Act, s.346: *cf.* extended provision in subs.(1)(b).
[99] *Ibid.* s.347.

in this context are open to appeal to the county court.[1] A local authority is obliged to publish a notice of intention to submit a registration scheme to the Secretary of State for confirmation.[2] For the purpose of assertaining whether a house is registrable and to ascertain registrable details concerning the house, the authority is able to require a person with an estate or interest in the house, or anyone living in the house, to provide in writing any information in his possession. Any failure to provide the information, or any misstatement knowingly made, is a summary offence.[3]

Standard of fitness and power to limit occupation

The Housing Act makes provision for a local housing authority to serve (normally on the person having control of the house) a notice requiring the execution of works in order to render the premises fit for the number of occupants.[4] Despite the absence of any criteria for the determination of what is adequate or satisfactory in connection with the fitness standard here, advisory guidance is to be found elsewhere. The circular in question[5] indicates a number of factors to be considered in evaluation of the fitness of a house in multiple occupation. These factors are as follows:

(a) facilities for storage, preparation and cooking of food;
(b) the number of water-closets, suitably located, for the exclusive use of the occupants;
(c) the number of fixed baths or showers and hand-basins, suitably located, with a satisfactory supply of hot and cold water, for the exclusive use of the occupants;
(d) means of escape from fire; and
(e) other fire precautions, if any.

The Circular recognises that there may be circumstances suggesting that higher or lower standards may be appropriate.

While a section 352 notice may be used to secure provision of the foregoing facilities, or some of them, for the benefit of the number of people in occupation, a direction under section 354 can be used to determine the maximum number of occupants, taking account of existing facilities.

Section 352 notices and section 354 directions

Either set of powers may be resorted to individually. However, if the local housing authority chooses to use both sets of powers, the action taken will seek to secure the maximum number of persons who may occupy the house following

[1] *Ibid.* s.348.
[2] *Ibid.* s.349.
[3] *Ibid.* s.350.
[4] *Ibid.* s.352.
[5] Circular 12/92.

completion of works referable to the fitness of the premises. The practicalities attending a local authority's decision here may present a complex picture, particularly if it appears that present arrangements affecting the house are in breach of planning control.[6] Action in respect of a house in multiple occupation under the foregoing powers in Part XI does not preclude action by means of repair notice under section 189 or 190 of the Act, depending on whether or not the house is unfit for human habitation. Indeed, there are requirements under section 189 including lighting and ventilation that are not required under section 352.[7]

The foregoing action may, however, be premature, particularly in view of the fact that, while there may often be considerable overlap between section 352 requirements and the section 604 fitness standard, failure of the fitness standard may suggest a need for other action, such as demolition.[8]

Management requirements

A person who is managing a house in multiple occupation may be served with a management order for the purpose of ensuring that that person observes proper standards of management.[9] These standards are prescribed by the Secretary of State[10] and extend to include matters such as the state of repair, condition and cleanliness of certain common parts of a house, as well as the maintenance and repair of means of escape from fire.

Failure to comply with these prescribed requirements knowingly or without reasonable excuse is a summary offence.[11] An alternative course of action for the local housing authority is to serve on the person managing a house a notice indicating works required to make good a neglect of management following a failure to comply with a management order.[12] Such a notice is subject to appeal to the county court.[13]

Means of escape from fire

Under section 352, a stipulated requirement is that a house in multiple occupation be provided with adequate means of escape from fire. Nevertheless, other provisions in the Housing Act reinforce what is essentially a discretionary requirement. More particularly, the local authority with the power to serve a section 352 notice by virtue of a failure to provide adequate means of escape from fire has the additional power to accept an undertaking or make a closing order by virtue of section 368.[14] Furthermore, that authority may be obliged to exercise

[6] *Ibid.* para. 4.2.3.
[7] *Ibid.* para. 4.3.1.
[8] *Ibid.* para. 4.5.
[9] Housing Act, s.369.
[10] S.I. 1990 No. 830.
[11] *Neville v. Marroghemis, The Times*, October 29, 1983.
[12] Housing Act, s.372.
[13] *Ibid.* s.373.
[14] *Ibid.* s.365(1).

those powers if the Secretary of State prescribes by order houses and modes of occupation for present purposes.[15] Prior to any action under section 352 in respect of a failure to provide adequate means of escape from fire, or under section 368, the local housing authority is obliged to consult with the fire authority.[16]

Control orders

The local housing authority is able to secure possession of a house in multiple occupation for any period up to five years for the purpose of acting in a variety of ways to bring the house up to a satisfactory standard. More particularly, the power is available if notices under sections 352 and 372 have been served, if a direction under section 354 has been given or it appears to the authority that the state or condition of the house is such as to call for the taking of action under any of these provisions. Whatever the situation, a control order can be made only if it appears to the authority that the living conditions in the house are such that it is necessary to make the order in order to protect the safety, welfare or health of persons living in the house.[17] It is often the case that control orders are required quickly for these protective purposes, suggesting a need for local authorities to have suitably streamlined arrangements in place.[18] The width of the term "house" for present purposes allows action in a variety of cases that traditionally pose problems. For example, the control order powers are applicable to common lodging houses, against a background in which it has been said that it would be difficult to conceive of a way of saying that a common lodging house is not a "house".[19]

As soon as a control order is made, it is in force and the local authority responsible is required, as soon as is practicable, to take possession and to take steps to protect the safety, welfare and health of the occupants. Those steps are required to be "immediate" steps.[20] As soon as practicable after the making of the order, the authority is required to post a copy of the order in an accessible position in the house, together with a notice setting out the effect of the order, the right of appeal and the principal grounds on which the authority considered it necessary to make the order.[21] An order gives the local housing authority a right to possession for as long as the order is in force, as well as a right to do anything which a person with an estate or interest in the premises would be entitled to do without incurring liabilities except as provided for by Part XI of the Act. The authority also has a right to create certain limited leasehold arrangements.[22] Various statutory notices, directions or orders[23] are no longer of legal effect, except in so far as they involve residual matters of criminal enforcement.[24]

[15] *Ibid.* subs.(2). *Cf.* the limitation in subs.(2A) and note the terms of S.I. 1981 No. 1576.
[16] *Ibid.* s.365(3).
[17] *Ibid.* s.379.
[18] Circular 12/93, para. 4.8.6.
[19] *R. v. Southwark London Borough Council, ex p. Lewis Levy* (1983) 8 H.L.R. 1, *per* Brown J. at 15.
[20] Housing Act, s.379(2).
[21] *Ibid.* subss.(3), (4).
[22] *Ibid.* s.381. An order is registrable as a local land charge: *ibid.* subs.(5).
[23] *Ibid.* ss.352, 354, 366, 370 and 372.
[24] *Ibid.* s.381(4).

With a control order in force, the local authority is under a duty to exercise the powers conferred by that order for the purpose of maintaining proper standards of management, and to take such action as is needed to remedy all matters considered to require remediation if no control order had been made, and to make reasonable provision for insurance of the premises against destruction or damage by fire.[25] The realisation of proper standards of management is by means of a management scheme to be made by the authority once a control order is in force.[26] In practice, it may be the case that more appropriate longer-term housing facilities can be provided through compulsory acquisition. If this option is considered, it may be possible in some circumstances for the local housing authority to delay preparation of a management scheme.[27]

The Housing Act makes provision for appeals to the county court. This appeal facility applies to control orders, management schemes and decisions against revocation of control orders.[28]

Overcrowding

Overcrowding, as provided for generally in Part X, must be distinguished from overcrowding under Part XI in relation to houses in multiple occupation. Unlike the approach in Part X, Part XI overcrowding depends on whether the local housing authority considers that the number of occupants is "excessive". Furthermore, the Part XI powers are discretionary only and ultimately enforceable only following a written warning and service of a notice.[29]

If the local housing authority considers that the numbers being accommodated are excessive, or that that situation will arise, in both cases by reference to the number of rooms available, an overcrowding notice may be served on the occupier or on the person managing the premises, or both.[30] Any person aggrieved by the notice may appeal to the county court.[31] The overcrowding may be dealt with by reference either to existing residents[32] or new residents.[33] A person who contravenes a Part XI overcrowding notice is guilty of a summary offence.[34]

[25] *Ibid.* s.385.
[26] *Ibid.* s.386. Matters to be provided for via a scheme are to be found in Sched. 13 of the Act.
[27] *Ibid.* Sched. 13, Pt. IV.
[28] *Ibid.* s.384, Sched. 13, para. 3 and s.393, respectively.
[29] Circular 12/93, para. 4.11.5. *Cf.* the facility provided by s.354.
[30] Housing Act, s.358.
[31] *Ibid.* s.362.
[32] *Ibid.* s.360.
[33] *Ibid.* s.361.
[34] *Ibid.* s.358(4).

Area Renewal

The Local Government and Housing Act 1989, Part VII

Earlier in the present chapter, reference was made to concerns to ensure that judgments and determinations about the fitness of individual dwellings in particular were arrived at in the broadest context possible for the purpose of pursuing action to deal with the adverse conditions. Introducing the area renewal approach, the Department of the Environment, referring to the new provisions in Part VII (and Part VIII) of the Act of 1989, describes the philosophy as follows:

> "The intention . . . is to focus attention on the use of a broader based strategy which may include environmental and socio-economic regeneration. The aim should be to secure a reduction in the number of unfit houses, whether by repair or demolition, as part of such a strategy. In addition . . . Part VIII [provides for] . . . the user of group repair schemes . . . and renovation grants [as] part of this strategy."[35]

Against this background, the Act of 1989 provides for a new "concept", the "renewal area", encouraging local housing authorities to assess the need for clearance and renovation on a systematic and area basis, declaring renewal areas where concentrated action is required. Any such declaration confers wide powers on a local authority and attracts contribution towards expenditure from the Secretary of State for the Environment. The local authority is nevertheless expected to undertake a thorough appraisal of the options available to deal with areas of poor quality private sector housing before declaring a renewal area. The essence of the approach is stated to be a comprehensive approach covering renovation and redevelopment of housing, alongside action on social, economic and environmental problems.[36] The Housing Act seeks to focus the local authority's attention on the action outlined above. At least once per year, the authority is required to consider housing conditions in the area in order to determine what action to take in performance of the functions associated with, *inter alia*, renewal areas.[37]

The identification and declaration of renewal areas

The Act of 1989 sets a template by reference to which the local housing authority may arrive at a formal declaration. The present section of the chapter outlines the essential nature of the template—as defined by section 89 of the Act—before examining the approaches recommended for the purpose of systematically appraising the variables that may affect the ultimate declaration.

[35] Circular 6/90, para. 16.
[36] *Ibid.* paras. 19 and 20.
[37] Housing Act, s.605(1).

Renewal area declaration

The starting point for present purposes is the local housing authority's consideration of a report prepared by a person who appears to be suitably qualified for the purposes.[38] That report must address six matters:

(a) living conditions in the area;
(b) approaches to improvement of those conditions;
(c) powers available to the local authority if a renewal area is declared;
(d) the authority's detailed proposals for the exercise of the available powers during the currency of any declaration;
(e) the cost of proposals; and
(f) the availability of financial resources.

The report should also contain a recommendation on whether a renewal area should be declared. That report and any other matters considered to be relevant by the local authority will form the basis for the authority's determination. However, before a resolution for declaration can have effect, the authority must be satisfied that the living conditions in an area consisting primarily of housing accommodation are unsatisfactory and that those conditions can most effectively be dealt with by declaring the area to be a renewal area.[39]

Identification of a possible renewal area

The local housing authority is obliged to have regard to guidance published by the Secretary of State in approaching its task in section 89. That guidance is published as part of a circular,[40] and stresses the importance of the "neighbourhood renewal assessment", stressing a multi-disciplinary, corporate approach.[41] The process is based "... on a series of logical steps which, when taken together, provide a thorough and systematic appraisal for considering alternative courses of action for an area".[42] Before proceeding to a declaration, the local authority is required to comply with any directions from the Secretary of State in connection with publicity for a proposed exercise of the Part VII powers, as well as requirements for dealing with invited representations in relation to the proposal.[43]

[38] That person may be an officer of the authority.
[39] Local Government and Housing Act, s.89(1), (3).
[40] Circular 6/90, Annex B. *Cf.* Annex G, in relation to individual unfit premises.
[41] *Ibid.* paras. 26 and 27.
[42] *Ibid.* para. 28.
[43] Local Government and Housing Act, s.89(5). *Cf.* the directions set out at Annex E of Circular 6/90, para. 2.

Conditions for a declaration

An area declared as a renewal area is subject to certain restrictions[44] and conditions.[45] These conditions are set out in broad terms in the Act, and in more detail in the Secretary of State's directions,[46] as follows. An area may not be declared a renewal area unless:

(a) that area contains not less than a specified number of dwellings (300);
(b) of the dwellings in the area, not less than a specified proportion are privately owned (75 per cent.);
(c) such conditions as may be specified in relation to the physical condition of the dwellings (at least 75 per cent. to be unfit or qualifying for mandatory and discretionary grants) and the financial circumstances of those living in the area (at least 30 per cent. of the households must appear to be dependent to a significant extent on receipt of one or more State benefits) are fulfilled; and
(d) any other specified conditions are fulfilled.

The reference to dwellings here includes houses in multiple occupation.[47]

Publicity and information availability after declaration

Once a renewal area declaration is in force, the local authority is obliged to publicise the renewal area in local newspapers and to bring the matter to the attention of owners and residents in the locality, who will also benefit from the requirement for the authority to establish an information and advice facility.[48] In addition, the local authority is obliged to publish information as an ongoing duty in relation to action proposed or to be taken in the area, as well as information on assistance, such as grant-aid, that may be available for works carried out in the area.[49]

Local authority powers

A local housing authority is empowered to acquire compulsorily or by agreement any land on which there are premises comprising housing accommodation for the purpose of achieving or securing their improvement or repair, their proper management and use or the well-being of residents in the area. The objectives of improvement, repair and proper management may be realised by some other person to whom the authority would propose to dispose of the premises; a housing association, for example.[50] Land may also be acquired compulsorily or by

[44] *Ibid.* s.89(2).
[45] *Ibid.* s.90.
[46] Circular 6/90, Annex E, para. 3.
[47] Local Government and Housing Act, s.90(4).
[48] *Ibid.* s.91. *Cf.* the direction under subs.(2): Circular 6/90, Annex E. para. 4.
[49] *Ibid.* s.92. *Cf.* the direction under s.92(2): Circular 6/90, Annex E, para. 5.
[50] *Ibid.* s.93(2), (3).

agreement in a renewal area for the purpose of improving amenities. Again, the authority is able to dispose of such land to some other person for the realisation of this objective, which typically might include the provision of public amenity open space.[51] These powers are without prejudice to any power possessed by the local authority for the acquisition of land relevant to a use referable to a renewal area.[52]

In the case of land already in the ownership of the local housing authority, the Act empowers that authority to undertake works, including demolition, within a renewal area. This power extends to allow the authority to contract out the performance of such works to a housing association or some other person.[53] In the same way, the authority may assist in relation to works in the renewal area which are not in its ownership by the giving of aid including grants, loan or guarantees.[54]

Group repair schemes funded under Part VIII of the Act of 1989 are potentially important devices for the treatment of adverse housing conditions. Such schemes, often referred to in the past as "enveloping", involve the renovation of groups of property in order to secure their external fabric.

Grant-Aid for Repair and Improvement

Categories of grant-aid

Part VIII of the Local Government and Housing Act 1989 provides for four categories of grant:

(a) the "renovation grant" for the improvement, repair or conversion of dwellings;
(b) the "common parts grant" referable to the common parts of a building;
(c) the "disabled facilities grant" for the provision of facilities for the disabled in a dwelling or in the common parts of a building containing one or more flats; and
(d) the "HMO grant" providing aid for the improvement or repair of a house in multiple occupation by the conversion of a house or other building.[55]

Formal requirements

Unless at the date of the application the dwelling, common parts or house or other building is 10 or more years old, the local housing authority is unable to entertain a grant application unless that application relates to a disabled facilities

[51] *Ibid.* subs.(4).
[52] *Ibid.* subs.(8).
[53] *Ibid.* subss.(5), (6).
[54] *Ibid.* subs.(5).
[55] *Ibid.* s.101.

grant.[56] Similarly, the authority is unable to entertain any application, except one relating to a common parts grant, unless:

(a) the applicant has or proposes to acquire an owner's interest;
(b) (in the case of a renovation grant) the applicant is a tenant of the dwelling who does not have, or propose to acquire, an owner's interest;
(c) (in the case of a disabled facilities grant for works to a dwelling) the applicant is a tenant but does not have or propose to acquire an owner's interest; or
(d) (in the case of a disabled facilities grant for works to the common parts of a building containing one or more flats) the applicant is a tenant of a flat in the building but does not have or propose to acquire an owner's interest.[57]

Mandatory and discretionary grant examples

Where the local authority receives an application from an owner-occupier or tenant and determines that the dwelling is unfit but that works will render that dwelling fit for human habitation, the application must be approved. However, any such mandatory grant is payable only if the authority is also satisfied that completion of the relevant works is the most satisfactory course of action.[58]

In the case of a renovation or other grant, an application by a landlord will also attract a mandatory grant if completion of relevant works is necessary to comply with notices under section 189, 190 and 352 of the Housing Act.[59] On the other hand, where the authority considers that relevant works go beyond or are other than those which will render the dwelling fit for human habitation, but that the works are necessary to put the dwelling in reasonable repair, for example, the application may be approved as a matter of discretion.[60]

The Local Government and Housing Act indicates that, in some circumstances, a grant application must be refused. Among such circumstances is the case of any application in respect of a dwelling or house which is not fit for human habitation, where the authority considers that the execution of relevant works will not render the dwelling or house fit.[61] A further example of significance relates to works to be undertaken as part of a group repair scheme approved by the Secretary of State.[62]

Conditions

Part VIII is very prescriptive in relation to the conditions that may be attracted to grant-aid, despite a statement in the Act that no conditions may be imposed

[56] *Ibid.* s.103.
[57] *Ibid.* s.104(1). As to an "owner's interest", see subs.(2).
[58] *Ibid.* s.112.
[59] *Ibid.* s.113.
[60] *Ibid.* s.115.
[61] *Ibid.* s.107(2)(a).
[62] *Ibid.* s.107(3). Group repair schemes generally are governed by s.127.

except with the consent of the Secretary of State or as provided for elsewhere in the Act.[63] The Act provides for conditions relating to the completion of works, availability for letting, repayment of grant in certain circumstances and conditions concerning the HMO grant.

Minor works

Provision is made for grant-aid in respect of so-called minor works,[64] which cover:

(a) the provision or improvement of thermal insulation in a dwelling;
(b) the execution of repairs to a dwelling in a clearance area or a dwelling intended to be included in a clearance area in the next 12 months;
(c) the execution of works for the repair, improvement or adaptation of a dwelling occupied by an elderly owner or tenant;
(d) the adaptation of a dwelling for the care of an elderly resident who is neither the owner nor tenant; and
(e) any other purpose prescribed by the Secretary of State.[65]

[63] *Ibid.* s.118(1).
[64] *Ibid.* ss.118–126.
[65] *Ibid.* s.131.

CHAPTER 13

FOOD SAFETY

Food Safety and Related Legislation

The essential emphasis of the present chapter is the legislation governing food safety to be found in the Food Safety Act 1990 and accompanying legislation. That accompanying legislation comprises a variety of provisions, including matters relating to meat, milk and dairies.

The Food Safety Act 1990

The Act of 1990 is dealt with under a variety of headings, beginning with preliminary matters underpinning legislation that is, in large part, enabling legislation.[1] Accordingly, frequent emphasis is given to the many regulations made under this and preceding legislation, such as the Food Act 1984. The government's White Paper[2] anticipated that the Act of 1990 would continue to cover food hygiene and the protection of the consumer against injurious or unfit food, as well as protection against food that is not of the "nature, substance or quality" demanded by the purchaser, protection against false or misleading labelling and powers to make regulations on the composition, labelling and hygiene of food.[3]

"Food" and other terminology

The Act of 1990 does not define "food", but indicates that the expression includes drink, articles and substances of no nutritional value which are used for human consumption, chewing gum and other products of a like nature and use, and articles and substances used as ingredients in the preparation of food, or anything falling within the above descriptions.[4] In proceedings under the former Food and Drugs Act 1955, it was held that a purported sale of lemonade was sufficient to constitute a sale of "food", although something quite different was in fact provided (caustic soda) entirely unknown to both the waiter and the

[1] As to the background to the legislation, see the White Paper, "Food Safety—Protecting the Consumer", Cm. 732 (1989).
[2] *Ibid.*
[3] *Ibid.* p.31.
[4] Food Safety Act, s.1(1).

customer.[5] Water is necessarily included in the expression "drink" but note that there is a limit to its inclusion (up to the point where the supply is made available to premises).[6]

Various items are not included as "food" under the Act:

(a) live animals or birds (or live fish which are not used for human consumption while alive);
(b) fodder or feeding stuffs for animals, birds or fish;
(c) controlled drugs under the Misuse of Drugs Act 1971; and
(d) (subject to exceptions prescribed by order) certain medicinal products within the Medicines Act 1967.[7]

"Business", "food business" and other expressions

"Business" is stated to include the undertaking of a canteen, club, school, hospital or institution, whether carried on for profit or not, and any undertaking or activity carried on by a public or local authority. Frequent reference is made to the term "food business", particularly in the numerous regulations made under the legislation, such as the Food Hygiene (Markets, Stalls and Delivery Vehicles) Regulations 1966.[8] The term is interpreted to mean any business in the course of which commercial operations with respect to food or food sources are carried out. In turn, "food premises" are those premises used for the purpose of a food business. "Commercial operation" in relation to any food or "contact material" is stated to mean:

(a) selling, possessing for sale and offering, exposing or advertising for sale;
(b) consigning, delivering or serving by way of sale;
(c) preparing for sale or presenting, labelling or wrapping for the purpose of sale;
(d) storing or transporting for the purpose of sale; and
(e) importing and exporting.

Furthermore, in relation to any food source, a "commercial operation" means deriving food from that source for the purpose of sale or for purposes connected with sale. "Contact material" referred to here means any article or substance (such as packaging) which is intended to come into contact with food. A "food source" is defined to mean any growing crop or live animal, bird or fish from which food is intended to be derived, whether by harvesting, slaughtering, milking, collecting eggs or otherwise. Finally, "premises" are stated to include any place, any vehicle, stall or movable structure and, for such purposes as may be specified by the Ministers,[9] any ship or aircraft of a description so specified.[10]

[5] *Meah v. Roberts* [1977] 1 W.L.R. 1187: see particularly *per* Wien J. at 1195.
[6] Food Safety Act, ss.55 and 56. *Cf.* Chap. 1, "Water Resources and Supply".
[7] *Ibid.* s.1(2).
[8] S.I. 1966 No. 1426.
[9] Food Safety Act, s.4(1).
[10] *Ibid.* s.1(3).

Scope of the term "sale"

The term "sale" is crucially important for a variety of purposes under the Food Safety Act: sections 8, 9, 14, 15, 21 and 22. Respectively, these sections deal with:

(a) the sale of food not complying with food safety requirements;
(b) the inspection and seizure of suspected food intended for human consumption and sold or offered or exposed for sale;
(c) the sale of food not of the nature or substance or quality demanded;
(d) the false description or presentation of food which is sold or offered or exposed for sale;
(e) the successful operation of the defence of due diligence where a sale or intended sale (as a basis for an offence under the Act) is proved not to be a sale or intended sale under the defendant's name or mark; and
(f) the operation of the defence of publication of advertisements in the course of business in respect of an offence of the advertising of food for sale.

Although the term "sale" is crucial, the White Paper[11] anticipated application of certain enforcement powers ". . . to possession for sale as well as sale itself, so that the powers can be exercised before . . . goods are put on sale".[12] A significant example of enforcement by reference to "sale" and "possession for sale" is to be found in section 8, above.

The term "sale" in relation to food is extended by the Act so that the supply of food, otherwise than on sale, in the course of a business, as well as any other thing which is done with respect to food as specified in an order made by the Ministers, is deemed to be a sale of the food.[13] The term "business" for present purposes is central to this extended definition of sale, stressing, *inter alia*, the irrelevance of profit-making.

By way of elucidation, a number of situations is listed, indicating that the Act will apply because the situation in question is to be identified with the exposure of food for sale. These situations fall into three categories:

(a) where food is offered as a prize or reward or is given away in connection with any entertainment[14] to which the public is admitted, whether on payment or not;
(b) where food, for the purpose of advertisement or in furtherance of any trade or business, is offered as a prize or reward or given away; and
(c) where (in relation to either of the two situations above) food is exposed or deposited in "any" premises "for the purpose of being offered or given away".[15]

[11] See n.1, *supra*.
[12] *Ibid.* p.32.
[13] Food Safety Act, s.2(1).
[14] "Entertainment" includes any social gathering, amusement, exhibition, performance, game, sport or trial of skill: *ibid.* subs.(2).
[15] *Ibid.* s.2(2).

The presumption that food is intended for human consumption

The Act of 1990 in section 3 seeks to perpetuate the rebuttable presumption that food is intended for human consumption. Operation of the presumption in aid of enforcement may be assisted by the Act's reference to any food "commonly" used for human consumption. Any fishmonger, for example, would be unable to rebut the presumption by reference to the dietary needs of his cats! Failure of the fish to comply with food safety requirements in these circumstances would attract criminal enforcement under section 8. That the presumption may be rebutted otherwise than by the defendant's own words was confirmed by the High Court in proceedings relating to the "Fairy Belle" restaurant:

> "I would not for a moment go so far as to say that in a case of this kind the presumption can only be rebutted by evidence out of the mouth of the defendant ... [there may be, for example] food unfit for human consumption found in a dustbin ..."[16]

It is also presumed that any food commonly used for human consumption which is found on premises used for the preparation, storage or sale of that food, and any article or substance commonly used in the manufacture of food for human consumption which is found on premises used for the preparation, storage or sale of that food, is intended for sale or for the manufacturing of food, for sale, for human consumption.[17] It is also presumed that any article or substance capable of being used in the composition or preparation of any food commonly used for human consumption which is found on premises on which that food is prepared is intended for such use.[18]

Enforcement

Sections 4–6 of the Act of 1990 concentrate on the identity of the enforcing agencies and their possible relationship with other statutory agencies. The essential foundation of the Act is the distribution of functions between one or more responsible Ministers and various food authorities, subject to ministerial direction and control. The identity of the Ministers responsible under the Act is of significance for a variety of purposes, particularly in relation to regulation-making powers under Part II of the Act (sections 16–19 and 26), certain matters of administration and enforcement under Part III of the Act and certain powers found in Part IV, dealing with matters such as defaulting food authorities.

[16] *Per* Lord Widgery C.J. in *Hooper v. Petron* (1973) 71 L.G.R. 347 at 352.

[17] Food Safety Act, s.3(3).

[18] *Ibid.* subs.(4).

The Ministers responsible

References in the Act to "the Ministers" are references to the Minister of Agriculture in England and Wales and, in Scotland, to the Secretary of State for Scotland. References in the Act to "the Ministers" in the plural are references to the Minister of Agriculture, the Secretary of State responsible for health in England and food and health in Wales, acting jointly and, in Scotland, the Secretary of State for Scotland.[19] Where the Act (in section 13) refers to the making of emergency control orders, any reference to "the Ministers" is a reference to the Minister of Agriculture or (somewhat "open-endedly") "the Secretary of State".[20] No doubt the need for expedition in relation to emergency control orders justifies the failure to specify which Secretary of State may have responsibility for action here.

Food authorities and authorised officers

Although subject to some modification, as explained below, in England and Wales a food authority is principally a London borough council or a district or county council. Food authority functions may also be assigned, by order, to a port health authority under section 2 or 7 of the Public Health (Control of Disease) Act 1984, a joint board for a united district under section 6 of the Public Health Act, or a single authority for a metropolitan county under paragraph 15(6) of Schedule 8 to the Local Government Act 1985. In so far as particular functions are exercisable concurrently by authorities, the Ministers are empowered, by order, to assign a function to the district or county council, as the case may be.[21] Both in relation to the inspection and seizure of suspected food under section 9 of the Act and in relation to powers of entry for enforcement purposes under section 32, an "authorised officer" of a food authority exercises important functions. An authorised officer may or may not be an officer of the food authority, but he must be authorised by that authority in writing, either generally or specially, to act in matters arising under the Food Safety Act. The Act gives the Ministers the power to provide, through regulations, that no person may be authorised unless he holds prescribed qualifications.[22]

Enforcement responsibilities

It is normally the case that the food authority for an area will also be the enforcement authority. The Act divides its references to the food authority and

[19] *Ibid.* s.4(1).
[20] *Ibid.* subs.(2).
[21] See the Food Safety (Enforcement Authority) (England and Wales) Order 1990 (S.I. 1990 No. 2462), dividing responsibility in non-metropolitan counties for emergency prohibition notices and orders, and enforcement of prohibitions on false description and presentation of food, between district and county council, respectively.
[22] Food Safety Act, s.5.

the enforcement authority by reference to a distinction between the administrative functions of the former and the executive, enforcement functions of the latter.[23] The constituent orders and regulations made under the Food Safety Act or its predecessors refer to the relevant food authority, whose powers of enforcement are referable back to the Act and the powers available *qua* enforcement authority. For example, the Imported Food Regulations 1984[24] describe the food authority either as the relevant district council or London borough council, or even a port health authority as previously referred to, particularly in relation to food unloaded at the subject port. Every food authority is obliged to enforce and execute within their area the provisions of the Act, except in so far as any such duty is imposed expressly or by implication on some other authority. If any duty is imposed on a food authority, the Ministers may direct that it be discharged by them or, alternatively, one of the Ministers. The institution of proceedings under the Act, or any regulations or orders made under it, is in the hands of the enforcement authority, with a power to the Minister or Ministers to take over proceedings instituted "by some other person".[25]

Food rendered injurious to health

The first specific offence relates to the act of any person who thereby renders "any" food injurious to health, by means of various operations, with intent that it should be sold for human consumption.[26] The operations comprise:

(a) any addition of an article or substance to the food;
(b) the use of any such article or substance as an ingredient in food preparation;
(c) the abstraction of any constituent from food; and
(d) the subjection of food to any other process or treatment.

The specification of an operation of some kind stresses the centrality of the positive act which renders food injurious to health. Mere passivity in selling food without such an intervening act is not an offence here, although it could amount to an offence under other provisions in Part II of the Act. The adulteration of food in supermarkets as part of a programme of "consumer terrorism" would be caught by the present provision, although the modesty of the penalties on conviction would no doubt suggest a prosecution under "mainstream" criminal offences. Nevertheless, it seems likely that interference with milk, for example, whereby milk deficient in fat is drawn from the bottom of a container when the fat has risen to the top would fall within the confines of the present offence.[27] The proof of intention by the prosecution should lead to a conviction even if the food be rendered injurious quite innocently. In determining whether food is injurious

[23] Contrast ss.9, 23, 24, 27, 28, 40–42, 44 and 49 with ss.10–12, 18, 19, 29, 30, 32 and 45.
[24] S.I. 1984 No.1918.
[25] Food Safety Act, s.6.
[26] "Human consumption" includes use in the preparation of food for human consumption: *ibid.* s.53(1).
[27] *Bridges v. Griffin* [1925] 2 K.B. 233.

to health, regard must be had to the probable effect of the food on the person consuming it, as well as the probable cumulative effect of food of substantially the same composition on the health of a person consuming it in ordinary quantities. "Injury" for this purpose in relation to matters of health includes any permanent or temporary impairment.[28]

The first of the operations identified relates to the addition of any "article or substance" to the food in question. An "article" for this purpose does not include a live animal or bird, or a live fish except any live fish (such as eels) used for human consumption. In turn, an "animal" is any creature, such as an insect, which is not a bird or fish. A substance is stated to include any natural or artificial substance or other matter, whether it is in solid or liquid form or in the form of a gas or vapour: a very wide category.[29]

The second of the operations refers to the use of any article or substance as an ingredient in the "preparation" of food. The Act again seeks to avoid a comprehensive definition, but identifies preparation as including manufacture and any form of processing or treatment, while the term "preparation for sale" is regarded as including packaging and the term "prepare for sale" is construed accordingly.[30]

The fourth operation involves subjection of food to "any other" process (as seen previously) in relation to the word "preparation" or "treatment". Treatment includes subjection of food to heat or cold, reflective of many modern processes such as chilling and cooking, as well as freezing.

Sale of food without compliance with food safety requirements

The offence of selling food which fails to comply with food safety requirements is widely defined. The offence is aimed at any person who sells for human consumption, or offers, exposes or advertises for sale for such consumption, or has in his possession for the purpose of such a sale or for preparation for such a sale, food that fails to comply, as well as any person who deposits with, or consigns to, any other person for the purpose of such a sale, or for preparation for such a sale, food that fails to comply.[31] The width of the offence is to be seen in its extension to a variety of situations short of actual sale and, in turn, the extended meaning of the term "sale".[32] Although less significant compared with the situation in law prior to the Act of 1990, where an offence of selling contaminated food arose only on sale of the food, it may still be important to identify the point of sale. In some instances, the point of sale will be determined through the terms of an agreement indicating, for example, that property will pass, along with the risk, at the "place of delivery".[33]

[28] Food Safety Act, s.7.

[29] *Ibid.* s.53(1).

[30] In proceedings under the Food Act 1984 it was held in *Leeds City Council v. Dewhurst* [1990] Crim.L.R. 725 that the slicing of cooked meats was not "preparation" within s.16 of the Act and that "preparation" should be distinguished from "preparation for sale" under s.17.

[31] *Ibid.* s.8(1).

[32] *Ibid.* s.2. *Cf.* n.13, *supra.*

[33] *Watson v. Coupland* [1945] 1 All E.R. 217.

One element of the offence may be exposure for sale of food that fails to comply. Again, arguably, that requirement of exposure is widely drawn. Food may, for example, be wrapped but still be capable of exposure for sale even though it is invisible to the purchaser.[34]

Failure to comply with food safety requirements is defined in three ways by the Act, in so far as food is rendered injurious to health by means of any of the operations defined for the purpose of the offence under section 7, or is unfit for human consumption, or is so contaminated (whether by extraneous matter or otherwise) that it would not be reasonable to expect it to be used for human consumption in that state.[35] A number of cases point up the question of whether it is appropriate to prosecute under the present section or section 14 relating to the sale of food which is not of the nature or substance or quality demanded, particularly where food is found to contain some foreign object or substance. The presence of such an object or substance may not necessarily render food injurious to health, unfit for human consumption or so contaminated that it would not be reasonable to expect human consumption in that state. Where a piece of metal entered a child's mouth from a cream bun, there was a prosecution under section 9 of the Food and Drugs Act 1938 for selling food unfit for human consumption. The court's view was that the section 9 offence related to food which was unsound because it was putrid or unwholesome. Consequently, the presence of the metal in the bun did not mean that the bun was unfit for human consumption.[36] On the other hand, the court has said that where a bottle of milk contained a mouse and others contained slivers of glass, the justices had misdirected themselves because there was credible evidence constituting a prima facie case that the milk was unfit for human consumption.[37]

There is a presumption, for present purposes, and for the purposes of section 9 of the Act relating to the inspection and seizure of suspected food, that where food failing to comply forms part of a batch, lot or consignment, all the food in the batch, lot or consignment fails to comply.[38]

The inspection and seizure of suspected food

Powers relating to inspection and seizure are referable to two sets of circumstances in which an authorised officer of a food authority may be operating. In the first place, an authorised officer may "at all reasonable times" inspect any food intended for human consumption which has been sold or offered or exposed for sale or is in the possession of, or has been deposited with or consigned to, any person for the purpose of sale or preparation for sale.[39] In the second place, and outside any inspection just referred to, an authorised officer

[34] *Wheat v. Brown* [1892] 1 Q.B. 418.
[35] Food Safety Act, s.8(2).
[36] *Miller v. Battersea Borough Council* [1956] 1 Q.B. 43.
[37] *Barton v. Unigate Dairies* (1987) 151 J.P. 128.
[38] Food Safety Act, s.8(3).
[39] *Ibid.* s.9(1). *Cf.* Code of Practice No. 4 on the inspection, detention and seizure of suspected food, made under s.40 of the Act.

may operate under the powers provided by the Act where it appears to him that any food is likely to cause food poisoning or any disease communicable to human beings.[40]

An authorised officer has an option either to give notice to the person "in charge" of food that until that notice is withdrawn the food (or any specified portion) is not to be used for human consumption and may not be removed or removed only to a place indicated in the notice, or to seize that subject food and remove it so that it may be dealt with by a justice of the peace. A person who knowingly contravenes any of these requirements commits an offence.[41] One critical element of this provision concerns identification of a person "in charge", who will normally have some specific managerial responsibility *qua* owner of the food business or a manager thereof.[42]

If an authorised officer uses the first option and serves a notice, he must, as soon as practicable and in any event within 21 days, determine whether or not he is satisfied that the subject food complies with food safety requirements. If the authorised officer is so satisfied, the notice must be withdrawn forthwith. If not so satisfied, the authorised officer must seize the food and remove it so that it can be dealt with by a justice of a peace.[43] In any of the above circumstances in which there is proposed resort to a justice of the peace, the person in charge of the food must be advised of the intention and any person who might be liable to prosecution under section 7 or 8 in respect of the food is entitled to be heard before the justice of the peace and to call witnesses.[44] Where a justice of the peace deals with a referral here and it appears to him, on the basis of such evidence as he considers appropriate in the circumstances, that any food fails to comply with food safety requirements, he is obliged to condemn that food. Furthermore, the justice of the peace is obliged to order destruction or disposal to prevent the food being used for human consumption: any expenses reasonably incurred here are defrayed by the owner of the food.[45] If a justice of the peace refuses to condemn the food or if a notice is withdrawn, as previously described, the food authority will be liable to pay compensation to the owner in respect of the depreciation of the food resulting from the action of their officer.[46] Disputes about the right to or amount of compensation will be determined by arbitration.[47]

Improvement notices and prohibition orders

Notices and orders here are important elements of the enforcement process.[48] Both enforcement devices relate to various food-processing and food hygiene

[40] *Ibid.* subs.(2).
[41] *Ibid.* subs.(3).
[42] *Tesco Supermarket Ltd v. Nattrass* [1972] A.C. 153. *Cf.* s.11(11) of the Act of 1990.
[43] Food Safety Act, s.9(4).
[44] *Ibid.* subs.(5).
[45] *Ibid.* subs.(6).
[46] *Ibid.* subs.(7).
[47] *Ibid.* subs.(8).
[48] *Ibid.* ss.10 and 11.

regulations which have effect by virtue of provisions in Part II of the Act. Prominent examples from practice would include the Food Hygiene (General) Regulations 1970[49] and the Code of Practice on the use of improvement notices.[50]

Improvement notices

If an authorised officer of an enforcement authority has reasonable grounds for believing that the proprietor of a food business is failing to comply with any regulations, he may serve an improvement notice on the proprietor stating grounds for the belief, the matters constituting failure to comply and the measures required to secure compliance, and requiring such measures (or at least their equivalent) to be taken in not less than 14 days. Failure to comply is an offence.[51] A proprietor under the Act is any person who carries on the subject food business.[52] Facilities for an appeal against an improvement notice are also provided for by the Act.[53]

Prohibition orders

The prohibition order is a widely applicable enforcement device extending to:

(a) food processing or treatment;
(b) the use of premises generally or in relation to particular elements of a food business;
(c) the use of equipment; and
(d) prohibitions on a proprietor participating in the management of a food business.

If the proprietor of a food business is convicted of an offence by virtue of food-processing or food hygiene regulations and the court is satisfied that certain health risk conditions (of the sort listed above) are fulfilled in relation to the subject business, the court[54] must order the imposition of an "appropriate prohibition".

Prohibitions fall into three categories,[55] the first of which is a prohibition on the use of a process or treatment for the purposes of the business in question. The second prohibition relates to the use of premises or equipment for the purposes of the business, or any food business of the same class or description. The third

[49] S.I. 1970 No. 1172.
[50] Code of Practice No. 5 (April 1994).
[51] Food Safety Act; s.10.
[52] *Ibid.* s.53(1).
[53] *Ibid.* ss.37 and 39.
[54] *Ibid.* s.11(1).
[55] *Ibid.* subs.(3).

prohibition relates to the use of subject premises or equipment for the purposes of any food business. While these prohibitions are mandatory, the court has a discretion to impose a prohibition on a proprietor who has been convicted of acting in breach of food hygiene regulations to the extent that such a person may not be permitted to participate in the management of any food business, or any food business of a class or description specified in the court's order.[56]

Whether it is a mandatory or discretionary prohibition, an enforcement authority is obliged to serve a copy of the order on the proprietor of the business and, in the case of a mandatory order, must affix a copy of the order on a conspicuous part of the premises. Any person who knowingly contravenes such an order commits an offence.[57]

A number of provisions govern the cancellation of prohibition orders.[58] An order ceases to have effect where the enforcement authority certifies that a proprietor has taken sufficient measures to secure the health risk condition in relation to the state of food preparation equipment, for example, in the case of a mandatory order, or where the court gives a cancellation direction, in the case of a discretionary order.[59]

Emergency prohibition notices and orders

While the court may impose a prohibition upon conviction where satisfied that a health risk condition is satisfied, as seen above, a similar power is given to an authorised officer of an enforcement authority.[60] Imposition of the prohibition here is also on the proprietor of a food business, but by means of an emergency prohibition notice.[61] Any such officer may apply to the magistrates' court, so that if the court is satisfied that the health risk condition is fulfilled in relation to any food business, it is obliged to impose an emergency prohibition order.[62] If such an order is made, the court is able to impose an appropriate prohibition, even if the proprietor has not been convicted of an offence.[63] For present purposes, any reference to a risk of injury (which includes any temporary or permanent impairment)[64] is a reference to an "imminent" risk of such injury.

As soon as practicable after the service of a notice, the enforcement authority is obliged to affix a copy of the notice in a conspicuous position on the subject premises.[65] The same requirement applies in the case of the making of an emergency prohibition order, with the addition of a requirement to serve a copy

[56] *Ibid.* subs.(4). These provisions apply to the manager of a food business in the same way as they apply to a proprietor.
[57] *Ibid.* subs.(5).
[58] *Ibid.* subss.(6)–(8).
[59] *Ibid.* subs.(6). The procedures are set out in subss.(7) and (8), respectively.
[60] *Ibid.* s.7(3).
[61] *Ibid.* s.12(1). In non-metropolitan counties, the enforcement authority is a district council: Food Safety (Enforcement Authority) (England and Wales) Order 1990 (S.I. 1990 No. 2462).
[62] *Ibid.* s.12(2): note that the officer can apply within three days of a notice served on the proprietor.
[63] *Ibid.* s.11(9). *Cf.* n.55, *supra.*
[64] *Ibid.* s.7(3).
[65] *Ibid.* s.12(5).

on the proprietor of the business.[66] In both cases, any person who knowingly contravenes a notice or order commits an offence.[67]

A notice or order will cease to have effect where the enforcement authority certifies that the health risk condition no longer applies.[68] The authority is obliged to so certify within three days of being satisfied about the health risk condition. This period extends to 14 days on an application by a proprietor, although it is open to the authority to refuse to certify, in which case an appeal is available under section 37.[69] The enforcement authority may be vulnerable to a compensation claim from a proprietor where an application for an emergency prohibition order is not made within the period of three days referred to by section 12(7). However, the court must be satisfied of an absence of any imminent risk to health upon service of the notice.[70] Disputed matters concerning any right to or the amount of compensation are determined by arbitration.[71]

Emergency control orders

The White Paper[72] refers to a need to address potentially serious problems such as adulterated wine imports where, hitherto, reliance has been placed on the co-operation of manufacturers and traders. In these circumstances, the Minister of Agriculture has powers to make an emergency control order if it appears that, in carrying out commercial operations concerning food, food sources or contact materials involve or may involve imminent risk of injury to health. Any such order may prohibit the carrying out of such operations.[73] Any person who knowingly contravenes an order is guilty of an offence, although a defence is available in so far as it is shown that the Minister has consented to otherwise proscribed activities or that any condition of such a consent has been complied with.[74] To maintain the flexibility which may be required in these circumstances, the Minister may give directions which appear to him to be necessary or expedient for the purpose of preventing the carrying out of commercial operations in connection with any food, food sources or contact material which he believes, on reasonable grounds, to be subject to an emergency control order. Furthermore, the Minister may do anything which appears to him to be necessary or expedient for that purpose.[75] Failure to comply with a direction is an offence.[76] Where a person fails to comply with an order or a direction, as the consequence of

[66] *Ibid.* subs.(6).
[67] *Ibid.* subss.(5) and (6).
[68] *Ibid.* subs.(7).
[69] *Ibid.* subss.(8) and (9).
[70] *Ibid.* subs.(10).
[71] *Ibid.*
[72] See n.1, *supra.*
[73] Food Safety Act, s.13(1).
[74] *Ibid.* subss.(2), (3) and (4).
[75] *Ibid.* subs.(5).
[76] *Ibid.* subs.(6).

which the Minister does "anything", the Minister may recover from that person any expenses reasonably incurred.[77]

The sale of food not of the nature, substance or quality demanded

Any person who sells to the purchaser's prejudice any food which is not of the nature, substance or quality demanded by that purchaser is guilty of an offence.[78] Any sale must be a sale for human consumption and, furthermore, there is no defence that the purchaser was not prejudiced because he bought food for analysis or examination. "Food" for present purposes may include drink, as well as any item supplied in the mistaken belief that it is food or drink.[79]

In proceedings for an offence here, an important issue may be the extent to which quantitative evidence by analysts is evidence of the nature, substance or quality of the article demanded by the purchaser. This issue was addressed in *Goldup v. John Manson Ltd*,[80] a case relating to proceedings under the similar terms of section 2 of the Food and Drugs Act 1955. Ormerod L.J. commented:

> "The standard prescribed . . . is defined in terms of the purchaser's demand which, ultimately, is a question of fact. It may be determined by the express terms of the contract . . . More often the nature or substance or quality demanded by the purchaser will be a matter of implication or inference from all the surrounding circumstances . . . In other cases of absence of evidence of circumstances, it will be inferred that the purchaser demanded an article which corresponds in substance or quality with that normally sold in the trade . . . In that case evidence from the trade established the standard of commercial quality or merchantability. When the article is sold by description . . . the purchaser impliedly demands a product which is of merchantable quality . . . the disparity between the composition of the article sold and the description may be so great as to raise a prima facie case of unmerchantable quality and, in the absence of evidence to the contrary, prove the case for the prosecution . . . [A] *bare* statement by the analyst . . . [may be] irrelevant since by itself it is not evidence of the quality demanded by the purchaser . . ."[81]

The section creates three distinct offences. Consequently, an information charging that the food is not of the nature, or not of the substance, or not of the quality demanded is bad for uncertainty.[82] If there is doubt about this matter, the better option is to prefer more than one information.[83]

The presence of some foreign object in food, in so far as it is the basis for a prosecution under the present section, need not be shown to be deleterious:

[77] *Ibid.* subs.(7).
[78] *Ibid.* s.14(1).
[79] *Meah v. Roberts, supra.*
[80] [1981] 3 All E.R. 257.
[81] *Ibid.* at 264.
[82] *Bastin v. Davies* [1950] 2 K.B. 579.
[83] *Moore v. Ray* [1951] 1 K.B. 98.

"It is sufficient for the prosecution to prove that the presence of the extraneous matter will give rise to the consequence that a purchaser could, in the context of the particular transaction, reasonably object to the presence of that matter in the article of food supplied, though if the presence of the extraneous matter was deleterious, it is difficult to see how in such circumstances the article could be of the requisite quality."[84]

Where a purchaser gets an article inferior to that which he demands and pays for, he is necessarily prejudiced.[85] On the other hand, if a material fact about the food is brought to the knowledge of the purchaser, as where, for example, there was a notice in a public house indicating the sale of "mixed spirits", and there is a purchase notwithstanding that, the court will not interfere with that transaction.[86] The crucial test for present purposes is whether a purchaser without the special knowledge would be prejudiced:

"I think the words 'to the prejudice of the purchaser' are used in the sense that there is a sale to the prejudice of the purchaser if a purchaser in the abstract would be prejudiced, although the actual purchaser may for some reason peculiar to himself not be prejudiced."[87]

Despite some confusion in judicial thinking, it seems clear that the present offence is one of strict liability at least. In *Smedley's Ltd v. Breed*,[88] the House of Lords was confronted by facts which described the finding of a caterpillar in a can of peas. Lord Hailsham observed:

"Whilst I accept that the system was as good as reasonable skill and diligence on the part of management could make it, on the construction which I am constrained to place upon the relevant provisions of the Act [section 2 of the Food and Drugs Act 1955], the absence of any finding that the failure to eliminate the caterpillar was unavoidable is, in my opinion, fatal to the appeal."[89]

Two members of the House considered that "unavoidable" means unavoidable by an exercise of a reasonable standard of care, while one member of the House (equally ambiguously) refers to a "high standard of reasonable care".

The false description and presentation of food

The Act provides for three groups of offences under the present heading. The first group of offences arises where any person gives a label (whether or not attached to or printed on a wrapper or container) which falsely describes the food or is likely

[84] *Per* Robert Goff L.J. in *Barber v. Co-operative Wholesale Society Ltd* (1983) 81 L.G.R. 762 at 767–768.
[85] *Per* Mellor J. in *Hoyle v. Hitchman* (1879) 4 Q.B.D. 233 at 237.
[86] *Sandys v. Small* (1878) 3 Q.B.D. 449.
[87] *Per* Darling J. in *Pearks, Gunston & Tee Ltd v. Ward* [1902] 1 K.B. 1, at 9–10.
[88] [1974] A.C. 839.
[89] *Ibid.* at 848.

to mislead as to the nature or substance or quality of the food. However, the person giving a label must have sold the food with the subject label or have displayed the label with any food offered or exposed for sale. The offences of display even extend to food in the defendant's possession for the purpose of sale where, for example, food is in a factory or warehouse pending distribution.[90] The present provision defines two separate offences of falsely describing food and labelling food so that it is likely to mislead. The fact that a label contains an accurate statement of the composition of the food in question does not preclude the court from finding that the offence was committed.[91]

The second group of offences also relate to false description and misleading labelling but apply to any person who publishes or is party to a publication of an advertisement which is not a label given or displayed for the purposes of the former group of offences.[92] Once again, the fact that an advertisement contains an accurate statement of the composition of the food in question does not preclude the court from finding that the offence was committed.[93]

A third offence applies to any person who sells, or offers or exposes for sale, or has in his possession for the purposes of sale, any food the presentation of which is likely to mislead as to the nature or substance or quality of the food.[94]

Enforcement of the foregoing provisions is the responsibility of county councils in the case of non-metropolitan counties.[95]

Regulations under the Food Safety Act

As indicated previously, the Act rests to a considerable degree on detailed requirements to be spelt out in regulations to be made by the Ministers.[96] Such flexibility facilities, *inter alia*, a timely response to fast-moving developments in relation to food safety and hygiene, including requirements emanating from the European Community and requirements relating to novel foods and novel food ingredients.

Food safety and consumer protection regulations

The Act lists an extensive number of purposes for which regulations may be made, including specification of which residues, if any, may be allowed in food or food sources, observation of hygienic conditions and practices in connection with the carrying out of commercial operations, and the labelling, marking, presentation or advertising of food.[97] Regulations may also be made in

[90] Food Safety Act, s.15(1).
[91] *Ibid.* subs.(4).
[92] *Ibid.* subs.(2).
[93] *Ibid.* subs.(4).
[94] *Ibid.* subs.(3).
[95] Food Safety (Enforcement Authority) (England and Wales) Order 1990 (S.I. 1990 No. 2462).
[96] The powers are found in ss.16–19 of the Food Safety Act, together with supplementary provision in s.26. As to the obligation to consult, see s.48(4).
[97] *Ibid.* s.16(1).

connection with a wide variety of activities concerning contact material such as food packaging.[98] Without prejudice to the generality of these regulation-making powers, the Act also provides further, detailed catalogues of matters that may be subject to regulation.[99] These additional matters relate to the composition of food, the fitness of food, the processing and treatment of food, food hygiene and the inspection of food sources. Of future significance in particular are the provisions that may be included in regulations, relating to the processing and treatment of food. Provision may be made, *inter alia*, for the issue by enforcement authorities of licences in respect of the use of any process or treatment in the preparation of food.[1] Such enabling powers will be of significance in relation to the irradiation of food and the development and marketing of novel foods.

Food irradiation

The White Paper referred to at the outset[2] anticipated centralised licensing of irradiation facilities and informative labelling of irradiated foods. Some, if not all of these requirements may be achieved through the regulation-making powers here referred to. In addition to licensing, for example, there is reference to a power to include in regulations provision for specialist opinion about the use of a particular process or treatment and to prohibit use of that process or treatment except in accordance with specialist opinion.[3]

Novel foods

Novel foods are characterised (despite a limited definition in section 18(3)) as those foods or food ingredients which have not hitherto been used for human consumption to a significant degree and which may have been produced by processes that result in a significant change in their composition (probably by means of artificial techniques of genetic manipulation) or nutritional value. The regulation of novel foods is still very much in its infancy, particularly in comparison with the regulation of food additives such as colouring matter and preservatives. Food additives have been subject to E.C. regulation for many years, under the terms of various directives. Preservatives, for example, have been subject to regulation since 1964,[4] so that only those preservatives that are authorised may be used in foodstuffs for human consumption. The same broad approach applies in relation to a long list of foods and food ingredients. For example, natural mineral waters may only be exploited and marketed in compliance with standards and requirements set out in the relevant Directive.[5]

[98] *Ibid.* subs.(2).
[99] *Ibid.* Sched. 1.
[1] *Ibid.* para. 4(6).
[2] See the White Paper, *op. cit.*, p.35.
[3] Food Safety Act, Sched. 1, para. 4(a). See now the Food (Control of Irradiation) Regulations 1990 (S.I. 1990 No. 2490).
[4] Directive 64/54: [1963–64] O.J. L99, as amended.
[5] Directive 80/777: [1980] O.J. L229, implemented by the Natural Mineral Waters Regulations 1985 (S.I. 1985 No. 71).

In the case of novel foods, there exists no similar E.C.-wide regulatory regime. It is conceivable that many of the offences under the Food Safety Act could well apply to novel foods that have an adverse impact on the health of the public, but the statutory framework does not presently assume that the food in question is safe following some regulatory determination. Until regulations are made under the Food Safety Act provisions now under discussion, novel foods will not be subject to such control. At the time of writing, the European Community has a proposal for a regulation on novel foods and novel food ingredients which would put in place a system of regulatory approvals. In the meantime, liability for damage caused by food, again in so far as damage or injury is caused after an event such as sale, may arise under the Consumer Protection Act 1987 where a food product is the result of an industrial process.[6] The European Community's product safety directive[6a] will remove the requirement for an industrial process presently in place.

Enforcement of E.C. requirements

Hitherto the European Communities Act has been used to justify some regulations such as the Natural Mineral Waters Regulations.[7] The Food Safety Act now provides widely defined empowering provisions in respect of food, food sources and contact materials. Accordingly, the Ministers are empowered to make such provision here "... as appears to them to be called for by any Community obligation".[8] The Drinking Milk Regulations,[9] for example, supplement E.C. Regulation 1411/71[9a] (as amended) in restricting the delivery of milk on sale for human consumption to certain categories. More recently, the Quick-frozen Foodstuffs Regulations 1990[10] implement Directive 89/108[10a] on the approximation of laws on quick-frozen foodstuffs for human consumption through certain restrictions to be satisfied as a prerequisite to the sale of such products.

The Act also makes provision for directly applicable Community regulations which have the force of law automatically in Member States.[11] The Ministers are empowered to make such provision as they consider necessary or expedient for the purpose of securing that the Community provision is administered, executed and enforced under the Act. Furthermore, the Ministers may make modifications to the provisions of the Act for present purposes. However, the Ministers are not obliged to consult prior to the making of regulations under this provision arising from a directly applicable Community provision.[12]

[6] Consumer Protection Act 1987, Pt. I.
[6a] [1985] O.J. L210/29.
[7] S.I. 1985 No. 71: see n.5, *supra*.
[8] Food Safety Act, s.17(1).
[9] S.I. 1976 No. 1883.
[9a] [1971] O.J. L148.
[10] S.I. 1990 No. 2615.
[10a] [1989] O.J. L40/34.
[11] Food Safety Act, s.17(2).
[12] *Ibid.* s.48(4).

Special provision for particular foods

The power to make regulations in relation to novel foods was referred to previously. The Ministers may provide for prohibitions in respect of the carrying out of commercial operations with respect to novel foods or food sources and with respect to genetically modified food sources,[13] as well as in respect of the importation of such foods. Special designations may also be made by means of regulations in relation to milk, specifying, for example, untreated milk. Such regulations may require that any person producing untreated milk be licensed by the Minister of Agriculture, while distribution of and dealing in such milk is subject to local authority licensing.[14] These powers[15] relating to novel foods and foods which are genetically modified are significantly supplemented by the regulation-making power to be found in section 16 and Schedule 1.

Registration and licensing of food premises

The Ministers are empowered to make regulations for the registration by enforcement authorities of premises used or proposed to be used for the purposes of a food business through a licensing regime. However, the power is exercisable only for the purposes of securing that food complies with food safety requirements, the interests of public health or the protection and promotion of consumer interests.[16] Accordingly, if, for example, the display of fish in a shop is not such as to be injurious to public health, an exercise of powers for that purpose could well be *ultra vires*.[17]

The Food Premises (Registration) Regulations 1991[18] have been made under the authority of this and other sections of the Food Safety Act. The Regulations provide for the registration of food premises by food authorities according to registration criteria which refer to premises being in use for the purpose of a food business on five or more days in any period of five weeks. Various categories of premises are exempt from registration, including certain domestic premises used for the purposes of a food business. A public register is provided for, in addition to a supplementary record available only to police officers and authorised officers of the enforcement authorities. Various criminal offences are provided for, including, in particular, the use of unregistered premises.

[13] *Ibid.* s.18(4). *Cf.* s.16(1)(c).
[14] See the Milk and Dairies (General) Regulations 1959 (S.I. 1959 No. 277), as amended.
[15] Food Safety Act, s.18.
[16] *Ibid.* s.19: *cf.* the Milk and Dairies (General) Regulations.
[17] *Mac Fisheries (Wholesale and Retail) Ltd v. Coventry Corporation* [1957] 3 All E.R. 299.
[18] S.I. 1991 No. 2825.

Defences to Proceedings under the Act

Defences fall into three categories, relating to offences due to the fault of some person other than the defendant,[19] due diligence,[20] and (in proceedings relating to advertisement for sale of any food) publication in the ordinary course of business.[21]

Offences due to the fault of another person

If it is shown that the commission of an offence under Part II (sections 7–19) was due to an act or default of some other person, that other person is guilty of the subject offence. Proceedings can be taken against the latter person and a conviction recorded whether or not proceedings are taken against the "original" party. The facility for such prosecutions is not uncommon and is found in a variety of legislation with relevance to environmental health law enforcement, for example, the Control of Pollution Act 1974,[22] the Control of Pollution (Amendment) Act 1989[23] and the Environmental Protection Act 1990.[24]

Due diligence

The Government's White Paper "Food Safety: Protecting the Consumer"[25] stated the importance of striking "... the right balance between the interests of consumers, manufacturers, retailers and importers, a balance that is now translated into a defence of due diligence or (in broader terms) reasonable care".

However, the Act refers to a defendant who took all reasonable precautions and exercised all due diligence to avoid commission of an offence under the preceding provisions of Part II either by himself or by a person under his control.[26] The conjunction between reasonable precautions and due diligence appears to suggest an onerous, objective standard of behaviour often referable to the systems operating within a food business. Where a defence founded on the act or default of another person or information supplied by that other person is relied on, that reliance is dependent on satisfaction of certain prerequisites that would assist the prosecutor in the identification of the alleged third party.[27]

Special requirements govern reliance on the present defence (without prejudice to the generality of the defence of due diligence) where the offences charged are those relating to the sale of food not complying with safety requirements (section 8), the sale of food not of the nature, substance or quality

[19] Food Safety Act, s.20.
[20] *Ibid.* s.21. *Cf. Carrick District Council v. Taunton Vale Meat Traders Ltd, The Times*, February 15, 1994.
[21] *Ibid.* s.22.
[22] Control of Pollution Act, s.87(2).
[23] Control of Pollution (Amendment) Act 1989, s.7(5).
[24] Environmental Protection Act 1990, s.158.
[25] See n.1, *supra*.
[26] Food Safety Act, s.21(1).
[27] *Ibid.* subss.(5), (6).

demanded (section 14) or the false description or presentation of food (section 15). In these cases, any person charged may be able to establish the defence where it can be shown that he neither prepared the subject food nor imported it into Great Britain.[28] However, the defence will only be available if further requirements can be established. Those further requirements are stated in the alternative.

The first alternative is built around proof that commission of the offence was due to:

(a) the act or default of another person not under the defendant's control (or reliance on information from such a person);
(b) the execution of reasonable checks on the food by the defendant; and
(c) the fact that the defendant did not know and had no reason to suspect that the act or omission amounted to an offence at the time of its commission.[29]

The second alternative is built around proof of the first and third of the above elements, but with the substitution of the second element with proof that the sale or intended sale of which the alleged offence consisted was not a sale or intended sale under the defendant's name or mark.[30] The critical difference in practice arises from those transactions which are or are not referable to the defendant's own name or mark as the "badge" of the subject sale. Arguably, the second alternative defence is less onerous, since fewer substantive checks appear to be expected in law, compared with a situation where the defendant is selling by reference to his own name or mark.

Publication in the ordinary course of business

This defence is referable to an offence relating to the advertisement for sale of any food. In this case, it is a defence to prove that it is the business of the person charged to publish or arrange for the publication of advertisements and that that person received the advertisement in the ordinary course of business and did not know and had no reason to suspect that its publication would amount to an offence.[31]

[28] *Ibid.* subs.(2).
[29] *Ibid.* subs.(3).
[30] *Ibid.* subs.(4).
[31] *Ibid.* s.22.

Administration and Enforcement of the Food Safety Act

Sampling and analysis

An authorised officer of an enforcement authority has broad powers to undertake sampling.[32] The Act also provides detailed requirements in connection with the collection, treatment and analysis of samples.[33] The Ministers are empowered to require those who carry on a relevant business to afford facilities for the taking of samples of any food, substance or contact material and to furnish prescribed information in relation to any such food, substance or contact material.[34] However, information relating to an individual business obtained by means of an order made by the Ministers may not be disclosed without the previous consent in writing of the person carrying out that business. The only exceptions to the obligations of confidentiality, breach of which is an offence, arise where a Minister issues directions necessary for the purposes of the Act or for the purpose of complying with any European Community obligation, or where disclosure is necessary for the purposes of any proceedings for an offence against an order or any report of those proceedings.[35] The Act clarifies the circumstances in which disclosure is necessary for the purposes of the Act by including the purpose of securing that food complies with food safety requirements or public health interests, or the purpose of protecting or promoting consumer interests.[36]

In relation to sampling, an authorised officer of the enforcement authority is empowered to purchase a sample of any food or any substance capable of being used in the preparation of food. Additionally, an authorised officer is able to take samples in three different situations. First, an officer may take a sample of any food or "any substance" that appears to be intended for sale or to have been sold for human consumption or is found by him on or in any premises which he is authorised to enter. This latter power is obviously important in the defence of hygiene standards, where it may be necessary to collect samples of dirt found in kitchens, for example. Secondly, an officer may take a sample from any food source or of any contact material found in or on any premises which he is authorised to enter. Thirdly, an officer may take a sample of any article or substance which is found by him on or in any premises which he is authorised to enter, where he has reason to believe that that article or substance may be required as evidence in proceedings under the Act or any of its regulations or orders.[37]

Where a sample has been procured under the foregoing powers, the officer is obliged to submit it to the public analyst[38] for analysis,[39] or to a food examiner for

[32] *Ibid.* s.29.
[33] *Ibid.* ss.30 and 31.
[34] *Ibid.* s.25(1), (2). The requirements are prescribed by order.
[35] *Ibid.* subs.(3).
[36] *Ibid.* subs.(4).
[37] *Ibid.* s.29.
[38] As appointed by a food authority under s.27.
[39] As defined by s.30(9).

examination, according to his view of the way in which the sample should be treated.[40] Any person other than such an officer who has purchased any food or any substance capable of being used in the preparation of food may also submit a sample to the public analyst or a food examiner.[41] Upon examination or analysis of a sample, the examiner or analyst will be required to give a certificate specifying the result of the examination or analysis.[42] Normally, production of a certificate by one of the parties in proceedings under the Act is treated as sufficient evidence of the facts stated in it.[43]

The foregoing provisions distinguish between "analysis" and "examination". The term "analysis" is stated to include microbiological assay and any technique for establishing the composition of food.[44] "Examination", on the other hand, is defined to mean a microbiological examination.[45] To facilitate analysis, each food authority is obliged to appoint a public analyst.[46] Detailed requirements governing these various activities are to be found in the Food Safety (Sampling and Qualifications) Regulations 1990,[47] made under, *inter alia*, section 31 of the Food Safety Act. This section empowers the making of regulations by the Ministers for a wide variety of purposes in the present context, including the method of dealing with samples and (where appropriate) their division into parts. Although division into three parts is the norm, such a division is not required where it is not reasonably practicable or where it might impede analysis.[48] However, some regulations contain their own requirements for sampling: the Natural Mineral Waters Regulations, for example.[49] Further specific guidance is contained in the Code of Practice on sampling for analysis or examination.[50]

Powers of entry and obstruction

If an authorised officer of an enforcement authority is able to establish his authority, the Act gives rights of entry at all reasonable hours to a variety of premises. The exception relates to any private dwelling-house where entry as of right may not be demanded: in this case, the occupier is entitled to 24 hours' notice before entry as of right can be demanded. Otherwise, entry as of right is permitted in three sets of circumstances.[51] The first right of entry is to any premises in the area of the authority for the purpose of ascertaining whether there is or has been on the premises any contravention of the Act or of regulations or orders made under it. The second right of entry is restricted to business premises

[40] Food Safety Act, s.30(1).
[41] *Ibid.* subs.(2).
[42] *Ibid.* subs.(6).
[43] *Ibid.* subs.(8).
[44] *Ibid.* s.53(1).
[45] *Ibid.* s.28(2).
[46] *Ibid.* s.27.
[47] S.I. 1990 No. 2463, as amended by S.I. 1991 No. 2843.
[48] *Ibid.* reg.6(1), (4).
[49] See n.7, *supra.*
[50] Food Safety Act, s.40.
[51] *Ibid.* s.32(1).

which may, nevertheless, be within or outside the area of the enforcement authority. In this case, the right of entry is provided for the purpose of ascertaining whether there is on the premises any evidence of contravention. The third right of entry extends to an authorised officer of a food authority who is authorised to enter any premises for the purpose of performance of the authority's functions under the Act.[52]

In any of the three situations above, if admission to premises is refused or a refusal is apprehended, a justice of the peace may by warrant authorise entry if satisfied that there are reasonable grounds for entry and notice of an intention to apply for a warrant has been given to the occupier. Such a warrant may also be issued but without any requirement for a notice of intention where (again) there are reasonable grounds for entry but where an application for entry would defeat the object of entry, or the matter is one of urgency, or the occupier is temporarily absent from premises that are unoccupied.[53]

Whether or not entry to premises be secured by means of a warrant, an authorised officer is able to take with him such other persons as he considers necessary. If entry is by means of a warrant to unoccupied premises, those premises must be left as effectively secured against unauthorised entry as they were found.[54] Entry under a warrant or otherwise also empowers the inspection of any records relating to a food business, including computerised records.[55] Furthermore, an authorised officer exercising these powers of inspection may seize and detain any records which he has reason to believe may be required as evidence in proceedings under the Act, its regulations or orders, and demand that computerised records are produced in a form that allows them to be taken away.[56] Any disclosure of information so obtained in relation to a trade secret is an offence, unless that disclosure was undertaken in the performance of the authorised officer's duty.[57]

The Food Safety Act creates two offences of obstruction.[58] The first offence arises where a person intentionally obstructs a person acting in the execution of his duties under the Act.[59] The second offence arises where a person, without reasonable excuse, fails to give to any person acting in the execution of his duties under the Act any assistance or information which that person may reasonably require of him for the performance of such duties.[60] Any person who for this purpose knowingly or recklessly furnishes information which is false or misleading in a material particular also commits an offence.[61] However, the

[52] *Ibid.*
[53] *Ibid.* subs.(2). Any warrant remains in force for one month.
[54] *Ibid.* subs.(4).
[55] *Ibid.* subs.(5).
[56] *Ibid.* subs.(6).
[57] *Ibid.* subs.(7).
[58] *Ibid.* s.33.
[59] *Ibid.* subs.(1)(a).
[60] *Ibid.* subs.(1)(b).
[61] *Ibid.* subs.(2).

obligation to give assistance or information does not extend to require a person to answer any question or give any information which might incriminate him.[62]

Offences

In the case of any offence under the Act other than the obstruction offences in section 33(1), a prosecution may not be commenced after three years from the commission of the offence or one year from its discovery by the prosecutor, whichever is the earlier.[63] The former offences are triable only in summary proceedings, whereas all other offences under the Act are triable both ways, summarily and on indictment.[64] The Food Safety Act addresses, in common with many other areas of legislation, the matter of those who may be identified with corporate operations sufficiently to be criminally responsible for acts or omissions that might otherwise be identified with the company alone. If an offence has been committed by a body corporate but it is proved that that offence was committed with the consent or connivance of, or was attributable to any neglect on the part of, any director, manager, secretary or other similar officer, or any person purporting to act in such a capacity (a director not properly appointed according to law, for example), that person as well as the company is deemed to be guilty of the offence and therefore liable to be proceeded against and punished accordingly.[65]

There are circumstances in which common law principles will operate for the purpose of imposing criminal responsibility on an employer for the acts or omissions of an employee. It is possible, for example, that an employer could be a "seller" of milk for the purposes of a relevant offence.[66] It has been said that:

> ". . . the legislation in question has the effect of imposing an absolute duty so that a principal would be liable for the acts of his servant, or agent, done within his authority . . . The principle applies [also] . . . to the distributor who is selling milk in bottles [who] sub-contracts the bottling and delivery to another."[67]

Appeals

An appeal to the magistrates' court is available in three situations where a person is aggrieved by:

(a) the service of an improvement notice;
(b) the decision of an enforcement authority to refuse to issue a certificate, as a result of which a prohibition order, emergency prohibition notice or emergency prohibition order remains in force; and

[62] *Ibid.* subs.(3).
[63] *Ibid.* s.34.
[64] *Ibid.* s.35(1), (2).
[65] *Ibid.* s.36.
[66] *Brown v. Foot* (1892) 66 L.T.(N.S.) 649.
[67] *Per* Parker J. in *Quality Dairies (York) Ltd v. Pedley* [1952] 1 K.B. 275.

(c) a decision of an authority to refuse, cancel, suspend or revoke a licence required by any regulations made under Part II of the Act, in so far as those regulations do not make provision for an appeal to a tribunal.[68]

The procedure applicable for any such appeal is by way of a complaint for an order.[69]

A person who is aggrieved by the dismissal of an appeal brought by way of a complaint for an order, or a decision of the court to make a prohibition order or an emergency prohibition order, or to withdraw a licence described in section 35(4), on conviction can appeal to the Crown Court.[70]

Special provision is made by the Act in connection with appeals against improvement notices. On appeal, the court may either cancel or affirm the notice. If there is affirmation of the notice the court has a discretion to maintain the original terms, or to modify the notice.[71]

Ministerial Control of Local Authorities

The Act contains three significant provisions allowing central control of local authorities. In the first place, every food authority is required to send to the Minister such reports and returns and give such information about the exercise of statutory functions as may be required by him.[72] If the Minister is satisfied that a food authority has failed to discharge any duty imposed by the Act and that that failure affects the general interests of consumers of food, he may exercise his default powers by order, empowering another food authority[73] or one of his officers to discharge the subject duty.[74] As a prerequisite to the exercise of any default powers, the Minister may convene a public local inquiry.[75] The substitute authority or the Minister is able to recover any expenses reasonably incurred from the authority in default.[76]

For the guidance of food authorities, the Ministers are empowered to issue codes of recommended practice in relation to the execution and enforcement of the Act, its regulations and orders. Each authority is obliged to have regard to any relevant provision of a code and to comply with any direction from the Minister (or Ministers). Any such direction is enforceable by an order of mandamus. Particular codes are referred to elsewhere in the present chapter. Prior to the issue of a code, the Minister (or Ministers) are obliged to consult with such

[68] Food Safety Act, s.37(1), (2).
[69] *Ibid.* subs.(3). As to time limits for appeals, see subss.(5), (6).
[70] *Ibid.* s.38.
[71] *Ibid.* s.39.
[72] *Ibid.* s.41.
[73] Referred to as "the substitute authority".
[74] Food Safety Act, s.42(1).
[75] *Ibid.* subs.(2). The provisions of s.250(2)–(5) apply to any such inquiry.
[76] *Ibid.* subs.(4).

organisations as appear to be representative of interests likely to be substantially affected by the code. Following issue, a code must be laid before Parliament.[77]

Miscellaneous Liabilities

The Food Safety Act contains various provisions broadly concerned with matters of liability relating to:

(a) the circumstances in which a registration or licence may continue on the death of a person holding a registration or licence[78];
(b) the application of the Act to the Crown[79];
(c) the protection of officers of a food authority acting in good faith in the execution of the Act within the scope of their employment[80]; and
(d) the application of charges through regulations in respect of the discharge of functions by enforcement authorities.[81]

In the case of the continuation of a registration or licence, that registration or licence will subsist on the death of the person registered or holding a licence under the Act, by virtue of Part II, for a limited period in favour of the deceased's personal representative, or his widow or any other member of his family.

The Crown is bound by the Act, its regulations and orders but with the exception that does not permit the imposition of criminal liability. Nevertheless, the High Court (or the Court of Session in Scotland) may declare unlawful any contravention of the Act by the Crown. Otherwise, the Act and its obligations apply to persons in the service of the Crown as they apply to other persons.

An officer of a food authority is not liable personally if, in the exercise or purported exercise of his duties under the Act, within the scope of his employment, he does an act in the honest belief that such duties required him or entitled him to do it. This does not relieve the food authority of its own vicarious liability for the acts of its officers. The food authority may indemnify an officer in respect of any action against him in respect of an act undertaken in the exercise or purported exercise of the Act but outside the scope of his employment.

[77] *Ibid.* s.40.
[78] *Ibid.* s.43.
[79] *Ibid.* s.54.
[80] *Ibid.* s.44.
[81] *Ibid.* s.45.

Documentary requirements

The form and authentication of documents is specified by the Act,[82] which indicates a requirement for documents to be in writing. Regulations may also prescribe the form of documents such as improvement and prohibition notices and orders.[83] The Act also lays down requirements for the service of documents, indicating that postal delivery is normally sufficient.[84]

The Food and Environment Protection Act 1985

Contaminated food

Part I of the Act of 1985 authorises the making of orders in an emergency, specifying activities which are to be prohibited as a precaution against the consumption of food rendered unsuitable for human consumption as a consequence of the escape of "substances" such as radioactivity following incidents such as that at Chernobyl. Local authorities are not entitled to be consulted in connection with a designated incident. As to pesticide residue in food, the limits are set under Part III and by reference to the Pesticides (Maximum Residue Levels in Crops, Food and Feeding Stuffs) Regulations 1994.[84a]

Emergency orders

Responsibility for emergency orders is with the "designating authority", namely the Minister of Agriculture and the Secretary of State for the Environment, or either of them.[85] The Act gives the designating authority an important discretionary power whereby if, in the opinion of that authority, there exists or may exist circumstances which are likely to create a hazard to human health through human consumption of food which is in the United Kingdom or within British fishery limits which is, or may be, or may become, unsuitable for human consumption, that authority may by statutory instrument designate the area and impose emergency prohibitions.[86] Any emergency order is referable to the escape or suspected escape of a substance affecting food so that, in the opinion of the authority, that food is, or may be, or may become, unsuitable for human consumption.

Where an emergency order has been made, either of the Ministers is empowered to consent to the doing of a prohibited act.[87] The considerable

[82] *Ibid.* s.49.

[83] *Ibid.* subs.(2). *Cf.* the Food Safety (Improvement and Prohibition—Prescribed Forms) Regulations 1991 (S.I. 1991 No. 100).

[84] *Ibid.* s.50.

[84a] S.I. 1994 No. 1985.

[85] Food and Environment Protection Act, s.24(1).

[86] *Ibid.* s.1(1). As to the scope and nature of emergency prohibitions, see Sched. 1.

[87] *Ibid.* s.2(1).

discretion of the Ministers is further extended by a widely drawn power to issue directions considered necessary or expedient for the purpose of preventing human consumption of food following a designated incident, such as a polluting discharge.[88] Failure to comply with any such direction permits the Minister to take action in default and to recover the cost from the person responsible.[89]

Investigating and enforcement officers

The Act provides for the authorisation of investigating officers to conduct investigations in order to determine whether the powers in Part I of the Act should be exercised and the manner in which they should be exercised.[90] Enforcement officers, on the other hand can be authorised to enforce emergency orders and any directions given.[91] Significantly, the Act goes on to state that either of the Ministers may authorise an investigating officer or an enforcement officer who is not an officer of his department to perform any of the Minister's functions under Part I of the Act.[92] This would allow, for example, a fisheries officer to be employed in enforcement duties by the Secretary of State.

The powers available to the officers are prescribed by the Act.[93] An investigating officer's power of entry to any land, vehicle, vessel, aircraft, hovercraft or marine structure depend largely on reasonable grounds for suspecting that prescribed food is present.[94] The enforcement officer, on the other hand, can enter for any one of three reasons, including reasonable grounds for suspicion that there exists, for example, some record which would assist in determining the whereabouts of prescribed foods.[95] These powers are supported by further powers, which include the power of both investigating and enforcement officers to seize things for the purpose of the performance of their functions under the Act.[96] Further supporting powers are to be found in Schedule 2, and include significant powers to enable acquisition of information and entry into dwellings. Where the acquisition of information is concerned, an officer may demand from any person details of substances or articles on board or lost from a vessel, aircraft, hovercraft or marine structure. To facilitate the exercise of such powers, the officer may, for example, require a vessel to stop and direct it to (say) the nearest port or even take it there himself, probably for detention pending investigation.[97] Entry to a dwelling is permitted only "... for the purpose of performing ... functions under [the] Act" and where "... a Justice has issued a warrant authorising [the officer] to enter and search [the] dwelling".[98]

[88] *Ibid.* subs.(3).
[89] *Ibid.* s.1(6).
[90] *Ibid.* s.3(1)(a).
[91] *Ibid.* subs.(1)(b).
[92] *Ibid.* subs.(2).
[93] *Ibid.* s.4 and Sched. 2.
[94] *Ibid.* s.4(1).
[95] *Ibid.* subs.(2).
[96] *Ibid.* subs.(3). *Cf.* subss.(4) and (5).
[97] *Ibid.* Sched. 2(3).
[98] *Ibid.* Sched. 2(7).

Criminal enforcement

The foregoing functions are enforceable by reference to offences of intentional obstruction, failure (without reasonable excuse) to comply with officers' requirements and directions and the giving of false or misleading information.[99] Another offence arising under Part I of the Act is found in section 1 and applies to any person who contravenes an emergency prohibition or causes or permits any other person to do so.[1] This offence is subject to a variety of defences. First, where the charge alleges contravention of an emergency order's prohibition on the movement of food or on activities prohibited throughout the United Kingdom, or where it alleges that a person caused or permitted another to contravene the prohibition, it is a defence to show that contravention took place on a foreign vessel, foreign aircraft, foreign hovercraft or foreign marine structure, and nothing to which the prohibition related was landed from it in the United Kingdom.[2]

A second defence arises from the provisions of section 2, where it is shown that consent was given under that section allowing contravention of any prohibition or that any attached conditions have been complied with.[3] A third defence is also referable to section 2 and arises where any person fails to comply with a direction issued under that section or causes or permits another to do so.[4]

The most general defence, applying to any proceedings for an offence under the Act,[5] appears in section 22 and covers due diligence. The defence enables the person charged to prove that he took all reasonable precautions and exercised all due diligence to avoid commission of the offence.[6] It is possible to establish this defence by proving either that the defendant acted under his employer's instructions or that he acted in reliance on information supplied by another person without any reason to suppose that the information was false or misleading and, in either case, that he took all such steps as were reasonably open to him to ensure that no offence would be committed.[7] Finally, where there is reliance on the general defence by reference to the allegation that the offence was committed through the act or omission of another person, other than by reference to an employer's instructions or reliance on information supplied by another person, information identifying or assisting in the identification of that other person in the defendant's possession must be notified to the prosecutor within a period ending seven days before the hearing.[8]

[99] *Ibid.* Sched. 2(10).
[1] *Ibid.* s.1(6).
[2] *Ibid.* subs.(7).
[3] *Ibid.* s.2(2).
[4] *Ibid.* subs.(4).
[5] As to the penalties for offences, see s.21.
[6] *Ibid.* s.22(1).
[7] *Ibid.* subs.(2).
[8] *Ibid.* subs.(3).

Civil liability

Part I of the Act makes no provision for compensation to be paid where, for example, an order under section 1 is found to impose prohibitions over too wide an area, or where no "escape" had in fact occurred and prohibitions imposed loss-making restrictions on farmer's stock or produce for example. The legislation enshrines the "polluter pays principle" and the expectation appears to be that those who may suffer loss would insure for that contingency.[9]

Miscellaneous Primary Legislation

The International Carriage of Perishable Food Stuffs Act 1976

The Act empowers the government to accede to the Agreement on the International Carriage of Perishable Foodstuffs,[9a] introducing European thermal efficiency standards for refrigerated and heat-insulated transport deployed for international carriage of perishable foodstuffs.

The Local Government (Miscellaneous Provisions) Act 1982

The Act allows for closing orders to be made by a district council in respect of take-away food shops operating between midnight and 5 a.m. The local authority may require establishments to close for the whole of or part of that period in the interests of the amenity of local residents.[10]

Prevention of Damage by Pests Act 1949

Part II of the Act[11] contains an obligation by which every person whose business consists of or includes the manufacture, storage, transport or sale of food must notify the Minister of Agriculture of any infestation as soon as that infestation comes to his knowledge. "Infestation" is defined as the presence of rats, mice, insects or mites in numbers or under conditions which involve an immediate or potential risk of substantial loss of or damage to food.[12] The infestation may occur in a wide variety of locations defined by the Act: premises, vehicles or equipment used or likely to be used in the manufacture, storage, transport or sale of food, for example.[13] The Minister is invested with wide powers of direction in connection with infestation,[14] although any such direction is subject to appeal to a magistrates' court.[15] Any failure to comply with the requirements of Part II is an

[9] *Hansard*, H.C. Deb. Vol. 80, col. 709; H.L. Deb. Vol. 459, col. 123.
[9a] Cmnd. 6441 (1970).
[10] Local Government (Miscellaneous Provisions) Act 1982, ss.4–6 and 49.
[11] ss.13 to 18. *Cf.* Chap. 14, "Miscellaneous Controls".
[12] Prevention of Damage by Pests Act 1949, s.28(1).
[13] *Ibid.* s.13(1)(a).
[14] *Ibid.* s.14.
[15] *Ibid.* s.15.

offence[16] but, without prejudice to such criminal proceedings, the Minister may order measures to be taken in the event of a default to comply with any requirements laid down in directions.[17] As to a prohibition on the delivery of infested food for three working days following notification without the Minister's consent, the Minister has made regulations to that effect.[18] Any of the Minister's functions under Part II may be delegated to a local authority where that authority consents to such delegation.[19]

Public Health (Control of Disease) Act 1984

The legislation provides that a "proper officer"[20] of a local authority is obliged to inform the Chief Medical Officer for England (or for Wales, as the case may be) of any serious outbreak of any disease, including food poisoning.[21] The requirement is for an "immediate" reporting of any incidence of food poisoning.

Miscellaneous Secondary Legislation

Milk and Dairies (General) Regulations 1959[22]

These Regulations are subject to certain provisions in the Food Safety Act and are enforced by food authorities (principally district councils and London borough councils), although a registration function in relation to dairy farms and farmers is undertaken by the Minister of Agriculture. The Regulations define the term "dairy" for present purposes, as well as defining the term "milk".[23] The Regulations deal with:

(a) the inspection and health of cattle (supported by an offence relating to the sale of milk from diseased cows);
(b) standards for buildings and water supplies;
(c) standards and requirements for the production, treatment, handling and storage of milk; and
(d) prescriptions in relation to the infection of milk.[24]

In the case of this last provision, where a medical officer of health for a district has evidence in respect of any milk supplied in that district from registered premises, indicating that a person is suffering from a disease caused by consumption of such milk, or that the milk is infected with disease communicable to man, he may by

16 *Ibid.* s.17.
17 *Ibid.* s.16.
18 Prevention of Damage by Pests (Infestation of Food) Regulations 1950 (S.I. 1950 No. 416).
19 Prevention of Damage by Pests Act 1949, s.18.
20 Public Health (Control of Disease) Act 1984, s.74.
21 Public Health (Infectious Diseases) Regulations 1988 (S.I. 1988 No. 1546), reg.6.
22 S.I. 1959 No. 277, as amended.
23 *Ibid.* reg.2(1).
24 *Ibid.* Pts. II, IV, V, VI and VII, respectively.

notice in writing to the occupier specify the evidence and require that either restrictions are put in place on sales for human consumption or that sales should not occur without specified treatment.

Milk (Special Designation) Regulations 1989[25]

Implementation of E.C. Directive 85/397[25a] is achieved by these Regulations. The Directive relates to health and animal health problems affecting intra-Community trade in heat-treated milk. The Regulations prescribe special designations for use in relation to the sale of milk and provide for the grant, refusal, suspension and revocation of licences authorising such use.

Meat Inspection Regulations 1987[26]

Food authorities have a range of duties under these Regulations. Such authorities are empowered:

(a) to control the times of slaughter;
(b) to carry out post-mortem inspections of animal carcasses slaughtered for human consumption;
(c) to require prior notification of slaughter;
(d) to carry out ante-mortem health inspections of animals to be slaughtered at slaughterhouses;
(e) to require notification of any disease or unsoundness in a carcass;
(f) to impose restrictions on the movement of carcasses and the use of slaughterhouses;
(g) to require the marking of carcasses in certain circumstances;
(h) to make provision for notices to be given to the food authority; and
(i) to specify the responsibilities of those who slaughter animals for human consumption.

Each food authority is obliged to keep records of ante-mortem and post-mortem health inspections. The Regulations provide for appeals to the magistrates' court in the case of certain action taken. Enforcement is by criminal offences triable either summarily or on indictment.

Meat (Sterilisation and Staining) Regulations 1982[27]

The requirement here is that meat be stained or sterilised prior to removal in various circumstances, for example, meat which is unfit for human consumption which, as yet, has not been removed from a slaughterhouse. In this and a variety of other circumstances, failing to comply on removal of meat is a criminal offence triable either summarily or on indictment.

[25] S.I. 1989 No. 2383.
[25a] [1985] O.J. L186/23.
[26] S.I. 1987 No. 2236.
[27] S.I. 1982 No. 1018.

Bovine Offal (Prohibition) Regulations 1989[28]

These Regulations apply to specified bovine offal from any animal slaughtered in the United Kingdom, normally over the age of six months. There is a prohibition on the sale for human consumption or use in the preparation of food for sale for human consumption of any specified bovine offal or material derived wholly or partly from it. It is a general requirement that the offal should be sterilised immediately at a slaughterhouse or placed in a room or container for the purpose of sterilisation. Accordingly, there are statutory restrictions on the removal or movement of such offal, including its movement into England and Wales.

The Regulations provide for prescribed destinations to which offal may be removed under the authority of food authority movement permits. Criminal enforcement is by means of offences triable either summarily or on indictment.

Poultry Meat (Hygiene) Regulations 1976[29]

The Regulations prescribe the conditions that must be satisfied for the production, cutting up and storage of poultry meat intended for sale for human consumption.

[28] S.I. 1989 No. 2061.
[29] S.I. 1976 No. 1209.

CHAPTER 14

MISCELLANEOUS CONTROLS

The Range of Regulatory Controls

The present categorisation emphasises substantive controls, usually administered and enforced by a local authority. In some cases that control—as in the Health and Safety at Work Act—will be shared with another enforcing agency. Much of the control stresses licensing or registration, enforced by criminal sanctions. There are often, in addition, powers of direct intervention, usually in the event of default.

The categories

The categories of miscellaneous controls are as follows:

(a) the control of disease and environmental intrusions;
(b) the control of pests;
(c) health and safety at work;
(d) entertainment, theatre, cinema and sex establishment licensing;
(e) animal welfare;
(f) street trading;
(g) scrap metal dealers;
(h) skin-piercing;
(i) nursing agencies;
(j) rag flock; and
(k) camp and caravan sites.

Control of Disease and Environmental Intrusions

Coverage

The present category covers:

(a) the control of disease;
(b) the treatment of filthy or verminous premises;
(c) the removal of noxious matter;
(d) offensive trades; and
(e) the removal and disposal of abandoned vehicles, together with the removal and disposal of abandoned refuse.

Each area is covered in turn.

The control of disease

The district councils and London boroughs are the local authorities principally responsible for enforcement of the main legislation here, the Public Health (Control of Disease) Act 1984.[1] The Secretary of State is empowered by order to designate a port health authority for the purposes of the Act so that such an authority replaces the responsible local authority in the discharge of defined functions and responsibilities.[2]

Local authority powers

The Act of 1984 contains a variety of powers available to the local authority responsible for enforcing the Act,[3] in addition to various powers available by virtue of statutory instrument.[4] The foregoing powers in the Act create an extensive list of powers dealing with various matters arising from contact with a person suffering from a notifiable disease extending, for example, to:

(a) an order from the proper officer of the local authority requiring a person to stop work with a view to preventing the spread of such a disease;
(b) the protection of children;
(c) the treatment of infected premises;
(d) the use of public conveyances;
(e) the control of persons infected;
(f) common lodging houses; and
(g) the death of infected persons.

For present purposes, the Act defines what is comprised in the term "notifiable disease" for present purposes, with supplementary detail to be found in accompanying statutory instruments.[5]

Whether any of the particular powers above apply to particular diseases may be discovered from the terms of the relevant regulations. The powers under section 17 of the Act, for example, apply to scarlet fever. Consequently, where a person knowing that he is suffering from this notifiable disease, exposes others to the risk of infection by his presence or conduct in a street or other public place, for example, he is liable to summary conviction. Many of the powers found in Part II are enforceable by criminal sanctions. Prosecution by anyone other than a party

[1] s.1.
[2] *ibid.*, ss.1–5. *Cf.* ss.6–8 in relation to the Port of London.
[3] *Ibid.* Pt. II.
[4] See, *inter alia*, the Public Health (Infectious Diseases) Regulations 1988 (S.I. 1988 No. 1546), Scheds. 3 and 4.
[5] See in particular S.I. 1988 No. 1546. Where, *e.g.*, an *ex parte* order is made for a person's removal to hospital, it is against the public interest and the fair administration of justice to allow publication of the name and address of the person with the notifiable disease: *Birmingham Post and Mail Ltd. v. Birmingham City Council*, *The Times*, November 25, 1993.

aggrieved or a local authority is possible only with the consent of the Attorney-General.[6]

The notification of diseases

Where a registered medical practitioner becomes aware, or suspects, that a patient is suffering from a notifiable disease or from food poisoning, he is subject to a duty to send to the proper officer of the local authority details relating to *inter alia*, the disease or suspected disease and the date of its onset.[7] Where certain infectious diseases are notified to the proper officer of the local authority, there are additional obligations to inform the appropriate medical officer of the appropriate district health authority or (as the case may be) the Chief Medical Officer of England or Wales.[8]

Facilities and powers for dealing with infection

A local authority is empowered to provide a disinfecting station and to cause any article to be brought there to be disinfected, free of charge.[9] The local authority is also empowered to notify the occupier of premises that they will, at his cost, cleanse and disinfect the premises and its contents unless that occupier does so himself. The power here is very wide, referring as it does to any infectious disease and not just a notifiable disease.[10] There are also powers in the Act permitting the local authority to remove persons from a house in which an infectious disease has occurred or where the authority deems it necessary to disinfect that house. The authority may itself provide temporary accommodation in these circumstances.[11]

Compensation and enforcement

The Public Health (Control of Disease) Act provides that a local authority shall make full compensation to any person who has sustained damage by reason of an exercise of its powers under the Act, as long as that person is not himself in default. Disputes here are referable to arbitration.[12] A claim here (which must relate to the direct consequences of the act causing loss, damage or injury) may not be sustainable unless the local authority's act would have been actionable but for the existence of the statutory power.[13] Any negligent exercise of statutory powers will not attract compensation under the present provision: an action in tort is appropriate for this purpose.[14]

[6] Public Health (Control of Disease) Act 1984, s.64. As to continuing offences, see s.65.
[7] *Ibid.* ss.11 and 12.
[8] Public Health (Infectious Diseases) Regulations 1988 (S.I. 1988 No. 1546), reg.6.
[9] Public Health (Control of Disease) Act, s.27.
[10] *Ibid.* s.31. *Cf.* s.83 of the Public Health Act 1936.
[11] *Ibid.* s.32. As to various powers and other notification requirements affecting common lodging-house, see ss.39–42.
[12] *Ibid.* s.57.
[13] *Ricket v. Metropolitan Railway* (1867) L.R. 2 H.L. 175.
[14] *Geddis v. Proprietors of Bann Reservoir* (1878) 3 App.Cas. 430.

The Act confers a right of entry on authorised officers of a local authority, with the authority of a justice's warrant:

(a) if entry is refused or if refusal is apprehended;
(b) if the premises in question are unoccupied or the occupier is temporarily absent;
(c) where there is a need for urgency; or
(d) where an application for admission would defeat the object of entry.[15]

Wilful obstruction of an execution of the Act is an offence punishable on summary conviction.[16]

The treatment of filthy or verminous premises

If a local authority is satisfied that "any premises" are in such a filthy or unwholesome condition as to be prejudicial to health, or are verminous, a notice must be served on the owner or occupier of those premises. Among other things, a list of remedial measures, including cleansing, and disinfecting, must be specified, together with the destruction or removal of vermin in appropriate cases. The local authority has power to act in default and to recover expenses reasonably incurred. Without prejudice to the local authority's exercise of its default powers, the person on whom the notice is served may be liable to summary conviction, the financial penalty including provision for continuing fines. In any such proceedings for a failure to comply with a notice, the person on whom the notice is served may question the reasonableness of the local authority's requirements or their decision to address the notice to him and not the occupier or, as the case may be, the owner of the premises.[17] There is no appeal against a notice served here by the local authority whose powers extend, with one exception, to all premises.

Noxious matter

Where a proper officer of a local authority considers that any accumulation of noxious matter should be removed by the occupier of premises in an urban district, a notice to this effect (against which there is no appeal) will require the owner or occupier to remove the offending material. The local authority has default powers and may recover any reasonably incurred expenses in the exercise of those powers.[18]

[15] Public Health (Control of Disease) Act, ss.61 and 62.
[16] *Ibid.* s.63..
[17] Public Health Act 1936, s.83, as amended by the Public Health Act 1961, s.35. *Cf.* s.31 of the Act of 1984.
[18] *Ibid.* s.79, prospectively repealed from a day yet to be appointed: Control of Pollution Act 1974, Sched. 4.

Accumulations of rubbish and refuse

If it appears to the local authority that, on land in the open air, there is rubbish which is seriously detrimental to the amenities of the neighbourhood, that authority is empowered to take such steps for removing the rubbish as it considers necessary in the interests of amenity. A notice served on the owner and the occupier of the subject land will advise of the action proposed. The notice must be served not less than 28 days from the date of the action proposed. The person served with the notice may serve a counter-notice, indicating the action he proposes to take for present purposes: alternatively, he may appeal to the magistrates' court on the ground that the action proposed is not justified or is not reasonable. "Rubbish" for present purposes means rubble, waste paper, crockery and metal, and any other kind of refuse (including organic matter), but not any material accumulated for, or in the course of, any business, or waste deposited under the terms of a waste disposal licence.[19]

The present provision is one of a variety of statutory provisions allowing control over what can be described generally as activities having an adverse impact on amenity. Perhaps the most significant provision is that to be found in the Environmental Protection Act 1990 relating to statutory nuisance, where the definition of a statutory nuisance includes "... any accumulation or deposit which is prejudicial to health or a nuisance".[20] Powers to control rubbish and other accumulations adverse to amenity also reside with a number of other agencies, although most powers reside with local authorities, including local planning authorities (see, for example, sections 215–219 of the Town and Country Planning Act 1990) and local highway authorities (see, for example, sections 148 and 171 of the Highways Act 1980).

Amenity and refuse disposal

An important part of the law here is to be found in the Refusal Disposal (Amenity) Act 1978. The Act contains provisions for controlling the dumping of refuse, requiring local authorities to provide sites for the disposal of non-commercial refuse and to remove and dispose of abandoned vehicles and other refuse. The Act also confers incidental powers of compulsory purchase, powers of entry to land, and powers to provide plant and apparatus for treatment and disposal of refuse and for the disposal of abandoned motor vehicles.

The Act of 1978 requires local authorities (principally county councils and London boroughs) to provide free of charge to residents in their area sites at reasonably accessible locations for the deposit of non-commercial refuse.[21] The Act specifies that the unauthorised dumping on any land in the open air or

[19] Public Health Act 1961, s.34. See now the provision for waste management licences under Pt. II of the Environmental Protection Act 1990.

[20] Environmental Protection Act 1990, s.79(1)(e): see Chap. 10, "Statutory Nuisance".

[21] Refuse Disposal (Amenity) Act, s.1.

otherwise forming part of a highway, of a motor vehicle or parts dismantled from it on the land is an offence.[22]

Where it appears to a local authority that a motor vehicle in its area is abandoned without lawful authority on any land in the open air or on any other land forming part of a highway, it is the duty of that authority to remove the vehicle. If it appears that the land in question is occupied, the authority is obliged to notify the occupier of its intention to remove the abandoned vehicle.[23] If the licence for a car is still current, the authority is unable to dispose of it. If there is no licence or the licence has expired, there may be immediate disposal following expiration of a prescribed period extending from attachment to the vehicle of a notice stipulating the authority's intention to remove and destroy it. Otherwise disposal can occur only following efforts to trace the vehicle owner.[24] Where the owner seeks to reclaim his vehicle, a prescribed fee is payable to the local authority.[25]

While there is a duty to remove motor vehicles, such a duty does not extend to other "things" abandoned in the area of a local authority. Subject to this restriction the Act clearly indicates that it extends beyond noxious or insanitary deposits referred to in other legislation. However, where the abandoned article is on occupied land, its removal by the authority must be preceded by a notice of intention given to the occupier which does not then attract an objection from him.[26]

Offensive trades

The Public Health Act 1936 has provided for a regulatory control of offensive trades for which local authority consent has been required.[27] The primary concern of the regulatory requirements, achieved by means of byelaws, has been either to prevent or to diminish any noxious or other injurious effects of a subject trade. Under Part I of the Environmental Protection Act 1990, the foregoing regulatory framework is gradually superseded by local authority air pollution control as various processes are designated for that purpose.[28]

[22] *Ibid.* s.2.
[23] *Ibid.* s.3.
[24] *Ibid.* s.4.
[25] Removal, Storage and Disposal of Vehicles (Prescribed Sums and Charges etc.) Regulations 1989 (S.I. 1989 No. 744), as amended by S.I. 1992 No. 385. As to recovery of charges for removal, storage and disposal, see s.5.
[26] Refuse Disposal (Amenity) Act, s.6.
[27] Public Health Act 1936, ss.107 and 108. *Cf.* Local Government Act 1972, Sched. 14, para. 11.
[28] See Chap. 6, "Atmospheric Pollution".

Control of Pests

The range of controls

Various statutes provide for action directed at the control of pests, either specifically or more generally. The primary focus of the present section of this chapter is the control of rats and mice under the Prevention of Damage by Pests Act 1949. Towards the end of the present section, brief reference will be made to a selection of other statutory provisions of particular significance to local authorities.

The control of rats and mice

The Prevention of Damage by Pests Act 1949 deals in Part I with the control of rats and mice, while Part II deals with the infestation of food by rats, mice, insects or mites. Primary responsibility for enforcement of these provisions lies principally with district councils and London borough councils.

Local authority duties

It is the duty of every local authority to take such steps as may be necessary to secure so far as practicable that its district is kept free from rats and mice.[29] Although such a general duty is probably unenforceable by mandamus, if the Secretary of State is satisfied, following a complaint or otherwise, that any of a local authority's functions are not being satisfactorily performed, he may order that those functions be performed on behalf of the local authority by some other person, but only after the local authority has had an opportunity to make representations and to demand a local inquiry.[30]

Beyond the general duty set out above, the Act of 1949 includes three more specific duties directly linked to the general duty:

(a) to carry out inspections of the district from time to time;
(b) to destroy rats and mice on land of which they are the occupier; and
(c) to enforce Part I of the Act,

and also to carry out operations authorised by the Act.[31]

Occupiers' obligations

The occupier of any land is obliged "forthwith" to give a local authority notice in writing if it comes to his knowledge[32] that rats or mice are living on or resorting to the land in substantial numbers. What are "substantial numbers" must of course

[29] Prevention of Damage by Pests Act 1949, s.2.
[30] *Ibid.* s.12.
[31] *Ibid.* s.2(1).
[32] Significantly the Act does not refer to mere notice.

be a matter of fact and degree. The notice requirement here does not apply to agricultural land. Equally, the notice requirement does not apply if notice has been given to the Secretary of State for the purposes of Part II of the Act dealing with the infestation of food.[33]

Local authority power to require action

If in the case of any land it appears to the local authority, whether as a result of the notice provisions described previously or otherwise, that steps should be taken for the destruction of rats or mice "... on the land" or otherwise for keeping the land free from rats and mice, it may serve a notice for these purposes on the owner or the occupier. Such a notice will require such reasonable steps as may be specified to be taken within a reasonable period, again as may be specified by the notice. If the owner and occupier are not the same person, separate notices may be served by the local authority. Any such notice must be sufficiently precise to allow compliance and, if necessary, enforcement. For example, a notice served by one local authority set out the following steps: "Poison treatment of infested land, such measures to be carried out to the approval of the local authority, or other work, of a not less effectual character, to be executed for the destruction of the rats." This notice was defective because the "other work" was not particularised and did not require any "specified" steps as required by the terms of section 4(1).[34]

Apart from requiring application to the land of any form of treatment specified, the notice may also require the carrying out on the land of any structural repairs or other works. Whatever the form and content of the notice, if any owner complains to the magistrates' court that an occupier has prevented his completion of work required by a notice, the court may order that occupier to permit completion of the work. In respect of any notice requiring the carrying out of any structural works, there is an appeal to the magistrates' court.[35]

Failure to comply with steps required by a notice empowers the local authority to take action in default and to recover any expenses reasonably incurred. Without prejudice to this power, but subject to the facility for a limited appeal described previously, a person who fails to comply with a notice is guilty of an offence punishable in summary proceedings.[36]

Where the local authority concerned finds that rats and mice are in substantial numbers on land comprising premises in the occupation of different persons, instead of serving a number of section 4 notices, action considered necessary or expedient may be taken (except in respect of any structural work) by the authority. Each occupier must be given notice of intended action by the authority and, in turn, the authority may recover expenses reasonably incurred from the several occupiers of the premises in question according to what is considered just by reference to the cost of the works.[37]

[33] Prevention of Damage by Pests Act, s.3.
[34] *Perry v. Garner* [1953] 1 Q.B. 335.
[35] Prevention of Damage by Pests Act, s.4.
[36] *Ibid.* s.5.
[37] *Ibid.* s.6.

Any expenses recoverable in these circumstances where there are premises in the occupation of different persons are recoverable as a simple contract debt in any court of competent jurisdiction. In any proceedings for recovery where there has been a failure to comply with the requirements of a section 4 notice, it is not open to a defendant to raise by way of defence any question which he could have raised through an appeal.[38]

Infestation of food

Part II of the Prevention of Damage by Pests Act 1949 deals with matters of infestation, defined as "... the presence of rats, mice, insects or mites in numbers or under conditions which involve an immediate or potential risk of substantial loss of or damage to food ...".[39] Part II of the Act obliges every person whose business consists of or includes the manufacture, storage, transport or sale of food to provide the Minister of Agriculture, Fisheries and Food with notice of any infestation that comes to his knowledge. The duty extends also to any person whose business consists of or includes the manufacture, sale, repair or cleaning of containers.[40] The Minister is empowered to give any directions considered expedient, whether or not as a consequence of any notice just referred to, for the purpose of preventing or mitigating damage to food.[41] An appeal to the magistrates' court is available for the benefit of any person aggrieved by directions here, in so far as those directions require the execution of structural works, or the destruction of any food or container. Notification of the availability of an appeal must be contained in the direction issued by the Minister.[42] Where there is a failure to comply with directions then, subject to the above appeal facility, the Minister may nominate a person to take action in default and recover any expenses reasonably incurred in taking such action. Any proceedings for the recovery of such expenses may not be used to raise a matter that should have been raised in appeal proceedings.[43] Any criminal proceedings may not be instituted except by or with the consent of the Minister or a local authority.[44] Subject to the facility for an appeal, any contravention or failure to comply with Part II requirements or any direction issued is an offence punishable in summary proceedings.[45]

The Minister may, by statutory instrument, delegate to a local authority any of his functions under Part II, with one exception.[46] Any such delegation requires the consent of the local authority in question.

[38] *Ibid.* s.7.
[39] *Ibid.* s.28(1).
[40] *Ibid.* s.13.
[41] *Ibid.* s.14.
[42] *Ibid.* s.15.
[43] *Ibid.* s.16.
[44] *Ibid.* s.26.
[45] *Ibid.* s.17.
[46] *Ibid.* s.18. As to the exception, see s.13(3).

Powers of entry under Parts I and II

Various powers of entry are provided by the Act and enforced by offences of wilful obstruction. If damage to land is caused in the exercise of the power of entry, any person interested in the land may recover compensation from the local authority or the Minister, as the case may be.[47]

Other controls

Part III of the Environmental Protection Act 1990 dealing with statutory nuisance represents a particularly important vehicle for local authority treatment of problems arising from the presence on land of rats and mice, as well as the problems of infestation. This matter is dealt with in Chapter 10, "Statutory Nuisance".

The Housing Act 1988 permits the Secretary of State to confer on a housing action trust specified local authority environmental health functions in so far as they are relevant to housing matters. Those functions may be conferred either concurrently with or instead of the local authority's exercise of those functions. The environmental health functions in question include those that arise under Part I of the Act of 1949, as well as those relating to statutory nuisances.[48]

Health and Safety at Work

General duties

The Health and Safety at Work Act 1974 contains a variety of general duties[49] in addition to a framework of detailed regulations whose substance and effect is better explored through the pages of more specialised publications on the law relating to health and safety at work. Of particular significance generally for the purposes of environmental health are sections 2–5. Section 2 requires employers to safeguard the health, safety and welfare of their employees. This is achieved through a duty to ensure employees' health so far as is reasonably practicable. The existence of a universal practice does not necessarily exempt an employer from the necessity of proving that some other, safer method was not reasonably practicable to use.[50] Whether a course of action is reasonably practicable depends on physical and financial viability, as well as a balancing of the degree of risk with any sacrifice that may be involved.

Section 3 defines a general duty caste on employers—and the self-employed—to conduct their respective undertakings in such a way as to ensure, so far as is reasonably practicable, that persons not in their employment who may

[47] *Ibid.* s.22.
[48] Housing Act 1988. s.68.
[49] ss.2 and 7.
[50] *Martin v. Boulton and Paul (Steel Construction) Ltd* [1982] I.C.R. 366. *Cf.* Guidance notes issued from time to time by the Health and Safety Executive.

be affected are not exposed to risks to their health or safety: legionella, for example. The legionella organism is generated through aerosols from water systems. Cooling towers and other water systems may provide a sympathetic environment for proliferation of the organism, usually where there has been poor or inadequate maintenance.

Section 4 of the Health and Safety at Work Act creates a duty resting on any person with the right of control over premises, for the benefit of those who are not employees. The duty here is to take reasonably practicable measures to ensure that means of access to or egress from the premises, as well as any plant or substance provided for use in the premises, are safe and without risk to health.

Section 5 imposes a duty on persons having control of premises to use best practicable means for preventing emission into the atmosphere from the premises of noxious or offensive substances and for rendering harmless and inoffensive such substances emitted.

Allocation of functions

The Health and Safety (Enforcing Authority) Regulations[51] allocate an enforcement function to local authorities, principally district councils and London borough councils.[52] Each local authority made responsible for enforcement is subject to a duty to make adequate arrangements for enforcement of the relevant statutory provisions within its area.[53] The Health and Safety (Enforcing Authority) Regulations stipulate a distinction between functions to be enforced by the Health and Safety Executive, on the one hand, and local authorities, on the other. In the case of the local authorities, their enforcement functions relate to a list set out in the Regulations: any "main activity carried out in non-domestic premises" is subject to local authority enforcement.[54] Remaining functions are the responsibility of the Health and Safe Executive. Among the areas of enforcement assigned to a local authority are the sale or storage of goods for retail or wholesale distribution, "office activites" and catering services.[55] Provision is also made for determinations in the event of uncertainty about division and distribution of enforcement responsibilities.[56]

Administration

Each enforcing authority is empowered to appoint inspectors. Each instrument of appointment must stipulate the precise powers to be exercised by an inspector so appointed.[57] With this in mind, the Act goes on to provide a variety of powers available to an inspector, including powers of entry and search and seizure, as well

[51] S.I. 1989 No. 1903.
[52] *Ibid.* reg.2(1). As to the Secretary of State's default powers, see s.45.
[53] Health and Safety at Work Act, s.18(4).
[54] Health and Safety (Enforcing Authority) Regulations, reg.3(1).
[55] *Ibid.*
[56] *Ibid.* reg.6.
[57] Health and Safety at Work Act, s.19.

as important powers to require that premises or any part of premises entered are left undisturbed, and to take samples of articles and substances and of the atmosphere "... in or in the vicinity of any such premises".[58] In the case of any article or substance found by an inspector, in premises which he has the power to enter, which he has reasonable cause to believe in the circumstances is a cause of imminent danger of serious personal injury, he may seize that article or substance and cause it to be rendered harmless.[59]

Enforcement

Enforcement measures under the Act cover prosecution and the use of improvement and prohibition notices. The duties described previously are binding on the Crown, although the foregoing enforcement measures do not apply.[60]

Improvement and prohibition notices

Where an inspector is of the opinion that a person is contravening one or more of the relevant statutory provisions, such as the foregoing duties, or has contravened one or more of these provisions in circumstances that make it likely that contravention will continue or be repeated, he may serve an improvement notice requiring the situation to be remedied within a stipulated period of time.[61] If, on the other hand, the inspector is of the opinion that activities to which the Act's statutory provisions (such as the foregoing duties) will apply involve or will involve a risk of serious personal injury, he may serve a prohibition notice. Among other things, the notice will specify that the subject activities may not be pursued until the situations specified in the notice are remedied.[62]

The Act provides for an appeal against an improvement and a prohibition notice to an industrial tribunal. In the case of an improvement notice, an appeal has the effect of suspending the operation of that notice whereas, in the case of a prohibition notice, an appeal suspends the notice only on the direction of the tribunal.[63] Any notice served under the foregoing provision will be placed in a public register by virtue of the Environment and Safety Information Act 1988.[64]

Prosecution

The Health and Safety at Work Act provides for the definition and prosecution of a number of offences, including failure to discharge any one of the duties referred to previously, contravention of any requirement set by an inspector under section

58 *Ibid.* s.20.
59 *Ibid.* s.25.
60 *Ibid.* s.48.
61 *Ibid.* s.21.
62 *Ibid.* s.22.
63 *Ibid.* s.24. *Cf.* the Industrial Tribunals (Improvement and Prohibition Notices Appeals) Regulations 1974 (S.I. 1974 No. 1925).
64 s.2 and Schedule. *Cf.* Chap. 9, "Access to Environmental Health Information".

20 (requiring entry to premises, for example) or section 25 (concerning cases of imminent danger), and contravention of any requirement or prohibition imposed by an improvement or prohibition notice.[65] While some offences listed in the Act are triable summarily, including in the above sample the offence of contravening an inspector's requirements under section 20, other offences (including the remainder of the above sample) are triable either summarily or on indictment.[66] If so authorised by the enforcing authority, an inspector, although not of counsel or a solicitor, may prosecute before a magistrates' court for an offence under any of the relevant statutory provisons.[67] Directors, managers and secretaries of bodies corporate whose consent, connivance or neglect causes hazards are open to prosecution.[68] Whatever the context of the criminal proceedings, the burden of proving that something is reasonably practicable is on the accused: a reversal of the normal onus of proof.[69]

Where a person is convicted in respect of matters which appear to the court to be within the power of the defendant to remedy, the court may, in addition to or instead of imposing any punishment, order that defendant to take such steps as may be specified for remedying the matters in question.[70]

Entertainment, Theatre, Cinema and Sex Establishment Licensing

Statutory regulation

The present category deals with public and private entertainment licensing under the Local Government (Miscellaneous Provisions) Act 1982, theatre licensing under the Theatres Act 1968, cinema licensing under the Cinemas Act 1985 and the licensing of sex establishments also under the Act of 1982 above.

Public entertainment licensing

The Local Government (Miscellaneous Provisions) Act 1982[71] imposes a statutory framework for the licensing of "public entertainments" outside Greater London. The licensing regime covers public dancing or music or any other public entertainment of like kind, but not music in a place of public religious worship, an entertainment held in a pleasure fair or an entertainment taking place wholly or mainly in the open air.[72] The local authorities responsible for implementation and enforcement of these provisions are district councils. Merely because there exists a formal scheme of club membership does not necessarily mean that those

[65] Health and Safety at Work Act, s.33.
[66] *Ibid.* s.33(2), (3).
[67] *Ibid.* s.39.
[68] *Ibid.* s.37.
[69] *Ibid.* s.40.
[70] *Ibid.* s.42.
[71] s.1 and Sched. 1. Paras. 3 and 4 of Sched. 1 only have effect if a local authority so resolve: *ibid.* s.1.
[72] *Ibid.* Sched. 1, para. 1(2), (3).

attending an event cease to be members of the public for present purposes. Accordingly, the council responsible may be able to enforce that part of the Act, described below, relating to organisation or management of an unlicensed public entertainment.[73]

The licensing process

A local authority

> "... may grant to ... and from time to time renew ... a licence for the use of any place specified in it for all or any of the entertainments [specified by Schedule 1] on such terms and conditions and subject to such restrictions as may be so specified".[74]

In imposing conditions, the local authority is obliged to take account of:

(a) the safety of performers;
(b) the adequacy of access for emergency services;
(c) the adequacy of sanitary appliances; and
(d) the prevention of unreasonable disturbance by noise.[75]

An applicant is obliged to give notice of his intention to apply to the local authority, the chief officer of police and the fire authority. Fees are normally payable to the local authority.[76] Provision is also made for provisional licence grants and the variation of licences.[77] Appeals against adverse decisions go to the magistrates' court.[78]

Enforcement

Criminal enforcement is by reference to two particular offences, one of being concerned in the organisation of a public musical entertainment and one of letting a place, etc., be used for such a purpose.[79] The former offence is one of strict liability.[80] The statute must be regarded for present purposes as being concerned with "social policy", regulating a specific activity rather than the general conduct of citizens. The court does not regard the conduct as being truly

[73] *Lunn v. Colston-Hayter* (1991) 89 L.G.R. 754.
[74] Local Government (Miscellaneous Provisions) Act 1982, Sched. 1, para. 1(4).
[75] *Ibid.* para. 4(4).
[76] *Ibid.* paras. 6 and 7.
[77] *Ibid.* paras. 15 and 16.
[78] *Ibid.* para. 17.
[79] *Ibid.* para. 12: punishable summarily.
[80] *Chichester District Council v. Sylvester* [1992] Crim.L.R. 886.

criminal. The offences included were created essentially for enforcement of the licensing provisions to ensure public safety and welfare. Decisively, the present area of the Act distinguishes between persons concerned in the organisation and management of unlicensed entertainment and others who, knowing or having reasonable cause to believe that such an entertainment would be provided, permit a place to be used for the provision of entertainment. The former offence is wide enough to include anyone who takes part in running entertainment and contributes significantly to the whole unlicensed entertainment.[81]

The offence of permitting a place to be used for the purpose of unlicensed public entertainment attracts a defence where it can be established that reasonable precautions and due diligence were used to avoid commission of the offence. In the event of the holder of a licence being convicted of this or the other offence, the local authority is empowered to revoke the licence.

Whether or not a licence is in force, there are powers of entry and inspection available under the Act. Where, for example, a licence is not in force and there is a suspicion that an offence is being committed, a constable or authorised officer of the local authority may enter the premises with a warrant granted by a justice of the peace.[82]

In the event of a conviction, the court has powers of confiscation by virtue of the Criminal Justice Act 1988.[83]

Private entertainment licensing

The Private Places of Entertainment (Licensing) Act 1967 may be adopted by a local authority for the purpose of imposing licensing control where premises are to be used for dancing, music or other entertainment of the like kind which is not a public entertainment but is promoted for "private gain", as defined by section 5A of the Act.[84]

The licensing process

The local authority may grant to any applicant and from time to time renew a licence "... on such terms and conditions (including conditions for securing entry to and inspection of the premises) and subject to such restrictions as may be specified ...".[85] The authority also enjoys a wide discretion in determining whether or not the transfer of a licence should be permitted, either on an application from the licence holder or a proposed transferee.[86] Equally wide is the authority's discretion to determine an application from the licence holder for a variation of the licence.[87]

[81] *Ibid.*
[82] Local Government (Miscellaneous Provisions) Act 1982, Sched. 1, para. 14.
[83] s.71 and Sched. 4.
[84] Private Places of Entertainment (Licensing) Act, s.2: this section also contains exemptions from the licensing requirements.
[85] *Ibid.* s.3. As to appeals (normally to the magistrates' court), see s.5.
[86] *Ibid.*
[87] *Ibid.* s.3A.

Enforcement

Both the holder of a licence and any other person knowing or having reasonable cause to suspect that an unlawful entertainment has taken place on premises in contravention of licence terms, conditions or restrictions are guilty of an offence under the Act and are punishable in summary proceedings. Equally, if any person is concerned in the organisation or management of an entertainment that should be, but is not, licensed commits an offence which, again, may be punished in summary proceedings. Also guilty of such an offence is any other person who, knowing or having reasonable cause to suspect that an unlawful entertainment would be provided at premises, allows the premises to be used or lets those premises or otherwise makes them available for the purpose.[88] If a licence holder is convicted of the offence described above, the local authority concerned may revoke his licence.[89]

Any duly authorised officer of the local authority or any constable is empowered, at all reasonable times, to enter and examine premises used (or which either officer has reasonable cause to believe are used) or intended to be used for entertainment. However, a justice's warrant is required for these purposes and may even authorise entry by force, although the justice's powers here are carefully constrained so that, for example, there should normally be an indication of notice having been given to the occupier of the premises of an intention to apply for a warrant.[90]

In the event of a conviction, the court has powers of confiscation by virtue of the Criminal Justice Act 1988.[91]

Theatre licensing

The Theatres Act 1968 stipulates that no premises, whether or not licensed for the sale of intoxicating or excisable liquor, shall be used for the public performance of any play except under and in accordance with the terms of a licence granted by the licensing authority: a London borough council or a district council.[92] An appeal against an adverse licensing decision lies to the magistrates' court and, beyond that, to the Crown Court.[93]

In terms of enforcement, the Act of 1968 provides for two main categories of offence according to whether the above activity occurs without a licence or, alternatively, under a licence but in contravention of its terms and other requirements. In this latter offence, it is a defence to prove that the contravention took place without the consent or connivance of the defendant and that he exercised all due diligence to prevent commission of the offence. Proceedings for

[88] *Ibid.* s.4.
[89] *Ibid.* s.4(4).
[90] *Ibid.* s.4A.
[91] s.71 and Sched. 4.
[92] Theatres Act, s.12(1). As to the definition of crucial terms like "play" and "public performance", see s.18.
[93] *Ibid.* s.14.

both these summary offences may be instituted by the licensing authority.[94] The Act of 1968 also provides powers of entry and inspection.[95]

Cinema licensing

The Cinemas Act 1985 provides that no premises shall be used for a "film exhibition" unless licensed for the purpose by the licensing authority: either a London borough council or a district council.[96] The licensing authority may grant a licence to "... such a person as they think fit" to use any premises specified in the licence on such terms, conditions and restrictions as they may determine. However, in granting a licence, it is the duty of the authority to impose conditions or restrictions prohibiting the admission of children to exhibitions involving the showing of works designated by that authority or any other body specified by the licence as works unsuitable for children or, indeed, satisfying any other designated category for this purpose.[97] The British Board of Film Censors serves as a non-statutory classification agency for present purposes. However, the local authority as licensing authority is required by law to exercise its statutory licensing discretion and must not blindly follow the Board's classification.[98] In addition to the central requirement for a licence, any film exhibition may not be given unless statutory requirements for the safety, health and welfare of children are complied with.[99]

Any person proposing to apply for the grant, renewal or transfer of a licence is required to give notice of his intention to the licensing authority, the fire authority and the chief officer of police. The licensing authority "shall have regard to" any observations submitted by the fire authority or the chief officer of police.[1]

The Act prescribes a wide range of offences, most importantly in relation to failure to obtain a licence or, alternatively, failure to comply with the terms, conditions and restrictions of any licence actually granted.[2] Any person found guilty of the prescribed offences is liable to conviction in summary proceedings. Furthermore, the court may order anything produced to that court, and shown to its satisfaction to relate to the offence, to be forfeited and dealt with in such manner as the court may order.[3] Conviction of a licence holder in respect of a range of offences under the Act and related legislation concerning children and young persons empowers the licensing authority to revoke the licence.[4] Various

[94] *Ibid.* s.13.
[95] *Ibid.* s.15.
[96] Cinemas Act, ss.1 and 21. A video amusement game does not fall within the Act: *British Amusement Catering Trades Association v. Westminster City Council* [1988] A.C. 147, H.L.
[97] *Ibid.* s.1(3). *Cf.* s.2, relating to controls on exhibitions for children. As to appeals against adverse decisions, see s.16 (appeals to the Crown Court).
[98] *Ellis v. Dubowski* [1921] 3 K.B. 621.
[99] S.I. 1955 No. 1129, as amended.
[1] Cinemas Act, s.3.
[2] *Ibid.* s.10.
[3] *Ibid.* s.11.
[4] *Ibid.* s.12.

powers of entry are conferred on a constable or on an authorised officer of the local authority or the fire authority.[5] Powers of arrest are conferred on a constable who has reasonable cause to suspect that an offence under the Act has been committed. Any such constable or authorised officer of the local authority has power to enter and search premises under the authority of a warrant and may seize and remove any apparatus or equipment "or other thing whatsoever" found on the premises which he has reasonable cause to believe may be subject to forfeiture by the court.[6]

The licensing of sex establishments

The provisions of the Local Government (Miscellaneous Provisions) Act 1982 governing the licensing of sex establishments may be adopted and applied by a local authority.[7] The term "sex establishment" means a sex cinema, a sex encounter establishment or a sex shop.[8] These provisions are implemented and enforced by those district and London borough councils adopting them.[9] Any such local authority is required to give local publicity to any adoptive resolution: this is a mandatory legal requirement.[10]

The core of licensing control is that no person shall use any premises, vehicle, vessel or stall as a sex establishment except under and in accordance with the terms of a licence granted by the local authority. The use or proposed use of any premises, vehicle, vessel or stall as a sex establishment may benefit from a waiver of the licensing requirement on an application for that purpose and where the authority considers that the requirement of a licence would be unreasonable or inappropriate.[11] Otherwise, the local authority may grant and from time to time renew a licence on such terms and conditions and subject to any restrictions as may be specified. Where a licence is subject to renewal, the local authority is obliged to take account of any change of circumstances. If there is no such change of circumstances and the authority refuses a renewal on the ground of the character of the locality, reasons must be given. If those reasons are properly relevant to the locality, the court will not interfere with the decision.[12]

An applicant for the grant, renewal or transfer of a licence is required to give local publicity to the application. In turn, any objections to the application must be communicated to the local authority within a prescribed time limit and identified to the applicant. In coming to a decision, the local authority "shall have regard to" any observations of the chief officer of police and any objections submitted. Prior to any refusal, the authority is obliged to give the applicant or

[5] *Ibid.* s.13.

[6] *Ibid.* s.14.

[7] Local Government (Miscellaneous Provisions) Act 1982, s.2 and Sched. 3. As to Greater London, see the Greater London Council (General Powers) Act 1986, s.12.

[8] *Ibid.* Sched. 3, para. 2.

[9] *Ibid.* s.2(5).

[10] *Ibid.* s.2(2): *cf. R. v. Swansea City Council, ex p. Quietlynn Ltd, The Times*, October 15, 1983.

[11] *Ibid.*, Sched. 3, para. 7.

[12] *R. v. Birmingham City Council, ex p. Sheptonhurst* (1989) 87 L.G.R. 830.

licence holder (as the case may be) an opportunity of being heard by a committee or sub-committee of that authority.[13] Any such hearing is not judicial in nature such as to allow application of the rule in natural justice against bias.[14] There is a discretion available to allow the objector or objectors a hearing also.[15]

Apart from the need for a refusal of a licence application on specific grounds because the applicant is under the age of 18 or has had a licence revoked previously,[16] there are various other general grounds available for a licence refusal. Among these general grounds are the following: that the applicant would be an unsuitable licence holder by virtue of having been convicted of an offence or that the number of sex establishments in the locality at the time of the application is equal to or exceeds the number considered by the local authority to be appropriate.[17]

A local authority may, if it so wishes, make regulations prescribing standard conditions applicable to licences for present purposes in relation to terms, conditions and restrictions. Amongst other things, these standard requirements may relate to displays, advertisements and hours of opening.[18]

The local authority is empowered to revoke a licence. However, revocation can occur only after an opportunity has been given to the holder to appear before and be heard by the authority. Thereafter, if revocation occurs, the holder will be disqualified from holding another licence under these provisions in the area for a period of 12 months.[19]

Offences fall into two categories and apply either to a person who knowingly uses or knowingly causes or permits the use of unlicensed premises, or to a licence holder who among other things may have employed a disqualified person in the subject premises or knowingly contravened the terms and conditions of a licence. All offences prescribed by the legislation are triable summarily.[20]

Both constables and authorised officers of the local authority have powers of entry and inspection. If the purpose of entry is not to determine licence compliance but rather to ascertain whether there is justification for a suspicion that certain offences under the present provisions have been or are being committed, a justice's warrant is required.[21]

A particular problem of law enforcement in the present context arises where the relevant criminal statutory provisions described in outline above are subject to challenge before the European Court of Justice. Despite such challenge, a civil court may grant an injunction to prevent the existing law being broken even where the criminal proceedings have been interrupted for the above reason.[22]

[13] Local Government (Miscellaneous Provisions) Act 1982, Sched. 3, para. 11.
[14] *R. v. Reading Borough Council, ex p. Quietlynn Ltd* (1987) 85 L.G.R. 387.
[15] *R. v. Chester City Council, ex p. Quietlynn Ltd* (1987) 85 L.G.R. 308.
[16] Local Government (Miscellaneous Provisions) Act 1982, Sched. 3, para. 12(1).
[17] *Ibid.* para. 12(3).
[18] *Ibid.* para. 13.
[19] *Ibid.* para. 17.
[20] *Ibid.* paras. 20 to 23.
[21] *Ibid.* para. 25.
[22] *Portsmouth City Council v. Richards* (1989) 87 L.G.R. 757, C.A.

Following the conclusion of criminal proceedings and a conviction in those proceedings, the court has powers of confiscation by virtue of the Criminal Justice Act 1988.[23]

Animal Welfare

Categorisation of controls

Many areas of statute law in the present context are based on local authority control, exercised through a licensing regime, supported by various enforcement facilities. This form of control is to be found in:

(a) the Pet Animals Act 1951;
(b) the Animal Boarding Establishments Act 1963;
(c) the Riding Establishments Act 1964;
(d) the Breeding of Dogs Act 1973;
(e) the Slaughterhouses Act 1974;
(f) the Dangerous Wild Animals Act 1976; and
(g) the Zoo Licensing Act 1981.

A range of controls also involve local authorities under the Animal Health Act 1981 and (in relation to dogs specifically) the Environmental Protection Act 1990 and the Dogs Act 1906. These latter provisions dealing with dogs have to be seen in the context of additional provisions in the Dangerous Dogs Act 1991.

Local authority licensing control and enforcement

The seven Acts referred to previously are set out below in summary form, indicating the main features of local authority legal responsibilities. Overall, the scope of local authority legal responsibilities is considerable. The discharge of those legal responsibilities falls principally to the district councils and London borough councils.

Pet Animals Act 1951

The framework for licensing controls under the Act of 1951, is the keeping of pet shops: "... the carrying on at premises of any nature (including a private dwelling) of a business of selling animals as pets ..."[24] No person may keep a pet shop without a licence from the local authority. Among other things, the local authority is required to have regard to a number of matters, including the suitability of accommodation for animals, the provision of suitable food and drink and the taking of reasonable precautions to prevent the spread of infectious diseases. The authority may attach to the licence such conditions as are considered to be necessary or expedient in the particular case. Any adverse

[23] s.71 and Sched. 4.
[24] Pet Animals Act, s.7(1).

decision following an application may be taken by way of appeal to the magistrates' court.[25] Among various offences created by the Act, the offence of failing to comply with the foregoing licensing requirements is punishable on summary conviction.[26] Another offence relates to the wilful obstruction of or delay to an inspection of premises by the enforcing authority.[27]

Animal Boarding Establishment Act 1963

The framework for licensing controls under the Act of 1963 is the keeping of boarding establishments for animals: "... the carrying on by [any person] at premises of any nature (including a private dwelling) of a business of providing accommodation for other people's animals ..."[28] The local authority dealing with an application for a licence here is unable to grant a licence if the applicant is disqualifed under this Act or is disqualified from having the custody of animals or from keeping a pet shop. Otherwise, the licensing regime under the Act of 1963 is broadly similar to that described previously in relation to the Pet Animals Act 1951.

Riding Establishments Act 1964

The framework for licensing controls under the Act of 1964 is the keeping of riding establishments:

> "... the carrying on of a business of keeping horses for either or both of the following purposes, that is to say, the purpose of their being let out on hire for riding or the purposes of their being used in providing, in return for payment, instruction in riding ..."[29]

Once again, the licensing regime is very similar in many respects to that described previously in relation to the Acts of 1951 and 1963. However, the licensing discretion of the local authority is also subject to the requirement that regard be had to whether the applicant appears to be suitable and qualified, either by experience in the management of horses or by being the holder of an approved certificate, or by employing in the management of the establishment a person qualified to be the holder of such a licence.[30]

Breeding of Dogs Act

The framework for licensing controls under the Act of 1973 is the keeping of breeding establishments for dogs:

[25] *Ibid.* s.1.
[26] *Ibid.* s.5. On conviction a person may be disqualified from keeping a pet shop.
[27] *Ibid.* s.4.
[28] Animal Boarding Establishments Act 1963, s.5.
[29] Riding Establishments Act 1964, s.6.
[30] *Ibid.* ss.1(4) and 6.

> "... the carrying on by [any] person at premises of any nature (including a private dwelling) of a business of breeding dogs, with a view to their being sold in the course of such business, whether by the keeper thereof or by any other person ..."[31]

The licensing regime is very similar in many respects to those for the foregoing Acts of 1951, 1963 and 1964. However, the powers of inspection available to the local authority under the Act extend to premises not covered by a licence.[32]

Slaughterhouse Act 1974

The Act of 1974, as amended by the Welfare of Animals at Slaughter Act 1991, deals with slaughterhouses and knacker's yards and their licensing. Failure to comply with the licensing requirements is an offence, punishable on summary conviction. An applicant for a licence must be an occupier or proposed occupier of slaughterhouse premises. The local authority in its licensing capacity must be satisfied that certain requirements are met for the purpose of statutory control: constructional requirements, for example. However, no licence can be granted until there has been an inspection of and report on the premises and facilities by an officer of the local authority. In certain cases, application must be refused where, for example, a slaughterhall is to be part of a dwelling. Adverse decisions of a local authority are subject to an appeal to the magistrates' court. Failure to comply with the foregoing licensing requirements is a summary offence.[33] For the purposes of enforcement, the Act gives a local authority extensive powers of entry and inspection.[34]

Methods of slaughter are prescribed by the Act and (subject to certain exceptions) no animal in a slaughterhouse or knacker's yard can be slaughtered otherwise than instantaneously by means of a mechanically operated instrument in proper repair.[35] The Act empowers the making of regulations for the purpose of prescribing humane conditions for slaughter[36] and also contains a requirement that slaughtermen should be licensed.[37]

Slaughter of Poultry Act 1967

This Act relates to the slaughter of turkeys kept in captivity, as well as the slaughter of a number of other varieties, such as duck, geese and guinea fowl. Such varieties may be slaughtered only by humane methods, subject to certain exceptions.

[31] Breeding of Dogs Act, s.5.
[32] Breeding of Dogs Act 1991.
[33] Slaughterhouses Act, ss.1–7.
[34] *Ibid.* s.20.
[35] *Ibid.* s.36.
[36] *Ibid.* s.38. *Cf.* the Slaughter of Animals (Humane Conditions) Regulations 1990 (S.I. 1990 No. 1242).
[37] *Ibid.* ss.39 and 40.

Dangerous Wild Animals Act 1976

No person is able to keep any dangerous wild animal except under the authority of a licence granted by a local authority.[38] A local authority may not grant a licence unless the application specifies the species and the number of animals of each species proposed to be kept, and specifies the premises where any animal will normally be held. Furthermore, a licence may not be granted unless the local authority is satisfied that it is not contrary to the public interest on the grounds of safety, nuisance or otherwise to grant the licence. A licence may not be granted unless the application is made by a person who both owns and possesses, or proposes both to own and possess, any animal concerned, except where the circumstances are, in the authority's opinion, exceptional. No licence can be granted by the local authority until the subject premises have been inspected and reported on. The authority may grant or refuse a licence as it thinks fit but, where it decides to grant a licence, certain conditions must be specified, but without prejudice to the inclusion of such other conditions as the authority thinks fit. Among the "mandatory" conditions, it must be specified that any animal or animals should be kept by no person other than the person or persons identified in the licence and that the animal or animals should be kept on the premises identified in the licence.[39]

Adverse decisions of the local authority are subject to appeal to the magistrates' court.[40] The local authority is empowered to undertake the inspection of premises where any animal is held or where it is proposed to hold an animal.[41] The Act also provides powers to seize, retain or destroy any animal in the event of a breach of the regulatory requirements without payment of compensation. In so far as non-compliance with the requirements of the Act is an offence, such an offence is punishable on summary conviction with the additional possibility of a cancellation of the licence by the court.[42]

Zoo Licensing Act 1981

It is unlawful to operate a zoo except under the authority of a licence from the local authority for the area within which the whole or any major part of the zoo is situated. A zoo is defined as an establishment where wild animals are kept for exhibition to the public otherwise than for purposes of a circus and otherwise than in a pet shop. The Act applies to any zoo to which members of the public have access, with or without charge for admission, on more than seven days in any period of 12 consecutive months.[43] Notice of an intention to apply for a licence must be publicised locally and to the local authority in advance, giving a

[38] Dangerous Wild Animals Act, s.1. As to the definition of dangerous wild animals, see the Schedule to the Act.
[39] *Ibid.*
[40] *Ibid.* s.2.
[41] *Ibid.* s.3.
[42] *Ibid.* s.6.
[43] Zoo Licensing Act, s.1.

number of prescribed details. The local authority is obliged to take into account any representations made by a range of prescribed individuals and organisations in considering any application. Prior to any decision on an application, the local authority must consider a report on an inspection of the zoo or consult certain prescribed individuals if no inspection is undertaken. A licence will be refused if the local authority is satisfied that the establishment or continuance of the zoo would injuriously affect the health or safety of persons living in the neighbourhood, or would seriously affect the preservation of law and order. Refusal may also be required if the authority remains dissatisfied with standards of accommodation, staffing or management. Equally, conviction of the applicant of certain prescribed offences relating to animal welfare may justify refusal. If the local authority is uncertain about the planning control issues affecting the site because, for example, it is not certain that there is appropriate planning permission in force, there may be a refusal of the zoo licence or an appropriate suspension of its operation.[44]

An original licence granted remains valid for a period of four years. Licences are capable of renewal and may be transferred, with the approval of the local authority.[45] The local authority is empowered to alter a licence if it is considered necessary or desirable to ensure proper conduct of the zoo during the currency of the licence. The licence may also be revoked on specified grounds but only after providing the licence holder with an opportunity to be heard.[46] Adverse decisions on applications are subject to an appeal to the magistrates' court.[47] Various failures to comply with the regulatory requirements of the Act are punishable as summary offences.[48]

Animal health

The Animal Health Act 1981, as amended by the Animal Health and Welfare Act 1984, makes provision to empower the Ministers to make orders in the interests of animal health, to control, eradicate and prevent disease and infection, to control cleansing and movement of animals and to control dogs, among other things. Much of the Act is built on the authority of statutory orders which empower the Minister (of Agriculture) or the Ministers and (on occasions) the local authorities to act for the various purposes of the Act.[49] In so far as the provisions of the Act confer powers on, or otherwise relate to, any local authority, its inspectors or officers, they refer to district councils.[50] Each local authority is obliged to appoint as many inspectors and other officers as it thinks necessary for the execution and enforcement of the Act.[51]

[44] *Ibid.* ss.2–4.
[45] *Ibid.* ss.5–7.
[46] *Ibid.* ss.16 and 17.
[47] *Ibid.* s.18.
[48] *Ibid.* s.19.
[49] The Minister of Agriculture and the Secretaries of State for Scotland and Wales.
[50] Animal Health Act, s.51.
[51] *Ibid.* s.52.

General powers

Parts I and II of the Act contain a miscellany of powers dealing with, *inter alia*:

(a) the separation of diseased animals and attendant notification to a local authority in the case of rabies, for example[52];
(b) the declaration of infected areas[53];
(c) the examination of sheep in connection with sheep scab (any such order may authorise entry to premises by local authority inspectors)[54]; and
(d) the control of dogs.[55]

The most recent order under this latter provision[56] deals with the wearing by dogs of collars, the prescription of related offences and the provision of powers of seizure, enforceable by a district council.

The export of horses

Part III of the Act again contains a miscellany of provisions, including requirements governing the export of horses. Each local authority may be required, if directed by the Minister under an order made by virtue of the Act, to execute and enforce the specific requirements governing the export of horses.[57]

Offences

The Act contains two categories of offence. In the first category,[58] it is an offence without lawful authority or excuse (proof of which lies with the defendant) to undertake an act or to omit to do an act in a manner declared by the Act to be an offence or declared by an order under the Act not to be lawful, as in the case of the Control of Dogs Order, for example. More general offences including failure to observe the terms of a licence are also provided for.[59]

Dangerous and stray dogs

Dangerous dogs are subject to a variety of controls under the Dangerous Dogs Act 1991, which designates certain types of dog for the purpose. After any day appointed, no person may have in his possession or custody any dog of these types unless such a dog complies with a scheme of exemption in an order made by the Secretary of State for Home Affairs, or the dog has been seized under powers in the Act or is being dealt with under an order for its destruction. Failure to comply

[52] *Ibid.* s.15.
[53] *Ibid.* s.17.
[54] *Ibid.* s.14.
[55] *Ibid.* s.13.
[56] Control of Dogs Order 1992 (S.I. 1992 No. 901).
[57] Animal Health Act, s.49.
[58] *Ibid.* s.72.
[59] *Ibid.* s.73.

with these requirements is an offence punishable on summary conviction.[60] The foregoing provision relates to dogs bred for fighting, although any other types may be similarly designated if it is considered that they pose a serious danger to the public. An order made for this purpose may also define an appropriate summary offence in respect of a failure to comply with the requirements of the order.[61]

It is an offence to have a dog—no matter what the breed—dangerously out of control[62] in a public or private place where it is not permitted.[63] If the dog injures a person, the owner must be convicted of an aggravated offence under section 4. The Act provides powers of seizure and entry to premises in favour of a police officer or any authorised officer of the local authority. Those powers of seizure arise in a variety of situations, including a situation where it appears to the officer that the dog is of a type covered by section 1, is not exempted and is in a public place at a time when it is unlawful for any person to have possession or custody of such a dog.

Dogs that are seized may be destroyed on the order of the court, whether or not a prosecution is brought. If the dog is a specially controlled dog or has been seized when dangerously out of control in a public place, but no prosecution is to be brought, the court may order destruction on an application by the police or the local authority. If the owner is prosecuted and convicted, the court is unable to order destruction immediately. In these circumstances, the court is obliged to wait until any notice of appeal is given: destruction may not occur until the appeal is determined or withdrawn. The court also has power to order that a person convicted of various offences[64] be disqualifed from having custody of a dog.[65]

The Dogs Act 1906 has provided for a duty on the part of the police to accept and detain any stray dog left at a police station by a member of the public. Both police and local authorities have relied on discretionary powers for the purpose of rounding up stray dogs.[66] Local authorities are now subject to a duty to collect and detain stray dogs and to dispose of such dogs if they are not collected.[67] In support of this duty is the Control of Dogs Order made under the Animal Health Act 1981 and referred to previously.

[60] Dangerous Dogs Act, s.1. Note also *R. v. Knightsbridge Crown Court, ex. p. Dunne* [1993] 4 All E.R. 491, and *Britton v. Lambourne*, 1994 (unreported).

[61] *Ibid.* s.2.

[62] Where there are grounds for reasonable apprehension that the dog will injure any person: *ibid.* s.10(3).

[63] A path leading to a person's front door is not a "public place" for present purposes in s.10(2): *Fellowes v. Crown Prosecution Service, The Times*, February 1, 1993.

[64] Under s.1, 3(1) or (3) or by virtue of an order under s.2.

[65] *Ibid.* s.4.

[66] Dogs Act 1906, ss.3 and 4.

[67] Environmental Protect Act 1990, ss.149–151.

Street Trading

The development of statutory control

Prior to the enactment of section 3 and Schedule 4 of the Local Government (Miscellaneous Provisions) Act 1982, there was generally no regulation of street trading (apart from powers that may have been obtained under Private Acts of Parliament, such as the Croydon Corporation Act 1927), except to the extent that offences of obstructing the highway or causing inconvenience could have been prosecuted under the Town Police Clauses Act 1847.

The provisions of the Act of 1982 apply across the country and are implemented and enforced by district councils.[68] Although described as a complicated piece of legislation,[69] the law governing street trading cannot be described (as was the closely allied law relating to markets) as "abstruse and somewhat archaic".[70] The distinction between a pedlar and a street trader was explored by the court in *Watson v. Malloy*.[71] In that case the court, referring to the definition of a "pedlar" in section 3 of the Pedlars Act 1871, concluded that such a person sells items on the move and not from a stall, so that a pedlar trades as he travels whereas a street trader travels to trade. Street trading is defined to mean "... the selling or exposing or offering for sale of any article (including a living thing) in a street".[72] However, certain activities are expressly stated not to be included in this definition of street trading, including:

(a) trading by a person acting as a pedlar and holding a pedlar's certificate under the Pedlars Act 1871;
(b) the sale or exposure for sale of items by a roundsman;
(c) the process of trading as a news vendor; and
(d) provision and operation of facilities under Part VIIA of the Highways Act 1980 for recreation or refreshment.[73]

Controls under the Act of 1982

Section 3 of the Act stipulates that a district council may resolve to adopt the provisions of Schedule 4. The Schedule contains a detailed set of provisions forming the regulatory framework for licensing, other forms of control and their enforcement. Streets for these purposes may fall into three different categories: "consent" streets, "licensed" streets or "prohibited" streets: a licensed street is one in which it is prohibited to undertake street trading without a licence from the district council, a consent street is one where street trading is prohibited without

[68] As to the position in Greater London, see the London Local Authorities Act 1990.
[69] *Per* Forbes J. in *R. v. Liverpool City Council, ex p. Reid*, 1984 (unreported).
[70] *Per* Glidewell L.J. in *Jones v. Lewis*, *The Times*, June 14, 1989.
[71] [1988] 1 W.L.R. 1026.
[72] Local Government (Miscellaneous Provisions) Act, s.1(1).
[73] *Ibid.* subs.(2).

the consent of the council, and a prohibited street is one in which street trading is absolutely prohibited.[74]

The distinction between licence and consent

The distinction between licence and consent has been explained thus, in the absence of any precise specification in the Act:

> "... licensing relates to persons trading from stalls in fixed and regular positions on a permanent basis, whereas consents are intended to cover itinerant traders or intermittent traders perhaps operating from small moveable stalls or vehicles ... The code with regard to licences is much more elaborate. It provides specifically for there to be an opportunity for representations to be made by the applicant and there is an opportunity for appeal.[75] So far as consents are concerned, there is no corresponding provision either for the making of representations or for appeal ..."[76]

Whatever code applies, it is necessarily limited to trading in a "street", defined to include any road, footway, beach or other area to which the public have access without payment, and a service area defined by section 329 of the Highways Act 1980. If it is intended to alter the code applicable, the procedures in Schedule 4 must be followed,[77] including detailed notification requirements. If it is intended to designate a street for the purpose of the above codes, notification requirements apply, as well as a requirement to copy such notification to the chief officer of police and the highway authority.[78] If, on the other hand, the intention is to introduce the code for the licensed street, the consent of the highway authority is required.[79] More generally, notification of the local authority's intention to adopt the provisions of the Act of 1982 for present purposes is not required.

The licence code The local authority is subject to a duty to grant an application for a licence or its renewal unless there exist one or more grounds for refusal, as listed in Schedule 4.[80] However, the Act does allow an important discretion in indicating that, despite the existence of grounds for refusal, the licence may nevertheless be granted.[81] The licence is required to specify certain "principal conditions", breach of which may lead to criminal enforcement. These conditions relate to the street in which and the days on which and times between which the licence holder is permitted to trade, the description of articles in which the licence holder is permitted to trade and (if necessary) the place in the

[74] *Ibid.* s.1(1).
[75] There is a facility for an appeal to the magistrates' court, with a further appeal to the Crown Court by either party: Sched. 4, para. 6(5), (6).
[76] *Per* Taylor J. in *R. v. Penwith District Council, ex p. May*, 1985 (unreported).
[77] *Ibid.* paras. 15 and 16.
[78] *Ibid.*
[79] *Ibid.*
[80] *Ibid.* para. 3(4), (5) and (6).
[81] *Ibid.* para. 3(5).

street where trading can occur.[82] The local authority may also add so-called "subsidiary conditions" (including, for example, a prohibition on the leaving of refuse), breach of which, though not attracting criminal sanctions, may be taken into account for the purpose of any renewal or revocation of the subject licence.[83]

The consent code The discretion available to the local authority in respect of an application for consent is considerable: "... the council may grant a consent if it thinks fit."[84] In granting or renewing a consent, the local authority may attach "... such conditions as it considers reasonably necessary".[85] More specific conditions permitted relate to obstruction of the street or danger to persons using it, as well as to nuisance or annoyance.[86] The local authority is empowered to permit a street trader to trade in a "consent street" from a stationary van, car, barrow or other vehicle, or from a portable stall.[87]

Although there is no statutory obligation requiring the local authority to give reasons for its decision, it may be open to the court to conclude that the absence of reasons indicates that there is, in law, no good reason for the decision.[88] At the outset also, it will be a matter of importance that the local authority seek relevant, pertinent information from applicants if it is to be fair as between applicants, particular where the provisions of the Act of 1982 are first adopted.[89]

If there appears to be a large measure of freedom in relation to the substantive grounds which may support a decision on an application for a licence, there appears to be an even greater freedom in the case of consent applications. As indicated previously, there is no procedure in the case of consent applications for the making of representations by an applicant, no procedure for receiving objections and no procedure for notification of the applicant of any objections. In the absence of an appeal facility here, the only remedy is an application for judicial review.[90] An order may be made by the court on such an application if the local authority has taken irrelevant considerations into account or ignored relevant considerations, acted in breach of natural justice or perversely, or is otherwise guilty of some procedural irregularity, as explained in *Council of Civil Service Unions v. Minister for the Civil Service*.[91] Although the process here in relation to decision-making under the consents code has been characterised as one involving application for a licence with no expectation that it will be granted, it has been

[82] *Ibid.* para. 4(1)–(3).
[83] *Ibid.* paras. 4(4) and (5) and 10(5).
[84] *Ibid.* para. 7(2).
[85] *Ibid.* para. 7(4).
[86] *Ibid.* para. 7(5).
[87] *Ibid.* para. 7(8) and (9).
[88] *R. v. Penwith District Council, ex p. May*, 1985 (unreported), applying *Padfield v. Minister of Agriculture* [1968] 2 W.L.R. 924, H.L.
[89] *R. v. Liverpool City Council, ex p. Reid*, 1984 (unreported).
[90] Ord. 53, R.S.C.
[91] s.71 and Sched. 4.

held that the rules of natural justice are applicable, requiring the local authority to act fairly.[92] Accordingly:

> "... a local authority committee, considering applications for consent ... which decides to receive and entertain letters of objection or representations of any sort from persons other than its own officers, or officers of the police or county highway authority, is under a duty normally to tell the applicant the substance of those objections, not necessarily actually to send them to him, but to tell him at least what they contain and to give him some opportunity to comment."[93]

Fees for applications

Schedule 4 to the Act indicates that a local authority may charge such fees as it considers reasonable for the grant or renewal of a licence or consent.[94] This power does not permit the local authority to take account of market considerations when determining fees.[95] On the other hand, the local authority is no longer confined to the cost of issuing licences and may take account of the costs incurred in operating a street-trading scheme, including the prosecution of those who trade unlawfully, without licences. However, the weighing and placing of a monetary value on the various facets of a street-trading scheme and the determination of a "reasonable" fee are matters for the authority's own judgment.[96]

Scrap Metal Dealers

Registration requirements

The Scrap Metal Dealers Act 1964 requires every district council and London borough council to maintain a register of persons carrying on business in their area as scrap metal dealers. Any person proposing to carry on a business as a scrap metal dealer may apply to the local authority for entry of a range of particulars on the authority's register, such particulars relating to the identify of the applicant and the nature of the business. Any variation in the particulars recorded must be advised to the local authority within a stipulated time limit. Failure to comply with these requirements is an offence, punishable in summary proceedings.[97]

The term "scrap metal" is defined by the Act[98] to include any old metal, and any broken, worn-out, defaced or partly manufactured articles made wholly or

[92] Theatres Act, s.12(1). As to the definition of crucial terms like "play" and "public performance", see s.18.
[93] *Ibid. per* Glidewell J. at 715.
[94] Local Government (Miscellaneous Provisions) Act 1982, Sched. 4, para. 9(1).
[95] *R. Manchester City Council, ex p. King* (1991) 89 L.G.R. 696.
[96] *Ibid.*
[97] Scrap Metal Dealers Act 1964, s.1.
[98] *Ibid.* s.9.

partly of metal, among other things. Such is the construction of this part of the Act that scrap from new metal, in the form of swarf or off-cuts, for example, is included in the regulatory framework of the Act.[99]

Records of dealings

At each place occupied by a scrap metal dealer as a scrap metal store, there is a requirement that a record book be maintained, indicating all scrap metal received at that place, and all scrap metal either processed at, or dispatched from, that place. Failure to comply with the requirement is an offence punishable summarily.[1] Although detailed specifications are required in respect of scrap metal on the individual site, it may suffice that what is provided by way of a description is a general description only, as long as it can be said to be a "fair" description.[2]

Enforcement

In the event of a conviction for an offence of unlicensed scrap metal dealing, for failure to maintain records or for an offence which in the court's opinion is an offence of dishonesty, the court may impose various requirements and restrictions on operations at the defendant's scrap metal store, including restrictions on the hours of operation.[3]

Both constables and authorised officers of a local authority have powers of entry to and inspection of premises for the purposes of the Act.[4]

Skin-Piercing

The scope of regulation and control

The term "skin-piercing" extends to cover four activities, acupuncture, tattooing, ear-piercing and electrolysis, and is regulated under the Local Government (Miscellaneous Provisions) Act 1982.[5] None of the foregoing expressions is defined by the Act. The local authorities may, if they wish, adopt these provisions but subject to the requirement that the appropriate resolution is publicised locally, indicating, *inter alia*, which provisions are to come into force in the area concerned. The local authorities responsible for implementation and enforcement are district councils and London borough councils.[6]

[99] *Jenkins v. A. Cohen and Co. Ltd* [1971] 1 W.L.R. 1280.
[1] Scrap Metal Dealers Act, ss.2 and 3.
[2] *Jenkins v. A. Cohen and Co. Ltd, supra.*
[3] Scrap Metal Dealers Act, s.4.
[4] *Ibid.* s.6.
[5] Local Government (Miscellaneous Provisions) Act, 13 to 17.
[6] s.13.

Acupuncture

Where the Act's provision on acupuncture are in force, such a practice may be undertaken only by acupuncturists registered with the local authority. The registration process relates both to personal registration and registration of the subject premises. Additionally, a local authority may impose requirements by means of byelaws in relation to the cleanliness of premises, the cleanliness of persons registered and assisting in the practice, and the cleanliness and sterilisation of instruments, materials and equipment.[7]

Tattooing, ear-piercing and electrolysis

The control and regulation of these activities is on a similar basis to that relating to acupuncture. Unlike the provisions on acupuncture, the present provisions refer to the carrying on of a "business" indicating (possibly) that any non-commercial undertaking would be beyond regulation and control.[8]

Enforcement

It is an offence, *inter alia*, for an unregistered person to carry on skin-piercing in its various forms or for any person, whether registered or not, to carry on such activities from unregistered premises. Contravention of byelaws referred to previously is also an offence. In addition to the imposition of a fine for any one of the (summary) offences, the court is also empowered to cancel or suspend a person's registration or the registration of premises where an offence was committed. The statutory provisions contain a right of appeal to the Crown Court.[9]

An authorised officer of the local authority is empowered to enter any premises if there is reason to suspect that an offence has been committed in relation to the present provisions. The power of entry is exercisable only under a justices's warrant.[10]

Nursing Agencies

The conduct of agencies

Any person carrying on an agency for the supply of nurses is obliged, in carrying on that agency, to supply only registered nurses and midwives, and such other classes of persons as may be prescribed. In supplying a nurse or midwife, the person carrying on an agency is also obliged to give a statement of the qualifications of the person supplied. Selection of persons supplied must be

[7] *Ibid.* s.14.
[8] *Ibid.* s.15.
[9] *Ibid.* s.16.
[10] *Ibid.* s.17.

undertaken by or under the supervision of a registered and qualified nurse or registered medical practitioner. These requirements are contained in the Nurses Agencies Act 1957.[11] An agency for the supply of nurses is defined as a business (whether not carried on for gain and whether or not carried on in conjunction with another business) for the supply of nurses and midwives.[12]

Licensing

The licensing authority under the Act of 1957 is principally a London borough council, a county council or a metropolitan district council. A licence from such an authority is required for the purpose of carrying on an agency as previously described. The authority is obliged to grant an application made in the prescribed form, subject to such conditions as they may think fit for securing the proper conduct of that agency. On the other hand, any licence application may be refused and any licence granted revoked on various grounds, including unsuitability of the subject premises or of the applicant to hold a licence.

An appeal lies to the magistrates' court in respect of adverse decisions of an authority: the court is empowered to make any order as it considers just.

Where a licence application is made in respect of an agency already subject to a licence, that application may not be refused and any other licence may not be revoked without the licence holder being heard by the authority or a committee of that authority.[13]

Enforcement

Various powers of entry to and inspection of premises are provided by the Act, exercisable by any registered and qualified nurse or other authorised officer of the local authority.[14]

The Act of 1957 provides for a range of summary offences either where a person has been carrying on an unlicensed agency or has been operating a licensed agency otherwise than in compliance with conditions attached to the licence. The Act also makes provision for continuing fines and empowers the court to revoke a licence in addition to or in lieu of any penalty imposed.[15]

Rag Flock

Registration requirements

Flock is a generic description for locks or tufts of wool, cotton or similar materials used for quilting, upholstery and similar processes. "Rag flock" is defined by the

[11] s.1.
[12] Nursing Agencies Act, s.8.
[13] *Ibid.* s.2.
[14] *Ibid.* s.3.
[15] *Ibid.* s.4.

Rag Flock and Other Filling Materials Act 1951 as flock which has been produced wholly or partly by tearing up spun or woven knitted or felted materials, whether old or new. However, the term does not include flock obtained wholly in the process of the scouring, milling or finishing of newly woven, newly knitted or newly felted fabrics.[16]

The Act of 1951 declares that it is unlawful in the course of a business to use filling materials to which the Act applies in any activity identified by the Act in premises that are not registered by a local authority.[17] The local authorities responsible are district councils and the councils of London boroughs.[18] The principal activities identified by the Act include upholstery and the stuffing of bedding, subject to some exemptions such as the remaking or reconditioning of any article.

Licensing

The premises covered by the Act's requirements are those where rag flock is manufactured or stored. The Act sets out the circumstances in which a local authority may refuse a licence, including the absence from premises of necessary manufacturing facilities (in the case of a manufacturing proposal). Before a licence may be granted, an officer of the local authority must inspect and report on the premises described in the application.[19]

Enforcement

There are various prescribed offences relating to the presence on licensed premises of unclean rag flock or the presence on registered premises of unclean filling materials,[20] in addition to an offence of selling, or offering or exposing for sale, articles containing materials.[21] Powers of sampling are available to any local authority concerned with enforcement of the statutory requirements.[22] An authorised officer of a local authority has powers of entry to and inspection of premises, as well as various powers to secure materials that are believed to be associated with the commission of an offence committed under the Act.[23]

An offence against the Act may be tried summarily.[24] In addition, the court has a power of forfeiture in respect of any material or article owned by the person convicted and in respect of which the court convicts him.[25]

[16] s.35. As to the definition of "rags" for the purpose of the narrowly worded definition in s.1 of the Rag Flock Act 1911, see *Cooper v. Swift* [1914] 1 K.B. 253 and *Balmforth v. Chadburn* [1927] 1 K.B. 663. See now the Rag Flock and Other Filling Materials Regulations 1981 (S.I. 1981 No. 1218).

[17] *Ibid.* s.1.

[18] *Ibid.* s.35.

[19] *Ibid.* ss.6 and 7.

[20] *Ibid.* ss.3, 6(8), 7(8).

[21] *Ibid.* s.10. Standards of cleanliness here are defined by the 1981 Regulations, *supra.*

[22] *Ibid.* s.15.

[23] *Ibid.* s.13.

[24] *Ibid.* s.18.

[25] *Ibid.* s.20.

Camp and Caravan Sites

Camp sites

Local authorities and, more particularly, district and London borough councils are empowered to control the use of "moveable dwellings".[26] In addition, a number of statutory provisions apply to tents, vans, sheds and similar structures used for human habitation.[27]

A "moveable dwelling" is defined to include any tent, any van or other conveyance whether on wheels or not and any shed or similar structure, being a tent, conveyance or structure which is used either regularly or at certain seasons only, or intermittently, for human habitation. Not included is any structure to which the Building Regulations apply. A local authority has power to issue licences authorising the stationing of movable dwellings (other than caravans), as well as a power to authorise the use of a site as a site for movable dwellings. Any adverse decision of the local authority in respect of a licence application is subject to an appeal to the magistrates' court. Any conditions imposed must be referable to matters of environmental health.[28] Failure to comply with the regulatory requirements of these provisions is an offence punishable in summary proceedings.[29]

Various provisions and, more particularly, the statutory nuisance provisions in Part III of the Environmental Protection Act, as well as the provisions of Part II of the Public Health Act relating to filthy or verminous premises or articles and verminous persons, are applied to tents, vans, sheds and similar structures used for human habitation. A local authority may also make byelaws in this context for the promotion of cleanliness and habitable condition. Where proceedings in respect of any statutory nuisance or breach of any byelaw are brought, the court may prohibit use of the tent, etc., for human habitation.[30]

Caravan sites

Many local authority responsibilities under Part II of the Caravan Sites Act 1968 are now repealed by The Criminal Justice and Public Order Act 1994. Since the repeal occurred when this book was going to press the following description of elements of Part II of the Act of 1968 are retained.

A caravan site is defined as land on which a caravan is stationed for the purpose of human habitation and land which is used on conjunction with land on which a caravan is so stationed, thus excluding sites used for storage or display of caravans. It is provided by the Caravan Sites and Control of Development Act 1960 that no occupier of land shall cause or permit any part of the land to be used as a caravan

[26] Public Health Act 1936, s.269.
[27] *Ibid.* s.268.
[28] *Pilling v. Abergele District Council* [1950] 1 K.B. 636.
[29] Public Health Act, s.269(7).
[30] *Ibid.* s.268(4).

site unless he holds a site licence.[31] a prerequisite to the grant of a site licence is a grant of planning permission under the Town and Country Planning Acts.[32] Possession of planning permission means that the grant a site licence should follow automatically unless, for example, the applicant has had a licence revoked. The crucial matter for present purposes is the attachment of conditions to a site licence.[33] The discretion of the authority is widely drawn, although any conditions must be referable to physical use of the subject land and not, for example, to the rents payable or the terms on which security of tenure may be available.[34] The requirement is that any conditions must be either necessary or desirable in the interests of caravan dwellers on the site itself or any other class of person or the public at large. An appeal to the magistrates' court is available in respect of any conditions attached, although the court is limited to determining whether any condition is "unduly burdensome", an expression not defined in the Act.[35]

Once granted, the conditions in a licence may be altered and for this purpose the local authority may take the initiative at any time, although the licence holder must be given an opportunity to make representations. The fire authority also must be consulted. The licence holder may apply for an alteration of conditions and may appeal to the magistrates' court in respect of an adverse decision relating to new conditions or a refusal to alter existing conditions.[36]

Enforcement

Failure to comply with any condition attached to a licence is an offence, punishable in summary proceedings. Revocation can occur only through an order of the court before whom a person is convicted for breach of a condition and then only when it is shown that that person has already been two or more times previously convicted for breach of site licence conditions.[37]

A local authority is obliged to maintain a register of licences. Such a register must be maintained for public inspection.[38] Powers of entry to premises are available to any authorised officer of the local authority, reinforced as necessary by a justice's warrant in appropriate cases.[39]

Gipsy encampments

It is the duty of county councils, London borough councils and metropolitan district councils in the exercise of their powers under section 24 of the Caravan Sites and Control of Development Act 1960 to provide caravan sites so far as may be necessary to provide adequate accommodation for gipsies residing in or

[31] Caravan Sites and Control of Development Act, s.1.
[32] *Ibid.* s.3.
[33] *Ibid.* s.5.
[34] *Babbage v. North Norfolk District Council, The Independent*, August 10, 1989.
[35] Caravan Sites, etc., Act 1960, s.5.
[36] *Ibid.* s.8.
[37] *Ibid.* s.9. *Cf.* s.3(6), in relation to the issue of any further licence.
[38] *Ibid.* s.25.
[39] *Ibid.* s.26.

resorting to their area.[40] The Secretary of State is empowered to direct a local authority to provide a site or sites for present purposes. Through a process of area designation (following an application under section 12 to the Secretary of State for that purpose by a responsible local authority), section 10 of the Act is triggered for the purpose of enabling the application of certain offences. More particularly, it is an offence in a designated area if a gipsy stations a caravan for the purpose of residing for any period on land within the boundaries of a highway, on any other unoccupied land or any unoccupied land without the consent of the occupier. The offence is triable summarily. The court may also impose a continuing fine, in addition to the standard penalty.[41]

The duty to provide caravan sites

Unless and until a local authority is subject to directions from the Secretary of State to provide a caravan site under section 6,[42] that local authority is not in breach of its statutory duty under that section. Because the Minister has sole responsibility for this matter, the court will not intervene by way of mandatory injunction, for example.[43] The fact that a local authority may be in breach of the duty under section 6 may not affect the court's view of proceedings for judicial review in respect of eviction from an unauthorised site where the authority pursues eviction proceedings only where specific criteria are met, such as the existence of an intolerable nuisance or public health conditions.[44] The fact of there being a breach of the section 6 duty may not be a ground for refusal of an injunction to secure compliance with an enforcement notice.[45] However, the court has confirmed the correctness of a decision to adjourn possession proceedings by a district council pending judicial review proceedings against it where the propriety of possession proceedings might be in issue in circumstances where the county council was in breach of its duty under section 6.[46]

Unlawful presence on land

The Criminal Justice and Public Order Act 1994 provides for orders to be made by a magistrates' court on an application by a local authority where the court is satisfied that persons and vehicles are unlawfully on land in contravention of a direction issued under section 77 of the Act.[47] A local authority also has power to direct that unauthorised campers leave land.[48] The Act repeals Part II of the Caravans Sites Act 1968, dealt with previously.

[40] Caravan Sites Act 1968, s.6. *Cf.* the definition of 'gipsy' as substituted in the Act of 1960 by the Criminal Justice and Public Order Act 1994, s.80.
[41] *Ibid.* s.10.
[42] *Ibid.* s.9.
[43] *Kensington and Chelsea LBC v. Wells* (1974) 72 L.G.R. 289.
[44] *R. v. Gloucester City Council, ex p. Dutton* (1991) 24 H.L.R. 246, C.A.
[45] *Mole Valley District Council v. Smith* (1992) 24 H.L.R. 442, C.A.
[46] *South Hams District Council v. Slough, The Times*, December 8, 1992.
[47] s.78.
[48] s.77.

INDEX

QM LIBRARY
(MILE END)